DICTIONARY OF
RUSSIAN
SLANG
and Colloquial Expressions

Third Edition

Vladimir Shlyakhov and Eve Adler

BARRON'S

All inquiries should be addressed to:
Barron's Educational Series, Inc.
250 Wireless Boulevard
Hauppauge, New York 11788
http://www.barronseduc.com
ISBN-13: 978-0-7641-3033-5
ISBN-10: 0-7641-3033-1

Library of Congress Cataloging-in-Publication Data

Shlyakhov, Vladimir.
    Dictionary of Russian slang & colloquial expressions = Russkii sleng /
Vladimir Shlyakhov, Eve Adler. – 3rd ed.
        p. cm.
    Includes bibliographical references.
    ISBN-13: 978-0-7641-3033-5 (alk. paper)
    ISBN-10: 0-7641-3033-1 (alk. paper)
    1. Russian language – Slang – Dictionaries – English. 2. Russian language –
New words – Dictionaries – English. 3. Russian language – Idioms – Dictionaries
– English. I. Title: Russian slang. II. Title: Dictionary of Russian slang. III. Title:
Russkii sleng. IV. Title: Dictionary of Russian slang and colloquial expressions.
V. Adler, Eve. VI. Title.

PG2752.S57 2006
491.73'21-dc22
                                                                2005052401
Library of Congress Control Number 2005052401

Printed in the United States of America

9 8 7 6 5 4 3

Table of Contents

ACKNOWLEDGMENTS

We are grateful to Middlebury College for generous financial assistance in preparing the manuscript for publication.

Ivan and Fyodor Shlyakhov helped in collecting youth and army expressions. Olga Shlyakhov gave invaluable help with Russian stress and punctuation. Toma Tasovac helped with typing.

Jane Chaplin and Bill and Peggy Nelson gave help and encouragement from start to finish.

Ray and Shirley Benson of the American Collegiate Consortium read and commented on the earliest version of the dictionary. Professors Kevin Moss and Sergei S. Davydov read parts of the manuscript and made many helpful suggestions.

We are grateful to A. Akishina, V. Zanin, and M. Vyatyutnev, all colleagues from the Pushkin State Institute of Russian, who helped with advice and shared their vast knowledge of slang.

We are grateful to my friend Bill Nelson for his help with the usage examples for the letters П, Р, С, Т, which he translated with his characteristic sensitivity to nuance.

We are grateful to Marine Corps Captain Kristen Lasica, who, as a student at the Pushkin Russian Language Institute in Moscow, devoted a great deal of time and energy to translating the Russian examples into English.

The Pushkin State Institute of Russian generously supported Vladimir Shlyakhov with leave from teaching duties to work on this dictionary.

PREFACE

Russian Slang and Russian Lexicography in Our Time

Russian, like every language, has a considerable stock of slang and colloquial words and expressions. Although everyone knows that slang is widely used, the Soviet regime attempted to outlaw it. Official Soviet linguistic scholarship and censorship made every effort to prevent the appearance of slang in literary works and in the pages of newspapers and magazines. For decades, slang was off-limits to dictionaries and no research was conducted in this field.

As a result, Russian lexicography has shown large gaps in this area. For more than half of the twentieth century, beginning in the 1920s, not a single adequate dictionary of Russian slang was published, and it has been extremely difficult to find any scholarly literature on the subject. During the Soviet period the only dictionary of slang available in Russia was V.F. Trachtenberg's *Блатная музыка* (*Thieves' Cant*), published in St. Petersburg in 1908. Aside from Trachtenberg's work, dictionaries of criminal slang, such as the *Dictionary of Thieves' Cant* published in Baku in 1971, were produced only for official police use.

In Russia, then, twentieth-century dictionaries have excluded the vast areas of contemporary youth slang, army slang, criminal slang, children's slang, and professional slang, as well as colloquial words and expressions—street language—in wide use at all levels of the population.

Interest in slang has increased considerably in Russia in recent years. One sign of this interest is the fate of A. Flegon's *За пределами русских словарей* (*Beyond the Bounds of Russian Dictionaries*), originally published in London (Flegon Press) in 1973. This dictionary, in spite of its lexicographic defects, became a best-seller when it was reprinted in Russia in 1991. Russians' increasing interest in slang is also evidenced by the appearance of many collections of youth slang and criminal slang in newspapers and magazines. Since the beginning of the 1990s, the following works on slang have been published in Russia.

V.V. Makhov, *Словарь блатного жаргона в СССР* (*Dictionary of Criminal Slang in the USSR*) (Kharkov: 1991).

F.I. Rozhansky, *Hippie Slang: Materials for a Dictionary* (St. Petersburg: European House, 1992).

D.S. Baldayev et al., *Словарь тюремно-лагерно-блатного жаргона* (*Dictionary of Prison/Labor-Camp/Criminal Slang*) (Moscow: Kraya Moskvy, 1992).

V.P. Belyanin and I.A. Butenko, *Толковый словарь современных разговорных фразеологизмов и присловий* (*Explanatory Dictionary of Contemporary Colloquial Idioms and Sayings*) (Moscow: Rossisskij Institut Kulturologii, 1993).

I. Yuganov and F. Yuganova, *Русский жаргон 60-90-х годов* (*Russian Slang from the '60s to the '90s*) (Moscow: Pomovskij i partnery, 1994).

The most lexicographically professional and complete Russian slang dictionary to date is V.S. Yelistratov, *Словарь московского арго* (*Dictionary of Moscow Argot*) (Moscow: Russkie slovari, 1994).

Thus, recent years have shown marked activity within Russia aimed at filling the lexicograpical gaps of the Soviet years.

At the same time, several useful publications in the field of Russian slang have appeared in the United States, including such specialized works as D.A. Drummond and G. Perkins, *A Short Dictionary of Russian Obscenities* (Berkeley, Calif.: Berkeley Slavic Specialties, 1973); V. Carpovich, *Solzhenitzyn's Peculiar Vocabulary: Russian–English Glossary* (New York: Technical Dictionaries, 1976); V. Kozlovsky, *A Collection of Russian Thieves' Dictionaries* (New York: Chalidze Publications, 1983); and I. Corten, *Vocabulary of Soviet Society and Culture* (Duke University Press, 1992).

The present dictionary is based on the recording and collecting of Vladimir Shlyakhov in the years 1987 through 1994, mostly in Moscow. The author was guided by one chief principle: all words and expressions, in whatever social stratum of the Russian-speaking population they may originate, have a claim to appear in the pages of dictionaries. During the long process of collecting the materials and composing the articles, he was sustained by his sense of performing a duty, as an inheritor, lover, and scholar of the Russian language, to preserve an endangered part of that language and bear witness to its use. The negative attitude of Soviet scholarship toward slang resulted in significant losses for lexicography; many words of "low style" have been lost forever. In this dictionary, the author has striven to record Russian slang of the second half of the twentieth century in a manner conforming to the standards of scholarly lexicography.

The Russian–English version of the dictionary was composed in close collaboration by Vladimir Shlyakhov and Eve Adler. This work attempts to take account not only of the realities of Russian slang and colloquial speech, but also of the special needs and interests of English-speaking students and scholars. Its goal is to provide such readers with a reliable and convenient key to this previously inaccessible area of Russian life and language. In adapting the dictionary for this Russian–English edition, special efforts have been made to render the explanatory material and the usage examples as transparent as possible, particularly where words and expressions reflect those areas of Russian and Soviet experience that are likely to be most foreign to English speakers.

Chief Sources of the Words and Expressions in this Dictionary

This dictionary draws on the speech in use in several specific spheres of life, but includes primarily expressions that have entered into the usage, or at least the passive recognition, of a wide spectrum of the Russian-speaking population. The chief sources are:

1. *Widely used colloquialisms and street language.* In many cases, such idioms and expressions fall into a gray area covered neither by standard dictionaries nor by specialized slang dictionaries. Special attention has been given to fixed forms of banter, rhyming phrases, and so on. For example, Она девушка что надо. = "She's quite a gal." Что-то стало холодать, не пора ли нам поддать? = An invitation or suggestion to have a drink (lit., "It seems to be getting a little chilly—shouldn't we have a drink?").

2. *Criminal slang.* A thieves' argot, unintelligible to the general population, is for obvious reasons the distinguishing feature of communication among criminals. In Stalin's time a great many people were condemned to terms in prisons and camps, where they were compelled to adopt the language in use. Thus hundreds of words of criminal slang have penetrated the Russian colloquial and written language—perhaps to a greater extent than in any other language. Today many of these words are no longer felt to belong to criminal slang, such as алкаш (drunkard), башли (money), водяра (vodka), вышка (death sentence), дешёвка (traitor), косой (drunk), лажа (nonsense), and so on.

Of course, other words still belong more strictly to criminal usage, such as бан (train station), верхи (outer pocket), and скрип (basket).

3. *Army slang.* Most of those who serve in the army are of course young people, who are the most receptive to slang and the most fertile in creating new words and expressions. Many words of army slang have entered the national language, such as салага (new recruit), полкан (colonel), лейт (lieutenant), and губа (place of disciplinary punishment). Words still belonging more strictly to army usage include шнурок (a new recruit) and гаситься (to shirk duty).

4. *Youth slang.* Youth slang has become a vast and productive system influencing the development of contemporary Russian speech. It manifests all the processes that attend the emergence of new words and expressions. Youth slang interacts with other slangs; it includes, for instance, a great number of criminals' expressions. Many words and expressions from youth slang have come into general use.

In the last ten to fifteen years, youth slang has adopted a great many words from the west European languages, modifying them in accordance with the rules of Russian word formation. Some foreign words have kept their meanings, such as фейс (face), баксы (dollars), дринкать (to drink), файновый (fine); others have taken on different shades of meaning: мейкаться (to turn out all right); френдиться (to be friends with someone).

5. *School and university, sports, and musical slang.*

6. *Obscenities* and the expressions and wordplays derived from them.

Role of this Dictionary in Linguistics and Sociolinguistics

The study of slang-word usage reveals the propensity of slang words and expressions to penetrate from one social sphere into another, and, particularly, into standard Russian. Youth slang, army slang, and criminal slang are, in turn, open systems. The mutual influence of different slangs is obvious: each adds to its own lexicon from the stocks of the others. Slang is one of the sources of increase to the lexical stock of the Russian language.

The processes of word formation and shifts of meaning that take place in standard speech proceed very rapidly in slang systems. These processes can be studied and classified. With this dictionary, linguists can investigate the laws of the birth and spread of slang expressions in the Russian-speaking milieu.

For scholars and students of Russian language and culture, this dictionary will make it possible to open or extend important areas of study:

1. The processes by which slang penetrates the standard national language.

2. The processes by which different spheres of slang borrow from one another.

3. The processes of morphological and semantic adaptation of words borrowed from the European languages.

4. The development of new meanings of words in common use, for example, колебать/заколебать = lit., to vibrate; colloquially, to irritate, exasperate. Ты меня заколебал своими просьбами, "You've exasperated me with your constant requests" (cf. English "vibes").

5. The formation of new slang idioms from widely used proverbs and sayings.

На бабца и зверь бежит, "Men simply run into a woman's traps," from На ловца и зверь бежит, "The game simply runs to the trapper."

Водка наш враг и мы её уничтожаем, "The enemy is vodka, so we'll utterly consume it," from the well-known saying of the Stalin years regarding enemies of the people: Если враг не сдаётся, мы его уничтожаем, "If the enemy won't surrender, we'll utterly consume him."

6. Culture through the prism of words, that is, how culture and everyday life are reflected in words.

Скоммуниздить, to steal, "communize," by rhyme-play on спиздить, an obscene expression for "steal," and коммунизм, "communism." The expression reflects the sardonic popular stance on stealing from plants and factories: there is nothing dishonest in it since, according to communist doctrine, property belongs to all, that is, to no one.

Глубешник, a KGB agent. From глубокий, "deep," and кагебешник or гебешник, "KGB-agent". The expression is based on a jocular interpretation of the abbreviation KGB

(КГБ — Комитет государственной безопасности, "Committee on State Security") as standing for Контора глубокого бурения, "Office of Deep Drilling"—a place where people are occupied in "digging," conducting deep investigations.

Прихватизация, corrupt exploitation of unstable policies on the privatization or denationalization of plants, factories, and stores. Punning on прихватить, "grab," and приватизация, "privatization." In the absence of stable and enforceable policies, everyone who had the power started to appropriate, or grab, government property—Moscow real estate, factory equipment, and so on— by dishonest means.

Organization of the Dictionary

Contents and Organization of Each Entry

A typical entry consists of:

1. The Russian word or phrase, its accentuation, and its chief grammatical forms.
2. Identification of its grammatical category, social sphere, and emotional tone.
3. A definition in standard English, sometimes with suggestions of slang counterparts.
4. A Russian sentence or sentences illustrating the usage of the word or phrase.
5. An English translation of the Russian example. Where possible, corresponding English slang expressions are suggested. In the many cases where the two languages and cultures present no such correspondences, the English translations use standard English or literal renditions of the Russian.

Verbs are listed as imperfective/perfective pairs when possible:

БА́НИТЬ/ПОБА́НИТЬ, *crim.* To interrogate (lit., to give someone a steam bath). *Нас банили четыре часа, но мы молчок.* "They grilled us for four hours, but we held our tongues."

In long verb entries, expressions are organized in the following order: (1) fully conjugable expressions, (2) expressions limited to the infinitive, past, present, future, and imperative.

Nouns are listed in the nominative, followed by their genitive ending.

БУ́ХТА, -ы, *f., crim.* A dive, den, shabby or illegal establishment (lit., a bay, harbor). *Кто держит эту бухту?* "Who's the proprietor of this joint?"

In long noun entries, expressions are organized by the case of the noun in the traditional order (nom., acc., gen., dat., instr., prep.) and in alphabetical order within each case.

Adjectives are listed in the masculine singular, followed by their feminine and neuter singular endings.

БЕСПРЕДЕ́ЛЬНЫЙ, -ая, -ое, *neg.* Illegal, immoral (cf. **беспреде́л**). *Ты читал беспредельную статью о русских фашистах? О них пишут как о героях.* "Have you read this outrageous article about the Russian Fascists, praising them as if they were heroes?"

Phrases and Idioms

This dictionary not only explains individual words but gives special attention to colloquial phrases and idiomatic expressions. How should the user find an idiomatic expression in this dictionary?

1. If the expression is governed by a conjugable verb, it is listed under the main entry for that verb. For example:

дать по шара́м is listed under дава́ть/дать.

забива́ть мозги́ is listed under забива́ть/заби́ть.

мета́ть икру́ is listed under мета́ть/замета́ть.

In many cases a cross-reference to the relevant verb is provided under another significant word in the phrase. For example, a reference to дава́ть is given under шары́; to забива́ть, under мозги́; and to мета́ть, under икра́.

a. If the verb is optional in the expression, the main entry appears under the noun or adjective, with a cross-reference from the verb. For example:

(пить/вы́пить) из го́рла is listed under го́рло, with a cross-reference from пить/вы́-пить.

b. If the verb occurs in a conjugated form (usually imperative) at the head of a fixed expression, then the main entry is given under the conjugated form, with a cross-reference from the main listing of that verb. For example:

возьми́ с по́лки пирожо́к is listed under возьми́, with a cross-reference from брать/взять.

да́ли, догна́ли и ещё раз да́ли is listed under да́ли, with a cross-reference from дава́ть/дать.

2. An expression consisting of the nominative form of a noun with an accompanying adjective is listed under the word beginning the expression. For example:

асфа́льтовая боле́знь is listed under асфа́льтовая

иша́к по́тный is listed under иша́к

3. An expression consisting of a declined form of a noun, with or without a preposition or accompanying adjectives, is listed under the nominative of that noun. For example:

на бровя́х is listed under бровь

до порося́чьего ви́зга is listed under визг

всю доро́гу is listed under доро́га

4. A fixed expression not governed by a conjugable verb and including more than a noun phrase is listed under its first word, regardless of the grammatical class of that word. Such expressions are, where possible, cross-referenced from a keyword. For example:

го́лый Ва́ся ночева́л is listed under го́лый, with a cross-reference from Ва́ся

на бабца́ и зверь бежи́т is listed under на, with a cross-reference from бабе́ц

без ка́йфу не́ту ла́йфу is listed under без, with a cross-reference from кайф

5. An expression containing any of the following obscene nouns is listed under that noun: говно́, жо́па, пизда́, хер, хрен, хуй, яйцо́.

PREFACE TO THE SECOND EDITION

Four years have passed since the appearance of the first edition of this work. During this time, standard Russian has become more receptive to elements of "low" style. The stream of slang and colloquial expressions has become very powerful in the mass media and the literary language.

On television, in political speeches, and in newspapers we now hear and read that somebody put someone on a hit list (заказал), that the president was deceived (подставить), that there are unsolved murder cases (висячие заказные дела), that banks have collapsed (легли), that profits (навар) are being smuggled abroad (за бугор).

Business language has borrowed from English such terms as кастомер (customer), дилер (dealer), юзер (user), брокер (broker), сайт (site) and so on.

One cannot fail to notice how many new words and expressions portray Russia's political and economic situation in dark colors. Besides already familiar terms like прихватизация and дерьмократ, we now find большой хлопок (the "big grab" for privatized property), депутант (combining "deputy" and "prostitute"), and прачечник (money launderer). Almost all the terms referring to well-known political figures have a negative character.

Previously, the dominant sources of slang and colloquial expressions were the worlds of criminals and drunks. Nowadays, the worlds of business, drugs, homosexuality, and prostitution contribute a greater share.

Thus, over the last 10 years, the colloquial and slang elements have expanded the Russian language with words previously excluded from print and public speech. Speakers and scholars of contemporary Russian have the unusual opportunity to see the birth and death of words, and in some cases the revival of forgotten words, condensed from a very short historical period.

This dictionary will be useful for students of Russian as well. The time has passed when a knowledge of standard Russian could open the doors to the worlds of politics, literature, and journalism. Today, without a familiarity with the corpus of words presented in this dictionary, without this "second language" that has not yet reached the pages of textbooks, access to contemporary Russian political and cultural life will be severely limited.

This dictionary records and explains all the phenomena in the life of the modern Russian language.

Vladimir Shlyakhov, Eve Adler
Moscow/Middlebury, 1999

PREFACE TO THE THIRD EDITION

Several years have passed since the second edition of this dictionary was published. During this time there have been many events of a violent and warlike character, such as the wars in Chechnya, Afghanistan, Yugoslavia, and Iraq, as well as the terrorist attacks of September 2001. Words about war and terror have entered our lives and become familiar to us. All this is reflected in the colloquial language of everyday. That is why the colloquial words and expressions newly collected for this edition are to some extent connected to the world of violence, war, and suffering – "the soldier's world." It is a known fact that military slang absorbs words generously from the worlds of business, politics, race, youth, and organized crime.

Naturally the main corpus of new words was composed of youth, criminal, business, and computer colloquialisms.

The authors
Moscow/Middlebury 2006

ABBREVIATIONS

abbr.=	abbreviation, abbreviated
acc. =	accusative case
adv. =	adverb
cf. =	compare
collect.=	collective noun
crim.=	criminal
dat. =	dative case
Eng. =	English
esp. =	especially
euph.=	euphemism
f. =	feminine
Fr. =	French
gen. =	genitive case
Ger. =	German
Heb.=	Hebrew
imperf.=	imperfective aspect
indecl.=	indeclinable
instr.=	instrumental case
interj.=	interjection
joc. =	jocular
lit. =	literally
loc. =	locative case
m. =	masculine
n. =	neuter
neg. =	negative
nom.=	nominative case
obs. =	obsolete
perf. =	perfective aspect
pl. =	plural
pos. =	positive
pred.=	predicate, predicative
prep.=	prepositional case
sg. =	singular
Ukr. =	Ukrainian
usu. =	usually

А В ГРÉЦИИ ВСЁ ЕСТЬ, *idiom, obs.* A deflating reply to someone's claim to have visited the West (lit., In Greece they have everything, with the sense "Big deal," "So what?").

А ЕБÁЛО НЕ ТРÉСНЕТ?, *idiom.* You're being too greedy, you're asking for or taking too much (lit., But won't your mouth split?). ◆*И ты все эти конфеты хочешь только себе взять, а ебало не треснет?* "You mean you're going to take all that candy just for yourself? But won't your mouth split?"

А ЗÁДНИЦА НЕ СЛÍПНЕТСЯ?, *idiom, rude.* See **А жóпа не слíпнется?** under **жóпа.**

А ОЛÉНИ ЛУ́ЧШЕ, *idiom, joc.* From the words of a popular song: *"Самолёты хорошо, а олени лучше"* ("airplanes are okay, but reindeer are better"). ◆*Пойдём пешком? — Пешком хорошо, а олени лучше. Поедем на такси.* "Shall we go on foot? — "On foot is okay, but reindeer are better. Let's take a cab."

А ПО ГÓЛОЙ МÓРДЕ НЕ ХÓЧЕШЬ?, *idiom, joc.* A threat to hit someone in the face, to beat up. From a conflation of Ударить по голой жопе, " to hit on one's bare ass," and морда, "face." ◆*Тебе всё, а нам ничего, а по голой морде не хочешь?* "How come you're taking everything and leaving nothing for us? Watch out or you'll catch it on your bare face!"

А ПОТÓМ — СУП С КОТÓМ, *idiom, joc.* A rhyming nonsense phrase used in reply to the question "What will happen then?" with the sense "It's none of your business" or "I haven't the slightest idea" (lit., "And then, cat soup"). ◆*А что будет потом, когда ты вернёшься? — А потом — суп с котом.* "And then what will happen when you come back? — And then, cat soup."

А ТЕБÉ ПО ГУБÉ, *idiom.* A rhyming phrase (lit., You'll get it on the lip). You won't get any, there's none for you! Used in answer to the question А мне? "What

about me?"

АБАЖУ́Р, -а, *m.* Lit., a lampshade. **1.** Head. ◆*Убери абажур, экран не видно.* "Move your head, I can't see the screen." **2.** Buttocks, behind. ◆*Скоро твой абажур в дверь не пройдёт.* [You're getting fat] "Soon your behind won't fit through the door."

АБÁС, -а, *m., crim., obs.* Twenty kopecks, a twenty-kopeck piece. ◆*Дай ему абас на хлеб.* "Give him a twenty to buy bread."

АБЗÁЦ, -а, *m.* Lit., paragraph or end of paragraph. **1.** End, death, "curtains." ◆*Ну, теперь нам абзац, мы пропали.* "It's curtains for us; we've had it now." **2.** Damn it! ◆*Он, абзац, так и не отдал мне деньги!* "He hasn't returned my money, damn it!" **3.** Excellent, good, terrific. ◆*Ну, как фильм? — Абзац!* "How was the movie? — Awesome!"

АБИТÁ, -ы́, *f., collect., youth.* People under age 35 who are competing for entrance to a college (abbr. of абитуриенты). ◆*Где здесь списки абиты?* "Where's the applicant list?"

АБОРДÁЖ, -а, *m.* Abortion (from resemblance of *аборт,* "abortion," to абордаж; lit., boarding an enemy ship in battle, with reference to the gravity and irrevocability of the decision to have an abortion). ◆*Что, решила рожать? — Нет, пойду на абордаж.* "So, have you decided to have the child? — No, I'm going to board the enemy ship (have an abortion)."

АБОРТÍРОВАТЬСЯ, *imperf. and perf., gay.* To go to the bathroom (cf. **аборт,** "an abortion"). ◆*Где бы можно поскорее абортироваться?* "Where can a person relieve himself around here?"

АБРÉК, -а, *m., neg.* A Caucasian; a dishonest person, thief, cheater (lit., an armed horseman of the Caucasus). ◆*На базаре здесь абрек на абреке, все норовят обмануть.* "In this market it's just one thief after another, all trying to rip you off."

АБРО́ТНИК, -а, *m., crim., obs.* A horse thief. ♦*У нас в камере два абротника сидят из цыган.* "There are two gypsy horse thieves doing time in our cell."

АВ-А́В, *indecl., crim.* Oral sex (lit., 'bow-wow', baby talk for the sound of a dog's bark.) ♦*Знаю, они там ав-ав занимаются.* "They're making 'bow-wow' over there."

АВТОГРАЖДА́НКА, -и, *f.* Compulsory civil liability insurance for vehicle owners. ♦*Не вижу никакой пользы от автогражданки.* "I don't see any use in having compulsory liability insurance."

АВТОМА́Т, -а, *m., youth.* A passing grade earned in the nonfinal semester(s) of a two- or three-semester university course by a student who, because of good performance in the course, is exempted from the end-of-semester pass–fail examination (from автоматический, "automatic"). ♦*Тебе хорошо, у тебя одни автоматы, а мне всю сессию ещё сдавать.* "You've got it easy with all your exemptions, but I've still got to take all the finals."

АВТОПИЛО́Т: На автопило́те, *idiom, joc.* In a drunken stupor (lit., on automatic pilot). ♦*Домой пришёл на автопилоте, ничего не помню.* "I must have come home on automatic pilot; I can't remember a thing."

АВТОПО́ЙЛКА, -и, *f.* A (self-service) gas station (lit., an automatic watering device for cattle). ♦*Бензин на нуле, где здесь автопоилка?* "The gas gauge is on zero — is there a service station around here?"

А́ВТОР, -а, *m., youth.* A person in authority over young people (from авторитет, "authority"). ♦*Чего он командует, он у вас что, автор?* "Why is he giving orders? Is he some sort of authority among you?"

АВТОСБРО́С, -а, *m.* Diarrhea, the runs (from автоматически and сброс, to throw down automatically). ♦*А что, после молока с абрикосами будет понос?* "Do milk and apricots really make one sick?"

АГДА́М СУХЕ́ЙН, *m., idiom, joc.* A dry wine. From Агдам, the name of a wine, and **сухе,** "dry wine" (by wordplay on "Saddam Hussein"). ♦*Почём сейчас "Агдам Сухейн"?* "How much does "Agdam Sukhein" cost these days"?

АГЕ́НСТВО «НЕ БОЛТА́Й!», *idiom.* A name of any special service, e.g., Federal Security Service (ФСБ, Федеральная служба безопасности). Lit., "a mum's-the-word agency." ♦*Ну, сам знаешь, откуда он – агенство «...Не болтай».* "Well, you know very well that he works for a hush-hush agency!"

АГЕНТЕ́ССА, -ы, *f., gay, neg.* An informer (fem. form of agent, "secret agent"). ♦*При этой агентессе — молчок!* "Mum's the word when this 'agent' is around."

АГРЕ́ССОР, -а, *m., joc.* Womanizer, Don Juan (lit., an agressor). ♦*Этот агрессор ради баб готов на всё.* "This skirt-chaser will do anything to get women into bed."

АГУ́-АГУ́, *adv., youth, joc.* On sexually intimate terms (lit., a baby-talk expression commonly used by adults cooing at babies; cf. агукать, "to talk baby talk"). ♦*Вы с ней уже агу-агу или ещё нет?* "Are you sleeping with her yet or not?"

АГУ́ШКА, -и, *f., youth, neg.* A girl, girlfriend; a disparaging word suggesting that the girl is silly. *Ты ещё ходишь с этой агушкой?* "Are you still going out with that lightweight?"

АДИЁТ, -а, *m., neg., joc.* (Distorted form of идиот, "idiot"). A silly person. ♦*Хватит шептаться, адиёты — спать пора.* "Cut out the whispering, you ninnies! It's time to go to sleep."

А́ЗЕР, -а, *m.* An Azerbaijani. ♦*У меня есть один знакомый азер, ничего мужик.* "I've got an Azerbaijani friend who's quite a fellow."

АЙ ЭМ ВРО́ТЭБАЛ, *idiom, students, rude, pred.* A distorted form of я в рот ебал, (see under **ебать**), imitating the sound of English words ("I am…"), in the sense of "the hell with…" ♦*Ай эм вротэбал такие разговоры.* "The hell with that kind of talk."

АЙЗЫ́, -о́в, *pl., youth, obs. (1970s).* Eyes (from Eng. "eyes"). ♦*Какие у него айзы? — Голубые.* "What color eyes does he have? — Blue."

А́ЙСБЕРГ, -а, *joc.* A Jew (lit., iceberg, playing on the "-berg" ending of many Jewish surnames). ♦*У них на работе синагога: Айсберги, Вайсберги, Цукерманы.* "They've got a whole synagogue in their office — Icebergs, Weisbergs, Zuckermans…"

АКАДЕ́МИК, -а, *m., crim.* An experienced recidivist. ♦*Ты ещё не говорил с академиком, может быть, он посоветует, как быть.* "You haven't talked with the 'academician' yet; maybe he'll advise you what to do."

АКАДЕ́МИЯ, -и, *f., crim.* Prison (with reference to its being a training ground for robbers). ♦*Попадёшь в академию — выйдешь спецом.* "If you go to prison (the "academy") you'll come out a specialist."

АКАДЕ́МКА, -и, *f., youth.* Academic leave (академический отпуск) taken by a student because of illness or family circumstances. ♦*Он уже месяц в академке.* "He's been on academic leave for a month now." •**Брать/взять академку,** see under **брать.**

АКВА́РИУМ, -а, *m., joc.* A place of compulsory overnight incarceration and sobering up for drunks. ♦*Он опять в аквариум попал?* "You mean he's landed in the 'aquarium' again?"

АКВЕДУ́К, -а, *m.* Penis (lit., aqueduct). ♦*Акведук работает как сумасшедший, второй раз бегаю в туалет.* "My aqueduct is working like crazy, that's the second time I've been to the toilet."

АКТИ́В, -а, *m., youth, neg.* The active partner in homosexual relations; a homosexual. ♦*Он что, актив, ко всем мужикам пристаёт?* "What is he, an 'active' or something, coming on to all the guys like that?"

АКТИ́РОВАТЬ, *imperf. & perf., crim.* To give sick leave from prison labor. ♦*Меня актировали на две недели.* "They've given me two weeks' sick leave."

АКТИРО́ВКА, -и, *f., crim.* Sick leave from prison labor, or early release from a prison term because of illness (cf. **акти́ровать**). ♦*Он по актировке не работает уже месяц.* "He's been on sick leave for a month now."

АКТУА́ЛЬНЫЙ, -ая, ое, *youth.* Popular, fashionable. ♦*На сегодня он самый актуальный дизайнер.* "He's the most fashionable designer these days."

АЛЕКСА́НДРОВСКИЙ ЗА́ДИК, -ого, -а, *idiom, Petersburg, joc.* A gay/lesbian meeting place. From Александровский сад, the "Alexander Gardens" near the Admiralty in St. Petersburg, by wordplay on сад, "garden," and зад, "buttocks."

А́ЛИК, -а, *m.* A drunkard. ♦*Он — алик законченный.* "He's a confirmed drunk."

АЛК, -а, *m., neg.* A drunkard. ♦*Он превращается в настоящего алка.* "He's turning into a real drunk."

АЛКА́РИК, -а, *m., joc.* A drunkard. ♦*Все вы-алкарики.* "You guys are just a bunch of drunks."

АЛКА́Ш, -а́, *m., rude.* A drunkard. ♦*Что с него взять, он же алкаш!* "What can you expect of him? He's just a drunk."

АЛКМЭ́Н, -а, *m., youth, joc.* A heavy drinker, drunkard (from алкоголь and Eng. "man"). ♦*Алкмэны у магазина уже с утра крутятся.* "Those 'alc-men' have been hanging around the liquor store since the crack of dawn."

АЛКОНА́ВТ, -а, *m., joc.* A drunkard ("alconaut," by wordplay from "astronaut"). ♦*Ну что, алконавты, пора в полёт.* "Well, alconauts, time for take-off" (cf. **в полёте** under **полёт**).

АЛКОТА́, -ы́, *f., collect., rude.* Drunks, a group of drunks. ♦*А ну, быстро из подъезда, алкота проклятая, здесь вам не пивная!* "Get out of the lobby, you damned drunks. This isn't a bar!"

АЛКОФА́Н, -а, *m., youth, joc.* A heavy drinker, habitual drinker (from алкоголь and Eng. "fan"). ♦*Спроси у алкофанов, где купить портвейн.* "Ask the 'alco-fans' where to get some cheap wine around here" (referring to local experts on the sources of liquor).

АЛКУ́ШНИК, -а, *m., rude.* A drunkard. ♦ *Он обязательно подведёт; на таких алкушников не надейся.* "You can be sure he'll let you down; you can't rely on drunks like him."

АЛЛА́Х: Алла́х с кем-л.! *idiom.* Let someone have it his own way (lit., Allah be with someone). ♦ *Не хочешь идти в гости, Аллах с тобой.* "So you don't want to pay a visit? Okay, have it your way." **Ну тебя́ к Алла́ху,** *idiom.* The hell with you, damn you (lit., "To Allah with you!"). ♦ *Сколько можно тебя просить, ну тебя к Аллаху!* "How many times do I have to ask you, damn you!"

А́ЛЛЕС! *interj., youth.* That's all! Enough! (from German "alles"). ♦ *Ты всё сказал, больше слушать тебя не могу, аллес!* "You've already said your say. I won't listen to another word — enough!"

АЛО́РЕЦ, ало́рца, *m.* (f. **ало́рка, -и**), *youth.* An Italian. ♦ *Что тебе сказал вчера тот алорец?* "What did that Italian guy say to you yesterday?"

АЛТА́РЬ, -ря́, *m., crim.* A judge's bench (lit., church altar). ♦ *Кто там сегодня за алтарём?* "Who's behind the altar (on the bench) today?"

АЛЬФО́НС, -а, *m., neg.* A man living at a woman's expense. ♦ *Как ты терпишь этого альфонса, он тебя разорит!* "How can you bear that parasite? He's milking you dry!"

АЛЬФОНСИ́РОВАТЬ, *imperf. only, neg.* To live at a woman's expense (cf. **альфо́нс**). ♦ *И давно он альфонсирует?* "Has he been 'Alphonsing' long?"

АЛЮ́РА, -ы, *f., crim.* A female member of a gang. ♦ *У тебя знакомых алюр много, попроси кого-нибудь продать эти вещи.* "You know a lot of molls; ask one of them to fence these things."

АЛЯ́СКА, -и, *f.* A warm coat with a fur-trimmed hood (from "Alaska"). ♦ *Я вижу, у тебя новая аляска.* "I see you've got a new 'Alaska.'"

АМА́РА, -ы, *f., crim.* A prostitute. ♦ *Это место стоянки амар.* "This is a regular beat for prostitutes."

АМБА́Л, -а, *m., neg.* A strong, thickset fellow, thug, muscle-man. ♦ *Открываю дверь — стоит амбал.* "So I open the door, and there's this big brute standing there."

АМБА́ЛИСТЫЙ, -ая, -ое, *neg.* Coarse, strong, thickset (cf. **амба́л**). ♦ *Муж у неё уж больно амбалистый.* "Her husband is awfully brawny."

АМБА́ЛЬНЫЙ, -ая, -ое, *youth, neg.* Coarse, strong, thickset (cf. **амба́л**). ♦ *Все друзья у него амбальные чуваки.* "All his friends are real jocks."

АМБРАЗУ́РА, -ы, *f., joc.* Buttocks, behind (lit., embrasure). ♦ *Амбразуру прикрой, гости идут.* "Cover up your ass, we're having visitors."

АМЁБА, -ы, *m. & f., neg.* A dull, boring person (lit., an amoeba). ♦ *Опять надо с этим амёбой разговаривать, от скуки сойдёшь с ума.* "Talking to that drip can drive you out of your mind with boredom."

АМЕРИКА́Н, -а, *m., joc.* An American. ♦ *Делать им там американам в Боснии нечего.* "The Americans have no business meddling over there in Bosnia."

АМЕРИКА́НСКИЕ ГО́РКИ, АМЕРИ-КАНСКИХ ГОРОК, *idiom, army.* Heavy seas (lit., "American mountains," referring to a roller coaster). ♦ *Опять ветер, опять американские горки, у всех уже морская болезнь.* "There goes the wind again, and these heavy seas—everyone's seasick."

АММОНА́Л, -а, *m., crim.* Bread (lit., explosives). ♦ *Аммонал есть, лук есть, что ещё надо?* "We've got bread and onions — what more could we need?"

АМОРА́ЛКА, -и, *f., obs., Soviet.* Publicly punishable immoral behavior, usually drunkenness or sexual irregularities. ♦ *Его надо гнать с работы за аморалку.* "He'll have to be fired for moral turpitude."

АМО́РОМ, *adv., crim.* Quickly. ♦ *Это надо сделать амором, пока никого нет.* "We've got to get this done fast, while the coast is clear."

А́МПУЛА, -ы, f. A bottle of liquor (lit., an ampule). ♦ *Ещё бы пару ампул на всех, тогда бы хватило.* "I think another few bottles of booze will do for all of us."

АМУ́РЧИК, -а, *m., crim.* The protector of a gang of women thieves (from Fr. "amour"). ♦ *У тебя амурчик есть, надо помочь одному человеку.* "You've got a protector — can you get help for a guy I know?"

АНАКО́НДА, -ы, *f., neg.* A nasty, venomous woman, a scolding wife (lit., anaconda). ♦ *Твоя анаконда ругать тебя не будет за мальчишник?.* "Is your anaconda going to bawl you out for out stag party?"

АНАЛИЗА́ТОР, -а, *m., joc.* A toady, ass-licker (from анальное отверстие, "anus," and лизать, "to lick"; punning on анализ, "analysis"). ♦ *Он у нас главный анализатор.* "He's the head ass-licker in our department."

АНАЛОГИ́ЧНЫЙ СЛУ́ЧАЙ был. . . , *idiom, joc.* The opening of an expression of mocking disbelief (lit., "something similar happened"). ♦ *Ты слышал, на прошлой неделе у нас над Москвой тарелки летали. Аналогичный случай был в Африке с моей коровой.* "Have you heard? We had flying saucers here over Moscow last week. — Oh, yeah? Something similar happened in Africa with my cow."

АНАНА́С, -а, *m., youth, neg.* A masturbator (lit., a pineapple; by wordplay on онанист, "onanist"). ♦ *Почему он с девушками не ходит, в ананасы записался, что ли?* "How come he doesn't go out with girls? Has he joined up with the onanists or something?"

АНГА́Р, -а, *m., joc.* Buttocks, behind (lit., hangar). ♦ *Смотри, какой ты себе ангар отрастил.* "Look how fat your behind has got!"

АНГИДРИ́Т ТВОЮ́ ПЕ́РЕКИСЬ МА́Р-ГАНЦА, *idiom, joc.* Euphemistic swear-word playing on the similarity between chemical terms and the obscenity "едрит твою мать." ♦ *Куда я дел часы, ангид-рит твою перекись марганца!* "Where the anhydrite did I put my watch?!"

АНДЕРГРА́УНД, -а, *m.* (From Eng. "underground".) **1.** *obs.* Non-conformist art of the Soviet period. ♦ *Андерграунд уже всем на Западе надоел.* "In the West this 'underground' kind of art is out of fashion." **2.** Writers or artists considered counter-cultural, marginal, or oppositional. ♦ *Наш андерграунд сейчас использует во всю интернет и ругает всё и вся.* "Our counter-culture is using the internet to denounce everything."

АНДРЕ́Й — ВОРОБЕ́Й, *idiom, joc.* A teasing rhyming phrase for people named Andrei (lit., Andrei the sparrow).

АНДРЕ́Й! ДЕРЖИ ХЕР (ХУЙ) БОДРЕ́Й!, *idiom, rude.* A teasing rhyming phrase for people named Andrei (lit., Andrei, carry your prick more boldly!)

АНДРО́ПОЛЬ, -я, *m., joc., obs., Moscow.* The KGB building in Lubyanka Square, built in the 1970s (by wordplay on акрополь, "acropolis," and Андропов, "Andropov").

АНДРЮ́ХА! ХЕР ТЕБЕ́ В У́ХО, *idiom, rude.* A teasing rhyming phrase for people named Andrei (lit., Andrei, a prick in your ear!)

АНОНИ́МКА, -и, *f., obs., Soviet.* An anonymous letter of denunciation. ♦ *В последнее время его замучили аноним-ками, пишут, что он спит с амери-канкой.* "There've been some 'anonym-kas' against him recently saying that he's been having an affair with an American."

АНТА́БУС, -а, *m., youth.* A medication for alcoholism. ♦ *Ты же принимал антабус и опять за своё, пьёшь сутками.* "There you go drinking round the clock again, even after your treatment."

АНТЕ́НЩИК, -а, *m., youth, neg.* A masturbator. ♦ *Ему бабы до лампочки, вид-но, антенщик.* "Women are nothing to him; apparently he's an onanist."

АНТИЗНОБИ́Н, -а, *m.* Vodka (lit., anti-chills). ♦ *Прими стакан антизнобину, не простудишься.* "Take a glass of vodka to avoid catching cold."

АНТИПОЛИЦÁЙ, -я, *m.* Pills that neutralize the smell of alcohol (lit., antipoliceman). ♦ *На таблетку антиполицая и за руль.* "Take an anti-police pill and hit the road."

АНТИФÉЙС, -а, *m.* The behind, buttocks (from Eng. "face"). ♦ *Такой антифейс ни в какие джинсы не влезет.* "A behind like that won't fit into any pair of jeans."

АНТÓШКА — КАРТÓШКА!, *idiom, joc.* A teasing rhyming phrase for boys named Anton (lit., Anton is a potato!)

АНТРАЦИ́Т, -а, *m., crim.* Narcotics (lit., anthracite). ♦ *Угощайся, это — антрацит.* "Help yourself to some 'anthracite.'"

АППАРÁТ, -а, *m.* **1.** An automobile. ♦ *Чей это аппарат стоит во дворе?* "Whose car is that in the yard?" **2.** *joc.* Male genitals. ♦ *Что-то аппарат болит, надо к врачу сходить.* "I've got a pain in the 'apparatus'; I've got to see a doctor."

АППЛИКУ́ХА, -и, *f.* An applied computer program. ♦ *Такую аппликуху и мне надо поставить.* "I need to install this very program on my computer."

АПРОПИНДÓС, -а, *m., youth, neg.* A mess, disaster, trouble. ♦ *У него в семье полный апропиндос.* "His family is falling apart."

АПРОПИНДÓСИТЬСЯ, *perf. only, youth, neg.* To be cheated, tricked. ♦ *Будешь продавать машину, смотри, апропиндосишься.* "Make sure you don't get ripped off when you try to sell your car."

АПТÉКА, -и, *f.* A personal supply of narcotic drugs (lit., a pharmacy). ♦ *Какая у тебя аптека, давай поймаем кайф.* "What do you have that we can get high on?" •**Как в аптéке,** *idiom.* Exactly, accurately (lit., as in a pharmacy, with reference to pharmaceutical scales). ♦ *Вот все деньги, пересчитай. — Хорошо, здесь как в аптеке.* "Here's the money. Count it. — Good. You're running things as accurately as in a pharmacy." **Дружи́ть с аптéкой,** see under **дружи́ть.**

А́РА, -ы, *m.* A Caucasian (i.e., a person from the Caucasus; from a Georgian term of address, "pal" or "buddy"). ♦ *Ты знаешь того ару?* "Do you know that Caucasian fellow?"

АРÁП, -а, *m., crim. & youth, neg.* A cheeky, insolent person. ♦ *Этот арап своего добьётся, наглый как танк.* "That brazen fellow will always get what he wants; he's as pushy as a tank."

АРÁХИСЫ, -ов, *pl., joc.* Scrotum, balls (lit., peanuts). ♦ *Не отморозь арахисы, на улице мороз.* "It's cold out, don't let your balls get frostbitten!"

АРБÁТ, -а, *m., youth.* Work (from Ger. "Arbeit"). ♦ *Сейчас арбат кончу и пойдём.* "I'm going to finish work in a minute and then we'll leave."

АРБУ́З, -а, *m., joc.* Lit., a watermelon. **1.** A potbelly, big paunch. ♦ *Когда ты успел такой арбуз отрастить?* "When did you manage to put on such a potbelly?" **2.** One billion rubles. ♦ *Это уже стоит не лимон, а арбуз.* "With our inflation that costs a billion now, not a million."

АРБУ́З РАСТЁТ, А КÓНЧИК СÓХНЕТ, *idiom, joc.* Lit., "The melon's growing but the stem is shriveling." Said of an aging man who gains weight and loses sexual potency.

АРИСТОКРÁТ, -а, *m., crim.* A high-ranking thief. ♦ *Пусть аристократ скажет своё мнение.* "Let's hear the aristocrat's opinion."

АРКÁНИТЬ/ЗААРКÁНИТЬ. (From аркан, "lasso.") To catch, force, lasso into. ♦ *Меня заарканили на две недели работать на даче.* "They've roped me into working at the dacha for a couple of weeks."

А́РКТИКА, -и, *f., joc.* A bald crown (lit., arctic). ♦ *У тебя самая большая арктика среди нас всех.* "You've got the biggest bald patch of all of us!"

АРМÁДА, -ы, *f.* The army (lit., the armada). ♦ *Ну кто сейчас хочет служить в армаде?* "Nobody wants to serve in the army today."

АРМÉН, -а, *m., neg.* An Armenian.

АРМЯ́ШКА — В ЖÓПЕ (ПÓПЕ) ДЕРЕВЯ́ШКА, *idiom, rude.* A teasing rhyming phrase for an Armenian (lit., An Armenian with a piece of wood up his ass).

АРНО́ЛЬД, -а, *m., youth, joc.* A brawny bodybuilder, a muscular but dumb fellow (from Arnold Schwarzenegger). ♦*У этого Арнольда один спорт на уме.* "That jock has nothing in his head but sports."

АРТЕ́ЛЬ «НАПРА́СНЫЙ ТРУД», *idiom.* A useless job (lit., the "wasted labor" team). ♦*Копать в песке ямы— артель «Напрасный труд».* "Digging ditches in this sand is simply wasted labor."

АРТИЛЛЕ́РИЯ, -и, *f., crim., joc.* Lice (lit., artillery). ♦*У нас артиллерия завелась, надо в баню сходить.* "We've got lice; we'd better go have a bath."

АРШИ́Н, -а, *m.* **1.** *joc.* A tall, thin person. **2.** *youth.* A measure of marijuana.

АСК! *interj., youth.* Of course! It goes without saying! (from Eng. "ask"). ♦*Ты придёшь слушать попсу? — Аск!* "Are you going to the pop concert? — Of course!" •**Жить на а́ске,** see under **жить.**

АСКА́ТЕЛЬ, -я, *m., youth, neg.* Someone who is always asking to borrow things. ♦*Этому аскателю хватит давать взаймы.* "Don't loan any more money to that moocher."

А́СКАТЬ/А́СКНУТЬ, *youth.* Cf. **аск.** **1.** To ask for. ♦*Аскни у него полтинник.* "Ask him to loan you fifty rubles." **2.** To ask. ♦*Пойдём аскнем, где мотель.* "Let's ask where the motel is."

А́СКЕР, -а, *m., youth.* Someone who habitually borrows money or things (cf. **аск**). ♦*Ты у нас аскер что надо, достань немного денег.* "You're the master moocher here, so see if you can raise some cash for us."

А́СКИ, -ов, *pl., youth.* Problems, questions, objections (cf. **аск**). ♦*Какие могут быть аски? Идём в гости и всё.* "What objections could there be? We're going to the party and that's all there is to it."

АСКОРБИ́НКА, -и, *f.* A vitamin C tablet (lit., an ascorbic). ♦*Купи аскорбинки, у* всех авитаминоз. "You'd better buy us some 'ascorbettes' — we all have a vitamin deficiency."

АСТРА́Л, -а, *m., youth.* An eccentric, an unsociable person who acts strangely (from астральный, "astral"). ♦*Ты совсем живёшь, как астрал, никого месяцами не видишь.* "You've turned into a regular space cadet, going for months without seeing anyone."

АСФА́ЛЬТОВАЯ БОЛЕ́ЗНЬ, *idiom, joc.* "Pavement sickness." Used of one with facial bruises from falling or fighting while drunk. ♦*У тебя всё лицо в царапинах, это что — асфальтовая болезнь?* "Your face is all scratched up — what's wrong, a little pavement sickness?"

АТА́, *interj., crim.* So long, good-bye. ♦*Ну, ата, увидимся через день.* "So long. See you tomorrow."

АТАНДЕ́! *interj., crim.* Watch out! A warning of danger (from Fr. "attendez"). ♦*Атанде! Кто-то идёт!* "Watch out! Someone's coming!"

АТА́С, *interj., youth.* A warning of danger. ♦*Атас! Милиция! — закричал кто-то.* "'Watch out! The police!', someone cried."

АТА́СНЫЙ, -ая, -ое, *youth, pos.* Excellent, extraordinary. ♦*У него атасная машина.* "He's got a fantastic car."

А́ТОМНЫЙ, -ая, -ое, *youth, pos.* Lit., atomic. **1.** Strong. ♦*Это атомные сигареты.* "Those are strong cigarettes." **2.** Excellent, extraordinary. ♦*Когда ты купил это атомное пальто?* "When did you buy that fabulous coat?"

А́УТ, -а, *m., crim. & youth.* Death, end (from Eng. "out"). ♦*Ему скоро аут будет, он всех заложил.* "He's in for it now — he's betrayed everyone." •**В а́уте,** *idiom.* Out cold, unconscious. ♦*Он уже в ауте, много выпил.* "He's out cold already from all that liquor."

АФГА́НЕЦ, афга́нца, *m.* A veteran of the Afghanistan war. ♦*А разве ты не знал, что он афганец?* "Didn't you know he's an 'Afganetz'?"

АФГА́НКА, -и, *f., army.* A type of army

jacket with a lot of pockets. ♦*Сигареты возьми там, в афганке.* "Get the cigarettes from my 'afganka'."

АФИ́ША, -и, *f., crim., neg.* A fat face (lit., a poster). ♦*Ну и афиша у него, жрёт, наверное, хорошо.* "Look at the fat face on him — evidently he's eating plenty." •**Афи́ша жёванная,** *idiom, joc.* A good-for-nothing, incompetent person (lit., a chewed-up poster). ♦*Что с тебя взять, афиша жёванная, так и знали, что ты не сумеешь достать вина.* "You schlemiel, I should have known you were incapable of getting hold of a bottle of wine."

АЭРОВА́ФЛЯ, -и, *f., youth.* Oral sex. ♦*Эта — специалист по аэровафлям.* "She specializes in blowjobs."

АЭРОДРО́М, -а, *m., joc.* A large, round, flat cap worn by Caucasians (lit., an airfield). ♦*Зачем ты этот аэродром купил?* "What did you buy that airfield-cap for?" •**Аэродро́м в лесу́,** *idiom, joc.* A bald spot (lit., a landing strip in the woods). ♦*А у тебя аэродром в лесу появился.* "You're getting a noticeable bald spot."

БА́БА, -ы, *f., neg.* A woman. ◆*Бабы его любят.* "Dames like him." ●**Как наде́нешь Адида́с, тебе́ люба́я ба́ба даст,** see under **как.**

БАБА́ХА, -и, *f.* A blow, stroke (from бабах, the sound of an explosion). ◆*Недолго и бабаху получить за гря́зный воротничок от сержанта.* "With that dirty collar, you're in for a slap from the sergeant."

БАБА́ХНУТЫЙ, -ая, -ое, *youth.* Crazy (from бабах, the sound of an explosion). ◆*Он слегка бабахнутый, не обижайся на него.* "He's a little crazy — don't be offended by him."

БАБА́ХНУТЬСЯ, *perf. only, youth.* To go crazy. ◆*Он совсем бабахнулся.* "He's completely taken leave of his senses."

БАБЕ́Ц, бабца́, *m., joc.* A woman. ◆*Она бабец ничего.* "She's not a bad-looking woman." ●**На бабца́ и зверь бежи́т,** see under **на.**

БАБЕ́ШНИК, -а, *m., joc.* A women's get-together, coffee-klatsch, girl-talk. ◆*Они устраивают бабешник в среду.* "They're having a girl-talk session on Wednesday."

БА́БКИ, ба́бок, *pl.* Money. ◆*На эти бабки ничего сейчас не купишь.* "You can't get anything for that money any more." ●**Отбива́ть/отби́ть ба́бки,** see under **отбива́ть.**

БАБЛО́, -а, *n.* Money, cash (from "бабки," money). ◆*Без бабла сейчас ни умереть, ни родиться.* "Nowadays you can neither die nor be born without money."

БА́БОЧКА: Ночна́я ба́бочка, see under **ночна́я.**

БАБУИ́Н, -а, *m., joc.* A woman. (Playing on ба́ба and бабуин, "baboon." ◆*Этот бабуин — страшна как смерть.* "That 'baboon' is ugly as hell."

БА́БУШКА, -и, *f., homosexual.* An elderly homosexual (lit., a grandmother).

БАБЦА́, -ы́, *f., rude.* A woman. ◆*А это что за бабца?* "Who's that woman?"

БАБЬЁ, -я́, *n., collect., neg.* Women. ◆*Собралось вчера одно бабьё, начались сразу сплетни.* "As soon as the women got together yesterday they started up with the gossip."

БАГА́ЖНИК, -а, *m., joc.* Rear end, behind (lit., trunk of a car). ◆*Убери свой багажник, сесть негде.* "Move your behind; there's no room to sit."

БА́ЗА, -ы, *f., crim.* **1.** A (thieves') den. ◆*Пойдём на базу, там выпьем.* "Let's go back to base-camp and have a drink." **2.** A powder for throwing into the eyes of pursuers (typically made of ground tobacco and pepper). ◆*На всякий случай возьми с собой базу.* "Take some 'baza' with you just in case."

БАЗА́Р, -а, *m., neg.* Noise, commotion. ◆*Кончай базар, ничего не слышно.* "Cut out the noise. I can't hear myself think."

БАЗА́Р-ВОКЗА́Л, -а, *m., collect., joc.* Lit., bazaar-station. **1.** A mess, a dirty place. ◆*Давай уберём этот базар-вокзал.* "Let's clean up this pigsty." **2.** Chatter, empty talk. ◆*Надоел ваш базар-вокзал, пора спать.* "Enough of your yakkety-yak, it's time to go to sleep."

БАЗА́РИТЬ/ПОБАЗА́РИТЬ. Cf. **база́р.** **1.** To quarrel, argue. ◆*Они уже базарят полдня.* "They've been arguing half the day already." **2.** To talk, converse. ◆*О чём базарите?* "What are you guys talking about here?"

БАЗА́РНЫЙ, -ая, -ое. Cf. **база́р. 1.** Noisy, disorderly. ◆*На такие базарные сборища я не ходок.* "I don't like this sort of noisy gathering." **2.** Quarrelsome, hostile. ◆*Ну раз пошли базарные разговоры, жди драки.* "Once the angry words start there are sure to be fistfights."

БАЗЛ, -а, *m., youth.* An argument, a loud conversation. ◆*За вашим базлом ничего не слышно.* "I can't hear a thing over your yelling."

БАЗЛА́НИТЬ/ЗАБАЗЛА́НИТЬ, *neg.* To yell, bawl (cf. **базл**). ◆*Хватит базланить, не глухой!* "Stop yelling. I'm not deaf!"

БАЗЛА́ТЬ/ЗАБАЗЛА́ТЬ, *neg.* See **базла́нить.**

БА́ЙДА, -ы, *f.* Nonsense, fantasy; чушь,

ерунда. ♦*Твоя байда всем надоела, никаких пришельцев не было и нет.* "We're sick and tired of your bullshit! There aren't any aliens and there never were."

БАЙКА́Л, -а, *m., crim.* Weak tea (from Lake Baykal, a large, clear lake in Siberia). ♦*Завари чай, да не делай Байкал, как в прошлый раз.* "Put up some tea, but don't make 'Baykal' like last time."

БАК: Забива́ть/заби́ть ба́ки, see under **забива́ть.**

БА́КЕНЫ, -ов, *pl.* Sideburns (by wordplay on бакен, "buoy," and бакенбарды, "sideburns"). ♦*Подровняй бакены, они разные.* "Even up your sideburns, one side is longer than the other."

БАКЛАЖА́Н, -а, *m., rude.* Penis (lit., an eggplant). ♦*Баклажан у тебя вырос, а ума не прибавилось.* "You've got an adult penis but an infantile mind."

БАКЛА́Н, -а, *m., neg.* **1.** *crim.* A hooligan, a rude or thuggish person. ♦*Эх вы, бакланы, у вас одни драки на уме.* "Hey, you thugs, brawling is the only thing you've got on your mind." **2.** *south.* A provincial; an ignoramus. ♦*О чём говорить с таким бакланом, как ты.* "What can a person talk about with a country bumpkin like you!"

БАКС, -а, *m.* A dollar; money (from Eng. "bucks"). ♦*Баксы нужны до зарезу.* "I need some money very badly."

БАКШИ́Ш, -а, *m.* **1.** A bribe (from Persian). ♦*Если хочешь, чтобы он помог тебе, без бакшиша к нему не ходи.* "If you want him to help you, you'd better bring him a tip." **2.** *Army.* The explosion of an enemy shell (lit., gift). ♦*Еще один бакшиш, но далеко, лепят наугад.* "There's another gift, but it's far off— just aimless shelling."

БА́ЛА, -ы, *f., crim.* Bread. ♦*Садись, ешь; вот бала, сало.* "Sit down and eat — here's some bread and sausage."

БАЛАБА́С, -а, *m., crim.* Sausage. ♦*Передай своим, пусть пришлют кило балабаса.* "Tell the folks to send me a kilo of sausage."

БАЛАБО́Л, -а, *m., neg.* A babbler, liar. ♦*Не верь этому балаболу!* "Don't believe that liar."

БАЛАБО́ЛИТЬ/ПОБАЛАБО́ЛИТЬ, *joc. or neg.* To babble, to talk nonsense. ♦*Тебе бы только балаболить.* "You just like to run off at the mouth."

БАЛАБО́ЛКА, -и, *m. & f., neg.* Someone who babbles a lot. ♦*Не слушай ты эту балаболку!* "Don't be taken in by that babbler."

БАЛА́КАТЬ/ПОБАЛА́КАТЬ, *joc.* To talk, have a conversation (from Ukr. балакать). ♦*Отойдём, побалакать надо.* "Let's step outside; I need to have a talk with you."

БАЛАМУ́Т, -а, *m., neg.* Someone who stirs up trouble, a practical joker, a tease, a telltale. ♦*Что ещё придумал этот баламут?* "What prank has that joker thought up this time?"

БАЛА́Н, -а, *crim.* Timber, logs. ♦*Скоро пошлют нас баланы катать, там не сахар.* "They're sending us to roll logs down the river — that's no picnic."

БАЛА́НДА, -ы, *f., neg.* Bad-tasting food, soup. ♦*Сама ешь эту баланду, кто так готовит!* "Eat that stuff yourself! That's no way to cook."

БАЛДА́, -ы́, *f., crim.* **1.** Drugs, marijuana (from **балде́ть**). ♦*У тебя балда неплохая, где брал?* "Your dope is pretty good — where did you get it?" **2.** The moon. ♦*Балды нет, ничего не видно.* "There's no moon; you can't see a thing." •**Без балды́,** *idiom.* Seriously, without kidding. ♦*Я говорю без балды.* "I'm not kidding about this."

БАЛДЁЖ, -а, *m.* Cf. **балде́ть. 1.** A drinking bout, drinking party. ♦*Вчера у нас был балдёж до ночи.* "Last night we drank until the small hours." **2.** *pred. use.* Something excellent or outstanding, someone impressive or pleasing. ♦*У него все концерты — сплошной балдёж!* "All his concerts are terrific."

БАЛДЁЖНИК, -а, *m., neg.* A drunkard or drug addict (cf. **балде́ть**). ♦*Опять этот балдёжник дома не ночевал.* "That drunk didn't come home again last night."

БАЛДЁЖНЫЙ, -ая, -ое. Good, excellent. ♦*Сейчас балдёжная погода, идём погуляем.* "The weather's gorgeous — let's take a walk."

БАЛДЕ́НЬ, -я, *m., neg.* A nickname for the rightist newspaper *День,* (by wordplay on балда, "blockhead"). ♦*От Балденя обалдеть можно, всякую чушь несут.* "The Balden can drive you crazy with all the nonsense they print!"

БАЛДЕ́ТЬ/ЗАБАЛДЕ́ТЬ. 1. To get drunk. ♦*Ты совсем забалдел, иди домой.* "You're completely drunk. You'd better go home." **2.** To be ecstatic, enraptured. ♦*Я от его песен балдею.* "I'm crazy about his songs."

БАЛДО́ХА, -и, *f., crim.* The sun (cf. **балда́ 2.**). ♦*Пока балдоха светит, надо работать.* "We've got to do the job while the sun's shining."

БАЛЕРИ́НА, -ы, *f., crim.* A set of thieves' tools (lit., a ballerina). ♦*Возьми балерину, пригодится.* "Take the 'ballerina'; we'll need it."

БАЛЕРУ́Н, -а, *m.* **1.** A male ballet dancer. ♦*Он работает в оперном театре, он — балерун.* "He's a dancer with the opera company." **2.** *neg.* A light-minded, unserious person. ♦*Этот балерун работать не любит.* "That flighty fellow doesn't like to work."

БАЛКО́Н, -а, *m., joc.* A large behind, large buttocks. ♦*У неё не зад, а балкон.* "That's not a behind she's got — it's a balcony."

БАЛЛО́Н, -а, *m., business.* **1.** Credit to be returned in full (not by installments) (lit., balloon). ♦*Мы наберём к среде деньги, надо весь баллон отдать.* "We'll raise the money by Wednesday, when the whole balloon comes due." **2.** Big belly, potbelly (lit., container, tank). ♦*Худеть надо, баллон в штаны не влезает.* "I've got to lose weight; I can't get my pants up over my potbelly."

БАЛТИ́ЙСКИЕ ТРУСЫ́. See **семе́йные трусы́.**

БАЛТИМО́Р КЭ́МЭЛ, *idiom, youth, joc.* The name of a Russian brand of cheap cigarettes. Lit., "Baltimore Camel," giving an English-sounding twist to the brand-name Беломор-канал, "White Sea Canal." ♦*У меня только Балтимор Кэмэл, будешь?* "All I've got are some 'Baltimore Camels,' would you like one?

БАМБУ́КОВЫЙ, -ая, -ое, *joc.* Stupid, foolish (by wordplay on дундук, "fool," and бамбук, "bamboo"). ♦*Давно не слышал таких бамбуковых речей.* "That's the stupidest thing I've heard in ages."

БАМО́Н, -а, *m., crim.* A gathering of homosexuals. ♦*Когда у гомиков бамон собирается?* "When are the gays having their get-together?"

БА́МПЕР, -а, *m., neg.* Buttocks (lit., bumper of a car). ♦*Весь бампер отсидел, пока к вам доехал.* "The trip to your place took so long that my behind fell asleep."

БАН, -а, *m., crim.* A train station (from Ger. "Bahn"). ♦*Встретимся на бане в семь.* "Let's meet at the station at seven."

БАНА́Н, -а, *m., youth.* **1.** A penis (lit., banana). ♦*Чем ты женщин берёшь? У тебя кроме банана ничего нет.* "How do you manage to attract women? You've got nothing going for you but your 'banana.'" **2.** A bad grade (a 1 or 2 in the five-point system). ♦*Как тебе удалось нахватать столько бананов?* "How did you manage to get so many poor grades?"

БАНА́НЫ, -ов, *pl., obs.* Trousers that taper at the ankles (lit., bananas). ♦*Сейчас никто не носит бананы.* "No one wears those banana pants any more."

БАНА́НЫ В УША́Х, *idiom, joc.* Of someone with poor hearing. Lit., Bananas in the ears. This is the punchline of the following joke: One man approached another in the street: "You've got bananas in your ears!" The other said, "What?!" "You've got bananas in your ears!" The other took the bananas out of his ears and said: "Excuse me, I can't hear you. I've got bananas in my ears!"

БА́НБЕР, -а, *m., crim.* A crowbar for

break-ins. ◆*Подай банбер, замок не могу открыть.* "Give me the crowbar — I can't open the lock."

БА́НДА, -ы, *f., youth.* A rock band (play on Eng. "band" and Russian банда, "gang"). ◆*Кто играет в вашей банде?* "Who's playing in your band?"

БАНДА́Н, -а, *m., youth.* A neckerchief, bandana.

БАНДЕРЛО́Г, -а, *m., joc.* A monkey (from Kipling's *Mowgli*). ◆*Вы, бандерлоги, хорош кричать.* "Stop carrying on like a bunch of monkeys!"

БАНДЕРО́ЛЬ, -и, *f., crim.* A roll of bills, bankroll (lit., a postal parcel) ◆*Ты что, разбогател? Я заметил, у тебя бандеролей штуки три.* "What happened, you struck it rich? I noticed you were carrying three rolls of bills."

БА́НДЕРША, -и, *f., neg.* The madam of a whorehouse or the female proprietor of a place for gambling, drinking, and so on; generally, a woman of dubious respectability. ◆*Чтоб я эту бандершу в моём доме не видел!* "I don't want to see that madam in my house."

БАНДИ́ТСКАЯ ПУ́ЛЯ ДОСТА́ЛА, *idiom, joc.* Lit., "I was hit by a bandit's bullet"; used as a banteringly evasive explanation of a wound. ◆*У тебя голова забинтована, что с тобой? — Бандитская пуля достала.* "How come your head is bandaged like that? — Oh, I was hit by a bandit's bullet."

БАНДУ́РА, -ы, *f.* A big, heavy thing (from бандура, a Ukrainian musical instrument). ◆*Ну и бандура этот шкаф, как ты думаешь затащить его в дом?* "This chest is a back-breaker! How do you plan to get it into the house?"

БА́НИТЬ/ПОБА́НИТЬ, *crim.* To interrogate (lit., to give someone a steam bath). ◆*Нас банили четыре часа, но мы молчок.* "They grilled us for four hours, but we held our tongues."

БА́НКА, -и, *f.* A bottle of liquor. ◆*Идём ко мне, у меня есть две банки.* "Let's go to my place; I've got two bottles." •**Под ба́нкой,** *idiom.* Drunk. ◆*Вчера ты сильно был под банкой.* "Yesterday you were really stewed." **Держа́ть ба́нку,** see **держа́ть вес** under **держа́ть. Раздави́ть ба́нку/ба́ночку,** see **раздави́ть.**

БА́НКИ, ба́нок, *pl., youth.* A woman's breasts (lit., jars, jugs). ◆*Посмотри, какие у неё банки!* "Look at the boobs on her!"

БАНКИ́Р, -а, *m., homosexual.* 1. A rich lover. 2. An active homosexual.

БА́ННАЯ ДЕ́ВКА, -и, *f., idiom, homosexual.* A homosexual who looks for partners in public baths.

БА́ННО-СТАКА́ННЫЙ ДЕНЬ, *idiom, army.* A bath day (lit., a bath and glass day, used as a reference to the possibility of a drink after bathing). ◆*Завтра банно-стаканный день, надо затариться пивом.* "Tomorrow's a bath day, we've got to stock up on beer."

БА́НЯ, -и, *f., crim.* Interrogation (lit., steam bath). ◆*Завтра у него баня, подскажи, что ему говорить.* "He's going in for a grilling tomorrow. What do you think he should say?"

БАОБА́Б, -а, *m., joc.* A fool (lit., a baobab-tree). ◆*Ничего ты этому баобабу не втолкуешь, не тот случай.* "There's no way that baobab will understand what you're trying to say."

БАРАБА́Н, -а, *m., joc.* A belly (lit., a drum). ◆*Набили свои барабаны, марш спать!* "Okay, you've stuffed your bellies, now off to bed!"

БАРАБА́НИТЬ/ОТБАРАБА́НИТЬ. To serve in the army (lit., to drum). ◆*Я на границе отбарабанил 10 лет, хочу служить поближе к дому.* "I served for ten years as a frontier guard, now I'd like to serve closer to home."

БАРАБА́ННАЯ ПА́ЛОЧКА, *idiom, crim., neg.* A woman who has a venereal disease (lit., a drumstick). ◆*Я давно подозреваю, что она — барабанная палочка.* "I've suspected for a long time that she's got the clap."

БАРАБА́НЩИК, -а, *m., youth.* An informer, betrayer. ◆*Мы всё равно узнаем, кто здесь барабанщик.* "We're going to find out who's the informer here."

БАРА́Н, -а, *m., neg.* A stupid and stubborn person (lit., a ram). ♦*Ты бараном был, бараном и остался; тебя трудно в чём-либо убедить.* "You've always been a mule and you still are; it's hard to convince you of anything."

БАРА́НКА, -и, *f.* Lit., a small bagel. **1.** *drivers.* A steering wheel. ♦*Он всю жизнь за баранкой.* "He's been behind the wheel his whole life" (i.e., he's always worked as a driver). **2.** *sports.* A zero score. ♦*Вы хорошо выступили, а у нас — баранка за неявку.* "You did well, but we were given a zero by disqualification." •**Крути́ть бара́нку,** see under **крути́ть³. Получа́ть/получи́ть бара́нку,** see under **получа́ть.**

БАРА́НКИ ГНУ!, *idiom, joc.* A rhyming phrase used in evasive response to a question introduced by "Ну!" (lit., I'm bending bagels). ♦*Ну, и зачем она тебе нужна? — Ну, ну, барабки гну!* "What you you need her for?!" — "It's none of your business."

БАРА́ТЬСЯ/ПОБАРА́ТЬСЯ, *rude.* **1.** To copulate. ♦*Хватит бараться, пора за ум браться.* "Enough screwing around — it's time to get down to business." **2.** To be deeply occupied with something, to work on a difficult matter. ♦*Устал я бараться с этими бумагами.* "I'm exhausted from messing around with these papers."

БАРБО́С, -а, *m., crim., neg.* A prosecutor (lit., a mutt, mongrel). ♦*Меня опять к барбосу вызывают.* "They've summoned me before the prosecutor again."

БАРДА́К, -ка́, *m., neg.* **1.** A whorehouse. ♦*Сейчас в Москве много бардаков.* "There are a lot of whorehouses in Moscow nowadays." **2.** A disorderly place, a mess. ♦*Что за бардак у тебя здесь?* "What a pigsty you're living in here!" •**Разводи́ть/развести́ (устра́ивать/устро́ить) барда́к,** see under **разводи́ть.**

БАРДА́ЧИТЬ/НАБАРДА́ЧИТЬ, *neg.* **1.** To make a mess. ♦*Кто здесь набардачил?* "Who made this mess here?" **2.** To have a wild party, esp. with sex.

♦*Они бардачат у него на квартире.* "They're having a bash over at his apartment."

БАРДА́ЧНЫЙ, -ая, -ое, *neg.* **1.** Dirty, disorderly. ♦*Почему такой бардачный вид, почисти одежду.* "Why are you looking so sloppy? Fix up your clothes." **2.** Disorganized, absentminded. ♦*Человек он бардачный, ничего не помнит.* "What an absentminded fellow! He never remembers anything."

БАРДАЧО́К, бардачка́, *m.* The glove compartment of a car (from бардак, something completely disorganized). ♦*Бардачок забит всякой дрянью, не мог найти даже права, когда меня остановили.* "I had so much junk in my glove box that I couldn't find my registration when I got pulled over."

БАРКАШИ́, -е́й, *pl., neg.* Members of the rightist nationalistic organization led by A. Barkashov (by wrorldplay on **алка́ш**).

БА́РМА, -ы, *f., youth, neg.* Cheap wine, home brew. ♦*У нас бармы — хоть залейся!* "All we've got is cheap wine, but at least there's plenty of it."

БАРМАЛЕ́Й, -е́я, *m., school.* An unpleasant person (lit., Бармалей, the name of a character in a fairy tale by K. Chukovsky). ♦*Этот бармалей не учит, а мучит.* "That nasty guy is a torturer, not a teacher."

БАРСУ́К, -ка́, *m., crim.* **1.** A young homosexual (lit., a badger). ♦*Ты что, в барсуки записался?* "What's with you — have you joined up with the 'badgers'?" **2.** An enemy sharpshooter (lit., a badger). ♦*За барсуком наши охотятся уже две недели, всё не могут выследить.* "Our men have been tracking that badger for two weeks, but they haven't managed to flush him out."

БАРУ́ХА, -и, *f., youth, neg.* A woman of loose behavior, an easily available woman, a prostitute. ♦*Ты знаешь вон ту баруху?* "Do you know that floozy over there?"

БА́РХАТНАЯ РЕВОЛЮ́ЦИЯ, *idiom.* Recent bloodless revolutions in former Soviet Republics such as Ukraine and

Georgia (lit., Velvet Revolution, referring to "soft" revolutions or revolutions without bloodshed).

БАРЫ́ГА, -и, *m., peg.* **1.** A vendor, merchant. ♦ *Купи сигареты у того барыги.* "Buy some cigarettes from that huckster over there."

БАСМА́Ч, -á, *m., peg.* An inhabitant of Central Asia (lit., a bandit).

БАСТИ́ЛИЯ, -ии, *f.* The skyscraper of Moscow State University.

БАСЫ́, -óв, *pl., youth.* A woman's breasts (lit., bass notes, as on an accordion). ♦ *У неё басы что надо.* "She's got quite a pair of boobs."

БАТЛ, -a, *m., youth.* A bottle (from Eng. "bottle"). ♦ *У нас как раз на батл вина.* "We've got just enough money for a bottle of wine."

БА́ТНИК, -a, *m., youth.* See **ба́тон.**

БАТО́Н, -a, *m., youth.* **1.** A father. ♦ *Батон дома?* "Is your dad home?" **2.** A passerby, outsider, bystander. ♦ *Откуда этот батон к нам прибился?* "Where did that guy come from? He's not one of us." •**Кроши́ть бато́н,** see under **кроши́ть. 3.** A rubber police truncheon (lit., a French bagette). ♦ *Тебя еще не отоваривали батоном, того ты такой смелый.* "You've never tasted the 'long loaf,' that's why you're so brave."

БА́ТОН(-ДА́УН), -a, *m., youth, obs.* A button-down shirt (from Eng. "button-down"). ♦ *У тебя неплохой батон.* "That's a nice button-down shirt you're wearing."

БА́ТЬКА, -и, *m.* Ukr. **1.** A father. ♦ *Твой батька не болеет?* "Is your dad sick?" **2.** A boss, manager. ♦ *Наш батька повысил нам зарплату.* "Our boss gave us a raise."

БА́ХАТЬ/БА́ХНУТЬ. To drink. ♦ *Давай за тебя бахнем.* "Let's drink to your health."

БА́ЦАТЬ/СБА́ЦАТЬ. 1. To play (a musical instrument) (from бац, the sound of striking). ♦ *Сбацай нам что-нибудь весёлое.* "Play us something cheerful." **2.** To dance. ♦ *Этот танец я сбацаю с*

подругой. "I'm going to dance this one with my girlfriend." **3.** To make, prepare (food). ♦ *Мы сейчас сбацаем что-нибудь закусить.* "Let's make ourselves something to eat."

БАЦИ́ЛЛА, -ы, *f., youth.* A cheap type of cigarette. ♦ *Дай хоть одну бациллу, у меня все кончились.* "Let me just have a 'bacilla' — I'm completely out of cigarettes." •**Баци́лла с ни́ппелем,** *idiom, youth, joc.* A filter cigarette (from ниппель, a mechanical nipple.) ♦ *У тебя бациллы с ниппелем? Дай покурить.* "Do you have filter cigarettes? Let's have a smoke."

БАШ, -a, *m., youth.* Profit, income. ♦ *Твой баш — лимон.* "Your share of the profits is a million rubles."

БАШКА́, -и́, *f.* A head. ♦ *Что-то у меня башка трещит.* "I've got a splitting headache." •**Секи́(р) башка́ кому́-л.,** *idiom.* (Someone) is in hot water, is in danger of severe punishment (lit., cut off someone's head; a grammarless phrase mimicking Tatar language). ♦ *Мне за это секир башка.* "Uh-oh — it's going to be off-with-my-head for this."

БА́ШЛИ, -ей, *pl.* Money. ♦ *Зачем тебе башли?* "What do you need money for?"

БАШЛЯ́ТЬ/ЗАБАШЛЯ́ТЬ, *crim.* To pay. ♦ *Сколько ты забашлял за костюм?* "How much did you pay for that suit?"

БА́ШНЯ, -и, *f.* **1.** A tall building (lit., a tower). ♦ *Он живёт в башне около рынка.* "He lives in that tower near the market." **2.** A tall person. ♦ *Он по сравнению с этой башней прямо карлик.* "He's a midget compared with that 'tower'." **3.** Head (lit., tower). ♦ *Башню береги, здесь низкие потолки.* "Watch your head; the ceilings are low in here." •**Башню снесло,** *idiom* (lit., to lose one's tower, head). О не нормальном поведении, о безумных поступках. About abnormal or crazy behavior. ♦ *У него, что, башню снесло, кто за грибами ночью ходит?* "What's with him, has he lost his head, who goes to pick mushrooms in the middle of the night?"

БАЯ́Н, -a, *m., crim.* A syringe (lit.,

an accordion). ♦*Дай мне свой баян, а то мой сломался.* "Let me have your syringe; mine is broken."

БЕ́ГАТЬ¹/ПОБЕ́ГАТЬ по со́ннику, *idiom, crim.* To rob sleeping passengers at night in railroad stations or trains. ♦*Он ещё бегает по соннику?* "Is he still specializing in robbery of sleeping passengers?"

БЕ́ГАТЬ²/СБЕ́ГАТЬ по-бы́строму. See **ходи́ть/сходи́ть по-бы́строму** under **хо́дить.**

БЕГУ́Н, -а, *m., business.* A messenger in the stock exchange (lit., runner). ♦*Пошли бегуна к Газпрому, беру бумаги на 10,000.* "Send a gofer over to Gasprom, I want 10,000 rubles' worth of shares."

БЕДА́, -ы́, *f., crim.* Drugs, narcotics (lit., troubles). ♦*Беда кончилась, надо ещё прикупить.* "We're out of dope; we'll have to buy some more."

БЕЗ БУЛДЫ́, *idiom.* Joking aside, in all seriousness. ♦*Ладно, без булды, где ты был вчера?* "Okay, all joiking aside, where were you last night, really?"

БЕЗ БУМА́ЖКИ ТЫ КАКА́ШКА, *idiom.* "Without documents you're shit." ♦*Чтобы получить паспорт, у меня нет всех документов. — Да, без бумажки ты какашка.* "I haven't got all the papers necessary for getting a passport. — Well, without documents, you're shit."

БЕЗ КА́ЙФА НЕ́ТУ ЛА́ЙФА, *idiom.* "Without fun there's no life" (cf. **кайф**). ♦*Что с тобой? Кажется, у тебя одни гульки на уме? – Без кайфа нету лайфа.* "What's with you? It seems all you think about is having fun. — Without fun there's no life."

БЕЗ ПО́Л-ЛИ́ТРА НЕ РАЗОБРА́ТЬ-СЯ, *idiom, joc.* Lit., "It can't be understood without half a liter (of liquor)." Used in protest at difficulties, complications. ♦*Вы так напутали в чертежах, что теперь без пол-литра не разобраться.* "You've made such a mess of the drawings that now I can't understand them without half a liter."

БЕЗ ПОНЯ́ТИЯ, *idiom.* Stupid, ignorant. ♦*Он без понятия в сельском хозяйстве.* "In agriculture he's an ignoramus."

БЕЗ ПЯТИ́ КАК СПЁРЛИ (КАК СВИ́СТНУЛИ), *idiom, joc.* Lit., Five minutes to when-they-stole-it. Used in reply to "What time is it?" in the sense "I don't have a watch, I don't know."

БЕЗ РУБА́ШКИ — БЛИЖЕ К МА́ШКЕ, *idiom, rude.* A rhyming phrase referring to sexual relations. Lit., Without one's shirt one it's closer to Mary, playing on the proverbial expression Своя рубашка — ближе к телу, "One's own property/interests come first" (lit., one's own shirt is closest to one's body). ♦*Ну как там у них, без рубашки — ближе к Машке?* "What's going on between them? Is it a case of 'The less clothes, the closer to Mary'?"

БЕЗ ШУ́МА И ПЫ́ЛИ, *idiom.* **1.** With caution, discreetly (lit., without noise and dust). ♦*Этих мафиози надо взять без шума и пыли.* "We have to take every precaution in arresting those mafiosi." **2.** Carefully, accurately, precisely. ♦*Вы всё провернули без шума и пыли.* "You negotiated that business just right."

БЕЗАЛКОГО́ЛЬНАЯ БОРМОТУ́ХА, *idiom, obs.* A nickname for M. Gorbachev (lit., alcohol-free cheap wine).

БЕЗАНДЕСТЕ́НД, *indecl., pred., youth.* Ignorant, incompetent (from Eng. "understand"). ♦*Я в физике безандестенд.* "In physics I'm an ignoramus."

БЕЗАРБУ́ЗИЕ, -я, *n., joc.* Disorder (lit., watermelonlessness, by wordplay on арбуз, "watermelon," and безобразие, "disorder"). ♦*Что за безарбузие вы здесь устроили? Соберите игрушки и идите обедать.* "What a mess you've made here! Pick up your toys and come to dinner."

БЕЗБА́ШЕННЫЙ, -ая, -ое. Crazy, reckless (lit., without a tower). ♦*Не пойму, почему молодёжь такая безбашенная пошла?* "I don't get it. Why have teenagers become so reckless?"

БЕЗВО́РКОВЫЙ, -ая. Unemployed (from Eng. "work"). ♦*И давно ты безворковый?* "Have you been out of work for long?"

БЁЗДНИК, -а, *m., youth.* Birthday (by wordplay from Eng. "birthday" and праздник, "holiday"). ◆*У тебя сегодня бёздник?* "Is today your birthday?"

БЕЗДО́ННЫЙ, -ого, *m., crim., neg.* A tirelessly active, unrelenting homosexual (in prison life) (lit., bottomless). ◆*Сейчас этот бездонный опять приставать начнёт.* "Here's that bottomless pit making advances again."

БЕЗДОРО́ЖЬЕ, -я, *n.* Silliness, stupidity (lit., impassable roads). ◆*Но это полное бездорожье, — в болоте копать траншеи.* "But this is sheer idiocy! We're digging trenches in a swamp!"

БЕЗЛОША́ДНЫЙ, -ая, -ое. 1. Poor, without resources (lit., horseless). ◆*Он всё продал, теперь безлошадный, ни дачи, ни дома.* "He's sold everything, now he's a complete pauper: no house, no dacha." **2.** Without one's car. ◆*Сегодня я безлошадный, выпить можно.* "I'm not on wheels today, so I can have a few drinks."

БЕЗМАЗНЯ́К, -а́, *pred. use, youth, neg.* Something pointless, useless (cf. **ма́за**). ◆*Туда ехать — безмазняк!* "There's no sense in going there."

БЕЗМА́ЗОВЫЙ, -ая, -ое, *youth, neg.* **1.** Useless, pointless. ◆*Это безмазовая поездка.* "This is a pointless trip." **2.** Bad, unpleasant. ◆*Подруга у тебя — безмазовая.* "Your girlfriend is not a nice person." **3.** Unlucky. ◆*У нас совсем безмазовый день.* "We've had terrible luck today."

БЕЗНАДЁГА, -и, *f., youth.* A hopeless situation. ◆*Насчёт женитьбы у меня полная безнадёга.* "I haven't got a chance of marriage."

БЕЗНА́Л, -а, *m.* A non-cash transaction (by bank transfer, check, credit card, etc.) (from безналичный, not in cash [cf. **наличма́н**]; in Russia it is usual for all private transactions, even the purchase of a car or home, to be conducted in cash). ◆*Я расплачусь безналом.* "I'll pay you on account."

БЕ́ЙЦЫ, -о́в, *m., youth, rude.* Testicles (from Heb. "beytzim," eggs; cf. **я́йца**). ◆*Тебе надо бейцы оторвать за твои дела.* "You deserve to have your balls

ripped out for what you've done." •**Крути́ть бе́йцы,** see **крути́ть я́йца** under **яйцо́**.

БЕЛИ́НСКИЙ, -ого, *m., youth & army.* White bread (by wordplay on белый, "white," and Белинский, "Belinsky"). ◆*Сегодня праздник, — значит, будет белинский на обед.* "Today's a holiday — there'll be white bread for dinner."

БЕ́ЛОЕ — НЕСМЕ́ЛОЕ, КРА́СНОЕ — НАПРА́СНОЕ, ВО́ДКА — В СЕ́РД-ЦЕ ПРЯМА́Я НАВО́ДКА, *idiom, joc.* A rhyming phase used in praise of vodka (lit., white wine is timid, red wine is in vain, but vodka goes straight to the heart).

БЕ́ЛОЧКА, -и, *f. and m.* **1.** A fussy person (lit., a little squirrel). ◆*Сегодня я, как белочка, бегаю весь день, то в детский сад, то за покупками, то на работу.* "I'm running around like a squirrel today — taking the kids to kindergarten, doing the shopping, and going to work." • **Бе́лочка больна́я,** *idiom, usu. in women's speech.* Mad, crazy (lit., a sick squirrel). ◆*А я всё работаю, стираю, убираю, как белочка больная, ни минуты отдыха.* "Here I am madly working, cleaning, doing laundry… not a minute's rest." **2.** Delirium tremens, the shakes (from белая горячка, a wordplay on "белочка," a squirrel, and "белый," white). ◆*У него белочка, всю ночь кричал, командовал.* "He's got the DTs—he's been yelling commands all night."

БЕ́ЛОЧНИК -а, *m., crim.* A thief specializing in stealing linens off clotheslines (from бельё, "linens"). This specialty has been particularly lucrative at times of linen shortages, as in the early 1980s. ◆*Это работа белочника, унесли всё бельё со двора.* "This is a professional job — all the linens have been stolen from the yard."

БЕЛУ́ГА, -и, *f., crim.* Silver. (Playing on белый, "white," and белуга, "beluga"). ◆*Ножи из белуги?* "Are the knives silver?"

БЕ́ЛЫЕ КОЛГО́ТКИ, *idiom, army.* A female mercenary sharpshooter in Chechnya (lit., white pantyhose; from a rumor that such mercenaries wore white panty-hose). ♦*Если русские солдаты ловят белые колготки, — убивают на месте.* "Whenever Russian soldiers catch a female sharpshooter, they kill her on the spot."

БÉЛЫЕ НÓЧИ, idiom. Poorly brewed, weak tea (lit., white nights, referring to a period of summertime in Northern Russia where it remains light outside almost all night long). ♦*Разве это чай, ни цвета, ни вкуса, белые ночи, одним словом.* "That's not tea; it doesn't have any color to it, let alone taste. The best word for that is 'white nights.'"

БÉЛЫЙ МЕДВÉДЬ, idiom. A mixture of vodka and champagne (lit., a white bear). ♦*Приготовь «белый медведь», хочет-ся опьянеть.* "Make a 'white bear' and let's get drunk."

БÉЛЬМА, бельм, pl., rude. Eyes (lit., white spots, cataracts). ♦*Бельма у неё злые.* "She's got nasty eyes." •**Выка́ты-вать/вы́катить бÉльма,** see under **вы-ка́тывать. Убира́ть/убра́ть бÉльма,** see under **убира́ть.**

БЕМС. 1. interj. Exclamation at something unexpected. ♦*Стали играть в карты, бемс, — сто рублей как не бывало.* "We started a card game, and, poof! — I lost a hundred rubles." **2.** m., indecl. Tumult, alarm, ruckus. ♦*Вчера на танцах такой бемс устроили, милиция растас-кивала.* "At the dance last night there was such a row that the police came."

БЕНЦ, indecl. **1.** Noise, disorder. ♦*Бенц не поднимай, может быть, доку-менты еще найдутся.* "Don't start car-rying on! We may still find your papers." **2.** Bad luck, trouble. ♦*Тут, бенц, два солдата с автоматами сбежали из части.* "And then, shit! A couple of sol-diers with automatics just ran out of our unit."

БЕРДÁНА, -ы, f., crim. A package sent to a prisoner from relatives or friends. ♦*Что у тебя в бердане? Колбаса есть?* "What's in your package? Is there any sausage?"

БЕРЁЗА, -ы, f., collect. youth, neg., obs. A citizens' auxiliary police squad; the mem-bers of such a squad (lit., a birch tree). ♦*На улицах сегодня берёзы много.* "There are a lot of 'birches' patrolling the streets today."

БЕРЁЗКА, -и, f., obs. In Soviet times, a store selling goods for hard currency (lit., little birch tree). ♦*"Берёзки" закрылись в 1988.* "The 'beryozkas' were closed in 1988."

БЕРЕЗНЯ́К, -а, m. Girls, chicks (from берёза, birch tree). ♦*А березняк на тусне будет?* "Will there be chicks at the party?"

БЕРЁЗОВЫЙ, -ая, -ое, obs. Purchased for hard currency in a beryozka (cf. **берёзка**). ♦*Это берёзовый видик.* "This video player is from a beryozka."

БЕРÉЧЬ/УБЕРÉЧЬ ФÁЗУ, idiom. To avoid trouble, to stay calm (lit., to watch the electric phase). ♦*Не ссорься ты с женой каждый день, береги фазу.* "Don't fight with your wife every day, it's bad for your nerves."

БЕРМУ́ДЫ, -ов, pl., youth. A type of swimming trunks (from Eng. "Bermuda shorts"). ♦*У тебя бермуды что надо!* "That's a nice pair of Bermudas you're wearing!"

БÉРТА, -ы, f., homosexual. The Belorussia Railroad Station in Moscow, as a meeting place for gays (lit., Bertha).

БЕС, -а, m., neg. A boss, director, manager (lit., devil, demon). ♦*Что это за бес поехал на "мерсе"?* "Who's that 'demon' in the Mercedes?"

БÉСКА, -и, f., army. A sailor's cap. ♦*Летом бески белые, зимой чёрные.* "In summer they wear white caps, and in winter black."

БЕСПЛÁТНИК, -а, neg. A passenger on public transportation who hasn't bought a ticket. ♦*Сейчас все в автобусах бесплатники, дорого платить.* "These days, tickets have become so expensive that everybody tries to freeload."

БЕСПЛÁТНО: За беспла́тно тебé и в лицó не плю́нут, see under **за.**

БЕСПРЕДÉЛ, -а, m., neg. Lawlessness, violence (lit., unlimitedness). ♦*У них в роте — беспредел.* "In their unit complete lawlessness reigns."

БЕСПРЕДÉЛОВО, *n.*, *indecl.*, *pred. use*, *neg.* See **беспредéл**.

БЕСПРЕДÉЛЬНЫЙ, **-ая**, **-ое**, *neg.* Illegal, immoral (cf. **беспредéл**). ♦ *Ты читал беспредельную статью о русских фашистах? О них пишут, как о героях.* "Have you read this outrageous article about the Russian Fascists, praising them as if they were heroes?"

БЕСПРЕДÉЛЬЩИК, **-а**, *m.*, *neg.* A criminal, lawbreaker (cf. **беспредéл**). ♦ *Этот беспредельщик и убить может.* "That criminal is capable of murder."

БЕССРÓЧНЫЙ ДÉМБЕЛЬ, *idiom*, *army*. A death (lit., an indefinite discharge). ♦ *А ты не знал, он в бессрочном дембеле уже год.* "Didn't you know he was killed a year back?"

БЕТОНОМЕШÁЛКА, **-и**, *f.*, *army, joc.* A helicopter (lit., a cement mixer). ♦ *Эта бетономешалка к нам?* "Is that helicopter coming our way?"

БÉШЕНСТВО МÁТКИ, *idiom*, *neg.* Nymphomania (lit., womb madness). ♦ *У неё что, бешенство матки, на всех мужиков кидается?* "What's with her, a case of womb-madness? Look how she's throwing herself at all the guys!"

БЖÍКАТЬ/БЖÍКНУТЬ. **1.** To flick repeatedly, as a cigarette lighter. ♦ *Хватит бжикать, газ кончится.* "Stop flicking the lighter; it's running out of lighter fluid." **2.** To spray, as cologne, insect repellent. ♦ *Бжикни на меня твой одеколон.* "Spray some of your cologne on me."

БЗДЕЛÓВО, *n.*, *indecl.*, *youth, rude.* Cf. **бздеть**. **1.** Verbal abuse, insult. ♦ *На меня твоё бзделово не действует.* "Your insults don't affect me at all." **2.** Report, denunciation. ♦ *Чьё это бзделово дошло до директора?* "Who's the rat who reported to the director?"

БЗДЕТЬ/НАБЗДÉТЬ, *crim. and rude.* **1.** To fart. ♦ *Кто здесь так набздел?* "Who laid that fart?" **2.** To be afraid. ♦ *Не надо бздеть, тебе ничего не будет.* "Don't be scared — nothing's going to happen to you."

БЗДИЛОВÁТЫЙ, **-ая**, **-ое**, *rude.* Cowardly (cf. **бздеть**). ♦ *Таким бздиловатым у нас в роте делать нечего.* "There's no place for such a coward in our unit."

БЗДНУТЬ: **Ни бзднуть, ни пёрднуть**, see under **ни**.

БЗДÓШНЫЙ, **-ая**, **-ое**, *rude.* Cf. **бздеть**. **1.** Frightening, horrifying. ♦ *Это бздошный фильм.* "That's a terrifying movie." **2.** Unpleasant, repellent. ♦ *Эти бздошные речи слушать не хочу.* "I don't want to listen to your disgusting talk."

БЗДУН, **-на́**, *m.*, *rude.* **1.** One who farts. ♦ *Выгони этого бздуна, дышать нечем.* "Get that farter out of here. It's impossible to breathe." **2.** A coward. ♦ *Я этого бздуна в разведку не возьму.* "I'm not taking that chickenshit fellow on this mission."

БЗДЫК, *interj.*, *youth, neg.* Exclamation about an unexpected and unpleasant event. ♦ *А тут, бздык, она требует жениться.* "And then, out of the blue, she asked me to marry her."

БЗДЫМÓ: **Не бздымо!** *idiom*, *rude.* There's nothing to be afraid of. ♦ *Не бздымо, прорвёмся!* "Don't worry — we're going to make it!"

БÍВЕНЬ, **бивня**, *m.* Tooth (lit., tusk). ♦ *Посмотри на его бивни, он их чистит, наверное, раз в месяц.* "Get a look at those teeth! I'd be surprised if he brushed them once a month!"

БÍГОВЫЙ, **-ая**, **-ое**. Big (from Eng. "big"). ♦ *Какая биговая дача!* "What a big country house!"

БИЗНЕСВУ́МЕН, **-а**, *f.* Businesswoman (usually used ironically or with a negative connotation). ♦ *Хоть она и называет себя бизнесвуменом, но для нас непонятно, чем это она занята целый день.* "She calls herself a businesswoman but none of us can figure out what it is she does all day."

БИЗНЕСМÉНТ, **-а**, *m.* Corrupted policeman (a wordplay on "бизнесмен" and "мент," businessman and a cop). ♦ *Мне надо бизнесмента найти, за бабки без очереди техосмотр пройти.* See **мент**.

"I need to find me a dirty cop who will take a little incentive and get me my car inspection certificate without me having to stand in line." (In Russia, car inspection certificates are handled by the police).

БИКИ́ЦЕР, *adv., crim.* Quickly (from Heb./Yiddish "bekitzer"). ♦*Давай отсюда бикицер, скоро здесь будут менты.* "Let's get out of here quick; the police will be here any minute."

БИ́КСА, -ы, *f., crim.* A prostitute. ♦*Ты эту биксу знаешь? Сколько берёт?* "Do you know that prostitute? How much does she charge?"

БИКСОСЪЁМ, -а, *m.* A casual acquaintance with a woman, a pick-up (see **би́кса** and **снима́ть**). ♦*Я займусь биксосъёмом на вечер, а ты, как хочешь.* "You do whatever you like, I'm going to pick up some girls for the night."

БИ́НБЕР, -а, *m., crim.* A thieves' crowbar for forcing doors and windows. ♦*Давай бинбер, окно не открывается.* "Let me have the crowbar; I can't open the window."

БИР, -а, *m., youth.* Beer (from Eng. "beer").

БИРКО́, -á, *n., youth, joc.* Beer (from Eng. "beer"). ♦*Бирко ещё не завозили?* "Didn't they ship in any more beer?"

БИРЛЯ́ТЬ/ПОБИРЛЯ́ТЬ, *youth, joc.* To eat. ♦*Что-то бирлять хочется.* "Let's have a bite to eat."

БИССЕКТРИ́СА, -ы, *f.* A bisexual (lit., a bisector, playing on бисексуал, "bisexual").

БИТЛАЗА́, БИТЛА́З, *collect.* Long hair (from the Beatles). ♦*Даже мы, офицеры, битлаза не носим, так что придется тебе эту красоту убрать.* "Even we officers can't wear our hair that long—you'll have to trim those tresses."

БИ́ТЫЙ, -ая, -ое. Experienced, toughened by experience. ♦*Он так просто на это не пойдёт: он битый.* "He won't agree to that so easily — he's an old hand."

БИТЬ по мозга́м, *idiom, neg.* To annoy (lit., to beat in the brains). ♦*Выключи эту музыку, так и бьёт по мозгам.* "Turn off that music; it's annoying me."

БИ́ТЬСЯ, *imperf. only.* To match to, to correspond. ♦*Ты говоришь, что не трогал его, но это не бьётся с его синяками.* "You say you didn't lay a hand on him, but that doesn't square with his bruises."

БИТЮ́Г, -гá, *m., joc.* A man of strong build (lit., a type of draft horse). ♦*А ты, такой битюг, хоть бы помог!* "Why don't you give me a hand, a big strong fellow like you!"

БИЧ, -чá, *m., neg.* A vagrant (from Eng. "beachcomber"). ♦*Он давно бич, у него денег нет.* "He's been bumming around for a long time; he has no money."

БИЧЕВА́ТЬ/ЗАБИЧЕВА́ТЬ, *joc.* Cf. **бич. 1.** To be a vagabond, live as a tramp, bum around. ♦*Давно бичуете?* "Have you been bumming around like this for a long time?" **2.** To be idle, live in idleness. ♦*Ты, я вижу, бичуешь, на работу не ходишь.* "I see you're a bum; you don't go to work."

БИЧЁВКА, -и, *f., youth, neg.* A female vagabond (cf. **бич,** with play on бичёвка, a hempen rope). ♦*Ты кто такая, бичёвка, что ли?* "What are you, some kind of tramp?"

БИЧЕ́ВСКИЙ, -ая, -ое. Vagabond (cf. **бич**). ♦*Надоела мне бичевская жизнь.* "I'm tired of this hobo life."

БЛАТ, -а, *m.* **1.** Secret thieves' language, thieves' cant, argot. ♦*А ты этот блат знаешь?* "Do you understand this argot?" **2.** Connections, influence, protection. ♦*У меня есть блат в магазине: достану всё, что надо.* "I've got connections at that store; I can get whatever I need there." •**По бла́ту,** *idiom.* Illegally, by circumventing rules or laws through personal influence, bribes, and so on. ♦*Меня устроят по блату на работу, я не волнуюсь.* "I'm not worried — I've got connections at work." **Блат в го́роде,** *idiom, crim.* An official who takes bribes (lit., a connection in town). ♦*У тебя блат в городе есть? Мне нужен новый паспорт.* "Do you have a connection in town? I need a new passport."

БЛАТАТА́, -ы́, *f. collect., neg.* Gangsters,

hooligans, criminals. ♦*Опять эта блатата дебоширит.* "There go those
hooligans making a row again."

БЛАТНОЙ, -ого, *m., neg.* **1.** A criminal.
♦*От блатных нет прохода.* "There are
so many criminals around that it's impossible to go out on the streets." **2.** One who
uses influence, connections, or bribes to
get a job, obtain entrance to college, and
the like. ♦*Он экзамены сдаст, он же
блатной.* "He'll do fine on his entrance
exams — his connections are taking care
of him."

БЛАТОВИК, -а, *m.* See **блатной.**

БЛАТ-ХАТА, -ы, *f., crim.* A place of illegal or seedy activities, such as gambling,
prostitution, and drinking. ♦*Тут недалеко есть блат-хата, там можно отдохнуть.* "There's a den around here
where we can take a break."

БЛАТЯГА, -и, *m., neg.* See **блатной.**

БЛЕВАТЬ/БЛЕВАНУТЬ, *rude.* To
vomit. ♦*Меня блевать тянет, когда
его слушаю.* "I feel like vomiting whenever I hear his voice."

БЛЕВОНТИН, -а, *m., rude.* Vomit; any
disgusting, nauseating substance. ♦*Это
не суп, а блевонтин.* "This isn't soup;
it's vomit."

БЛЕВОТИНА, -ы, *f., rude.* **1.** Vomit.
♦*Чья в туалете блевотина? Убрать
надо.* "Whose vomit is this in the toilet?
It has to be cleaned up." **2.** Trash, junk.
♦*Эта книга — блевотина.* "This book
is trash."

БЛЕКОТА, -ы, *f., rude.* **1.** Vomit. ♦*Не
ходи туда, там блекота.* "Don't go
over there; someone vomited." **2.** Trash,
garbage, nonsense. ♦*Я эту блекоту о
ней слушать не хочу.* "I don't want to
listen to that trash about her."

БЛИЖЕ К ТЕЛУ, *idiom, joc..* Request to
speak more directly, more to the point.
Lit., closer to the body, by wordplay on
Ближе к делу, "more to the point." ♦*Ну
давай, ближе к телу, чем дело
кончилось?* "Come on, don't beat
around the bush, what was the outcome?"

БЛИН, -а, *m., rude, euph.* **1.** An expression
of annoyance, displeasure (lit., pancake;

by alliteration with **блядь**). ♦*Опять
деньги забыл — вот блин!* "I forgot the
money again — oh, sugar!" ♦**Блин
горелый,** *idiom, joc., euph.* Damn it (lit.,
burnt pancake). ♦*Ты, блин горелый,
почему не позвонил вчера?* "Why the
hell didn't you call yesterday?" **2.** Compact disk, CD (lit., pancake). ♦*Что на
этом блине, фильм?* "What's recorded
on this CD, a movie?"

БЛИНЫ, -ов, *pl., crim.* Counterfeit bills
(lit., pancakes, from the method of "cooking them up"). ♦*Он по-прежнему делает блины?* "Is he still cooking up 'pancakes'?"

БЛОНДА, -ы, *f., youth.* A blond. ♦*Подойди вон к той блонде, спроси телефончик.* "Ask that blond over there for
her phone number."

БЛОНДИНКА, -и, *f.* Vodka. ♦*Что ты
взял? — Блондинку.* "What did you
buy? — Vodka."

БЛУДУАР, -а, *m.* A bedroom (wordplay
on будуар, boudoir, and блудить, to
have promiscuous sex). ♦*В блудуаре у
нее музыка, притушенные лампы, всё
для интима.* "She's got soft music and
dimmed lamps in her bedroom—everything for an intimate atmosphere."

БЛУЁВЫЙ, -ая, -ое. Light blue. ♦*Юбку
блуёвую не надевай, не в тон.* "Don't
put on that blue skirt, the color is not
right."

БЛЫМАТЬ/БЛЫМНУТЬ, *rude.* Ukr.
1. To blink the eyes (as in confusion, perplexity.) ♦*Не блымай глазами, говори,
что надо.* "Don't stand there blinking
your eyes — say what you want." **2.** To
blink, flicker (of an electric light, flashlight, etc.). ♦*Смотри, там фонарь
блымает.* "Look — there's a light blinking."

БЛЭК, -а, *m., youth.* A black person,
African (from Eng. "black"). ♦*На этом
этаже наших нет, одни блэки.* "None
of our kind live on this floor — only
blacks."

БЛЯ. See **блядь.**

БЛЯДКИ: Ходить/пойти на блядки, see
under **ходить.**

БЛЯДОВА́ТЬ/ПОБЛЯДОВА́ТЬ, *rude.* To whore around (cf. **блядь**). ♦*Ну ты и любишь блядовать.* "You're too fond of whoring around."

БЛЯДОВИ́ТЫЙ, -ая, -ое, *rude.* Sexually active or overactive (cf. **блядь**). ♦*Муж у неё такой блядовитый, ни одной юбки не пропустит.* "Her husband is such a tail-chaser, he can't let a single skirt go by."

БЛЯДОХО́Д, -а, *rude.* Spring fever, spring as the season of stepped-up erotic activities (by wordplay on ледоход, the breaking up of river ice in the spring, and **блядь**). ♦*Скоро в мае блядоход начнётся, будет не до занятий.* "Spring fever will begin soon, in May — how will anyone be able to study?!"

БЛЯ́ДСТВО, -а, *n., rude.* 1. Sexual promiscuity (cf. **блядь**). ♦*Она блядством уже давно занимается.* "She's been sleeping around for a long time already." 2. Immorality. ♦*С его стороны так поступать — настоящее блядство.* "That kind of behavior on his part is simply immoral."

БЛЯДУВА́Р, -а, *m., youth, rude.* An avenue (бульвар) for promenading, girl-watching, picking up girls (cf. **блядь**). ♦*Ты будешь на блядуваре?* "Will you be out on the avenue looking for a pickup?"

БЛЯДУГА́Н, -а, *m., rude.* A womanizer, skirt-chaser (cf. **блядь**). ♦*Зачем ты меня познакомила с этим блядуганом, он сразу начал ко мне приставать.* "Why did you introduce me to that skirt-chaser? He started coming on to me right away."

БЛЯДУГА́НТСВО, -а, *n., rude.* Cf. **блядь**. 1. Sexual immorality, sexually immoral behavior. ♦*Сколько можно заниматься блядуганством?* "It's about time to cut out this libertine life!" 2. Any kind of immoral behavior; difficult, obstructive social conditions. ♦*Везде одно блядуганство, никто не считает нас за людей.* "We're getting screwed from every side; no one treats us like human beings."

БЛЯДУ́Н, -на́, *m., rude.* A womanizer, skirt-chaser. ♦*Зачем он тебе нужен блядун этот?* "What do you see in that womanizer?"

БЛЯДУ́НЬЯ, -ьи, f. See **блядун**.

БЛЯДЬ, -и, f., rude. 1. A loose woman. ♦*Эта блядь спит со всеми подряд.* "That slut sleeps with everybody." 2. Exclamation of extreme annoyance. ♦*Замолчи, ты мне надоел, блядь!* "Shut up, damn it, I'm sick of you!" •**Не блядь, а голу́бчик**, *idiom, rude.* Used in response to the word **блядь**. Don't talk that way, don't call me names (lit., [I'm] not a whore but a darling). ♦*Вот, блядь, ты опять чепуху говоришь. — Не блядь, а голубчик.* "There you go with your nonsense again, damn you! — Don't damn me, I'm a darling." **Порто́вая блядь**, see under **порто́вая. После́дняя блядь**, see under **после́дняя**.

БЛЯДЬ НЕРУ́ССКАЯ, *idiom, rude.* A stupid person, an idiot (lit., a non-Russian whore).

БЛЯЖ, -а, *m., joc.* A beach where girls can be picked up (by wordplay on пляж, "beach," and **блядь**). ♦*Давай снимем кого-нибудь на бляже?* "Shall we go pick up some girls at the beach?"

БЛЯ́КАТЬ/БЛЯ́КНУТЬ, *neg.* To talk inadvisedly or out of turn, to chatter, babble irresponsibly. ♦*Не знаешь толком, в чём дело, — не блякай.* "You don't know what it's all about, so don't just babble."

БЛЯ́МБА, -ы, f. 1. A whatchamacallit, esp. something round. ♦*Что это за блямба? — Это телефонный адаптер.* "What's that thing-a-ma-jig?" — "It's a telephone adapter." 2. A bump, a swollen bruise. ♦*Кто тебе поставил блямбу?* "Who gave you that bump?" 3. A stamp, a seal. ♦*Поставь блямбу на бумагу.* "Stamp that document."

БЛЯНДИ́НКА, -и, f., rude. A whore, prostitute (by wordplay on **блонди́нка**, "blond," and **блядь**). ♦*Видишь ту бляндинку, тащи её в постель.* "See that blond floozy? You can get her into bed."

БЛЯ́ХА-МУ́ХА, *interj.* Damn it (an

expression of extreme annoyance, euph. for **блядь**; cf. **блин**). ♦*Вот, бляха-муха, опять автобус опаздывает!* "Damn it all, that bus is late again!"

БОБ, -á, *m., crim.* A cartridge, round of ammunition (lit., a bean). ♦*У тебя сколько бобов к автомату?* "How many rounds of ammunition do you have for your automatic?"

БÓБИК, -а, *m., neg.* An unknown and unattractive person (from a widespread pet name for a dog). ♦*Каждому бобику давать выпить я не обязан, не приводи незнакомых людей в дом.* "I don't have to serve drinks to any stray who happens along! Don't bring strangers to the house."

БÓБИК СДОХ (И ЛÁПКИ КВÉРХУ), *idiom.* It's all over, it's the end (lit., Bobik is dead, [with his paws in the air]). ♦*Всё с делами на сегодня, бобик сдох, по домам.* "Okay, enough of this business for today. Bobik is dead, let's go home."

БÓБКА, -и, *f., crim.* A shirt. ♦*Ты мне бобку порвал, плати!* "You've ripped my shirt — you'll have to pay for it."

БÓ-БÓ, *interj., joc.* Painful, sore (imitating baby talk for **больно**, "painful"; cf. Eng. "boo-boo"). ♦*Ты мне сделал бо-бо, извинись.* "You gave me a boo-boo. Say you're sorry."

БОБР, -á, *m., crim.* A manifestly rich person, as an object of theft (lit., a beaver). ♦*Этого бобра хорошо бы подоить в карты.* "This 'beaver' would be a good mark for a card game."

БОБЫ́, -ов, Money (lit., beans). ♦*Бобы позарез нужны.* "I am in desperate need of money."

БОГ: В Бóга дýшу мать, see under **в. Всё не слáва Бóгу,** see under **всё.**

БОГОДÉЛЬНЯ, -и, *f., neg.* Lit., a poor-house. **1.** A disorderly, undisciplined workplace. ♦*У вас не завод, а богодельня, когда хочешь — приходи, когда хочешь — уходи.* "This isn't a factory, it's bedlam, everyone coming and going at will." **2.** A shabby, underfunded office. ♦*Бросай свою богодельню, лаборато-рию — переходи в банк работать.* "Quit that poorhouse of a laboratory of yours and go to work in a bank."

БОДÁТЬСЯ, *imperf. only, neg.* To butt in, interfere (from **бодать/боднуть**, "to butt with the horns"). ♦*Любишь ты бодаться, когда не нужно.* "You like to butt in where you're not wanted."

БОДУ́Н: С бодунá, *idiom.* Having a hang-over, suffering from a hangover. ♦*Ты, я вижу, со страшного бодуна, где вы вчера пили?* "You seem to have an awful hangover! Where did you guys go drinking last night?"

БОДУ́ЧИЙ, -ая, -ое. Obstreperous, irritable. ♦*Что ты сегодня такой бодучий?* "Why are you so out of sorts today?"

БОДЯ́ГА, -и, *f., neg.* Nonsense, a bore, a drag. ♦*Он ничего интересного не сказал, одна бодяга.* "He didn't say anything interesting, just a lot of hot air."

БОДЯ́ЖИТЬ/РАЗБОДЯ́ЖИТЬ, *youth.* To prepare narcotics for use. ♦*Кто разбодяжит это на всех?* "Who'll get this stuff ready for us to use?"

БОЕГОЛÓВКА, -и, *f.* A penis (lit., warhead). ♦*Боеголовка к бою готова!* "My warhead is ready for battle!" (i.e. "I have an erection.")

БОЕКОМПЛÉКТ, -а, *m.* Liquor (lit., military kit). ♦*Боекомплект в поезд берём?* "Are we taking some liquor for the train trip?"

БОÉЦ, бойцá, *m., pos.* A brave fellow, good soldier; said of one who drinks a lot without ill consequences, who carries on with his work the next morning. ♦*Интересно, он опоздает на работу после вчерашнего? —Нет, он — боец.* "I wonder if he'll be late to work after yesterday's party? — Certainly not, he's a real trouper."

БÓЖЬЯ КОРÓВКА, *idiom, crim.* Narcotics (lit., ladybug). ♦*У кого есть божья коровка? Покурить хочется.* "Who has some 'ladybug'? I feel like a smoke."

БОЙ, -я, *m., crim.* Playing cards, a pack of cards (lit., a battle). ♦*У кого бой есть,* сыграем? "Who's got a pack of cards? Let's have a game."

БОЙ-БА́БА, -ы, *f., idiom.* An agressive, decisive woman. ♦*Эта бой-баба всего сама добьётся.* "That battle-ax gets whatever she sets her mind on."

БОЙНИ́ЦА, -ы, *f.* Buttocks, ass (lit., embrasure, gun-hole). ♦*Всю бойницу отсидел, пока доехали.* "The trip was so long that my ass got numb."

БОКА́, -о́в, *pl., crim.* A watch (lit., sides, from the rounded shape of a pocket watch). ♦*Который час, у тебя бока есть?* "What time is it? Have you got a watch?"

БОКОВИ́К, -а, *m., business.* An additional "side" contract for spurious services (from бок, "side"). ♦*Тут боковик нужно придумать, напрямую дорогая сделка получается.* "We'll have to come up with a 'side' contract, otherwise the deal will cost us too much."

БОКСЁР, -а, *m., crim.* A police official, the head of a residential district (lit., boxer, prize-fighter). ♦*Приходил боксёр, интересовался тобой.* "The 'boxer' came by here asking about you."

БОЛДУИ́Н, -а, *m.* An idiot, a fool (from балда, idiot). ♦*В журналистике сейчас болдуин на болдуине.* "Nowadays journalists are one idiot after another."

БОЛТ, -а́, *m., rude.* A penis (lit., bolt, as in nuts and bolts). ♦*У меня что-то болт болит.* "I've got a pain in my tool." •Забива́ть/забить болт на что-л., see under забива́ть.

БОЛТ ТЕБЕ́ В ГЛО́ТКУ, *idiom, rude.* Damn you! Up yours! ♦*Болт тебе в глотку, а не бутылки.* "No one's going to give you a bottle, damn you!"

БОЛТА́НКА, -и, *f.* **1.** Turbulence, rough air. ♦*Сколько ни летаю, такой болтанки ещё не видел.* "I've never seen such turbulence in all my years of flying." **2.** *youth.* Homemade narcotics.

БОЛТА́ТЬ (ЧЕСА́ТЬ, ТРЕПА́ТЬ) языко́м, *idiom.* To babble, talk nonsense. ♦*Тебе лишь бы языком поболтать.* "You babble too much."

БОЛТ-МА́СТЕР, -а, *m., crim.* A penis (lit., bolt-master). ♦*Что-то с болт-мастера каплет, не триппер ли?* "I've got a discharge from my 'bolt-master' — maybe it's the clap?"

БОЛТУ́Н — НАХО́ДКА ДЛЯ ШПИО́НА, *idiom, joc.* Lit., "A chatterbox is a godsend for a spy." This was the caption of a widely known World War II poster; used colloquially to mean "Don't gossip," "I won't gossip," "I won't tell." ♦*Ты знаешь, с кем он спит? — Болтун — находка для шпиона.* "Have you heard who he's sleeping with? — Don't gossip! A chatterbox is a godsend for a spy."

БОЛТУ́ШКА, -и, *f., youth.* A narcotic substance, drug. ♦*Они достали немного болтушки.* "They got hold of a little dope."

БОЛЬНА́Я ДРЯНЬ, *idiom, crim., neg.* Drugs of poor quality (lit., sick trash). ♦*Ты это грызло не трогай, больная дрянь, я пробовал.* "Don't buy that dope. I tried it — it's trash."

БО́ЛЬШЕ СКО́РОСТЬ — МЕ́НЬШЕ ЯМ, *idiom.* It's better to go fast. Lit., the higher the speed, the fewer the potholes. Used as a retort to the saying Тише едешь — дальше будешь, "The slower you go, the further you get." ♦*Куда ты так гонишь? — Больше скорость — меньше ям.* "Where are you speeding like that?! — "The more speed, the less potholes."

БО́ЛЬШЕ СКО́РОСТЬ — МЕ́НЬШЕ ЯМ И РЕССО́РЫ ПО ХУЯ́М, *idiom, obs.* A rhyming phrase used as a retort to the preceding entry. Lit., The higher the speed, the fewer the potholes — but your suspension gets fucked up.

БОЛЬШЕВИ́К, -а, *m., business.* A big, well-established bank (lit., a Bolshevik, playing on большой, "big"). ♦*Инкомбанк — большевик, ему никакой кризис не страшен.* "Inkombank is a real Bolshevik — no financial crisis can shake it."

БОЛЬШО́Й ХАПО́К, большо́го хапка́, *m., idiom, neg.* Lit., the big steal, by wordplay on Большой Скачок, the Chinese "Great Leap Forward." **1.** The

Revolution of 1917. **2.** The unfair privatization of the 1990s. ♦*После большого хапка родились новые русские.* "The big steal of state property gave birth to the New Russians."

БО́МБА, -ы, *f., neg.* An obese woman (lit., a bomb). ♦*Жена у него — бомба.* "His wife is a 'bomb.'"

БОМБИ́ТЬ/ПРОБОМБИ́ТЬ, *youth.* To engage in dishonest business, to make money by deceit. ♦*Они пошли на рынок бомбить приезжих.* "They went to the vegetable market to rip off the farmers." •**Бомби́ть/пробомби́ть фирму́,** *idiom, youth.* To do business with foreigners, to practice extortion, to defraud. ♦*Там в углу наши бомбят фирму, хотят им сдать офицерскую форму.* "Over there in the corner our boys are doing a bomb job, selling a secondhand officer's uniform."

БОМЖ, -а́, *m., neg.* A tramp, vagrant, homeless person. (Acronym for без определённого места жительства, the official status of being without a fixed place of residence.) ♦*Сейчас в городе полно бомжей.* "Nowadays the city is full of vagrants."

БО́НДАРЬ, -я, *m., crim.* A gang leader (lit., a barrel-maker). ♦*Кто у них сейчас бондарь?* "Who's the leader of that gang now?"

БОРДЕ́ЛЬ, -я, *m., rude.* A whorehouse, bordello; used metaphorically of a place or situation of disorder. ♦*Не жизнь, а бордель.* "This is no a life, it's a bordello."

БОРДЮ́Р, -а, *m., joc.* **1.** Buttocks, ass. **2.** Thigh.

БОРЗЕ́ТЬ/ОБОРЗЕ́ТЬ, *neg.* To behave in a demanding, aggressive, pushy manner (from борзая собака, a type of hunting dog). ♦*Ты не борзей, а то быстро успокоим.* "Don't be so pushy or we'll find means to calm you down."

БОРЗО́Й, -ая, -ое, *neg.* (From борзая, "a borzoi-hound"). **1.** Fast, decisive. ♦*У него на все вопросы борзые ответы.* "He's got quick answers to any questions." **2.** Pushy, aggressive. ♦*Эти*

борзые всё делают в наглую. "These borzois are pushy about everything."

БОРЗОТА́, -ы́, *f., collect., neg.* Pushy, aggressive people. ♦*Эта твоя борзота, все твои дружки мне страшно надоели.* "I'm sick of your pushy friends."

БОРИ́С — БАРБАРИ́С, *idiom, joc.* A rhyming phrase used to tease people named Boris. Барбарис is a type of berry or bush. ♦*Борис — барбарис, идёшь в кино?* "Boris-berry, are young going to the movies?"

БОРИ́С ФЁДОРОВИЧ, *m., crim., joc.* A type of glue, sold under the trademark БФ, used as an intoxicant. ♦*Ты Бориса Фёдоровича достал?* "Did you manage to get some 'Boris Fyodorovich'?"

БОРИ́С — НА ГОВНЕ́ ПОВИ́С, *idiom, rude.* A rhyming phrase used to tease people named Boris. Lit., Boris is hanging from shit.

БОРМОТА́, -ы́, *f., neg.* Strong, cheap wine of inferior quality. ♦*Посидели, выпили какой-то бормоты.* "They sat around and drank some rotgut."

БОРМОТУ́ХА, -и, *f., neg.* See **бормота́.**

БО́РОВ, -а, *m., neg.* A fat, healthy, but lazy man (lit., a boar, pig). ♦*Смотри, какой боров, а работать не хочет.* "Look what a boar — and he won't do any work."

БОРОДА́, -ы, *f., joc.* A bearded man (lit., a beard). ♦*Спроси у бороды, где магазин.* "Ask the beard over there if he knows where the store is."

БОРО́ТЬСЯ/ПОБОРО́ТЬСЯ С УНИ-ТА́ЗОМ, *idiom, joc.* To vomit (lit., to wrestle with the toilet). ♦*Кажется, пора побороться с унитазом, много выпил.* "Uh-oh, I've drunk too much, it's time to wrestle with the toilet."

БОРТАНУ́ТЬ, *perf. only, neg.* To refuse, reject, repel. ♦*Меня бортанули с работой.* "They refused to give me a job."

БО́ТАЛО, -а, *n., crim.* Lit., a cowbell. **1.** tongue. ♦*Придержи ботало, много говоришь.* "Hold your tongue. You talk too much." **2.** A chatterbox, babbler. ♦*Ты не слушай, что он треплет,* *ботало известное.* "Don't listen to his nonsense, everyone knows he's a chatterbox."

БОТА́НИК, -а, *m., school, neg.* A bookworm, grade grubber, nerd, Goody Two-shoes. ♦*Он время с нами терять не станет, он же ботаник.* "He wouldn't waste his time on us — he's too much of a bookworm."

БОТАНИ́ЧЕСКИЙ, -ая, -ое, *joc.* Primitive, backward (lit., botanical). ♦*Что ты всё читаешь эти ботанические книги?* "How come you're always reading those Neanderthal books?"

БО́ТАТЬ/ЗАБО́ТАТЬ, *crim.* To talk, speak. ♦*Ты по-русски ботаешь?* "Do you speak Russian?" •**Бо́тать/забо́тать по/на фе́не,** *crim.* To speak thieves' cant. ♦*Он на фене ботает?* "Does he speak thieves' cant?"

БОТВА́, -ы, *f.* Petty merchandise (lit., the inedible part of plants). ♦*Они торгуют ботвой: мыло там всякое, порошки.* "They're dealing in trifles — all sorts of soaps and powders."

БОТЛ, -а. See **батл.**

БОЧА́РА, -ы, *f.* Belly (from бочка, "barrel"). ♦*В бочаре что-то болит.* "I've got a pain in my belly."

БОЧА́РЫ, -ов, *pl., crim.* A watch. ♦*У тебя бочары наши или японские?* "Is your watch Soviet-made or Japanese?"

БО́ЧКА, -и, *m. and f., neg.* A fat person (lit., a barrel). ♦*Ты стала бочкой, надо сесть на диету.* "You've become a regular barrel, you'd better go on a diet."

БО́ШКА, и, *f.* A head. ♦*Как бошка после вчерашнего?* "How's your head feeling after last night's party?"

БРА́ЗЕР, -а, *m., youth.* A brother (from Eng. "brother"). ♦*Кем твой бразер работает?* "What does your brother do for a living?"

БРАКОДЕ́Л, -а, *m., joc.* A man who has daughters rather than sons (lit., a maker of defective goods). ♦*Наш бракодел уже третью дочь рожает.* "That sloppy workman has already produced his third daughter."

БРАНДАХЛЫ́СТ, -а, *m., joc.* A drunkard. ♦*Этот брандахлыст не остановится, пока всё не выпьет.* "That drunk won't stop until he's drunk it all."

БРАСЛЕ́ТЫ, -ов, *pl., crim.* Handcuffs. ♦*По тебе браслеты плачут.* "Handcuffs are calling out for you" (i.e., you are committing a crime and will be caught).

БРАТА́Н, -а, *m., pos.* Brother. ♦*У меня братан дома остался.* "My brother stayed at home."

БРАТВА́, -ы, *f., collect.* Gangsters (from брат, "brother"). ♦*Местная братва сильно шалит?* "Are the local hoods active around here?"

БРА́ТКА, -и, *m., crim.* A small pistol, ladies' gun (lit., little brother). ♦*Вот братка, возьми, пригодится.* "Take this 'little brother'; it'll come in handy."

БРАТО́К, братка́, *m.* **1.** A gangster. **2.** A pal, friend.

БРА́ТСКОЕ ЧУВЫ́РЛО, *idiom, crim., neg.* An ugly person (lit., a fraternal monstrosity). ♦*У неё мужик — братское чувырло.* "Her boyfriend is ugly as sin."

БРА́ТЦЫ-КРО́ЛИКИ, -ов, *pl., joc.* Friends, buddies (lit., brother rabbits). ♦*Ну, братцы-кролики, что делать будем?* "Well, guys, what should we do?"

БРАТЬ/ВЗЯТЬ. To intoxicate, affect with drunkenness. ♦*Что-то меня водка сегодня не берёт.* "Somehow I'm not getting high from the vodka today." •**Брать/взять акаде́мку,** *idiom, youth.* To take academic leave. ♦*Наверное, он возьмёт академку, он всё время болеет, не может учиться.* "He'll probably take academic leave — he's constantly sick and can't study." **Брать/взять ва́флю,** *idiom.* To perform fellatio (lit., to take a wafer). ♦*Она берёт вафли?* "Does she give blow jobs?" **Брать/взять но́ги в зу́бы,** *idiom.* To collect oneself, get ready to go. ♦*Бери ноги в зубы и давай в магазин.* "Get yourself together and let's go to the store." **Брать/взять за жа́бры,** *idiom, neg.* To catch someone red-handed (lit., to take by the gills). ♦*Тебя скоро возьмут за жабры, если не перестанешь воровать.* "One of these days they'll catch you in the act if you keep on stealing." **Брать/взять за зя́бры,** *idiom, joc.* To catch, capture, apprehend, suppress, apply pressure on (distorted from **брать за жа́бры**). ♦*Я его взял за зябры, он всё рассказал.* "I put the screws on him, and he confessed everything." **Брать/взять за хо́бот,** see **брать/взять за жа́бры. Брать/взять за шки́рку,** *idiom, neg.* To catch, apprehend (lit., to take by the scruff of the neck). ♦*Когда его возьмут за шкирку, он всё время берёт взятки.* "Will they ever catch him for constantly taking bribes?" **Брать/взять на гло́тку,** *idiom, neg.* To shout down, to try to win over by shouting, without arguments (lit., to take by the throat). ♦*Ты меня на глотку не бери, всё равно я туда не пойду.* "Don't try to shout me down, you still won't persuade me to go." **Брать/взять на ку́мпол,** *idiom.* To butt, hit with one's head. ♦*Он его правильно взял на кумпол, иначе бы не победил.* "He made the right move by hitting him with his head — he'd have lost otherwise." **Брать/взять на понт,** *idiom.* To deceive, cheat. ♦*Меня на понт не возьмёшь.* "It's not so easy to trick me." **Брать/взять на пупо́к,** *idiom, joc.* Lit., to take on the navel; from the idea that the navel is the center of a person's strength. **1.** To lift a heavy weight. ♦*Ты возьмёшь этот мешок на пупок?* "Can you lift this sack?" **2.** To undertake responsibility for something, have something within one's power. ♦*Я эту сумму на пупок не возьму.* "I can't manage this cost." **Возьми́ с по́лки пирожо́к,** see under **возьми́. Не бери́ в го́лову (бери́ в рот),** see under **не.**

БРЕВНО́, -а́, *n., neg.* A cold, uncaring person (lit., a log, beam). ♦*Разве ты кого-нибудь пожалеешь, бревно несчастное?* "So you don't care about anyone, do you, you wretched log?"

БРЕ́ДНИ, -ей, *pl., neg.* Nonsense, ravings. ♦*Что за бредни, этого не может быть.* "What nonsense! That can't be true."

БРЕХА́ЛО, -а, *n., rude.* Mouth (from брехать, "to bark"). ♦*Ты когда-нибудь*

заткнёшь своё брехало? "Can't you ever shut up your mouth?"

БРЕХА́ТЬ/СБРЕХА́ТЬ, *neg.* To lie (lit., to bark pointlessly, of a dog). ♦*Не бреши, всё равно в это не поверю.* "There's no use lying about it — I don't believe it anyhow."

БРЕХНЯ́, -и́, *f., neg.* Twaddle, idle chatter. ♦*Это всё брехня.* "That's a bunch of twaddle."

БРИГА́ДА, -ы, *f., crim.* A gang, a group of armed gangsters. ♦*А что мы можем против бригады сделать, вот они и берут в киосках, что хотят.* "We're helpless against the gang. They just take whatever they want from the kiosks."

БРИГА́ДА "УХ!" РАБО́ТАЕТ ДО ДВУХ , *idiom, joc.* A rhyming phrase used to reproach inefficient workers. Lit., The 'Ugh' Brigade only works until 2:00.

БРИГАДИ́Р, -а, *m.* **1.** A common term of address to a taxi driver, merchant, and the like (lit., brigadier). ♦*Бригадир, а почему такие дорогие помидоры?* "Hey, chief, how come these tomatoes are so expensive?" **2.** A bodyguard (lit., foreman). ♦*У нас на фирме бригадир нужен. Может быть, пойдёшь к нам?* "Our company is looking a bodyguard. Are you interested?"

БРИ́ТИШ, -а (*pl.* **бритиша́, -е́й),** *m., youth.* An Englishman or Englishwoman (from Eng. "British"). ♦*Он кто, бритиш?* "What is he, a Brit?"

БРИЦ, -а, *m., crim.* A Jew. ♦*С нами сидел один бриц.* "There was a Jew serving time with us."

БРОВЬ: На бровя́х, *idiom, neg.* Drunk (lit., on one's eyebrows). ♦*Они пришли вчера на бровях.* "They crawled in on their faces yesterday."

БРОД, -а, *m.* The main shopping/promenading/meeting street of a town or city (e.g., Tverskaya Ulitsa in Moscow; from Eng. "Broadway"). ♦*Пойдём на Брод?* "Let's go over to 'Broadway.'"

БРО́ЙЛЕР, -а, *m.* A fat man, a fatso (lit., a broiler). ♦*Этот бройлер кил на сто пятьдесят.* "That fatso must weigh about 330 pounds."

БРОНЕТЮФЯ́К, -а́, m., army. Bullet-proof vest (lit., armored mattress). ♦*Бронетюфяки у всех надеты, тогда вперед в атаку.* "Everyone got their vest on? Okay, let's roll."

БРОНЯ́, -й, f., army. A tank or an infantry vehicle (lit., armor). ♦*Раненые на броню садятся, остальные пешком.* "We'll take the wounded on the tanks, and the rest will follow on foot."

БРОСА́ТЬ/БРО́СИТЬ: Броса́ть/бро́сить кость, idiom. To conciliate, pacify, pay off (lit., to throw someone a bone). ♦*Ему тоже надо бросить кость, долларов сто, чтобы молчал.* "We'll have to pay him off too, a hundred dollars or so, to keep him quiet." **Броса́ть/бро́сить па́лку, idiom, rude.** To have sex with a woman (lit., to throw a stick). ♦*Ты ей уже бросил палку?* "Have you screwed her yet?"

БРО́СИТЬ/ПОДБРО́СИТЬ подля́нку, idiom, neg. To do something secretive and malicious. ♦*Кто же мог такую подлянку подбросить?* "Who could have done such a sneaky, nasty thing?"

БРЫ́ЗГИ, брызг, pl., crim. Eyes (lit., drops). ♦*Убери брызги, не смотри в карты.* "Hey, get your eyes off my cards."

БРЫКА́ТЬСЯ/ЗАБРЫКА́ТЬСЯ, neg. To refuse, object (lit., to kick [of a horse]). ♦*Не брыкайся, слушай, что тебе советуют.* "Don't be recalcitrant; listen to the advice you're being given."

БРЭНДО́ВЫЙ, -ая, -ое, youth, obs. New, unused (from Eng. "brand-new"). ♦*Это совсем брэндовый батон.* "This is a brand-new button-down shirt."

БРЮ́ЛИК, -а, m., crim. A diamond. ♦*А брюлики у тебя в кольце хороши.* "Ooh, what nice diamonds you've got in your ring!"

БУ́БЕН, -а, m. Face (lit., tambourine). ♦*Бубен вымой, весь в саже.* "Go wash your mug; it's full of soot."

БУБЕНЦЫ́, -о́в, pl. Balls, crotch (lit., jingle bells). ♦*Не тряси бубенцами, оденься.* "Don't go around with your bells dangling, put on some pants!"

БУГА́Й, -ая́, m., crim. A wallet (lit., a bull). ♦*Ты не видел моего бугая? Найти не могу.* "Have you seen my wallet? I can't find it."

БУГО́Р, бугра́, m. A foreman, boss (lit., a hump, hillock, bump). ♦*Где наш бугор?* "Where's the boss?" •**За бугро́м, idiom.** Abroad (lit., on the other side of the hillock). ♦*Ну, как там жизнь за бугром?* "So, what's it like to live abroad?"

БУГРОВО́З, -а, m., joc. A government car (lit., boss-conveyer, from **бугор** and возить, "to convey"). ♦*Кого там бугровозы повезли?* "Who's riding in the boss-conveyers?"

БУ́ДЕТЕ РЯ́ДОМ — ПРОХОДИ́ТЕ МИ́МО, idiom, joc. Don't bother me, stay away from me (lit., If you're in the neighborhood, pass by, playing on the conventional phrase Будете рядом, заходите, "If you're in the neighborhood, drop in").

БУ́ДЕШЬ ИМЕ́ТЬ БЛЕ́ДНЫЙ ВИД, idiom, neg. "You'll look pale"; used as a threat meaning "things will be hot for you." ♦*Возьмёшь машину без разрешения — будешь иметь бледный вид.* "If you take the car without permission, you'll be sorry."

БУ́ДКА, -и, f., neg. A big, fat face (lit., a shed). ♦*Ну и будка у тебя после курорта.* "What a fat face you've got after your rest cure."

БУДЬ: Будь здоро́в! A great deal, very much (lit., "Be healthy!"). ♦*Там денег платят, будь здоров!* "They pay a lot there." **Будь здоро́в, расти́ большо́й, не будь лапшо́й, idiom, joc.** An expression used in addressing children when they sneeze; lit., "Be healthy, grow big, don't be a noodle." **Будь здоро́в, не ка́шляй!, idiom, joc.** So long! Be seeing you! (lit., "Be well, don't cough"). **Будь про́ще, и к тебе́ потя́нутся лю́ди, idiom, joc.** Don't overcomplicate things (lit., be more direct, and people will reach out to you). ♦*Им, наверное, наш приход не понравится? — Будь проще, и к тебе потянутся люди.* "He probably won't be pleased to see us. — Don't make complications; be more direct, and people will reach out to you." **Будь спок!** *idiom.* Don't worry (abbr. from Будь спокоен, "Be calm"). ♦*Твои деньги никуда не денутся, будь спок!* "Don't worry, nothing's going to happen to your money!"

БУЗА́, -ы́, *f., neg.* Noise, commotion. ♦*Что там за буза, куда люди идут с плакатами?* "What's the commotion over there, where they're carrying those placards?"

БУЗИ́ТЬ/ЗАБУЗИ́ТЬ. To make a commotion, to riot, agitate. ♦*Ребята бузят, отказываются выходить на работу.* "The fellows are making a disturbance and refusing to go to work."

БУЗОТЁР, -а, *m., neg.* A troublemaker, agitator. ♦*Здесь на заводе бузотёрам не место, здесь работать нужно.* "There's no place for troublemakers here at this plant; we've got work to do."

БУК, -а, *m.* A store selling used and rare books. ♦*Смотри, я в буке нашёл первый номер журнала Галковского!* "Look what I found in the used-book store — the first issue of Galkovsky 's journal."

БУКА́ШКА, -и, *m. and f., neg.* Lit., a bug. **1.** A small, insignificant person. ♦*Этот букашка тебя обижает, не смеши меня.* "*That* little insect offended you?! Come off it!" **2.** (Moscow) The "Б" trolley running on the Garden Ring Road. ♦*На букашке туда не доедем.* "You can't get there on the Bukashka."

БУКЕ́Т, -а, *m., crim.* A set of multiple violations of the criminal code for which someone is convicted (lit., a bouquet). ♦*У него букет: и ограбление, и насилие, и вымогательство.* "He's been convicted of a bouquet: robbery, rape, and racketeering." •**Буке́т Абха́зии,** *idiom, joc.* A venereal disease (lit., Abkhazian Bouquet, a Georgian wine). ♦*У этого парня букет Абхазии.* "That boy's got the clap." **Буке́т-дубле́т,** *idiom, crim.* Syphilis and gonorrhea at the same time (lit., a double-barreled bouquet). ♦*У неё букет-дублет.* "She's got the double-barreled bouquet."

БУКСОВА́ТЬ/ЗАБУКСОВА́ТЬ, *joc.* **1.** To hem and haw, mutter, mumble. ♦*Чего ты там буксуешь, говори всё как есть.* "What are you mumbling about? Just tell it like it is." **2.** To scold repeatedly or lecture, to harp on or rag on (lit., to skid or slip, referring to wheels spinning without gaining traction). ♦*Буксуй не буксуй, от этого я не буду быстрей работать, так что успокойся.* "Chill out! Ragging on me isn't going to make me work any faster."

БУЛДА́, -ы́, *f., youth.* Homosexual activity. ♦*Там у них булда, я к ним не хожу.* "There's homosexual activity going on at their place; I won't go there." •**Без булды́,** *idiom.* Just as it really is, without fabrication. ♦*Я тебе говорю без булды, там уже никого нет, все разошлись по домам.* "Look, I'm telling you straight out: there's no one there, everyone's gone home."

БУ́ЛКИ, бу́лок, *pl.* Buttocks, backside. ♦*Подставляй булки, укол надо сделать.* "You'll have to present your backside for this injection."

БУЛЬ-БУ́ЛЬ, *interj.* **1.** To drown (from the sound of bubbles rising to the surface). ♦*Он буль-буль и ко дну!* "He drowned — went down to the very bottom." **2.** To pour (from the sound of a liquid being poured from a bottle). ♦*Что вы там всё время буль-буль да буль-буль?* "Why are you pouring yourself one drink after another like that?" •**Буль-бу́ль кара́сик,** *idiom, joc.* Gone, disappeared, left (lit., the carp went glug-glug, imitating the sound of drowning). ♦*А где твой жених? Буль-буль карасик?* "Where's your fiancé? Gone bye-bye?"

БУ́ЛЬКАТЬ/ЗАБУ́ЛЬКАТЬ, *neg.* To speak (lit., to gurgle). ♦*Кто там булькает, вашего совета никто не просил.* "Cut out the yakking over there, nobody asked your advice."

БУ́ЛЬКИ: Разлива́ть по бу́лькам, see under **разлива́ть.**

БУМА́ГА, -и, *f., youth.* Money (lit., paper). ♦*У тебя бумага на водку есть?* "Have you got money for vodka?"

БУМА́ЖКА/БАМА́ЖКА, -и, *f., joc.* Documents, papers, official authorization (lit., little paper). ♦*У тебя бамажка есть на вывоз товара с базы?* "Do you have authorization papers for shipping merchandise from the warehouse?" •**Без бума́жки ты кака́шка**, see under **без.**

БУМ-БУ́М: Ни бум-бу́м, see under **ни.**

БУ́НДЕС, -а, (*pl.* **бундеса́**), *m., youth.* A citizen of Germany. ♦*Что там бундеса делают? Строят завод?* "What are those Germans doing? Building a plant?"

БУНДЕСО́ВЫЙ, -ая, -ое, *youth.* German. ♦*Смотри, я купила бундесовые сапоги.* "Look at the German boots I bought."

БУ́НКЕР, -а, *m., youth.* A stomach (lit., a bunker). ♦*В бункере пусто, надо поесть.* "The bunker's empty — gotta eat."

БУР: Идти́/пойти́ бу́ром, see under **идти́.**

БУРА́К, -ка́, *m., rude.* A penis (from Ukr. for beet). ♦*Поправь плавки, бурак видно.* "Pull up your shorts — your dick is showing."

БУРДЮ́К, -а, *m., neg.* A paunch, a big belly. ♦*Наел себе бурдюк, ходить трудно.* "You've grown such a paunch that you can hardly even walk any more."

БУРЕ́ТЬ/ЗАБУРЕ́ТЬ. To get drunk (from бурый, "beet-red"). ♦*Ты совсем забурел, пора домой.* "You're completely drunk; you'd better go home."

БУРИ́ТЬ/ПРОБУРИ́ТЬ, *neg.* To persuade, talk into something (lit., to drill, bore). ♦*Вы меня не пробурите, никуда я не пойду.* "It's no use trying to persuade me. I'm not going anywhere."

БУ́РКАЛЫ, -ов, *pl., neg.* Eyes (from буркалить, an obsolete word for "to look"). ♦*Отверни буркалы!* "Don't look!"

БУРО́ВИТЬ/ЗАБУРО́ВИТЬ/НАБУРО́-ВИТЬ. To mumble, to babble. ♦*Чего он набуровил, никак не пойму.* "What was it he was babbling about? I couldn't understand a thing."

БУ́РОСТЬ, -и, *f., neg.* Insolence, cheek, pushiness. ♦*Твоя бурость хоть кого достанет.* "Your pushy behavior would get on anyone's nerves."

БУ́РЫЙ, -ого, *m., army.* A mature, experienced soldier. ♦*Туда берём только бурых, зелёных перестреляют сразу.* "This is strictly a mission for old hands — greenies would get shot at once."

БУ́РЫЙ, -ая, -ое, *youth, neg.* Insolent, pushy, fresh. ♦*Не будь слишком бурым, не таких видели.* "Don't be so fresh. I'm not impressed by it."

БУ́САТЬ/ЗАБУ́САТЬ по-чёрному, *idiom, youth.* To drink alone. ♦*Он в компании не пьёт, бусает по-чёрному.* "He doesn't drink socially, only when he's alone."

БУ... СДЕ..., *idiom, joc.* An expression indicating readiness to carry out a request (abbr. from будет сделано, "it shall be done"). ♦*Ты почему не сходил за хлебом? — Минуту, бу. . . сде. . .* "Why haven't you gone out to buy the bread?— Just a minute, it's as good as done."

БУТЫ́ЛКА: Лома́ть/полома́ть буты́л-ку, see under **лома́ть²**.

БУФЕРА́, -о́в, *pl., rude.* A woman's breasts (lit., buffers). ♦*У неё, знаешь, буфера ничего.* "She's got quite a pair of buffers."

БУФЕРИ́СТАЯ, *adj., f., rude.* Chesty, big-breasted. ♦*Она баба буферистая.* "She's really stacked."

БУ́ХАЛО, -а, *n.* Liquor. ♦*Этого бухала на всех не хватит.* "This won't be enough liquor for everyone."

БУХА́ЛОВКА, -и, *f.* A party, drinking party. ♦*Сегодня у нас бухаловка, ты придёшь?* "We're having a party today. Are you coming?"

БУХА́РИК, -а, *m., neg.* A drunkard. ♦*Не ходи с этими бухариками, толку не будет.* "Don't associate with those drunks. Nothing good will come of it."

БУХА́РИТЬ/ЗАБУХА́РИТЬ. To get drunk, be drunk. ♦*Они бухарили всю ночь.* "They were drinking all night long."

БУХА́ТЬ/ЗАБУХА́ТЬ, БУХНУ́ТЬ. To drink. ♦*Они забухали на весь день.* "They drank all day."

БУ́ХАТЬСЯ/БУ́ХНУТЬСЯ. To fall, to throw oneself, to collapse. ♦*Вчера я* пришёл с работы, сразу бухнулся в постель и спал 10 часов. "When I got home from work yesterday I fell into bed and slept for ten hours."

БУХЕНВА́ЛЬДСКИЙ НАБА́Т, *idiom, army.* Alarm (lit., a Buchenwald alarm bell). ♦ *Опять Бухенвальдский набат, вторую ночь поспать не дают.* "There goes that alarm again—this is the second night they won't let us sleep."

БУХЛО́, -а́, *n.* See **бу́хало.**

БУХО́Й, -а́я, -о́е. Drunk. ♦ *Ты уже бухой, а нам ещё в гости идти надо.* "Here you are drunk already, just when we're supposed to be going to pay a visit."

БУ́ХТА, -ы, *f., crim.* A dive, den, shabby or illegal establishment (lit., a bay, harbor). ♦ *Кто держит эту бухту?* "Who's the proprietor of this joint?"

БУХТЕ́ТЬ/ЗАБУХТЕ́ТЬ, *neg.* To scold, reprimand. ♦ *Хватит бухтеть, я не виноват.* "Stop yelling at me! I'm not the one who did it."

БУХТИ́ЛА, -ы, *f., neg.* A grumbler, griper. ♦ *Не обращай внимания на этого бухтилу, он всегда так.* "Don't pay attention to that grumbler. He's always like that."

БУ́ЦАТЬ/ПОБУ́ЦАТЬ. To beat up (lit., to kick a ball). ♦ *Жить будешь, побуцали тебя немного, это ничего.* "You'll survive—they just roughed you up a bit."

БЫВА́ЕТ ХУ́ЖЕ, НО РЕ́ЖЕ, *idiom, joc.* "Worse things happen, but more rarely." Used in reply to the dismissive comment Бывает хуже, "Worse things happen." ♦ *Мне сын нахамил. — Бывает хуже. — Бывает хуже, но реже.* "My son insulted me." — "Well, worse things happen." — "Worse things happen, but more rarely."

«БЫВА́ЮТ В ЖИ́ЗНИ ЗЛЫ́Е ШУ́ТКИ,» — сказа́л пету́х, слеза́я с у́тки, *rhyming phrase, rude.* Lit.. "'There are wicked tricks in this life,' said the rooster, dismounting from the duck." Used in sardonic dismissal of other people's complaints or troubles.

БЫВА́ЮТ В ЖИ́ЗНИ ОГОРЧЕ́НЬЯ, ВМЕ́СТО ХЛЕ́БА КУ́ШАЕШЬ

ПЕЧЕ́НЬЕ, *idiom, joc.* Things are good, the situation is pleasing (a rhyming phrase). ♦ *Нам вчера икры из Астрахани прислали, бывают в жизни огорченья, вместо хлеба кушаешь печенье.* "Yesterday we received some caviar from Astrakhan. Well, life has its little sorrows; sometimes you have to eat cake instead of bread."

БЫДЛА́, -ы́, *f., crim., neg.* A large woman or girl. ♦ *Чья эта быдла там сидит?* "Whose girl is that big dame sitting over there?"

БЫ́ДЛО, -а, *n., neg, rude.* Silently obedient, worthless people (lit., cattle). ♦ *Что у тебя общего с этим быдлом?* "What do you have in common with those sheep?"

БЫК, -а́, *m., youth.* **1.** A strong fellow (lit., an ox). ♦ *Не связывайся с ним, он известный бык.* "Don't mess with him. He's a real 'ox'." **2.** A killer or a bodyguard in a criminal gang. ♦ *К нему не подойдешь даже, возле него пара быков крутится.* "You can't get near him, with that pair of bodyguards hanging around."

БЫКОВА́ТЬ, *imperf.* To bull the market (from **бык,** "bull"). ♦ *Эти ребята всегда быкуют, видишь, как цены взлетели!* "Those guys are always bulling the market! See how prices have skyrocketed?!"

БЫКОВА́ТЬ/ЗАБЫКОВА́ТЬ, *youth, neg.* To act rudely, throw one's weight around, act superior (cf. **бык).** ♦ *Кончай быковать, это не интересно.* "Stop showing off; it's not interesting."

БЫЛ ДА СПЛЫЛ, *idiom, joc.* Lit., "He was here and he floated off." ♦ *Директор был? — Был да сплыл.* "Was the director here? — He was, but he drifted off (i.e., I have no idea where he is now)."

БЫ́ЛО Б ЗА ЧТО, УБИ́Л БЫ, *idiom, joc.* Used in ironic justification of unjust treatment. Lit., If there had been a justification, I'd kill him/you. ♦ *За что ты его ругаешь? Что он такого сделал? — Было бы за что, убил бы.* "What are bawling him out for? What did he do so terrible?" — "If he *had* done something, I'd kill him!"

БЫ́ЛО ВА́ШЕ, СТА́ЛО НА́ШЕ, *idiom, joc.* A rhyming phrase used in justification of appropriating someone else's property. Lit., "It was yours, now it's ours." ♦*Подожди, это же моя книга! — Было ваше, стало наше.* "Hey, wait a minute, that's *my* book!" — "It was yours, now it's ours."

БЫ́СТРЫЙ: По-бы́строму, *adv., youth.* Quickly. ♦*Это надо сделать по-быстрому.* "This has to be done quickly." •**Ходи́ть/сходи́ть (бе́гать/ сбе́гать) по-бы́строму,** see under **ходи́ть.**

БЫТОВИ́К, -ка́, *m., crim.* Someone convicted for domestic crimes. ♦*Вчера в лагерь ещё бытовиков привезли.* "Yesterday they brought some more domestic offenders to the camp."

БЫЧКОВА́ТЬ/ЗАБЫЧКОВА́ТЬ, *youth.* To smoke only part of a cigarette, so as to save the butt (cf. **бычо́к**). ♦*Я забычковал на завтра пару окурков.* "I saved a couple of butts for tomorrow."

БЫЧО́К, бычка́, *m.* The butt of a cigarette (lit., a bullock). ♦*Дай докурить бычок.* "Let me smoke the butt." •**Бычо́к до́енный,** *crim.* Home-brewing apparatus, a still (lit., a dairy bullock). ♦*У тебя рабо-тает бычок доенный?* "Is your dairy bullock working?"

БЭ, *f., indecl., neg.* A prostitute (from the first letter of **блядь**). ♦*Я эту бэ знать не хочу.* "I don't want to have anything to do with that whore."

БЭ ТО́ЖЕ ВИТАМИ́Н И ЦЭ НЕ ОТРА́ВА, *idiom, rude.* Used in response to an inquisitive "a?," as if continuing to recite the alphabet, alluding to the euphemistic abbreviations "бэ" for блядь, "whore," and "цэ" for целка, "hymen." Lit., "B" is a vitamin and "ts" is no poison, either.

БЭ́БИК, -a, *m., youth, joc.* A baby (from Eng. "baby"). ♦*А где твой бэбик?* "And where's your baby?"

БЭ́БИС, -a, *m.* See **бэ́бик.**

БЭГ, -a, *m., youth.* A bag, purse, case (from Eng. "bag"). ♦*Ты бэг взял?* "Did you bring your bag?"

БЭКСА́ЙД, -a, *m., youth, rude.* Buttocks, behind (from Eng. "backside"). ♦*По-двинь свой бэксайд.* "Move your ass (i.e., get out of the way)."

БЭУ́, *abbr.* Old, worn out (from **бывший в употреблении**, used). ♦*Новых грузо-виков не дают, ездим на бэу.* "They don't supply any new trucks, so we drive these old jalopies."

◆ В ◆

В БО́ГА ДУ́ШУ МАТЬ, *idiom.* A euphemism for **ёб твою́ мать** (see under **еба́ть**).

В ГО́СТИ, ГЛОДА́ТЬ КО́СТИ, *rhyming phrase, joc.* Lit., On a visit, to gnaw at bones. Used in reply to the words Пойдём в гости, "Let's visit [someone]," in the sense that one can't expect anything good from such a visit.

В КА́ЖДОЙ И́СТИНЕ ЕСТЬ ДО́ЛЯ ПРА́ВДЫ, *idiom, joc.* Lit., There's a grain of 'pravda' in every 'istina' (playing on the two Russian words for "truth"). Distorted from В каждой сказке есть доля правды, "There's a grain of truth in every fairy tale." Used to express doubt of some assertion.

В ПО́ЛНЫЙ РОСТ, *idiom, youth.* Fully, to one's heart's content. ◆*Мы в Сочи отдохнули в полный рост.* "We had a perfect vacation in Sochi."

В РОТ ТЕБЕ́ ПАРОХО́Д, *idiom, euph., rude.* Up yours, the hell with you (lit., a steamboat in your mouth). ◆*Что ты орёшь, в рот тебе пароход?* "What are you shouting about? The hell with you!"

В СОЮЗПЕЧА́ТЬ — ГОВНО́ КАЧА́ТЬ, *obs. (Sov.), rude.* Lit., To Soyuzpechat', to pump shit. A rhyming phrase used to express distaste in reply to a mention of going to Союзпечать, a network of kiosks or shops distributing newspapers, magazines, stationery, etc.

В ТЕМНОТЕ́, ДА НЕ ОБЕ́ДАЛ, *idiom, joc.* Lit., In the dark, but haven't had dinner. Distorted from В тесноте, да не в обиде, "It's crowded, but friendly." Used to accept an offer of dinner.

ВАГО́Н И МА́ЛЕНЬКАЯ ТЕЛЕ́ЖКА, *idiom, joc.* Very much, a lot (lit., a wagon and a little side cart). ◆*Ого, сколько фруктов принесли! — Да, вагон и маленькая тележка.* "Wow, look at all the fruit they brought! — Yeah, a wagonload and then some."

ВАЖНЯ́К, -ка́, *m.* **1.** An important person, bigwig, VIP. ◆*Ты этого важняка знаешь?* "Do you know that big shot?"

2. *youth.* Something important, significant. ◆*Для меня эта новость — важняк!* "This news is a big deal for me."

ВАЙН, -а, *m., youth.* Wine (from Eng. "wine"). ◆*Дай хлебнуть вайна.* "Let me have a sip of wine."

ВАЛА́НДАТЬСЯ/ПРОВАЛА́НДАТЬ-СЯ, *neg.* To dawdle, dilly-dally, lag. ◆*Хватит валандаться, пора идти.* "Stop dawdling — it's time to go."

ВАЛИ́ТЬ/СВАЛИ́ТЬ. To leave (lit., to dump, unload, as from a truck). ◆*Он уже свалил домой.* "He's gone home already." ●**Вали́, но то́лько не в штаны́**, *idiom, rude.* (Playing on literal meaning, "dump"). "Dump away, but not in your pants." ◆*Мне пора валить домой. —Вали, но только не в штаны.* "It's time for me to dump off. — Okay, dump away, but not in your pants."

ВАЛИ́ТЬ/ЗАВАЛИ́ТЬ To kill (lit., to knock, to pull down). ◆*Его так просто не завалишь, надо для этого человека три.* "It won't be easy to kill him—we'll need about three guys for the job."

ВАЛИ́ТЬ/ПОВАЛИ́ТЬ па́чками, *idiom.* To go in a group, go in packs. ◆*В этот магазин люди пачками валят.* "Crowds of people go to that store."

ВАЛТУ́РИТЬ/ИЗВАЛТУ́РИТЬ. To beat, to bruise. ◆*Кто тебя так извалтурил, весь в синяках?* "Who beat you up with all those black-and-blue marks?"

ВАЛЯ́Й! *idiom.* Go ahead, proceed. ◆*Можно я возьму твой словарь? — Валяй!* "May I borrow your dictionary? — Go ahead."

ВАЛЯ́ТЬ/СВАЛЯ́ТЬ ва́ньку, *idiom, neg.* From the name of a children's game, Ванька — встанька, involving a doll. **1.** To feign stupidity, play the fool. ◆*Не валяй ваньку, ты всё прекрасно понимаешь.* "Don't play dumb, you understand perfectly well what's going on." **2.** To make a mistake. ◆*Я свалял ваньку, когда купил эту машину.* "I made a big mistake when I bought this car."

ВАМП, -а, *т., neg.* A vampire. ♦ *Это настоящий вамп, ему нравится мучить людей.* "He's a real vampire — he likes to torment people."

ВАМПИРÉЛЛА, -ы, *т. & f., joc.* A greedy person. ♦ *Пока не наворует, эта вампирелла не успокоится.* "That vampire isn't happy unless she steals a big haul."

ВАН, -а, *т., youth, obs.* One ruble (from Eng. "one"). ♦ *Ещё вана не хватает на сигареты.* "I need another ruble for cigarettes."

ВАНТАЖИ́СТ, -а, *т., crim.* A cardsharp. ♦ *С ним не садись, он вантажист.* "Don't play with him — he's a cardsharp."

ВÁНЬКА: Валя́ть/сваля́ть ва́ньку, see under **валя́ть.**

ВАРГÁНИТЬ/СВАРГÁНИТЬ. To prepare or cook something very quickly. ♦ *Сваргань что-нибудь поесть.* "Throw something together to eat."

ВÁРЕЖКА, -и, *f., rude.* A mouth (lit., a mitten). ♦ *Закрой варежку!* "Shut up!" •**Разева́ть/рази́нуть ва́режку,** see under **разева́ть.**

ВАРЁНКА, -и, *f.* Bleach-stained denim (fashionable in the 1980s). ♦ *У него куртка из варёнки.* "He's got a bleached-denim jacket."

ВАРЁНКИ, варёнок, *pl.* Jeans made from bleach-stained denim. ♦ *Классные у него варёнки.* "He's got a classy pair of bleached-denim jeans."

ВАРИ́ТЬ/СВАРИ́ТЬ МЫ́ЛО, idiom (lit., to boil soap, refers to how soap used to be made). To perform, compose, or produce a cheesy soap opera or a low-quality drama.

ВАРИ́ТЬСЯ/ПОВАРИ́ТЬСЯ. Lit., to boil, to steam. To remain for a long time in a certain group of people or at a certain job. ♦ *Я варился в их компании года три, всё о них знаю.* "I hung out with them for three years, so I know everything about them."

ВАРЯ́Г, -а, *т.* A manager brought into an organization from outside. (From the Scandinavian warriors invited to rule ancient Kievan Rus.) ♦ *К нам в институт директором придёт варяг.* "We're having a 'varyag' as the next director of our Institute."

ВАСЬ-ВÁСЬ: (На) вась-ва́сь, *idiom, joc.* On friendly terms, on a first-name basis (from Вася, nickname for "Vasily"). ♦ *Он в министерстве со всеми вась-вась.* "He's on first-name terms with everyone at the ministry."

ВÁСЬКА, -и, *т., crim.* A guard, lookout in illegal games of cards or "thimbles" (cf. **наперсток**). ♦ *Если смотреть, как идёт игра в наперсток, сразу можно обнаружить васек, которые высматривают милицию.* "If you watch carefully at a game of thimbles, you'll see some 'vaskas' on the lookout for the police."

ВÁСЯ, -и, *т., neg.* A stupid person (lit., nickname for "Vasily"). ♦ *Эх ты, Вася, кто так делает?* "You dumbbell, what do you think you're doing!" •**Го́лый Ва́ся ночева́л,** see under **го́лый. Гуля́й, Ва́ся (жуй опи́лки)!** see under **гуля́й.**

ВАТРУ́ШКА, -и, *f., youth, neg.* A woman of loose morals (lit., a cheese tart). ♦ *Возьми пару ватрушек и подъезжай ко мне.* "Pick up a couple of tarts and bring them over to my place."

ВÁУЧЕР, -а, *т., neg.* Lit., a voucher — a very foreign-sounding word introduced with reference to the unsuccessful plan for privatization of state-owned property in 1991. **1.** A penis. ♦ *Как ваучер, ещё функционирует?* "How's your 'voucher' — still working?" **2.** Mouth. ♦ *Закрой свой ваучер, несешь чёрт знает что!* "Shut your 'voucher,' you're spouting rubbish!"

ВÁФЛЯ: Дава́ть/дать ва́флю, see under **дава́ть. Брать/взять ва́флю,** see under **брать.**

ВАХЛÁК, -ка́, *т., neg.* An idler, milksop, do-nothing. ♦ *Наш вахлак ничего в жизни не добьётся.* "That milksop will never accomplish anything in life."

ВАЩÉ, *interj., youth.* Distorted form of вообще, "altogether." **1.** *neg.* Oh, come on! Are you kidding?! ♦ *Ну, ты ваще, как ты поверил?* "Oh, come on! How

could you have believed such a thing?!"
2. *pos.* Wow! Amazing! ♦ *Столько пива
отхватил? Ну ты даёшь, ваще!* "How
did you manage to get so much beer!
Wow! Good for you!"

ВДОЛБИ́ТЬ, *perf., rude.* To engage in a
vigorous sex act (lit., to chisel). ♦ *Как
ты думаешь, он уже вдолбил ей?* "Do
you think he's screwed her yet?"

**ВДРАБАДА́Н (ВДРЕБАДА́Н, ВДРЕ-
БЕДЕ́НЬ, ВДРЫЗГ).** See **вдребезину.**

ВДРЕБЕЗИ́НУ, *adv., neg.* Extremely
drunk (by wordplay from **вдрезину** and
вдребезги, "to pieces," "in smither-
eens"). ♦ *Он там вдребезину пьяный
лежит.* "He's lying there dead drunk."

ВДРЕЗИ́НУ, *adv., neg.* Extremely, too
much (of degrees of drunkenness; from
дрезина, "[railway] trolley"). ♦ *Он пьян
вдрезину.* "He's drunk out of his mind."

ВДРУГ БЫВА́ЕТ ТО́ЛЬКО ПУК,
rhyming phrase, rude. Lit., A fart is the
only thing that happens suddenly. A
rhyming phrase used in reply to a
question beinning with "Вдруг…?",
("what if…?"). ♦ *А вдруг он просту-
дится и заболеет? — Вдруг бывает
только пук.* "But what if he suddenly
catches cold and develops pneumonia?"
— "A fart is the only thing that happens
suddenly."

ВДУВА́ТЬ/ВДУТЬ, *youth.* To smoke narcotics by taking the lit end of a cigarette
into one's mouth and breathing out the
smoke for someone else to inhale.
♦ *Хочешь ещё вдуну?* "Do you want
another drag?"

ВДУПЕЛИ́НУ, *adv., neg.* In a very drunk
condition. ♦ *Мой с твоим опять вдупе-
лину пришли с получки.* "It's a payday
again — my husband and yours have
come home drunk."

ВДУТЬ, *rude.* To have sex with a woman
(lit., to inflate). ♦ *Ты собираешься ей
вдуть?* "Are you going to sleep with
her?"

ВЕДРО́, -а́, *n.* Head (lit., bucket). ♦ *Стой,
не крути своим ведром. Дай причешу
тебя.* "Stop twisting your head around,
I'm trying to comb your hair."

ВЕК ВО́ЛЬВЫ НЕ ВИДА́ТЬ, *idiom, joc.*
An oath attributed to "New Russians"
(lit., May I never see a 'Volvo'!, playing
on the criminal oath Век воли (свободы)
не видать, "May I never see freedom!").

ВЕК СВОБО́ДЫ НЕ ВИДА́ТЬ, *idiom,
crim.* On my word of honor (lit., [may I]
never see freedom [if I'm lying]). ♦ *Мы
тебе не верим, не может быть, что
вы вдвоём взяли такие деньги. — Век
свободы не видать, нам пофартило.*
"We don't believe that the two of you
managed to steal that much money. —
Cross my heart we did — we just got
lucky."

ВЕ́ЛИК, -а, *m.* A bicycle (from велосипед).

ВЕЛИ́КИЙ: Наш вели́кий и могу́чий,
see under **наш.**

ВЕ́НИК, -а, *m.* A bouquet or bunch of
flowers (lit., a broom). ♦ *Поставь веник
в воду.* "Put the flowers into water."

ВЕ́НТИЛЬ, -я, *m., rude.* A mouth (lit., a
large tap). ♦ *Закрой вентиль, надоел.*
"Shut your mouth. You're boring me."

ВЕНЯ́К, -а́, *m., youth.* A vein. ♦ *Не знаю,
куда колоть, веняка не видно.* "I don't
know where to make an injection — I
can't find a vein."

ВЕРБАНУ́ТЫЙ, -ая, -ое, *police, crim.*
Recruited (from завербованный). ♦ *Он
давно вербанутый?* "Was he recruited a
long time ago?"

ВЕРБЛЮ́Д: От верблю́да, *idiom, joc.* It's
none of your business (lit., from a camel,
used by rhyme play in answer to the question Откуда? "From where?"). ♦ *Откуда у тебя эти часы? —От верблюда.*
"Where did you get that watch? —From a
camel." **Докажи́, что ты не верблю́д,**
see under **докажи́.**

ВЕРБЛЯ́ДЬ, -и, *f., rude.* A prostitute (by
wordplay on верблюд, "camel," and
блядь, "whore"). ♦ *Откуда взялась
эта верблядь?* "Where did that prostitute come from?"

ВЕРЁВКА, -и, *f.* A wire, a cable (lit., a
горе). ♦ *Эта верёвка не подходит к
этому сканеру.* "That cable won't connect to this scanner."

ВЕРЗА́ТЬ/ПОВЕРЗА́ТЬ, *neg., rude.* **1.** To defecate. ♦*Ты уже поверзал?* "Have you taken a shit yet?" **2.** To be frightened. ♦*Не верзай, прорвёмся.* "Don't be scared. We're going to make it all right."

ВЕРЗО́, -а́, *n., rude.* Behind, rear end. ♦*Мне сделали укол в верзо.* "They gave me the injection in my butt."

ВЕРЗО́ХА, -и, *f., rude.* Behind, rear end. ♦*Всё время пишу, верзоху отсидел.* "I've been sitting here writing so long that I've worn out my behind."

ВЕРМУ́ТЬ, -и, *f., joc.* Cheap wine of poor quality (by wordplay on вермут, "vermouth," and муть, "dregs," "mud"). ♦*Зачем вы пьёте эту вермуть?* "Why are you drinking that rotgut?"

ВЕРНЯ́К, *pred. use, youth, pos.* Something certain, a sure thing (from верный, "true," "precise"). ♦*Поверь мне, это дело верняк.* "Believe me, it's in the bag."

ВЕРТЕ́ТЬ¹/ВЕРТАНУ́ТЬ, *crim.* To steal (lit., to turn, twist). ♦*Последнее дело у своих вертеть.* "The worst thing is to steal from your own friends."

ВЕРТЕ́ТЬ²/ЗАВЕРТЕ́ТЬ за́дом, *idiom, neg.* To seek attention, flirt (lit., to wiggle one's behind). ♦*Она уже давно перед ним задом вертит.* "She's been flaunting herself at him for ages already."

ВЕРТИКА́ЛЬ ВЛА́СТИ, *idiom* Hierarchy of political authority, the strict subordination of all levels of authority (lit., an authority vertical). ♦*Укрепили вертикаль власти, а порядка больше не стало.* "They have centralized the political regime, but it hasn't become more orderly."

ВЕРТИХВО́СТКА, -и, *f., neg.* A flirtatious woman (from вертеть хвостом, "wag the tail"). ♦*Эта вертихвостка ни одних брюк не пропустит.* "That flirt can't pass up any pair of pants."

ВЕРТУХА́Й, -я, *m., crim.* A prison guard.

ВЕРТУХА́ТЬСЯ/ЗАВЕРТУХА́ТЬСЯ, *crim.* To fuss, be jittery, be nervous. ♦*Не вертухайся, сиди тихо, всё будет как надо.* "Don't jitter around, sit still, and everything will be okay."

ВЕРТУ́ШКА, -и, *f.* **1.** *army.* A helicopter (from вертолёт). ♦*Туда добраться можно только на вертушке.* "The only way to get there is by helicopter." **2.** A government telephone, direct connection to high government officials. ♦*Я сразу по вертушке связался с Кремлём.* "I phoned direct to the Kremlin."

ВЕРХА́, -о́в, *pl., crim.* Outer pockets of slacks or jacket. ♦*Деньги в верха не клади, вытащат.* "Don't put money in your outer pockets — it'll be stolen."

ВЕС: Держа́ть вес, see under **держа́ть.**

ВЕСЛО́, -а́, *n.,* **1.** *crim.* A spoon (lit., a paddle). ♦*Бери весло, мечи кашу.* "Pick up your spoon and eat your kasha." **2.** *army.* A machine-gun. ♦*Весло без патронов, что палка.* "Without ammunition, a tommy-gun is just a stick."

ВЕСТИ́СЬ, *imperf., youth.* To go along with, be compliant. ♦*Она никак не ведётся на постель.* "She'll never agree to go to bed with anyone."

ВЕ́ТЕР: Ходи́ть/пойти́ до ве́тру, see under **ходи́ть.**

ВЕ́ТКИ, ве́ток, *pl., youth, neg.* Hands, arms (lit., branches). ♦*Куда ты тянешь свои ветки, всем дам бутерброды по очереди.* "Don't wave your branches! Everyone will get a sandwich."

ВЕТРО́ВКА, -и, *f.* A windbreaker; light, hooded jacket of nylon or other synthetic material. ♦*Возьми ветровку и сапоги.* "Take your windbreaker and your boots."

ВЕЧЕРИ́НА, -ы, *f.* A party. ♦*Некогда мне бегать по вечеринам, мне работать надо по вечерам.* "Going to parties is not my thing; I have to work in the evenings."

ВЕЧЁРКА, -и, *f.* A nickname for the Moscow newspaper Вечерняя Москва.

ВЕ́ШАЛКА, -и, *f., neg.* **1.** Gallows, death, calamity (lit., a clothes hanger). ♦*Если он потребует долг, для меня это — вешалка.* "If he demands his money back it will be all over for me." **2.** A skinny girl (lit., a coat rack, a hat rack). ♦*Смотри, как на ней пальто висит, ну и худющая, чистая вешалка.* "Look at how that dress hangs off of her, she's not just skinny, she's a coat rack."

ВЕ́ШАТЬ/ПОВЕ́СИТЬ: Ве́шать/пове́-сить лапшу́ на́ уши, *idiom, neg.* To deceive, fool (lit., to hang a noodle from someone's ears). ♦*Не вешай мне лапшу на уши, я в это всё равно не верю.* "Don't try to pull the wool over my eyes! I don't believe a word of it." **Ве́шать/пове́сить лы́чки,** *idiom, army.* To promote in rank (lit., to hang stripes). ♦*Ему ещё одну лычку повесили, теперь он сержант.* "They hung another stripe on him, so now he's a sergeant." **Ве́шать/пове́сить спаге́тти на у́ши,** *idiom, joc.* To kid, fool, deceive (lit., to hang spaghetti from someone's ears; formed on the older idiom **ве́шать лапшу́ на у́ши,** "to hang a noodle on someone's ears"). ♦*Не вешай мне спагетти на уши, я знаю, где ты был.* "Don't try to kid me. I know where you've been."

ВЗБРЫ́КИВАТЬ/ВЗБРЫКНУ́ТЬ, *neg.* To object, contradict, behave arbitrarily or unpredictably (lit., to kick). ♦*Опять она взбрыкнула и не пришла, как договорились.* "Again she's been undependable — she didn't keep our appointment."

ВЗВОД: На взво́де, *idiom.* Drunk (lit., cocked [of a gun]). ♦*Не наливай ему, он и так на взводе.* "Don't give him any more to drink. He's half-cocked already."

ВЗДРА́ГИВАТЬ/ВЗДРО́ГНУТЬ, *joc.* To drink (lit., to shudder, be startled). ♦*Не хочешь вздрогнуть?* "Let's have a drink."

ВЗДРО́ЧЕННЫЙ, -ая, -ое, *neg., rude.* On edge, testy, nervous (from **дрочи́ть**). ♦*Что ты сегодня такой вздроченный?* "Why are you so touchy today?"

ВЗДРЮ́ЧЕННЫЙ, -ая, -ое, *neg.* See **вздро́ченный.**

ВЗДРЮ́ЧИВАТЬ/ВЗДРЮ́ЧИТЬ, *neg.* To scold, reprimand (lit., to beat up, abuse). ♦*Мать его вздрючила за пьянку.* "His mother bawled him out for getting drunk."

ВЗДРЮ́ЧИВАТЬСЯ/ВЗДРЮ́ЧИТЬ-СЯ, *neg.* To worry, fret, be anxious. ♦*Не надо так вздрючиваться, всё не так плохо.* "There's no call to worry like that

— things aren't so bad."

ВЗДРЮ́ЧКА, -и, *f., neg.* A scolding, reprimand. ♦*Теперь жди вздрючки, я лыжи сломал.* "I'm going to get a tongue-lashing now — I've gone and broken the skis."

ВЗЛЁТКА, -и, *f., army.* An aisle between beds in barracks (from **взлётная полоса,** "runway").

ВЗЛЯ́ГИВАТЬ/ВЗЛЯГНУ́ТЬ, *neg.* To be contrary, headstrong. ♦*Что-то она взлягивает, не хочет идти в ресторан.* "She's just being obstinate — she doesn't want to go to the restaurant." ♦*Не взлягивай, успокойся, не возьму я твои деньги.* "Relax, don't be so touchy! I'm not going to take your money."

ВЗРО́СЛЫЙ ВОР, *idiom, crim.* An experienced thief. ♦*Он не подведёт, он взрослый вор.* "You can count on him — he's an experienced thief."

ВЗРЫВА́ТЬ/ВЗОРВА́ТЬ, *youth.* To begin smoking a narcotic cigarette (lit., to burst). ♦*Ну, кто взорвёт первый?* "Who's going to light this joint?"

ВЗЪЁБКА, -и, *f., rude.* A punishment. ♦*Мне будет взъёбка от жены за то, что не принёс зарплату.* "I'm going to get it from my wife for not bringing home my paycheck."

ВИБРИ́РОВАТЬ/ЗАВИБРИ́РОВАТЬ, *joc.* To be upset, worried (lit., to vibrate). ♦*Не надо вибрировать, всё будет хорошо.* "Don't worry. Everything's going to be all right."

ВИДА́К, -ка́, *m.* A VCR. ♦*У тебя видак есть?* "Do you have a VCR?"

ВИ́ДЕТЬ: Ви́деть кого́-что-л. в гробу́, *idiom, neg.* To despise, spit on (lit., to see someone or something in the grave). ♦*В гробу я видел эту работу.* "I despise that work." **Ви́деть кого́-л. в гробу́ в бе́лых та́почках,** *idiom, neg.* To despise (lit., to see someone in the grave with white slippers on). ♦*Я эту бабу видел в гробу в белых тапочках.* "I despise that broad." **В упо́р не ви́деть,** *idiom.* To give the cold shoulder (lit., not to recognize even face-to-face). ♦*Раньше мы были друзья, а теперь он меня в упор *не видит.* "We used to be friends, but now he doesn't acknowledge my existence."

ВИ́ДИК, -а, *m.* See **вида́к.**

ВИДЮ́ШНИК, -а, *m.* See **вида́к.**

ВИЗГ: До порося́чьего ви́зга, *idiom.* Too much (esp. of drinking) (lit., to a piglet's squeal). ♦*Вчера они напились до поросячьего визга.* "Yesterday they got squealing drunk."

ВИ́ЛКА, -и, *f., business.* A profit margin (lit., fork). ♦*Какая сегодня вилка по долларам?* "What's the margin on dollars today?"

ВИНДЫ́, -о́в, *pl.* Windows software. ♦*На твоём компьютере винды стоят?* "Do you have Windows on your PC?"

ВИНИ́Л, -а, *m., youth, south.* A (vinyl) record.

ВИНТ, -á, *m., youth.* A type of narcotic. ♦*Я пользую только винт.* "'Vint' is the only kind of dope I use." • **БЫТЬ НА ВИНТА́Х,** *idiom.* To be tense, nervous. ♦*Ты на винтах всю неделю, так нельзя.* "You've been so wound up all week, you can't go on like this." •**От винта́,** *joc.* Stand aside! Get out of the way! ♦*От винта! Не трогайте машину!* "Stand aside! Don't touch that car!" **Во́дка с винто́м,** see under **во́дка. Идти́/пойти́ винто́м,** see under **идти́. Нама́тывать/намота́ть на винт,** see under **нама́тывать.**

ВИНТИ́ЛОВО, -а, *n., youth.* Police detention, arrest. ♦*Не ходи туда, там сейчас идёт винтилово.* "Don't go over there. They're taking everyone into custody."

ВИНТИ́ТЬ/ПОВИНТИ́ТЬ, *youth.* **1.** To arrest. ♦*Вчера наших много повинтили.* "Yesterday a bunch of our guys were arrested." **2.** To run away, to go away. ♦*Они свинтили уже по домам.* "They've already gone home."

ВИСКА́РЬ, -ря́, *m., youth.* Whisky, a bottle of whisky. ♦*Знаешь, сколько вискарь сейчас по-чёрному стоит?* "Do you know the current price of a bottle of whisky on the black market?"

ВИ́СКИ ИЗ ПИПИ́СКИ, *neg.* A rhyming phrase used to describe bad liquor (lit., whisky from pee-pee-sky).

ВИСЮ́К, -а, *m.* A computer freeze-up. ♦*Опять висюк, вирус попал через сеть, что ли?* "My PC has frozen up again, I wonder if it has caught a virus from the Internet."

ВИСЯ́К, *pred. use, youth.* **1.** An uncertain situation (from висеть, "to hang," "to hover"; cf. **зависа́ть**). ♦*У меня с работой — висяк.* "Things are shaky with my job." ♦*С деньгами пока — висяк.* "The money situation just now is precarious." **2.** *m., crim.* An unsolved case. ♦*Сколько у нас висяков по угону машин?* "How many unsolved cases do we have on stolen cars?"

ВИТАМИ́Н В, *idiom, business.* A bribe (by wordplay on "vitamin V" and взятка, "bribe"). ♦*А сколько витамина "В" ему дать?* "How much vitamin V should we give him?"

ВИТРИ́НА, -ы, *f.* A woman's breasts, bosom (lit., window). ♦*У неё витрина ничего.* "She's got a nice bust."

ВКА́ЛЫВАТЬ, *imperf. only, neg.* To work hard and long (lit., to inject). ♦*Нам пришлось вкалывать с утра до ночи.* "We had to drudge from morning to night."

ВКАТИ́ТЬ ПРОМЕ́Ж ГЛАЗ, *idiom.* To hit in the face (lit., to roll between the eyes). ♦*Быстро он тебе вкатил промеж глаз, без разговоров.* "He punched you in the face without any preliminaries."

ВКЛЕ́ИВАТЬ/ВКЛЕ́ИТЬ. To hit, beat up. ♦*Тебе вклеить или сам уйдёшь?* "Do I have to give you a licking, or will you leave on your own?"

ВКЛЕ́ЙКА, -и, *f.* Punishment. ♦*За все дела будет тебе вклейка от матери!* "You're really going to get it from your mother for the things you've done!"

ВКЛЮЧА́ТЬ/ВКЛЮЧИ́ТЬ дурака́, *idiom.* To play the fool, play innocent. ♦*Включай дурака, делай вид, что ничего не знаешь.* "Play dumb — make like you don't know a thing."

ВКЛЮЧИ́ТЬСЯ, *perf. only, youth.* To

crash, collide. ♦ *Вчера они включились на "Жигуле" в дерево, не вписались в поворот.* "Yesterday they missed a turn in the road and crashed their Zhiguli into a tree."

ВКУСНЯ́ЧИЙ, -ая, -ее, *pos.* Very tasty, delicious. ♦ *Кто это приготовил такой вкуснячий суп?* "Who made this delicious soup?"

ВЛА́ЖНЫЙ, -ого, *m., joc.* A drunk (from влажный, "moist").

ВЛА́МЫВАТЬ/ВЛОМИ́ТЬ, *neg.* To beat up, give a beating. ♦ *Ему вчера Колька вломил как следует.* "Yesterday Kolka gave him quite a thrashing."

ВЛЕЗТЬ: Чем да́льше влез, тем бо́льше интере́с, see under **чем.**

ВЛЕПЛЯ́ТЬ/ВЛЕПИ́ТЬ, *neg.* To hit, to strike; used in any quick, decisive action. ♦ *Учитель влепил ему пару.* "The teacher smacked him with a failing grade."

ВЛЕТА́ТЬ/ВЛЕТЕ́ТЬ. 1. To get into an unpleasant situation. ♦ *Опять ты влетела на друзьях, который раз они тебя обманули.* "Again you've got into trouble through those friends of yours, how many times they've deceived you!" **2.** To get pregnant (see **залете́ть**).

ВЛИВА́НИЕ, -я, *n., joc.* A reprimand, punishment (lit., enema; cf. **кли́зма**). ♦ *Сейчас нам за драку будет вливание.* "Now we're going to catch it for that fight."

ВЛИВА́ТЬ/ВЛИТЬ, *joc.* To punish, scold (lit., to give an enema). ♦ *Ему за прогулы сейчас вольют.* "He's going to get it for missing work." • **ВЛИВА́ТЬ/ВЛИТЬ под шку́ру,** *idiom.* To scold, to punish (lit., to pour under the skin). ♦ *Ну хватит вливать под шкуру, всё я уже понял.* "Quit scolding me already! I've got the point."

ВЛИПА́ЛОВО, -a, *n., youth.* An unpleasant, dangerous situation. See **влипа́ть.**

ВЛИПА́ТЬ/ВЛИ́ПНУТЬ. To get into an unpleasant situation. ♦ *Кажется, мы влипли, сейчас нас будут бить.* "It looks like we're in trouble. They're going to beat us up."

ВЛЫ́НДИТЬ (ЗАЛЫ́НДИТЬ). See вманди́чить.

ВМА́ЗКА, -и, *f., youth.* A dose of a narcotic. ♦ *Ещё одна вмазка осталась.* "There was still one hit of the stuff left."

ВМА́ЗЫВАТЬ/ВМА́ЗАТЬ, *youth.* **1.** To strike, hit. ♦ *Вмажь ему за всё.* "Beat him up to get back at him for everything." **2.** To give someone a dose of a narcotic. ♦ *Кому ещё вмазать?* "Who still needs a hit of this stuff?"

ВМАНДЯ́ЧИТЬ, *perf., rude.* To hit, to beat. See **манда́.** ♦ *Я его вчера вмандячил камнем, аж кровь пошла.* "Yesterday I beat him bloody with a stone."

ВМА́ЩИВАТЬ/ВМАСТИ́ТЬ. To do something opportunely, come to someone's rescue (from масть, "suit" [of cards]). ♦ *Ты мне вмастил, что деньги отдал.* "You saved me in the nick of time by returning that money."

В-МО́РДУ-ТРЕ́НИНГ, *idiom, army.* Violence, blows, slaps to the face (lit., in-your-face training). ♦ *Ты прямо просишь в-морду-тренинг, нагло ведёшь себя.* "You're just asking for some in-your-face training by acting so cheeky."

ВМОЧИ́ТЬ, *neg.* To hit, bloody (lit., to make wet). ♦ *Сейчас вмочу!* "Now I'm going to bloody your face."

ВНАГЛЯ́К, *adv., neg.* In a pushy, aggressive, self-serving manner. ♦ *Ты всё привык делать внагляк.* "You're always acting offensive."

ВНАРЕ́ЗКУ, *adv.* In a very drunk condition. Cf. **вре́занный.**

ВНИМА́НИЕ! ГОВОРИ́Т ГЕРМА́НИЯ!, *rhyming phrase, joc.* Lit., Attention! Germany speaking! A rhyming phrase used in response to the words Внимание! Прошу внимания!

ВНУ́ЧКА, -и, *f., homosexual.* Lit., granddaughter. A greeting used by an old homosexual to a young one.

ВО ДАЁТ! An expression of amazement, admiration. ♦ *Смотри, как Славка бежит, во даёт!* "Wow! Look at Slavka run!"

ВО́ВКА-МОРКО́ВКА, *idiom, joc.* A teasing rhyming phrase for a boy named Vladimir (nickname Vova, Vovka).

♦*Вовка-морковка, иди к нам играть.* "Vovka-carrot, come play with us."

ВОДИ́ЛА, -ы, *m., joc.* A driver (from во-дить машину). ♦*Он водилой работа-ет?* "Does he work as a driver?"

ВОДИ́ТЬ ЖА́ЛОМ, *idiom, neg.* To be capricious, difficult (lit., to move one's string [mouth]). ♦*Не води жалом, реши-ли работать, значит работать без разговоров.* "Don't be difficult! We decided to work, and that means work, not chat."

ВО́ДКА: Во́дка с винто́м, *idiom.* A bottle of vodka with a screwcap (considered more desirable than bottles sealed with lead caps). ♦*Купи эту водку с винтом, она лучше.* "Buy that screw-cap bottle of vodka — it's better." **Пья́нствовать во́дку,** see under **пья́нствовать.**

ВО́ДКА БЕЗ ПИ́ВА — ДЕ́НЬГИ НА ВЕ́ТЕР, *idiom.* Vodka should be drunk with beer (lit., Vodka without beer means money's to the wind).

ВО́ДКА — НАШ ВРАГ, И МЫ ЕЁ УНИЧТОЖА́ЕМ, *idiom, joc.* "Vodka is our enemy, so we'll utterly consume it." (This expression is a play on the well-known saying of the Stalin years regarding enemies of the people: Если враг не сдаётся, мы его уничтожаем, "If the enemy won't surrender, we'll utterly consume him.") ♦*Зачем вы пьёте? Это вредно для здоровья. — Водка — наш враг, и мы её уничтожаем.* "Why do you drink? It's bad for your health. — Vodka is our enemy, so we'll utterly consume it!"

"ВО́ДКА — Э́ТО ВИТАМИ́Н!" — СКАЗА́Л ХО ШИ МИН, *joc.* Lit., Ho Chi Minh says: Vodka is a vitamin! A rhyming phrase used in praise of liquor.

ВОДОЛА́З, -а, *m., youth, neg.* Someone who wears eyeglasses (lit., an underwater worker, from the image of wearing goggles or a mask). ♦*Я в очереди стою вон за тем водолазом.* "My place in line is behind that four-eyes over there."

ВОДОПРОВО́ДЧИК, -а, *m., joc.* Someone who urinates frequently (lit., a plumber). ♦*Ну ты и водопроводчик, полчаса*

не посидишь. "What a 'plumber' you are! You can't sit still for half an hour without going to take a leak."

ВОДЯНО́Й. A plumber (lit., a water sprite, from a fairy tale in pagan times, refers to a creature who lives in a marsh). ♦*Вызови водяного, кран опять течёт.* "Call the plumber; our tap is leaking again."

ВОДЯ́РА, -ы, *f., rude.* Vodka. ♦*Водяра у вас есть?* "Have you got any vodka?"

ВОЗБУХА́ТЬ/ВОЗБУХНУ́ТЬ, *rude.* To stir up trouble, be defiant, make objections (from бух, the sound of a crash; cf. **бухте́ть**). ♦*Сиди тихо, не возбухай!* "Sit down and don't make a ruckus."

ВО́ЗДУХ, -а, *m., youth.* **1.** Money (lit., air, perhaps from the expression деньги нужны как воздух, "money is as neces-sary as air"). ♦*С воздухом у меня слож-ности.* "I'm having money problems." **2.** *m., army.* A civilian.

ВОЗДУ́ШКА, -и, *f.* An air gun, pneumatic gun (from воздух, "air"). ♦*Пойдём по-стреляем из воздушки.* "Let's fire the air gun."

ВОЗИ́ТЬ/ПОВОЗИ́ТЬ мо́рдой об ас-фа́льт (об стол), *idiom, neg.* To bawl out, abuse verbally (lit., to push some-one's face onto the ground, or table). ♦*Хватит меня возить мордой об асфальт, все могут ошибаться.* "Stop rubbing my nose in it — anyone can make a mistake."

ВОЗМУДЕ́ТЬ, *perf., rude.* A word used to deflate the pretensions of young people to maturity, adulthood. By wordplay from возмужать, "to become a man," and **муда́к.** ♦*Ты, я вижу, возмудел, роди-телей ни в грош не ставишь.* "I see you've grown up into quite a baby, ignoring your parents like that."

ВОЗЬМИ́ С ПО́ЛКИ ПИРОЖО́К, *idiom, joc.* A sarcastic response to some-one's boasts about his achievements (lit., "Take a cookie from the pantry," i.e., as a reward.) ♦*Ты знаешь, сколько у меня девушек? — Молодец! Возьми с полки пирожок.* "Do you know how many girls I'm going out with? — What a hero!

Take yourself a cookie from the pantry."

ВОКЗА́ЛЬНАЯ ДЕ́ВКА, *idiom, homosexual.* A homosexual who looks for partners in train stations.

ВОЛГА́РЬ, -ря́, *m.* Owner of a Volga, a big car used by officials and rich people (lit., an inhabitant of the Volga region). ◆ *Где здесь гараж волгаря, с бородкой такой?* "Where's the parking space of the 'Volga man' — you know, that guy with the beard?"

ВОЛЖА́НКА, -и, *f.* A Volga automobile. ◆ *Здесь проезжала голубая "волжанка"?* "Did a blue Volga pass by here?"

ВОЛК: Во́лки позо́рные, *idiom, neg., rude.* Scum, riffraff (lit., vicious wolves). ◆ *Опять вы, волки позорные, обыграли пьяного в карты.* "You scum, again you've beaten a drunk man at cards." **Ско́лько во́лка ни корми́, а у слона́ всё равно́ (я́йца) бо́льше,** see under **ско́лько. Тамбо́вский волк тебе́ това́рищ,** see under **тамбо́вский.**

ВОЛНА́: Гнать волну́, see under **гнать**[1].

ВОЛОСА́ТИК, -а, *m., neg., obs.* Someone with long hair (usually referring to a hippie). ◆ *В этом кафе одни волосатики собираются.* "The only people who go to that café are hippies."

ВОЛОСЯ́НКА, -и, *f., rude.* Female genitals (lit., hairy one). ◆ *Она волосянку любому подставляет.* "She'll put out for just anyone."

ВОЛО́ЧЬ, *imperf. only, youth.* To understand, grasp (lit., to drag). ◆ *Ты в машине, вижу, совсем не волочёшь.* "It's obvious you don't understand a thing about cars."

ВОЛТУ́ЗИТЬ/ПОВОЛТУ́ЗИТЬ. To beat. ◆ *За что его так волтузят, как бы не изуродовали.* "Why are they beating him so hard? They'll maim him like that."

ВОЛЫ́НА, -ы, *f., crim.* A pistol, gun (lit., bagpipe). ◆ *Он без волыны не ходит.* "He never goes anywhere without his gun."

ВОЛЫ́НИТЬ/ПРОВОЛЫ́НИТЬ. To procrastinate, postpone, delay (from волынка, "bagpipes"). ◆ *Он проволынил це-*

лый день, так и не починил машину. "He procrastinated all day and never got the car fixed."

ВОЛЬТ, -а (*pl.* **вольты́**), *m., neg., youth.* Abnormality, insanity (pl. only, lit., volts). ◆ *У тебя опять вольты?!* "Have you taken leave of your senses again?" **•Вольты́ прилете́ли,** *idiom.* Someone has gone crazy (lit., the volts have arrived, after the title of Savrasov's famous painting "Грачи прилетели", "The Rooks Have Arrived"). ◆ *Вы что всё время смеётесь, вольты прилетели?* "Why do you keep laughing like that? Bats in the belfry?" **Прики́дываться/прики́нуться вольто́м,** see under **прики́дываться.**

ВОЛЬТАНУ́ТЬСЯ, *perf. only, neg.* To go crazy (lit., to be electrocuted). ◆ *Ты совсем вольтанулся, говоришь такие вещи ребёнку?* "Have you completely flipped out, saying such things to a child?"

ВОЛЬТОВА́ТЬ/ЗАВОЛЬТОВА́ТЬ, *youth.* To shirk, avoid, circumvent work. ◆ *У нас не завольтуешь!* "There'll be no malingering here in this outfit."

ВОНЬ ПОДРЕЙТУ́ЗНАЯ, *idiom, rude.* A bad person, scoundrel (usually of a woman). (From рейтузы, women's long underwear; lit., stench under the panties). ◆ *А твоей, вонь подрейтузная, чтоб ноги даже не было!* "Never set foot in this house again, you piece of filth!"

ВОНЮ́ЧКА, -и, *f., neg.* A nasty, disgusting person (lit., stinker). ◆ *Эта вонючка опять ругалась.* "That skunk yelled at us again."

ВООБРАЖА́ЛА, ХВОСТ ПОДЖА́ЛА, *rhyming phrase, neg.* Said to people with too high an opinion of themselves, their looks, their clothes (mainly in children's speech). Lit., "Stuck-up fellow, you've got your tail between your legs." ◆ *Вы что не видите? У меня платье новое! — Воображала, хвост поджала.* "Look at my new dress! — Don't be so stuck-up!"

ВОР В ЗАКО́НЕ, *idiom, crim.* A thief who observes the thieves' code of honor, the main articles of which are (1) don't work in prison, (2) don't report to or otherwise cooperate with prison authorities, and (3) obey orders of criminal authorities. ♦ *Он вор в законе, он работать не будет.* "He's a law-abiding thief; his code forbids him to work."

ВОРК, -а, *m., youth, obs.* Work (from Eng. "work"). ♦ *Сегодня неохота идти на ворк.* "I don't feel like going to work today."

ВОРКОВА́ТЬ/ЗАВОРКОВА́ТЬ. To work (from Eng. "work"). ♦ *Кто сегодня воркует на кухне, моет посуду?* "Who's on dish-washing duty today in the kitchen."

ВО́РОН(О́К), -а, (-нка́), *m.* A dark blue police cr (lit., a crow).

ВОРО́НА, -ы, *f.* An absent-minded person. ♦ *Опять ты не то купил, ворона.* "Again you've bought the wrong thing, you featherbrain."

ВОРОТИ́ТЬ/ОТВОРОТИ́ТЬ ры́ло, *idiom, neg.* To turn up one's nose at something, reject. ♦ *Ешь, не вороти рыла, больше нет ничего.* "You'd better not turn up your nose at the food — it's all there is."

ВОРОТНИ́К: Попра́вь воротни́к, врать меша́ет, see under **попра́вь.**

ВОСЬМИДЕРА́СТ, -а, *m., neg.* A member of the generation of the 1980s, alluding to the "New Russians" (by wordplay on восемьдесят, "80," and педераст, "pederast"). ♦ *Среди висьмидерастов мало порядочных людей.* "There aren't many honest people of the 80s generation."

ВО́ШКАТЬ ЧЕРЕПАНА́МИ, *idiom, army.* To turn one's head from side to side (lit., to turn one's skull). ♦ *Кто там вошкает черепанами, уже была команда «смирно!».* "Who's that rubbernecking over there? You've been called to attention!"

ВО́ШКАТЬСЯ/ПРОВО́ШКАТЬСЯ, *neg.* To waste time, take a long time, dawdle (lit., to pick nits). ♦ *Кончай вошкаться, опаздываем.* "Stop dawdling, or we'll be late."

ВОШЛЯКИ́, -о́в, *pl., crim.* Crabs, pubic lice (from вошь, "louse"). ♦ *Надо бы*

мазь достать, вошляки завелись. "I've got to get some ointment, I've got crabs."

ВОШЬ: Скака́ть, как вошь на гребешке́, see under **скака́ть. Ядрёна вошь,** see under **ядрёна.**

В ПА́ДЛУ, *idiom.* Contrary to one's wishes, involves negative feelings. See **западло́.**

ВПА́РИВАТЬ/ВПАРИ́ТЬ, *neg.* To palm off (defective goods). ♦ *Смотри, там могут впарить фальшивые доллары.* "Watch out that they don't palm off any counterfeit dollars on you."

ВПАЯ́ТЬ, *perf.* To beat, to punish (from паять, "to solder"). ♦ *Видно, сильно тебе впаяли, еле ходишь.* "It looks like they really beat you up, you can hardly walk. **Впаять по чайнику,** *idiom.* To hit in the head or in the face. ♦ *Так и хочется впаять тебе по чайнику как следует.* "Oh, how I'd like to smack you in the face!"

ВПАЯ́ТЬСЯ, *perf. only, neg.* To crash (from паять, "to weld, solder"). ♦ *Сейчас туман, запросто можно впаяться во встречную.* "In this fog you could easily crash into an oncoming vehicle."

ВПЕНДЕ́РИВАТЬ/ ВПЕНДЕ́РИТЬ, *neg.* To reprimand, to call on the carpet (lit., to fuck). See **вставля́ть.** ♦ *Любит он впендерить просто так для профилактики.* "He likes to bawl people out for no special reason—'just in case'."

ВПЕРЁД, ДРУЗЬЯ́, А Я ЗА ВА́МИ. Я ГРУ́ДЬЮ ПОСТОЮ́ ЗА ВА́ШИМИ СПИНА́МИ, *rhyming phrase, joc.* Used in response to an exhortation to do something difficult or demanding, mimicking the exhorter. Lit., "Forward, friends, I'm behind you! I'll lay down my life for you — behind the cover of your backs!" ♦ *Ну что, вперёд, ещё немного, и мы закончим этот ремонт. — Вперёд, друзья, а я за вами. Я грудью постою за вашими спинами.* "Come on, fellows, we're almost done with this job. — Forward, friends, I'm behind you! I'll lay down my life for you — behind your backs."

ВПЕРЕ́ТЬСЯ, *perf. only, neg.* To enter unexpectedly, to burst in without permission or invitation. ♦ *Мы не знали, что там заседание, вот и впёрлись.* "We didn't realize there was a meeting in session, so we just burst in."

ВПИ́ЛИВАТЬСЯ/ВПИЛИТЬ/ВПИЛИ́Т ЬСЯ. 1. To run into, meet unexpectedly (пилить, "to saw"). ♦ *Будешь уходить с работы, смотри, не впились в начальника.* "If you slip out of the office be careful not to run into the boss." **2.** To collide with something in a car. ♦ *Он на своей машине впилился в столб.* "He ran into a pole with his car." **3.** To beat up, to hit. ♦ *Я тебе сейчас так впилю, своих не узнаешь.* "I'm going to hit you so hard you won't recognize your own mother."

ВПИ́СКА, -и, *f., youth, obs.* A place to spend the night (cf. **пропи́ска**). ♦ *Как насчёт вписки, на две ночи нужна.* "What about a pad? I need a place for two nights."

ВПИ́СЫВАТЬ/ВПИСА́ТЬ, *youth.* To permit someone to live or spend nights in one's apartment. ♦ *Он нас впишет на пару дней?* "Will he put us up for a couple of days?"

ВПИ́СЫВАТЬСЯ/ВПИСА́ТЬСЯ, *youth.* To fit, match; to meet no objection; to be opportune. ♦ *Мы в компанию впишемся?* "Will we fit in with that group?"

В ПОЛНОГИ́, *idiom.* Not in full swing, half-heartedly (lit., half-legged). ♦ *В полноги будешь английский учить – никогда не выучишь.* "If you study English half-heartedly – nothing will come of it."

ВПРАВЛЯ́ТЬ/ВПРА́ВИТЬ мозги́, *idiom.* To correct, set right. ♦ *Ему мозги не вправишь, раз решил уехать, значит, уедет.* "Don't try to set him straight; once he's decided to go, he'll go."

ВРАТА́РЬ, -я, *m., joc.* A bouncer in a restaurant or bar (lit., goalkeeper) ♦ *Туда так просто не войдёшь, надо зарядить вратаря.* "It's not easy to get in there, we'll have to bribe the bouncer."

ВРЕ́ЗАННЫЙ, -ая, -ое, *neg.* Drunk. ♦ *Ещё утро, а он уже врезанный идёт.* "It's still morning, and he's already going around drunk."

ВРЕЗА́ТЬ/ВРЕ́ЗАТЬ. To drink a large amount of alcohol. ♦ *Он врезать ой как любит!* "How he likes to swill it down!" •**Вре́зать по стопа́рику,** *idiom.* To drink a shot-glass each. ♦ *Давай врежем по стопарику.* "Come on, let's have just a little drink." •**Вреза́ть/вре́зать по са́мое не хочу́,** *idiom, joc.* To strike, to punish. ♦ *Кризис врезал нам всем по самое не хочу.* "The economic crisis has hurt everyone."

ВРУБА́ТЬ/ВРУБИ́ТЬ. To turn on, turn up (from рубильник, an electric switching mechanism). ♦ *Вруби музыку посильней!* "Turn up the volume of the music!"

ВРУБА́ТЬСЯ/ВРУБИ́ТЬСЯ. 1. To understand. ♦ *Что-то я не врублюсь, о чём разговор.* "I really don't understand what you're talking about." **2.** To crash into something. ♦ *Они в мотоцикле врубились в дерево.* "They ran into a tree on their motorcycle."

ВРУ́БЕЛЬ, -я. *m.* A person who's quick on the uptake (lit., Vrubel, a famous Russian artist, a wordplay on "Врубель" and "врубаться" – to understand. ♦ *Он сразу понял что к чему, нашему Врубелю объяснять два раза не нужно.* See **вруба́ться.** "He quickly understood everything, our 'Vrubel' doesn't need things to him explained twice."

ВРУБО́Н, -а, *m., youth.* Understand, grasp. ♦ *У тебя врубона нет, а это всё просто.* "You don't get it at all, and yet it's so simple."

ВРУНО́К, врунка́, *m., joc.* A radio set, radio receiver (a Sovietism from врун, "a liar," alluding to the assumption that official radio news is all lies). ♦ *Включи врунок, скоро новости.* "Turn on the lie-machine; it's time for the news."

ВСА́ЖИВАТЬ/ВСАДИ́ТЬ. 1. To beat, to hit. **2.** To have intensive sex with a woman. ♦ *Вот кому надо всадить, видишь, как на мужиков смотрит?* "There's a woman you should screw — look how she ogles all the men." •**Вса́живать/Всади́ть по ты́кве (по пле́ши, по жба́ну),** *idiom, neg.* To hit in the head (lit., to plunge in the pumpkin [bald spot, jug]). ♦*Вчера ему всадили по тыкве, попал в больницу.* "Yesterday he got such a bash in the head that he landed in the hospital."

ВСА́СЫВАТЬ/ВСОСА́ТЬ, *army.* To understand (lit., to suck in). ♦*Что-то я не всосу, что ты хочешь.* "I don't understand exactly what you want."

ВСЁ НЕ СЛА́ВА БО́ГУ, *idiom.* Things aren't right, something's wrong (lit., not everything is to the glory of God). ♦*Опять у тебя всё не слава Богу: то ты деньги потеряла, теперь заболела.* "Again something's the matter with you — first you lost the money, now you're sick."

ВСЁ ПОНИ́ЖЕ ПО́ЯСА, *idiom, neg.* It doesn't matter, it's all the same (lit., it's all below the belt; euph. for **по́ ху́й**). ♦*Ваши проблемы меня не волнуют, мне всё это пониже пояса.* "I don't care about your problems; to me it's all the same."

ВСЁ ПУТЁМ, *idiom.* Everything is O.K., all is going as it should, all is well (lit., everything's on the right path). ♦*Ну что у тебя с учёбой? – Всё путём.* "Well how are your studies going? – All is well."

ВСЁ РАВНО́ ВОЙНА́, *idiom.* There's nothing to lose, you might as well (lit., there'll be war anyhow). ♦*Давай последние, купим водку, всё равно война.* "Come on, let's buy some vodka with the rest of the money — we might as well."

ВСЁ СХВА́ЧЕНО (у кого́-л.), *idiom.* (Someone has) good (Mafia) connections, reliable protection. ♦*У них в этом магазине всё схвачено.* "The people in that store have reliable connections."

ВСЁ ТЕЧЁТ, ВСЁ ИЗ МЕНЯ́, *idiom, joc.* Lit., Everything is flowing from me. By wordplay from the phrase Всё течёт, всё изменяется, "Everything is in flux, everything changes". **1.** A deflating response to the phrase Всё течёт, всё изменяется. **2.** "I need to take a piss."

ВСЕ ТРИ́ДЦАТЬ ТРИ УДОВО́ЛЬ-СТВИЯ, *idiom.* A good time, a lot of fun (lit., all thirty-three enjoyments).

♦*Пойдём в баню, получим все тридцать три удовольствия: и попаримся и пивка попьём.* "Let's go to the steam bath. We'll have a great time there, steaming ourselves and having some beer."

ВСЕМ ДАВА́ТЬ, ТАК СЛОМА́ЕТСЯ КРОВА́ТЬ, *rhyming phrase, joc.* Used in refusing a request, with allusion to sexual refusal; lit., "if I give to everyone, the bed will collapse." ♦*Дай немного печенья. — Всем давать, так сломается кровать.* "Let me have some cookies. — If I give some to everyone, the bed will collapse."

ВСЕХ ПЕРЕЕБА́ТЬ НЕЛЬЗЯ́, НО К Э́ТОМУ СТРЕМИ́ТЬСЯ НА́ДО, *idiom, rude.* Lit., You can't fuck them all, but you ought to try.

ВСОСА́ТЬ, *perf.* To drink (lit., to suck in). ♦*Ты уже свой стакан всосал, оставь другим.* "You've already had your drink, leave some for the others!"

ВСПРЫ́СКИВАТЬ/ВСПРЫ́СНУТЬ. To drink in celebration of a holiday or a new purchase (lit., to besprinkle). *Ты, я слышал, машину купил? Это дело надо вспрыснуть!* "I hear you just bought a new car — that's something we have to drink to!"

ВСТАВА́Й, ВСТАВА́Й, ДРУЖО́К, С ПОСТЕ́ЛИ НА ГОРШО́К! *rhyming phrase, joc.* Lit., Get up, get up, buddy, from bed to the potty! A rhyming phrase that means "Time to get up!" (Derived from pioneer camp life.)

ВСТАВА́ТЬ/ВСТАТЬ сранья́, *idiom, rude.* To get up early (by wordplay on **сраньё** and рано, "early"). ♦*Надо завтра встать сранья и сразу на рыбалку.* "I've got to get up shit-early to go fishing tomorrow."

ВСТАВЛЯ́ТЬ/ВСТА́ВИТЬ. 1. To have sex. ♦*Кажется, ты вставил всем, кому можно.* "You seem to have been to bed with everybody." **2.** To hit, to beat. ♦*Как бы нам не вставили за наши шутки.* "I'm afraid, we're going to get it for our jokes." ●**Вставля́ть/вста́вить пистóн,** *idiom.* To scold, to punish. (Cf.

under **писто́н**). ♦*Тебе вставили писто́н, если мало, можно повторить.* "If that's not enough punishment for you, we can do it again." •**Вставля́ть/Вста́вить фити́ль**, *idiom.* To scold, bawl out (lit., to replace the wick of a lamp; with sexual connotation). ♦*Тебе за это такой фитиль вставят, не обрадуешься.* "You're going to get such a tongue-lashing for this, you won't enjoy it!"

ВСТРЕВА́ТЬ/ВСТРЯТЬ, *neg.* To interfere, to interrupt. ♦*Не встревай в разговор.* "Don't butt in on our conversation."

ВСТРЕ́НУТЬСЯ, *perf. only, joc.* To meet, get together. ♦*Встренулись они давеча и налакались.* "Recently they got together and had a lot to drink."

ВСТРЕ́ЧКА, -и, *f.* Oncoming traffic. ♦*За выезд на всречку—большой штраф.* "Don't cross the line into oncoming traffic—there will be a big fine."

ВСЮ ДОРО́ГУ. See under **доро́га.**

ВСЯ́КОМУ О́ВОЩУ СВОЙ ФРУКТ, *idiom, joc.* Everything in good time (lit., "Every vegetable has its fruit," playing on Всякому овощу своё время, "Every vegetable has its season"). ♦*Наконец-то он решил жениться. — Всякому овощу свой фрукт.* "So he finally decided to get married. — Well, every vegetable has its fruit."

ВТИРА́ТЬ/ВТЕРЕ́ТЬ в ко́жу, *idiom, neg.* To insist repetitively (lit., to rub into someone's skin). ♦*Хватит втирать в кожу о ценах, не хочу больше о них слышать.* "Stop harping on the cost of living; I don't want to hear any more about it."

ВТИРА́ТЬСЯ/ВТЕРЕ́ТЬСЯ, *youth.* To inject a drug. ♦*Ты хочешь ещё втереться, на сегодня хватит.* "You want another shot, but you've had enough for today."

ВТОРО́Й СТАКА́Н РОССИ́И, *idiom, joc.* Yeltsin's right-hand man (lit., The second glass of Russia). ♦*А кто сейчас у нас второй стакан России?* "Who's Yeltsin's second these days?"

ВТОРЯ́К, -а, *m.* Old tea, tea made from used tea-leaves. ♦*Там вторяк остался,* погрейся. "There's some old tea there, have some and warm yourself up."

ВТРЕ́СКИВАТЬСЯ/ВТРЕ́СКАТЬСЯ, *joc.* To fall in love (lit., to crack). ♦*Он в неё сразу втрескался.* "He suddenly fell head over heels in love with her."

ВТЫК, -а, *m., neg.* A reprimand, punishment. ♦*Давно втык не получал?* "You're really asking for it!"

ВТЫКА́ТЬ/ВОТКНУ́ТЬ. To scold, reprimand. ♦*Мне вчера воткнули за опоздание.* "Yesterday they bawled me out for being late."

ВТЫКА́ТЬСЯ/ВОТКНУ́ТЬСЯ, *rude.* To interfere in someone else's business, meddle. ♦*Не твоё дело, сиди и не втыкайся!* "It's none of your business — don't butt in."

ВТЮ́РИВАТЬСЯ/ВТЮ́РИТЬСЯ, *joc.* To fall in love. ♦*Когда он успел в неё втюриться?* "When did he manage to fall in love with her?"

ВУ́ЛЬВА, -ы, *f., rude.* A woman's thick pubic hair. ♦*У неё вульва — запутаться можно.* "She has such thick pubic hair you can get stuck in it."

ВУ́МНЫЙ, КАК ВУ́ТКА, *idiom, neg.* (Lit., Clever as a duck). Regional variant of **У́мный, как у́тка** Foolish, dumb. ♦*Ну, ты вумный, как вутка, зачем пьёшь кофе на ночь?* "You fool, why do you drink coffee at night?"

ВУ́СМЕРТЬ, *adv.* Extremely, very much (lit., to death). ♦*Вчера все устали вусмерть.* "Yesterday everyone got dead tired." •**Ву́смерть ката́ться,** *idiom, crim.* To drink one's fill, drink to one's satisfaction. ♦*В субботу вусмерть катались, спирта было, сколько хочешь.* "On Saturday they drank their fill — there was all the alcohol you could ask for."

ВХУЯ́ЧИВАТЬ/ВХУЯ́ЧИТЬ, *rude.* **1.** To have sex with a woman. ♦*Пора ей вхуячить.* "It's time to get her into bed." **2.** To hit. ♦*Ему вхуячили камнем в спину.* "They hit him in the back with a brick."

(НО) ВЧЕРА́, И ПО ПЯТЬ, *idiom, joc.* An ironic reply to regrets about inflation (lit., But that was yesterday, and it only cost five rubles). ♦*Зря мы не купили летом стиралку. — Да, это было вчера и по пять.* "We should have bought the washing machine last summer." — "Yes, it would have been cheaper, but that's already history."

ВШИ́ВНИК, -а, *m., army.* Longjohns, underwear for extra warmth, often a jogging outfit. ♦*Без вшивника на посту холодно.* "It's cold on sentry duty without a pair of longjohns."

ВШИВОТА́, -ы́, *f., coll., neg.* Insignificant people (lit., lice). ♦*Зачем тебе эта вшивота, не друзья они тебе.* "What are you doing with those nonentities? They're not suitable friends for you."

ВШИ́ВЫЙ, -ая, -ое, *neg.* Bad, dirty, cheap. ♦*Концерт какой-то вшивый, совсем не понравился.* "That was a lousy concert, I didn't like it at all."

ВЪЕБА́ТЬ, *imperf. only, rude.* Cf. **ёб-.** **1.** To have sex with a woman. ♦*Ты её когда-нибудь въебёшь?* "Aren't you ever going to fuck her?" **2.** To hit. ♦*Отойди, а то въебу.* "Get out of here or I'll hit you." •**Въеба́ть по са́мые я́йца,** *idiom, rude.* To have sex with a woman (lit., to fuck her up to one's balls). ♦*Такую надо въебать по самые яйца и забыть.* "With that sort of woman you should just fuck her and forget about her."

ВЪЕЗЖА́ТЬ/ВЪЕ́ХАТЬ, To understand (lit., to drive in). ♦*Я не въехал, повтори.* "Would you repeat that? I didn't get it."

ВЫ НЕ ЛЮБИ́ЛИ, ВАМ НЕ ПОНЯ́ТЬ, *idiom, joc.* You can't understand what you haven't experienced (lit., "You haven't loved, so you can't understand"). ♦*Хорошо бы сейчас зимой отдохнуть в Италии. Правда, вы не любили, вам не понять.* "How nice it would be to spend the winter vacation in Italy. Of course you wouldn't understand, you've never been there."

ВЫ ПЕ́СНЕЙ ХОТИ́ТЕ, ИХ ЕСТЬ У МЕНЯ́, *idiom, joc.,* imitating illiterate speech. Lit., You want songs? I've got some. **1.** I have my opinion, I have something to say. ♦*Ну скажи, что ты думаешь об этом? — Вы песней хотите, их есть у меня.* "Tell us what you think." — "You want to know? I'll tell you!" **2.** I can provide what you want. ♦*Ты принёс билеты в Большой? — Вы песней хотите, их есть у меня.* "Have you brought tickets for the Bolshoi?" — "You want? I have."

ВЫ́БЛЯДОК, вы́блядка, *m., rude.* Cf. **блядь. 1.** An illegitimate child, bastard. ♦*Она своего выблядка в детдом отдала.* "She put her bastard in an orphanage." **2.** Idiot, scum. ♦*Я с этим выблядком знаться не буду, он меня уже сто раз подвёл.* "I won't have anything to do with that bastard, he's let me down a thousand times already."

ВЫ́БЛЯДЫШ, -а, *m.* See **вы́блядок.**

ВЫБРА́СЫВАТЬ/ВЫ́БРОСИТЬ (в прода́жу), *idiom, obs.* To put deficit goods on sale, to make available for sale previously unavailable merchandise (lit., to throw out). ♦*Иди скорее, там выбросили летние туфли.* "You'd better hurry — they've just started selling a shipment of summer shoes."

ВЫ́БРОС, -а, *m., joc.* The political party Выбор России ("Russia's Choice") (lit., emission).

ВЫ́ВЕРНУТЬ рабо́ту, *idiom, crim.* To rob an apartment. ♦*Давно видно не было, что делал? — Да недавно вывернули работу, пересиживали.* "I haven't seen you for a long time. What've you been up to? — We robbed an apartment recently and then went underground for a while."

ВЫГИБО́НИСТЫЙ, -ая, -ое, *youth, neg.* Vain or conceited, having too high an opinion of oneself. ♦*Будешь таким выгибонистым, я за себя не отвечаю.* "Don't act so stuck-up or I'll be tempted to smack you."

ВЫГОРА́ТЬ/ВЫ́ГОРЕТЬ. To be successful, to turn out well. ♦*У него с лотереей ничего не выгорело.* "He's had no luck with the lottery."

ВЫГУ́ЛИВАТЬ/ВЫ́ГУЛЯТЬ, *joc.* To butter up (lit., to walk [a dog]). ♦*Я* *своего шефа давно выгуливаю, хочу взять большой отпуск.* "I've been buttering up my boss for a long time because I want to apply for a long leave."

ВЫДАВА́ТЬ/ВЫ́ДАТЬ. 1. To perform. ♦*Когда он выпьет, он выдаёт балдёжные анекдоты.* "When he drinks he tells very funny stories." **2.** To speak out, declare straight out. ♦*А ну, выдай ему всё, что ты о нём думаешь.* "Well, tell him straight out exactly what you think of him."

ВЫДВИГА́ТЬСЯ/ВЫ́ДВИНУТЬСЯ. To leave, pull out, move out. ♦*Нам пора выдвигаться, а то опоздаем на работу.* "Well, we've got to move along now or we'll be late for work."

ВЫ́ДОХНУТЬ, *perf.* To feel relief, to be relieved. ♦*Выдохни, всё уже кончилось.* "It's over, you can relax now."

ВЫДРЮ́ЧИВАТЬСЯ/ВЫ́ДРЮЧИТЬ-СЯ, *neg.* **1.** To be capricious, contrary, uncooperative. ♦*Не выдрючиваться, одевайся и пошли в гости.* "Don't be obstreperous. Get dressed and let's go out." **2.** To annoy, torment, offend. ♦*Он любит выдрючиваться над слабыми.* "He likes to torment weak people." **3.** To be boastful, to act conceited. ♦*Он стал артистом и начал выдрючиваться перед друзьями.* "He became an actor and started putting on airs with his friends."

ВЫ́ЕБАТЬ И ВЫ́БРОСИТЬ, *idiom, rude.* Worthless, useless (of things or people) (lit., "fit to be fucked and thrown out"; cf. **ёб-**). ♦*Зачем мне эта куртка, выебать и выбросить.* "What do I need that coat for? It's just a piece of junk."

ВЫЁБИСТЫЙ, -ая, -ое, *rude.* Stuck-up, capricious, willful (cf. **ёб-**). ♦*С ним нелегко разговаривать, слишком выёбистый.* "It's hard to talk to him, he's so stuck-up."

ВЫЕБО́Н, -а, *m., rude, neg.* A prank, trick (cf. **ёб-**). ♦*Мне твои выебоны надоели.* "I'm sick and tired of your tricks."

ВЫ́ЕБОНА, -ы, *f., rude, joc.* A pothole (from выбоина, "pothole," by wordplay on вы́ебать, "to fuck"; cf. **ёб-**). ♦*На дороге одни выебоны.* "This road is full of fucking potholes."

ВЫЁБЫВАТЬСЯ/ВЫ́ЕБНУТЬСЯ, *rude.* To be willful, abusive (cf. **ёб-**). ♦*Не выёбывайся, нам пора ехать.* "Don't be obstreperous, it's time for us to go." ♦*Он привык над всеми выёбываться.* "He's in the habit of abusing everybody." •**Не́ хуй выёбываться,** *idiom, rude.* Don't be naughty, don't play pranks (cf. **хуй**). ♦*Не хуй выёбываться, жри, что дают.* "Don't carry on like that. Just eat what you're given."

ВЫЁЖИВАТЬСЯ, *imperf. only, neg.* **1.** To be capricious, uncooperative. ♦*Не выёживайся, я терпеть капризы не буду.* "Don't mess around. I won't put up with any nonsense." **2.** To be offensive, disrespectful. ♦*Он всё время выёживается, а жена всё ему прощает.* "He's constantly acting obnoxious, but his wife keeps forgiving him."

ВЫЕЗДНО́Й, -о́го, *obs., Soviet.* A Soviet citizen having the right to travel abroad (hence, officially certified as loyal and reliable). ♦*Когда это он стал выездным, раньше он за границу не ездил.* "When was he declared travel-certified? He never used to travel abroad."

ВЫЖИРА́ТЬ/ВЫ́ЖРАТЬ (буты́лку, полли́тра), *idiom, rude.* To drink a bottle of liquor. ♦*Ты уже с утра выжрал бутылку — остановись.* "You've already gulped down a bottle since this morning — it's time to stop."

ВЫКА́ТЫВАТЬ/ВЫ́КАТИТЬ бе́льма, *idiom, rude.* To stare, look hard at something (lit., to roll one's whites). ♦*Ты чего бельма выкатила: мужиков, что ль, не видела?* "What are you staring at? Haven't you ever seen a man before?"

ВЫКИ́ДЫВАТЬ/ВЫ́КИНУТЬ: Выки́дывать/вы́кинуть трюк, *idiom, neg.* To behave strangely, pull a stunt. ♦*Вот какой он выкинул трюк: бросил жену, детей и уехал на север.* "He pulled quite a stunt — suddenly left his wife and children and went north." **Выки́дывать/вы́кинуть фо́ртель,** *idiom, neg.* To behave unpredictably, to pull a stunt. ♦*Он может выкинуть любой фор-*

тель, не надейся на него. "He's capable of any stunt; you can't rely on him.'"

ВЫКОБЕ́НИВАТЬСЯ, *imperf., neg.* To be capricious, to be difficult. ♦*Не выкобенивайся, сказал, что идёшь с нами, иди.* "Don't be difficult! You said you'd come with us, so come.'"

ВЫ́КОЛОТЬ МОРГА́ЛЫ, *idiom, rude.* To punish, to beat (lit., to puncture someone's eyes). Cf. **морга́лы.** ♦*Будешь жаловаться, выколю моргалы.* "If you tell on me, I'll smash your face in.'"

ВЫ́КРАСИТЬ ДА ВЫ́БРОСИТЬ, *idiom, neg.* Said of something junky or worthless (lit., paint it and throw it out). ♦*У тебя лампа настольная — выкрасить да выбросить.* "Your table lamp is a piece of junk.'"

ВЫКРУТА́СЫ, -ов, *pl., neg.* Tricks, whims, capricious behavior. ♦*Как ты надоел со своими выкрутасами.* "I'm sick of you and your tricks.'"

ВЫКУПА́ТЬ/ВЫ́КУПИТЬ, *crim.* To steal, as by picking pockets (lit., to ransom). ♦*А это я у него выкупил, здесь деньги, часы.* "Here's what I stole from him — some money and a watch.'"

ВЫЛА́МЫВАТЬСЯ, *imperf.* To give oneself airs, to be capricious, to be fretful. ♦*Хорош выламываться, говори, ты идёшь или нет с нами?* "Quit being so capricious, just tell us whether you are coming with us or not.'"

ВЫ́НЕСТИ (ПОНЕСТИ́), *perf.* **1.** To beat up. ♦*Там за углом наших несут.* "Our boys are being beaten up around the corner there." **2.** To win, to score. ♦*Мы вынесли их со счётом 3:2.* "We beat them 3 to 2.'"

ВЫ́НОС, -а, *m., youth.* A loss at cards or sports. ♦*Вынос состоялся, наши больше не играют в футбол на первенство.* "Our team lost the game, so they won't be playing in the championships.'"

ВЫ́НОС ТЕ́ЛА, *idiom.* To be out cold, dead drunk (lit., the carrying of a body to the cemetery). ♦*Вчера состоялся вынос тела у Володьки, ему кинули капитана.* "Our Volodya got really smashed yesterday to celebrate his promotion to captain.'"

ВЫНОСИ́ТЬ/ВЫ́НЕСТИ нога́ми вперёд кого́-л., *idiom.* To bury someone (lit., to carry someone out feet-first). ♦*Все вы ждёте, когда меня вынесут ногами вперёд.* "You're all waiting for them to carry me off to my grave.'"

ВЫ́ПАВШИЙ, -ая. Unconscious (lit., dropped out). ♦*Не трожь его, он выпавший.* "Don't bother him, he's stoned out of his mind.'"

ВЫПАДА́ЛОВО, -а, *n., youth.* A shock, a big surprise. ♦*Для меня его смерть — выпадалово.* "His death was a big shock to me.'"

ВЫПАДА́ТЬ/ВЫ́ПАСТЬ в оса́док, *idiom.* Lit., to precipitate out. **1.** To lose consciousness. ♦*Смотри, он уже выпал в осадок, совсем пить не умеет.* "Look, he's already out cold — apparently he doesn't know how to drink." **2.** To go into hiding. ♦*Тебя давно не видно. — Выпал в осадок на неделю.* "I haven't seen you in a while. — I went underground for a week.'"

ВЫПАДНО́Й, -а́я, -о́е. Outstanding, unusual, unbelievable (from "падать," to fall, meaning to fall out of order, to stand out, always used in a positive sense). ♦*Это выпадной случай, встретиться в метро через десять лет.* "It's amazing to meet you like this in the subway after not having seen you for ten years!'"

ВЫПЕНДРЁ́Ж, -а, *m., neg.* **1.** Capriciousness, naughtiness. ♦*Кончай свой выпендрёж, вставай и иди на работу.* "Stop being naughty; get up and go to work." **2.** Boasting, bragging. ♦*Мне их выпендрёж по поводу загранки надоел.* "I'm sick of their boasting about their trip abroad.'"

ВЫ́ПЕ́НДРИВАТЬСЯ/ВЫ́ПЕНДРИТЬ-СЯ, *neg.* **1.** To be contrary, capricious, unreliable. ♦*Не выпендривайся, ты сама обещала, а теперь не делаешь.* "Don't be so irresponsible! You promised, and now you're not delivering!" **2.** To mock, ridicule. ♦*Хватит выпендриваться над нами.* "Stop laughing at us." **3.** To boast, show off. ♦*Она любит выпендриваться своими связями.* "She's always bragging about her connections in high places."

ВЫ́ПИВО́Н, -а, *m.* Liquor. ♦*Какой у нас выпивон есть?* "What do we have to drink?" **2.** A (drinking) party. ♦*У нас будет выпивон в субботу, ты придёшь?* "We're having a party on Saturday. Will you come?"

ВЫ́ПИВО́ХА, -и, *m. and f., neg.* A drunkard.

ВЫПИ́ЗЖИВАТЬСЯ. See **выёбываться.**

ВЫПИ́ЛИВАТЬСЯ, *imperf., neg.* **1.** To work hard, to slave. ♦*Мне надоело выпиливаться целый день на солнце.* "I'm exhausted from working in the sun all day." **2.** To be capricious, uncooperative.

ВЫПИ́СЫВАТЬ/ВЫ́ПИСАТЬ, *youth.* To evict, kick out, forbid someone to live in one's apartment. ♦*Сегодня нас выпишут, надо искать, где жить.* "Today they're going to kick us out; we'll have to look for another place to live." •**Выпи́сывать/вы́писать (де́вушек . . .).** To ask (girls) out on a date. ♦*Давай выпишем пару чувих на вечер.* "Let's ask a couple of girls out for the evening."

ВЫПУ́ЛИВАТЬСЯ/ВЫ́ПУЛИТЬСЯ, *joc.* To flee, leave quickly (from пуля, "bullet"). ♦*Выпуливаемся отсюда, пока не поздно.* "Let's get out of here before it's too late."

ВЫ́РВАТЬ НО́ГИ ИЗ ЗА́ДНИЦЫ, *idiom, rude.* To beat, to punish (lit., to tear someone's legs from his buttocks). ♦*Будешь ходить к ней, вырву ноги из задницы.* "You go near her and I'll tear your legs off."

ВЫ́РВИ ГЛАЗ, *idiom, joc., neg.* Very sour (lit., tear-your-eyes-out). ♦*Где ты взял эту гадость? Не вино, а вырви глаз!* "Where did you get that nasty stuff? That's not wine, that's rotgut."

ВЫРУБА́ТЬ/ВЫ́РУБИТЬ. 1. To turn off, switch off. ♦*Выруби свет, глазам больно.* "Turn off the light, it's hurting my eyes." **2.** To knock unconscious, knock out. ♦*Он его вырубил с первого удара.* "He knocked the guy out with a single punch."

ВЫРУБА́ТЬСЯ/ВЫ́РУБИТЬСЯ. To lose consciousness (lit., to be switched off). ♦*После первого удара он вырубился.* "He lost consciousness after the first punch."

ВЫРУБО́Н, -а, *m., youth.* **1.** Astonishment, amazement. ♦*Такой вырубон получишь от фильма, дальше некуда.* "That movie is a real knockout!" **2.** Extreme exhaustion. ♦*Не могу даже сидеть, вырубон после работы наступил.* "I'm so exhausted after work that I can't even sit up."

ВЫ́СЕРОК, вы́серка, *m., rude.* A worthless person (lit., a turd, a piece of shit). ♦*Если ты, высерок, ещё раз сюда придёшь, смотри у меня тогда!* "You piece of shit! If you show up here again I'll really let you have it!"

ВЫСИРА́ТЬ/ВЫ́СРАТЬ, *rude.* To get, acquire (lit., to shit). ♦*Где я тебе высру новые ботинки?* "Where do you expect me to get you new boots — do you think I can shit them?" •**Что я тебе́, вы́сру?** *idiom, rude.* How do you expect me to get it? A response to someone's complaining or nagging. ♦*У меня нет водки. Что я тебе, высру?* "I have no vodka; what do you want me to do, shit it?"

ВЫСИРА́ТЬСЯ/ВЫ́СРАТЬСЯ, *rude.* To defecate. ♦*Долго тебя не было, высрался наконец.* "It took you a long time to shit."

ВЫСКРЕБА́ТЬ/ВЫ́СКРЕСТИ. To perform an abortion on someone (lit., to scrape out). ♦*Её сегодня должны выскрести.* "She's supposed to be having an abortion today."

ВЫСКРЕБА́ТЬСЯ/ВЫ́СКРЕСТИСЬ, *youth.* To leave. ♦*Пора нам из этого города выскребаться.* "It's time for us to get out of this town."

ВЫСО́ТКА, -и, *f.* A tall building, skyscraper.

ВЫССЫВА́ТЬСЯ/ВЫ́ССАТЬСЯ, *rude.* To empty out one's bladder. ♦*После пива никак выссаться не могу.* "When I drink beer I just can't stop pissing."

ВЫСТАВЛЯ́ТЬ/ВЫ́СТАВИТЬ. To pressure or deceive someone into spending money. ♦*Надо бы его выставить на поддачу.* "Let's try to get him to pick up the tab for the drinks."

ВЫСТАВЛЯ́ТЬСЯ/ВЫ́СТАВИТЬСЯ. To spend money in order to throw a party (from "поставить стол," to prepare a table with dishes, food, and drinks). ♦*Я на пару тысяч выставился, когда получил орден.* "I shelled out 2 Gs hosting a celebration party when I was awarded my medal."

ВЫСТУПА́ЛА, -ы, *m. and f., neg.* **1.** A troublemaker, hooligan. ♦*Этот выступала не успокоится, пока не подерётся с кем-либо.* "That hooligan always has to be fighting with someone." **2.** Someone who likes to make speeches before an audience. ♦*Этот выступала будет теперь говорить часами.* "That long-winded speechifier is going to be talking for hours."

ВЫСТУПА́ТЬ/ВЫ́СТУПИТЬ, *neg.* To pick quarrels, be provocative. ♦*Не выступай, а то получишь.* "Don't provoke me or you'll get it." •**Выступа́ть/вы́ступить (не) по де́лу,** *idiom.* To make a just (unjust) claim to something, to be right (wrong) in an argument. ♦*Ты выступил по делу, они уступили.* "You were in the right; they had to give in." ♦*Извини, старик, в этот раз ты выступил не по делу, всё было не так.* "Sorry, old boy, this time you're simply wrong — it wasn't like that at all."

ВЫСУ́ШИВАТЬ/ВЫ́СУШИТЬ. To be tired out, to be fed up (lit., to dry out, from сушить, to dry). ♦*Ты меня высушил своим нытьём.* "I am fed up with your whining!"

ВЫ́СШИЙ ПИЛОТА́Ж! *idiom.* Excellent, first-class. ♦*Он делает шашлыки — высший пилотаж!* "He can make first-class shishkebab."

ВЫСЫПО́Н, -а. *m.* A restful sleep (lit., rest in a dream, from высыпаться, to sleep soundly). ♦*О высыпоне можно только мечтать, не успеваю в сроки сдать книгу.* "I can only dream of a peaceful night's sleep, I'm not going to be able to finish writing this book on time."

ВЫ́ХЛОП, -а, *m.* Breath reeking with liquor (lit., exhaust from an automobile). •**На вы́хлопе,** *idiom.* Exhausted, worn out. ♦*Я делаю это уже на выхлопе, надо отдохнуть.* "I'm already running on empty, I need to take a rest."

ВЫ́ХОД, -а, *m.* Connections, influential acquaintances. ♦*У тебя есть выход на горсовет?* "Do you have connections on the city council?"

ВЫХОДИ́ТЬ/ВЫ́ЙТИ в тира́ж, *idiom.* To retire, leave the scene, become obsolete or superfluous. ♦*Ещё год поработает, а потом выйдет в тираж.* "He'll work for another year, and then he'll be pensioned off."

ВЫЧИСЛЯ́ТЬ/ВЫ́ЧИСЛИТЬ. To deduce logically, figure out, calculate. ♦*Я вычислил место, где они встречались.* "I figured out where they must have been meeting."

ВЫША́К, -ка́, *m., crim.* A death sentence. ♦*За убийство ему дали вышак.* "They gave him the death sentence for murder."

ВЫ́ШЕ КРЫ́ШИ, *rhyming phrase.* The best, supreme (lit., higher than the roof). ♦*Мы стол накрыли на Новый год – выше крыши.* "We had a real feast for New Year's Eve—it was tops!"

ВЫШИБО́Н, -а, *m., youth, joc.* The last dance at a restaurant or club, after which the establishment closes (from вышибать, "to kick out"; вышибала, "bouncer"). ♦*Давай станцуем вышибон и по домам.* "Let's dance the last number and go home."

ВЫ́ШКА, -и, *f., crim.* See **выша́к.**

ВЬЕТ, -а, *m.* A Vietnamese.

ВЬЮ́ГА, -а, *f., homosexual.* A passive homosexual (lit., snowstorm; cf. **вью́житься**).

ВЬЮ́ЖИТЬСЯ/ЗАВЬЮ́ЖИТЬСЯ, *m., homosexual.* To flirt, to get acquainted.

ВЭНТА́ТЬ/ПОВЭНТА́ТЬ, ВЭНТА- НУ́ТЬ, *youth, obs.* To go, leave, slip out, get out (from Eng. "went"). ♦*Когда вы вэнтанули с работы?* "When did you get out of work?"

ВЯЗА́ТЬ/ПОВЯЗА́ТЬ. Lit., to tie up. **1.** To apprehend, arrest. ♦*Их вчера всех* *повязали, сидят в изоляторе.* "They were all rounded up yesterday and put into a detention cell." **2.** To force, enlist forcibly for a task. ♦*Меня мать повязала на уборку дома.* "My mother roped me into cleaning the house."

ВЯ́КАЛКА, -и, *f., neg.* Mouth (cf. **вя́кать**).

ВЯ́КАТЬ/ВЯ́КНУТЬ, *neg.* To chatter, make noise. ♦*Сиди, не вякай.* "Sit down and shut up."

◆ Г ◆

ГА́ВКА, -и, *f., joc.* Mouth. Cf. **га́вкаться**.

ГА́ВКАТЬСЯ/ПОГА́ВКАТЬСЯ, *neg.* To quarrel (from гавкать, "to bark"). ◆*Я с ним не разговариваю, мы вчера погавкались.* "I'm not talking with him; we quarreled yesterday."

ГА́ВРИК, -а, *m.* **1.** *neg.* A petty criminal, sneak thief (from a man's nickname). ◆*Знаю я этих гавриков, оглянуться не успеешь, что-нибудь натворят.* "I know those crooks — before you can look about you they're up to some mischief." **2.** *pl., joc.* Buddies, guys. ◆*Ну, гаврики, пошли в кино.* "Come on, guys, let's go to the movies."

ГАД, -а, *m., neg.* Lit., a reptile, snake. **1.** A repellent, disgusting person. ◆*Опять этот гад нас подвёл!* "That snake let us down again!" **2.** *crim.* A police officer. ◆*Смотри, сколько гадов нагнали, бежим отсюда!* "Look at all the cops on duty. Let's get out of here!" ◆**Гад ползу́чий,** *idiom, rude.* A bastard, scoundrel (lit., creeping snake). ◆*А он, гад ползучий, обещал мне помочь и не помог.* "That snake promised to help me and never came through."

ГАДЁНЫШ, -а, *m., neg.* A bad. nasty person (lit., a young snake). Cf. **гад**.

ГАДИ́ЛЬНИК, -а, *m., crim., neg.* A police station (lit., a snake den). ◆*Где у них здесь гадильник? Надо знать на всякий случай.* "Where's the police station around here? We'd better find out just in case."

ГА́ДИТЬ/ПОГА́ДИТЬ. To defecate. ◆*Я давно хочу погадить.* "I really need to take a shit."

ГА́ДСКИЙ, -ая, -ое, *rude.* Bad, disgusting, repellent. ◆*Когда кончится эта гадская погода?* "When is this crappy weather going to end?"

ГА́ДЫ, га́дов, *pl.* Heavy navy boots (lit., snakes). ◆*Эти гады и за три года не износишь.* "These clodhoppers won't wear out in three years."

ГАДЮ́ШНИК, -а, *m., neg.* Lit., a snake nest. **1.** A dirty, messy place. ◆*Здесь не комната, а гадюшник.* "Your room is a pigsty." **2.** A beer bar, a cheap bar. ◆*В гадюшнике много народа, туда не пойдём.* "It's too crowded in that beer bar; let's not go in."

ГАЗ, -а, *m.* Liquor, alcoholic drink. ◆*У нас газ на вечер есть?* "Do we have any liquor for the party?"

ГАЗИРО́ВКА, -и, *f., neg.* Champagne, sparkling wine (lit., gassy stuff). ◆*Я эту газировку не пью, мне водки налейте.* "I don't drink that fizzy stuff. Pour me some vodka."

ГАЗОВА́ТЬ/ЗАГАЗОВА́ТЬ. To drink, get drunk. ◆*Он газует уже целую неделю.* "He's been on a drunk for a week already."

ГА́ЙШНИК, -а, *m.* A traffic officer (from ГАИ, abbr. of Госавтоинспекция, "Government Traffic Surveillance"). ◆*Смотри, там гаишник стоит. Сбавь скорость.* "Look, there's a traffic cop. Slow down."

ГА́ЛИКИ, галиков, *pl.* A hallucination. See **глюк**. ◆*Примешь дозу, галики начинаются, всю нашу житуху в этой дыре забудешь.* "Take a hit of this—it'll give you such dreams you'll forget about this hole we're living in."

ГА́МА, -ы, *f.* Chewing gum (from Eng. "gum"). ◆*Дай гаму, во рту противно.* "Give me some gum — I've got a bad taste in my mouth."

ГАМА́К, -а́, *m., crim., neg.* A homosexual (lit., a hammock). ◆*Чего к тебе гамак вяжется?* "Why does that homo keep hanging around you?"

ГАМБА́Л, -а, *m., south.* A strong, heavily built man (cf. **амба́л**). ◆*Этот гамбал может поднять не только чемоданы, а и тебя вместе с ними.* "That ox can carry you and your suitcases too."

ГАМБА́ЛИТЬ/ПОГАМБА́ЛИТЬ, *south.* To work long and hard. ◆*Мне надоело гамбалить на его даче, он даже мне фрукты не даёт за это.* "I'm sick of slaving away for him in his garden; he never even gives me any of the produce."

ГАМИ́РА, -ы, *f.* Strong wine. ◆*Налей ещё гамиры.* "Pour me some more of that wine."

ГАНДЕ́ЛИК, -а, *m.* An underground (cellar) wine tavern. ◆*Зайдём в ганделик, пропустим по стакану.* "Let's just stop in at the wine tavern and have a glass."

ГАНС, -а, *m.* A German (lit., a Hans). ◆*О чём там этот Ганс лопочет?* "What's that Kraut babbling about over there?"

ГАРАНТИ́ЙКА, -и, *f.* A shop where appliances are repaired under warranty. ◆*Телевизор сломался, надо отнести его в гарантийку.* "The TV isn't working. We'll have to take it to the warranty shop."

ГАСАНУ́ТЬ, *perf.* To put someone in his place, to humble someone (from гасить, to beat). ◆*Гасануть его недолго, всем надоел своими приколами.* "We'll soon take him down a peg—we've had enough of his practical jokes."

ГАСА́ТЬ/ГАСАНУ́ТЬ. To move fast, to jump (lit., to prance). ◆*А тебе приходилось гасать по горам с тридцатью кило выкладки?* "Have you ever had to high-tail it over the mountains with a 60-pound pack?"

ГАСИ́ СВЕТ, БРОСА́Й ГРАНА́ТУ, *idiom.* There's nothing to lose, it doesn't matter, come what may (lit., "Turn off the light and throw the grenade"). ◆*Пить так пить, гаси свет, бросай гранату.* "If we're going to drink we might as well really drink; what have we got to lose?!"

ГАСИ́ЛОВО, -а, *n., youth, obs.* A beating, a fight. ◆*Мы не успели затанцевать, сразу началось гасилово.* "We had hardly even started dancing when a fight broke out."

ГАСИ́ЛЬЩИК, -а, *m.* A killer, a trigger man (from гасить, to extinguish). ◆*У него пара гасильщиков всегда найдётся, если надо кого успокоить.* "He can always call on a couple of trigger men if there's someone he needs to quiet down."

ГАСИ́ТЬ/ПОГАСИ́ТЬ. To knock out, beat into unconsciousness (lit., to put out, turn off). ◆*Они разговаривать не стали, начали всех гасить подряд и всё.* "Before anyone could say a word they started beating people unconscious left and right."

ГАСИ́ТЬСЯ/ЗАГАСИ́ТЬСЯ, *army.* To shirk, dodge, give the slip, make oneself scarce (lit., turn oneself off). ◆*Ты опять гасишься, а работать кто будет?* "There you go sneaking off again — who do you think is going to do the work?"

ГАСТАРБА́ЙТЕР, -а, m. An illegal immigrant (from the German *Gastarbeiter,* guest worker). ◆*Без гастарбайтеров Москва уже не может ни строить, ни убирать улицы.* "Without illegal immigrants Moscow can neither build nor clean the streets."

ГАСТРИ́Т, -а, *m., joc.* A meat-filled pastry (lit., gastritis, in reference to the likelihood of poor quality). ◆*Давай хоть гастрит купим, есть хочу.* "I'm so hungry, let's at least buy a 'gastritis.'"

ГАСТРОЛЁРША, -и, *f., homosexual.* A homosexual visiting from a different city (from гастролёр, "performer on tour"). ◆*Это не наш человек, наверное, гастролёрша.* "He's not one of our set. He must be touring."

ГАШЁННЫЙ, -ая. Drunk (lit., extinguished, put out). ◆*Куда вам ещё глотать, уже совсем гашённые.* "Where is there for you to swallow more booze, you are already done, you're completely drunk."

ГВОЗДИ́ТЬ/ПОГВОЗДИ́ТЬ. To fire (lit., to nail). ◆*Сейчас наши начнут гвоздить по деревне, туда духи вошли.* "Our troops are going to fire on that village where the guerrillas went."

ГВОЗДОДЁР, -а, *m., neg.* Cheap strong wine or tobacco (lit., a crowbar). ◆*Этот гвоздодёр душа не принимает.* "I can't stomach that rotgut."

ГВОЗДЬ, -я́, *m., pos.* A good, reliable person, a capable, resourceful fellow (lit., a nail). ◆*Он не пропадёт, он парень — гвоздь.* "He'll make out all right; he's a resourceful fellow." •**Гвоздь бере́менный,** *idiom, joc.* Lit., a pregnant nail. **1.** A useless, incompetent person. ◆*Да что он может, гвоздь беременный?* "That pregnant nail can't do anything right." **2.** A weak man who tries to give others an impression of physical strength. ♦*Тебе с ним не справиться, гвоздь беременный.* "You'll never be able to beat him, you weakling."

ГДЕ РАЗГИЛЬДЯ́Й, ТАМ И НЕ-СЧА́СТЬЕ, *idiom.* That's what I expected from such a bungler! (lit., Where there's a bungler, there's bound to be trouble). Cf. **разгильдя́й.**

ГЕБЕ́ШНИК, -а, *m., neg., obs.* A KGB-agent (from initials of Комитет Государственной Безопасности, "Committee on State Security"). ♦*Не знаешь, где он работает? — Да он гебешник.* "Do you know where he works? — Yes, he's KGB."

ГЕБИ́СТ, -а, *m., obs.* See **гебе́шник.**

ГЕГЕМО́Н, -а, *m., joc.* The working class; a worker (from класс-гегемон, lit. the "leading class," by sarcastic reference to communist theory). ♦*Сейчас в метро гегемон едет на работу. Давай поедем через час, будет народу поменьше.* "Right now the subway is full of the leading class on its way to work. Let's wait an hour until there's less of a crowd."

ГЕЕВА́ТЫЙ, -ая. Homosexual (by wordplay on Eng. "gay" and Гайевата, "Hiawatha"). ♦*Он у вас гееватый или как?* "Is that guy a Hiawatha, or what?"

ГЕЙ, -я, *m.* A homosexual (from Eng. "gay").

ГЕНЕРА́Л, -а, *m., crim.* Syphilis. ♦*Он где-то умудрился подцепить генерала, сейчас лечится.* "He managed to pick up a case of syphilis somewhere; he's under treatment for it now."

ГЕ́НИЙ СРЕДИ́ УДОБРЕ́НИЙ, *rhyming phrase, joc.* A phrase used to puncture someone's pretensions to cleverness (lit., a genius in a dung heap). ♦*Смотри, это же гениальное решение! — Да, ты гений среди удобрений.* "Look what a brilliant solution I came up with! — Yeah, you're a genius in a dung heap."

ГЕРА́КЛ ЗАСУ́ШЕННЫЙ, *idiom, joc.* Someone who has an inflated opinion of his physical powers (lit., a dried-up Hercules). ♦*Мне ничего не стоит под-*

нять эти чемоданы. — Ладно, Геракл засушенный, не хвастай. "It's child's play for me to lift these suitcases. — Oh, come off it, you dried-up Hercules."

ГЕРЛА́, -ы́, *f., youth.* Girl (from Eng. "girl"). ♦*А это что за герла, не знаю такую.* "Who's that girl? I don't know her." ♦*За геройские дела / Даст нам каждая герла.* "For our heroic deeds / Every girl will put out for us" (popular song of the 1970s).

ГЕРЛИ́ЦА, -ы, *f., youth.* Girl, woman, girlfriend (from Eng. "girl"). ♦*Чья эта герлица?* "Whose girlfriend is that?" (This word occurs in the popular rhyme ♦*"Кабы я была кингица," — спичет первая герлица,* "'If I were queen,' said the first girl," a takeoff on Pushkin's lines "Кабы я была царица", — говорит одна девица.) See xxxxxx

ГЕРЛО́ВЫЙ, -ая, -ое, *youth.* Female, girls', women's (from Eng. "girl"). ♦*Это герловый туалет.* "This is the women's bathroom."

ГЕРОИ́Н, -а, *m., joc.* A father of many children (from мать-героиня, the official honorific title of a woman with more than five children.) ♦*Ты у нас один героин на весь институт.* "You're our only father-hero at this institute."

ГИББО́Н, -а, *neg.* A strong, hairy man (lit., a gibbon ape). ♦*Я таких гиббонов не люблю.* "I don't like that sort of hairy ape."

ГИБУ́ЧЕСТЬ, -и, *f., neg.* Submissiveness, compliance (lit., flexible honor, by wordplay on гибкий, "pliant," and **ебу́чий**). ♦*Не нравится он мне за свою гибучесть.* "I don't like him because he's too much of a yes-man."

ГИБУ́ЧИЙ, -ая, -ое, *rude.* **1.** Highly sexed, having a lot of sexual stamina. ♦*Она, знаешь, какая гибучая!* "Wow, she's really dynamite in bed!" **2.** Compliant, spineless (cf. **гибу́честь**). ♦*Слишком ты гибучий, скажи, что ты думаешь?* "Don't be so ingratiating; say what you actually think."

ГИГ, -а, *m.* Gigabyte.

ГИ́ГАТЬСЯ/ГИ́ГНУТЬСЯ.   To   be

spoiled, to be messed up, to die. ♦*Компьютер у неё гигнулся, она в него чай пролила.* "Her computer broke down when she spilled tea on it."

ГИДРА́ВЛИК, -а, *m.* A thick head (lit., a hydraulic brake). ♦*Ты что, совсем гидравлик, не знаешь, что можно, а о чем нельзя с ним говорить?* "Are you a complete meathead? Don't you have any idea what's safe to discuss with him and what's not?"

ГИДРАВЛИ́ЧЕСКИЙ БУДИ́ЛЬНИК, *idiom, joc.* A full bladder (lit., hydraulic alarm clock). ♦*Меня гидравлический будильник поднимает в 6 утра.* "My hydraulic alarm clock gets me up at six in the morning."

ГИМНЮ́К, -а, *m., rude.* A nickname for S. Mikhalkov, author of the national anthem of the USSR (by wordplay on гимн, "anthem," and **говнюк**).

ГИПНО́З, ГИПНО́З — ХВАТЬ ТЕБЯ́ ЗА НОС! A children's rhyming phrase used to fool someone by offering to hypnotize him. Lit., Hypnosis, hypnosis, grab your nose!

ГИ́РЯ С ГАРМО́ШКОЙ, *idiom, army.* An army boot (lit., a weight with an accordion, referring to the heaviness and shape of army boots). ♦*Гири с гармошкой не надевай, жарко, кроссовки будут в самый раз.* "It's too hot for boots—running shoes will be just the thing."

ГИ́ТЛЕР, -а, *m., joc.* **1.** A large bottle of strong wine (lit., a Hitler). ♦*Маленьких бутылок не было, только гитлеров продают.* "There weren't any small bottles. They're only selling 'Hitlers.'" **2.** Strong drink. ♦*Вот это гитлер, сразу пьянеешь!* "That stuff is real 'Hitler' — you get drunk the minute you touch it."

ГКЧП, *abbr., joc.* Properly, the State Emergency Committee (Государственный комитет чрезвычайного положения) formed in 1991 to remove Gorbachev from power. Jokingly deciphered as Государственный комитет чрезвычайных придурков, "State

Committee of Extreme Idiots."

ГЛА́ДИТЬ/ПОГЛА́ДИТЬ шнурки́, *idiom, joc.* To be oversolicitous, to do too much (lit., to iron someone's shoelaces). ♦*Ты мне поможешь убрать постель? — А шнурки тебе не погладить?* "Will you help me make the bed? — Next thing you'll be asking me to iron your shoelaces."

ГЛАЗ: Дава́ть/дать проме́ж глаз, see under **дава́ть. Му́тный глаз,** see under **му́тный.**

ГЛАЗ-АЛМА́З or **ГЛАЗ-ВАТЕРПА́С,** *idiom.* An acute sense of sight, a good ability to estimate measurements by sight; a person with this ability (lit., diamond-eye or an eye like a level). ♦*Ну у тебя глаз-алмаз, разливаешь всем поровну.* "What an eagle eye you've got! You managed to pour equal portions for everyone."

ГЛАЗА́ В КУ́ЧУ, *idiom.* Said about an expression of surprise or astonishment on one's face (lit., the eyes are lumped together, from "куча," a pile, a heap). ♦*Ты бы видела его, глаза в кучу, как только я сказала ему, что я о нем думаю.* "You should have seen it; his eyes about popped right out of his head when I gave him a piece of my mind."

ГЛА́ЗА ЗАМЫ́ЛИЛИСЬ, *idiom, army.* "My eyes are tired," alluding to a special kind of eyestrain after long observation of targets (lit., My eyes feel soapy). ♦*На тебе бинокль, понаблюдай, я ничего не вижу, глаза замылились.* "You take the binoculars — my eyes are so strained, I can't see a thing."

ГЛАЗЕ́Т, -а, *m., youth, joc.* An eye (playing on глаз, "eye," and клозет, "toilet"). ♦*Дай ему в глазет, чтоб не выступал.* "Give him one in the eye for showing off like that."

ГЛИНОМЕ́С, -а, *m., crim.* A homosexual man playing the active or dominant role (lit., a potter). ♦*Кого это там глиномес высматривает?* "Who's that homo over there staring at?"

ГЛИССОВА́ТЬ/ГЛИССОНУ́ТЬ, *youth & crim.* To steal (from Fr. "glisser," to

slip off). ♦*Кто глиссонул мою рубашку?* "Who slipped off with my shirt?"

ГЛИСТА́, -ы́, *f., neg.* A skinny, weak person (lit., a tapeworm). ♦*Где ты нашла
эту глисту?* "Where'd you pick up that
90-pound weakling?" •**Глиста́ в
скафа́ндре,** *idiom, neg.* Same as **глиста́**
(lit., a tapeworm in scuba gear).

ГЛО́БУС, -а, *m., army.* A new recruit, a
soldier in his first year of service (lit.,
globe, referring to the short haircut).

ГЛО́ТКА, -и, *f., neg.* A loud voice. ♦*Ну и
глотка у тебя, не кричи так.* "Your
voice is too loud — don't shout like that."
•**Брать/взять на гло́тку,** see under
брать. Драть гло́тку, see under **драть.**

ГЛО́ТНИЧАТЬ, *imperf. only, neg.* To
shout. ♦*Не надо глотничать, поговорим
спокойно.* "There's no need to
shout; let's talk calmly."

ГЛО́ХНУТЬ/ЗАГЛО́ХНУТЬ, *neg.* To
keep silent, shut up. ♦*Когда вы там
заглохнете, спать хочется!* "Hey, shut
up. You're keeping me awake."

ГЛУБЕ́ШНИК, -а, *m., neg., obs.* A KGB
agent. (From глубокий, "deep," and
кагебешник or **гебе́шник,** a KGB-agent,
by a jocular interpretation of the abbreviation KGB, Комитет государственной
безопасности, "Committee on State
Security," as standing for Контора глубокого бурения, "Office of Deep
Drilling" — a place where people are
occupied in digging, or conducting deep
investigations.) ♦*А как вели себя глу-
бешники во время путча?* "So how did
the KGB-agents behave during the
putsch?"

ГЛУМА́РЬ, -ря́, *m., youth, neg.* One who
scoffs, jeers, taunts at others' tender or
serious feelings (from глумиться, "to
scoff"). ♦*Опять этот глумарь к нам
идёт, добра не жди.* "Is that scoffer
coming to see us again? Nothing good
can come of it."

ГЛУМЁЖ, -ежа́, *m., neg.* Scoffing, taunting, derision. ♦*Я терпеть этот глумёж не собираюсь.* "I'm not going to
put up with that taunting."

ГЛУП, КАК ТУ́ЛЬСКИЙ ПРЯ́НИК,
idiom, neg. Dumb as a Tula cookie (a
type of gingerbread, a specialty of the city
of Tula). ♦*Он ничего решить не
может, он же глуп, как тульский пряник.* "He can't figure anything out; he's
as dumb as a Tula cookie."

ГЛУПА́НТ, -а, *m., youth, neg.* A fool, idiot
(from глупый, "stupid"). ♦*Если ты глу-
пант, то это надолго.* "You're a fool
and you've always been one."

ГЛУ́ПИЗДИ, -ей, *pl., joc.* Nonsense, foolishness (playing on глупость, "silliness,"
and **пизда́**). ♦*Всё это большие глу-
пизди.* "That's all a lot of nonsense."

ГЛУПИ́СТИКА, -и, *f., neg.* Useless stuff,
pointless studies (playing on the ending
-истика, "science" or "study"). ♦*Всё,
что мы сейчас учим на первом курсе,
— глупистика.* "Everything we're studying in that introductory course is inane."

ГЛУ́ПЫЙ: Глупе́е парово́за, *idiom, joc.*
Very stupid, doltish (lit., more stupid than
a steam engine). ♦*Не считай меня глу-
пее паровоза, я понимаю всё не хуже
тебя.* "Don't take me for an idiot! I
understand it all as well as you do."

ГЛУХА́РЬ, -я́. *m.* An unsolved crime (lit.,
wood-grouse, from глухой, deaf). See
глу́хо. ♦*У нас сколько глухарей за
год? Раскрываемость хуже некуда.*
"How many unsolved crimes do we have
in a year? Our rate of solving crimes has
never been worse."

ГЛУХА́Я ТЕТЕ́РЯ, *idiom, rude.* Someone who is hard of hearing (lit., a deaf
grouse). ♦*Я тебе звоню, звоню в
дверь, а ты, глухая тетеря, ничего не
слышишь.* "I've been ringing your door-
bell for ages! You must be stone-deaf."

ГЛУ́ХО, *pred. use.* Unpromising, hopeless,
desperate. ♦*С реформами сейчас глухо.*
"There's no hope for the success of the
present reforms." •**Глу́хо как в та́нке,**
idiom. Utterly hopeless, past cure. ♦*У
нас на работе глухо как в танке.* "The
situation at work is completely hopeless."
Глу́хо де́ло, *idiom.* A hopeless situation,
a bad business. ♦*Глухо дело, ничего мы
не заработаем в этом месяце.* "It's a
poor outlook; we're not going to earn a

penny this month."

ГЛУША́РЬ, -ря́, *m., crim.* A sand-filled bag used for stunning blows to the head (from глушить, "to deafen"). ♦*Приготовь глушарь, пора мочить его, пока спит.* "Bring a stunner — let's knock him out while he's asleep."

ГЛУШИ́ТЬ, *imperf.* To fire on, to beat (lit., to stun). ♦*Глуши их, снаряды не жалеть!* "Smash them up, don't hold back on the shells!"

ГЛЮК, -а, *m., youth.* A hallucination, figment of the imagination, pipe dream. ♦*Кажется, кто-то стучит в дверь. — У тебя глюки.* "I think someone's knocking at the door. — You're just imagining things." (Cf. the popular lines *В потолке открылся люк — это глюк. На стене большой паук — тоже глюк:* "A hatchway opened in the ceiling — that was a hallucination. On the wall was a big spider — also a hallucination.")

ГЛЮКОГЕ́Н, -а, *m., youth, joc.* Hallucinatory drugs. ♦*Я этот глюкоген ненавижу.* "I can't stand this acid."

ГЛЮ́ЧИТЬСЯ/ПРИГЛЮ́ЧИТЬСЯ, *youth, obs.* To imagine, dream. ♦*Мне приглючилось, что я один в Москве.* "I imagined that I was alone in Moscow."

ГЛЮ́ЧНЫЙ, -ая, -ое, *youth, obs.* Outstanding, extraordinary. ♦*Это глючный концерт.* "That was a terrific concert."

ГЛЯ! Look! (shortened from гляди). ♦*Гля! Снег пошёл!* "Look! It snowed!"

ГЛЯДЕ́ЛКИ, гляде́лок, *pl., neg.* Eyes. See **бу́ркалы.**

ГЛЯ́КОСЬ! *joc.* Look! Wow! ♦*Глякось, кто к нам пришёл!* "Wow, look who's here!"

ГНАТЬ¹, *imperf. only, youth.* To lie, fib. ♦*Что ты гонишь, никто этого не говорил.* "Don't lie; no one said that." •**Гнать волну́,** *idiom, neg.* To be abusive, make a scene (lit., to make waves). ♦*Не гони волну, успокойся.* "Calm down, don't make a scene." **Гнать ду́ру,** *idiom, neg.* To talk nonsense; to deceive. ♦*Не гони дуру, что ты был в Штатах.* "Don't try to kid people into thinking you've been in the States." **Гнать**

майда́н, *idiom, crim.* To travel on trains in order to rob passengers. ♦*Кто ещё с нами гонит майдан?* "Who else is going to be with us on this train job?" **Гнать в ше́ю (в три ше́и),** *idiom, rude, neg.* To get rid of. ♦*Они бездельники, их надо гнать в три шеи.* "They're useless. Let's get rid of them once and for all." **Гони́ что-л.,** *idiom.* Give, give back. ♦*Гони деньги!* "Give me my money!"

ГНАТЬ²/ПОГНА́ТЬ туфту́, *idiom, crim.* To lie. ♦*Я следователю гнал туфту всю дорогу.* "I lied to the prosecutor from start to finish."

ГНАТЬ³/ПРОГНА́ТЬ, *youth.* To inject a narcotic into a vein, to make an injection. ♦*Прогоню ещё раз по вене, мне мало.* "I need to run it through my vein again. I didn't get much the first time." •**Гнать/прогна́ть теле́гу,** *idiom, youth, neg.* To lie, tell tall tales. ♦*Это ты явно прогнал телегу.* "It's perfectly obvious that you're spinning yarns."

ГНИ́ДА, -ы, *f., rude.* A scoundrel, bastard (lit., nit, louse). ♦*Я тебя, гнида, за это убью.* "You louse! I'm going to give it to you for what you did."

ГНИДЮ́ШНИК, -а, *m., neg.* A cheap or shabby bar, dive, joint. ♦*Тут рядом где-то есть гнидюшник, там и выпьем.* "There's a joint somewhere around here — let's stop in and have a drink."

ГНИ́ЛИТЬ/ЗАГНИ́ЛИТЬ, *crim., neg.* To lie, deceive (from **гнило́й,** "rotten"). ♦*Тебе нет веры, много гнилишь.* "You're such a liar, you can't be believed."

ГНИЛО́Й, -а́я, -о́е, *neg.* Rotten, spoiled, gone bad (of a person). ♦*Ты совсем гнилой стал, только о бабах и думаешь.* "You've completely gone to the dogs — all you think about is dames." •**Гнило́е нутро́ у кого́-л.,** *idiom, neg.* Lit., someone has rotten insides; used to describe a corrupt person. ♦*У тебя нутро какое-то гнилое, ты нас не поймёшь.* "A corrupt person like you wouldn't be able to understand us."

ГНО́ЙНЫЙ, -ая, -ое. Bad, repulsive (lit., purulent). ♦*Когда же эта гнойная жара кончится?* "When is this disgusting heat wave going to end?"

ГНУС, -а, *m., neg.* A boring or annoying person (lit., gnat). ♦*Это такой гнус, пристанет, всё — не отстанет.* "This guy is such a pain in the ass, once he gets hold of you, he'll never let go."

ГНУ́ТЫЙ, -ого, *m., rude.* Lit., bent, crooked. **1.** A scoundrel, bastard. ♦*А ты, гнутый, вали отсюда!* "Get out of here, you bastard!" **2.** A venal person; a yes-man. ♦*Этого гнутого все начальники любят.* "All the bosses love that boot-licker."

ГНУТЬ/ЗАГНУ́ТЬ ма́том, *idiom.* To abuse, to swear at someone (lit., to bend with abuse). ♦*Он сразу загнул матом и весь разговор.* "He started swearing, and that was the end of the discussion."

ГНУТЬ ПА́ЛЬЦЫ, *idiom.* To make threatening gestures with one's hands (lit., to bend one's fingers). See **па́льцы ве́ером.**

ГНУ́ТЬСЯ под на́ры, *idiom, crim.* To hide in order to avoid blows; lit., to cringe under a plank bed (as in prison). ♦*Не гнись под нары, от нас не уйдёшь.* "There's no use hiding, you won't get away from us."

ГОВЁННЫЙ, -ая, -ое, *rude.* Bad (lit., filthy; cf. **говно́**). ♦*Преподаватель он говённый, да и человек не очень.* "He's a crappy teacher and not much of a human being either."

ГОВНИ́СТЫЙ, -ая, -ое, *rude.* Bad, having a bad character (cf. **говно́**). ♦*К этому преподавателю не ходи сдавать, он самый говнистый.* "Don't take your exams with that teacher — he's the very worst."

ГОВНО́, -а́, *n., rude.* **1.** Feces, excrement. ♦*Не ходи туда, там куча говна.* "Watch your step! There's a pile of shit over there." **2.** A worthless or bad person, thing, or event. ♦*И не подумаю извиниться перед этим говном!* "I wouldn't dream of apologizing to that turd."

•**ГОВНО́** (*пот.*): **Говно́ соба́чье,** *idiom, rude.* A bastard, scoundrel (lit., dog shit). ♦*Он оказался говном собачьим, а мы ему верили.* "We trusted him, and then he turned out to be a scoundrel." **По́лное говно́,** *idiom, rude.* Someone or something terrible (lit., complete shit). **Говно́ на па́лочке,** *idiom, rude.* A conceited, stuck-up person (lit., shit on a stick). ♦*Подумаешь, говно на палочке, слова ему не скажи.* "Look at that guy! Shit on a stick — you can't say a word to him." **Говно́ на по́стном ма́сле,** *idiom, rude.* Nonsense, trash (lit., shit in vegetable oil). ♦*Этот фильм — говно на постном масле.* "That film is a crock." **Своё говно́ не па́хнет,** *idiom, rude.* "One's own shit doesn't smell." ♦*Она от него без ума, а он — такое говно. Правда, своё говно не пахнет.* "She's crazy about him, and he's just a piece of shit. Of course, one's own shit doesn't smell." **Болта́ться/проболта́ть-ся, как говно́ в про́руби,** *idiom, rude.* To idle about, to cool one's heels (lit., to bob about like a turd in an ice-fishing hole). ♦*Я здесь болтаюсь, как говно в проруби, никто моим делом не занимается.* "I've been hanging around here like a turd in a fishing hole, and no one at all has has taken care of me." **ГОВНО́** (*асс.*): **Окуну́ться в говно́,** *idiom, rude.* To feel bad (lit., to take a dip in shit). ♦*С ним пообщаешься, как в говно окунёшься.* "When you hear the way he talks with people, it makes you feel soiled." **Попа́л в говно́, так не чири-ка́й,** *idiom, rude.* Don't try to justify yourself if you're guilty (lit., "You've landed in the shit, so don't chirp"). ♦*Не хочу ничего слышать, проворовался, попал в говно, так не чирикай.* "You've been embezzling funds and I don't want to hear any of your excuses — you're in the shit, so don't chirp."

ГОВНА́ (*gen.*): **Для дру́га и говна́ не жа́лко,** *idiom, rude, joc.* Used as a jocularly modest deflection of gratitude for a small favor: it's nothing, don't mention it (lit., "For a friend I wouldn't grudge even [my] shit"). ♦*Спасибо за книгу. — Для друга и говна не жалко.* "Thanks for the book. — Oh, for a friend I wouldn't grudge even shit." **Кто спо́рит, тот говна́ не сто́ит,** *idiom, rude.* Betting is a pointless thing; used in response to a suggestion to bet on something (lit., "He who bets isn't worth shit"). ♦*Спорим, наша команда выиграет! — Кто спорит, тот говна не стоит.* "I'll bet you that our team will win! — Someone who bets isn't worth shit." **Как говна́ нае́лся,** *idiom, rude.* Soiled, degraded (lit., as if one had eaten shit). ♦*Я с ним поговорил пять минут и весь день чувствовал себя, как говна наелся, он обо всём нарассказывал столько гадостей.* "I only spoke to him for five minutes and for the rest of the day I felt as if I had eaten shit — he said such disgusting things about everyone." **Ло́жка говна́ в бо́чке мёда,** *idiom, rude.* An unpleasant or unexpected difficulty (lit., a spoonful of shit in a barrel of honey). ♦*Это требование — ложка говна в бочке мёда.* "Everything's been fine, but this new demand is a fly in the ointment." **Де́лать/сде́лать из говна́ конфе́тку,** *idiom, rude.* To improve something (lit., to make a piece of candy out of shit). ♦*Сейчас я сделаю из говна конфетку, давай сюда статью.* "Give me the draft of your article and I'll make a silk purse from that sow's ear." **ГОВНО́М** *(instr.):* **Мешо́к с говно́м (дерьмо́м),** *idiom, rude.* A person with a nasty character (lit., a sack of shit). ♦*Это надо же быть таким мешком с говном, всех оскорбляет.* "He's so incredibly nasty, he offends everyone." **ГОВНЕ́** *(prep.):* **По го́рло в говне́,** *idiom, rude.* Overwhelmed with troubles (lit., up to one's neck in shit). ♦*После проверки магазина заведующая по горло в говне.* "Since her store was audited, the manager's been up to her neck in shit." **Сиде́ть по́ уши в говне́,** *idiom, rude.* To experience strong negative feelings (lit., to be sitting in shit up to one's ears). ♦*После его выступления все сидят по уши в говне, всех опозорил.* "He's disgraced everyone by his behavior; they're all up to their ears in shit." **Ковыря́ться/поковыря́ться в чужо́м говне́,** *idiom, rude.* To meddle, stick one's nose in someone else's business (lit., to pick around in someone else's shit). ♦*Не люблю я в чужом говне ковыряться.* "I don't like to mess around in other peo-

ple's affairs." **На говне́ заме́шан,** *idiom, rude.* Fundamentally defective, having a poor character (lit., with shit kneaded in as a basic ingredient). ♦*С ним одни проблемы, видно, на говне замешан.* "With him it's just one problem after another — I guess he just came from the mold that way." **Тащи́ться как лом в говне́,** *idiom, rude.* To go slowly, drag along (lit., to drag like a scrap in shit). ♦*Прибавь шагу, не тащись как лом в говне.* "Shake a leg! You're as slow as molasses."

ГОВНОВО́З, -а, *m., rude.* A cart or truck for removing excrement, waste (lit., a shit transporter; cf. **говно́**). ♦*Он работает на говновозе.* "He works in waste removal."

ГОВНОДА́ВИНА, -ы, *f., rude, joc.* The market in Luzhniki, a Moscow district (from **говно́,** "shit," and давить, "to crush"). ♦*На говнодавину народ ездит, как сумасшедший.* "People are going to Luzhniki in droves."

ГОВНОДА́ВЫ, -ов, *pl., rude.* Awkward-looking rough boots (lit., shit-crushers; cf. **говно́**). ♦*Я эти говнодавы носить не буду.* "I'm not going to wear those clodhoppers."

ГОВНОЕ́Д, -а, *m., rude.* A bastard, scoundrel (lit., shit-eater; cf. **говно́**). ♦*Что этому говноеду надо?* "What does that bastard want?"

ГОВНОПРОТИ́ВНЫЙ, -ая, -ое, *rude.* Disgusting, loathsome (cf. **говно́**). ♦*Я этот суп говнопротивный есть не буду.* "I'm not going to eat that disgusting soup."

ГОВНОЧИ́СТ, -а, *m., rude.* A latrine cleaner (cf. **говно́**). ♦*Он работает говночистом.* "He works cleaning latrines."

ГОВНЮ́К, -а́, *m., rude.* A bad or worthless person (lit., a turd; cf. **говно́**). ♦*На этого говнюка надеяться не стоит.* "You can't rely on that turd."

ГОВНЯ́ДИНА, -ы, *f., rude.* Spoiled meat (by wordplay on говядина, "beef," and **говно́**). ♦*Зачем ты купила эту говнядину?* "What did you buy that shitty meat for?"

ГОВНЯ́НЫЙ, -ая, -ое. See **говённый.**

ГОВНЯ́ТЬ/НАГОВНЯ́ТЬ, ИЗГОВ-НЯ́ТЬ, *rude.* To harm, spoil (cf. **говно́**). ♦*Ты весь рисунок изговнял.* "You've smudged up my whole drawing." ♦*Любишь ты наговнять другому человеку.* "You're always trying to harm others."

ГОВНЯ́ТЬСЯ¹/ИЗГОВНЯ́ТЬСЯ, ЗА-ГОВНЯ́ТЬСЯ, *rude.* Cf. **говно́.** **1.** To soil oneself, get involved in dirty business. ♦*Я в этом деле говняться не хочу.* "I don't want to dirty my hands in this affair." **2.** To become corrupted, go bad. *Он стал говняться на глазах, когда стал начальником.* "The minute they made him boss, he went bad."

ГОВНЯ́ТЬСЯ²/ОБГОВНЯ́ТЬСЯ, *rude.* To mess up, do something wrong (cf. **говно́**). ♦*Наши в хоккей совсем обговнялись.* "Our hockey team messed up completely."

ГОВОРИ́ТЬ — НЕ ДЕ́ЛАТЬ, *idiom.* Lit., Talk isn't action. ♦*Ему хорошо давать советы, говорить — не делать.* "He likes to give advice. Well, talk is cheap."

ГОВОРИ́ТЬ/СКАЗА́ТЬ прямы́м те́кстом, *idiom.* To speak openly, directly (lit., to speak in uncoded text). ♦*Я тебе говорю прямым текстом: ничего он для тебя не будет делать, так и знай.* "I'm telling you straight out: you've got to realize that he's never going to do anything for you."

ГОВОРЛИ́ВЫЙ, ВЫ́ТРИ НОС СОП-ЛИ́ВЫЙ, *rhyming phrase, rude.* Don't gossip, don't tattle (lit., "You chatterbox — wipe your runny nose"). ♦*Я много могу рассказать о том, что никто не знает. — Говорливый, вытри нос сопливый.* "I could tell you a lot that no one else knows. — Don't run off at the mouth."

ГОВОРЯ́Т — КУР ДОЯ́Т, *idiom, joc.* A rhyming phrase used in skeptical reply to Говорят…, "people say…". Lit., People say you can milk chickens.

ГОВЯ́ШКА, -и, *f., mainly in children's speech.* **1.** A turd. ♦*Осторожно, здесь говяшка.* "Watch out! There's a pile over there." **2.** A worthless or pathetic person. ♦*Зачем же ты, говяшка, это сделал?* "You schlemiel, what did you do that for?"

ГОДО́К, годка́, *m., army.* **1.** A soldier in his first year of service (from год, a year). ♦*Что делать, терпи, сначала годок, а потом и дедок.* "You're just a rookie now, but just wait, you'll soon be an old hand." **2.** Soldiers enlisted in the same year. ♦*Он мой годок, вместе в армию пришли, вместе и на дембель.* "He's my 'classmate'—we enlisted together, we'll be released together."

ГОЛДЫ́РЬ, голдыря́, *m.* A drunkard (lit., a naked man). ♦*Зачем дал деньги, этот голдырь их донесет до первого магазина.* "Why did you give him money? That soak'll spend it in the first liquor store."

ГОЛИ́МЫЙ, -ая, -ое, *youth, pos.* Complete, absolute, extreme. ♦*Он — голимый меломан.* "He's completely wild about music."

ГОЛОВА́, -ы́, *f.* A clever, competent person. ♦*Он — голова, сам всё сообразит.* "He's a real brain; he thinks of everything." •**Брать/взять в го́лову,** see under **брать. Ни в голове́, ни в жо́пе,** see under **жо́па. Что в голове́, что в жо́пе,** see under **жо́па.**

ГОЛОВА́ В ШТАНЫ́ ПА́ДАЕТ, *idiom, joc.* Said of someone very sleepy (lit., his head is falling into his pants). ♦*Больше не могу работать, голова в штаны падает.* "I can't work any longer — my head is falling into my pants."

ГОЛОВА́, КАК ДОМ СОВЕ́ТОВ, *idiom, obs. joc.* Very smart, very clever (lit., a head like the House of Soviets). ♦*Он решит эту задачу, голова у него, как Дом Советов.* "He'll solve the problem — he's really got brains."

ГОЛОВА́СТИК, -а, *m., joc.* (Lit., a tadpole). **1.** A child. **2.** A small, fussy person. ♦*Этот головастик целый день носится по коридорам.* "That tadpole has been bustling around in the corridor all day long."

ГОЛОВЕ́ШКА, -и, *f., youth, joc.* A black person, African (lit., charcoal). ♦*У этой* *головешки есть вещи на продажу?* "Is that African selling something?"

ГОЛО́ВКА БО́-БО́, ДЕ́НЕЖКИ ТЮ-ТЮ́, *idiom, joc.* Said of a person with a hangover, whose head is aching and who has spent all his money (lit., in baby talk, something like "head boo-boo, money bye-bye"). ♦*Понимаю, головка бо-бо, денежки тю-тю, сколько тебе надо?* "I understand your situation: head boo-boo, money bye-bye. How much do you need?"

ГОЛОВОЧЛЕ́Н , -а, *m.* A skinhead (from "голый," naked, and "член," penis). ♦*Форма такая у головочленов, всё чёрное и кожаное.* "Skinheads have a kind of uniform – everything is black and leather."

ГОЛОЖО́ПЫЙ, -ая, -ое, *rude.* Poor, impoverished (lit., bare-assed). ♦*Он ничего не нажил, голожопым был, голожопым и остался.* "He never managed to earn anything — he started poor and he stayed poor."

ГО́ЛОС, -а, *m., homosexual.* A penis (Lit., voice). ♦*У него знаешь, какой голос, тебе и не снилось.* "You know how big his 'voice' is? You can't imagine it in your wildest dreams!"

ГОЛУБА́Я ФИ́ШКА, *idiom, business.* A well-known company and its shares (lit., blue chip). ♦*Даже голубые фишки перестали брать, кризис, — ничего не поделаешь.* "They won't even take blue chips now. Well, that's the crisis for you."

ГОЛУБИЗНА́, -ы́, *f, joc.* Homosexuality (lit., blueness). ♦*У него повышенная голубизна.* "You can see he's homosexual."

ГОЛУБО́Й, -о́го, *m.* A homosexual man (lit., light blue). ♦*Ты не знал, что он голубой?* "Didn't you know he was gay?"

ГО́ЛУБЬ, -я, *m., joc.* Gay, homosexual (by wordplay on голубь, "dove" and голубой, "gay").

ГО́ЛЫЙ ВА́СЯ НОЧЕВА́Л, *idiom, joc.* There's nothing on the shelves (lit., naked Vasya spent the night). ♦*У тебя в*

холодильнике голый Вася ночевал. "Looks like naked Vasya spent the night in your refrigerator."

ГОЛЯ́К, -а́, *m.* Empty shelves in a store (lit., nakedness). ♦*В магазин не ходи, там голяк.* "Don't bother going to that store, the shelves are empty there." •**Голя́к на ба́зе,** *idiom.* "Nakedness in base camp," nothing to eat at home. ♦*Бери на рыбалку колбасу, хлеб, консервы. У меня голяк на базе.* "Bring along some sausages and bread for our fishing trip — my cupboard is bare."

ГО́МИК -а, *m.* A homosexual. ♦*Там у него собираются одни гомики.* "The only people who go to his place are gay."

ГОМОФО́Б, -а, *m., joc.* Homophobe, hater of homosexuals.

ГОН, -а, *m., youth.* Nonsense, twaddle. ♦*Опять начали гон на два часа.* "They spent another couple of hours chattering."

ГОНДО́Н ШТО́ПАНЫЙ, *idiom, rude.* A worthless or repellent man (lit., a darned [mended] condom). ♦*Ты, гондон штопаный, когда деньги отдашь?* "When are you going to pay me back, you bastard?"

ГОНЕ́Ц, гонца́, *m., joc.* One sent to buy liquor for friends (lit., a herald). ♦*Надо послать поскорее гонца, а то магазины закроются.* "We'd better send out a herald right now before the stores close."

ГО́НИВО, -а, *n.* Nonsense, fiction (from гнать, to tell tall tales). ♦*Пойдем послушаем, там гониво идет об экстрасенсах и другой лабуде.* "Let's go listen to their bullshit about extrasensory perception and the rest of that nonsense."

ГО́НКИ, гонок, *pl., youth, joc.* See **гон.**

ГОНО́РА, -ы, *f., youth.* Gonorrhea. ♦*С ней поосторожней, у неё гонора.* "Watch out for her; she's got gonorrhea."

ГОНОШИ́ТЬСЯ/ЗАГОНОШИ́ТЬСЯ, *neg.* **1.** To worry. ♦*Не гоношись, всё будет в порядке.* "Don't worry; everything will be all right." **2.** To make a scene, an outburst. ♦*Не гоношись, делай, как было сказано.* "Don't make a scene — keep to our agreement!"

ГО́НЩИК, -а, *m., youth, neg.* A liar, idle babbler (lit., race driver). ◆ *Ну что, гонщик, всё рассказал?* "Enough of your stories! I don't believe you anyhow."

ГОНЯ́ТЬ/ПОГОНЯ́ТЬ, *rude.* To have long-lasting sex. (Cf. **пили́ть**). ◆ *Ты же гонял всю ночь, не надоело?* "Didn't you get tired of screwing all night?"

ГОНЯ́ТЬ Ду́ньку Кулако́ву, *idiom, crim., joc.* To masturbate (lit., to drive Dunka Kulakova. This is a play on the regular expression гонять в кулак, "to drive it into one's fist"). ◆ *Там баб нет, приходится гонять Дуньку Кулакову.* "There aren't any women there, so they drive Dunka Kulakova."

ГОП СО СМЫ́КОМ, *idiom, crim., obs.* A criminal (from the title phrase of an old song), esp. as marked by such fashions as a shaved head, tattoos, and gold rings. ◆ *А что это за гоп со смыком?* "Who is that criminal-looking guy?"

ГО́ПА, -ы, *f., youth.* A group, set of people.

ГО́ПНИК, -а, *m., crim.* A criminal. ◆ *Где эти гопники собираются?* "Where do those crooks hang out?"

ГО́П-СТО́П, *idiom, crim.* An armed holdup. ◆ *Его взяли на гоп-стоп.* "They held him up at gunpoint."

ГОРА́: На куды́кину го́ру (ворова́ть помидо́ры). See under **на.**

ГОРБА́ТИТЬ(СЯ), *imperf. only, neg.* To work hard, toil (from горб, "hump," "hunchback," with suggestion of back-breaking labor). ◆ *Я не буду на тебя больше горбатить(ся).* "I'm not going to slave for you any more."

ГОРБА́ТЫЙ: Лепи́ть/залепи́ть горба́того. See under **лепи́ть.**

ГОРБУ́ХА, -и, *f., youth.* **1.** A joke, anecdote. ◆ *Ну, давай ещё горбуху, у тебя здорово получается.* "Tell another joke — you're so good at it!" **2.** *pred. use.* Good, excellent. ◆ *Погода — горбуха, пойдём на лыжах.* "The weather's perfect. Let's go skiing!"

ГОРЕ́ТЬ си́ним пла́менем, *idiom, neg.* To be in trouble, to be in difficulties. ◆ *Горю синим пламенем, выручайте.*

"I'm in trouble — give me a hand."

ГОРИ́ (ВСЁ) СИ́НИМ ПЛА́МЕНЕМ, *idiom.* The hell with it, I don't care, I don't give a damn (lit., let it burn with a blue flame). ◆ *Гори эта работа синим пламенем, надоело.* "The hell with this job; I'm sick of it."

ГО́РКА, -и, *f., army.* A steep take-off (lit., a hill). ◆ *Потом быстро горку делай, чтобы не засекли.* "Then do a vertical take-off, so they won't have time to take aim at you."

ГО́РЛО: (Пить/вы́пить) из горла́, *idiom.* To drink from the bottle. ◆ *Будешь из горла, стакана нет.* "Have some from the bottle; there's no glass."

ГОРЧИ́ЧНИК, -а, *m., youth.* A hundred rubles (lit., a mustard plaster; from the color of the old hundred-ruble bills). ◆ *Кто разменяет горчичник?* "Can someone change a hundred for me?"

ГОРЧИ́ШНИК, -а, *m.* See **горчи́чник.**

ГОРШО́К, горшка́, *m., joc.* A head (lit., pot). ◆ *Здесь низкие двери, не разбей горшок.* "That door is low — don't bump your head."

ГОРЮ́ЧЕЕ, -его, *n.* Alcohol, liquor (cf. **горю́чка**). ◆ *Горючего хватит на вечер?* "Is there enough liquor for the party?"

ГОРЮ́ЧКА, -и, *f.* Gas (for an automobile). ◆ *Горючка кончилась, где здесь можно заправиться?* "We're out of gas. Where can we tank up around here?"

ГОСТ: По го́сту! *idiom, youth.* Okay, fine (lit., up to standards, from ГОСТ, acronym of государственный стандарт, "government standard"). ◆ *Как жизнь? — По госту!* "How's life? — Okay."

ГОСТИ́НИЦА, -ы, *f., joc.* A train station (lit., hotel). ◆ *Где сегодня ночуешь? — Конечно, на Курском, в гостинице.* "Where are you staying tonight? — At the Kursk Railway Station, of course."

ГОСУДА́РСТВО: Игра́ть с госуда́рством в аза́ртные и́гры. See under **игра́ть.**

ГО́ЦАТЬ/ЗАГО́ЦАТЬ, *crim.* To dance. ◆ *Слышишь, гоцают наверху, свадьба у них, что ли?* "Listen to them dancing upstairs. What are they having, a wedding?"

ГРА́БКИ, гра́бок, *pl.* Hands (from **гра́бли**). ♦*Убери грабки, не твоё, не трогай!* "Hands off. It's not yours, don't touch it!"

ГРА́БЛИ, -ей, *pl.* Hands (lit., rake).

ГРАЖДА́НКА, -и, 1. Civilian life. ♦*Что ты собираешься делать на гражданке?* "What are you planning to do when you get out of the army?" **2.** The Russian Civil War (1918–1920). ♦*Он участник гражданки.* "He fought in the Civil War."

ГРАНА́ТА: Гаси́ свет, броса́й грана́ту. See under **гаси́.**

ГРАНИ́ЦА НЕ ЗНА́ЕТ ПОКО́Я, *idiom, army.* Said of a fence around a military unit (lit., the name of a movie, "It's Never Quiet on the Frontier"). ♦*Опять полезли через забор за водкой, граница не знает покоя.* "There they go over the fence again for vodka, really it's never quiet on the frontier."

ГРАНТ, -а, *m., crim.* A robbery, armed robbery. ♦*Не каждый пойдёт на такой грант.* "Not everyone could pull off a holdup like this."

ГРАНЬ: На гра́ни фо́ла, *idiom.* Barely acceptable, at the outer limits of law or right (lit., on the verge of an error). ♦*Ты ездишь на грани фола.* "You're asking for a speeding ticket the way you're driving."

ГРАФЬЁ, -я́, *n., neg.* See **графья́.**

ГРАФЬЯ́, -ёв, *pl., joc., neg.* VIP's, directors, chiefs, bosses, the management (lit., princes, though the regular plural of the prerevolutionary variety is графы). ♦*Графья идут, сейчас начнутся речи.* "Here come the big guns; now they'll start up with the speeches."

ГРЕ́БЕНЬ, гре́бня, *m., crim., neg.* A homosexual man (lit., a big cockscomb). ♦*Что этому гребню надо?* "What does that homo want?"

ГРЕБИ́ ОТСЮ́ДА! *idiom.* Get out of here! Scram! (lit., row away). ♦*Греби отсюда, ты лишний!* "Get out of here! You're in the way!"

ГРЕВ, -а, *m.* A parcel with food and clothes (lit., warmth). ♦*Грев тебе пришел, что там у тебя?* "You got a parcel? What's in it?"

ГРЕМЕ́ТЬ/ЗАГРЕМЕ́ТЬ костя́ми, *idiom.* To make a lot of noise (lit., to rattle one's bones). ♦*Не греми костями, ребёнок спит.* "Don't make a racket, the baby's sleeping."

ГРИН, -а́, *m., youth.* A dollar (from Eng. "greenback"). ♦*У тебя сколько гринов осталось?* "How many dollars do you have left?"

ГРИ́ППЕР, -а, *m., joc.* The flu, a headcold (by wordplay on грипп, "influenza" and три́ппер, "gonorrhea"). ♦*Кашляю, вот, где-то гриппер подхватил.* "I've got a cough. I must've caught a cold somewhere."

ГРОБ: Ви́деть кого́-что-л. в гробу́ (в бе́лых та́почках). See under **ви́деть.**

ГРОБАНУ́ТЬ/УГРО́БИТЬ, *perf.* To kill (from гроб, "coffin"). ♦*Сколько ребят зря угробили в Чечне.* "How many boys they've killed in Chechnya, and all for nothing!"

ГРОМ ГРЕМИ́Т, ЗЕМЛЯ́ ТРЯСЁТСЯ, ПОП НА КУ́РИЦЕ НЕСЁТСЯ, *joc.* A children's rhyming phrase (lit., Thunder is rumbling, the earth is quaking, a priest is riding a chicken). Used in reaction to thunder or any loud noise.

ГРОМКОГОВОРИ́ТЕЛЬ, -я, *m., joc.* A mouth (lit., loudspeaker). ♦*Ты бы лучше не открывал свой громкоговоритель!* "Keep your mouth shut!"

ГРО́ХНУТЬ, *perf.* **1.** To kill. ♦*Сегодня в Чечне троих солдат грохнули.* "Today three soldiers were killed in Chechnya." **2.** To hit. ♦*Грохни его чем-нибудь, слишком умный.* "Hit him with something, he's a smart-aleck."

ГРУЗ 200, *idiom, army.* Corpses transported by air (lit., load-200). ♦*Груз двести когда домой отправляем?* "When are we going to fly the load-200 home?"

ГРУЗИ́ЛО, -а, *n., army, neg.* A sailor serving on a submarine (lit., a sinker, lead weight used in fishing). ♦*С грузилами* *драться — себе дороже.* "It's more than your life is worth to get into a fight with submarine sailors."

ГРУЗИ́ТЬ, *imperf., youth.* To teach (lit., to load). ♦*Не надо меня грузить, без вас учёный.* "You needn't lecture me, I know it without your help."

ГРУ́ЗЧИК, -а, *m., crim.* Someone who takes the blame or punishment for another's crime (lit., a porter). ♦*Они нашли грузчика, сами легко отделаются.* "They've found a fall guy. They themselves will get off easy."

ГРУ́ППЕНСЕКС, -а, *m., youth.* Group sex; an orgy. ♦*Мне группенсекс ни к чему.* "I have no interest in group sex."

ГРУППЕ́ШНИК, -а, *m., youth.* See **гру́ппенсекс.**

ГРУППОВУ́ХА, -и, *f., youth.* See **гру́ппенсекс.**

ГРУППОВЩИ́НА, -ы, *f., neg.* Gang rape. ♦*Им дали 10 лет за групповщину.* "They were sentenced to 10 years for gang rape."

ГРУ́ША, Я́БЛОКО, ЛИМО́Н — ВОТ ТЕБЕ́ И МИЛЛИО́Н. A children's rhyming phrase used in counting. Lit., A pear, an apple, a lemon — and there's a million. Cf. **лимо́н.**

ГРУ́ШИ ОКОЛА́ЧИВАТЬ, *idiom.* To hang around, to do nothing (lit., to knock pears off a tree). ♦*Всё лето околачивали груши, пора и делами заняться.* "You've been hanging around idly all summer; now it's time to get down to work."

ГРЫЗЛО́, -а́, *n., youth.* **1.** Ground poppy-heads for chewing as a narcotic. ♦*Не скучай, вот возьми грызла.* "If you're bored, chew some poppyheads." **2.** A mouth (from грызть, "to gnaw").

ГРЫЗУ́Н, -а́, *m.* **1.** A child (lit., a rodent). ♦*Грызунов у них трое, а денег нет.* "They've got three kids and no money." **2.** A louse.

ГРЫ́МЗА, -ы, *f., neg.* An ugly, unkempt, sloppily dressed woman. ♦*Это что за грымза там сидит?* "Who's that dog over there?"

ГРЯЗЬ, -и, *neg.* **1.** Scum, dregs of society (lit., dirt, filth). ♦*Ну и друзья у тебя, грязь какая-то!* "Your friends are scum." **2.** Worthless stuff, triviality. ♦*Деньги для него, что грязь.* "Money is nothing to him." •**Чего́-л. как гря́зи,** *idiom.* Something is plentiful, cheap. ♦*Там этих магнитофонов как грязи.* "Those tape recorders are sold cheap as dirt there." **Пья́ный как грязь,** see under **пья́ный.**

ГУБА́, -ы́, *f., army.* A guardhouse, place of military punishment. ♦*Опять он на губе сидит.* "He's in the guardhouse again."

ГУБА́РЬ, -ря́, *m., army.* A soldier serving a sentence in the guardhouse. ♦*Где сейчас губарь? — Как где, на губе.* "Where's the prisoner now? — What do you mean, where? In the guardhouse, of course."

ГУДЁЖ, гудежа́, *m.* A drinking party, drinking bout (cf. **гуде́ть**). ♦*Мне надоел бесконечный гудёж.* "I'm sick of this endless drinking bout."

ГУДЕ́ТЬ/ЗАГУДЕ́ТЬ, *neg.* **1.** To complain, whine. ♦*Не гуди, всё равно я не могу пойти с тобой.* "There's no use whining. I just can't go with you." **2.** To drink, get drunk. ♦*Они гудят со вчерашнего дня.* "They've been on a drunk since yesterday."

ГУЖЕВА́ТЬСЯ/ПОГУЖЕВА́ТЬСЯ, *youth, obs. (1960s).* To party, have a good time. ♦*Мы гужевались до утра.* "We partied all night."

ГУЖЁВКА, -и, *f., youth, obs.* A party, get-together. ♦*У нас гужёвка намечается, придёшь?* "We're having a party. Will you come?"

ГУЛЬБА́, -ы́, *f.* A drinking party. ♦*Гульба там у них идёт уже три дня с утра до вечера.* "They've been carrying on a drinking bout over there for three whole days already."

ГУЛЬБА́РИЙ, -я, *m., youth, joc.* A party. ♦*Когда у вас гульбарий по поводу дня рождения?* "When are you having your birthday party?"

ГУ́ЛЬКИ, гу́лек, *pl., joc.* Fun, entertainment. ♦*У тебя одни гульки на уме.*

"All you can think of is having a good time."

ГУЛЯ́Й, ВА́СЯ, *idiom.* "Johnny Walker" whisky (lit., Have fun, Vasya). ◆*Вот тебе «Гуляй, Вася», как никак день рождения.* "Here's some Johnny Walker for you—after all, it's your birthday."

ГУЛЯ́Й, ВА́СЯ (, жуй опи́лки)! No matter how bad things are, we'll have a good time (lit., "Enjoy yourself, Vasya — chew sawdust!"). ◆*Выпьем, что ли? — А то нет! Гуляй, Вася, жуй опилки!* "What do you say we have a drink? — Sure, why not! Enjoy yourself, Vasya, chew some sawdust!"

ГУМАНИТА́РКА, -и, *f.* Humanitarian aid from the West, especially food. ◆*В это лето мы выжили на гуманитарке.* "We made it through the summer on humanitarian aid."

ГУМО́ЗНЫЙ, -ая, -ое, *neg.* Disgusting, repulsive. ◆*Что за гумозная колбаса!* "What disgusting sausage this is!"

ГУНДО́С(КА), -а (-и), *m. (f.), rude.* Someone who speaks indistinctly or unintelligibly. ◆*Этого гундоса не поймёшь.* "You can't understand a word that mumbler says."

ГУНДО́СИТЬ/ЗАГУНДО́СИТЬ, *rude.* To speak indistinctly or unintelligibly. ◆*Не слышу, что ты там гундосишь.* "I can't hear what you're mumbling over there."

ГУНЯ́ВИТЬ/ЗАГУНЯ́ВИТЬ, *youth, neg.* **1.** To gossip about, badmouth. ◆*Её гунявить не надо, не такой она плохой человек.* "You shouldn't spread that sort of gossip about her; she's a fine person." **2.** To say indistinctly, mutter (cf. **гундо́сить**). ◆*Ты понимаешь, что она гундосит?* "Can you understand what she's muttering?"

ГУТАЛИ́Н, -а, *m., joc.* A black person (lit., black shoe polish). ◆*Здесь живёт мой знакомый гуталин.* "This is where that black guy I know lives."

ГЭ, *n., indecl.* Shit (from the initial letter of **говно́**). ◆*Ну и гэ эта колбаса!* "This sausage is crap."

«ДА БУ́ДЕТ СВЕТ!» — сказа́л монтёр и сде́лал замыка́ние, *idiom, joc., neg.* An expression used to blame or ridicule failure (lit., "Let there be light," said the electrician, as he short-circuited the line). ◆*Я что-то не так сделал, у меня сломался телевизор. — «Да будет свет!» — сказал монтёр и сделал замыкание.* "I seem to have done something wrong — the TV's not working. — Yeah, 'Let there be light,' said the electrician, as he shortcircuited the line.'"

ДА ЗДРА́ВСТВУЕТ НА́ША КРА́СНАЯ ИКРА́, СА́МАЯ ЧЁРНАЯ ИКРА́ В МИ́РЕ, *idiom, joc.* "Long live our read caviar, the blackest caviar in the world." A jocular way of commenting on the poor quality of domestic Russian products.

ДАВА́Й, СКИ́ДЫВАЙ! *idiom, joc.* Get started, get going (lit., come on and take off your clothes; imitating dialectal form for давай снимай). ◆*Давай, скидывай, начали работать!* "Come on, get going! The job is under way!"

ДАВА́ЛКА, -и, *f. rude.* **1.** A loose, sexually available woman (from давать, "to give"). ◆*Познакомь, она, говорят, давалка.* "Would you introduce me to her? I hear she's available." **2.** The female genitals. ◆*У тебя давалка есть, тогда ляжем.* "If you have a cunt, let's go to bed."

ДАВАНУ́ТЬ ХРАПАЧКА́, *idiom.* To sleep (from храпеть, to snore). ◆ *Давануть бы храпачка часов восемь.* "I wish I could sleep for eight hours."

ДАВА́ТЬ/ДАТЬ, *rude.* To grant sexual favors. ◆*Он за ней ходил целый год, а она ему так и не дала.* "He went with her for a whole year, but she would never go to bed with him." ●**Дава́ть/дать ва́флю,** *idiom.* To have fellatio performed on oneself (lit., to give a wafer). Cf. **брать/взять ва́флю** under **брать. Дава́ть/дать дра́ла,** *idiom.* To flee. ◆*Как только он появился, они сразу дали драла.* "As soon as he showed up, they took to their heels." **Дава́ть/дать жи́зни,** *idiom, neg.* To punish. ◆*Ещё раз принесёшь двойку, отец даст тебе жизни.* "If you get another failing grade, your father is going to give it to you." **Дава́ть/дать ма́ху,** *idiom, joc.* To make a mistake. ◆*Ну, в этом деле ты дал маху.* "Well, you were wrong about that." **Дава́ть/дать Ма́ху и Фейерба́ху,** *idiom, youth, joc.* To make a mistake, do something wrong (lit., to sleep with both Mach and Feuerbach). ◆*Ой, я дала маху, забыла тетрадь! — Да, ты дала Маху и Фейербаху заодно.* "Oh, how stupid of me. I forgot my notebook! — Yeah, you put out for both Mach and Feuerbach." **Дава́ть/дать оборо́тку,** *idiom, crim.* To respond in kind, pay back. ◆*Чего он к тебе лезет? Дай ему оборотку.* "Why do you let him yell at you? Yell back at him." **Дава́ть/дать пизды́,** see under **пизда́. Дава́ть/дать (наве́шивать/наве́сить, отве́шивать/отве́сить) пиздюле́й,** *idiom.* To beat up, hit. ◆*А ты дай ей пиздюлей, не будет приходить домой так поздно.* "If you give her a spanking, she'll stop coming home so late." **Дава́ть/дать плю́ху,** *idiom, neg.* To hit, beat. ◆*Дай ему плюху, чтоб успокоился.* "Sock him one to make him act nicer." **Дава́ть/дать прочуха́нку,** *idiom, joc.* To scold, take to task. ◆*Отец даст тебе прочуханку за твою учёбу.* "Your father's going to scold you for your poor grades." **Дава́ть/дать в нюх,** *idiom, neg.* To hit in the face. ◆*Дай ему в нюх за наглость.* "Give it to him in the face for his presumptuousness." **Дава́ть/дать в па́чку,** *idiom.* To hit, beat. ◆*Дай ему в пачку, чтобы не выступал.* "Give him a punch in the face so he'll stop acting up." **Дава́ть/дать в торе́ц,** *idiom, rude.* To hit in the face. ◆*Дай ему в торец, чтоб много не болтал.* "Give him a smack in the face to shut him up." **Дава́ть/дать за́ щеку,** *rude.* To have fellatio performed on oneself (lit., to give it in the cheek). ◆*Надо попробовать дать ей за щеку.* "I'll have to try getting a blow job from her." **Дава́ть/дать на ла́пу**, *idiom, neg.* To give a bribe. ♦*Сейчас, чтобы землю получить, всем надо на лапу давать.* "In order to get land these days, you've got to grease everybody's palm." **Дава́ть/дать по мозга́м**, *idiom, neg.* To punish (lit., to give it in the brains). ♦*Ему дали по мозгам за аферы.* "They really gave it to him for his scams." **Дава́ть/дать по рога́м**, *idiom, rude.* To hit, punch (lit., give it on the horns). ♦*Дай ему по рогам, чтоб не приставал.* "Let him have it, or he'll keep getting on your case." **Дава́ть/дать по ты́кве**, *idiom.* To hit in the head. ♦*Сейчас дам по тыкве, тогда будешь знать, как оскорблять мать!* "I'll give you such a punch in the head, you'll never insult your mother again!" **Дава́ть/дать по ша́пке**, *idiom, neg.* To hit, beat (lit., give it on the cap). ♦*Ему пора дать по шапке за всё враньё, что он пишет в газетах.* "He should get a pummeling for all the lies he's published in the papers." **Дава́ть/дать по шара́м**, *idiom, rude.* **1.** To hit, strike (in the head). ♦*Иди отсюда, а то как дам по шарам!* "Get out of here, or I'll let you have it between the eyes!" **2.** To intoxicate. ♦*Крепкая водка, сразу по шарам дала.* "That's strong vodka — it went to my head immediately." **Дава́ть/дать проме́ж глаз**, *idiom.* To punch in the face (lit., give between the eyes). ♦*Дать бы тебе за эти слова промеж глаз!* "I'm going to give it to you between the eyes for saying that!" **Дава́ть/дать све́рху**, *idiom.* To pay a premium, pay above the usual or fixed price. ♦*Сверху не дам ни копейки.* "I won't pay a penny extra." **Дава́ть/дать просра́ться**, *idiom, rude.* To defeat. ♦*Наши вчера в футбол дали «Спартаку» просраться.* "Our team beat the Spartak team yesterday." **Дать ду́ба**, *idiom.* To die. ♦*От такой работы можно дать дуба.* "You could drop dead from work like that." **Дать по рука́м**, *idiom, neg.* To punish, to catch red-handed, to slap someone's wrists. ♦*Нашему мэру дали по рукам за взятки.* "Our mayor got punished for taking

bribes." **Всем дава́ть, так слома́ется крова́ть**, see under **всем**. **Если ка́ждому дава́ть, не успе́ешь и встава́ть**, see under **е́сли**. **Ле́гче дать, чем объясни́ть**, see under **ле́гче**. **Ни дать ни взять**, see under **ни**. **Да́ли, догна́ли и ещё раз да́ли**, see under **да́ли**. **Дашь на дашь**, see under **дашь**. **Так дам, всю жизнь на апте́ку бу́дешь рабо́тать**, see under **так дам**. **Так дам, ни оди́н до́ктор не почи́нит**, see under **так дам**. **Так дам, ни одна́ больни́ца не при́мет**, see under **так дам**. **Ну ты даёшь!** see under **ну**. **Во даёт!** see under **во**.

ДАВА́ХА, -и, *f.* See **дава́лка**.

ДАВИ́ЛОВКА, -и, *f.* A crowd, throng. ♦*Я в эту давиловку не полезу, давай подождём другой автобус.* "I'm not getting into that can of sardines — let's wait for the next bus."

ДАВИ́ТЬ/ЗАДАВИ́ТЬ (НА-, ПО-, ПРО-): Дави́ть/надави́ть на пси́хику, *idiom, joc.* To irritate, get on someone's nerves (lit., to press on someone's psyche). ♦*Не дави на психику, не ной!* "Stop nagging; you're getting on my nerves!" **Дави́ть/подави́ть ли́вер**, *idiom, crim.* To be an observer, stay on the sidelines, be a non-participant (lit., to press one's liver). ♦*Вы делайте, я буду ливер давить, не верю я, что у вас что-нибудь толковое выйдет.* "You do the job and I'll stay on the sidelines. I don't think anything worthwhile will come of this job anyhow." **Дави́ть/подави́ть клопа́**, *idiom, joc.* To sleep (lit., to crush the bedbugs). ♦*Хватит давить клопа, пора завтракать.* "Enough of your sleeping. It's time for breakfast." **Дави́ть/продави́ть ток**, *idiom, youth.* To speak in a foreign language, to try to pass oneself off as a foreigner, especially in order to gain admittance to foreigners-only establishments (lit., to squeeze one's talk; cf. **ток**). ♦*Когда будем в гостях, продави ток.* "Talk like a foreigner when we go out." **Дави́ть на ма́ссу**, *idiom, youth, joc.* To sleep. ♦*Любишь ты давить на массу, пора вставать.* "You shouldn't sleep so much! It's time to get up." **Дави́ть

сачка́, *neg.* To be idle, play truant. ◆*Не дави сачка, иди в школу. Ты и так много прогулял.* "Enough goofing off — go to school. You've missed enough classes as it is." **Всех ежей го́лым за́дом задави́ть**, *idiom, rude, joc.* An expression used to deflate someone who is overly self-confident (lit., to crush all the hedgehogs with one's bare behind). ◆*Я его не боюсь, я всё скажу, что я о нём думаю. — Ты у нас всех ежей голым задом задавил.* "I'm not afraid of him; I'm going to tell him exactly what I think of him. — Sure, we know. You've crushed all the hedgehogs with your bare ass."

ДАВИ́ТЬСЯ, *imperf. only.* To be crowded, to throng (lit., to be pressed). ◆*Они там давятся у банка, хотят получить дивиденды.* "They're jam-packed at the bank waiting to collect their dividends."

ДА́ЛИ, ДОГНА́ЛИ И ЕЩЁ РАЗ ДА́ЛИ, *idiom, joc.* A punning answer to the question "Did they give you (what you wanted)?" Lit., "They gave it to me (i.e., they beat me), they caught me, and they gave it to me again." ◆*Тебе дали тринадцатую зарплату? — Как же, дали, догнали, и ещё раз дали.* "Did they give you your end-of-the-year bonus salary? — Yeah, they gave it to me, they grabbed me, and they gave it to me again."

ДАЛЬНОБО́ЙЩИК, -а, *m., drivers.* A long-distance trucker (lit., member of a long-range artillery unit). ◆*Он перешёл из таксистов в дальнобойщики.* "He used to be a taxi driver but now he's a long-distance trucker."

ДАЛЬНОБО́ЙЩИЦА, -ы, *f., drivers.* A prostitute who specializes in a clientele of truckers (cf. **дальнобо́йщик**). ◆*У него кабина занята, он с дальнобойщицей развлекается.* "He's in his cab entertaining a long-distance prostitute."

ДАЛЬНЯ́К, -а́, *m., crim.* A faraway prison camp. ◆*Кажется, нас везут в дальняк.* "Looks like they're shipping us off to never-never land."

ДА́МКА: Раз-ра́з и в да́мки, see under **раз-ра́з.**

ДА́ТЫЙ, -ая, -ое. Drunk. ◆*Он пришёл сильно датый.* "He arrived completely drunk."

ДА́УН, -а, *m., youth.* (From Eng. "down"). **1.** Depression, low spirits. ◆*Он сейчас в дауне, от него девушка ушла.* "He's in a bad mood right now because his girlfriend left him." **2.** A surprise, shock, jolt. ◆*Я в дауне от твоих слов.* "What you said really gave me a jolt." **3.** An idiot. ◆*Он что, даун, простых вещей не понимает?* "What is he, some kind of idiot? He doesn't understand the simplest things."

ДА́ШКА-ПРОМОКА́ШКА. A children's rhyming phrase, used for girls named Dasha (lit., Dahka — blotting-paper).

ДАШЬ НА ДАШЬ, *idiom, neg.* For mutual advantage, exchange of benefits, quid pro quo. ◆*У них не дружба, а всё строится на дашь на дашь.* "They're not friends; their relationship is strictly on a quid pro quo basis."

ДВА НА ДВА ЛЕЧЬ, *idiom, youth.* To die (lit., to lie 2 x 2 [meters], alluding to the size of a grave). ◆*Мне ещё рано два на два лечь.* "My time hasn't come yet."

ДВА́ДЦАТЬ ПЕ́РВЫЙ ПА́ЛЕЦ, *idiom, joc.* A penis (lit., twenty-first digit). ◆*Штаны узкие, двадцать первый палец жмут.* "These pants are too tight; they're squeezing my twenty-first digit."

ДВА́ЖДЫ ЕВРЕ́Й СОВЕ́ТСКОГО СОЮ́ЗА, *idiom, obs., joc.* A Jew who had returned to the Soviet Union after emigrating (lit., twice a Jew of the Soviet Union, playing on the expression "twice a hero of the Soviet Union"). ◆*Он у нас дважды еврей Советского Союза: уехал, приехал, значит, не понравилось.* "He's twice a Jew of the Soviet Union — he left and came back, so apparently he didn't like it over there."

ДВЕ КО́СТИ СЛО́ЖЕНЫ (, ме́жду ни́ми пизда́ вло́жена), *idiom, rude.* A skinny woman (lit., two bones [with a cunt between them]). ◆*Что ты в ней нашёл, две кости сложены.* "What do you see in that walking skeleton?"

ДВИ́ГА, -и, *f., youth.* A dose of narcotics,

an injection. ♦*Он уже получил свою двигу.* "He's already had his shot."

ДВИГАНУ́ТЫЙ, -ая, -ое, *neg.* Crazy, eccentric, behaving in a bizarre manner. ♦*Директор наш какой-то двигану́тый в последнее время.* "Our manager has been acting rather weird lately."

ДВИ́ГАТЬ/ДВИ́НУТЬ. 1. To leave, go away (lit., to move). ♦*Двигай отсюда и побыстрее.* "Get out of here, fast." **2.** To hit, beat up. ♦*Двинь его как следует, он по-другому не понимает.* "Give him a good beating; that's the only way you'll get him to understand." **3.** To sell. ♦*За сколько ты двинул машину?* "How much did you sell your car for?" •**Дви́гать/дви́нуть фуфло́,** *crim., neg.* To lie. ♦*Ты мне фуфло не двигай, не на того напал.* "Don't lie to me! You've picked the wrong person for that."

ДВИ́ГАТЬСЯ/ДВИ́НУТЬСЯ, *youth.* To take narcotics by injection. ♦*Он давно двигается?* "Has he been shooting up for a long time?"

ДВИ́НУТЬСЯ, *perf. only, youth, neg.* To go crazy, go out of one's mind. ♦*Он совсем двинулся, ни с кем не разговаривает, что-то бормочет.* "He's gone completely bonkers — he doesn't talk to anyone, just mutters like that."

ДВОРТЕРЬЕ́Р, -а, *m.* A mixed breed, not pedigree, a mutt (lit., a yard-terrier; wordplay on "двор," yard, and "терьер," a terrier). ♦*У меня хоть и двортерьер, но поумней многих будет.* "Though my dog is a mutt, he is smarter than many others."

ДЕ́ВИЧЬЯ ПА́МЯТЬ (кому́ дала́, не по́мню), *idiom, joc.* A bad memory, forgetfulness (lit., a girl's memory, alluding to the idea that girls quickly forget their lovers). ♦*Что-то не помню, когда они должны прийти? — У тебя девичья память.* "I don't remember what time they're supposed to arrive. — Yes, you always did have a poor memory."

ДЕ́ВКА, -и, *f., homosexual.* A passive homosexual (lit., a girl).

ДЕ́ВОЧКИ: Ме́жду на́ми, де́вочками (говоря́), see under **ме́жду.**

ДЕ́ВЯТЬ ГРА́ММ(ОВ), *idiom.* A bullet (lit., nine grams, the weight of a bullet). ♦*Он свои девять грамм получит.* "He'll get his nine grams," (that is, he's inviting death by his behavior).

ДЕ́ВЯТЬ НА ДВЕНА́ДЦАТЬ, *idiom, joc.* Wide open in astonishment (of eyes) (lit., nine by twelve [centimeters], referring to the standard size of a snapshot). ♦*Я им сказала, что уезжаю в Штаты, а у них глаза — девять на двенадцать.* "I told them I was going to the States and their eyes got round like saucers."

ДЕД, -а, *m., army.* A soldier in his last year of service (lit., a grandfather; cf. **дедовщи́на**). ♦*Что ты за дед, тебя молодые не слушаются.* "What kind of a 'grandfather' are you?! The new recruits don't pay any attention to you."

ДЕД ПИХТО́, *joc.* A nonsense-rhyme evasion of the question "Who is it?" (lit., Grandpa Pikhto). ♦*Это кто с тобой на концерте был? — Кто, кто, дед Пихто.* "Who was that at the concert with you? — Grandpa Pikhto, that's who."

ДЕДОВЩИ́НА, -ы, *f., army.* Irregular conduct in the army; beating, ridiculing, hazing of new recruits by older soldiers (cf. **дед**). ♦*В стройбатах одна дедовщина.* "The construction brigades are hotbeds of hazing by 'grandfathers.'"

ДЕЖУ́РНЫЙ, -ая, -ое. Constant, repeated, regular (lit., on duty). ♦*Мне твои дежурные шутки надоели.* "I'm sick of your constant shenanigans."

ДЕЗА́, -ы́, *f.* Rumors, lies (abbr. of дезинформация, "disinformation"). ♦*Зачем ты распустил эту дезу?* "How come you spread that story around?"

ДЕЗОДОРА́НТ, -а, *m.* Pepper spray (lit., deodorant). ♦*Возьми дезодорант, какое никакое, а оружие, пригодится.* "Take some spray with you—it's not a real weapon, but it may come in handy."

ДЕЛА́, дел, *pl.* Menstrual period (lit., business, affairs). ♦*У меня дела, я с вами не пойду плавать.* "I'm having my period so I'm not going swimming with you."

ДЕ́ЛАТЬ/СДЕ́ЛАТЬ: Де́лать/сде́лать

дум-ду́м, *idiom, joc.* To think something over (from думать). ♦*Не торопи меня, надо сделать дум-дум, а потом соглашаться.* "Don't rush me. I have to think it over before I decide." **Де́лать/сде́лать котле́ту (шашлы́к, отбивну́ю),** *idiom.* To beat up (lit., to make into hamburger). ♦*Да он из тебя котлету сделает, если узнает!* "He'll grind you into mincemeat if he finds out about this!"

Де́лать/сде́лать но́ги, *idiom.* To leave (lit., to make feet). ♦*Мы их не поймали, они давно сделали ноги.* "We couldn't catch them; they left long ago." **Де́лать/сде́лать со́лнечное затме́ние,** *idiom, youth, joc.* To knock out, strike so as to make someone lose consciousness (lit., to cause a solar eclipse). ♦*Вы доиграетесь, вам сделают солнечное затмение за эти дела.* "You're playing with fire there; you'll get knocked out cold for what you're doing." **Де́лать пого́ду (не де́лать пого́ды),** *idiom.* (Not) to be decisive, (not) to make an important difference (lit., [not] to make the weather). ♦*Один миллион погоды не делает, если ты хочешь купить квартиру.* "A million rubles cuts no ice if you're thinking of buying an apartment." **Де́лать телодвиже́ния,** *idiom, neg.* To show some activity, take some initiative (lit., to make body movements). ♦*Не буду я делать никаких телодвижений, сам устраивайся.* "I'm not going to put any effort into it. Take care of it yourself." **Сде́лать яи́шницу,** *idiom, rude.* To hit or kick in the balls (lit., to make scrambled eggs; cf. **я́йца**). ♦*Я ему сделал яишницу, будет помнить!* "I gave it to him in the balls so that he won't forget it!" **Сде́лать,** *perf. only, youth, neg.* To punish someone, get one's own back against someone. ♦*Я этого не забуду, я тебя ещё сделаю.* "I won't forget this, and I'll get you for it."

ДЕ́ЛО: Де́ло таба́к, *idiom, neg.* A bad or dangerous situation. ♦*Кажется, дело табак, сейчас стрелять начнут.* "Things look bad — they're going to start shooting." **Де́ло я́сное, что де́ло тёмное,** *idiom, joc.* Said of a situation that is hard to figure out, obscure, or ambiguous (lit., "it's clear that the matter is murky"). ♦*Дело ясное, что дело тёмное, поди разберись, кто прав, кто виноват.* "It's clear as mud — just you try to figure out who's right and who's wrong!" **Де́ло в шля́пе,** *idiom.* Things are under way; everything's fine. ♦*Дело в шляпе, я получил отпуск.* "I got my leave, so things are fine now." **Де́ло па́хнет кероси́ном,** *idiom, joc.* "The business smells of kerosene," used of a situation that seems unpleasant or dangerous. ♦*Они заметили, как мы сюда пробрались, дело пахнет керосином.* "They saw us sneak in; it's a bad lookout for us." **Де́ла (все) в па́пках,** *idiom.* Everything's fine, all is in order (lit., the whole business is in the files). Used in response to the question "How are things?" ♦*Как дела? — Дела в папках.* "How are things? — Everything's fine." **Дела́ иду́т, конто́ра пи́шет (рубль даду́т, а два запи́шут),** *rhyming phrase.* Used in response to the question "How are things?" (lit., "Things are normal; the office is working; they give you one ruble and charge you two"). **Выступа́ть/ вы́ступить (не) по де́лу,** see under **выступа́ть.** **Дура́цкое де́ло не хи́трое,** see under **дура́цкое. Мо́крое де́ло,** see under **мо́крое. Шить де́ло,** see under **шить. Сде́лал де́ло, слеза́й с те́ла,** see under **сде́лал.**

ДЕЛОВА́Р, -а, *т., neg.* An excessively materialistic, profit-minded person. ♦*За так этот деловар ничего не сделает.* "That wheeler-dealer isn't going to do anything for you just as a favor."

ДЕЛОВО́Й, -а́я, -о́е, *neg.* Overefficient, excessively businesslike, smart-alecky. ♦*Ну ты, деловой, меня не обманешь.* "Don't try to put one over on me, you smart-aleck."

ДЕЛЯ́ГА, -и, *f., neg.* A hustler, go-getter. ♦*Этот деляга своего не упустит.* "That hustler is always looking out for number one."

ДЕЛЯ́Ш, -а́, *т., neg.* See **делово́й.**

ДЕ́МБЕЛЬ, -я, *т., army.* **1.** *sg. only.* Demobilization, discharge from the armed services (from демобилизация). ◆*Жду я не дождусь дембеля.* "I can hardly wait for my discharge." **2.** (*pl.* **дембеля́**). An already discharged soldier still in uniform. ◆*Там сидят дембеля, курят.* "Some discharged soldiers are sitting around there having a smoke."

ДЕМБЕЛЯ́ТЬ/ДЕМБЕЛЬНУ́ТЬ. To discharge from the army. ◆*Начинают дембелять, кто из наших первыми уходит на гражданку?* "They've started demobbing, I wonder which of our guys will be discharged first?"

ДЕМОКРАТИЗА́ТОР, -а, *m., joc.* A rubber truncheon (lit., a democratizer; in Russia, police officers began carrying them during the perestroika period when public discussion of democratization was beginning to take place). ◆*Митинг опять разгоняли демократизаторами.* "They've used democratizers to break up another meeting."

ДЕМШИЗА́, -ы́, *f., collect., joc.* Democrats (from демократ and **шиза́**). ◆*А где на митинг демшиза собирается?* "Where are the democrats having their meeting?"

ДЕ́НЬГИ: Не в де́ньгах сча́стье, а в их коли́честве, see under **не.**

ДЕПРЕСНЯ́К, -á, *m., youth.* Depression, melancholy. ◆*У неё опять депресняк начался.* "She's got the blues again."

ДЕПУТА́НТ, -а, *m., joc.* A deputy (by wordplay on депутат, "deputy," and **пута́на.**

ДЕРБАЛЫ́ЗНУТЬ, *perf. only, joc.* To drink a lot of liquor out of joy or grief. ◆*Мы на радостях, что встретились, дербалызнули как следует.* "We had a regular drinking bout from joy at meeting each other."

ДЕРБА́Н, -а, *m., youth.* The harvesting of opium poppies. ◆*Они уехали на дербан.* "They've left for the poppy harvest."

ДЕРБА́НИТЬ/НАДЕРБА́НИТЬ, *youth.* To collect poppies for opium. ◆*Ты хоть кило надербанил?* "Did you manage to collect a kilo at least?"

ДЕРБАНУ́ТЬ, *perf. only, joc.* To drink, esp. to drink quickly. ◆*Давай дербанём по одной.* "Let's toss back a glass together."

ДЁРГАТЬСЯ/ЗАДЁРГАТЬСЯ, To be worried, to feel jumpy (lit., to twitch). ◆*Не дёргайся, никуда он не денется, придёт, раз обещал.* "Don't start getting antsy—he promised to come, and he'll come."

ДЕРЕ́ВЬЯ УМИРА́ЮТ СТО́Я, *idiom, army.* Said of a soldier standing on duty on a single spot (lit., trees die standing, from the title of a movie). ◆*Я уже два часа у знамени, что делать, деревья умирают стоя.* "I've been standing here at the colors for two hours straight, but what can you do—that's the job."

ДЕРЕВЯ́ННЫЙ, -ого, *m., joc.* A ruble (lit., a wooden one, in reference to its worthlessness as a result of inflation or perhaps to its being backed by wood rather than gold). ◆*У меня одни деревянные, валюты нет.* "I've only got wooden guys — no hard currency."

ДЕРЕВЯ́ННЫЙ БУШЛА́Т, *idiom.* A coffin, grave (lit., a wooden peacoat). ◆*Все они надели деревянные бушлаты.* "They all put on their wooden pea coats" (i.e., they all died).

ДЕРЖА́ТЬ: Держа́ть вес, *idiom.* To hold one's liquor (lit., to hold the weight). ◆*Он умеет держать вес.* "He can hold his liquor all right." **Держа́ть де́ньги в ба́нке ... стекля́нной,** *idiom, joc.* It's safer to keep your money in a jar than in a bank. (By wordplay on в банке, "in a bank," and в банке стеклянной, "in a glass jar.") **Держа́ть ма́зу,** *idiom, youth.* To be important, have influence. ◆*Он у них держит мазу, сначала надо с ним поговорить, а потом делать.* "He's the big honcho there — you've got to talk with him before you do anything." **Держа́ть па́узу,** *idiom.* To be patient, keep still. ◆*Ты не умеешь держать паузу, вечно спешишь.* "You're always in such a hurry; you just can't keep still." **Держа́ть петуха́** or **ударя́ть/уда́рить по петуха́м,** *idiom.* To greet someone with a handshake (by wordplay on петух, "rooster," and пять, "five") ◆*Держи петуха, давно тебя не видел.* "Let me shake your hand. I haven't seen you for ages." **(Не) держа́ть све́чку/свечу́,** *idiom.* (Not) to know for sure whether a couple are having sexual relations (lit., [not] to hold up a candle, [not] to investigate what is hidden). ♦*Откуда ты знаешь, что она его любовница? Ты что, свечку держал?* "How do you know that she's sleeping with him? Did you hold up a candle, or what?" **Держа́ть у́шки топо́риком,** *joc.* To be alert, attentive (lit., to hold one's ears like a hatchet). ♦*Он держит ушки топориком, когда речь заходит о деньгах.* "He pricks up his ears whenever there's any talk about money." **Держа́ть фасо́н,** *idiom, joc.* To keep up appearances. ♦*Нам надо держать фасон, пусть никто не догадывается, что у нас неприятности.* "We've got to keep up appearances so no one will guess that we're in trouble." **Держа́ть фи́гу в карма́не,** *idiom, joc.* To have secret reservations, to disagree inwardly (lit., to make a fig in one's pocket; cf. **фи́га**). ♦*Я знаю, хотя он и согласился с нами, но фигу держит в кармане.* "Even though he went along with us, I know he really objects." **Держи́(те) меня́!** *idiom.* An exclamation of amazement or incredulity (lit., "Hold me up!"). ♦*Ты знаешь, что Колька женился? — Ой, держите меня!* "Did you hear that Kolka got married? — Are you kidding?! I'm going to faint!" **Держи́ карма́н ши́ре,** *idiom.* Don't believe it, it's impossible (lit., "Open your pocket a little wider!") ♦*Мне скоро купят видак. — Держи карман шире, как же, купят.* "They're going to buy me a TV soon. — Don't be so gullible! They're not going to buy you anything."

ДЕРЖИ́СЬ ЗА ВО́ЗДУХ, *idiom, joc.* A jokey piece of advice to someone who is falling down. ♦*Ты на катке в первый раз, будешь падать — держись за воздух.* "If you start falling when you try to ice-skate, just hold on to the air!"

ДЁРНУТЬ, *perf. only.* Lit., to pull. **1.** To take a drag of a cigarette. ♦*Дай дёрнуть пару раз.* "Let me have a couple of drags." **2.** To drink. ♦*Дёрнем по стакану и по домам.* "Let's have a glass before we go home."

ДЕРЬМО́, -а́, *m., rude.* **1.** Excrement, filth. ♦*Осторожно, там дерьмо.* "Watch out — there's a pile over there." **2.** A worthless or bad person. ♦*Он такое дерьмо, хуже не бывает.* "He's such a shit — he's really awful." ●**(По́ уши) в дерьме́,** *idiom, rude.* To be in an extremely unpleasant situation (lit., to be [up to one's ears] in shit). ♦*После этой истории все по уши в дерьме.* "Ever since that business, they've all been up to their ears in shit." **Понесло́сь дерьмо́ по тру́бам,** see under **понесло́сь.**

ДЕРЬМО́ВЫЙ, -ая, -ое, *rude.* Nasty, bad, repulsive (cf. **дерьмо́**). ♦*Он дерьмовый человек.* "He's a nasty fellow."

ДЕРЬМОКРА́Т, -а, *m., rude.* A pun on демократ, "democrat," and **дерьмо́**; used in disparagement of so-called democrats. The word first appeared in 1991, when the Democratic Russia Party conducted a currency revaluation that wiped out people's unprotected savings. ♦*Дерьмократы проклятые, ограбили народ.* "Those damned shitocrats have robbed the nation." ●**Ка́чество (воровства́) дерьмокра́тов не зна́ет грани́ц,** *idiom, rude.* Lit., "The quality of the shitocrats('robbery) knows no limits." By wordplay on the text of a widely publicized advertisement for foreign goods: Качество не знает границ, "Quality recognizes no borders."

ДЕРЮ́ГА, -и, *m. & f., neg.* A director, manager (lit., burlap, rough canvas; by sound play on директор). ♦*Тихо, дерюга идёт!* "Sh-h-h — the boss is coming!"

ДЕРЯ́БНУТЬ, *perf. only, joc.* To drink quickly in order to warm up. ♦*Хорошо бы дерябнуть по сто грамм.* "A hundred-gram warm-up would be good right now." ●**Что́-то ста́ли но́жки зя́бнуть, не пора́ ли нам деря́бнуть,** see under что́-то.

ДЕСЮ́Н, -а, *m.* **1.** A ten-kopeck coin. **2.** Ten rubles.

ДЕ́ТИ: Де́ти — цветы́ жи́зни на моги́ле

роди́телей, *idiom, joc.* Used in sardonic response to complaints about children's bad behavior; lit., "Children are the flowers of life — on their parents' graves." ♦*Сын вырос и совсем перестал мать слушать. Не зря говорят: "Дети — цветы жизни на могиле родителей."* "Her son has grown up and won't listen to her anymore. It's not for nothing that they say children are the flowers of life on their parents' graves." **Де́ти — цветы́ жи́зни, но пуска́й они́ расту́т на чужо́м подоко́ннике,** *idiom, joc.* Although it's true that there is great joy in having children, it's so difficult to raise them that it would be better not to have them at all. ♦*Тебе хорошо: у тебя детей нет. Ты не знаешь наших проблем. — Ну, конечно, дети — цветы жизни, но пусть они лучше растут на чужом подоконнике.* "You have it easy without children; you don't know how hard it is for us. — Sure, children are the flowers of life, but let them grow on someone else's windowsill."

ДЕФЕКТИ́В, -а, *m., joc.* A detective story, mystery story (by wordplay on детектив and дефективный, "defective"; with the idea that such literature is trashy, "defective"). ♦*У тебя есть какой-нибудь дефектив почитать?* "Have you got some 'defective story' to read?"

ДЕФЕКТИ́ВНЫЙ, -ая, -ое, *joc.* See **дефекти́в.**

ДЕШЁВЫЙ ПО́ТРОХ, *idiom, rude.* A traitor (lit., cheap giblets). ♦*А ты дешёвый потрох, за всё это получишь.* "You're going to get it, you stooge."

ДЖАПА́Н, -а́, *m., youth.* A Japanese person (from Eng. "Japan"). ♦*Мне сегодня нужно встретиться с джапанами.* "I have to meet with the Japanese guys today."

ДЖАПА́НСКИЙ, -ая, -ое, *youth.* Japanese (cf. **джапа́н**). ♦*Этот джапанский видик — просто класс.* "This Japanese VCR is first-class."

ДЖЕФ, -а, *m., youth.* Narcotics, drugs. ♦*Он принёс джеф, это хорошо.* "He's

brought the dope — that's good."

ДЖИНСА́, -ы́, *f.* Ordered and incorrect TV and newspaper material, prepaid propaganda (from jeans, referring to material that is cheap and manufactured). ♦*Я джинсу не буду делать ни за какие деньги.* "I will not write false propaganda, not for any sum of money."

ДЖИНЫ́, -о́в, *pl., youth.* Jeans (the standard word is джинсы). ♦*Отхватил вчера новые джины?* "Were you able to buy new jeans yesterday?"

ДЖИП ШИРО́КИЙ, *idiom.* Jeep Cherokee (from "Днепр широкий," a popular song). ♦*Какие проблемы? Как, и Джип Широкий может сломаться?* "What's the problem? How could a Jeep Cherokee have a breakdown?"

ДЖОРЖ, -а, *m., youth, joc.* A Georgian (from Eng. "Georgian"). ♦*Ты знаком с тем джоржем?* "Do you know that Georgian?"

ДИ́ЗЕЛЬ, -я, *m., army.* Disciplinary unit, military unit for soldiers convicted of crimes. ♦*Мне не привыкать служить в дизеле.* "I'm used to serving time in the brig."

ДИ́КАН, -а, *m., army, obs.* Ten rubles, a ten-ruble note. ♦*Дай дикан до завтра.* "Loan me a ten until tomorrow."

ДИНАМИ́СТКА, -и, *f., neg.* A woman who flirts with men but won't have sex with them (from the idea of revving up an engine, динамо, without using it for anything). ♦*Ничего у меня с ней не получилось, она чистая динамистка.* "I got nowhere with her, she's just a cockteaser."

ДИНАМИ́ТЧИК, -а, *m., business.* A broker selling unreliable securities (from динамит, "dynamite"). ♦*Все динамитчики сейчас в панике, кому нужны их бумажки?* "All the dynamiters are in a panic. No one wants their stuff now."

ДИНА́МИТЬ/ПРОДИНА́МИТЬ, *neg.* Cf. **динами́стка. 1.** To flirt with or encourage a man sexually while refusing sex. ♦*Она меня продинамила всю ночь.* "She led me on all night." **2.** To make someone wait for a long time. ♦*Ты* *меня динамишь целый час, почему ты опаздываешь?* "Why are you so late? You've kept me idling here for a whole hour."

ДИНА́МО: Крути́ть дина́мо, see under **крути́ть.**

ДИСК, -а, *m., youth.* A recording, a record. ♦*У тебя есть клёвые диски?* "Do you have any good records?"

ДИСКА́Ч, -á, *m., youth.* A disc jockey. ♦*Кто сегодня дискач?* "Who's the DJ today?"

ДИСКОТЕ́КА, -и, *f., army.* A place for washing dishes, canteen (lit., a disco-thèque). ♦*На дискотеке не соску-чишься, пока не перемоешь тысячу тарелок, спать не пойдешь.* "There's never a dull moment at this disco—a thousand dishes before you can go to sleep."

ДИСКОТНЯ́, -и́, *f., youth, joc.* **1.** A dis-cotheque. ♦*Ты пойдёшь в дискотню?* "Are you going to the disco?" **2.** Disco-style music. ♦*Нам на вечер нужна хорошая дискотня.* "We need some good disco music for the party."

ДИ́ССЕР, -а, *m.* A dissertation. ♦*Он всё никак не закончит диссер.* "He'll never finish his dissertation."

ДИССИДА́, -ы́, *f., collect., obs., Soviet.* Dissidents, the dissidents as a group or movement. ♦*Он давно в диссиду пошёл?* "How long ago was it that he went over to the dissidents?"

ДИСТРО́Ф, -а, *m., neg.* A weak, uncoor-dinated person (from Eng. "dystrophy"). ♦*Тебе помочь, дистроф, или сам до-тащишь этот ящик?* "Hey, you invalid, do you need some help or can you carry that box yourself?"

ДИСТРОФА́Н, -а, *m., neg.* See **дистро́ф.**

ДИХЛОФО́С, -а, *m., neg.* Cheap, nasty liquor (from the chemical name of a flea powder). ♦*От этого дихлофоса тош-нит.* "This rotgut is nauseating."

ДНО: Ложи́ться/лечь на дно, see under **ложи́ться.**

ДО ПОТЕ́РИ ПУ́ЛЬСА, *idiom, joc.* To the point of exhaustion. ♦*Вчера танце-вали до потери пульса.* "Yesterday we danced till we dropped."

ДО СВА́ДЬБЫ ЗАЖИВЁТ, *idiom, joc.* Don't worry, it's not serious (esp. of a wound; lit., "it will heal in time for the wedding"). ♦*Не плачь, это всего лишь царапина, до свадьбы заживёт.* "Don't cry, it's just a scratch; it'll heal in time for the wedding."

ДО УПА́ДА, *idiom.* To the point of exhaustion. ♦*Вчера хохотали до упада.* "Yesterday we laughted till we dropped."

ДОБИВА́ТЬ/ДОБИ́ТЬ. To finish, finish off. ♦*Ну что, добьём эту бутылку и пора спать.* "Well, let's finish off this bottle and go to bed."

ДОГОНЯ́ТЬ/ДОГНА́ТЬ. Lit., to catch up. **1.** To understand. ♦*Что-то я вас не догоню, что вам надо?* "I don't exactly get you. What is it you want?" **2.** To catch up with someone else in the amount of liquor drunk. ♦*Догоняй, вот тебе стакан.* "We're already drunk. Here's a glass — catch up with us!"

ДОГОНЯ́ТЬСЯ/ДОГНА́ТЬСЯ, *youth.* **1.** To drink in order to get drunk, to try to catch up with the amount of drinking that others have already done. ♦*Нам надо догоняться, смотри, все уже пьяные, а мы — ни в одном глазу.* "We have to catch up — look, everyone else is drunk already, and we haven't had a drop." **2.** To take an additional dose of narcotics. ♦*Ты будешь догоняться?* "Are you going to take some more dope?"

ДО́ДИК, -а, *m., students.* **1.** A physically weak student. ♦*Этот додик не пробежит и ста метров.* "That 90-pound weakling can't run a hundred meters." **2.** Smart-aleck **3.** *crim.* A passive homosexual.

ДОДО́, *indecl., students, neg.* A fool. ♦*Ты совсем додо, простых вещей не понимаешь.* "You, idiot, can't you understand anything?"

ДОЕБА́НЕЦ, доеба́нца, *m., rude.* An irri-tating person, pest. ♦*Ну ты и доебанец, никого в покое не оставишь.* "What a pest you are! You can't leave anyone in peace."

ДОЁБЫВАТЬСЯ/ДОЕБА́ТЬСЯ, *rude.*

1. To pester, annoy. ♦*Не доёбывайся со своими вопросами.* "Don't pester me with your questions." **2.** To nag, criticize. ♦*Он ко мне доебался, всё не так делаю.* "He chewed me out — according to him, I never do anything right."

ДОЖДЕВИ́К, -а, *m.* A condom, a rubber (lit., a raincoat). ♦*С дождевиком трахаться, что здороваться в перчатках.* "Screwing with a rubber on is like shaking hands with gloves on."

ДО́ЗА, -ы, *f.* **1.** A blow or kick (lit., a dose). ♦*Ты свою дозу ещё не получил, так получишь.* "You'll get yours!" **2.** A portion of vodka. ♦*Давай по дозе тяпнем.* "Let's have a dose." **3.** One's limit in drinking, the most that one can drink. ♦*Я свою дозу знаю, двести грамм и всё.* "I know my limit — two hundred grams and that's it."

ДОЗНЯ́К, -а́, *m., youth.* A dose of narcotics. ♦*Принял дозняк, хватит.* "Lay off. You've already had a dose."

ДОЙТИ́, *perf.* To die (lit., to arrive). ♦*Этот раненный уже дошёл.* "That wounded soldier is dead already."

ДОК, -а, *m.* A doctor, physician. ♦*Ну, что сказал док, ничего у него нет серьёзного?* "So what did the doc say? Is it anything serious?"

ДОКАЖИ́, ЧТО ТЫ НЕ ВЕРБЛЮ́Д, *idiom.* It's hard to prove one's innocence (lit., "prove that you're not a camel"). This is the punch line of the following joke: A rabbit was running for its life through the desert. When asked by a fox what it was running from, the rabbit explained that a lion had threatened to eat any camel in its path. "But you're a rabbit," objected the other. "Yes, but just try to prove that you're not a camel!" ♦*Все знают, что я этого не делал, но попробуй докажи, что ты не верблюд.* "Of course everyone knows I didn't do it, but just try to prove that you're not a camel!"

ДО́КТОР: Как (то, что) до́ктор прописа́л, see under **как.**

ДОЛБАЁБ, -а, *m.* An idiot (cf. **долба́ть**). ♦*Не слушай ты этого долбаёба.* "Don't listen to that dickhead."

ДОЛБА́К, -а́, *m., rude.* An idiot (cf. **долба́ть**). ♦*Этот долбак ничего толком сделать не умеет.* "That shithead can't do anything right."

ДОЛБА́Н, -а, *m., army, youth.* A cigarette butt (cf. **долба́ть**). ♦*Дай долбан докурю.* "Let me have a butt to smoke."

ДОЛБАНА́ВТ, -а, *m., youth, neg.* An idiot (cf. **долба́ть**). ♦*Этому долбанавту ничего поручить нельзя.* "You can't trust that asshole with any job."

ДО́ЛБАННЫЙ, -ая, -ое, *rude.* Inferior, bad (cf. **долба́ть**). ♦*Я на этой долбанной машине не поеду.* "I'm not going anywhere in that crappy car."

ДОЛБАНУ́ТЫЙ, -ая, -ое, *neg.* Crazy, abnormal (cf. **долба́ть**). ♦*Ты что, долбанутый, за что ты её ударил?* "Are you crazy? What did you hit her for?"

ДОЛБА́ТЬ/РАЗДОЛБА́ТЬ, 1. To break, shatter. ♦*Раздолбайте этот камень!* "Break that stone!" **2.** To criticize, reprimand. ♦*Его раздолбали на собрании.* "They reprimanded him at the meeting."

ДОЛБЁЖ, -а, *m., neg.* Insistent lecturing. ♦*Мне твой долбёж надоел, что ты меня всё время учишь?* "I'm sick of your constantly lecturing me?"

ДОЛБЁЖНИК, -а, *m., neg.* **1.** A bookworm, nerd. ♦*Этот долбёжник все правила выучил, как всегда.* "That nerd learned all the rules, as usual." **2.** A bore.

ДОЛБЁЖНЫЙ, -а, -ое, *youth, neg.* **1.** Boring. **2.** Stupid, primitive. ♦*Прекрати свои долбёжные разговоры.* "Enough of that stupid conversation."

ДОЛБИ́ТЬ/ПОДОЛБИ́ТЬ, *rude.* To have sex with a woman (lit., to chisel). ♦*Он её целую ночь долбил.* "He screwed her all night." •**Долби́ть по те́мечку,** *idiom, neg.* To wear someone down with attempts to persuade (lit., to peck at the crown of someone's head). ♦*Она меня совсем задолбила по темечку: уговаривает уехать за границу.* "She's completely worn me down with her arguments that we should go abroad."

ДОЛБОЁБИСТЫЙ, -ая, -ое, *rude.* Dumb, stupid. ♦*Не надо быть таким* *долбоёбистым.* "Don't be so dumb."

ДОЛДО́Н, -а, *m., neg.* A stubborn, pig-headed person. ♦*Этому долдону ничего не докажешь.* "You can't tell that pig-headed guy anything."

ДО́ЛЬЧИК, -а, *m.* A dollar (from Eng. "dollar").

ДО́МА КТО ЕСТЬ?, *idiom, joc.* Are you crazy? (lit., Who's at home?). ♦*О чём ты думаешь? Дома кто есть? Зачем ты купил столько носков?* "What's wrong with you? Are you crazy? What did you buy all those socks for?"

ДОМУ́ШНИК, -а, *m., crim.* A thief who specializes in robbing apartments. ♦*Сейчас очень много развелось домушников.* "A lot of apartment thieves have been active lately."

ДОН ПЕ́ДРО, *indecl., joc.* A homosexual, pederast (lit., Don Pedro). ♦*Только что заходил Дон Педро, спрашивал тебя.* "That Don Pedro was just here looking for you."

ДОП, -а, *m. army.* An extra ration (from дополнительный паёк). ♦*Нам доп положен, мы в боевых условиях служим.* "We're serving in combat conditions, so we have the right to extra rations."

ДОРО́ГА, -и, *f., youth.* The track of a needle. ♦*У него на руках сплошь дороги.* "His arms are all covered with needle tracks." •**Всю доро́гу,** *idiom, youth.* Constantly, all the time. *Он керосинит всю дорогу, совсем спился.* "He drinks all the time."

ДОСКА́, -и́, *f., neg.* A thin, flat-chested woman (lit., a board). ♦*Что он нашёл в этой доске?* "What does he see in that skeleton?" •**Доска́ — два соска́,** *rhyming phrase, rude.* A flat-chested woman (lit., a board with two nipples). ♦*Мне она не нравится: доска – два соска.* "I don't find her attractive — just a board with two nipples."

ДОСТАВА́ТЬ/ДОСТА́ТЬ, *neg.* To irritate someone, get under someone's skin. ♦*Ты меня достал своими вопросами.* "You're annoying me with your demands."

ДОСТАЕ́ВЩИНА, -ы, *f., youth, joc.* (By wordplay on Достоевский and достава́ть). Insistence, persistence, obduracy. ♦*Мне твоя достаевщина надоела, всё равно буду делать как хочу.* "I'm sick of your insistence, and I'm going to do what I want anyhow."

ДОСТОЕ́ВЩИНА, -ы, *f.* (From Достоевский). Difficult, complicated literature. ♦*Мне что-нибудь попроще, я эту достоевщину читать не буду.* "I need something a little easier — I can't read this dry-as-dusty-evski stuff."

ДОСЧИТА́ТЬСЯ: Зубо́в не досчита́ешься! see under **зу́бы.**

ДОФЕНИ́СТ, -а, *m., joc.* Someone who doesn't give a damn, couldn't care less (from до фени, "who cares?"). ♦*Тебя, дофенист, наши проблемы не волнуют?* "You don't care about our problems, do you, Mr. What-me-worry?"

ДО́ХЛАЯ СОБА́КА, *idiom, neg., joc.* A low-quality frankfurter (lit., a dead dog). ♦*Сколько взять дохлых собак?* "How many hot dogs should I buy?"

ДО́ХЛЫЙ, -ая, -ое, *neg.* Weak (lit., dead). ♦*Муж у неё дохлый какой-то.* "Her husband is a weakling." ♦*Эти батарейки дохлые.* "These batteries are weak."

ДО́ХЛЫЙ ВО́ВА, *idiom, neg.* Lenin's body, preserved in the Mausoleum on Red Square.

ДО́ХНУТЬ как му́хи, *idiom, neg.* To die off in large quantities (lit., to drop like flies). ♦*Куры дохнут как мухи.* "The chickens are dropping like flies."

ДОХО́Д, -а, *m., neg.* A weak person (cf. **доходи́ть**). ♦*Ну ты и доход, даже мешок поднять не можешь.* "You 90-pound weakling — you can't even lift that sack!"

ДОХОДИ́ТЬ/ДОЙТИ́. 1. To die. ♦*Ты можешь совсем дойти, если не будешь есть как следует.* "You could actually die if you don't eat properly." **2.** To be exhausted. ♦*На новой работе я дохожу к вечеру.* "On this new job I'm completely wiped out by the end of the day." •**До кого́-л. дохо́дит как до жира́фа,** *idiom, joc.* Lit., "It gets to him as (slowly as) if he were a giraffe"; from a joke about a giraffe who takes a week to start sneezing after catching a cold. Used of someone dim-witted, slow to get the point. ♦*До тебя всё доходит как до жирафа.* "What are you, a giraffe? It takes you so long to get the point!"

ДОХОДЯ́ГА, -и, *m., crim.* Someone weakened in a prison or labor camp (cf. **дох-оди́ть**). ♦*Он его спас, тот был доходяга.* "He was a goner, but this fellow saved him."

ДРАЙВ, -а, *m., youth, pos.* From Eng. "drive." **1.** Energy, drive. ♦*Если он захочет, всего добьётся, знаешь, какой у него драйв.* "He'll achieve whatever he wants, he's got such drive." **2.** High volume or energy of music. ♦*У этой группы драйв что надо.* "That group has a really exciting sound."

ДРА́ЙВЕР, -а, *m., youth.* A driver (from Eng. "driver"). ♦*Где наш драйвер?* "Where's our driver?"

ДРАП, -а, *m., army.* Disorderly retreat (from драпать, see **драпать**). ♦*Скоро у них драп начнётся, патроны у них на исходе.* "They're running out of ammo—soon we'll see them running."

ДРА́ПАТЬ/ДРАПАНУ́ТЬ. To run away (from danger). ♦*Никого нет, куда все драпанули?* "Where'd everyone disappear to?"

ДРАТЬ[1] гло́тку, *idiom, neg.* To shout, quarrel. ♦*Чего вы дерёте глотку, о чём спор?* "What are you shouting your lungs out about?"

ДРАТЬ[2]/ОТОДРА́ТЬ, *rude.* To have sex with a woman (lit., to slap). ♦*Ты что, не видишь, её же драть надо!* "Look, what she needs is a good fuck!" ●**Драть/отодра́ть в два смычка́,** *idiom, rude.* For two men to have sex with the same woman (lit., to take with two [violin] bows). ♦*Вы её что, дерёте в два смычка?* "What's going on here, are both of you sleeping with her?"

ДРЕЙФЛО́, -á, *n.* A coward (from дрейфить, to be frightened). ♦*А ты оказался дрейфлом, таких нам и даром не надо, вали отсюда.* "You turned out to be a coward, get lost for all we care."

ДРИНК, -а, *m., youth.* An alcoholic beverage (from Eng. "drink"). ♦*В доме дринк есть?* "Is there anything to drink in the house?"

ДРИ́НКАТЬ/ДРИНКАНУ́ТЬ, *youth.* To drink (cf. **дринк**). ♦*Мне что-то дринкануть хочется.* "I'd like something to drink."

ДРИСТА́ТЬ/ПОДРИСТА́ТЬ, *rude.* To have diarrhea. ♦*Он съел несвежее мясо, теперь целый день дрищет.* "He ate some meat that wasn't fresh, and now he's had the runs all day."

ДРО́ЖЖИ: Продава́ть дро́жжи, see under **продава́ть**.

ДРОЧ, -а, *m.* Humiliation, torture (from дрочить). See **дрочи́ть**.

ДРОЧИ́ТЬ/ПОДРОЧИ́ТЬ, *rude.* **1.** To masturbate. ♦*В армии все дрочат.* "They all masturbate in the army." **2.** To irritate, annoy. ♦*Ты его не дрочи, он и так сердитый.* "Don't irritate him. He's mad enough as it is."

ДРУГА́Н, -а, *m., youth.* A friend, pal. ♦*А твой друган тебе будет помогать?* "Will your friend help you out?"

ДРУГО́Й КОЛЕНКО́Р, *idiom.* Something completely different, a different situation (lit., a different calico). ♦*Это совсем другой коленкор.* "That's a horse of a different color altogether."

ДРУЖИ́ТЬ с апте́кой, *idiom, youth.* To take drugs (lit., to be friends with the pharmacy). ♦*И давно он дружит с аптекой?* "Has he been doing drugs for a long time?"

ДРЫН, -а, *m.* A stick, post, club. ♦*А он сразу за дрын и давай его лупить.* "He grabbed a stick and started to beat him."

ДРЫ́ХАТЬ/ЗАДРЫ́ХАТЬ. To sleep deeply. ♦*Вы сразу как пришли, задрыхли.* "As soon as you got here, you fell sound asleep."

ДРЮ́ЧИТЬ/ЗАДРЮ́ЧИТЬ, *rude.* **1.** To have sex with a woman. ♦*Он её дрючит уже год.* "He's been sleeping with her for a year." **2.** To torment, bother, wear out. ♦*Он меня дрючит каждый день своими проблемами.* "He bothers me with his problems every day."

ДРЯНЦО́, -а́, *n., neg.* Someone or something bad, nasty, worthless (cf. дрянь). ♦*А директор ваш дрянцом оказался.* "Your boss turned out to be a piece of garbage."

ДРЯНЬ, -и, *f., youth.* Drugs, narcotics (lit., trash). ♦*Мне стало хорошо, я дрянь покурил.* "I felt good after smoking some dope."

ДУБ: Дать ду́ба, see under **дава́ть. Ру́хнуть с ду́ба,** see under **ру́хнуть.**

ДУБА́К, -а́, *m.,* **1.** *neg.* A fool, idiot (from дуб, "oak"). ♦*С таким дубаком и говорить не о чём.* "With a blockhead like that there's nothing you can even talk about." **2.** Intense cold (from the idea of "stiff as oak"). ♦*На улице такой дубак, околеть можно.* "It's so cold out, you could freeze to death."

ДУБА́РЬ, -ря́, *m.* A corpse. ♦*Там дубарь лежит.* "The stiff is lying over there."

ДУБИ́НА НЕОТЁСАННАЯ, *idiom, neg.* An uneducated, uncultured person (lit., an unworked oak club). ♦*А что от него, дубины неотесанной, можно ждать.* "Well, what can you expect of an ignoramus like that."

ДУБЛА́: Мо́края дубла́, *idiom, youth.* A sheepskin (дублёнка) finished with a water-repellent (lit., wet, from its slick appearance) surface. ♦*Сколько сейчас стоит мокрая дубла?* "How much does a water-repellent sheepskin cost?" **Обли́тая дубла́,** *youth,* see **мо́края дубла́.**

ДУБЛО́, -а́, *n.* A sheepskin. ♦*У тебя дубло есть?* "Do you have a sheepskin?"

ДУБО́ВЫЙ, -ая, -ое, *neg.* Stupid (lit., oaken). ♦*Кто такую дубовую статью написал?* "Who wrote that stupid article?"

ДУГА́: Пья́ный в дугу́, see under **пья́ный.**

ДУ́ЛЯ, -и, *f.* An obscene gesture, "the finger" (cf. **фиг, фи́га, шиш**). ♦*Не показывай дули.* "Don't give the finger." •**Ду́лю тебе́!** *idiom.* No; nothing doing. ♦*Дай мне твою машину. — Дулю тебе.* "Let me use your car. — Nothing doing."

ДУМА́К, -а, *m.* A member of the Duma, the Russian Parliament. A wordplay on Дума, the Duma, and дурак, an idiot. Duma came from the word думать, to think.

ДУНДУ́К, -а́, *m., neg.* A fool, idiot. ♦*Что ты хочешь от этого дундука?* "What do you expect from that idiot?"

ДУ́НУТЬ, *perf. only, joc.* To go away, run out (lit., to blow). ♦*Их нет дома, куда-то дунули.* "They're not home; they've gone out somewhere."

ДУ́НЬКА, -и, *f., neg.* A simple, uneducated, shallow woman. ♦*Этой дуньке доверять переговоры нельзя.* "You can't trust that bimbo with the negotiations." •**Гоня́ть Ду́ньку Кулако́ву,** see under **гоня́ть.**

ДУ́ПЕЛЬ: В ду́пель пья́ный, see under **пья́ный.**

ДУПЛИ́ТЬ/ПОДУПЛИ́ТЬ. To beat. ♦*Бежим, там наших дуплят.* "Let's get out of here; they're beating up our guys."

ДУПЛО́, -а́, *n.* An uneducated person (lit., a hollow, cavity; any tree, especially an oak tree, is a symbol of stupidity). ♦*Ты что, дупло последнее, не понимаешь, что так шутить нельзя?* "You, numbskull, don't you understand, it's disgusting to joke like that!"

ДУ́РА, -ы, *f.* **1.** *crim.* A pistol, revolver. ♦*Убери дуру, никто тебя не тронет.* "Take a pistol, so no one will mess with you." **2.** *neg.* Something big, outsize. ♦*Он приехал на новой дуре.* "He came in an enormous new car." •**Гнать ду́ру,** see under **гнать[1].**

ДУРАГО́Н, -а, *m., neg.* A fool. ♦*Ничего умного этот дурагон не скажет.* "That idiot won't have anything intelligent to say."

ДУРА́К, -а́, *m., rude.* The male genitals (lit., a fool). ♦*У него дурак еле в плавках помещается.* "His equipment hardly fits into his swimming trunks." •**Е́сли челове́к дура́к, то э́то надо́лго,** see under **е́сли. Обману́ли дурака́ на четы́ре кулака́,** see under **обману́ть.**

ДУРА́КА, -и, *m. & f.* An idiot, a fool (cf. **дура́к**). ♦*Ты, дурака, едешь на дачу в* *такой холод?* "You idiot, it's much too cold to go to the dacha!"

ДУРА́ЦКОЕ ДЕ́ЛО НЕ ХИ́ТРОЕ, *idiom, neg.* Said in disparagement of irresponsible actions (lit., foolish business isn't clever). ♦ *Вчера мы выпили всю водку. — Дурацкое дело не хитрое.* "We drank up all the vodka yesterday.—That's nothing to crow about."

ДУРДО́М, -а, *m., youth, neg.* An insane asylum. ♦ *Это не институт, а дурдом какой-то.* "This is no college — it's a madhouse."

ДУ́РИКОМ, *adv.* **1.** Without payment, for free. ♦ *Туда дуриком не попадёшь.* "You can't get in there without paying." **2.** By chance, by luck. ♦ *Он всех дуриком обыграл.* "He won against everyone by fool's luck."

ДУ́РКА, -и, *f., youth, neg.* A simple game, child's play, a game for fools. ♦ *В эту дурку я не играю.* "I don't play that silly game."

ДУ́РНИК, -а, *m.* Nausea, a hangover, a headache. ♦ *У меня такой дурник после коньяка, жить не хочется.* "That cognac gave me such a hangover, I just want to lie down and die."

ДУРНЫ́Е ДЕ́НЬГИ, *idiom.* Easily, quickly acquired money. ♦ *Это деньги дурные, как пришли, так и уйдут.* "A windfall like that is easy come, easy go."

ДУРНЯ́К: НА ДУРНЯ́К(А́), *idiom.* For free, gratis (cf. **халя́ва**).

ДУРОЛО́М, -а, *m., neg.* A boor. ♦ *Этот дуролом всё будет делать по-своему.* "That boor! He doesn't follow any of the social conventions."

ДУ́РОЧКА: На ду́рочку, *idiom, neg.* Without paying, by devious means. ♦ *Там на дурочку и выпьем.* "We'll manage to get a free drink there." **А ты, ду́рочка, боя́лась,** *idiom, joc.* Used of false fears or exaggerated dangers, in allusion to sex (lit., "And you were scared, you foolish thing!"). ♦ *Видишь, плавать совсем не страшно, а ты, дурочка, боялась.* "Well, you see, swimming isn't so dangerous after all, and you were afraid, you little fool!"

ДУРЦА́, -ы́, *f., neg.* A peculiarity of character, personal eccentricity. ♦ *Это у него дурца такая — кричать на всех.* "That's just a quirk of his, yelling at everyone."

ДУРЦИНЕ́Я, -и, *f., youth, joc.* A foolish woman (punning on Дульцинея, the heroine of Cervantes' *Don Quixote*). ♦ *Что этой дурцинее нужно?* "What does that Dulcinea-fool want?"

ДУРЬ, -и, *f., youth.* Narcotics, drugs. ♦ *Он уже без дури жить не может.* "He simply can't live without dope any more."

ДУ́РЬЮ МА́ЯТЬСЯ, *idiom, neg.* To waste time doing silly things. ♦ *Хватит дурью маяться, делай уроки.* "Stop wasting time and do your homework."

ДУ́СЕЧКА, -и, *f.* Dear, darling. ♦ *Тебе, дусечка, отдохнуть надо.* "You need a rest, dear."

ДУХ, -а, *m., army, joc.* A young soldier (lit., a spirit, ghost; in allusion to the unformed condition of the young). ♦ *Эй ты, дух, принеси воды.* "Hey, spook, bring some water over here." • **Ети́тский дух,** see under **ети́тский.**

ДУХА́НКА, -и, *f., army.* The first period of army service. See **дух.** ♦ *У тебя духанка кончается, слава богу, отмучился.* "Your tortures are over, you're not a young soldier any more."

ДУХА́РИК, -а, *m., youth.* A bold or reckless fellow. ♦ *Этот духарик их не побоится.* "That daredevil won't be scared of them."

ДУХАРИ́ТЬСЯ/РАЗДУХАРИ́ТЬСЯ, *neg.* To quarrel, be heated or violent. ♦ *В чём дело? Что вы так раздухарились?* "What's the matter? What are you so worked up about?"

ДУХАРНО́Й, -а́я, -о́е, *neg.* Impulsive, hotheaded. ♦ *Он парень духарной, сразу в драку лезет.* "He's a hothead; he gets into fights at the drop of a hat."

ДУХО́Й, -а́я, -о́е. Drunk. ♦ *Он уже не разговаривает — духой совсем.* "He can't even talk, he's so drunk."

ДУША́: Твою́ ду́шу так, see under **твою́.**

ДУША́РА, -ы, *m., neg., army.* A recruit,

young soldier.

ДУШМА́Н, -а, *m.* A Chechen terrorist, guerrilla.

ДЫМО́К, дымка́, *m., crim.* Tobacco (from дым, "smoke"). ◆ *Нет ли дымка?* "Do you have a smoke?"

ДЫМОПРОДУ́КТ -а, *m., business.* An advertised product that is not yet being produced (lit., smoke-product).

ДЫ́РКА, -и, *f., rude.* Lit., a hole. **1.** A woman. ◆ *Ты всё время о дырках думаешь.* "The only thing you can think about is broads." **2.** The female genitals. ◆ *Не поймёшь, у тебя дырка есть? Никак тебя в постель не уложишь.* "You're acting as though you don't realize you have a cunt!"

ДЫХА́ЛКА, -и, *f.* Breath, breathing, lungs. ◆ *У меня дыхалки нет, я километр не пробегу.* "I don't have the wind to run a kilometer."

ДЫША́ТЬ В ПУПО́К, *idiom.* To be shorter than someone (lit., to breathe into someone's navel). ◆ *Он тебе в пупок дышит, повыше не могла парня найти?* "He's so much shorter than you—couldn't you find a taller beau?"

ДЭРЭ́, *indecl., school, abbr.* Birthday (abbreviated from день рождения).

ДЯ́ДЯ, -и, *m.* A rich relative abroad, considered as a source of money (lit., an uncle). ◆ *У меня нет дяди в Америке.* "I don't have an uncle in America" (i.e., I'm on my own, I have to look out for myself).

ДЯ́ТЕЛ, дя́тла, *m., youth.* An informer, denouncer (lit., woodpecker, from the sound of knocking on doors; cf. **стука́ч**). ◆ *Особенно не болтай, у нас, кажется, дятел завёлся.* "Be careful not to chatter — there seems to be a stoolie among us."

ДЯХА́Н, -а, *m., school.* An adult (from дядя, "uncle").

ЁБ- [**ЕБ-**]. A common obscenity; see under **ебáть**. Many rude words are formed with this stem or a distorted (euphemistic) form of it.

ЁБ ТВОЮ́ МАТЬ. See under **ебáть**.

ЕБÁЛО, -а, *n., rude.* A mouth (cf. **хлебáло, ёб-**). ♦*Вытри ебало.* "Wipe off your mouth."

ЕБÁЛЬНИК, -а, *m., rude.* Cf. **ёб-**. **1.** A face. ♦*Набить бы тебе ебальник.* "I'd like to smash your face in." **2.** A mouth. ♦*Ты можешь заткнуть ебальник?* "Can't you shut your trap?"

ЕБАНУ́ТЬСЯ, *perf. only.* See **ёбнуться**.

ЁБАНЫЙ, -ая, -ое, *rude.* Worthless, bad, damned (lit., fucked; cf. **ёб-**). ●**Ёбаный по головé,** *idiom, rude.* **1.** An expression of surprise: Impossible! How can it be! ♦*Ёбаный по голове, когда же дождь кончится?* "How is it possible that it's still raining!" **2.** An idiot. ♦*Как же ты додумался это сделать, ёбаный по голове?* "You idiot, how did you get it into your head to do that!" **Ёбаная переёбаная мать,** *idiom, rude.* Damn it! ♦*Ёбаная переёбаная мать, когда сосед кончит играть на скрипке!* "Damn it all, when will that fellow next door be done practicing his violin?!" **До ёбаной (ебéней) мáтери,** *idiom, rude.* Very much. ♦*На концерте до ебеней матери народу, никто не ожидал.* "There was an enormous crowd at the concert — no one was expecting so many."

ЕБАНЬКÓ, -á, *n., rude.* An idiot (cf. **ёб-**). ♦*Ты что, ебанько? Кто так делает?* "What kind of idiot are you? No one does it like that!"

ЁБАРЬ, -я, *m., rude.* A sexually potent man (cf. **ёб-**). ♦*Этот ёбарь ещё не всех девок перепортил?* "Hasn't that lady-killer slept with all the girls yet?" ●**Грóзный ёбарь,** *idiom, rude.* A lady-killer, Don Juan (lit., awesome fucker). ♦*Он у нас грозный ёбарь, ты с ним поосторожней.* "He's our local Don Juan — watch out for him!"

ЁБАРЬ-КУ́БАРЬ. See **грóзный ёбарь** under **ёбарь**.

ЕБАТÓРИЯ, -и, *f., rude.* Nonsense, horseplay, ruckus (distorted from Евпатория, a resort town in the Crimea; cf. **ёб-**). ♦*Сколько ещё эта ебатория с ценами будет продолжаться?* "How long is this chaos with prices going to continue?"

ЕБÁТЬ/ПОЕБÁТЬ (**ЗА-**, **ПЕРЕ-**, **НЕДО-**, **ПРО-**, etc.), *obscene.* **1.** To fuck someone. ♦*Кого он ебёт сейчас?* "Who's he fucking these days?" **2.** To be contemptuous of, not to give a damn about. ♦*Я ебу ваши правила.* "I spit on your rules." ♦*Я ебал эти решения.* "These decisions don't make any difference to me." ●**Ебáть/заебáть мóзги,** *idiom, rude.* To wear out, tire out, pester beyond endurance (lit., to fuck someone's brains). ♦*Ты мне все мозги заебал своими жалобами.* "I'm sick and tired of your complaints." **В рот когó-л. ебáть/проебáть,** *idiom, rude.* To have contempt for someone, spit on someone. ♦*Он требует, чтобы ты уехал из города. — Я в рот его ебал и его требования.* "He says you have to leave town. — To hell with him and what he says." **Ебáть/проебáть по-офицéрски,** *idiom, rude.* To have sex with the woman's legs on the man's shoulders. ♦*Ты попробуй её проебать по-офицерски.* "Try screwing her officer-style." **Не ебáть дочь миллионéра,** *idiom, rude.* Not to be rich (lit., not to be fucking a millionaire's daughter); used in rejecting requests to spend money. *Ты поведёшь меня в ресторан? — Я ещё не ебу дочь миллионера.* "Will you take me out to dinner in a restaurant? — I can't afford it. I'm not sleeping with the boss's daughter yet." **Ебáть колхóзом,** *idiom, rude.* To have easy sexual access to a promiscuous woman (lit., to fuck someone with the whole collective farm). ♦*Её ебут колхозом, а ходит важная, как дама.* "She acts like a high-falutin' lady, but really the whole collective farm sleeps with her." **Ебáть мой лы́сый**

че́реп, *idiom*, *rude*. Damn it! (lit., "Fuck my bald head!") ♦ *Ебать мой лысый череп, куда же все гости делись?* "Damn it all, where have all the guests gone off to?" **Еба́ть-копа́ть**, *idiom*, *rude*. Damn it. ♦ *Ебать-копать, совсем времени нет.* "Damn it! There's just no time left." **Что-л. кого́-л. не ебёт**, *idiom*, *rude*. Something doesn't matter to someone. ♦ *Это меня не ебёт, какие слухи ходят обо мне.* "I don't care what kind of gossip they're spreading about me." **Когда́ ебу́т, фами́лию не спра́шивают**, *idiom*, *rude*. Lit., "When they fuck you, they don't ask your name"; used in sardonic response to complaints of ill treatment. ♦ *Директор материл всех за плохую работу и меня тоже. — Когда ебут, фамилию не спрашивают.* "I did good work, but the director bawled me out along with the slackers. — What do you expect? When they screw you, they don't ask your name." **Тебя́ не ебу́т, ты не подма́хивай**, *idiom*, *rude*. It's none of your business, don't stick your nose in (lit., you're not the one being fucked, so don't make the motions). **Коли́чество и ка́чество заебло́ (затра́хало) нас на́чисто**, *rhyming phrase*, *joc.*, *Soviet*. "With quantity and quality they've fucked us over royally." A sardonic expression of disbelief in the ability of Soviet industry to produce adequate amounts of acceptable goods. It refers to the slogan of the Khrushchev years, "Onwards and upwards with quantity and quality!" (Повышайте количество и качество!) and the five-year plans of quantity and quality. **Мы еба́ли парово́з**, *idiom*, *rude*. Used as a sarcastic rejoinder to boastful words (lit., we fucked a locomotive). ♦ *Мне дом за лето ничего не стоит построить. — Мы ебали паровоз.* "I can easily build a house in one summer. — Oh, sure." **Мы еба́ли, не пропа́ли, мы ебём, не пропадём**, *rhyming phrase*, *rude*. Nothing bad will happen; we've done it safely before, we know how to take care of ourselves. ♦ *Смотрите, не утоните на рыбалке. — Мы ебали, не пропали, мы ебём, не пропадём.* "Be careful not to drown when you go fishing. — Oh, don't worry, we've survived before and we'll survive again." **Ёб твою́ мать**, *idiom*, *rude*. Fuck you (lit., I fucked/would fuck your mother). **Ёб твою́ диви́зию мать (твою́ ду́шу в гро́ба до́ски мать)**, *idiom*, *rude*. Damn it! ♦ *Ёб твою дивизию мать, когда это кончится!* "Fuck it! When will this be over!" **Ты заебёшь кого́ хо́чешь**, *idiom*, *rude*. To annoy, wear out. ♦ *Ты заебёшь кого хочешь своими просьбами.* "You could drive anyone up the wall with your demands."

ЕБА́ТЬСЯ/ПОЕБА́ТЬСЯ (ЗА-, ПЕРЕ-, НЕДО-, ПРО-, etc.), *rude*. To have sex. ♦ *Я хочу ебаться.* "I want to get laid." •**Еба́ться/поеба́ться встояка́**, *idiom*, *rude*. To have sex while in a standing position. ♦ *Ебаться встояка я не привык.* "I'm not used to making love standing up." **Еба́ться как ко́шка**, *idiom*, *rude*. To be promiscuous (of a woman) (lit., to have sex like a cat). ♦ *Это она на вид скромная, а ебётся как кошка.* "She looks nice enough, but she's as promiscuous as a cat in heat." **Еба́ться-усра́ться**, *idiom*, *rude*. I'll be damned! ♦ *Ебаться-усраться, кто к нам пришёл.* "Well, I'll be damned! Look who's here!" **Вдруг отку́да не возьми́сь, появи́лся в рот еби́сь**, *idiom*, *rude*. All of a sudden, out of the blue. ♦ *Вдруг откуда не возьмись, появился в рот ебись.* "When did you get here, out of the blue like that?"

ЕБЁНА МАТЬ (вошь, ко́рень, Матрёна), *idiom*, *rude*. Damn it! (lit., "fucked mother [flea, root, Matryona]"; cf. **ёб-**). ♦ *Ебёна-матрёна, кончай трепаться по телефону!* "Damn it! That's enough of your yakking on the telephone!"

ЕБЁН-ТАТЬ, *idiom*, *rude*. Damn it! (cf. **ёб-**). ♦ *А я здесь при чём, ебён-тать?* "What did I do wrong, damn it?"

ЕБИМО́ТИТЬ/СЪЕБИМО́ТИТЬ, *rude*. **1.** To chatter. **2.** To drink.

Ё́БЛЯ, -и, *f.*, *rude*. Cf. **ёб-**. **1.** Sexual intercourse. ♦ *Я устал, а ты хочешь опять еблю устроить у меня на квартире.*

"I'm tired, and you want to use my apartment to sleep with women." **2.** Nonsense, fuss. ♦*Мне эта ебля с документами надоела, когда, наконец, всё будет готово?* "I'm tired of all this fuss with the documents. When will the business be done?" •**Ебля с пляской,** *idiom, rude.* Fuss, ruckus, trouble. ♦*Мне надоела эта ебля с пляской. Каждый день заводим машину целый час.* "I'm sick of this song and dance with the car — it takes an hour to get it started every day."

ЁБНУТЬСЯ, *perf. only, rude.* (Cf. **ёб-**). **1.** To fall down. ♦*Вчера я сильно ёбнулся на лестнице.* "Yesterday I took a nasty fall on the stairs." **2.** To go crazy. ♦*От новых цен ёбнуться можно.* "The new prices can drive you out of your mind."

ЕБНЯ́, -й, *f., rude.* See **ебля.**

ЕБО́Н, -а, *m., rude.* A nickname for Eltsin (from the abbreviation his initials: Ельцин Борис Николаевич; see **еб-**).

ЕБОТА́, -ы́, *f., rude.* A disturbance, trouble, a ruckus (cf. **ёб-**). ♦*Надоела мне ебота со старой машиной, надо покупать новую.* "I'm sick of all the trouble with the old car. It's time to buy a new one."

ЕБОТЕ́НЬ, еботни́, *f., rude.* Nonsense, trash (from тень and **ёб-**). ♦*Какую еботень ты несёшь.* "What nonsense you're talking!"

ЕБОТИ́ШКА, -и, *f., rude.* Cf. **ёб-. 1.** A girl or woman, viewed as a sexual partner. ♦*Когда же твоя еботишка придёт?* "When is your girl coming?" **2.** Sexual intercourse. ♦*Нам пора устроить еботишку.* "It's time we had a little roll in the hay."

ЕБОТРА́ХНУТЫЙ, -ая, -ое, *rude.* Crazy (cf. **ёб-**). ♦*Он становится совсем ебо-трахнутый, когда выпьет.* "He gets completely crazed when he's drunk."

ЕБСТЕ́СТВЕННО, *adv., rude, joc.* Naturally, of course (by wordplay on естественно, "naturally," and **ебать**). ♦*Ебстественно, я приду вовремя.* "Of course I'll fucking come on time."

ЕБУ́Н, -а. See **ебарь.**

ЕБУ́ЧИЙ, -ая, -ее, *rude.* Sexually potent and promiscuous (cf. **ёб-**). ♦*Он в общежитии самый ебучий.* "He's the stud of this dormitory." •**Ебучий козёл,** *idiom, rude.* Idiot (lit., fucking goat). ♦*Что ещё этот ебучий козёл натворил?* "What mischief has that idiot been up to now?"

ЕБУ́ШКА, -и, *f., rude.* A loose, sexually promiscuous woman (cf. **ёб-**). ♦*Вон Зинка, ебушка, идёт, давай её на танцы возьмём.* "There's Zinka. Let's take her to the dance hall — she's available."

ЕВРЕ́ЕЦ, еврейца, *m., joc.* A Jew (formed from еврей with the nationality-formative -ец, as in европеец, индеец). ♦*Муж у нашей Нинки евреец, что ли?* "Do you think Nina's husband may be a Jewman?"

ЕВРЕ́ИН, -а, *m., joc.* A Jew (formed from еврей with the family-name-formative -ин). ♦*Зачем ты взял ещё одного еврейна на работу, у нас и так их полно.* "How come you hired another Jewman? We've already got enough of that tribe at our office."

ЕВРЕ́Й: Два́жды евре́й Сове́тского Сою́за, see under **два́жды.**

ЁГНУТЬСЯ, *perf. only.* To go crazy, go out of one's mind (from йога, "yoga," with reference to an obsession with that doctrine or practice). ♦*Он у нас совсем ёгнулся.* "He's completely yoga'd out."

ЕГОЗА́ -ы́, *f., army.* Barbed wire (lit., a fidget). ♦*Егозу надо обойти справа, там проход сделан.* "You've got to get around the barbed wire from the right— there's a passage there."

ЕГО́Р, -а, *m., crim.* A thief who informs on or cheats his fellow thieves (from a proper name). ♦*Надо за ним посмотреть, уж не егор ли он.* "We'd better keep an eye on him in case he's an informer."

ЁЖ, ежа́, *m., army.* A board studded with nails for puncturing tires (lit., hedgehog). ♦*Побросай там ежей на всякий случай, чтобы никто на машинах не прорвался.* "Put down some nail-boards just in case anyone tries to break through by car." •**Ёж твою́ два́дцать!** *idiom, rude, euph.* Damn it! Damn you! (lit., "hedgehog yours twenty times over!", playing on **ёб твою мать**). ♦*Ёж твою двадцать, не ори!* "Stop shouting, damn you!" **Всех ежей голым задом задавить,** see under **давить.**

ЁЖИК: Пьяный ёжик, see under **пьяный.**

ЁЖИТЬСЯ, *imperf. only, joc.* To practice yoga, engage in yoga (lit., to bristle, shudder, shrink away; cf. **ёж, ёгнуться**). ♦*Он давно ёжится?* "Has he been doing yoga for long?"

ЁЖКИ-МОШКИ, *idiom, joc., rude, euph.* Damn it! (From **ёж** as a euphemism for **ёб-**, and **мошки,** "midges, gnats"). ♦*Когда жрать будем, ёжки-мошки?* "When the fuck are we going to eat?"

Ё-КА-ЛЭ-МЭ-НЭ, *euph., rude.* Damn it! (From **ё** as a euphemistic abbreviation for **ёб-**, and a garbled succession of letters of the alphabet.) ♦*Ё-ка-лэ-мэ-нэ, я забыл выключить утюг!* "Damn it, I forgot to turn the iron off!"

ЁКСЕЛЬ — МОКСЕЛЬ, *idiom, euph.* Damn it! (Cf. **ёлки-палки**).

ЕЛДА, -ы, *f., rude.* **1.** A penis. *Что-то елда отказывает.* "My 'yelda' somehow isn't responding." **2.** A gun on an artillery emblem (lit., a penis). ♦*Протри елду, окислилась.* "Polish your gun on the emblem; it's rusty."

ЁЛКИ ЗЕЛЁНЫЕ, *idiom, rude, euph.* Damn it! (lit., green fir trees, playing on **ёб-**). ♦*Когда же, ёлки зелёные, мы жить будем по-человечески!* "Damn it, when are we going to start living like human beings?"

ЁЛКИ-МОТАЛКИ, *idiom, rude.* See **ёлки зелёные.**

ЁЛКИ-ПАЛКИ, *idiom.* See **ёлки зелёные.**

ЁЛЫ-ПАЛЫ, *idiom.* See **ёлки зелёные.**

ЕМЕЛЯ, -и, *m.* E-mail (a wordplay on the old Russian name "Емеля" and e-mail). ♦*Скинь мне это всё на емелю.* "Send me those phone numbers by e-mail."

Ё-МОЁ, *idiom, rude, euph.* Damn it! (lit., fuck mine; cf. **ё-ка-лэ-мэ-нэ, ёб-**). ♦*Ё-моё, ты опять здесь!* "Damn it, you again!"

ЕНИСЕЙ: Перекрывать Енисей, see under **перекрывать.**

ЁРИКИ-МАЙОРИКИ!, *idiom, euph.* Damn it! ♦*Ёрики-майорики, иди быстрей!* "Go faster, damn it!"

ЁРШ, -ша, *m.* A mixture of vodka with beer or wine (lit., a small fish used in preparing soup stocks but too spiky to be eaten). ♦*Я ёрш пить не буду, это меня сразу вырубит.* "I'm not going to drink that 'yorsh'; it'll make me too drunk too fast."

ЕСЛИ КАЖДОМУ ДАВАТЬ, НЕ УСПЕЕШЬ И ВСТАВАТЬ, *idiom, joc.* Used in refusing a request; lit., "if you give to everyone, you won't be able to get up" (from bed, alluding to sexual exhaustion). ♦*Дай покататься на мотоцикле. — Если каждому давать, не успеешь и вставать.* "Let me take a ride on your motorcycle. — If I give to everyone, I won't be able to stand up."

ЕСЛИ (ЧЕЛОВЕК) ДУРАК, ТО ЭТО НАДОЛГО, *idiom, neg.* Don't expect anything good from a fool (lit., "If a man's a fool, he'll stay that way for good"). ♦*Неужели он отказался от работы в Штатах? — Если дурак, то это надолго.* "Did he really turn down a job in the States? — Well, what do you expect from an idiot!"

ЕТИ ТВОЮ МАТЬ, *idiom, rude, euph.* Damn it! (cf. **ёб-**). ♦*Не стой здесь, ети твою мать, ты мне мешаешь.* "Don't stand there, damn it! You're in my way."

ЕТИТСКИЙ ДУХ, *idiom, rude.* Used as a strong oath in the sense of "Damn it!" or "Devil take it!" (euph. for ебитский, "fucked"). ♦*Етитский дух, сколько денег!* "Damn, what a lot of money!"

ЁХАНЫЙ БАБАЙ!, *idiom, rude, euph.* Damn it! (cf. **ёб-**). ♦*Где же, наконец, мой галстук, ёханый бабай!* "Where the fuck is my necktie?!"

ЕХАТЬ/ПОЕХАТЬ: Ехать/поехать конём, *idiom, drivers.* To return from a taxi destination without a passenger (lit., to ride a horse). ♦*Я туда не поеду, оттуда придётся ехать конём.* "I won't take you there because I'd have to come back riding a horse." **Éхать/поéхать стóпом,** *idiom.* To hitchhike (from Eng. "stop"). ♦ *Он всё время стопом ездит.* "He hitchhikes all the time."

ÉХАТЬ/ПОÉХАТЬ/СЪÉХАТЬ ПО ФÁЗЕ, *idiom.* To be or go crazy (lit., to go along the phase). See **сдвиг по фáзе**. ♦ *Под такой бомбежкой съехать по фазе недолго.* "This kind of bombing would drive anyone crazy."

ЕЩЁ ТОТ (ТА), *idiom, neg.* Someone of bad character. ♦ *Это ещё тот кадр, вы с ним наплачетесь.* "That fellow's a cad; he'll give you plenty of grief."

ЖА́БА, -ы, *f., neg.* An ugly, repulsive person (lit., a type of large frog). ♦*Ну ты, жаба, прекрати дразниться.* "Stop teasing, you creep."

ЖА́БА ЗАДАВИ́ЛА, *idiom, south, joc.* Lit., to be run over by a toad. Epithet thrown at someone overcome by greed, miserliness. ♦*Что, жаба задавила, даже детям рубля не дашь на завтрак.* "Did a toad run you over that you won't even give the children a ruble for their lunch."

ЖА́БИТЬ/ПОЖА́БИТЬ. To eat (lit., to toad). ♦*Когда есть что жабить, их подгонять не надо, минута – и в тарелках пусто.* "You don't have to rush them when they've got something to eat—they'll lick their plates clean in an instant."

ЖА́БРЫ, -ов, *pl., joc.* Lungs (lit., gills). ♦*Что-то у меня жабры болят.* "I've got a pain in my lungs." •**Брать/взять за жа́бры,** see under **брать.**

ЖА́БРЫ КОРОТКИ́, idiom. Someone is unable, lacks the power (lit., someone's gills are too short). ♦*У нас ещё жабры коротки с ним тягаться.* "We don't have the strength to go after him."

ЖА́ВОРОНОК, жа́воронка, *m.* Someone who goes to sleep early and gets up early (lit., lark).

ЖА́ДИНА — ГОВЯ́ДИНА, *idiom, children's speech, neg.* A rhyming phrase used to reproach someone for miserliness (lit., miser — beef). ♦*Дай яблоко. — Самому мало. — Ах ты жадина-говядина.* "Give me an apple." — "I don't have enough for myself." — "You miser!"

ЖА́ДНОСТЬ ФРА́ЕРА ПОГУ́БИТ, *idiom.* Lit., "Greed will be a man's undoing"; used as a warning against or reproach for greedy actions. ♦*Я выиграл, пора остановиться. — Жадность фраера погубит.* "I'm going to quit playing while I'm ahead. — Don't be so greedy!"

ЖА́ЛКО У ПЧЁЛКИ, ЗНА́ЕШЬ ГДЕ,

В ЖО́ПКЕ, *idiom.* An expression used to reject an appeal for pity (by wordplay on жалко, "pity," and жало, "sting." Lit., A bee has pity/a sting in its ass.

ЖА́ЛО, -а, *n., neg.* A mouth (lit., sting). ♦*Убери жало, не болтай.* "Shut your mouth! Don't talk nonsense." •**Замочи́ть жа́ло,** see under **мочи́ть.**

ЖАЛЮЗИ́, *indecl., pl.* Eyes (lit., jalousie, blinds). ♦*Открой жалюзи, не видишь знак "кирпич", въезда нет.* "Open your eyes, don't you see the do not enter sign?" (Note: the sign "Do not enter" looks like a red brick, кирпич).

ЖА́РЕВО, -а, *n.* Sexual intercourse. Cf. **жа́рить.**

ЖА́РИТЬ/ПОЖА́РИТЬ, *rude.* To have sex with a woman (lit., to fry). ♦*Ты её не трогай, её жарит вон тот парень.* "Don't touch her, that fellow over there is her lover."

ЖА́РИТЬ/ПОЖА́РИТЬ КЛОПА́, *idiom.* To stall, to be slow (lit., to fry a bug). See **жарить.** ♦*Кончай жарить клопа, хочешь, не хочешь, а на пост пора.* "Stop stalling—like it or not, it's time to go on duty."

ЖБАНДЕ́ЛЬ, -я, *m., youth.* A bottle (from жбан, a large ceramic jug). ♦*Доставай жбандель, пора начинать.* "Get us a bottle. It's high time we had a drink."

ЖБА́НИТЬ/ЗАЖБА́НИТЬ. To drink a lot (from жбан; cf. **жбанде́ль**). ♦*Ну и что там делать в деревне? — А жбанить будем с утра до вечера.* "What is there to do out there in the country? — Oh, we'll swig it down from morning to night."

ЖВА́ХАТЬ/ЖВА́ХНУТЬ. To have a quick drink, to drink quickly. ♦*Жвахнем по кружке пива, а?* "Let's have a quick beer, okay?"

ЖВА́ЧКА, -и, *f., youth, neg.* Lit., cud. **1.** Chewing gum. **2.** A woman who prefers oral sex, a loose woman, a prostitute. ♦*Она жвачка, все знают, от неё подальше держись.* "Forget about her! Everyone knows she's a whore."

ЖЕ, *indecl.* **1.** *m.* A women's room (abbr. for женский туалет, "women's bathroom"). ◆*Где здесь же, мне надо зайти? — В конце коридора.* "Where's the bathroom around here? — Down there at the end of the hallway." **2.** *f., rude.* Buttocks (abbr. for **жопа**). ◆*Иди ты в же!* "Go to hell!"

ЖЕБА́БЕЛЬНЫЙ, -ая, -ое, *joc.* Edible, good to eat (by wordplay from жевать, "to chew," and **ба́ба**, "woman"). ◆*Ну, как плов? — Жебабельный.* "Well, how do you like the pilaf? — It's quite delicious!"

ЖЕВА́ЛО, -а, *n., neg.* A mouth (from жевать, "to chew"). ◆*Ты ещё не набил своё жевало?* "Haven't you finished stuffing your face yet?"

ЖЕВАНИ́НА, -ы, *f., neg.* Bad-tasting food (from жевать, "to chew"; lit., something already chewed over or chewed up). ◆*Кто как, а я эту жеванину в рот не возьму.* "I don't know about other people but I wouldn't put that junk in my mouth."

ЖЕЛЕ́ЗКА, -и, *f., army.* An automatic rifle (lit., a piece of iron). ◆*Железка у тебя не чищена, непорядок.* "Your metalware is awfully dirty."

ЖЕЛЕ́ЗКИ, -ок, *pl., crim.* Weapons, firearms. ◆*Обыщи их, железки сложи в угол.* "Search them, and pile their iron in the corner."

ЖЕЛЕ́ЗНО, *adv., pos.* For sure, without fail (from железо, "iron"). ◆*Раз он обещал, значит, железно придёт.* "If he promised, he'll certainly come."

ЖЕЛЕ́ЗНЫЙ ФРА́ЕР, *idiom, joc.* A tractor (lit., iron fellow). ◆*Сколько лет ты пашешь на железном фраере?* "How many years have you been working as a tractor driver?"

ЖЕЛЕЗНЯ́К, *pred. use, youth, pos.* Reliable, accurate, trustworthy (from железо, "iron"). ◆*Всё будет как надо, моё слово — железняк.* "Everything will be fine — you can take my word for it."

ЖЕЛЕ́ЗО, -а, *n.* **1.** *crim.* See **желе́зки**. **2.** *youth, business.* Computer hardware.

ЖЕЛОБО́К, желобка́, *m., youth, neg.* A greedy or self-serving young person (lit., a small ditch or trough; playing on **жлоб**). ◆*Этот желобок ещё себя покажет, от него жди всяких пакостей.* "You'll soon see that that young fellow is a pig — you can expect all sorts of nastiness from him."

ЖЕЛТО́К, желтка́, *m., joc.* An Asian (lit., a yolk).

ЖЕЛУ́ДОК: Темно́ как у не́гра в жо́пе/желу́дке, see under **жо́па.**

ЖЁЛУДЬ, -я, *m., neg.* A fool (lit., acorn, by wordplay **жлоб**). ◆*Не будь жёлудем, ты знаешь, о чём я говорю.* "Don't play dumb, you know what I'm talking about."

ЖЕНА́-ЕВРЕ́ЙКА — НЕ РО́СКОШЬ, А СРЕ́ДСТВО ПЕРЕДВИЖЕ́НИЯ, *idiom, joc.* Lit., A Jewish wife is not luxury, but a means of transportation (with reference to emigration to Israel).

ЖЕНА́ТИК, -а, *m., joc.* A married man, esp. a young person, student, or the like, who marries early. ◆*Среди наших знакомых он стал первым женатиком.* "He was the first fellow in our set to become a family man."

ЖЕНИ́ЛКА, -и, *f., joc.* A penis. ◆*Ты думаешь, женилка выросла, уже взрослым стал?* "You think you're grown-up just because your prick has grown?" •**У кого́-л. жени́лка не вы́росла,** *idiom, rude.* Said of a young, inexperienced person. ◆*Ему ещё рано ухаживать за женщинами, у него женилка не выросла.* "He's too young to be running after women, his prick hasn't grown up yet."

ЖЕНИ́Х И НЕВЕ́СТА ОБЪЕ́ЛИСЯ ТЕ́СТА, *rhyming phrase, joc.* Lit., "The bride and groom stuffed themselves with dough"; an absurd rhyming-phrase used to tease young couples. ◆*Смотри, идут жених и невеста. Жених и невеста объелися теста.* "Look, there go the lovebirds! Bride and groom ate the broom!"

ЖЕНИХА́ТЬСЯ, *imperf., joc.* To court a woman. ◆*Он уже женихается года два, а свадьбы не видно.* "He's been going out with her for a couple of years already, but there's still no wedding in sight."

ЖÉНЩИНА ЗА РУЛЁМ — ЧТО ОБЕЗЬЯНА С ГРАНÁТОЙ, *idiom, rude.* A woman behind the wheel is like a monkey with a grenade."

ЖÉНЩИНА РАЗВÓДИТ НОГÁМИ, А МУЖЧИ́НА РУКÁМИ, *idiom, joc.* A saying describing an occurrence of sexual impotence (lit., the woman spreads her legs and the man spreads [i.e., throws up in despair] his hands). ♦*У нас тот же случай: женщина разводит ногами, а мужчина руками.* "Well, you can see what's happened to me — it's a case of she spread her legs and he his hands."

ЖÉНЬШЕНЬ, -я, *f., joc.* A woman, girlfriend (by wordplay on женщина, "woman," and женьшень, "ginseng"). ♦*У него женьшень есть?* "Does he have a girlfriend?"

ЖЕРЕБÉЦ, жеребца́, *m., neg.* An oversexed man (lit., a stallion). ♦*Этот жеребец ни одной юбки не пропустит.* "That stallion can't let a single skirt go by without trying."

ЖÉРТВА АБÓРТА, *idiom, neg., rude.* A stupid or awkward person (lit., a victim of abortion, i.e., an aborted fetus). ♦*Ты, жертва аборта, даже чай не можешь заварить как следует.* "You aborted fetus! You can't even make a pot of tea properly!"

ЖИВИ́ — НЕ ХОЧУ́! Lit., "Live! — I don't want to!" Used to express exasperation at people's failing to appreciate their advantages in life. ♦*У него всё есть — дом, машина. Живи — не хочу. Что ещё ему надо?* "He's got everything — a house, a car. It's a case of 'Live! — I don't want to!' — What more could he possibly need?!"

ЖИВОДЁР, -а, *m., neg.* A surgeon (lit., one who skins animals alive). ♦*Кто сегодня режет? Если Иванов, — он настоящий живодёр.* "Who's operating today? If it's Ivanov, he's a real butcher."

ЖИВÓТНОЕ, -ого, *n., neg.* An unfeeling, cruel person (lit., animal). ♦*Эх ты,* животное, никогда не пожалеешь. "You monster! You never feel any pity."

ЖИГУ́ЛЬ, -ля́, *m.* **1.** A type of beer (from Жигулёвское пиво). ♦*"Жигуль" в магазине есть?* "Do they have any beer at the store?" **2.** *pl.* A type of car. ♦*Он ездит на "Жигулях".* "He drives a Zhiguli."

ЖИД, -á, *m.,* (*f.* **жидóвка, -и**), *neg.* From Yiddish "Yid," originally a neutral word but now used only negatively. **1.** A Jew. ♦*Жиды очень любят золото.* "The kikes are crazy about gold." **2.** A greedy person. ♦*Не будь жидом, дай хоть немного колбасы.* "Don't be such a Jew! Let me have a piece of the sausage." •**Жид пархáтый,** see under **пархáтый.** **За компáнию и жид повéсился,** see under **за.**

ЖИД ПО ВЕРЁВОЧКЕ БЕЖИ́Т, *rhyming phrase, neg.* A phrase used by children for taunting Jewish boys (lit., "There's a kike running along a tightrope").

ЖИДИ́ТЬСЯ/ПОЖИДИ́ТЬСЯ, *neg.* To be greedy or miserly (lit., to be Jew-like). ♦*Не жидись, доставай из холодильника всё, что у тебя есть.* "Don't be a Jew! Whatever you've got in the fridge, bring it out!"

ЖИДÓВИЯ, -и, *f., rude.* Israel. ♦*Что там сейчас происходит в жидовии, опять они воюют с арабами?* "What's going on in Jewland? Are they having another war with the Arabs?"

ЖИДОВНЯ́, -и, *f., collect., neg.* The Jews, Jewry. ♦*Жидовня открывает синагогу за синагогой в Москве.* "The Jews are opening one synagogue after another in Moscow."

ЖИДÓВСКАЯ МÓРДА, *idiom, neg.* A Jew (lit., a Jewish face). ♦*Что там говорит эта жидовская морда по телевизору?* "What's that Jew-face on TV saying?"

ЖИДÓВСКИЙ СУКОМÓЛЕЦ, *idiom, rude.* A twisted name of the popular newspaper "Moskovsky Komsomolets" (by wordplay on Московский and жидовский, комсомолец and сука).

ЖИДОМАСÓН, -а, *m., neg.* A Jew (lit., a Jew Mason, with special reference to the idea of a conspiracy of Jews to take over the world). ♦*Жидомасоны спаивают русский народ.* "The Jew Masons are getting the Russian people addicted to alcohol."

ЖИДОПРОДÁВЕЦ, жидопродáвца, *m., neg.* A Jew (lit., a Jew traitor, formed on the model of Христопродавец, a betrayer of Christ). ♦*Жидопродавцы уезжают в Израиль пачками.* "The Jew traitors are leaving for Israel in droves."

ЖИДОРВÁ, -ы́, *f., neg.* See **жидовня́**.

ЖИДОФИ́Л, -а, *m., neg., rude.* Someone who likes Jews.

ЖИДОФИ́ЛИЯ, -ии, *f., neg., rude.* Love for Jews or Jewish culture. ♦*У него все стены заклеены звездами Давида, демонстрирует свою жидофилию.* "All his walls are covered with Stars of David — he's showing his Yidophilia."

ЖИДУЛИ́, -éй, *pl., obs., neg.* A Zhiguli automobile, alluding to its being typically owned by rich people, that is, Jews (by wordplay on "Жигули" and **жид**). ♦*Чьи это "жидули"?* "Whose Yidoolee is that?"

ЖИДЫ́ ПРÓДАЛИ РОССИ́Ю, *idiom, neg.* Lit., "The Jews have betrayed Russia," originally a slogan of the Black Hundreds; today it often expresses the idea that Jews are supporters of American policies. ♦*Жиды продали Россию американцам! Посмотри, кто в правительстве — одни жиды!* "The Jews have betrayed Russia to the Americans. Look who's in our government — it's all a bunch of Jews!"

ЖИДЯ́РА, -ы, *m.* See **жид**.

ЖИЗНЬ: Жизнь трепанýла (потрепáла) когó-л., *idiom.* Life has worn someone out. ♦*Видно, трепанула жизнь мужика, весь седой, а ведь ещё не стар.* "Life has taken its toll on him — he's gray before his time." **Кучеря́вая жизнь,** see under **кучеря́вая**. **Давáть/дать жи́зни,** see under **давáть**.

ЖИ́ЛА: не в жи́лу, *idiom.* Said of something someone doesn't like, against the grain, against one's will (lit., not in a vein, from drug addict slang, refers to injected drugs). ♦*Мне не в жилу с ней встречаться, опять что-нибудь просить будет.* "It's against my will to meet with her again, she'll be asking for something as usual."

ЖИЛÉТКА, -и, *f., crim.* A ring set with a stone and equipped for cutting open pockets (lit., a small vest, with reference to the absence of sleeves, as if they had been cut off). ♦*Покажи свою жилетку.* "Let me see your razor-ring."

ЖИМ-ЖИМ, *idiom.* **1.** Said about cowardly behavior (from сжимать, to squeeze, to grab, also refers to the reaction of squeezing one's ass when scared). ♦*Как увидел братков, сразу у меня жим-жим начался.* "As soon as I saw those gang bangers, I got scared shitless." **2.** Also said about greediness. ♦*Кончай жим-жим, давай сюда деньги.* "Enough with the greediness, hand the money over."

ЖИРÁФ: До когó-л. дохóдит как до жирáфа, see under **доходи́ть**.

ЖИ́РИК, -а, *m., neg.* A nickname for V. Zhirinovsky (by wordplay on жир, "fat, grease").

ЖИРНЯ́К, -кá, *m., neg.* A fat person, fatty (from жир, "fat"). ♦*Ну ты и жирняк, сколько весишь?* "What a fatso you are! How much do you weigh, anyhow?"

ЖИРТРÉСТ, -а, *m., joc.* A fat person (from жир, "fat," and трест, "trust [company]"). ♦*Ты, жиртрест, иди сюда!* "Get over here, fat farm!"

ЖИСТЯ́НКА, -и, *f., neg., joc.* Life (by wordplay on жестянка, "tin can," and жизнь, "life"). ♦*Ну, как жистянка?* "How's life?"

ЖИТУ́ХА, -и, *f., joc.* Life (from жизнь). ♦*Что за житуха, жить не на что.* "What kind of a life is it when you've got nothing to live on?"

ЖИТЬ: Жить в тóнусе, *idiom, pos.* To live well, be well off, be doing all right. ♦*У меня всё в порядке, живу в тонусе.* "Things are okay with me. I'm living quite well." **Жить на áске,** *idiom, youth.*

To borrow, mooch, live on money acquired by constant wheedling. ♦ *Он давно не работает, живёт на аске.* "He hasn't had a job for a long time; he lives on what he can mooch." **Так они́ и жи́ли, гу́бы кра́сили, а ног не мы́ли,** see under **так. Так они и жи́ли, спа́ли врозь, а де́ти бы́ли,** see under **так. Живи́ — не хочу́!** see under **живи́.**

ЖЛОБ, -á, *m., neg.* **1.** A miser, greedy person. ♦ *Этот жлоб снега зимой не даст.* "That miser wouldn't give you a snowball in winter." **2.** A person, fellow. ♦ *Один жлоб мне сказал, что ты заболел.* "Some guy told me that you were sick."

ЖЛОБИ́НА, -ы, *m., neg.* See **жлоб.**

ЖЛОБИ́ТЬСЯ/ПОЖЛОБИ́ТЬСЯ, *neg.* To be miserly, greedy (from **жлоб**). ♦ *Не жлобись, дай немного.* "Don't be a miser; give me some."

ЖМОТ, -a, *m., neg.* See **жлоб.**

ЖМО́ТНИЧАТЬ/ПОЖМО́ТНИЧАТЬ, *neg.* See **жлоби́ться.**

ЖМУ́РИК, -a, *m., joc.* A corpse (from жмуриться, "to screw up one's eyes," "to squint"). ♦ *Ещё одного жмурика привезли, отправляй его в морг.* "They've shipped us another corpse. Send it over to the morgue."

ЖМУ́РКИ: Сыгра́ть в жму́рки, see under **игра́ть.**

ЖМУРКОМА́НДА, -ы, *f.* A funeral orchestra. See **жму́рик.** ♦ *А сколько жмуркоманда будет стоить?* "How much will a funeral orchestra cost us?"

ЖМУРО́ВКА, -и, *f., youth.* A morgue (cf. **жму́рик**). ♦ *Где в этой больнице жмуровка?* "Where's the morgue in this hospital?"

ЖО́ПА, -ы, *f., rude.* **1.** Buttocks, behind, rear end. ♦ *Ты чего жопой ко мне повернулся?* "Why did you turn your ass toward me?" **2.** A fool. ♦ *Ну и жопа ты, как же ты не догадался!* "What an ass you are, not to have figured it out!"

•**ЖО́ПА** *(nom.):* **Жо́па безро́дная,** *idiom, rude.* A common, simple person (lit., a behind without family). ♦ *У него вся семья профессоры, учёные, а ты*

— *жопа безродная.* "His whole family is full of professors and scientists, and you're just a nobody." **(Жо́па) не сли́пнется?** *idiom, rude.* An expression of disapproval of eating too much, especially too many sweets (lit., won't your ass get stuck shut?). ♦ *Я ещё съем шоколадку. — А не слипнется?* "I'll just have one more chocolate. — You've had too much already; you'll make yourself sick." **Жо́па с ру́чкой,** *idiom, joc.* Lit., an ass with a handle; used of someone awkward, uncoordinated. ♦ *Опять не так, вот жопа с ручкой!* "You got it wrong again, you ass with handles!"

ЖО́ПУ *(acc.):* **Брать/взять за жо́пу,** *idiom, rude.* To apprehend, catch someone doing something wrong (lit., take by the ass). ♦ *Нас не возьмут за жопу за то, что мы купили пистолет у солдат?* "Won't they haul us in for buying that pistol from the soldiers?" **Засу́нь (язы́к) себе́ в жо́пу,** *idiom, rude.* "Stuff it (your tongue) up your ass." ♦ *Эти подарки засунь себе в жопу, я их не возьму.* "You can stuff those presents up your ass. I'm not taking them." **Иска́ть [находи́ть/найти́] на свою́ жо́пу приключе́ний,** *idiom, rude.* To act recklessly, be asking for trouble, bring punishment upon oneself (lit., to look for [find] adventures for one's own behind). ♦ *Ну вот, нашли на свою жопу приключений, предложили перевести книгу, а сами не знаем языка.* "We've brought our own punishment on ourselves by offering to translate the book when we don't even know the language." **Лезть/ влезть без мы́ла в жо́пу (в зад),** *idiom, rude.* To be an apple-polisher, ass-licker (lit., to climb up someone's ass without soap). ♦ *Они все так и лезут к проректору без мыла в жопу, хотят получить прибавку к зарплате.* "All those guys are licking the rector's ass trying to get a raise in pay." **Лиза́ть жо́пу,** *idiom, rude,* see **лезть без мы́ла в жо́пу. На ка́ждую хи́трую жо́пу есть хуй с винто́м,** *idiom, rude.* He who cheats will be cheated (lit., for every smart-ass there's a prick with a bolt). **Нажира́ться/ нажра́ться в**

жóпу, *rude.* To drink oneself unconscious (lit., into one's ass). ♦*Ты вчера опять нажрался в жопу.* "Last night you drank yourself out cold again." **Натя́гивать/натяну́ть глаз на жóпу,** *idiom, rude.* To punish severely (lit., to pull someone's eye over his ass). ♦*Будешь брать сигареты без спроса, натяну глаз на жопу.* "I'm really going to give it to you if you keep taking my cigarettes without asking." **Прикрыва́ть/прикры́ть жóпу,** *idiom, rude.* To protect one's rear; to have insurance, take measures for safe retreat (lit., to cover one's ass). ♦*Ты подумал, как прикрыть жопу, если тебя спросят, почему ты не ходил на работу?* "Have you planned how to cover your ass if you're asked why you didn't go to work?" **Пья́ный в жóпу,** *idiom, rude.* Very drunk ("ass drunk"). ♦*Пришли пьяные в жопу, ещё и жрать требуют.* "They were dead drunk when they got here, and now they want to eat." **Че́рез жóпу,** *idiom, rude.* Wrongly, improperly, badly (lit., through the ass). ♦*Ты всё делаешь через жопу, суп не так варят.* "You do everything ass-backwards! That's not how to make soup!" **Язы́к в жóпу зали́п,** *idiom, rude.* Lit., one's tongue is stuck to one's ass; used of someone speechless from fear, embarrassment, and so on. ♦*Ну, что у тебя язык в жопу залип, рассказывай, что вы натворили в школе.* "Don't stand there with your tongue stuck to your ass! Tell me what kind of trouble you guys got into at school." **ЖÓПЫ** *(gen.):* **Мне до жóпы,** *idiom, rude.* I don't care, it doesn't concern me, it doesn't bother me. ♦*Ты ругайся, не ругайся, а мне до жопы.* "It's all the same to me whether you insult me or not." **Как из жóпы,** *idiom, rude.* Sloppy, wrinkled, unkempt (lit., as if from someone's ass). ♦*У тебя рубашка как из жопы, пойди погладь.* "Your shirt looks as though it came out of someone's ass — go iron it!" **Песóк из жóпы сы́пется,** *idiom, rude.* Lit., the sand is coming out of his ass, used of an old, decrepit person.

♦*У него песок из жопы сыпется, а он танцевать собрался.* "The stuffing's already coming out of his ass, but he still wants to dance." **Ру́ки из жóпы (из одногó ме́ста) расту́т,** *idiom, rude.* An expression used of someone's clumsiness (lit., someone's hands grow from his ass [from a certain place]). ♦*Кто так чистит ковёр, у тебя что, руки из одного места растут?* "You can't even clean the rug decently — what's wrong, are your hands growing from your ass?" **ЖÓПЕ** *(dat.):* **Пристава́ть/приста́ть как ба́нный лист к жóпе,** *idiom, rude.* To be persistent, to insist (lit., to stick like a bathhouse-leaf to someone's ass; from the practice of beating oneself with bunches of leaves in the steam bath). ♦*Ну что ты пристал как банный лист к жопе со своими книгами.* "Don't keep after me with those books of yours, like a leaf sticking to my ass!" **ЖÓПОЙ** *(instr.):* **Верте́ть жóпой,** *idiom, rude.* To flirt with men, attract men's attention (lit., to turn one's behind toward someone). ♦*Смотри, она перед нами жопой вертит, видно, ты ей понравился.* "Look how she's coming on to us! Apparently she finds you attractive." **Всех ежéй гóлой жóпой задави́ть,** *idiom, rude.* To be overconfident (lit., to crush all the hedgehogs with one's bare ass). ♦*Я женюсь на ней без проблем. — Ты всех ежей голой жопой задавил.* "I won't have any trouble getting her to marry me. — Oh, sure, you've crushed all the hedgehogs with your bare ass." **Ду́мать жóпой,** *idiom, rude.* To do something foolish (lit., to think with one's behind). ♦*Ты думал жопой, когда согласился работать почти даром.* "You must have been thinking with your ass when you agreed to do that job for practically nothing." **Жóпой кве́рху,** *idiom, rude.* How am I supposed to know? I don't know any more than you do (lit., ass-upwards; used in answer to the question "How?") ♦*Как мы достанем билеты? — Как? Жопой кверху.* "How will we manage to get tickets? — How should I know?" **Заверте́ть жóпой,** *rude.* To wheedle, prevaricate, be deceptive (lit., to twist one's backside). ♦ *Что ты жопой завертел, говори всю правду.* "Don't beat around the bush! Just tell the truth." **Хоть жóпой ешь,** *idiom, rude.* Very much, a lot (lit., [so much that] you could eat it with your behind [in addition to your mouth]). ♦ *Сейчас в магазинах колбасы — хоть жопой ешь, а цены кусаются, не купишь.* "Right now there's a real glut of sausage in the stores; only it's so expensive that you can't afford to buy it." **Чýять/почýять жóпой,** *idiom, rude.* To sense beforehand, sense instinctively (lit., to smell with one's behind). ♦ *Я жопой чую опасность.* "I smell danger." **ЖÓПЕ** (*prep.*): **В глубóкой жóпе,** *idiom, rude.* In danger, in an unpleasant position. ♦ *Знаешь, мы в глубокой жопе с финансами.* "We're in deep shit financially." **Ни в головé, ни в жóпе,** *idiom, rude.* There's no point, there's no result (lit., neither in the head nor in the ass). ♦ *От этих разговоров ни в голове, ни в жопе.* "There's no point to these conversations." **Нýжен как в жóпе зуб,** *idiom, rude.* Worthless, undesirable (lit., needed like a tooth in one's ass). ♦ *Мне эта поездка нужна как в жопе зуб.* "I need this trip like a hole in the head." **Рýки в жóпе,** *idiom, rude.* Lazy (lit., with one's hands in one's ass). ♦ *У тебя что, руки в жопе, сам не можешь позавтракать?* "What's wrong with you, too lazy to get yourself breakfast?" **Темнó как у нéгра в жóпе/желýдке,** *idiom, joc.* Very dark (lit., as dark as in a Negro's ass/belly). ♦ *Здесь темно как у негра в жопе, давайте включим свет.* "Let's find a light — it's as dark as a Negro's ass in here." **У когó-л. (в пóле вéтер), в жóпе дым,** *idiom, rude.* Someone is flighty, giddy, birdbrained (lit., someone has [wind in the field and] smoke in the ass). ♦ *Как ты ему веришь, не пойму. У него в поле ветер, в жопе дым.* "How could you believe that guy? He's such an airhead!" **Что в головé, что в жóпе,** *idiom, rude.* Said of a stupid or ignorant person (lit., what's in his head is also in his ass). ♦ *Что он может посоветовать? У него что в голове, что в жопе.*

"You can't get any sound advice from him — he's got the same thing in his head as he's got in his ass." **Рвать на жóпе вóлосы,** *idiom, rude.* To regret, be sorry (lit., to tear out the hair on one's behind). ♦ *Он сейчас на жопе волосы рвёт, что не купил до подорожания машину, а сейчас денег не хватает.* "Now he's kicking himself for not having bought that car before the prices went up; he can't afford it any more." **У когó-л. однá извúлина и та на жóпе,** *idiom, rude.* Someone is an idiot (lit., "Someone's got only one convolution, and it's not even in his brain, but on his ass!").

ЖОПÁСТЫЙ, -ая, -ое, *rude.* Having large buttocks (cf. **жóпа**). ♦ *Надо же быть таким жопастым, чтобы так на бабу походить.* "He looks like a woman with that big behind of his."

ЖОПÉНДИЯ, -и, *f., rude.* Large buttocks (cf. **жóпа**). ♦ *На эту жопендию никакие джинсы не лезут.* "You'll never find any jeans large enough to fit over that big behind."

ЖОПÉНЬ, -и, *f., rude.* Large buttocks (cf. **жóпа**). ♦ *Ну и жопень у неё!* "What a big ass she's got!"

ЖÓПНИК, -a, *m., rude.* A homosexual man (cf. **жóпа**). ♦ *Вон жопники на скамейке сидят.* "Those guys over on the bench are queers."

ЖОПОЛÚЗ, -a, *m., rude, neg.* An apple-polisher, ass-licker (from лизать, "to lick"; cf. **жóпа**). ♦ *Он известный жополиз, так и вертится перед начальством.* "He's a notorious ass-licker, always making up to the bosses."

ЖОПОРÓЖЕЦ, жопорóжца, *m., rude.* A Zaporozhetz automobile (by wordplay on **жóпа**). ♦ *Твой "жопорожец" ещё ездит?* "Is your 'Zhoporozhetz' still working?"

ЖÓПОЧНИК, -a, *m., rude.* A homosexual man (cf. **жóпа**). ♦ *В этом баре собираются жопочники.* "This bar is a hangout for buggers."

ЖОПУÁ: В жопуá, *youth, joc.* Very, extremely, to the last degree (from Папуа, "Papua [New Guinea]" and

жо́па). ♦ *Он пьян в жопу.* "He's dead drunk."

ЖОР, -а, *m.* Appetite (lit., feeding-frenzy of fish; from жрать, "to eat"). ♦ *На меня напал жор.* "I'm famished."

ЖОРЖ, -а, *m., crim.* A cardsharp, petty con artist. ♦ *Этот жорж меня надрал на лимон.* "That con artist took me for a million rubles."

ЖРАТВА́, -ы́, *f.* Food (cf. **жрать**). ♦ *Давай зайдём в магазин, купим какой-нибудь жратвы.* "Let's stop in at the store and pick up something to eat."

ЖРАТЬ/ВЫ́ЖРАТЬ: Жрать/вы́жрать во́дку, *idiom, rude.* To drink (lit., eat, devour) a lot of vodka. ♦ *Они там опять жрут водку.* "There they go again, devouring the vodka." **Жрать до по́та, срать до слёз,** *idiom, rude.* To do something with all one's might (lit., "eat till the sweat comes, shit till the tears come"). ♦ *Вы всё это выпьете? — А что? Жрать до пота . . .* "Are you guys really going to drink all that? — Of course! If you're going to drink, you might as well really drink!"

ЖРА́ЧКА, -и, *f., joc.* Food, portion of food (cf. **жрать**). ♦ *Опять вы в рабочее время жрачку устроили.* "There you go again, snacking during working hours!"

ЖУВА́ЧКА, -и, *f.* Chewing gum (cf. **жва́чка**).

ЖУЖЖА́ТЬ/ЗАЖУЖЖА́ТЬ, *neg.* To talk endlessly (lit., to hum). ♦ *Она жужжит и жужжит о своих покупках, не остановишь.* "You just can't stop her from droning on and on about the things she's bought."

ЖУЛЬЁ, -я́, *n., collect., neg.* Con artists, cardsharps. ♦ *В этом магазине работает одно жульё.* "All the guys who work in this store are con artists."

ЖУ́ХАЛО, -а, *m., youth, neg.* A deceiver, double-dealer (cf. **жу́хать**²). ♦ *Ну ты и жухало, опять обманул всех?* "What kind of a double-dealer are you, duping everyone again!"

ЖУ́ХАТЬ¹/ЗАЖУ́ХАТЬ, *youth, neg.* To hide. ♦ *Сколько вы от меня денег зажухали?* "How much money did you hide from me?"

ЖУ́ХАТЬ²/НАЖУ́ХАТЬ, *youth, neg.* To deceive, take in. ♦ *Не думай меня нажухать, я тебя вижу насквозь.* "Don't imagine you can take me in! I see right through you."

ЖУХЛО́, -а́, *n., youth, neg.* See **жу́хало**.

ЖУ́ЧИТЬ/ПОЖУ́ЧИТЬ, *joc.* To scold, abuse, insult. ♦ *Мать его жучит уже целый час.* "His mother's been yelling at him for an hour already."

ЖУ́ЧКА, -и, *f., crim.* A female thief (lit., a common name for a dog). ♦ *Ты знаешь эту жучку, ну ту, что работает на рынке?* "Do you know that woman thief — the one who works at the market?"

ЖУЧО́К, жучка́, *m., neg.* **1.** A small-time speculator, reseller. ♦ *Я купил эту куртку у одного жучка.* "I bought this coat from a huckster." **2.** A cheater, swindler. ♦ *И ты веришь этому жучку?* "How could you believe that faker?"

ЗА БЕСПЛА́ТНО ТЕБЕ́ И В ЛИЦО́ НЕ ПЛЮ́НУТ, *idiom, joc.* You can't get anything for free (lit., it costs money even to have someone spit in your face). ♦*Надо ему заплатить, за бесплатно тебе́ и в лицо не плюнут.* "He's got to be paid — there's no such thing as a free lunch."

ЗА КОМПА́НИЮ И ЖИД ПОВЕ́-СИЛСЯ, *idiom.* Lit., "Even a Jew hanged himself for the sake of company." Used to express the lengths to which people will go in order not to be alone. ♦*Все покупали часы и я купил, но они не работают. — За компанию и жид повесился.* "Everyone was buying these watches, so I bought one too; but it doesn't work. — Yeah, well, even a Jew would hang himself for the sake of company."

ЗА МНОЙ НЕ ЗАРЖАВЕ́ЕТ, *idiom.* I'll promptly reward you, I'll pay you (lit., it won't rust behind me, i.e., I won't neglect to make it worth your while). ♦*Вы только почините замок, а за мной не заржавеет.* "Go ahead and fix the lock for me — I'll make it worth your while."

ЗА МОЙ СЧЁТ, ЗА ТВОЙ ДЕ́НЬГИ, *idiom, joc.* Lit., "On my account, but on your money"; a jokingly self-deprecating way of indicating that one can't pay. ♦*Ну что, приглашаю тебя в ресторан за мой счёт, за твои деньги.* "I'd like to invite you out to eat — on my account, but on your money."

ЗА НЕЧА́ЯННО БЬЮТ ОТЧА́ЯННО, *idiom, joc.* A rhyming phrase used in rejection of an attempt to justify something; lit., For what one does in ignorance one gets beaten terribly. ♦*Это он сделал нечаянно. — За нечаянно бьют отчаянно.* "He did it by mistake!" — "Never mind, he'll catch it just the same."

ЗА ТЕХ, КТО ТАМ, А КТО ЗДЕСЬ — ТОТ САМ, *idiom, crim.* A toast to friends in prison: "To those who are 'there'; and as for those who are 'here' — they're on their own."

ЗАБЕЛДО́С, -а, *m., abbr., neg.* A defender of the White House of the Russian Parliament in October 1993 (Защитник Белого Дома). The suffix -ос conveys a pejorative connotation.

ЗАБИВА́ТЬ/ЗАБИ́ТЬ. To occupy. ♦*Там все места забиты.* "All the seats over there are taken." •**Забива́ть/заби́ть ба́ки,** *idiom, neg.* To deceive, take in. ♦*Он кому хочешь баки забьёт.* "That guy can con anybody." **Забива́ть/заби́ть болт на что-л.,** *idiom, rude.* To disregard, despise, not care about. ♦*Он забил болт на все сплетни.* "He completely ignored all the gossip." **Забива́ть/заби́ть верха́,** *idiom, crim.* To pin an outer pocket closed (cf. **верха́**). ♦*Забей верха, а то потеряешь документы.* "Pin your pocket shut or you'll lose the papers." **Забива́ть/заби́ть кося́к,** *idiom, youth.* To smoke drugs (cf. **кося́к**). ♦*Давай забьём косяк, а то скучно.* "Let's smoke some dope; there's nothing else to do." **Забива́ть/заби́ть ми́тинг,** *idiom, youth.* To make an appointment, arrange a meeting. ♦*Вы забили митинг на завтра?* "Did you make an appointment for tomorrow?" **Забива́ть/заби́ть мозги́,** *idiom, neg.* To occupy one's mind with something unnecessary (lit., to clog one's brains). ♦*Он забил себе мозги фантастикой.* "He's got his head filled with science fiction." **Забива́ть/заби́ть стре́лку,** *idiom, youth.* To make an appointment, set a time for a meeting (lit., to hammer down an arrow, referring to the dial of a watch). ♦*Мы забили стрелку на восемь.* "We agreed to meet at eight o'clock." **Забива́ть/заби́ть на что-л.,** *idiom, youth.* To lose interest in something. ♦*Студенты забили на учёбу, все занимаются бизнесом.* "The students have lost interest in their studies; they're all going into business."

ЗАБИРА́ТЬ/ЗАБРА́ТЬ. (Cf. **брать/взять**) **1.** To intoxicate, affect with drunkenness. ♦*Тебя уже водка заби-*

рает, уменьши дозу. "The vodka's going to your head already — you'd better not keep drinking so much." **2.** *impersonal.* To be worked up, upset. ♦*Смотри, как её забирает, она не говорит, а кричит.* "Look how worked up she is — she's shouting, not talking."

ЗАБОДА́ТЬ, *perf. only, neg.* To irritate, annoy (lit., to butt). ♦*Она меня совсем забодала разговорами о тряпках.* "She drove me to distraction with all her talk about her clothes."

ЗАБО́ЙНЫЙ, -ая, -ое, *youth.* Good, terrific (of music) (from забой, the end of a mine shaft, where the noisy work is done). ♦*У него много забойной музыки.* "He's got a lot of terrific music."

ЗАБО́РИСТЫЙ, -ая, -ое. Strong (of liquor; cf. **забира́ть**). ♦*А водка забористая, я уже пьяная.* "This is strong vodka! I'm drunk already."

ЗАБРИВА́ТЬ/ЗАБРИ́ТЬ. To induct into the army (lit., to shave). ♦*Тебя забривают осенью?* "Are you being inducted this autumn?"

ЗАБУГО́РНЫЙ, -ая, -ое. Foreign, from abroad, imported (cf. **за бугро́м** under **буго́р**). ♦*Никакой забугорный дядя нас не спасёт, мы сами должны решать свои проблемы.* "No uncle from abroad is going to save us; we have to solve our own problems."

ЗАБУРЕ́ТЬ, *perf.* To become tough and nasty. ♦*Он так забурел, пора и остановить.* "He's turned into such an aggressive bastard, we'll have to put a stop to it."

ЗАБУ́РИВАТЬСЯ/ЗАБУРИ́ТЬСЯ, *youth.* **1.** To go on the spur of the moment, drop in (cf. бурить, "to drill"). ♦*Не забуриться нам в какой-нибудь ресторан?* "Let's stop in at some restaurant." **2.** To hide (lit., to drill oneself in). ♦*Куда бы забуриться до отбоя, а то чистить снег заставят.* "We've got to find a place to hide until taps, or they'll make us shovel the snow."

ЗАВА́Л, -а, *m., students.* Lit., an obstruction, heap. **1.** Failure on an examination.

♦*У тебя сколько завалов?* "How many exams did you fail?" **2.** A lot of work. ♦*У нас работы — завал.* "We've got heaps of work to do."

ЗАВА́ЛИВАТЬ/ЗАВАЛИ́ТЬ. To kill (lit., to knock down). ♦*Он и без оружия кого хочешь завалит.* "He could kill a guy with his bare hands."

ЗАВЕРБОВА́ТЬ, *perf. only, youth, joc.* To meet a girl, pick up a girl, go to bed with a girl (lit., to recruit, as a spy). ♦*Он её уже давно завербовал, она к нему с месяц ходит.* "He picked her up a long time ago; she's been going with him for a month."

ЗАВЁРНУТЫЙ, -ая, -ое, *youth.* Complicated, hard to understand (lit., wrapped up). ♦*В этой пьесе ничего не понял, слишком завёрнутая.* "I didn't understand that play at all; it's too complicated."

ЗАВЕРНУ́ТЬСЯ на чём-л., *perf. only, youth, neg.* To be crazy about, wrapped up in. ♦*Он совсем завернулся на роке.* "He went completely wild for rock music."

ЗАВЕСТИ́СЬ (взя́ться) от сы́рости, *idiom, joc.* Lit., to result from dampness; an evasive answer to the question of where something came from. ♦*От кого у неё ребёнок? — От сырости завёлся.* "Who's the father of her child? — Oh, it's just a child of dampness."

ЗА́ВИДКИ БЕРУ́Т кого-л. To feel envy (зависть) (lit., feelings of envy grip someone). ♦*Его завидки берут, что у нас всё есть: и машина, и дача.* "He envies us because we have everything: a car, a dacha."

ЗАВИ́С, -а, *m., youth.* A drinking bout (lit., hanging, a suspended state in which one can't stop drinking). ♦*Он в зависе уже неделю.* "He's been on a drunk for a week already."

ЗАВИСА́ТЬ/ЗАВИ́СНУТЬ, *youth.* **1.** To be attracted by something, involved in something (lit., to hover over something). ♦*Они сейчас зависают на марках.* "They're very much interested in stamps." **2.** To wait a long time. ♦*Мы сильно зависли, его уже нет два часа.* "We've been cooling our heels for two hours already and he's still not here." **3.** To hesitate, waver, be uncertain. ♦*Он завис, не знает, жениться ему или нет.* "He's up in the air about whether to get married or not." **4.** To go on a drinking bout (cf. **зави́с**). ♦*Они встретились и, как всегда, зависли.* "When they met they went off on one of their usual sprees." **5.** To freeze up. Used when talking about a computer program (lit., to be suspended). ♦*У меня машина зависает каждые пять минут, не вирус ли?* "My computer freezes up every five minutes, maybe I've got a virus."

ЗАВИ́СНЫЙ, -ая, -ое. Lazy (lit., hanging, from завис, see **зави́с**). ♦*Если для работы люди нужны, этого воина не бери, самый зависный.* "If there's work to be done, take someone else; he's the laziest of the whole lot."

ЗАВОДИ́ТЬСЯ/ЗАВЕСТИ́СЬ. 1. To get angry (lit., to get cranked up, as of an engine). ♦*Он завёлся, когда ему сказали, что ему нет подарков.* "He got all worked up when they told him there were no presents for him." **2.** To cheer up, to get into a lively mood (lit., to be wound). ♦*Что-то они не заводятся, сидят хмурые, не разговаривают.* "For some reason they just won't cheer up; they're sitting there glumly, not even talking to each other."

ЗАВОДНО́Й, -а́я, -о́е. (From заводить, "to wind up," "to crank up"). **1.** Lively, cheerful, active. ♦*С ними всегда весело, они такие заводные.* "It's always fun with them, they're such live wires." **2.** Hotheaded, quarrelsome, violent. ♦*А твой друг заводной, сразу в драку полез.* "Your friend there seems to be quite a hothead — he got into a fistfight right away."

ЗАВСЕГДА́, adv. 1. Always willing, always ready. ♦*Поедешь за грибами? — Это я завсегда.* "Are you going mushroom-hunting? — That I'm always

glad to do." **2.** In one's daily life, regularly. ♦*Как оно завсегда?* "How's life?"

ЗАВЯ́ЗАНО! *idiom.* Agreed! Okay! It's a deal! (lit., tied up). ♦*Приходи ко мне завтра. — Завязано!* "Come over to my place tomorrow. — It's a deal!"

ЗАВЯ́ЗКА: Быть в завя́зке, see **завя́зывать.**

ЗАВЯ́ЗЫВАТЬ/ЗАВЯЗА́ТЬ. To stop, quit. ♦*Я с куревом завязал месяц назад.* "I quit smoking a month ago."

ЗАГАЗО́ВАННЫЙ, -ая, -ое, *youth, joc.* Drunk (cf. **газ, газова́ть**). ♦*Ложись спать, ты совсем загазованный.* "You'd better lie down; you're completely drunk."

ЗАГА́С: В зага́се, *idiom, army.* Shirking work, hiding so as not to work. ♦*Он где-то в загасе, посмотри в клубе.* "He's making himself scarce somewhere around here. Look in the clubhouse."

ЗАГАСА́ТЬ/ЗАГА́СНУТЬ, *army.* To arrange easy work for oneself. ♦*Ты давно загас на кухне?* "When did you get yourself that cushy kitchen job?"

ЗАГИБА́ТЬ/ЗАГНУ́ТЬ. To lie, fib (lit., to bend). ♦*Не загибай, это уже чересчур.* "Stop lying! You've gone too far already." •**Загиба́ть/загну́ть ко́рки,** *idiom, youth.* To talk entertainingly, tell good stories (lit., to bend a crust of bread). ♦*Ну ты корки загибаешь, рассмешил.* "What a raconteur you are! You really made me laugh."

ЗАГИБА́ТЬ ЛА́ПКИ КВЕ́РХУ, *idiom.* To die (lit., to bend one's paws up). ♦*Загибать лапки кверху никто здесь не собирается.* "Nobody's going to turn up his toes here."

ЗАГОГУ́ЛИНА, -ы, *f.* A riddle, an enigma, a problem, an unexpected circumstance (from the old Russian word загогулина that referred to a sudden curve or bend in the road, something not in its proper form). ♦*Кто же знал, что такая загогулина выйдет с банками, дефолт откуда-то взялся.* "Who could have known that such an unexpected disaster would happen with our banks, the default came out of nowhere."

ЗАГОЛУБЕ́ТЬ, *perf. only, youth.* To become a homosexual (cf. **голубо́й**). ♦*На девушек не смотришь, заголубел, что ли?* "You're not even looking at the girls. What's the matter — have you turned into a homosexual?"

ЗАГОНЯ́ТЬ/ЗАГНА́ТЬ дурака́ (шерша́вого) под ко́жу, *idiom, rude.* To have sex with a woman (lit., to stick the fool [the horny one] under someone's skin). ♦*Ты уже успел загнать шершавого под кожу?* "Have you managed to get her into bed yet?"

ЗАГРА́НКА, -и, *f., youth.* Something unacceptable or outrageous, behavior beyond the limits of acceptability (from за границей). ♦*Я всё терпел, но это уже загранка, ты меня ударил.* "I've put up with a lot from you, but this is really going too far! You hit me!"

ЗАГРЕМЕ́ТЬ, *perf.* To be sent fast (lit., to thunder, crash). ♦*После школы они все загремели в армию.* "They were drafted straight out of high school."

ЗАД: Верте́ть/заверте́ть за́дом, see under **верте́ть.**

ЗАДАВА́ТЬ/ЗАДА́ТЬ тя́гу, *idiom, joc.* To flee, escape (lit., to make a draft). ♦*Вон коты задали тягу, видно, собака рядом.* "Look how those cats ran off. There must be a dog around."

ЗАДАРМА́, *adv.* Gratis, for free. ♦*Эта вещь мне досталась практически задарма.* "I managed to get this for almost nothing."

ЗАДВИГА́ТЬ¹, *imperf. only, youth, neg.* To lie, speak untruthfully (lit., push something in). ♦*Хватит задвигать, так я тебе и поверил, что он уже за бугром.* "Cut the crap. I'm not such a fool as to believe that he's already gone abroad."

ЗАДВИГА́ТЬ²/ЗАДВИ́НУТЬ, *youth.* To quit, cease, leave off. ♦*Я давно задвинул пить.* "I gave up drinking a long time ago."

ЗАДВИГА́ТЬСЯ/ЗАДВИ́НУТЬСЯ, *youth.* To inject narcotics, give oneself an

injection. ♦*Они уже давно задвигаются.* "They've been mainlining dope for a long time."

ЗАДВИ́НУТЫЙ, -ая, -ое, *youth.* **1.** Beside oneself, out of one's mind. ♦*Только задвинутый мог это сделать.* "Only a lunatic could have done that." **2.** Unintelligible, complicated. ♦*Это для меня задвинутая книга.* "I couldn't make heads or tails of that book."

ЗАДЕ́ЛАТЬ, *perf. only.* **1.** *crim.* To kill. ♦*Наши вчера двоих заделали в перестрелке.* "Yesterday our boys did in two guys in the crossfire." **2.** *rude.* To have sex with someone. ♦*Тебе пора её заделать.* "It's really high time for you to do her."

ЗА́ДНИЦА, -ы, *f.* Buttocks (cf. **зад**). ♦*Убери свою задницу.* "Move your ass" (i.e., get out of the way). •**Иди́ в за́дницу,** *idiom, rude.* Go to hell, the hell with you. ♦*Иди ты в задницу со своим нытьём.* "Go to hell — you and your whining." **Че́рез за́дницу,** *idiom, rude.* Badly, awkwardly, incompetently. ♦*Ты всё делаешь через задницу.* "You do everything ass-backwards." **Рвать за́дницу,** see under **рвать.**

ЗАДО́ЛБЫВАТЬ/ЗАДОЛБА́ТЬ. 1. To bore (lit., to peck, to chisel). ♦*Ты всех задолбал своими шуточками.* "We're all bored by your little jokes." **2.** To torment by nagging, to pick at. ♦*Ты думал, меня совсем задолбал в сержантской школе, но скоро на передовую, там посчитаемся.* "You thought you wore me out with your nagging in sergeant school, but I'll get even with you at the battlefront."

ЗАДРА́ТЬ, *perf. only, youth, neg.* To bore, irritate. ♦*Не нуди, задрал жалобами на жизнь.* "Stop whining! I'm sick and tired of your complaints about life."

ЗАДРИ́ПАННЫЙ, -ая, -ое, *neg.* **1.** Good-for-nothing, incompetent, useless (from задрипать, "to soil," "to wear out"). ♦*Он инженер задрипанный.* "He's an incompetent engineer." **2.** Dirty, untidy. ♦*Он ходит в задрипанных брюках, опустился совсем.* "He's completely let himself go — walks around in dirty slacks."

ЗАДРО́ТЫШ, -а, *m., youth, rude.* A weakling, a worthless person (cf. **дро-чи́ть**). ♦*Твои мужики — все как один задротыши.* "Your friends are a bunch of nobodies."

ЗАДРО́ЧЕННЫЙ, -ая, -ое, *rude.* **1.** Depressed. ♦*Он ходит совсем задро-ченным. У него неприятности на работе?* "Why is he going around so depressed? Is something wrong at work?" **2.** Tired. ♦*Ты совсем задроченный, приляг отдохнуть.* "You're completely exhausted! Lie down and take a rest."

ЗАДРЫ́ГА, -и, *f., neg.* A persistent person (from дрыгать [ногами], "to kick"). ♦*Она такая задрыга, пока своего не добьётся, не отстанет.* "She's such a pest, she'll never leave you alone until she gets what she wants."

ЗАДУБЕ́ТЬ, *perf., youth, neg.* To get cold, to get chilled. ♦*Надо погреться, я совсем задубел.* "I'm frozen, I need to warm up."

ЗАДУВА́ТЬ/ЗАДУ́ТЬ, *rude.* To have sex with a woman (lit., to blow). ♦*Девка, видно, хочет, надо ей задуть как сле-дует.* "That girl's dying for it — give her the real thing."

ЗАДУ́МЧИВЫЙ, -ая, -ое, *youth, joc.* Expensive, hard to afford (lit., thought-ful). ♦*Да, эта куртка задумчивая.* "That's a very thoughtful coat" (i.e., one had better think carefully before spending so much money on it).

ЗАДУ́МЫВАТЬСЯ/ЗАДУ́МАТЬСЯ. To go bad, to spoil (lit., to fall into think-ing). ♦*Колбаса на солнце задумалась, есть нельзя, протухла.* "The sausage spoiled out in the sun, it already stinks, it can't be eaten."

ЗАЁБАНЫЙ, -ая, -ое, *rude.* Cf. **ёб-.** **1.** Frightened. ♦*Он всех боится, ходит совсем заёбаный.* "He's afraid of every-one; he goes around completely cowed." **2.** Tired. ♦*После матча все выглядят слишком заёбаными.* "Now that the game is over, they all look utterly exhausted."

ЗАЕБА́ТЕЛЬСКИЙ, -ая, -ое, *rude.* Cf. **ёб-.** Excellent, terrific. ♦*Дача у тебя заебательская.* "Your country house is fantastic."

ЗАЁБИСТЫЙ, -ая, -ое, *rude.* Cf. **ёб-.** **1.** Nasty, making trouble (of persons). ♦*Он всегда такой заёбистый?* "Is he always such a troublemaker?" **2.** Compli-cated. ♦*Это заёбистая задача.* "This is one hell of a complicated problem."

ЗАЁБЫВАТЬ/ЗАЕБА́ТЬ, *rude.* Cf. **ёб-.** **1.** To fuck into stupefaction. ♦*В эту ночь ты меня совсем заебала.* "You've fucked me into complete stupe-faction tonight." **2.** To tire someone out. ♦*Ты меня заебал своими вопросами.* "You've worn me out with all your ques-tions." •**Заёбывать/заеба́ть в до́ску,** *idiom, rude.* To bore or exhaust someone to the state of a dumb plank (lit., to fuck into a board). ♦*Я вижу, ты заебал его в доску своими анекдотами.* "I see you've bored him silly with your jokes." **Не заебёшь, так замучишь,** *idiom, rude.* I give in; okay, you've twisted my arm. ♦*Ну хорошо, пойдём гулять, ты не заебёшь, так замучишь.* "All right, we'll go for a walk — you've forced me into it." **Заеби́ нога́ ногу́, я рабо́тать не могу́,** *idiom, rude.* Used to express resistance to going to work (lit., "Let one foot fuck the other, but I can't work").

ЗАЁБЫВАТЬСЯ/ЗАЕБА́ТЬСЯ, *rude.* Cf. **ёб-.** **1.** To become tired. ♦*Спать охота, что-то я заебался.* "I feel sleepy; for some reason I'm exhausted." **2.** Not to have enough time for some-thing. ♦*Заёбываюсь со статьёй, надо завтра сдать в редакцию.* "I don't have time to finish the article by the dead-line tomorrow." •**Заеба́ться в до́ску,** *idiom, rude.* To become completely exhausted. ♦*Мы носим эти ящики три часа, заебались в доску.* "We've been hauling these cartons around for three hours; we're completely wiped out." **За-еби́сь!** *idiom, rude.* Great! Wonderful! ♦*Ну, как мороженое? — Заебись!* "How's the ice cream? — Fantastic!" **Заеби́сь в рот конём!** *idiom, rude.* Go to hell; up yours (lit., be fucked in the mouth by a horse). ♦*Заебись в рот конём, чтоб я тебя ещё раз послушал.* "Go to hell! I'm not going to listen to you any more."

ЗАЕДА́ТЬСЯ/ЗАЕ́СТЬСЯ, *neg.* To be naughty, ill-behaved, quarrelsome (lit., to gnash one's teeth). ♦*Отстань, не заедайся.* "Cut it out, don't be naughty." •**Кто-л. зае́лся,** *idiom, neg.* Said of one who acts superior to others. ♦*Они совсем заелись, не знают цену деньгам.* "They're completely above it all; they just don't know the value of money."

ЗАЖИГА́ТЬ/ЗАЖЕ́ЧЬ. To have a good time, to have fun (lit., to light a fire, to start a fire). ♦*Скучно здесь, никто не зажигает, не диско, а дом для пенсионеров.* "It's boring here, no one is having any fun, it's more like an old people's home than a disco."

ЗАЖИ́ЛИВАТЬ/ЗАЖИ́ЛИТЬ, *neg.* To appropriate; to keep for oneself what one has borrowed or what one owes to another. ♦*Ты, кажется, зажилил мой карандаш.* "It looks like you've appropriated my pencil."

ЗАЖИМА́ТЬ/ЗАЖА́ТЬ, *neg.* **1.** To steal, lift (lit., to squeeze). ♦*Ты зажал мои книги, так не пойдёт.* "You've made off with my books — that's not right." **2.** To hold back out of miserliness. ♦*Ты ресторан зажал, а обещал.* "You're such a tightwad — that's why you broke your promise to take me to the restaurant." **3.** To feel up, paw a woman. ♦*Он тебя опять зажимал?* "Did he feel you up again?"

ЗАЖО́ПИТЬ, *perf. only, rude.* To catch red-handed (cf. **жо́па**). ♦*Их зажопили на подделке документов.* "They were caught forging papers."

ЗАЖРА́ТЬСЯ, *perf. only, rude, neg.* To live too luxuriously (lit., to be overfed). ♦*Ты совсем зажрался, это для тебя уже не деньги.* "You've become altogether too soft — you don't know what money's worth anymore."

ЗАЗЕМЛЯ́ТЬСЯ/ЗАЗЕМЛИ́ТЬСЯ. To fall asleep (lit., to be grounded). ♦*Заземлюсь-ка я минут на полчаса.* "I'll do some blanket-drill for a half-hour."

ЗАЙ́ГРЫВАТЬ/ЗАИГРА́ТЬ, *neg.* To appropriate, not to return someone else's property. ♦*Я тебе дам книги, только не заиграй.* "I'll loan you the books, but just don't appropriate them."

ЗАКА́ПЫВАТЬСЯ/ЗАКОПА́ТЬСЯ. To be very busy, swamped with work (lit., to be dug in). ♦*Я совсем в бумагах закопался, конца и краю не видно.* "I'm completely swamped in paperwork with no end in sight."

ЗАКА́ТЫВАТЬ/ЗАКАТИ́ТЬ исте́рику, *idiom.* To make a scene (lit., to get hysterics going). ♦*Она мне закатила истерику, я опоздал на 10 минут.* "I was only 10 minutes late and she got hysterical."

ЗАКА́ШИВАТЬ/ЗАКОСИ́ТЬ. 1. To steal (lit., to mow down). See **коси́ть.** ♦*Это ты у меня закосил сигареты?* "Was it you that hooked my cigarettes?" **2.** To fake an illness. ♦*Вижу, закосить хочешь, не выйдет.* "I can see you're malingering. Nothing doing!"

ЗАКИ́ДЫВАТЬСЯ/ЗАКИ́НУТЬСЯ, *youth.* To take pills, drugs (lit., to throw in). ♦*Ты уже закинулся, а я ещё нет.* "You've already tossed some in, but I haven't had any yet."

ЗАКЛА́ДЫВАТЬ/ЗАЛОЖИ́ТЬ, *neg.* **1.** To drink a lot (shortened from the old expression закладывать за воротник). ♦*Он сильно закладывает в последнее время.* "He's really been swigging down a lot recently." **2.** To betray, inform on, denounce (cf. заложник, "hostage"). ♦*Это ты нас заложил, что мы курим?* "Are you the one who reported us for smoking?"

ЗАКЛИ́НИВАТЬ(СЯ)/ЗАКЛИ́НИТЬ-(СЯ), *neg.* **1.** To repeat, do again (from клин, "wedge"; lit., to get wedged in, get stuck). ♦*Не заклинивайся на этой идее, пойдём дальше.* "Don't keep repeating this same idea; let's get beyond that." **2.** To think constantly of one thing or person, be obsessed by something or someone. ♦*Она заклинилась на нём.* "She's really stuck on him."

ЗАКОЛА́ЧИВАТЬ/ЗАКОЛО́ТИТЬ де́ньги, *idiom.* To earn a lot of money, make big money (lit., to hammer money). ◆*Все они заколачивают неплохо на нефти.* "They're all raking it in from their oil dealings."

ЗАКОЛЕБА́ТЬ, *perf. only.* To irritate, annoy, wear out (cf. **колеба́ть, еба́ть**). ◆*Ты меня заколебал своими рассказами о бабах.* "You've worn my patience thin with your stories about your girlfriends."

ЗАКО́ННЫЙ, -ая, -ое, *obs.* Good, fine (lit., legal). ◆*Пойди посмотри, не пожалеешь, законный фильм.* "Go see it! You'll be glad you did — it's a fine film."

ЗАКОНСЕРВИ́РОВАТЬСЯ, *perf. only.* To look young, be well preserved. ◆*Смотри, наш начальник законсервировался, больше шестидесяти ему не дашь, а ему уже за семьдесят.* "Look how well-preserved our boss is — you wouldn't think he's more than sixty, but he's really on the wrong side of seventy."

ЗАКО́С, -а, *m., youth.* An act or instance of shirking work, slacking on the job. ◆*Ваши закосы прекратите, надо поднажать и закончить работу через неделю.* "Enough of your shirking; we've got to make a big push and finish this job within a week."

ЗАКРО́Й РОТ, КИШКИ́ ПРОСТУ́ДИШЬ, *idiom, rude.* Shut up! (lit., "shut your mouth, your guts will catch cold"). ◆*Закрой рот, кишки простудишь, хватит орать, никто тебя не слушает.* "Shut up! No one wants to hear your speeches."

ЗАКРОМА́ РО́ДИНЫ, *idiom, joc.* Storehouses for produce, where everything sits and rots (lit., granaries of the motherland). ◆*Весь урожай опять сдали в закрома родины, значит, голодать будем.* "Again they've dumped the whole harvest into the granaries of the motherland; we're in for starvation now."

ЗАКРЫВА́ТЬ/ЗАКРЫ́ТЬ: Закрыва́ть/ закры́ть дверь с той стороны́, *idiom, neg.* To leave a household, to be expelled (lit., to close the door from the other

side). ◆*Ты мне надоел, закрой дверь с той стороны.* "I'm sick and tired of you — get out and never darken my door again." **Закрыва́ть/закры́ть фонта́н,** *idiom, rude.* To keep silent, to shut one's mouth. ◆*Закрой фонтан и слушай, что тебе говорят.* "Shut up and listen to what's being said to you."

ЗАКУСО́Н, -а, *m., joc.* Appetizers (to accompany drinks) (from закуска). ◆*Закусон приготовили?* "Did you prepare some appetizers?"

ЗА́КУСЬ, -и, *f., joc.* See **закусо́н**.

ЗАЛЕПИ́ТЬ, *perf. only.* To say something strange, shocking, or unexpected. ◆*Как ты мог такое залепить, откуда ты взял, что она лезбианка?* "How could you say such a thing? Where did you get the idea that she's a lesbian?"

ЗАЛЁТ, -а, *m.* Trouble, difficulty (cf. **залета́ть**). ◆*У него залёт, он попал по пьянке в милицию.* "He's in trouble — he's been picked up by the police for drunkenness."

ЗАЛЕТА́ТЬ/ЗАЛЕТЕ́ТЬ. 1. To get into trouble, get caught (lit., to fly by mistake to the wrong place). ◆*Наш директор залетел на взятках.* "Our director got into trouble for taking bribes." **2.** To get pregnant unintentionally. ◆*Ты что, опять залетела?* "Don't tell me you got knocked up again?!" •**С кем поведёшься, от того и залети́шь,** see under **с.**

ЗАЛЁТНАЯ ШАЛА́ВА, *idiom, crim.* A traveling female thief, not one of the locals (lit., a whore flying off course). ◆*Я её что-то не знаю, залётная шалава, наверное.* "I've never seen her before; she must be an 'off-course whore.'"

ЗАЛЁТЧИК, -а, *m., neg.* Someone who keeps getting into difficulties. ◆*У этого залётчика одни несчастья!* "It's just one woe after the next with that poor schlemiel!"

ЗАЛИВА́ТЬ, *imperf. only, neg.* To lie, be untruthful (lit., to pour it on). ◆*Не заливай, что ты был в институте.* "Don't lie! You weren't at the institute."

ЗАЛИВА́ТЬ/ЗАЛИ́ТЬ ИЛЛЮМИНА́-

ТОРЫ, *idiom, army.* To drink heavily (lit., to flood potholes). ♦*Иди проспись, залил иллюминаторы, еле стоишь на ногах.* "Go get some sleep—you're so plastered you can hardly stand up."

ЗАЛИ́ЗАННЫЙ, -ая, -ое. Smooth, even. ♦*Мне не нравятся новые Жигули, совсем зализанные.* "I don't like the new Zhiguli model, it looks too flat."

ЗАЛИПУ́ХА, -и, *f., youth.* Falsehood, hoax, hokum. ♦*Ты уже читал залипуху о пришельцах?* "Have you read this hogwash about extraterrestrials?"

ЗАЛУДИ́ТЬ, *perf. only.* Lit., to tin, cover with tin. **1.** To hit, beat. ♦*Ну ты его и залудил, он до сих пор в больнице.* "Wow, you really gave it to him! — He's still in the hospital." **2.** To accomplish with hard work. ♦*Вы уже залудили план?* "You mean you've already slogged through that job?"

ЗАЛУ́ПА, -ы, *f., rude.* **1.** The head of the penis. ♦*Что-то залупа болит.* "My 'zalupa' hurts." **2.** A bastard, scoundrel. ♦*Вставай, залупа, это не твоё место!* "Get up, you bastard, this isn't your seat!"

ЗАЛУПА́НЕЦ, -нца, *m., rude.* A bastard, idiot (cf. **залу́па**). ♦*Чтоб я тебя здесь больше не видел, залупанец!* "I never want to see you here again, you bastard!"

ЗАЛУПА́ТЬСЯ/ЗАЛУПИ́ТЬСЯ, *rude.* Cf. **залу́па. 1.** To make a scene, get excited, get carried away. ♦*Не залупайся, он же сильнее!* "Don't get all worked up — he's stronger than you are!" **2.** To be stubborn, to object, refuse. ♦*Они залупились, не хотят работать за эти деньги.* "They've mutinied — they aren't willing to work for those wages."

ЗАЛЫ́СИТЬ, *perf. only, crim.* To cheat someone at cards (lit., to shave bald). ♦*Меня залысили на 300 долларов.* "I was ripped off to the tune of 300 dollars."

ЗАМА́ЗАННЫЙ СТВОЛ, *idiom, crim.* Weapons that have previously been in police custody and can be traced (lit., stained barrel). ♦*Надо проверить замазанный ствол, был в деле или нет?* "We've got to check whether this gun is already in the police records."

ЗАМА́ЗКА, -и, *f., crim.* Misfortune, trouble (lit., putty, caulk). ♦*Он остался в большой замазке, больше тысячи рублей.* "He was in big trouble; he lost more than a thousand rubles."

ЗАМА́ТЫВАТЬСЯ/ЗАМОТА́ТЬСЯ. To get tired from work or worries (lit., to spin, be wound up). ♦*Я совсем замотался, с утра на ногах.* "I'm exhausted after being on my feet all day."

ЗАМАЦО́ВЫВАТЬ/ЗАМАЦЕВА́ТЬ. To prepare marijuana for smoking ♦*Замацевать еще надо, а потом уже забить косяк.* See **кося́к.** "You've got to prepare it before you roll it."

ЗАМЕ́С, -а, *youth.* A fight (lit., kneaded dough). ♦*Вчера в замесе мне досталось.* "I really got my share in the brawl last night."

ЗАМЁТАНО! *idiom.* It's settled, agreed, so be it (lit., [the hand is] dealt). ♦*Замётано, ты ночуешь у меня.* "It's settled — you're sleeping at my house."

ЗАМКНУ́ТЬ НА МА́ССУ, *idiom.* To fall asleep (lit., to make ground fault). ♦*Когда это они успели замкнуть на массу, еще минуту назад песни орали.* "How did they manage to fall asleep already? A minute ago they were singing their lungs out."

ЗАМКНУ́ТЬ пасть, *idiom, neg.* To be quiet (lit., to lock one's mouth). ♦*Замкни пасть и чтобы я тебя весь вечер не слышал.* "Shut up and don't let me hear a word from you for the rest of the evening."

ЗАМО́К, замка́, *m., army.* The deputy of a commander (lit., a lock). ♦*Замок приказал строиться.* "The 'lock' gave orders to line up."

ЗАМОРО́ЗКА, -и, *f.* A local anaesthetic (lit., frost). ♦*Мне уже заморозку сделали, сейчас будут зуб рвать.* "They've already given me a 'freezing'; now they'll pull the tooth."

ЗАМОРО́ЧКА, -и, *f., joc.* **1.** An idée fixe, obsession. ♦*У неё давно заморочка — купить дачу.* "The idea of buying a dacha has been an obsession with her for a long time." **2.** Difficulties, complications, troubles. ♦*С обедом у нас заморочка, не успеваем к приходу гостей.* "We've been in a jam since lunchtime; we'll never be ready for the arrival of our dinner guests."

ЗАМОСТЫ́РИВАТЬ/ЗАМОСТЫ́РИТЬ. To make, prepare (food) (lit., to build a bridge [мост]). ♦*Давай кофейку замостырим.* "Let's put together some coffee."

ЗАМО́ТАННЫЙ, -ая, -ое. Tired (cf. **зама́тываться**). ♦*Ты совсем замотанный, отдохни.* "You're completely exhausted — take a rest."

ЗАМУДО́ХАННЫЙ, -ая, -ое, *rude.* Tired, exhausted (cf. **муде́**). ♦*Я прихожу с работы замудоханный, а ты ещё лезешь со своими советами.* "I come home from work exhausted, and you keep after me with your suggestions."

ЗАМУТИ́ТЬ ПОГА́НКУ, *idiom.* To make a mess (lit., to mud filth). ♦*Хочешь замутить поганку, помни, что всех в итоге сделают.* "Remember, if you make a mess in here, we're all going to get punished."

ЗАМЫ́ЛИВАТЬ/ЗАМЫ́ЛИТЬ. To steal (lit., to soap). ♦*Не вздумай замылить мой ремень, на нем выбита моя фамилия.* "Don't you even dream of pinching my belt! My name's engraved on it."

ЗАМЫКА́НИЕ, -я, *n., youth, joc.* Strange behavior, eccentricity (lit., short circuit). ♦*У него замыкание, перестал со всеми здороваться.* "He's acting really strange — he doesn't even say hello to anyone."

ЗАНА́ЧИВАТЬ/ЗАНА́ЧИТЬ. To hide, stash away. ♦*Я заначил от жены немного денег.* "I've hidden a little cache of money away from my wife."

ЗАНА́ЧКА, -и, *f.* A secret cache. ♦*Сколько у тебя в заначке денег?* "How much money have you got in your stash?"

ЗАНГ, -а, *m., crim.* Gold. ♦*Мне занг нужен, грамм двадцать.* "I need twenty grams of gold."

ЗАНИМА́ЙТЕ МЕСТА́ СОГЛА́СНО КУ́ПЛЕННЫМ БИЛЕ́ТАМ, *idiom, joc.* Take your seats (lit., take the seats for which you bought tickets). ♦*Гости дорогие, занимайте места согласно купленным билетам.* "Dear guests, please take seats at the table."

ЗАНИМА́ТЬСЯ гре́блей на конька́х, *idiom, joc.* To be incompetent at sports (lit., to row on skates). ♦*Он ходит на тренировки? — Он занимается греблей на коньках.* "Does he work out? — Oh, he rows on skates."

ЗАНУ́ДА, -ы, *m. & f., neg.* A whiner, complainer, nudnick (from **нуди́ть**). ♦*С тобой нельзя долго быть вместе, ты страшный зануда.* "It's impossible to spend time with you — you're such a nudnick."

ЗАНЫ́КИВАТЬ/ЗАНЫ́КАТЬ, *youth.* To hide away, steal, take on the sly (especially by taking advantage of confused circumstances). ♦*Я у родителей заныкал тридцатку.* "I lifted thirty rubles from my parents."

ЗАНЮ́ХАННЫЙ, -ая, -ое, *neg.* Plain-looking, ugly. ♦*У нас мужики все какие-то занюханные.* "All the available men here are ugly."

ЗАНЮ́ХИВАТЬ/ЗАНЮ́ХАТЬ, *joc.* To eat bread (lit., to sniff, smell). ♦*Чем бы занюхать, я так пить не могу?* "What is there to eat? I can't drink without some bread."

ЗА́ПАД: В запа́де, *idiom, youth.* Very interested, deeply involved (cf. **запада́ть**). ♦*Он будет помогать в этом деле? — Конечно, он уже в западе.* "Will he help out with the project? — Of course, he's already deeply involved in it."

ЗАПАДА́ТЬ/ЗАПА́СТЬ, *youth.* To fall for, fall in love with. ♦*Я запал на этот "Мерс".* "I've fallen in love with that Mercedes."

ЗАПАДЛО́, *n., indecl., youth, neg.* A worthless person, object of contempt or dislike (from падаль, "dead animal"). ♦*Он мне западло.* "He's scum as far as

I'm concerned."

ЗАПАКО́ВЫВАТЬ/ЗАПАКОВА́ТЬ В ЦИНК, *idiom., army.* To kill (lit., to pack someone in a zinc box). ♦*Я тебя в цинк всё равно запакую!* "I'll put you in your coffin all the same!"

ЗАПА́РКА, -и, *f.* Heavy work, exertion; especially, work that is stepped up in order to meet production norms in a sudden burst at the end of a month or year (from пар, "steam"). ♦*У нас сейчас на заводе запарка, конец года.* "We're steaming away at the plant because it's the end of the year."

ЗАПА́СКА, -и, *f.* A spare tire. ♦*Достань запаску, надо сменить правое колесо.* "Get me the spare. I have to change the right tire."

ЗАПЕНДРЯ́ЧИВАТЬ/ЗАПЕНДРЯ́- ЧИТЬ, *rude, neg.* **1.** To have sex with a woman. ♦*Они выпили, потом он ей запендрячил как следует.* "They had a drink, and then he balled her properly." **2.** To hit. ♦*"Спартак" уже вторую шайбу запендрячил.* "The Spartak team has already scored its second goal."

ЗАПИ́Л, -а, *m., youth, pos.* A guitar solo. ♦*Слушай, сейчас будет такой запил!* "Listen to this guitar solo!"

ЗАПИСТО́НИВАТЬ/ЗАПИСТО́- НИТЬ, *youth.* To have sex with a woman (cf. **писто́н**). ♦*Тебе её пора уже записто́нить.* "It's high time you took her to bed already."

ЗАПЛЫ́В, -а, *m., army.* Floor-washing. ♦*Сегодня ты на заплыве, беги за водой.* "It's your turn to wash the floor, run and get some water."

ЗАПО́Р, -а, *m., joc.* A Zaporozhets automobile (lit., constipation). ♦*"Запор" он и есть запор, никак не заведу.* "Well, what can you expect from a Zaporozhets! I can't start it."

ЗАПОРО́ТЬ, *perf. only.* **1.** *crim.* To cut with a knife, kill by knifing (lit., to rip). ♦*Запороть тебя мало за это!* "I ought to knife you for that!" **2.** To spoil, mess up. ♦*Я работал две недели, сегодня запорол всю картину.* "I've

been working on this painting for two weeks, and today I completely messed it up."

ЗАПОЧЁМ, *adv., youth.* For how much? ♦*Започём ты купил этот кейс?* "How much did you pay for that attaché case?"

ЗАПРАВЛЯ́ТЬ му́льки, *idiom.* To lie, speak untruthfully. ♦*Брось мне мульки заправлять, ты там не был.* "Don't lie to me! I know you weren't there."

ЗАПРЕ́ТКА, -и, *f.* An off-limits area, restricted area. ♦*В запретке рыбу ловить нельзя.* "Fishing is forbidden in the restricted area."

ЗАПУЗЫ́РИВАТЬ/ЗАПУЗЫ́РИТЬ, *joc.* To do something intensely or vehemently (from пузырь, "bubble"). ♦*Я уже запузырил пять бутылок пива, больше не могу.* "I've already tossed down five bottles of beer — I can't drink any more."

ЗАПУПО́К, *m., pred. use, army.* Fine, good, excellent (cf. **пупо́к**). ♦*Как дела? — Запупок.* "How're things? — Fine."

ЗАПУПЫ́РЬ, -я́, *m., youth, neg.* An irritating, unpleasant person. ♦*Ты можешь помолчать, запупырь чёртов?* "Can't you shut up, you creep?"

ЗАПУСКА́ТЬ/ЗАПУСТИ́ТЬ ПАРА́- ШУ, *idiom.* To misinform, lie (lit., to launch a chamber pot). ♦*Если кто запустит парашу про отступление, со мной дело будет иметь.* "Anyone who spreads stories about a retreat will have to deal with me."

ЗАРЖАВЕ́ТЬ: За мной не заржаве́ет, see under **за.**

ЗАРУ́БКА, -и, *f., crim.* An oath (lit., a notch, i.e., mark in wood, as a sign of a promise). ♦*Ты давал зарубку, значит, выполняй, что обещал.* "You gave your oath, so do what you promised."

ЗАРУ́ЛИВАТЬ/ЗАРУЛИ́ТЬ, *joc.* To come, enter (lit., to steer, as a car). ♦*Заруливай ко мне часов в семь.* "Come over to my place at about seven."

ЗАРЯЖА́ТЬ/ЗАРЯДИ́ТЬ, *youth.* To tip, bribe (lit., to load). ♦*Я зарядил швейца-*

ра, сейчас пройдём на диско. "I tipped the doorman, so we can go into the disco now."

ЗАСА́ДНЫЙ, -ая, -ое, *youth.* Good, interesting (from засадить, "to strike"). ♦ *Между прочим, посмотри телек, идёт засадная передача.* "By the way, there's an interesting program on TV."

ЗАСА́ЖИВАТЬ/ЗАСАДИ́ТЬ плю́ху (гол), *idiom, sports.* To score a goal. ♦ *Ты видел по телеку, какой гол засадили наши на последней минуте?* "Did you see on TV how our team scored a goal at the last minute?"

ЗАСАНДА́ЛИВАТЬ/ЗАСАНДА́ЛИТЬ, *joc.* **1.** To hit, thrash (from сандал, "sandal"). ♦ *И куда ты ему засандалил, в глаз?* "Where did you hit him — in the eye?" **2.** To do something intensely, vehemently. ♦ *Они засандалили не знаю сколько вина.* "They knocked down heaven only knows how much wine."

ЗАСВЕ́ЧИВАТЬСЯ/ЗАСВЕТИ́ТЬСЯ. To expose oneself, give oneself away. ♦ *Смотри, не засветись, когда будешь с ним говорить.* "Make sure you don't give yourself away when you speak with him."

ЗАСЕДА́ТЬ/ЗАСЕ́СТЬ (в туале́те), *idiom, joc.* To sit on the toilet for a long time (lit., to "preside" over the toilet, a Sovietism). ♦ *Хватит заседать, выходи!* "You've been presiding long enough — come on out now!"

ЗАСЕКА́ТЬСЯ/ЗАСЕ́ЧЬСЯ. To be caught red-handed (lit., to be located). ♦ *Смотри в оба, не засекись, когда проносить поддачу будешь через проходную.* "Play it safe and don't get caught when you bring the booze through the checkpoint."

ЗАСЕРА́ТЬ/ЗАСРА́ТЬ, *rude.* To shit on, to mess up. ♦ *Когда вы так успели засрать ковры в доме?* "When did you manage to mess up the carpets like that?" •**Засера́ть/засра́ть мозги́,** *rude.* To confuse, drive to distraction (lit., to shit on someone's brains). ♦ *Они ему совсем мозги засрали, решил эмигрировать.*

"They drove him to such a pitch of distraction that he decided to emigrate."

ЗАСЕ́РЯ, -и, *m. and f., rude.* A slob, dirty person (lit., shitter). ♦ *Приведи в порядок комнату, засеря!* "Clean up the room, you pig!"

ЗАСО́С, -а, *m.* The mark of a kiss on the skin (lit., a sucker). ♦ *Кто это тебе такой засос оставил?* "Who gave you that hickey?"

ЗАСРА́НЕЦ, засра́нца, *m., rude.* See **засе́ря.**

ЗАСРА́НСК, -а, *m., neg., rude.* Any small, provincial, remote town (by wordplay on Саранск, the town of Saransk, and **засра́нец**). ♦ *Он живёт где-то в Засранске, я этот город и на карте не вижу.* "He lives in some godforsaken hamlet somewhere, I can't even find it on the map."

ЗАССА́НЕЦ, засса́нца, *m., rude.* A bastard, good-for-nothing, idiot (from ссать, "to piss"). ♦ *Этот зассанец так и не принёс, что обещал.* "That bastard didn't bring what he promised."

ЗАССЫ́КА, -и, *m. & f., rude.* See **зассы́ха.**

ЗАССЫ́ХА, -и, *m. & f., rude.* **1.** Someone who urinates frequently. ♦ *У этой зассыхи недержание мочи.* "This pisser just can't hold it in." **2.** *neg.* A young woman. ♦ *Ишь ты, совсем ещё зассыха, а лезешь со своими советами.* "Oh, go on, you're just a squirt, but you keep after me with your advice." **3.** Feminine form of **засса́нец.**

ЗАСТРА́ИВАТЬ/ЗАСТРО́ИТЬ. To torment with formation drills (lit., to build, form). ♦ *Перед майскими совсем застроят, потом полегче будет.* "They'll drive us up the wall with drills until Veteran's Day, and then things will ease off."

ЗАСТРЕЛИ́СЬ! *idiom.* Terrific! Wonderful! (lit., shoot yourself). ♦ *Фильм вчера смотрела — застрелись!* "The film I saw yesterday was fantastic!"

ЗАСТРЕЛИ́ТЬСЯ: Застрели́ться мо́ж-

но! *idiom.* **1.** Terrible. ♦ *Скука здесь, застрелиться можно.* "You could die of boredom here." **2.** Wonderful. ♦ *Он рассказал такие анекдоты — застрелиться можно.* "He told such good jokes, you could have died laughing." **Застрелиться и не жить,** *idiom.* An expression used of an unexpected event. ♦ *Неужели эту бездарность выбрали директором института? Застрелиться и не жить.* "Did they really elect that fool director of the institute? You could knock me over with a feather!"

ЗАСТРÓЙКА, -и, *f.* A workout, drill. See **застрáивать.**

ЗАСТÚКАТЬ хови́ру, *idiom, crim.* To rob an apartment. ♦ *Эту ховиру надо срочно застукать.* "We'll have to rob this apartment soon."

ЗАСÚНЬ (ЯЗЫ́К) СЕБÉ В ЖÓПУ. See under **жóпа.**

ЗАСЫПÁТЬСЯ/ЗАСЫ́ПАТЬСЯ. To be caught at something, be apprehended (lit., to be sprinkled, as with sand, sugar, etc.). ♦ *Он слишком много воровал и, конечно, засыпался.* "He stole too much, so of course he got caught."

ЗАТÁРИВАТЬСЯ/ЗАТÁРИТЬСЯ. To stock up, buy up a lot of something (from тара, "carton, container"). ♦ *Я затарился сахаром на два месяца вперёд.* "I've stocked up on sugar — two months' worth."

ЗАТМÉНИЕ: Дéлать/сдéлать сóлнечное затмéние, see under **дéлать.**

ЗАТОРМÓЖЕННЫЙ, -ая, -ое, *neg.* Slow, passive (from тормоз, "brake"). ♦ *Ты сегодня заторможенный, не выспался, что ли?* "You're really sluggish today. What's the matter — didn't sleep enough last night?"

ЗАТРУХÁТЬ, *perf. only, rude.* To soil, smear. ♦ *Ты затрухал всё одеяло вареньем.* "You got jam all over the blanket."

ЗАТÚРКАННЫЙ, -ая, -ое, *neg.* Frightened, nervous, intimidated by harassing criticism (cf. **затÚркивать**). ♦ *Муж у неё совсем затурканный.* "Her husband

is really henpecked."

ЗАТÚРКИВАТЬ/ЗАТÚРКАТЬ, *neg.* To intimidate, unnerve (from Ukr. туркнуть, "to push, shove"). ♦ *Ты мальчишку совсем затуркала замечаниями.* "You've completely intimidated that boy with your comments."

ЗАТУСÓВАННЫЙ, -ая, -ое, *youth.* **1.** Socializing or partying a great deal, spending a lot of time at parties (cf. **тусóвка**). ♦ *Вы совсем затусованные, вам не надоело ходить по гостям?* "You guys have become quite the social butterflies — aren't you tired of partying so much?" **2.** Tired, exhausted. ♦ *Ты выглядишь затусованным, тебе надо отдохнуть.* "You look exhausted. Why don't you take a rest?"

ЗАТЫКÁТЬСЯ/ЗАТКНÚТЬСЯ. 1. To be quiet (lit., to be plugged up). ♦ *Ты не можешь заткнуться хоть на минуту?* "Can't you shut up for a single moment?" **2.** To be without communications (lit., to be choked). ♦ *Что мы заткнулись, чтоб связь была любой ценой.* "Why are we cut off? We've got to make contact at all costs!"

ЗАТЫ́РЩИК, -a, *m., crim.* A receiver of stolen goods, a fence. ♦ *Мне надо адрес затырщика, есть вещи.* "I need the address of a fence. I've got some stuff."

ЗАТЮ́КАННЫЙ, -ая, -ое, *neg.* Frightened, diffident, bullied (cf. **затю́кивать**). ♦ *Ты что ходишь последнее время совсем затюканный? Что-нибудь случилось?* "Why have you been going around so scared-looking lately? Has something happened?"

ЗАТЮ́КИВАТЬ/ЗАТЮ́КАТЬ, *neg.* (From the expletive тю! "Shame on you!"). **1.** To intimidate. ♦ *Ты дочь затюкала своими капризами.* "You've intimidated your daughter with your unpredictable behavior." **2.** To bully, harass. ♦ *В семье его совсем затюкали, ни во что не ставят.* "They harass him at home; they give him no respect."

ЗАУСÉНЕЦ, -нца, *m., neg.* An unpleasant, annoying person (from заусенец, "hangnail"). ♦ *Откуда ты такой заусенец взялся, покоя от тебя нет.*

"Where did you come from? You're cosntantly irritating me."

ЗА́ФИГОМ, *adv.* What for? Why? (cf. **фиг**). ♦*Зафигом он туда пошёл?* "What did he go there for?"

ЗАФИТИЛИ́ТЬ, *perf.* To hit (lit., to fuse). ♦*Зафитили его кирпичом, он слов не понимает.* "Hit him with a brick—he doesn't understand words."

ЗАХА́ПЫВАТЬ/ЗАХА́ПАТЬ, *neg.* To appropriate, take for oneself (lit., to grab). ♦*Ты все деньги себе захапал, а как же мы?* "You've taken all the money for yourself. What about us?"

ЗАХЕ́ЗЫВАТЬ/ЗАХЕ́ЗАТЬ всю мали́ну, *idiom, crim., neg.* To spoil a deal, ruin a project (lit., to shit on the whole raspberry patch; cf. **мали́на**). ♦*Ты нам всю малину захезал, проболтался о наших планах.* "You've ruined the whole deal by chattering about our plans."

ЗАХЕРА́ЧИВАТЬ/ЗАХЕРА́ЧИТЬ, *rude.* To hit, strike (cf. **хер**). ♦*У тебя кровь, в тебя камнем захерачили?* "You've got blood on you — did they hit you with a stone?"

ЗАХУЯ́РИВАТЬ/ЗАХУЯ́РИТЬ, *rude.* Cf. **худ́й. 1.** To hit, beat. ♦*Захуярь его палкой, может, успокоится.* "Beat him with a stick — maybe that'll quiet him down." **2.** To drink a lot or too much. ♦*Ну, мы вчера и захуярили, два литра, наверное, выпили.* "Yesterday we really belted it down — we drank about two liters."

ЗАЧЕ́М МНЕ ЧИНЫ́, КОГДА́ НЕТ ВЕТЧИНЫ́, *idiom, joc.* Lit., "What good is rank to me if I don't have ham." Used to express dissatisfaction with rewards considered insufficient, esp. with immaterial rewards as opposed to money. ♦*У тебя, кажется, всё в порядке, сидишь в большом кабинете. — Зачем мне чины, когда нет ветчины?* "I see you've got quite the position, with this big office and all. — Yes, but rank is no use to me if I don't have ham."

ЗАЧИ́СТКА, -и, *f., army.* A military operation against civilians to clear out an area (lit., cleanup). The term came into being during the Chechen war. ♦*После зачистки в деревне не осталось ни одной живой души.* "After the cleanup operation not a single living soul was left in the village."

ЗАЧУХА́НЕННЫЙ, -ая, -ое. Overtired, exhausted. See **чуха́н.** ♦*Вид у вас совсем зачуханенный, пара дней на отдых, а потом снова в разведку.* "You look dog-tired. Take a two-day break before you go back on recon again."

ЗАЧУ́ХАННЫЙ, -ая, -ое, *neg.* Unkempt, shabbily dressed (lit., scratched up). ♦*Сын ходит у неё всегда зачуханный.* "Her son always goes around looking like a slob."

ЗАШИБА́ТЬ/ЗАШИБИ́ТЬ. To earn a lot of money (lit., to strike). ♦*На приисках ещё зашибают деньги, у нас давно нет.* "They're striking it rich out in the gold mines, but there's no money in our line of work."

ЗАШИБЕ́Ц, *pred. use, youth.* Something excellent. ♦*Сегодня погода — зашибе́ц!* "The weather today is terrific!"

ЗАШИБИ́СЬ! *youth.* See **зашибе́ц.**

ЗАШИВА́ТЬ/ЗАШИ́ТЬ торпе́ду, *idiom.* To cure of alcoholism (lit., to sew in a torpedo; cf. **торпе́да**). ♦*Тебе надо зашить торпеду, а то ты станешь алкоголиком.* "You'd better go on Antabuse before you end up as a real alcoholic."

ЗАШИ́ТЬСЯ, *perf. only.* To receive treatment for alcoholism, especially the implanting under the skin of medication causing physical distress when alcohol is present (lit., to be sewn up). ♦*Он недавно зашился.* "He recently started taking anti-alcoholic drugs."

ЗАШИФРО́ВАННЫЙ, -ая, -ое, *joc.* Lit., in code. **1.** Secretive, mysterious. ♦*Что-то ты ходишь какой-то зашифрованный, что-нибудь случилось?* "You're going around looking very secretive. Has something happened?" **2.** Undercover, working for a secret service. ♦*Он что, зашифрованный?* "What is he, an undercover agent?"

ЗАШИФРО́ВЫВАТЬСЯ/ЗАШИФРОВА́ТЬСЯ, *joc.* To go underground by not answering the telephone, declining social invitations, and so on (cf. **зашифро́ван-ный**). ♦*Ты чего зашифровался, к тебе дозвониться нельзя.* "Have you gone underground? It's impossible to reach you by phone."

ЗАШКА́ЛИВАТЬ/ЗАШКА́ЛИТЬ, *impersonal.* **1.** To exceed the limits of something, go off the charts. ♦*Температура сегодня такая минусовая, что термометр зашкалило.* "It's so cold today, the temperature reading has dropped clean off the thermometer." **2.** To go crazy. ♦*Его совсем зашкалило.* "He's gone out of his mind."

ЗАШКЕ́РИВАТЬ\ЗАШКЕ́РИТЬ, *army.* To shirk, to dodge (lit., to hide behind rocks). ♦*И не мечтайте сегодня зашкерить, я сам буду проверять, что сделано.* "Don't you even think of dodging out today! I'm going to check the results myself."

ЗАШОКОЛА́ДЕНО! *idiom.* Okay, it's settled, agreed (from шоколад, chocolate). ♦*Зашоколадено, я буду у вас на шашлыках в субботу.* "It's a deal! I'll come to your shishkebab party on Saturday."

ЗАШТО́ПАТЬ, *perf.* To catch red-handed, to nail (from штопать, to darn, to stitch). ♦*Рано или поздно тебя заштопают за контрабанду.* "Sooner or later you'll be caught smuggling."

ЗАШУ́ГАННЫЙ, -ая, -ое. Scared, nervous, intimidated (from шугать, to scare away). ♦*Дети у них какие-то зашуганные, все время молчат, не играют.* "Their children seem kind of intimidated—they keep their mouths shut and never play any games."

ЗА́ЯЦ: Как за́йцу три́ппер, see under **как.**

ЗВЕЗДАНУ́ТЬ, *perf. only, neg.* To hit hard (lit., to make someone see stars). ♦*Кто тебя так звезданул?* "Who gave you such a walloping?"

ЗВЕЗДИ́ТЬ/ПОЗВЕЗДИ́ТЬ, *rude.* To lie, to chatter idly (by euphemistic wordplay on **[с]пизде́ть**). ♦*Не звезди, ничего такого, как ты говоришь, не было.*

"Stop lying. Nothing like what you're describing ever happened."

ЗВЕНЕ́ТЬ/ЗАЗВЕНЕ́ТЬ муди́ми, *idiom, rude.* To hang around idly (lit., to ring one's balls; cf. **мудозво́н**). ♦*Он ничего не делает, только звенит мудями.* "He's a real loafer — just hangs around ringing his balls."

ЗВЕРЁК, зверька́. See **зверь.**

ЗВЕРИ́НЕЦ, -нца, *m., rude.* The Caucasian Republics (lit., zoo, animal-house).

ЗВЕРЬ, -я, *m., neg.* A person from the Caucasus (lit., a wild animal). ♦*Ты этого зверя знаешь?* "Do you know that Caucasian fellow?"

ЗВОН, -а, *m., neg.* Empty chatter, lies (lit., ringing of bells). ♦*Это всё звон, не верь.* "That's all nonsense! Don't believe it."

ЗВОНА́РЬ, -я́, *m., neg.* A tongue-wagger, chatterer (lit., bell-ringer). ♦*Только ты этому звонарю ни слова, всё разболтает.* "But don't say a word to that tongue-wagger, or he'll spread stories all over town."

ЗВОНИ́ТЬ¹, *imperf. only, neg.* To lie (cf. **звон**). ♦*Что он там звонит?* "What kind of lies is he telling?"

ЗВОНИ́ТЬ²/РАЗЗВОНИ́ТЬ, *neg.* To divulge secrets, spill information (cf. **звона́рь**). ♦*Кто раззвонил?* "Who leaked it?"

ЗВОНО́К: Со звонко́м, *idiom, neg.* Crazy (lit., with a bell). ♦*Она уже давно со звонком, а всё ещё учит других.* "She's completely off her rocker, but she still goes around telling the others what to do."

ЗВЯ́КАТЬ/ЗВЯ́КНУТЬ. To call by telephone (lit., to clink, ring). ♦*Звякни мне вечером.* "Give me a buzz this evening."

ЗДО́РОВСКИ, *adv.* Strongly, excellently. ♦*Ребята играют здоровски, высший класс!* "The fellows are playing very strongly — really first-class!"

ЗДО́РОВСКИЙ, -ая, -ое. Excellent, fine. ♦*Вчера фильм здоровский смотрел!* "Yesterday I saw a terrific film!"

ЗДОРО́ВЫЙ ЛОБ, *idiom, neg.* A big,

strong man (lit., a big forehead). *Ты уже здоровый лоб, а всё у матери деньги просишь.* "You're already a big strong man, and you're still asking your mother for money!"

ЗДРА́ВСТВУЙ, ЗДРА́ВСТВУЙ, ХУЙ МОРДА́СТЫЙ. See under **хуй.**

ЗДРА́СТЕ-МОРДА́СТИ! *idiom.* An expression of surprise or incredulity. ♦*Здрасте-мордасти, как это может быть!* "Heavens! How could that be!"

ЗЕ́БРА, -ы, *f.* A pedestrian crossing. ♦*Его машина сбила прямо на зебре.* "He was hit by a car right in the middle of the zebra."

ЗЕЛЁНКА, -и, *f.* Bushes or trees suitable for an ambush (lit., greenery). ♦*Весной зеленка пойдет, труднее станет служить.* "Things will be tougher in the spring, when the vegetation thickens."

ЗЕЛЁНЫЕ ТОВА́РЫ, *idiom, business.* Environmentally harmless products.

ЗЕЛЁНЫЙ, -ого, *m.* A dollar (lit., green fellow). ♦*Зелёные есть?* "Do we have any greenbacks?"

ЗЕ́ЛЕНЬ, -и, *f.* Dollars (lit., greenery). ♦*У меня мало зелени осталось.* "I'm running low on greenbacks."

ЗЁМА, -ы, *m., army.* A person from one's hometown; a friendly greeting to any person. ♦*Зёма, дай закурить.* "Hey, buddy, give me a smoke."

ЗЕМЕ́ЛЯ, -и, *m., army.* See **зёма.**

ЗЕ́НКИ, зе́нок, *pl., rude.* Eyes. ♦*Протри зенки, не видишь, кто пришёл.* "Rub your eyes — look who's here!"

ЗЕРНО́, -а́, *n., crim.* Drugs in tablet form (lit., grain). ♦*Пора доставать зерно, у меня всё кончилось.* "It's time to get some more pills; mine are all gone."

ЗИМА́, -ы́, *f., crim.* A knife. ♦*Возьми, заточи мне зиму, совсем тупая.* "Sharpen my knife for me, would you? It's completely dull."

ЗИ́ПЕР, -а, *m., youth.* A zipper in trousers, fly (from Eng. "zipper"). ♦*У меня зипер сломался.* "My zipper is broken."

ЗЛОЕБУ́ЧИЙ, -ая, -ое, *rude.* Sexually insatiable (cf. **ёб-**). ♦*Она такая злоебучая, ночи не хватает.* "She's such a nympho, she can't get enough in a whole night."

ЗНА́КОВЫЙ, -ая, -ое. Very important, significant. ♦*Это знаковая речь, ясно, что он хочет стать президентом.* "This is a key speech, it means that he's going to run for President."

ЗНОЙ, -я, *m., crim.* A wound. ♦*Смотри, какой зной у него, от ножа, наверное.* "Look at that wound of his! It must be from a knife."

ЗОЛОТЫ́Е ВОРОТНИЧКИ́, *idiom, business.* High-class specialists in advanced materials and technology (lit., golden collars). ♦*Золотые воротнички тоже сейчас без работы сидят.* "The high-tech people are also out of work these days."

ЗОНТА́РЬ, -ря́, *m., crim.* A thief specializing in robberies through a breach in the ceiling (from зонт, as of someone who descends like a parachutist). ♦*Здесь работали зонтари.* "'Parachutists' have been at work here."

ЗРЯПЛА́ТА, -ы, *f., joc.* Salary (by wordplay on платить зря, "to pay at random" or "to pay pointlessly'; the idea is that the pay doesn't amount to much, but then, neither does the work). ♦*Когда у нас зряплата?* "When's playday around here?"

ЗУБИ́ЛО, -а, *n.* A model 9 car of the Zhiguli make. This is a prestigious and expensive but inconveniently delicate vehicle, which tends to meet with disaster on bumps or potholes. (By wordplay on Жигули and зубило, a metal cutter that is thought to resemble the front end of this car.) ♦*Он ездит на зубиле.* "He drives a tin-snip."

ЗУБО́В БОЯ́ТЬСЯ — В РОТ НЕ ДАВА́ТЬ, *idiom, joc.* Nothing ventured, nothing gained (lit., if you're afraid of teeth, you'll never get a blow job; from the proverb Волков бояться — в лес не ходить, "If you're afraid of wolves, you'll never go into the woods"). ♦*Не*

*надо бояться, а надо действовать. —
Я всё-таки боюсь. — Зубов бояться
— в рот не давать.* "Don't be scared.
This is a situation where you have to act.
— Well, I *am* scared. — If you're afraid
of teeth, you'll never get a blow job."

ЗУБÓВ НЕ ДОСЧИТÁЕШЬСЯ, *idiom,
neg.* I'll knock your teeth out (lit., you
won't get the full count of your teeth).
♦ *Сейчас как дам, зубов не досчи-
таешься!* "The way I'm going to give it
to you, you'll find some of your teeth
missing."

ЗУБР, -а, *m., crim.* **1.** An important person
in a prison, a boss of prison inmates (lit.,
a bison). ♦ *Он зубром стал, помогает
организовать работы.* "He's become a
boss, helping to organize the work
crews." **2.** A specialist, expert. ♦ *Он зубр
в математике.* "He's an expert in
mathematics."

ЗУБРИ́ЛА, -ы, *m. & f., students.* A dili-
gent student, a bookworm, nerd, grade
grubber (from зубрить, "to learn by
heart"). ♦ *Он гулять с нами не пойдёт,
это известный зубрила.* "A bookworm
like him wouldn't go out on the town

with us."

ЗУ́БЫ: Зубóв не досчитáешься! see
under **зубóв. Тебé зу́бы не жмут?** see
under **тебé.**

ЗУДÉТЬ/ЗАЗУДÉТЬ, *neg.* To speak
monotonously or boringly (lit., to buzz).
♦ *Слушай, не зуди, всё равно я сделаю
по-своему.* "Don't keep harping on it!
I'm going to do as I please anyhow."

ЗЫ́РИТЬ/ПОЗЫ́РИТЬ, *neg.* To stare,
gape. ♦ *Хватит зырить на витрины,
пора домой.* "Stop gaping at the shop
windows — it's time to go home."

ЗЫ́РКАТЬ, *imperf. only, neg.* To look
around. ♦ *Что ты по сторонам зырка-
ешь, сиди прямо.* "Why are you looking
around like that? Sit still!"

ЗЭК, -а, *m., crim.* A convict, prisoner
(abbr. of заключённый). ♦ *Этот завод
построили зэки.* "This plant was built
by convicts."

ЗЭ́ЧКА, -и, *f., crim.* A female convict.

ЗЯ́БРЫ: Брать/взять за зя́бры, see
under **брать.**

ЗЯ́МА, -ы, *m. & f., neg.* A Jew. ♦ *Он что,
зяма, что ли?* "What is he, a Jew?"

И ТО ХЛЕБ, *idiom.* Not bad; could be worse; nothing to sneeze at (lit., that's bread too). ♦*Тебе к зарплате добавили 10,000 рублей. — И то хлеб.* "You're getting a 10,000-ruble raise. — Well, it's not nothing."

ИВА́Н ИВА́НЫЧ, *idiom, crim.* A public prosecutor (lit., "Ivan Ivanovich"). ♦*Сейчас Иван Иваныч придёт, он тебе расскажет, куда тебя и на сколько определят.* "Now the prosecutor will come and tell you how long your sentence is and where you'll be serving it."

ИГРА́ТЬ/ЗАИГРА́ТЬ ПЯ́ТКАМИ, *idiom.* To run away (lit., to play with one's heels). ♦*Куда они денутся, танки пойдут и они заиграют пятками.* "There's no way out, they'll take to their heels when the tanks attack them."

ИГРА́ТЬ/СЫГРА́ТЬ: Игра́ть/сыгра́ть на гита́ре, *idiom, crim.* To break safes (lit., to play the guitar). ♦*Надо нам найти человека, чтоб умел играть на гитаре.* "We need to find someone who knows how to break safes." **Игра́ть/сыгра́ть на кларне́те,** *idiom, youth.* To engage in oral sex (lit., to play the clarinet). ♦*Она играет на кларнете?* "Does she 'play the clarinet'?" **Игра́ть/сыгра́ть на скри́пке,** *idiom, crim.* To saw through an iron bar (lit., to play the violin). ♦*Теперь ты играй на скрипке, я постою, посторожу.* "Now you do the sawing, and I'll stand guard." **Игра́ть/сыгра́ть на три ко́сточки,** *idiom, crim.* To play a game of chance where the stakes are life and death or where the loser must kill someone (lit., to play the three bones [skull and crossbones]). ♦*Он всем надоел, давай его сыграем на три косточки.* "Everyone's sick of him; come on, let's play for his life" (i.e., let's play to see who will kill him). **Игра́ть/сыгра́ть под очко́,** *idiom, crim.* To play at cards where the stakes are homosexual acts (lit., to play for one's ass, cf. **очко́**). ♦*Играл под* очко, проиграл, расплачивайся. "You played for your ass and lost; now pay up." **Игра́ть/сыгра́ть с госуда́рством в аза́ртные и́гры,** *idiom, joc.* Lit., to play games of chance against the government, that is, to buy government lottery tickets, bonds, and so on. ♦*Давай купим пару лотереек. — Я с государством в азартные игры не играю.* "Let's buy a couple of lottery tickets. — No thanks. I don't gamble against the government." **Игра́ть в молча́нку,** *idiom, neg.* To keep silent, give the silent treatment. ♦*Что вы играете в молчанку, пора помириться.* "Why are you still giving me the silent treatment? It's about time we made up." **Сыгра́ть в жму́рки,** *idiom.* To die (lit., to play hide-and-seek). ♦*Бабушка у него сыграла в жмурки на прошлой неделе.* "His grandmother kicked the bucket last week." **Сыгра́ть в я́щик,** *idiom, joc.* To die (lit., to play into the box). ♦*Не будешь беречь себя, быстро сыграешь в ящик.* "If you don't take care of yourself you'll drive yourself into the grave."

ИГРУ́ЛЯ, -и, *m. & f., sports, neg.* A bad athlete. ♦*Вот игруля, с пяти метров в ворота попасть не может.* "What an awful player he is — he couldn't score from just five meters away."

ИГРУ́ШКА, -и, *f., army.* An explosive device (lit., a toy). ♦*Не поднимай ничего на улице, сейчас этих игрушек полно везде.* "Don't pick up anything in the street—right now there are 'gimmicks' everywhere."

И́ДОЛ, -а, *m., crim.* A tooth. ♦*Мне идол выбили в драке.* "My tooth was knocked out in a fight."

ИДТИ́/ПОЙТИ́: Идти́/пойти́ бу́ром, *idiom, neg.* To be pushy, insolent. ♦*Ты всё время идёшь буром, о людях не думаешь.* "You're always so pushy! You don't consider other people." **Идти́/пойти́ винто́м,** *idiom, joc.* "To walk like a propeller"; used of the unsteady gait of a drunken person. ♦*Смотри, он выпил чуть, а уже пошёл винтом.* "Look! He's hardly had anything to drink but he's already walking like a propeller." **Иди́ ты!**, *idiom.* An expression of incredulity or surprise: Impossible! It can't be! You must be kidding! ♦*Ты знаешь, у них родилась тройня. — Иди ты!* "Did you hear they had triplets? — You must be kidding!" **Иди́ (ты) в одно́ ме́сто!** *idiom, rude, euph.* Go to hell! ♦*Иди ты в одно место со своими деньгами, я не продаюсь.* "Go to hell with your money. I'm not for sale." **Иди́ ты, зна́ешь куда́!**, *idiom.* Go to hell! (lit., go you-know-where, euph. for иди **на хуй** [**в жо́пу**].) ♦*Иди ты, знаешь куда, со своими сплетнями.* "Go to hell with your gossip!" **Иди́ ты в Катманду́!** *idiom, rude.* Get out of here, go to hell (lit., go to Katmandu; by wordplay on **манда́**.) ♦*Не приставай, иди в Катманду со своими делами.* "Don't keep pestering me! The hell with you and your problems!"

ИЗВИ́ЛИНА, -ы, *f., joc.* Intelligence, brains (lit., a bend, curve, as in a river; with reference to the convolutions of the brain). ♦*У него одна извилина.* "He's stupid" (lit., he's got only one convolution to his brain). ♦*Пошевели извилинами.* "Move your brains (Think!)!" •**У кого́-л. одна́ изви́лина и та на жо́пе,** see under **жо́па.**

ИЗГВА́ЗДЫВАТЬСЯ/ИЗГВАЗДА́ТЬ- СЯ, *neg.* To get dirty, soiled. ♦*Где это ты так изгваздался?* "Where did you get so dirty?"

ИЗГОВНЯ́ТЬСЯ, *perf. only, rude.* To become corrupted (cf. **говно́**). ♦*Он берёт взятки, изговнялся вконец.* "He takes bribes — he's completely corrupt."

ИЗГОЛЯ́ТЬСЯ, *imperf. only, neg.* To ridicule, abuse, humiliate. ♦*Уж как он надо мной изголялся, страшно вспоминать!* "It's awful to even think of how he humiliated me."

ИЗМЫВА́ТЬСЯ, *imperf. only.* See **изголя́ться.**

ИЗНАСИ́ЛОВАТЬ мёртвого, *idiom, neg.* To be persistent, insistent (lit., to rape a corpse). ♦*Она тебя всё равно заставит это сделать, она и мёртвого изнасилует.* "She'll get her way in spite of everything; she would even rape a corpse."

ИЗНО́С: Рабо́тать на изно́с, see under **рабо́тать.**

ИЗНОХРА́ЧИВАТЬ/ИЗНОХРА́ТИТЬ. To beat up (probably from нохр, *obs.,* a tricky person). ♦*Кто же тебя так изнохратил, места живого нет?* "Who beat you up like that? You don't have a good spot left."

ИЗОБРАЖА́ТЬ/ИЗОБРАЗИ́ТЬ шум морско́го прибо́я, *idiom, joc.* Not to get involved, to be a mere bystander (lit., to imitate the sound of the tide). ♦*Я не стал их мирить, изображал шум морского прибоя.* "I didn't try to reconcile them; I just made like the sound of the tide."

ИКОНОСТА́С, -а, *m., joc.* Badges and medals worn on the chest (lit., an iconostasis, the wall of icons over the altar of a church). ♦*Посмотри, какой у него иконостас, каких только наград нет!* "Look what an iconostasis he's wearing — every possible kind of medal!"

ИКРА́: Мета́ть икру́, see under **мета́ть.**

ИЛА́Й, -я, *m., crim.* An honest person. ♦*Он илай, он не подведёт.* "He's an honest fellow. He won't let us down."

ИМЕ́ТЬ/ПОИМЕ́ТЬ, *neg.* **1.** To have sex with a woman. ♦*Кто её только не имел!* "Is there anyone who hasn't had her?" **2.** To spit on, despise. ♦*Имел я твои угрозы!* "The hell with your threats!" •**Что име́ю, то и введу́,** *idiom, rude.* Never mind; none of your business; I have no intention of answering your question (lit., what I have, I insert). ♦*Он не придёт. — Что ты имеешь в виду? — Что имею, то и введу.* "He won't come. — What do you mean? — None of your business."

ИМПЕ́РИЯ, -и, *f., crim.* The female genitals (lit., empire). ♦*Штаны проносила, вся империя видна.* "You've got a hole in your slacks — the whole empire is showing."

И́МЯ: Полоска́ть чьё-л. и́мя, see under **полоска́ть.**

ИНДУ́С, -а, *m., crim.* A prisoner receiving punishment for bad behavior (lit., an [east] Indian). ♦*Бу́дешь так себя́ вести́, попадёшь в инду́сы.* "If you act like that you'll be put in a punishment cell."

ИНДЮ́К, -ка́, *m., neg.* An (east) Indian (lit., a turkey). ♦*Индюки́ нам бо́льше чай не поставля́ют.* "The Indians aren't exporting tea to us any more."

ИНОМА́РКА, -и, *f.* A foreign-made car. ♦*В Росси́и бум на инома́рки.* "There is a great demand for foreign-made cars in Russia."

ИНОСРА́НЬ, -и, *f., collect., youth, rude.* Foreigners (by wordplay on иностра́нный, "foreign," and **срать**). ♦*За таки́е де́ньги э́ту карти́ну ра́зве то́лько иносра́нь ку́пит.* "Only foreign shit would spend that much money on this painting."

ИНСА́ЙДЕР, -а, *m., business.* An inside-company spy (from Eng. "insider").

ИНСУ́ЛЬТНИК, -а, *m., youth, neg.* An elderly, weak man (lit., a stroke victim). ♦*Заче́м ты привела́ э́того инсу́льтника?* "Why did you bring that old geezer along?"

ИНСУ́ЛЬТ-ПРИВЕ́Т, *idiom, joc.* A greeting mocking the Soviet-style athletes' salutation Физкульт-привет! ("Phyzcult greetings!" [i.e., physical culture greetings!]), by wordplay on инсульт, "a stroke." The effect is something like "Hi, stroke victims!"

ИНТЕРДЕ́ВОЧКА, -и, *f.* A hard-currency prostitute (by wordplay on "international" and де́вушка, "girl"). ♦*Сейча́с преде́л её мечта́ний — стать интердево́чкой.* "What she's dreaming of now is to become a currency prostitute."

ИНТИ́М, -а, *m.* A cozy situation (from Eng. "intimate"). ♦*Зажги́ све́чи, дава́й устро́им инти́м.* "Light some candles; let's make ourselves cozy."

ИНТУИ́Т, -а, *m., youth.* A highly intuitive person, a person with a good ability to guess. ♦*В ка́рты ему́ везёт, он инту-

им. "He does well at cards because he's so intuitive."

ИНТУИ́ЧИТЬ/ПРОИНТУИ́ЧИТЬ, *youth.* To foretell, guess, divine. ♦*Как ты проинтуи́чила и забрала́ де́ньги из ба́нка, вчера́ он ло́пнул.* "How did you have the foresight to withdraw your money from the bank before it collapsed yesterday?"

ИРОКЕ́ЗЫ, -ов, *pl., youth.* A punk haircut, a cock's-comb (lit., Iroquois). ♦*У молоды́х сейча́с в мо́де ироке́зы.* "Punk haircuts are in fashion with the kids these days."

ИСКОЛБА́СИТЬ, *perf.* To beat up (from колбаса́, sausage). ♦*Исколба́сят тебя́, е́сли ска́жешь, кто пил в каза́рме.* "You'll be beaten up if you report who was drinking in the barracks."

ИСПЕ́ЧЬСЯ, *perf.* To get caught red-handed (lit., to be baked). ♦*Ещё оди́н из мили́ции испёкся на взя́тках.* "Another policeman has been caught taking bribes."

ИСПИЗДЯ́ЧИВАТЬ/ИСПИЗДЯ́ЧИТЬ, *rude.* To beat severely (cf. **пизда́**). ♦*Он тебе́ обеща́л испиздя́чить.* "He swore that he'd beat you to a pulp."

И́СПОВЕДЬ, -и, *f., crim.* A denunciation, informer's report (lit., confession). ♦*Кто-то на меня́ и́споведь написа́л, интере́сно кто.* "Someone informed on me — I wonder who."

ИСПО́РЧЕННЫЙ ТЕЛЕФО́Н, *idiom.* Distorted rumors, unreliable information. ♦*Кто тебе́ сказа́л, что це́ны повы́сятся, не верь, э́то про́сто испо́рченный телефо́н.* "Who told you that prices are going up? It's not true — it's just a distorted rumor."

ИСТЕ́РИКА: Зака́тывать/закати́ть исте́рику, see under **зака́тывать.**

ИСХОДИ́ТЬ/ИЗОЙТИ́ дерьмо́м, *idiom, rude.* To get angry, be beside oneself with anger (lit., to shit oneself out). ♦*Он це́лый час исходи́л дерьмо́м из-за твоего́ выступле́ния.* "He was in a rage for a whole hour about the way you walked out."

ИСХУЯ́РИВАТЬ/ИСХУЯ́РИТЬ, *rude.* To beat severely (cf. **хуй**). ◆*Его опять за баб исхуярили.* "Again they've beaten him up for his philandering."

ИША́К ПО́ТНЫЙ, *idiom, rude.* An idiot, ass (lit., sweaty mule). ◆*Ты когда-ни-будь уйдёшь, ишак потный?* "When are you going to get out of here, you ass?"

ИША́ЧИТЬ/ПОИША́ЧИТЬ, *neg.* To work hard (like a mule, ишак). ◆*Мне за тебя ишачить надоело.* "I'm sick of doing your work for you like a mule."

. Й .

ЙОК, *adv.* No, not, nothing (from Persian). ◆*Табак—йок, консервы—йок, совсем тоскливо.* "There's no tobacco, no canned food—total bummer."

КАБАКТÉРИЙ, -я, *m., youth, joc.* A restaurant (by wordplay on кафетерий, "cafeteria," and кабак, "bad restaurant"). ♦ *Этот кабактерий уже открыт?* "Is this restaurant open?"

КАБÁН, -á, *m., crim.* An aggressive, domineering lesbian (lit., a boar). ♦ *Раз у них этот кабан завёлся, она всех превратит в лесбиянок.* "If that 'boar' shows up among them she'll turn them all into lesbians."

КАБЫСДÓХ, -а, *m., neg.* A skinny man, a weakling. (From кабы, "if" and сдохнуть, "to die"). ♦ *От этого кабысдоха помощи не жди, он сам едва ходит.* "You won't get any help from this 90-pound weakling, he can hardly even walk."

КАГÁЛ, -а, *m., neg.* A large group, crowd (from Heb. "*kahal*"). ♦ *Что ты в дом привёл целый кагал?* "Why did you bring that whole crowd to the house?"

КАДÉТ, -а, *m.* A student in a military academy. ♦ *Он уже кадет два года.* "He's been in military school for two years."

КАДР, -а, *m., pos.* A girl or woman (lit., a qualified person or a frame of film). ♦ *Смотри, какой кадр идёт!* "Look at that sharp gal!"

КАДРÁ, -ы́, *f., pos.* See **кадр.**

КАДРÉВИЧ, *f., indecl., youth, joc.* See **кадр.**

КАДРÉЖ, -а, *m.* Flirtation, chasing girls, meeting and going out with girls (cf. **кадр**). ♦ *Ты, как всегда, занимаешься кадрёжем? Кто эта девушка?* "I see you've been chasing girls as usual. Who's that one you're with?"

КАДРИ́ТЬ/ЗАКАДРИ́ТЬ. To meet, become acquainted with, pick up a girl or woman. ♦ *Пойдём, закадрим кого-нибудь на танцах.* "Come on! Let's go pick up some girls at the dance."

КАДУ́ШКА, -и, *f., neg.* A fat woman (lit., a barrel). ♦ *Зачем тебе эта кадушка?* "What are you doing going around with that barrel?"

КÁЖДЫЙ СХÓДИТ С УМÁ ПО-СВÓЕМУ, *idiom.* Lit., "everyone goes crazy in his own way." ♦ *Он хочет, чтобы его дети стали монахами. — Ну что ж, каждый сходит с ума по-своему.* "He wants his children to become monks. — Well, everyone has his little quirks."

КАЗÁК КОЛÉНКАМИ НАЗÁД, *idiom.* A rhyming teasing phrase (lit., a Cossack with his knees on backwards).

КАЗÁНЬ ДА РЯЗÁНЬ, *rhyming phrase.* Two inseparable friends (lit., Kazan and Ryazan, Russian city names). ♦ *Куда это Казань да Рязань подались, никак в самоход?* "Where are Tweedledée and Tweedledum? Have they gone AWOL?"

КАЗÁЧИТЬ/КАЗАЧНУ́ТЬ, *crim.* To hold up, rob (from казак, "Cossack"). ♦ *Вчера казачнули одного, дублёнку сняли.* "Yesterday they stole someone's sheepskin coat in a holdup."

КАЙФ, -а, *m.* **1.** Enjoyment, good time (from Arabic). ♦ *Тебе здесь нравится? — Кайф!* "Do you like it here? — It's wonderful!" **2.** *pl., youth.* Pleasure, fun. ♦ *Поехали на юг в Крым, там будут кайфы.* "Let's go for a vacation in the Crimea. It'll be fun there." **3.** *pl., youth.* Profit, advantage. ♦ *Какие мне кайфы от этого будут?* "What's in it for me?" •**По кáйфу,** *idiom.* Pleasing, good, to one's taste. ♦ *Это пиво по кайфу.* "I like this beer." **Не в кайф,** *idiom.* Unpleasant, unsatisfactory. ♦ *Такие речи мне не в кайф.* "I don't like to hear that kind of talk." **Лови́ть/пойма́ть, слови́ть кайф,** see under **лови́ть. Лома́ть/слома́ть кайф,** see under **лома́ть.**

КАЙФ-БАЗÁР, -а, *m., crim.* A meeting place for drug users. ♦ *Здесь у них кайф-базар.* "This is where the druggies hang out."

КАЙФОВÁТЬ/КАЙФОНУ́ТЬ. To have a good time, have a party. ♦ *Мы получили премию и хорошо кайфонули.* "When we got our bonus we went out and had a night on the town."

КАЙФÓВЩИК, -а, *m.* A do-nothing, playboy, good-time Charlie. ♦*Этот кайфовщик работать не будет.* "That playboy will never do any work."

КАЙФОЛÓМ, -а, *m., youth, neg.* **1.** A heavy drinker. ♦*Он кайфолом известный.* "He's known to be a heavy drinker." **2.** A party-pooper, wet-blanket. ♦*Не приглашай этого кайфолома, он нам всё испортит.* "Don't invite that party-pooper; he'll spoil the whole occasion for us."

КАЙФОЛÓМСТВО, -а, *n., youth, neg.* Something that spoils the fun, depresses the spirits (from **кайф**, "good time," and ломать, "to break"). ♦*Это кайфоломство — работать в воскресенье.* "Bummer! I've got to work this Sunday."

КАЙФОМÁН, -а, *m.* A playboy, one who likes drinking and partying. ♦*Ну что, кайфоманы, пора погреться.* "Well, party people, time to warm up."

КАК БÉЛКА В КОЛЕСÉ, *idiom.* Very busily, actively (lit., Like a squirrel on a treadmill). ♦*Мать целый день как белка в колесе, а ты знай себе отдыхаешь.* "Mom runs around doing chores all day, while you just lie there."

КАК БÉЛЫЙ ЧЕЛОВÉК, *idiom, joc.* Comfortably, luxuriously (lit., like a white man). ♦*Давай поживём как белые люди, поедем в Крым, отдохнём.* "What do you say we live it up a little? Let's go to the Crimea for a vacation."

КАК В ЛÝЧШИХ ДОМÁХ Филадéльфии, *idiom, pos.* Properly (lit., as in the best homes in Philadelphia). ♦*Всё готово к приходу гостей? — Как в лучших домах Филадельфии.* "Is everything ready for the dinner party? — Sure, just like in the best Philadelphia families!" **Как в лýчших домáх Лондóна (и Конотóпа),** *idiom, joc.* An expression playing on the preceding idiom: "Good, but not all that good." (The stress on "London" is nonstandard; Konotop is a small provincial town in middle Russia.)

КАК В СКÁЗКЕ: ЧЕМ ДÁЛЬШЕ, ТЕМ СТРАШНÉЙ, *idiom, joc.* Things are going from bad to worse (lit., like a fairy tale — the further you go, the more

scary it gets). Used to answer the question "Как жизнь?" "How's life?"

КАК ДВА ПÁЛЬЦА ОБОССÁТЬ, *idiom, rude.* Easy as pie, a cinch. ♦*Тебе слабо выпить стакан водки? — Как два пальца обоссать.* "Can't you drink a glass of vodka? — Sure I can, easily."

КАК ДÓКТОР ПРОПИСÁЛ, *idiom, joc.* Properly, correctly (lit., "as the doctor prescribed"). ♦*Квартиру вам отремонтировали как доктор прописал.* "The way your apartment has been renovated is just what the doctor ordered."

КАК ЗÁЙЦУ ТРИ́ППЕР, *idiom, rude.* Unnecessary, irrelevant (lit., like gonorrhea to a hare). ♦*Мне эта работа нужна как зайцу триппер.* "I need that job like a hole in the head."

КАК КОРÓВЕ СЕДЛÓ, *idiom, neg., joc.* Unsuitable, out of place (lit., like a saddle on a cow). ♦*Ей новое пальто идёт как корове седло.* "That new dress suits her like a saddle on a cow."

КАК МÁЛЬЧИК ЮНЬ СУ, *idiom, youth.* Industriously, obediently, devotedly (lit., like the boy Yung Su). ♦*Я уже год работаю над словарём, как мальчик Юнь Су.* "I've been slaving away at this dictionary like a Chinaman for a year already."

КАК МЁРТВОМУ ПРИМÓЧКИ, *idiom, neg.* Useless, futile (lit., like an ice pack for a corpse). ♦*Эти лекарства я пить не буду, они — как мёртвому примочки.* "I'm not going to take this medicine — it would be like giving an ice pack to a corpse."

КАК НАДÉНЕШЬ АДИДÁС, ТЕБÉ ЛЮБÁЯ БÁБА ДАСТ, *rhyming phrase.* "If you wear Adidas (shoes) you can have any girl you want."

КАК ПÁПА КÁРЛО, *idiom, joc.* With effort and patience; laboriously, devotedly (lit., "like Papa Carlo," referring to the character in Collodi's "Pinocchio"). ♦*Ты спишь, а я, как папа Карло, обед готовлю.* "While you've been sleeping I've been making your dinner, like Papa Carlo."

КАК РЫ́БЕ ЗÓНТИК, *idiom.* Superfluous, out of place (lit., like an umbrella for a fish). ♦ *Мне твоя книга нужна как рыбе зонтик.* "I need your book like a hole in the head."

КАК С КУСТА́, *idiom, youth.* Easily, without effort (lit., as if [taken] from a bush). ♦ *Мы заработали миллион, как с куста.* "We earned a cool million like falling off a log."

КАК СОБА́КА ПОССАЛА́, *idiom, rude.* Uneven, crooked (lit., as if a dog pissed it). ♦ *Ты сама сшила чебе юбку? Сбоку шов как собака поссала.* "Did you make that skirt yourself? The side seam is cockeyed."

КАК УГОРЕ́ЛАЯ КО́ШКА, *idiom.* Excessively, to the point of stupefaction. ♦ *Я целый день ношусь как угорелая кошка, собираю его в дорогу.* "I've been running around like a madman all day, trying to get him ready for his trip."

КАК УГОРЕ́ЛЫЙ, *idiom.* Dizzy, giddy, confused. ♦ *Что ты носишься как угорелый, сядь, отдохни, успеем.* "How come you're acting so giddy? Sit down and take a rest — we've got plenty of time."

КАК У́МНАЯ МА́ША, *idiom, joc.* Like a fool (lit., like clever Masha). ♦ *Завтра праздники, все уже давно ушли, а я, как умная Маша, сижу, печатаю.* "Tomorrow is a holiday, everybody has gone home, and I sit here typing like a fool."

КА́КА, -и, *f., neg.* Junk, trash, poor-quality stuff (lit., shit, usu. in children's speech). ♦ *Зачем ты купил эту каку, это не котлеты, а чёрт знает что!* "What did you buy that crap for?! Those aren't cutlets, but heaven knows what!" •**Ка́кой кве́рху,** *idiom, joc.* An evasive or irritated reply to the question Как?, "How are things?", "How did it go?" (lit., shit upwards). ♦ *Ну как? — Какой кверху.* "So how did it go? — Never mind." **Хоте́ть/захоте́ть и ка́ку и ма́ку,** see under **хоте́ть.**

КАКА́Я МУ́ХА ТЕБЯ́ УКУСИ́ЛА? *idiom, neg.* What's gotten into you? What's wrong with you? (lit., what fly bit

you?). ♦ *Ты весь день ходишь злой, ругаешься, какая муха тебя укусила?* "You've been going around in a foul mood all day. What's gotten into you?"

КАКИ́Е ЛЮ́ДИ — И БЕЗ ОХРА́НЫ! *idiom, joc.* A greeting alluding to the pretensions of the people greeted (lit., "What [important] people — and walking around without their bodyguards!").

КА́КОМ КВЕ́РХУ, *idiom, joc.* Lit., ass-upwards; cf. **ка́кой кве́рху** under **ка́ка.**

КА́КТУС БРИ́ТЫЙ, *idiom, joc.* An unshaved man (lit., a shaved cactus).

КА́КТУС ЛЫ́СЫЙ, *idiom, joc.* A bald man (lit., a bald cactus).

КА́КЧЕСТВО, -а, *n., neg., joc.* Bad quality (by wordplay on качество, "quality," and **ка́ка**). ♦ *Как тебе это какчество нравится, неделю поносил туфли и отлетел каблук?* "How do you like the quality of these shoes! I've only been wearing them for a week, and the heel's already fallen off!"

КАЛАБА́ШКИ, калаба́шек, *pl.* Money. ♦ *Калабашек явно на билет не хватает.* "We don't have enough cash for a ticket."

КАЛА́Ш, -а́, *m., army.* A Kalashnikov (automatic rifle). ♦ *Ты стрелял из калаша?* "Have you ever used a 'Kalash'?"

КАЛГА́Н, -а, *m., neg.* Head. ♦ *Калган что-то болит.* "I've got a headache."

КА́ЛИКИ, ка́лик, *pl., youth.* Pills, narcotics. ♦ *Сколько ты уже заглотил калик?* "How many pills have you swallowed so far?"

КАЛИ́ТКА, -и, *f., joc.* A zipper in slacks, fly (lit., gate). ♦ *Затвори калитку!* "Close your fly!"

КАЛЫ́МИТЬ/ЗАКАЛЫ́МИТЬ. To earn, make money (from калым, "dowry"). ♦ *Мы хорошо закалымили на стройке.* "We earned a lot on that construction job."

КА́МЕШЕК, ка́мешка, *m., army.* A kilometer (lit., a little stone). ♦ *Ещё камешек, и мы дома.* "One more kilometer and we'll be home."

КАМСА́, -ы́, *f., collect., crim.* Young, inexperienced thieves (lit., small fish, typically eaten smoked and salted and accompanied by beer. ♦ *Этот киоск камса брала, много следов оставили.* "The people who robbed this kiosk were small fry — look at all the evidence they left."

КАНАРÉЙКА, -и, *f., youth, obs.* Police patrol car (lit., canary; from the yellow color of the cars). ♦ *Опять канарейка во дворе стоит, что случилось?* "How come there's a 'canary' in the yard again?"

КАНÁТЬ/ПОКАНÁТЬ, *youth.* To go. ♦ *Канай отсюда, пока цел!* "Get out of here while you still can!"

КАНИФÓЛИТЬ/ЗАКАНИФÓЛИТЬ МОЗГИ́, *idiom.* To try repeatedly to talk someone into doing something, to persuade. ♦ *Не надо мне мозги канифолить, не буду я продавать дом.* "You don't need to continue trying to talk me into it; I'm not going to sell the house."

КАНТОВÁТЬСЯ/ПЕРЕКАНТОВÁТЬ-СЯ. To spend time (lit., to maneuver or jockey something heavy or awkward). ♦ *Вы здесь ночь перекантуйтесь, а завтра в гостиницу.* "You can spend the night here tonight, but tomorrow you'll have to go to a hotel."

КАНТÓВЩИК, -а, *m., crim., neg.* One who avoids or shirks work. ♦ *Он давно в кантовщиках ходит, на него не рассчитывай, он работать не будет.* "He's a slacker. You can't count on him to do any work at all."

КÁНТРИ, *f., indecl., youth.* A country house, dacha (from Eng. "country"). ♦ *Что вы на кантри делали?* "What did you do in the country?"

КАНТРÓВЫЙ, -ая, -ое, *youth, neg.* Rural, provincial, from the sticks (cf. **кáнтри**). ♦ *Он же кантровый, что с ним говорить.* "He's such a hick, there's no use talking to him."

КАНТРУ́ШНИК, -а, *m., youth, neg.* A country bumpkin, hick, provincial (cf. **кáнтри**). ♦ *Кантрушники приехали на совещание.* "The country people came to the meeting."

КАНТРУ́ШНИЦА, -ы, *f., youth, neg.* See **кантру́шник.**

КÁНЦУР, -а, *m., rude.* A penis. ♦ *Таким канцуром ты насквозь проткнёшь.* "With a prick like that you'll puncture me right through." ●**Насáживать/насади́ть на кáнцур,** see under **насáживать.**

КАНЮ́ЧИТЬ/ЗАКАНЮ́ЧИТЬ, *neg.* To nag, to pester with requests (lit., to cry). ♦ *Не канючь, не куплю я тебе эту игру.* "Stop pestering me, I'm not going to buy that game."

КÁПАТЬ/НАКÁПАТЬ, *neg.* To inform on, report (lit., to drop [water] on someone). ♦ *Кто же мог накапать, что мы его избили, не пойму.* "I don't understand who could have informed on us for beating him up." ●**Кáпать на мóзги,** *idiom, neg.* To bore, be insistent, be wearisome (lit., to drip on someone's brains). ♦ *Не капай на мозги, всё равно я не поверю этому.* "Don't keep insisting — I won't believe it anyhow." **С концá кáпает у когó-л.,** see under **с.**

КАПÉЦ, *m.* Disaster, death (from конец, the end). ♦ *Если сейчас не подвезут снаряды, нам капец, не продержимся и часу.* "If they don't supply us with shells now, we won't hold out for even an hour—it's curtains for us."

КÁПЛЯ, -и, *f., army.* A bomb (lit., a drop).

КÁПОЧКА: По кáпочке, *idiom.* A little to drink, a glass (from капля, "a drop"). ♦ *Давай наливай всем по капочке!* "Pour everyone a glass!"

КАПУ́СТА, -ы, *f. youth.* Money (lit., cabbage). ♦ *Капусты нет, что делать будем?* "We're out of money. What should we do?" ●**Рéзать (руби́ть) капу́сту,** see under **рéзать.**

КАРАПÉТ, -а, *m., neg.* A short man. ♦ *Сначала в ВДВ только карапетов брали, а сейчас все парни рослые, техника позволяет брать всех.* "At first they only trained shorties as paratroopers, but modern equipment enables them to take tall guys as well."

КАРÁСИК: Буль-бýль карáсик, see under **буль-бýль.**

КАРÁСЬ, -ся́, *m., crim.* A wide-hipped

woman (lit., a carp). ♦*Ну ты и карася себе нашёл!* "What a broad-beamed gal you found yourself!"

КАРАЧУ́Н, -а, *m.* Death (lit., a Russian pagan evil spirit). ♦*Когда карачун придет, не угадаешь.* "No one knows when his number will come up."

КАРДА́Н, -а, *m., joc.* A hand (lit., an axle). ♦*Держи кардан!* "Let's shake hands on it!"

КАРДИ́Ф, -а, *m., crim.* Black bread. ♦*Мне кардиф надоел, у кого есть белый?* "I'm sick of black bread. Where can I get some white?"

КАРКАЛЫ́К, -а, *m., rude.* A penis. ♦*Каркалык отрастил, а ума всё нет.* "You've got a big prick but no mind." •**Наса́живать/насади́ть на каркалы́к,** see under **наса́живать.**

КАРМА́Н: Держи́ карма́н ши́ре, see under **держа́ть. Утю́жить карма́ны,** see under **утю́жить.**

КАРТА́ВЫЙ, -ого, *m., neg.* A nickname for Lenin, referring to his guttural speech. ♦*Когда же картавого уберут из Мавзолея?* "When are they going to move Old Funny Voice out of the Mausoleum?"

КАРТАФА́Н, -а, *m., army.* Potatoes. ♦*– Картафана ещё много, с голода не помрём.* "We've still got plenty of potatoes, so at least we won't starve to death."

КАРТЁЖ, -а, *m.* Card playing, card games. ♦*У них там всю ночь идёт картёж.* "They play cards there all night."

КАРТО́ШКА, -и, *f., crim.* A hand grenade. ♦*Нам бы пару картошек, тогда бы отбились от ментов.* "If we had some grenades we'd blast our way out of the police cover."

КА́РТЫ: Ре́заться в ка́рты, see under **ре́заться.**

КА́ССА: В ка́ссу, *idiom.* Opportunely, at the right time. ♦*Ты в кассу пришёл.* "You've come at just the right moment." **Не в ка́ссу,** *idiom, youth.* Mistaken, wrong. ♦*Это ты совсем не в кассу говоришь.* "What you're saying is completely off the mark." **Пролета́ть/про-**

лете́ть ми́мо ка́ссы, see under **пролета́ть.**

КАССЕ́ТНИК, -а, *m.* A cassette player. ♦*Не забудь взять свой кассетник.* "Don't forget to bring your cassette player."

КА́СТОМЕР, -а, *m., business.* A client, customer (from Eng. "customer"). ♦*Это наш старый кастомер, надо ему сделать скидку.* "He's an old customer of ours, so he gets a discount."

КАСТРЮ́ЛЯ, -и, *f., neg.* A head (lit., a saucepan). ♦*У тебя совсем кастрюля не варит!* "You're not thinking clearly!" **2.** *Army.* A helmet. ♦*Американские кастрюли легче наших.* "American helmets are lighter than ours."

КАТАВА́СИЯ, -и, *f.* **1.** A mess, hullabaloo, commotion. ♦*Продавали сапоги, там такая поднялась катавасия, я и ушёл.* "There was such a mob scene when they put the boots on sale that I simply left."

КАТАСТРО́ЙКА, -и, *f., joc.* Perestroika. Gorbachev's reforms (by wordplay on перестройка and катастрофа, "catastrophe"). ♦*Теперь все поняли, куда нас катастройка привела — к финишу.* "Now it's obvious to everyone that catastroika has brought us to ruin."

КАТА́ТЬ¹/ПОКАТА́ТЬ, *crim.* To play cards (lit., to roll). ♦*Ну, будем ещё катать или всё?* "Well, shall we keep playing, or have you had enough?"

КАТА́ТЬ²/НАКАТА́ТЬ. To write something quickly, to jot down. ♦*Я успел накатать два письма, пока ты брился.* "I managed to write two quick letters in the time it took you to shave."

КАТИ́ТЬ/ПОКАТИ́ТЬ балло́н, *idiom, neg.* To be annoyed with someone, pick on someone (lit., to roll a tire at someone). ♦*Что ты на меня баллон катишь, не брал я твои книги.* "Why are you picking on me? I'm not the one who took your books."

КАТИ́ТЬСЯ/ДОКАТИ́ТЬСЯ, *neg.* To go into decline, let oneself go, hit the skids. ♦*Он докатился до того, что уже попрошайничает на базаре.* "He's sunk so low that now he's actually begging in the marketplace." •**Кати́сь колба́сой (колба́ской) (кати́сь колба́ской по Ма́лой Спа́сской)**, *idiom, rude.* Get out of here! (lit., roll like a sausage). ♦*Ну-ка, катись колбасой, тебя сюда не звали.* "Get yourself out of here. You weren't invited!" **Кати́сь отсю́да**, *idiom, rude.* Scram, get out of here. ♦*Катись отсюда, пока по шее не получил.* "Get out of here before you get it in the neck."

КАТМАНДÉНЬ, -и, *f., rude.* Junk, something worthless or bad (by wordplay on **Катманду́** and **мандéнь**). ♦*Что это за катмандень? Я это пить не буду.* "What kind of junk is this? I'm not going to drink it."

КАТМАНДУ́: Иди́ ты в Катманду́! see under **идти́**.

КАТÓК, катка́, *m., joc.* A bald patch (lit., a skating-rink). ♦*Каток всё растёт, скоро совсем облысею.* "My bald patch is getting bigger and bigger, soon I'll be completely bald."

КАТРА́Н, -а, *m., crim.* A hangout of cardsharps. ♦*Ты в этот катран не ходи, тебя быстро обчистят.* "Don't go to that den of cardsharps — they'll pick you clean."

КАТУ́ШКА, -и, *f., neg.* An unshapely, unattractive woman (lit.. a spool, bobbin). ♦*Как можно любить такую катушку!* "How could anyone fall for that bobbin!" •**На всю кату́шку**, *idiom.* With all one's might, as much as possible. ♦*Жми на всю катушку!* "Drive as fast as you can!"

КА́ТЯ, -и, *f., obs.* A hundred rubles, a hundred-ruble bill (a "Katie," named for Catherine the Great, under whom the first such bills were issued). ♦*Дай ещё одну катю для ровного счёта.* "Add another hundred to make a round sum."

КА́ФА, -ы, *f., crim., obs.* A kopeck. ♦*У тебя кафа есть?* "Have you got a kopeck?"

КАЦА́П, -а, *m., neg., rude.* A Russian (from the point of view of non-Russians, esp. Ukrainians; with special reference to Russian pronunciation). ♦*На Украину сейчас кацапы почти не ездят.* "These days there are hardly any Russkies going to Ukraine." •**Шёл хохо́л, насра́л на пол, шёл кацáп, зубáми — цап!** A hostile rhyming phrase used by non-Russians, esp. Ukrainians, for taunting Russians; lit., "A Cossack went and crapped on the floor, along came a Russky and slurped it up" (cf. **хохо́л**).

•**Кацáп, за я́йца цап**, *idiom, rude.* A hostile rhyming phrase aimed against Russians (lit., If you see a Russky, grab him by the balls).

КАЦА́ПЩИНА, -ы, *f., joc.* Russia (cf. **кацáп**). ♦*Ну как у вас там в кацапщине жизнь?* "So how's life over there in Russkyland?"

КАЦÓ, *m., indecl.* A Georgian (from the Georgian word for friend). ♦*Где этот кацо живёт?* "Where does that Georgian guy live?"

КАЧА́ЛКА, -и, *f., youth.* A workout room, exercise center (cf. **кача́ться**). ♦*Кто вас тренирует в качалке?* "Who's your trainer at the workout center?"

КАЧА́ТЬ/НАКАЧА́ТЬ: Кача́ть/накача́ть му́скулы, *idiom.* To do bodybuilding exercises. ♦*Он начал качать мускулы, сейчас все качают.* "He started pumping iron, and now everyone's doing it." **Кача́ть права́**, *idiom, neg.* To be demanding, make a lot of demands. ♦*Ты здесь права не качай, никто тебя слушать не будет.* "Don't be so demanding! No one around here is going to pay attention to you."

КАЧА́ТЬ/СКАЧА́ТЬ. To get information with a computer (lit., to pump). ♦*Я из Интернета скачал его новый роман.* "I got his new novel on the internet."

КАЧА́ТЬСЯ/НАКАЧА́ТЬСЯ. To do gymnastic exercises, bodybuilding (cf. **кача́лка**). ♦*Тебе надо качаться по утрам, ты ослаб.* "You've gotten flabby; you should work out every morning."

КАЧÉЛЬ: Туда́/туды́ его́ (её, их) в качéль, see under **туда́**.

КАЧМА́Н, -а, *m., youth.* Someone who

goes in for athletics, gymnastics, body-building (cf. **кача́ться**). ♦*У нас в классе все качманы.* "Everyone in our class is a jock."

КАЧО́К, качка́, *m., youth.* See **качма́н.**

КА́ШЕЛЬ, ка́шля, *m., crim.* Complaints (lit., coughing). ♦*Кончай кашель, все так сейчас живут.* "Stop whining! Everyone has it hard nowadays."

КА́ШЛЯТЬ: Будь здоро́в, не ка́шляй! see under **будь.**

КАЩЕ́Й, -я, *m.* A thin, gaunt person (After Кащей Бессмертный, a bony, thin character in Russian folktales). ♦*Ты стал прямо как Кащей.* "You've turned into skin and bones."

КВА́КАЛО, -а, *n., neg.* A mouth. (From квакать, "to croak"). ♦*Квакало у тебя не закрывается, ты помолчал бы минуту!* "You never can keep your mouth shut.!"

КВА́КАТЬ/КВА́КНУТЬ. To drink quickly (lit., to croak). ♦*Где мы с тобой квакнем?* "Where can we go to toss back a quick one?"

КВАРТИРА́НТ, -а, *m., crim.* A convict, prison inmate (lit., a tenant). ♦*Новых квартирантов привезли.* "They've shipped in some new 'tenants.'"

КВА́СИТЬ/ЗАКВА́СИТЬ. To have a long drinking session (from the long process of preparing квас). ♦*С кем ты это вчера квасил?* "Who was that you were drinking with yesterday?"

КВЁЛЫЙ, -ая, -ое, *neg.* Limp, inert, slack. ♦*От жары все сидят квёлые.* "Everyone is drooping from the heat."

КВЕ́РХУ МО́РЕМ, *idiom, army.* Upside down. ♦*Поправь флаг, не видишь, висит кверху морем.* "Fix the flag, don't you see it's hanging upside down?"

КВИТА́ТЬСЯ/ПОКВИТА́ТЬСЯ. To pay back, in a positive or negative sense; to avenge oneself; to pay up, settle accounts. ♦*Я с тобой ещё за это поквитаюсь.* "I'll get back at you for this." ♦*Давай поквитаемся. Ты мне должен 30 долларов.* "Let's settle accounts. You owe me 30 dollars."

КВИ́ТЫ, *pred. use.* Even-steven, quits,

settled up (from Eng. "quits"; cf. квитанция). ♦*Вот тебе стольник и мы квиты.* "Here's another hundred, and now our accounts are settled."

КЕ́ГЛЯ, -и, *f., joc.* A fist (lit., skittles). ♦*Кегля у тебя не дай бог, убьёшь с одного удара.* "With that enormous fist, you could kill someone with a single blow."

КЕЙС, -а, *m.* Briefcase, attaché case (from Eng. "case"). ♦*Посмотри в кейсе, ты все бумаги взял?* "Look in the briefcase. Have you taken all the papers?"

КЕНА́Ф, -а, *m., crim.* Hashish. ♦*Идём к нему, у него можно по дешёвке купить кенаф.* "We can buy hash cheaper from him."

КЕГУРЯ́ТНИК, -а́, *m.* The high front bumper on a jeep. From кенгуру, kangaroo. ♦*Мне только кенгурятник в аварии помяли.* "I only smashed the front bumper in the accident."

КЕНТ, -а́, *m., youth.* A friend, pal. ♦*Это твой новый кент?* "Is that your new friend?"

КЕНТА́ВР, -а, *m., army.* A helicopter (lit., a centaur). ♦*Сколько для нас кентавров надо? Скажем, пять—в самый раз.* "How many choppers do we need? Five would be just right."

КЕНТОВА́ТЬ/ЗАКЕНТОВА́ТЬ. To be friendly with someone. See **кент.** ♦*Не первый год кентуемся, я тебе верю.* "We've been buddies for years, I trust you."

КЕРОСИ́Н, -а, *m., joc.* Liquor (lit., kerosene). ♦*Керосин купил?* "Did you buy the liquor?" ●**Де́ло па́хнет кероси́ном,** see under **де́ло.**

КЕРОСИ́НИТЬ/ЗАКЕРОСИ́НИТЬ. To drink, get drunk. ♦*А где они керосинят, в гараже?* "Where do they do their drinking — in the garage?"

КЕРЮ́ХА, -и, *m., obs.* A friend, acquaintance. ♦*Эй, керюха, иди сюда.* "Come over here, buddy."

КЕФ, -а, *m., crim.* A dose of drugs. ♦*Мне всего один кеф надо.* "I need just one fix."

КИДА́ЛА, -ы, *m., neg.* A cardsharp, con artist (cf. **кида́ть**). ♦*Будь осторожен, когда будешь продавать машину, на* *рынке полно кидал.* "Watch out when you go to sell your car. The market is full of con artists."

КИДА́ТЬ/КИ́НУТЬ, *youth.* To cheat, defraud (lit., to throw). ♦ *Меня вчера кинули на две тысячи.* "Yesterday I was cheated out of two thousand." •**Кида́ть/ки́нуть западло́,** *idiom.* To act dishonestly. See **западло** and **бросать подля́нку.** ♦ *Не вздумай кинуть западло, здесь сразу голову оторвут.* "Don't even think of trying something shady! In this outfit they'll tear your head off for it." •**Кида́ть/ ки́нуть на брига́ду,** *idiom, crim.* To gang-rape. ♦ *Они кинули её на бригаду, получили семь лет.* "They got seven years for gang-raping her." •**Кида́ть/ки́нуть через плешь,** *idiom.* To cheat, to deceive. ♦ *Он так и не понял, кто его так кинул через плешь и за что.* "He never found out who gypped him like that and why."

КИДА́ТЬСЯ/КИ́НУТЬСЯ В ШУРШ, *idiom, youth.* (Cf. **шурш**.) **1.** To quarrel, to make a scene. **2.** To run away. ♦ *Как услышишь сирену, кидайся в шурш.* "If you hear a siren, run for your life."

КИДНЯ́К, -а́, *m.* Cheating, deceit (from кидать, to cheat). See **кида́ть.** ♦ *Такого кидняка от тебя не ожидал.* "I never expected such cheating from you!"

КИ́НУТЬСЯ, *perf.* To die (lit., to rush). ♦ *Как бы он не кинулся с горя.* "I'm afraid he might die of grief."

КИ́ЛЛЕР-ПРО́ФИ, ки́ллера-про́фи, *m.* A professional killer. ♦ *Киллер-профи может пристрелить и за тысячу баксов.* "A professional hit-man will do a job for a mere thousand bucks."

КИМА́РИТЬ/ЗАКИМА́РИТЬ. To sleep, doze. ♦ *Хорошо бы закимарить на полчасика.* "A half hour's nap would be good right now."

КИНД, -а́, *m., youth.* A child (from Ger. "Kind"). ♦ *У неё кинды есть?* "Does she have any children?"

КИ́НДЕР, -а. See **кинд.**

КИ́ПЕШ, -а, *m., youth, neg.* Noise, disorder (from кипеть, "to boil"). ♦ *Что здесь за кипеш?* "What's the ruckus

here?" •**Поднима́ть/подня́ть ки́пеш,** see under **поднима́ть.**

КИР, -а, *m., youth.* Drink, liquor (cf. **киря́ть**). ♦ *Что-то кира мало.* "We haven't got much to drink."

КИРЗА́, -ы́, *f., army.* **1.** Imitation-leather boots. ♦ *Когда я уже сниму кирзу?* "I can't wait to get these boots off." **2.** Pearl barley, lumpy cooked grain. ♦ *Опять эта кирза на обед!* "Lumpy kasha for dinner *again*?!"

КИРЗАЧИ́, -е́й, *pl., army.* Boots made of artificial leather (from кирзовые сапоги, ки́рза, a surface of soil). ♦ *Мажь не мажь их салом, все равно воду кирзачи пропускают.* "These 'kirzachi' leak no matter how much you grease them."

КИРЮ́ХА, -и, *m.* **1.** A friend (lit., a nickname for Кирилл). ♦ *Он мой давний кирюха.* "He's an old friend of mine." **2.** A drinking buddy (from кир, кирять). ♦ *Эти кирюхи с тобой пришли, тогда налей им.* "If those guys who came with you are your drinking buddies, pour them something to drink."

КИРЯ́ТЬ/КИРНУ́ТЬ. To drink (cf. **кир**). ♦ *Что у тебя кирнуть есть?* "What do you have to drink?"

КИС, -а, *m., youth, obs.* A kiss (from Eng. "kiss"). ♦ *Ну ещё один кис и я пошёл.* "Give me another kiss and I'll be on my way."

КИ́СА, -ы, *f.* A girl, girlfriend (lit., cat; cf. **кис**). ♦ *Ты свою кису пригласил на танцы?* "Have you invited your girlfriend to the dance?"

КИ́САТЬСЯ/ПОКИ́САТЬСЯ, *youth, obs.* To kiss (cf. **кис**). ♦ *Прекратите кисаться.* "Enough kissing."

КИ́СЛО: Не ки́сло! *adv.* Excellently, very well (lit., not sourly). ♦ *Они в Сочи не кисло отдохнули.* "They had a great vacation in Sochi."

КИСЛОТА́, -ы́, *f., youth.* LSD (lit., acid). ♦ *У тебя ещё осталась кислота?* "Do you have any more acid?"

КИСТЕВО́Й, -а́я, -о́е, *youth.* **1.** Luxurious, plush (of things). ♦ *Куртка у него кистевая.* "He's got a very luxurious coat." **2.** Wealthy, rich (of people). ♦ *Я его знаю, он парень кистевой.* "I know him — he's a really rich guy."

КИТАЁЗА, -ы, *m., neg., rude.* A Chinese. ♦ *У китаёз реформы лучше идут, чем у нас.* "Those Chinks are doing better with their reforms than we are."

КИТА́ЙСКИЙ ТЕЛЕВИ́ЗОР, *idiom, business.* Manual examination of baggage at customs (lit., Chinese television).

КИ́ЧА, -и, *f., crim.* A prison. ♦ *Там в киче, много наших встретил.* "I ran into a lot of our friends in the prison there."

КИЧМА́Н, -а, *m., crim.* A prison. ♦ *В какой кичман нас везут?* "What prison are they taking us to?"

КИШКИ́ МАРШ ИГРА́ЮТ, *idiom, joc.* My stomach is growling with hunger (lit., my innards are playing a march). ♦ *Пойдём в столовую, что-то кишки марш играют.* "Let's go to the cafeteria — I'm famished."

КИШКОДРО́М, -а, *m., youth, neg.* A poor-quality cafeteria serving as the dining room of a school, plant, or other place of work (lit., gut-field). ♦ *Неохота идти в наш кишкодром, там сейчас очередь.* "I don't want to go to our cafeteria because there's a long line there at this hour."

КИШКОПРА́В, -а, *m., crim.* Switchblade (lit., gut-straightener, after костоправ, "bonesetter"). ♦ *Возьми кишкоправ на всякий случай.* "Take along your switchblade just in case."

КИШЛА́К, -á, *m., youth, joc.* A beer bar (lit., an eastern mountain village, with reference to the inferior sanitary conditions). ♦ *Заглянем в кишлак, пивка попьём.* "Let's stop in at the bar and have a beer."

КЛА́ПАН, -а, *m., youth, neg.* A mouth (lit., valve). ♦ *Закрой клапан!* "Shut up!"

КЛА́ССНЫЙ, -ая, -ое. Good, excellent (from Eng. "class"). ♦ *Это классный компьютер.* "That's a great computer."

КЛАСТЬ/ПОЛОЖИ́ТЬ: Класть/поло-жи́ть на кого́-л. (с прибо́ром), *idiom, rude.* To feel or express contempt for someone, spit on someone (lit., to put [excrement] on someone [with a whole set of tableware]). ♦ *Положил я на него.* "I felt the utmost contempt for him."

Класть/положи́ть глаз на кого́/что-л., *idiom.* To take a liking to, to be sexually attracted to, to notice with interest. ♦ *Кажется, он на тебя глаз положил.* "It looks like he's attracted to you."

• **Класть/положи́ть пода́льше, побли́же брать/взять,** *idiom.* Lit., The farther you hide something, the easier it is to get it back.

КЛЕВА́ТЬ/ПОКЛЕВА́ТЬ, *joc.* To eat a little, have a bite (lit., to peck). ♦ *Поклюй, вот мясо.* "Here's some meat — have a bite to eat."

КЛЁВО, *adv., youth.* Well, excellently. ♦ *Мы клёво отдохнули в горах.* "We had a wonderful vacation in the mountains."

КЛЕВОТА́, -ы́, *f., pred. use, youth, pos.* Something excellent, good. ♦ *Эти грибы — клевота!* "These mushrooms are fantastic!"

КЛЁВЫЙ, -ая, -ое, *youth.* Fashionable, classy (cf. **клёво**). ♦ *Клёвая у него рубашка!* "What a stunning shirt he's wearing!"

КЛЕ́ИТЬ/СКЛЕ́ИТЬ, *youth.* To become acquainted with a girl, pick up a girl, go out with a girl (lit., to glue). ♦ *Когда ты успел её склеить?* "When did you manage to start going out with her?"

КЛЕПА́ТЬ/НАКЛЕПА́ТЬ. To do or produce something quickly and carelessly (lit., to rivet). ♦ *Сколько же ты картин наклепал за неделю?* "How many pictures did you churn out in one week?"

КЛЁПОК НЕ ХВАТА́ЕТ у кого́-л., *idiom, neg.* Used of someone stupid or foolish (lit., his rivets aren't holding). ♦ *У него что, клёпок не хватает, ему же нельзя пить.* "He shouldn't drink; he just falls apart when he does."

КЛИ́ВЕР, -а, *m., crim. & youth.* A necktie (lit., a type of sail). ♦ *Где ты такой лохматый кливер купил?* "Where did you get this stylish tie!"

КЛИ́ЗМА: Ста́вить/поста́вить кли́зму, see under **ста́вить.**

КЛИ́КАТЬ/КЛИ́КНУТЬ. To click, to push a button on a computer. ♦ *Кликни "Мои документы", там найди файл "Письма".* "Click on 'My Documents,' then find the file called 'Letters'."

КЛИКУ́ХА, -и, *f., crim. & youth.* A name, nickname. ♦ *Как твоя кликуха?* "What's your nickname?"

КЛИКУ́ШНИК, -а, *m., crim. & youth,* A church robber. ♦ *Кликушники неплохо сегодня зарабатывают, иконы сейчас в цене.* "Church robbers are making big profits these days, with icons fetching so much on the market."

КЛИ́НИТЬ/ЗАКЛИ́НИТЬ. 1. To take a great interest in, to go mad about something. From клин, wedge. ♦ *Соседа заклинило на попсе.* "My neighbor is crazy about pop music." **2.** To repeat over and over. ♦ *Тебя что, клинит, ты уже сто раз вспомнил праздник.* "What's with you? You talk about it all the time. You've already recalled that holiday a hundred times."

КЛИНИ́ЧЕСКИЙ СЛУ́ЧАЙ, *idiom, joc., neg.* A crazy person (lit., a clinical case). ♦ *Он всё время говорит о себе, прямо клинический случай.* "He's constantly talking about himself — clearly a clinical case!"

КЛИПА́К, -а, *m.* A video clip. ♦ *Этот клипак видеть не могу, отморозки делали.* "I cannot watch that video clip, it was made by head cases."

КЛИФТ, -á, *m., crim.* A jacket, overcoat. ♦ *Где ты такой клифт купил?* "Where did you get that jacket?"

КЛО́П, -á, *m.* A hidden microphone (lit., a bug). ♦ *Как тут с клопами, чисто?* "What's the situation with bugs here? Is it clean?" ● **Дави́ть клопа́,** see under **дави́ть.**

КЛОПО́ВНИК, -а, *m., neg.* A dirty place (from клоп, "bedbug"). ♦ *Это не гостиница, а клоповник, я здесь ночевать не хочу.* "I don't intend to stay in this fleapit."

КЛО́УЗ, -а, *m., youth.* See **клоус.**

КЛО́УС, -а, *m., youth.* Clothes, a garment (from Eng. "clothes"). ♦ *Почём клоус?* "How much is that garment?"

КЛУБНИ́ЧКА, -и, *f.* An erotic scene or feature in a film or novel (lit., a strawberry). ♦ *Этот роман с клубничкой.* "This novel has some sexy stuff in it."

КЛЮКА́, -й, *f., crim.* A church (lit., walking stick, crutch, staff). ♦ *Там старая клюка стоит, недалеко живёт наш кореш.* "Our friend lives not far from where the old church is."

КЛЮКА́РЬ, -я́, *m., crim.* A church robber. ♦ *Это работа опытного клюкаря.* "This is the work of an experienced church robber."

КЛЮ́КАТЬ/КЛЮ́КНУТЬ. To have a drink. ♦ *Давай клюкнем по 100 грамм.* "Let's have us a little nip."

КЛЮ́ШКА, -и, *f., joc.* A foot (lit., hockey puck). ♦ *Убери свою клюшку, пройти нельзя.* "Move your foot — you're blocking the passage."

КЛЯ́ЧА, -и, *f., neg.* An ugly old woman (lit., an old mare). ♦ *Что ты в этой кляче нашёл?* "What do you see in that old hag?"

КНА́ЦАТЬ, *imperf. only, crim.* To guard. ♦ *Этот магазин, знаешь, как кнацают, забудь о нём, там делать нечего.* "Forget about that store; it's too heavily guarded for us to accomplish anything there."

КНО́КАТЬ/ЗАКНО́КАТЬ, НАКНО́-КАТЬ, *youth.* To see, notice. ♦ *Я тебя закнокал возле кинотеатра сразу.* "I noticed you right away near the movie theater."

КНУРЬ, -я́, *m., crim.* A member of a cooperative enterprise. ♦ *У этого кнуря деньги водятся.* "That entrepreneur is always flush with cash."

КОБЁЛ, -а, *m., crim., neg.* A lesbian who plays a masculine role (from **кобе́ль,** "dog"). ♦ *У них там уже есть свой кобёл.* "That set already has its butch member."

КОБЕЛИ́ТЬСЯ, *imperf. only, neg.* To run after women, be a skirt-chaser. ♦ *Они всё время на танцах, кобелятся.* "They're always trying to pick up girls at dances."

КОБЕ́ЛЬ, -я́, *m., neg.* A highly sexed or

oversexed man (lit., a he-dog). ♦*Он никак не успокоится, кобель несчастный.* "That poor dog just can't calm himself down."

КОБЕ́НИТЬСЯ/ЗАКОБЕ́НИТЬСЯ, *neg.* To be stubborn, resistant, uncooperative. ♦*Зря ты кобенишься, выходи за него замуж.* "Don't be so temperamental — go ahead and marry the guy!"

КОБЛУ́ХА, -и, *f., crim. & youth.* A passive or feminine lesbian (from каблук, "heel"). ♦*У неё подруги все коблухи.* "All her friends are 'heels.'"

КО́БРА, -ы, *f., crim.* **1.** A prostitute. ♦*Сколько эта кобра за час берёт?* "How much does that prostitute charge for an hour?" **2.** A debt-collection agency or agent. ♦*Пора кобру нанимать, так просто он деньги не вернёт.* "It's time to hire a 'cobra'. He's not going to return the money otherwise.

КОБЫ́ЛА, -ы, *f., neg.* A large girl or woman (lit., a mare). ♦*Ну и кобыла, когда она успела вырасти?* "When did she manage to turn into such a big girl?!" •**Кобы́ле под хвост,** *idiom, neg.* In vain, to no effect (lit., under a mare's tail). ♦*Деньги выбросили кобыле под хвост.* "With that purchase they were simply throwing their money under a mare's tail."

КОБЫ́ЛКА, -и, *f., crim.* A high-spirited gathering, jolly company. ♦*Там кобылка завелась, все ржут, веселятся.* "There's a high-spirited crowd there, laughing and having a good time."

КОВЫРЯ́ЛКА, -и, *f., crim., neg.* A female masturbator (from ковырять, "to pick", as at a wound). ♦*Ей мужиков не надо, она стала ковырялкой.* "She has no more need of men; she's taken to masturbating."

КО́ГТИ: Пока́зывать/показа́ть ко́гти, see under **пока́зывать. Рвать ко́гти,** see under **рвать.**

КО́ДЛА, -ы, *f., neg.* A group, gang. ♦*Что там за кодла во дворе?* "Who's that crowd in the yard?"

КО́ЖА: Втира́ть в ко́жу, see under **втира́ть. Ни ко́жи, ни ро́жи,** see under **ни.**

КОЖА́Н, -á, *m., youth.* A leather jacket. ♦*Сколько стоит такой кожан?* "How much does a leather jacket like that cost?"

КОЗА́, -ы́, *f.* Lit., a she-goat. **1.** A fidgety, restless girl. ♦*У тебя дочь — коза, на месте не сидит.* "Your daughter is so fidgety she just can't sit still!" **2.** A foolish, stupid girl or woman. ♦*Коза и есть коза, опять всё перепутала.* "What a nanny goat! She's gone and got everything mixed up again."

КОЗЁЛ: Козёл воню́чий, *idiom, rude.* A bastard, scoundrel (lit., smelly goat). ♦*Зачем ты его ударил, козёл воню́чий?* "What did you hit him for, you filthy bastard!" **Козёл шкребу́чий,** *idiom, rude.* A bastard, scoundrel (lit., scratching goat). ♦*Пошёл отсюда, козёл шкребучий!* "Get out of here, you bastard!"

КОЗЛЕТО́Н, -а, *m., joc.* A high, unpleasant voice (lit., goat-tone). ♦*У него козлетон, а не голос.* "He's got a goat-tone for a voice."

КОЗЛИ́НАЯ ПОРО́ДА, *idiom, rude.* A stubborn person (lit., goat-breed). ♦*А ты, козлиная порода, всё делаешь по-своему.* "You stubborn goat, you always have to do everything your own way."

КОЗЛИ́ТЬСЯ/ЗАКОЗЛИ́ТЬСЯ, *neg.* To be stubborn, difficult, contrary. ♦*Что ты козлишься, всё равно это делать надо.* "Don't be stubborn; you'll have to give in in the end anyhow."

КОЗЛОДО́Й, -я, *m., rude.* A stubborn person (lit., goat-milker). ♦*Сколько тебе, козлодой, можно говорить: убирай за собой!* "You stubborn goat — how many times do I have to tell you to clean up after yourself!"

КОЗЛОТЕ́НЬ, -и, *f.* Nonsense. ♦*Несёшь ты сплошную козлотень.* "You're talking sheer nonsense".

КОЗЫРЁК, козырька́, *m., army, neg.* An officer in charge of keeping a check on soldiers' reliability, loyalty (lit., a vizor or cap-peak). ♦*Тихо, не говори лишнего, козырёк идёт.* "Hush, not another word — here comes the 'vizor.'"

КОЗЯ́ВКА, -и, *f., neg.* An insignificant

person, cipher, mere child (lit., a gnat). ♦*А ты, козявка, цыц, не спорь со старшими.* "Shut up, small fry, don't argue with your elders."

КÓКИ, -ов, *pl., joc.* Testicles (lit., chicken eggs). ♦*На улице холодно, коки мёрзнут.* "It's cold enough out to freeze your balls."

КÓКНУТЬ, *perf.* To kill (from кока, an egg, something easy to break). ♦*Кокнули его за длинный язык, меньше болтаешь, дольше проживёшь.* "He was killed because he didn't know how to keep his mouth shut."

КОКÓСЫ, -ов, *pl., neg.* Testicles (lit., coconuts). ♦*Плохому танцору кокосы мешают.* "A poor dancer will blame his coconuts."

КОЛ, -á, *m., obs.* A ruble (lit., a club, post, stick). ♦*Гони кол!* "Give me a ruble!" •**Кол тебé в глóтку!** *idiom, rude.* Damn you! (lit., a stick in your throat). ♦*Кол тебе в глотку за всё, что ты натворил.* "Damn you for all the mischief you've done!" **Хоть кол на голóве теши,** see under **хоть.**

КОЛБАСИ́ТЬ¹/ЗАКОЛБАСИ́ТЬ, *joc.* To play excitedly, indulge in horseplay, be disorderly (cf. колбаса). ♦*Дети до сих пор колбасят, спать не хотят.* "The children are still horsing around and don't want to go to sleep."

КОЛБАСИ́ТЬ²/НАКОЛБАСИ́ТЬ. To do something poorly, carelessly (cf. колбаса). ♦*Что ты тут наколбасил, ну, кто так работает!* "What a mess you've made there — that's no way to work!"

КОЛБАСИ́ТЬ³/ПРИКОЛБАСИ́ТЬ. To go (cf. колбаса). ♦*Только к вечеру мы приколбасили домой.* "It was getting toward evening by the time we went home."

КОЛБАСНЯ́, -й, *f., neg.* Nonsense, baloney (cf. колбаса). ♦*Не хочу участвовать в этой колбасне с выборами.* "I don't want to take part in this nonsense about elections."

КОЛГОТИ́ТЬСЯ/ЗАКОЛГОТИ́ТЬСЯ. 1. To crowd. ♦*Не колготитесь в кори-*

доре, проходите в комнату. "Don't crowd around in the hallway; go on into the room." **2.** To make an uproar, be upset. ♦*Все сразу заколготились, когда узнали, что денег не будет.* "They all got upset when they found out that there wouldn't be any money."

КОЛДОЁБИНА, -ы, *f., joc.* A pothole, hole in pavement (by wordplay on колдобина and **ёб-**). ♦*Тормози, колдоёбины пошли.* "Slow down, here come some fucking potholes."

КОЛЕБÁТЬ/ЗАКОЛЕБÁТЬ, *neg.* To annoy, wear out (lit., to vibrate, with allusion to **ебáть**). ♦*Ты меня совсем заколебал просьбами.* "You've fucking worn me out with your requests."

КОЛЕНКÓР: Другóй коленкóр, see under **другóй.**

КОЛЁСА, колёс, *pl.* Lit., wheels. **1.** *neg.* Nonsense, garbage, baloney. ♦*Не верь ему, это всё колёса.* "Don't believe him, he's talking nonsense." **2.** *youth.* Shoes. ♦*Эти колёса тебе по размеру?* "Are these shoes your size?" **3.** *youth.* Pills, drugs. ♦*Мне колёса не нужны, я колюсь.* "I shoot up; I don't take pills."

КОЛЁСНИК, -a, *m., youth.* A drug addict, one who takes drugs in the form of pills (cf. **колёса 3**). ♦*Ты этого колёсника знаешь?* "Do you know that pill popper?"

КОЛЕСОВÁТЬ, *youth, neg.* To go, leave (from колесо, "wheel"). ♦*Колесуй отсюда подальше.* "Get out of here!"

КОЛИ́ЧЕСТВО И КÁЧЕСТВО ЗАЕБЛÓ (ЗАТРÁХАЛО) НАС НÁЧИСТО. See under **ебáть.**

КОЛЛЕКТИ́ВКА, -и, *f., crim.* Gang rape (lit., a collective). ♦*Он сидит за коллективку.* "He's serving time for gang rape."

КОЛОБÁХА, -и, *f.* A blow. ♦*Получил пару колобах, понял, кто здесь шеф, или повторить?* "OK, you've already taken two good blows, do you understand who's boss or do you need some more?"

КОЛÓДА, -ы, *f., youth.* A group, set of people (lit., pack of cards). ♦*Ты из чьей колоды, из мишкиной?* "Whose set do you belong to — Misha's?"

КОЛО́ДЕЦ: Упа́сть в коло́дец, see under **упа́сть.**

КОЛОТИ́ТЬСЯ/ПРОКОЛОТИ́ТЬСЯ. To bustle around, be busy (lit., to strike, hammer away). ♦ *Я с этими бумагами колочусь весь вечер, не могу разобраться.* "I've been fussing around with these papers all evening, and I can't make head or tail of them."

КОЛОТУ́Н, -а, *m.* Cold weather, freezing cold (lit., hammering, i.e., shivering from cold). ♦ *Ну и колотун сегодня!* "There's a real cold snap today."

КО́ЛОТЫЙ БОЙ, *idiom, crim.* Marked cards (from колоть, "to prick", referring to the practice of marking the cards with needles). ♦ *Это колотый бой, играть не буду.* "That's a marked deck; I'm not playing!"

КОЛОТЬЁ, -я́, *crim.* Cards, a deck of cards. ♦ *Передай колотьё, мне банковать.* "Hand me the deck; I'm banker."

КОЛО́ТЬСЯ/РАСКОЛО́ТЬСЯ ДО ЖО́ПЫ, *idiom.* To confess, to admit (lit., to be split up to one's ass). ♦ *Колись до жопы, что знаешь, а то ещё получишь!* "Spill it! Tell me everything you know or I'll beat you some more."

КОЛУ́Н, -а, *m., army.* A sentry (lit., a wood-chopper). ♦ *Сколько колунов поставим на ночь?* "How many sentries should we station for the night?"

КОЛУПА́ТЬ/КОЛУПНУ́ТЬ, *crim.* To rob (lit., to pick at, as locks). ♦ *Недавно в нашем доме колупнули квартиру.* "An apartment in our building was robbed recently."

КОЛХО́З: Всем колхо́зом, *idiom, joc.* All together (lit., with the whole collective farm). ♦ *Туда пойдём всем колхозом.* "Let's go there all together."

КОЛЫХА́ТЬ: Он лежи́т и е́ле ды́шет, то́лько яйцами колы́шет, see under **яйцо́. Это кого́-л. не колы́шет,** see under **э́то.**

КОЛЮ́ЧКА, -и, *f., army.* Barbed wire (lit., a thorn, a barb). ♦ *Колючки там везде понатыкали, не пройдёшь.* "It's not possible to simply pass through there,

there's barbed wire everywhere."

КОМЕНДА́НТ, -а, *m., crim.* An experienced prostitute managing younger ones. ♦ *Что-то комендант шумит, обманули её, что ли?* "What's the commandant so upset about? Did someone rip her off?"

КОМИССА́Р, -а, *m., crim.* A robber who impersonates a police officer. ♦ *Вчера комиссары взяли банк.* "Some 'commissars' robbed a bank yesterday."

КОМИССУ́ХА, -и, *f.* A secondhand shop trading on commission. ♦ *Отнеси костюм в комиссуху, пару штук за него дадут.* "If you take that suit to a commission shop, you can get a couple of thousand for it."

КОМИТЕ́ТЧИК, -а, *m.* A KGB-agent (lit., committee man). ♦ *А ты не знал, что это комитетчик?* "You mean you didn't know he's KGB?"

КОММУНЯ́КА, -и, *m., neg.* A communist. ♦ *Коммуняки опять ходят на митинги, хотят, наверное, снова построить коммунизм.* "There go the communists with their meetings again — apparently they want to rebuild communism."

КОМО́Д, -а, *m., army.* A platoon commander (lit., a cupboard). ♦ *Комод сейчас поведёт в наряд.* "The platoon commander is taking them on duty now."

КОМО́К, комка́, *m.* A store that sells on commission (by wordplay on комиссионный магазин, "commission store," and комок, "lump"). ♦ *Надо сдать в комок пару костюмов.* "I've got to bring a couple of suits over to the commission store."

КОМП, -а, *m.* A computer (abbr. of компью́тер). ♦ *Я в компах ни бум-бум.* "When it comes to computers, I don't have a clue."

КОМПА́ШКА, -и, *f.* A group of close friends, a set. ♦ *А что за компашка там собирается?* "What group is that hanging out over there?"

КОМПОЗИ́ТОР, -а, *m.* An informer (lit., a composer). ♦ *Мы вычислим, кто у нас композитор, кто оперу пишет.*

"We'll figure out who's been reporting us to authorities" (lit., who's been composing an opera).

КОМПÓT, -a, *m.* Lit., boiled fruit drink. **1.** *joc.* A bad situation. ♦*Такой компот, никто не пришёл на день рождения.* "Here's a nice kettle of fish! No one came for my birthday." **2.** *youth.* A broth made from poppyheads for use as a narcotic. ♦*Дай хлебнуть компота.* "Let me have a sip of the broth."

КОМПÓСТЕР, -a, *m.* A computer (lit., a ticket punch).

КОМПОСТИ́РОВАТЬ/ЗАКОМПОС-ТИ́РОВАТЬ мозги́, *idiom, neg.* To annoy, pester (lit., to puncture someone's brains, as in punching tram tickets). ♦*Не компостируй мне мозги, всё равно ничего не получишь.* "Stop addling my brain — there's no way you're going to get what you want."

КÓМПРА, -ы, *f.* Compromising materials (abbr. of компроментирующие материалы). ♦*Всю компру уничтожить надо, а то нам не сдобровать.* "Destroy all traces of these compromising materials; they could get us into trouble fast."

КОМПЬ́ЮТЕР, -a, *m., joc.* A computer (distorted from компьютер by wordplay on путать, "to entangle, perplex"). ♦*Ты на компутере можешь работать?* "Do you know how to work a compooter?"

КОМУТОХЕРОВÁТО, *indecl.* Said about an ambulance, imitating the sound of the Japanese language (lit., somebody's feeling bad). See **херовáтый.** ♦*Сзади комутохерово, пропусти, дай дорогу.* "Don't you see that ambulance behind us? Get off the road!"

КОНВÉРТ, -a, *m., crim.* Lit., envelope. A way of interrogating a detained person by making him lie down with his legs pulled up. ♦*Пора ему конверт делать, так он ничего не скажет.* "It's time for him to do the envelope, otherwise he won't talk."

КОНДРÁТИЙ ХВÁТИТ, *idiom.* Lit., paralysis will strike; a warning of dire consequences. ♦*Будешь так пить, кондратий хватит.* "If you drink like

that, you'll be struck down by paralysis."

КОНДЮ́К, -á, *m., crim.* A conductor (of a railroad train). ♦*Спроси у кондюка, чай будет?* "Ask the conductor whether they're going to be serving tea."

КОНÉЦ, концá, *m., rude.* A penis. ♦*Что-то конец болит, надо сходить к врачу.* "I've got a pain in my dick — I'll have to see a doctor." ♦**Конéц — тéлу венéц,** *idiom, joc., rude.* Everything ends up in bed; sex is what everything always leads to (lit., the end [i.e., extremity, prick] is the crown of the body; playing on the saying конец — делу венец, "the completion is the crown of a work"). ♦*Он её уломал, уложил в постель. Как говорится, конец — телу венец.* "He talked her into going to bed with him. As they say, 'the ending is the crown of the body.'" **С концá кáпает у когó-л.,** see under **c.**

КÓНИ, -éй, *pl.* Lit., horses. **1.** An army hockey team. **2.** Parents. ♦*Кони дома?* "Are your folks home?"

КОНИ́НА, -ы, *f.* Lit., horse meat. **1.** Brandy (by wordplay on коньяк). **2.** Meat of poor quality. ♦*Я пирожки с кониной не ем.* "I won't eat those lousy meat pies."

КОНКРÉТНО, *adv.* Excellent, good (lit., particularly). ♦*Мы там конкретно оттянулись.* "We definitely had a great time there."

КОНКРÉТНЫЙ, -ая, -ое. Aggressive, strong-minded. ♦*Там у нас все конкретные пацаны, с ними шутки в сторону.* "Here, with us, everyone is very strong-minded, you can't fool around with us."

КОНС, -a, *m.* A music school, conservatory. ♦*Ты идёшь сегодня в конс?* "Are you going to the conservatory today?"

КОНСÉНСУС, -a, *m., joc.* A penis (lit., consensus, a political term introduced by Gorbachev).

КОНСЕРВАТÓРИЯ, -и, *f., joc.* A factory producing preserved food (from консервы, "tinned food"). ♦*Он работает в консерватории по рыбе.* "He works in a fish conservatory."

КОНСЕ́РВЫ, -ов, *pl., army.* Mines (lit., tin cans). ♦*Консервы поставь на шоссе и уходи.* "Lay the tin cans on the road and get the hell out of here."

КОНСТАТИ́РОВАТЬ фак, *idiom, joc., rude.* To approve or confirm a sex act as a good one (from the idiom констатировать факт, "to confirm a fact"). ♦*Я констатирую удачный фак.* "I consider that a really good fuck!"

КОНТА́ЧИТЬ/ЗАКОНТА́ЧИТЬ. To be acquainted (from Eng. "contact"). ♦*С ним надо законтачить, он человек с весом.* "He's an influential guy — I've got to meet him."

КОНТО́РА, -ы, *f., joc.* **1.** An office. ♦*В какой конторе он работает?* "What office does he work in?" **2.** A security division of the police. ♦*Видишь, вывески нет, значит, контора.* "Look, there's no sign — it must be an office of the security forces."

КОНЦЕПТУА́ЛЬНО, *adv.* Good, excellent (lit., conceptually). ♦*По жизни он пишет музыку концептуально.* "He writes music excellently."

КОНЦЫ́: Концы́ в во́ду, *idiom.* In such a way as to escape notice (lit., with one's guy ropes in the water). ♦*Они недавно квартиру взяли и концы в воду.* "They robbed an apartment without leaving any traces." **С концами,** *idiom.* Completely, altogether (lit., with the guy ropes). ♦*Они уехали с концами.* "They've cleared out lock, stock, and barrel." **Отдава́ть/отда́ть концы́,** see under **отдава́ть.**

КОНЧИ́НА, -ы, *f., rude.* Semen, come (from кончать, "to have an orgasm"). ♦*Постирай простыню, она вся в кончине.* "Wash the sheet; it's all covered with come."

КОНЬ, -я́, *m., youth.* Father (lit., steed). ♦*Конь дома?* "Is your old man at home?" ●**Конь в кожа́ном пальто́,** *idiom, rude.* A penis (lit., stallion in a leather overcoat). The phrase is usually used as a response to the question "Кто?" ●**Конь с я́йцами,** *idiom, rude.* A strong, robust man (lit., a horse with balls).

♦*Ему не тяжело тащить мешок? — Да ты что! Он же конь с яйцами!* "Won't that sack be too heavy for him? — What are you talking about — he's a horse with balls!" **Ёхать/пое́хать конём,** see under **ёхать. Ста́рый конь борозды́ не по́ртит,** see under **ста́рый.**

КОНЬКИ́, -ов, *pl.* Feet (lit., skates). ●**Отбро́сить коньки́,** *idiom.* To die. ♦*Он скоро коньки отбросит.* "He's going to kick the bucket soon." **Занима́ться гре́блей на конька́х,** see under **занима́ться.**

КОНЬЯ́К "ТРИ СВЁКЛЫ", *idiom, joc.* Home brew from beets, esp. of a crude rural type (lit., three-beet cognac, by wordplay on коньяк "три звезды", "three-star cognac," i.e., three-year-old cognac). ♦*Будете пить? К сожалению, у меня только коньяк "три свёклы".* "Can I offer you a drink? Unfortunately, all I have is some three-beet cognac."

КОПА́ЛА, -ы, *f.* A tracker, "a tunnel rat," a person who digs up trenches and graves after WWII in search of weapons and other artifacts (from копать, to dig).

КОПА́ЛЬЩИК, -а, *m., crim.* A criminal investigator (cf. **копа́ть²**). ♦*Этот копальщик уже много нарыл.* "This detective has already dug up a lot of dirt."

КОПА́ТЬ¹, *imperf. only.* To undermine. ♦*Он под тебя копает, хочет сесть на твоё место.* "He's sabotaging you — he wants your job."

КОПА́ТЬ²/КОПНУ́ТЬ. To investigate (lit., to dig). ♦*Надо это дело копнуть как следует.* "This matter has to be properly investigated."

КОПА́ТЬСЯ/ПРОКОПА́ТЬСЯ, *neg.* To dawdle (from копать, "to dig"). ♦*Что ты копаешься? Опоздаем!* "What are you dawdling for? We're going to be late!"

КОПНА́, -ы́, *f., crim.* An old female robber (lit., a haystack). ♦*Что этой копне надо?* "What does that old robber woman want?"

КОПУ́ША, -и, *f., joc.* A slowpoke, dawdler. ♦*Тебя ждать — одно мучение, ну ты и копуша!* "What a slowpoke you are! It's a torture to wait for you!"

КОПЧЁНЫЙ, -ого, *m., neg.* A black person (lit., a smoked fellow). ♦*А копчёный сегодня придёт в гости?* "Is that black fellow coming to visit today?"

КОПЫ́ТА, копы́т, *pl., rude.* Feet (lit., hooves). ♦*Убери свои копыта с дивана.* "Get your hooves off the couch." •**С копы́т (доло́й),** *idiom.* Off one's feet (said of a hard fall). ♦*Ему чуть вмазали, он сразу с копыт.* "They barely touched him, and he fell right off his feet." **Откину́ть копы́та,** see under **отки́нуть.**

КОПЫ́ТИТЬ/НАКОПЫ́ТИТЬ, *neg.* To make a mess (from копыто, "hoof"). ♦*Вчера вы здесь накопытили, а кто убирать будет?* "Who's going to clean up the mess you made here yesterday?"

КО́РЕНЬ, ко́рня, *m., youth, neg.* An idiot, ignoramus, country bumpkin (lit., root). ♦*Эти корни в Москве ничего не знают.* "These provincials are clueless in Moscow."

КО́РЕШ, -а, *m.* A friend, pal. ♦*Есть у меня кореш, он поможет.* "I have a buddy who'll help out."

КОРЕШИ́ТЬСЯ/ЗАКОРЕШИ́ТЬСЯ. To be friendly, to get on friendly terms. ♦*Ты с кем-нибудь закорешиться успел?* "Did you have time to make friends with anyone?"

КОРИФА́Н, -а, *m., army.* A friend, pal. ♦*Корифан, скажи, который час?* "What's the time, buddy?"

КОРИФА́НИТЬСЯ/СКОРИФА́НИТЬ-СЯ, *youth.* To meet, become acquainted (cf. **корифа́н**). ♦*Они давно корифанятся.* "They've known each other for a long time."

КО́РКА, -и, *f., youth.* Lit., rind, crust. **1.** An adventure, occurrence. ♦*С тобой всегда какие-то корки случаются.* "You're always having some sort of adventure." **2.** An anecdote, story. ♦*Расскажи корку, что ты недавно рассказывал.* "Tell that story of yours again."

КОРМА́, -ы́, *f., joc.* Rear end (lit., aft part of a ship). ♦*Смотри, какая корма пошла, не охватишь.* "Look at the ass on her! You could never get your arms

around it."

КОРМИ́ЛЕЦ, корми́льца, *m., crim.* A shop paying protection money (lit., a bread-winner). ♦*Магазины закрываются, а мы теряем кормильца за кормильцем.* "The stores are going broke, and we're losing one breadwinner after another."

КОРМОВЫ́Е (ДЕ́НЬГИ), *pl.* Money put aside for food, a special fund for food (from корм, "fodder"). ♦*У меня остались только кормовые.* "I'm broke; all I've got left is my lunch money."

КОРМУ́ШКА, -и, *f., neg.* **1.** An official position that can be used to personal advantage (lit., a feeding trough). ♦*Министерство — это большая кормушка.* "That ministry is a regular feeding trough." **2.** *joc., obs.* A refrigerated display case in a store. ♦*Наверное, мясо выбросили, люди толпятся у кормушки.* "They must have put out some meat — look how the people are crowding around the feeding trough!"

КОРО́ВА, -ы, *f., crim.* A person taken with them by prison-camp escapees as food for the period of flight and hideout (lit., a cow). ♦*Захватили они с собой корову и в бега, но через месяц их поймали.* "They took a 'cow' and fled, but they were caught a month later."

КОРОЕ́Д, -а, *m., joc.* A child (lit., a bark-eating beetle). ♦*Сколько у тебя короедов?* "How many kids do you have?"

КОРО́ЛЬ: Куда́ коро́ль пешко́м хо́дит, see under **куда́.**

КОРО́НКА, -и. See **коро́нный но́мер.**

КОРО́ННЫЙ НО́МЕР, *idiom.* A person's favorite or regular trick or behavior (lit., the "crowning number"). ♦*Это у него коронный номер, пообещать и не сделать.* "That's his usual trick, to promise and not deliver."

КО́РОЧКИ, ко́рочек, *pl.* (From кора, "bark"). **1.** An entry pass. ♦*Смотри корочки в институт не забудь!* "Don't forget your entry pass when you go to the institute." **2.** A diploma. ♦*Не важно где учишься, главное — получить корочки.* "It doesn't matter where you study, as long as you get your diploma."

КО́РОЧНИК, -а, *m.* A fool, an idiot. ♦*Как ты ему веришь, это же известный корочник.* "Don't believe him — everyone knows he's an idiot."

КО́РЧИТЬ ИЗ СЕБЯ́ НЕ ЗНА́МО ЧТО, *idiom, neg.* To show off, give oneself airs, pose. ♦*Он корчит из себя не знамо чего, а на самом деле ни в чём не разбирается.* "He poses as an expert, but in fact he knows nothing about it."

КОРЯ́ГА, -и, *f.* A clumsy person (lit., a snag). ♦*Она такая коряга, всегда что-то да разобьёт.* "She's such a klutz, she breaks something every time she's here."

КОРЯ́ЧИТЬСЯ¹, *imperf. only.* To be in wait, in store for someone. ♦*Тебе отпуск корячится летом.* "You've got a vacation in store for you this summer."

КОРЯ́ЧИТЬСЯ²/НАКОРЯ́ЧИТЬСЯ, *neg.* To work hard in an awkward position (lit., to squat). ♦*Мы здесь корячимся, моем полы, а ты музыку слушаешь.* "Here we are slaving away on our knees, scrubbing the floors, while you're hanging around listening to music."

КОСА́Я, -о́й, *f., obs.* A thousand rubles. ♦*Ты мне должен косую.* "You owe me a thousand."

КОСЕ́ТЬ/ОКОСЕ́ТЬ, *joc.* To get drunk. ♦*Ты уже окосел, что ли?* "Drunk already, aren't you?"

КОСИ́ТЬ/ЗАКОСИ́ТЬ, *crim. & youth.* To hide, secrete, stash away (lit., to mow). ♦*Мы тут закосили пару килограмм яблок.* "We've got a couple of kilos of apples stashed away here." •**Коси́ть/закоси́ть на вольтану́того,** *youth, neg.* To act crazy or pretend to be crazy (from вольт, "volt," in reference to electric shock). ♦*Не коси на вольтануного, веди себя нормально.* "Don't act like a maniac—behave yourself!" • **Коси́ть на пси́ха,** *idiom.* (from псих, a madman). See **коси́ть/закоси́ть на вольтану́того.** •**Коси́ть на ши́зика,** *idiom.* (from шизофреник, a crazy person). See **коси́ть/закоси́ть под сумасшедшего.** •**Коси́ть/закоси́ть под**

сумасше́дшего (**под дурака́, под инвали́да),** *idiom.* To act or seem like a madman (an idiot, an invalid). ♦*Меня не обманешь, не коси под сумасшедшего.* "Don't play the fool; you can't take me in like that."

КОСИ́ТЬ/ОТКОСИ́ТЬ ОТ АРМА́ДЫ, *idiom.* To avoid being drafted into the army. ♦*Кто хочет откосить от армады, идёт в аспирантуру.* "Everyone who wants to avoid the draft goes to graduate school."

КОСО́Й, -а́я, -о́е, *neg.* Drunk (lit., crooked, cross-eyed). ♦*Там косой песни орёт.* "There's a drunk bawling some songs over there."

КОСОПУ́ЗЫЙ, -ого, *neg.* (From косой, "crooked," and пузо, "belly"). **1.** An unattractive, plain, insignificant person. ♦*Как она могла выйти замуж за такого косопузого?* "I can't understand why she married that hayseed." **2.** A poor person. ♦*Эти косопузые не могут даже игрушки детям купить.* "They're so poor, they can't even buy toys for their children."

КОСОРЫ́ЛОВКА, -и, *f., neg.* A cheap, inferior alcoholic drink (lit., face-twister). ♦*Видеть не могу эту косорыловку.* "I can't drink that rotgut."

КОСТЕРИ́ТЬ/ПОКОСТЕРИ́ТЬ. To scold, bawl out (lit., gnaw on). ♦*Мать его костерила почём зря за плохие отметки.* "His mother really chewed him out for getting such bad marks."

КО́СТИ, -ей, *pl.* Parents (lit., bones). ♦*Кости на даче, можно вечерину заделать.* "My parents are at the dacha, we can have a party."

КОСТЫЛИ́, -ей, *pl., neg.* Legs (lit., crutches). ♦*Подбери свои костыли, пройти негде.* "Move your legs; you're blocking the passage."

КОСТЫЛЯ́ТЬ/НАКОСТЫЛЯ́ТЬ, *neg.* To beat up, give a beating (from костыль, "crutch"). ♦*Тебе надо накостылять за такие дела, чтоб знал.* "We'll have to beat you up for that to teach you a lesson." •**Костыля́ть/накостыля́ть по нога́м,** *idiom, sports.* To hit in the legs. ♦ *Они только и делают, что костыляют по ногам, играть невозможно.* "They just keep going for the legs. It's impossible to play like that!"

КОСТЬ: Не в кость, *idiom.* Displeasing, not to one's taste. ♦ *Всё, что ты говоришь, мне не в кость.* "Everything you say is displeasing to me." **Бросáть/брóсить кость,** see under **бросáть. Две кóсти слóжены, (мéжду нúми пиздá влóжена),** see under **две.**

КОСУ́ХА, -и, *f., crim., obs.* One thousand rubles (cf. **косáя**). ♦ *Вот косуха, пока хватит тебе на жизнь.* "Here's a thousand — that should be enough for you."

КОСЯ́К, -á, *m., youth.* A "papirosa" cigarette emptied of tobacco and refilled with hash or any drug for smoking. (Originally a twist of paper [cf. **косóй**] for smoking tobacco). ♦ *Забил косяк (заряд) я в пушку туго / И думал: угощу я друга.* "I pushed a twist (a cartridge) tightly into the gun / And thought: 'I'll treat a friend to this.'" (Play on famous lines of Lermontov's poem "Borodino.") •**Забивáть/забúть кося́к,** see under **забивáть.**

КОТ, -á, *m., neg.* Lit., a tomcat. **1.** A pimp. ♦ *При ней всегда два кота.* "There are always two pimps hanging around her." **2.** A lover. ♦ *Она женщина богатая, держит двух котов: один — блондин, другой — брюнет.* "She's a rich woman — she keeps two lovers, a blond and a brunette." •**Коту́ под хвост,** *idiom, neg.* In vain, to no purpose (lit., under a cat's tail). ♦ *Вся наша работа пошла коту под хвост.* "All our work has gone for nothing." **А потóм — суп с котóм,** see under **а.**

КОТЁЛ, котлá, *m.* A head (lit., a boiler). ♦ *У тебя котёл совсем перестал работать.* "You're not thinking clearly."

КОТЕЛÓК, котелкá, *m., joc.* A head (lit., pot, cauldron). ♦ *Что-то котелок болит.* "I've got a bit of a headache." •**Котелóк не вáрит у когó-л.,** *idiom.* Someone isn't thinking clearly (lit., someone's pot isn't cooking). ♦ *Устал, котелок не варит, давай пройдёмся.* "I'm tired; my head isn't functioning. Let's go for a walk."

КОТЛЫ́, -óв, *pl., crim. & youth.* A wristwatch (lit., a large pot). ♦ *Надо ему подарить котлы.* "Let's give him a watch as a present."

КОФЕМÓЛИТЬ/ПОКОФЕМÓЛИТЬ, *neg.* To chat (from кофемолка, "coffee grinder"). ♦ *Хватит кофемолить, пора и поработать немного.* "Enough yakkety-yak, it's time to get some work done."

КÓЦАТЬ/ОТКÓЦАТЬ, *youth.* To admire, to appreciate. ♦ *Ты отцокал вон ту блондинку? Хороша!* "Did you get a load of that blonde over there? She's a real looker!"

КОЧÁН, -á, *m., joc.* Lit., a head of cabbage. **1.** A head. ♦ *Ты будешь думать своим кочаном?* "Use your head!" **2.** A revolver. ♦ *Продай мне кочан.* "Sell me your revolver." •**По кочану́,** *idiom, joc.* Rhyming nonsense answer to the question Почему? "Why?" ♦ *Почему ты не хочешь ехать? — Почему? По кочану!* "Why don't you want to go?" — "Why? Just because!"

КОЧЕВРЯ́ЖИТЬСЯ/ЗАКОЧЕВРЯ́-ЖИТЬСЯ, *neg.* To be stubborn, put up resistance, act naughty. ♦ *Ешь, не кочевряжься.* "Eat — don't be naughty."

КОЧУ́М, -а, *m., youth & crim.* Time off, leisure time, fun; esp., drunkenness. ♦ *Он, как всегда, в кочуме.* "He's on a spree, as usual."

КОЧУМÁТЬ, *imperf. only.* **1.** *crim.* To think, consider, deliberate. ♦ *Тут кочумать нужно, не всё просто.* "I need to think this over — it's not so simple." **2.** *youth.* To finish, stop. ♦ *Кочумай курить, пошли работать.* "Time to stop smoking and get to work."

КОШÁРЬ, -я́, *m., crim.* A sack, bag. ♦ *Пошарь в кошаре, там еда есть.* "Feel around in the sack — there should be something to eat there."

КОШЁЛКА, -и, *f., rude.* Lit., a sack with handles. **1.** A lesbian. ♦ *Все знают, она — кошёлка.* "Everyone knows she's a lesbian." **2.** An ugly woman. ♦ *У него девушка — кошёлка.* "His girlfriend is a bag."

КО́ШКА: Во рту, как ко́шки насра́ли, see under **срать.**

КО́ШКИ И СОБА́КИ, *idiom, business.* Risky, low-priced securities (lit., cats and dogs). ♦*Кошки и собаки уже месяц никому не нужны.* "No one's been interested in 'cats and dogs' for the last month."

КОШМА́ТЕРНЫЙ, -ая, -ое, *joc.* Horrible, dreadful (by wordplay on кошмар, "nightmare," and матерный, "obscene"). ♦*Со мной произошёл кошматерный случай.* "Something horrible happened to me."

КРАБ, -а, *m., joc.* **1.** A hand (lit., crab). ♦*Держи краба, давно не виделись.* "Let me shake your hand; it's been a long time since we've seen each other!" **2.** *Army.* A marine cockade, an insignia on a military cover (lit., a crab).

КРА́ЛЯ, -и, *f., joc.* A beautiful woman (from the Polish word for queen). ♦*Откуда ты эту кралю привёл?* "Where did you find that beauty-queen?"

КРАНТЫ́, *pl.* Curtains! The end! It's all over! ♦*За то, что я с ней переспал, мне — кранты.* "It'll be all over with me if they find out that I slept with her."

КРАСИ́В ДО БЕЗОБРА́ЗИЯ, *idiom, joc.* Lit., handsome to the point of ugliness (said of extreme good looks). ♦*Ну, как жених? — Красив до безобразия.* "So what's her beau like? — So handsome it hurts."

КРА́СКА, -и, *f.* **1.** *neg.* Cheap, strong red wine. ♦*Я эту краску пить не буду.* "I won't drink that rotgut." **2.** *youth.* Red Square in Moscow. ♦*Значит, на Краске в семь, смотри, не опаздывай.* "So, seven o'clock at Red Square — don't be late."

КРА́СКИ, кра́сок, *pl.* Menstrual period. ♦*Она в соревновании не участвует, у неё краски.* "She's not playing in the competition because she's got her period."

КРА́СНАЯ КРЫ́ША, кра́сной кры́ши, *f.* Illegal police protection of private enterprises, banks, etc. (lit., red roof). ♦*Ни под красную, ни под блатную крышу я не пойду.* "I'm not going to pay protection money either to the police or to the mob."

КРА́СНЕНЬКАЯ, -ой, *f., obs.* Ten rubles (from the red color of ten-ruble bills). ♦*Дай ещё красненькую на метро.* "Give me another ten rubles for the subway."

КРАСНОПУ́ЗЫЙ, -ого, *m., neg.* A communist (from красный, "red," and пузо, "belly"). ♦*О чём говорил этот краснопузый по телику?* "What was that redbelly talking about on the TV?"

КРА́СНЫЙ ПА́ПА, -ого, -ы, *m.* A nickname of Gennady Zyuganov, the leader of the Communist Party of Russia (lit., Red Daddy).

КРАСНЯ́К, -а́, *m., neg.* Cheap, strong red wine (cf. **кра́ска**). ♦*Вот купил красняка, хватит на всех.* "I've bought enough wine for everybody."

КРАСЮ́К, -а́, *m., crim., neg.* A good-looking man. ♦*Этот красюк только о бабах и думает.* "All that Adonis ever thinks about is dames."

КРЕВЕ́ТКА, -и, *f., youth, neg.* A small or short young person (lit., a shrimp). ♦*Пусть креветка сбегает за сигаретами.* "Send the shrimp out for cigarettes."

КРЕЙЗА́, -ы́, *f., youth, joc.* **1.** An insane asylum, psychiatric hospital (from Eng. "crazy"). ♦*Он лежит в крейзе.* "He's in a psychiatric hospital." **2.** *m. and f.* An insane person. ♦*Он полный крейза.* "He's completely out of his mind."

КРЕЙЗАНУ́ТЫЙ, -ая, -ое, *youth, neg.* Crazy (from Eng. "crazy"). ♦*Ты что, крейзанутый, чего орёшь?* "What are you, crazy, yelling like that?"

КРЕЙЗАНУ́ТЬСЯ, *perf. only, youth.* To be crazy about someone or something. ♦*Он крейзанулся на тяжёлом роке.* "He went crazy over hard rock."

КРЕЙЗО́ВЫЙ, -ая, -ое, *youth, joc.* Outstanding, extraordinary. ♦*Это крейзовая книга, почитай.* "This is an extraordinary book — you ought to read it."

КРЕМ, -а, *m., joc.* The Kremlin (lit., cream; a dialectal variant used for comic effect). ◆*Все в Крем рвутся, все хотят править.* "Everyone's running to the Kremlin these days — they all want to rule."

КРЕМЛЁВКА, -и, *f.* A special direct connection to high officials in the Kremlin. ◆*Тихо, шеф по кремлевке говорит.* "Keep it down, the boss is on the Kremlin line."

КРЕМЛЁВСКИЕ БРО́ВИ, *idiom, joc.* A nickname for Leonid Brezhnev or Victor Chernomyrdin, alluding to their bushy eyebrows (lit., Kremlin eyebrows).

КРЕПЫ́Ш ИЗ БУХЕНВА́ЛЬДА, *idiom, army, neg.* A skinny weakling (lit., a strong man from Buchenwald). ◆*Ты хоть раз на турнике подтянуться можешь, крепыш из Бухенвальда?* "Can you do even a single chin-up, you ninety-pound weakling?"

КРЕСТ, -а, *m., army, neg.* A stupid ignorant soldier (lit., a cross, from поставить крест на человеке, to consider someone so stupid that he ought to simply be crossed out). ◆*Ты уверен, что наш крест сделает всё, как объяснили?* "Are you sure that our fool will do everything as it was explained to him?"

КРИЧА́ЛКА, -и, *f.* A slogan repeated loudly by fans of a football or hockey team, a cheer (from кричать, to scream).

КРО́ВНАЯ МЕСТЬ, *idiom, joc.* Mentruation, as an excuse for interrupting sexual relations (lit., blood vengeance). ◆*Что-то ты часто применяешь кровную месть.* "It seems to me you've been having your period very often lately."

КРОВЬ: Ма́лой кро́вью, *idiom.* Without problems, without casualties (lit., with little bloodshed). ◆*Мне эта квартира досталась малой кровью.* "I managed to get this apartment without too much of a struggle."

КРОКОДИ́Л, -а, *m.* **1.** *army.* An army vehicle for transporting troops. ◆*Вот и наш крокодил, залезай, поехали!* "Here's our wagon — hop on, we're leaving." **2.** *joc., obs.* Fifty rubles, a fifty-ruble note. ◆*Мне надо крокодил до получки.* "I need to borrow fifty rubles

until payday." ●**Тако́й холо́дный, как крокоди́л голо́дный,** see under **такой.**

КРОПА́ЛИК, -а, *m.* A hashish dose (from кропить, to sprinkle, referring to a small size of any substance). ◆*Кропалик всегда для тебя найдется.* "For you, I can always find a dose of hash."

КРОССЫ́, -о́в, *pl.* Sports shoes, running shoes. ◆*Мои кроссы совсем развалились.* "My running shoes are completely worn out."

КРОШИ́ТЬ бато́н, *idiom, youth, neg.* To scold, reprimand (lit., to crumble a loaf of bread). ◆*Кончай батон крошить, ничего я не брал.* "Stop yelling at me! I didn't take anything."

КРОШИ́ТЬ/НАКРОШИ́ТЬ БАТО́Н НА ПЯ́ТКИ, *idiom.* **1.** To sleep. Lit., to crumble a loaf of bread on one's heels. ◆*Силён ты крошить батон на пятки, почти сутки спишь.* "You are a master when it comes to "rack-ups," you've been sleeping (racked out) for almost 24 hours." **2.** To boast and lie. ◆*Сейчас пойдёт крошить батон на пятки, как он положил голыми руками один пятерых.* "Now is when he'll start his bullshit bragging about how he killed five men at once with his bare hands."

КРУЖИ́ТЬСЯ, *imperf.* To be busy trying to make money (lit., to spin). ◆*Кручусь, кручусь, а денег всё равно не хватает.* "No matter how I work at it, I never have enough money."

КРУПА́, -ы́, *f., army.* Infantry (lit., grains of cereal, describing the view of infantry troops from above as being small, scattered, and of little importance). ◆*Крупа за нами идёт, а мы, ВДВ, всегда впереди, делаем всю опасную работу.* "We, the paratroopers, always go in first, and only after we've done all the dirty work does the infantry come in."

КРУПНЯ́К, -а́, *m., collect.* Large-denomination bills. ◆*У меня мелких нет, только крупняк.* "I haven't got any change, just large bills."

КРУТАНУ́ТЬ, *perf. only.* To interrogate, question (lit., to spin). ◆*Надо его крутануть как следует, что-то он скры-*

вает. "We'll really have to grill him — he's hiding something."

КРУТИЗНА́, -ы́, *f., youth, pos.* Strength, toughness, self-promotion (cf. **круто́й**). ♦ *Он парень с крутизной.* "He's a tough customer." •**С повы́шенной крутизно́й,** *idiom, youth, pos.* Strong, dangerous. ♦ *Его не заводи, он с повышенной крутизной.* "Don't start up with him — he's dangerous."

КРУТИ́ТЬ¹: Крути́ть дина́мо, *idiom, neg.* **1.** To flirt while refusing sex (lit., to spin the engine). ♦ *Она с ним только динамо крутит, не переживай.* "Don't worry, she's just leading him on." **2.** To stall, delay, deceive, renege. ♦ *Он мне крутит динамо уже месяц.* "He's been giving me the runaround for a month already." **Крути́ть ша́рики,** *idiom, neg.* To deceive, trick, cheat (lit., to spin someone's ball bearings). ♦ *Она ему шарики крутит, а сама гуляет с другим.* "She's cheating on him and going out with someone else." **Крути́ педа́ли, пока́ не да́ли,** *rhyming phrase, joc.* Get out of here! Scram! (lit., turn the pedals before you get beaten up). **Крути́ть я́йца,** see under **яйцо́.**

КРУТИ́ТЬ²/ЗАКРУТИ́ТЬ, *neg.* To prevaricate (lit., to spin, fishtail). ♦ *Ты не крути, говори правду.* "Don't beat around the bush — tell the truth." •**Крути́ть/закрути́ть любо́вь,** *idiom, joc.* To go out with someone, be someone's boyfriend or girlfriend (lit., to spin love). ♦ *С кем он сейчас любовь крутит?* "Who's he going out with now?"

КРУТИ́ТЬ³/ПОКРУТИ́ТЬ To interrogate (lit., to whirl, to twist, to spin). ♦ *Ты его здесь покрути, а я пока у него дома обыск сделаю.* "You grill him here, squeeze out all the information you can while I search his apartment." •**Крути́ть/покрутить бара́нку,** *idiom.* To work as a chauffeur (lit., to twirl the wheel). ♦ *Ты думаешь, легко крутить баранку целый день?* "You think it's so easy to twirl the wheel all day long?" •**Крути́ть/покрути́ть де́ньги,** *idiom.* To speculate in money. ♦ *В каком банке ты крутишь деньги?* "What bank are you investing your money in?"

КРУТНЯ́К, -а́, *m., youth.* **1.** A tense situation, quarrel, fight. *Скоро крутняк начнётся.* "Soon the fighting will start." **2.** See **круто́й.**

КРУ́ТО, *adv., youth.* Excellently, well. ♦ *Ну и круто он выдувает на саксе.* "Wow, he blows that sax really well."

КРУТО́Й, -а́я, -о́е, *pos.* **1.** Strong, strong-willed, strict, tough, pushy. ♦ *У тебя мужик крутой.* "Your husband is quite a tough guy." **2.** Making a strong impression, frightening, terrific. ♦ *Это фильм крутой, не для слабонервных.* "That was a powerful film — not for the weak-kneed!" •**Кру́че тебя́ быва́ют то́лько я́йца!** see under **яйцо́.**

КРУЧЁНЫЙ, -ая, -ое, *neg.* **1.** A sharp person (lit., twisted). ♦ *Этот новобранец непростой, крученый, из него получится командир.* "That recruit is 'locked-on,' he's smart, clever, he'll make a great leader." **2.** Treacherous, double-crossing. ♦ *Нет этой сволочи веры, крученый он, предаст.* "He cannot be trusted, he's a double-crossing bastard!"

КРЫСЯ́ТНИЧАТЬ/НАКРЫСЯ́ТНИ-ЧАТЬ, *neg.* To steal from fellow soldiers in the barracks (lit., to rat). ♦ *Давно у нас в роте никто не крысятничал, поймаем—конец.* "It's been a long time since we've had to worry about a rat (thief) among us, but don't worry, we'll catch this one and string him out to dry."

КРЫТЬ/ПОКРЫ́ТЬ: Крыть/покры́ть матюга́ми, *neg.* To swear at someone. ♦ *Не ходи сейчас к нему, он всех подряд кроет матюгами.* "Don't go near him just now; he's swearing at everyone in sight." **Крыть/покры́ть на чём свет стои́т,** *idiom.* To curse, abuse (lit., to cover the foundation of the world [with abuse]). ♦ *Он свою работу кроет на чём свет стоит.* "Now he's cursing his work." **Крыть/покры́ть ма́том,** see **гнуть/загну́ть ма́том.**

КРЫ́ША: Кры́ша пое́хала (потекла́) (кры́шу оторва́ло) у кого́-л., *idiom, neg.* Lit., someone's roof has flown off (used to describe strange or crazy behavior). ♦*У него, видать, крыша поехала, раз решил в свои годы ещё раз жениться.* "He seems to have flipped his lid. Imagine, deciding to remarry at his age!" **Крыша в пути,** *idiom, neg.* Lit., someone's roof is on the move; used to describe strange or crazy-seeming behavior. ♦*Что с него взять, у него давно крыша в пути.* "What can you expect from him? He's been off his head for a long time."

КРЫ́ШКА кому́-л., *idiom.* Someone is in for punishment or trouble (lit. cover, lid). ♦*Если об этом узнают, нам крышка.* "If they find out about this, it's curtains for us."

КРЯ́КНУТЬ, *perf.* To die (lit., to quack). ♦*Слышал, солдат, он сидел за измену, крякнул за месяц до трибунала.* "Didn't you hear? That soldier that was imprisoned for treason suddenly croaked about a month before his trial."

КСЕ́РЕВО, -а, *n., joc.* A photocopy (by wordplay on ксерокс, "xerox," and серево, "a turd"). ♦*Я положил тебе ксерево на стол, почитай!* "I already put the xerox on the table for you. Read it!"

КСЕ́РИТЬ/ПОКСЕ́РИТЬ, ОТКСЕ́РИТЬ. To make photocopies (cf. **ксе́рево**). ♦*Сколько тебе страниц ещё ксерить.* "How many more pages do you need xeroxed?"

КСИ́ВА, -ы, *f., crim.* A document, identification card (from Heb.). ♦*Показывай ксиву, а то не пройдёшь.* "Show your identification or you can't pass."

КТО НЕ ЗНА́ЕТ, ТОТ ОТДЫХА́ЕТ, *idiom.* Lit., He who doesn't know how [to make money] gets to rest.

КТО НЕ РИСКУ́ЕТ, ТОТ НЕ ПЬЁТ ШАМПА́НСКОГО, *idiom.* An expression used to urge or praise bold, decisive behavior (lit., "He who takes no risk drinks no champagne"). ♦*Не знаю, что делать, менять квартиру? — Решай, кто не рискует, тот не пьёт шампанского.* "I can't decide whether to move to another apartment or not. — Do it! Nothing ventured, nothing gained!"

КТО ОПОЗДА́Л, ТОТ НЕ УСПЕ́Л, *idiom.* "Whoever is late misses out." ♦*А мне осталось выпить? — Кто опоздал, тот не успел.* "Is there anything left for me to drink?" — "You're late, you're out of luck."

КТО СПО́РИТ, ТОТ ГОВНА́ НЕ СТО́ИТ. See under **говно́**.

КУБЛО́, -а́, *n., neg.* Bad company, a gang, den (of wolves). ♦*Их кубло мне не нравится, там они пьют, ширяются.* "I don't like that gang; they just drink and shoot dope."

КУГУ́Т, -а, *m., south, neg.* An unsophisticated, provincial person. ♦*Этого кугута не научишь вести себя прилично.* "That hick will never learn proper behavior."

КУДА́ КОРО́ЛЬ ПЕШКО́М ХО́ДИТ, *idiom, joc.* A toilet (lit., where even the king goes on foot). ♦*Мне надо, куда король пешком ходит.* "I need to go to the bathroom."

КУДА́ ТЫ ДЕ́НЕШЬСЯ, КОГДА́ РАЗДЕ́НЕШЬСЯ, *rhyming phrase, joc.* "There's no use getting dressed when you've already taken your clothes off." Used of a situation in which expectations established by previous compliance make it hard to extricate oneself later on. ♦*Я не буду больше печатать эти бумаги начальнику! — Куда ты денешься, когда разденешься.* "I'm not going to type any more of these papers for the boss. — No use getting dressed when you've already taken off your clothes."

КУКАРЕ́ШНИК, -а, *m., crim.* An isolation cell for holding prisoners pending trial (lit., a chicken coop). ♦*Кто у нас сидит сейчас в кукарешнике?* "Who've we got waiting in the coop?"

КУКАРЕ́КУ: Ни бэ, ни мэ, ни кукаре́ку, see under **ни**.

КУ́КЛА, -ы, *f., crim.* A roll of bills in which the inner bills have been replaced by worthless paper (lit., a doll). ♦*При расчёте ему вместо денег всучили куклу.* "When they paid up they slipped him a 'doll' instead of real money."

КУКНА́Р, -а, *m., youth.* 1. Ground poppyheads. 2. A decoction of poppyheads.

♦*Кукнар готов, начинай!* "The poppy brew is ready. Have some!"

КУКОВА́ТЬ/ЗАКУКОВА́ТЬ. To live alone (lit., to play the cuckoo; from the cuckoo's habit of slipping her eggs into other birds' nests for hatching; cf. **куку́шка**). ♦*Хватит куковать, пора жениться.* "Enough playing the cuckoo — it's time to get married."

КУ́КОЛЬНИК, -а, *m., crim.* Someone who passes bad money in the form of "dolls" (see **ку́кла**). ♦*Будешь продавать машину, берегись кукольников.* "Watch out for doll-passers when you sell your car."

КУ-КУ́, *idiom.* **1.** Crazy. ♦*Он что, совсем у тебя ку-ку?* "What is he, crazy?" **2.** So long! See you around! ♦*Ну, я пошёл, ку-ку!* "Well, I've got to go now. Ta-ta!"

КУКУ́ШКА, -и, *f., neg.* **1.** A mother who gives up her child to be raised by others (lit., a cuckoo). ♦*Эта кукушка и раз в неделю не зайдёт проведать сына.* "That cuckoo won't drop in to see her son even once a week." **2.** *f., army.* A sharpshooter (lit., a cuckoo, meaning that sharpshooters hide in the trees).

КУЛЁМА, -ы, *f., joc.* A dumb, awkward girl or woman (from куль, a big, heavy sack). ♦*Ты же не то купила, кулёма, я просил молоко, не кефир.* "You dumb sack! I told you to buy milk, not kefir!"

КУЛЬ С ДЕРЬМО́М, *idiom, neg.* A bad person (lit., a sack of shit). ♦*Меньше всего надо верить этому кулю с дерьмом.* "The last thing you should ever do is believe that sack of crap."

КУМ, -а, *m., crim.* A prosecutor, official who determines what offense a criminal is to be charged with (lit., a godfather). ♦*Кум мне шьёт убийство.* "The prosecutor is pinning a murder on me." •**Кум плетёт ла́пти,** *idiom, crim.* The prosecutor is putting together material against the accused (lit., the godfather is plaiting bast shoes). ♦*Смотри, веди себя осторожно, кум плетёт лапти.* "Watch out — the prosecutor is putting together a case against you."

КУМА́РИТЬ/ПЕРЕКУМА́РИТЬ, *youth.* To have a hangover from use of narcotics. ♦*Тебя кумарит, вот выпей.* "You're in a bad way — drink some of this!"

КУМЕ́КАТЬ/ПОКУМЕ́КАТЬ, *joc.* To think, consider. ♦*Вот я и кумекаю, стоит это делать или нет.* "I'm considering whether it's worth doing or not."

КУ́МПОЛ, -а, *m., joc.* A head (distorted from купол, "cupola"). ♦*У тебя на кумполе шишка.* "You've got a bump on your dome." •**Брать/взять на ку́мпол,** see under **брать.**

КУ́ПОЛ поехал. See **кры́ша поехала.**

КУРА́Ж, -а́, *m., crim.* Income, winnings, profits. ♦*Последнее время ты всё время в кураже.* "You're always flush these days."

КУ́РВА, -ы, *f., rude.* A prostitute, whore (term of abuse). ♦*От этой курвы держись подальше.* "Keep away from that prostitute." ♦*Ах ты курва!* "You whore, you!"

КУРВЁНЫШ, -а, *m., rude.* Good-for-nothing, worthless person (usually said of a young person; cf. **ку́рва**). ♦*Я тебя, курвёныш, чтобы здесь больше не видел.* "Don't let me see you around here again, you little bastard."

КУРВЕ́Ц, -а́, *m., rude.* A bastard, scoundrel. ♦*У этого курвеца ни стыда ни совести.* "That bastard has no shame and no conscience."

КУ́РВИТЬСЯ/СКУ́РВИТЬСЯ, *rude.* To become corrupted, go bad (of a person). ♦*Ты совсем скурвился, разговаривать противно.* "You've turned into such a creep, it's disgusting to even talk to you."

КУРВИ́ЩЕ, -и, *m. & f., irregular, rude.* A loose woman, slut (cf. **ку́рва**). ♦*Ты видишь эту курвищу? Так и просится в постель.* "See that floozy over there? You can see she's just asking to be taken to bed."

КУ́РЕВО, -а, *n., collect.* Cigarettes, "papirosi." ♦*Курево есть?* "Have you got anything to smoke?"

КУ́РЕВО-ПО́РЕВО, -а, *n., rude.* Sexual activity. ♦*Каждый день курево-порево мне уже не по силам.* "I haven't got the nergy to bed a woman evey day."

КУРОЛÉСИТЬ/ЗАКУРОЛÉСИТЬ, *neg.* To misbehave, to be naughty. ♦*Успокойтесь, не надоело куролесить?* "Calm down, aren't you tired of acting up?"

КУРОПÁТКА, -и, *f., crim.* An informer (lit., a wild chicken). ♦*Надо нам найти куропатку.* "We've got to find out who's ratting on us."

КУРÓЧИТЬ/РАСКУРÓЧИТЬ. To break. ♦*Кто это раскурочил мои часы?* "Who broke my watch?"

КУРС, -а, *m., army.* A cadet (abbreviated from курсант). ♦*Он ещё курс.* "He's still a cadet."

КУСМÁН, -а, *m.* A chunk, block, big piece. ♦*Вот тебе кусман колбасы, ешь.* "Here's a chunk of sausage for you. Eat up."

КУСÓК, куска́, *m.* **1.** *army, neg.* An ensign, an army officer usually working in provisions. ♦*Вон кусок идёт, опять надо строиться на работу.* "Here comes the ensign — better get back to work!" **2.** A thousand rubles, a thousand-ruble bill. ♦*Это тебе будет стоить кусок.* "That's going to cost you a thousand." **3.** *neg.* A greedy person (lit., a piece, from the saying Он не даст куска хлеба, "He won't even give you a piece of bread"). ♦*Этот кусок колбасы не даст.* "That hog wouldn't even share a piece of sausage."

КУСÓЧНИК, -а, *m.* **1.** A greedy person (from кусок, a piece of something). ♦*Здесь в армии я стал кусочником, надо всем надо дрожать, чтобы выжить.* "Serving in this detachment has made a miser out of me. Around here one has to 'scrounge' for food and goods to survive. **2.** *Army.* A cook. ♦*У кусочников жизнь трудная, но сытая.* "It's hard to work as a cook, but they never starve."

КУСÓЧНИЧАТЬ/ЗАКУСÓЧНИ-ЧАТЬ, *neg.* To be miserly, to hoard.

♦*Что уж ты так кусочничаешь, как нищий?* "Why are you hoarding crumbs like that, as if you were a beggar?"

КУСТ: Как с куста́, see under **как.**

КУТÓК, кутка́, *m., crim.* A thieves' den (from кут, a hiding place). ♦*У них в кутке всегда выпить найдётся.* "Over at their den there's always something to drink."

КУХ-ТРÉСТ, -а, *m., crim.* A gathering of prostitutes (lit., a kitchen consortium). ♦*Сегодня у них кух-трест, все будут там.* "The gals are having a get-together today; everyone will be there."

КÚЧЕР, -а, *m.* A driver, a taxi driver (lit., a coachman). ♦*Кто у него за кучера?* "Who's his driver?"

КУЧЕРЯ́ВАЯ ЖИЗНЬ, *idiom, pos.* Easy life, easy street (lit., curly life, with reference to luxurious, uncombed hair). ♦*У тебя сейчас отпуск, пошла кучерявая жизнь.* "Now that you're on leave, you're on easy street."

КУЧКОВÁТЬСЯ/ПОКУЧКОВÁТЬСЯ **1.** To get together, meet, have a gathering (from куча, "heap, pile"). ♦*Где они сегодня кучкуются?* "Where are they getting together today?" **2.** To be on friendly terms. ♦*Она с ним давно кучкуется.* "She's been friends with him for a long time."

КУЧУМÁРИТЬ/ЗАКУЧУМÁРИТЬ, *youth, crim.* To sleep, to dream. ♦*Я лягу на полчасика закучумарить.* "I'll just lie down for a half-hour nap."

КУЧУМÁТЬ/ЗАКУЧУМÁТЬ. To have a good time.

КÚШАЙТЕ, ГÓСТИ ДОРОГÍЕ, ВСЁ РАВНÓ ВЫБРÁСЫВАТЬ! *idiom, joc.* Don't stand on ceremony; make yourselves at home. Lit., "Help yourselves, dear guests, we were going to throw it out anyway!" ♦*Ну, что вы сидите, кушайте, гости дорогие, всё равно выбрасывать.* "Don't just sit there. Dig in! Make yourselves at home!"

ЛАБА́ТЬ/СЛАБА́ТЬ, *youth.* To play a musical intrument. ◆*Слабай что-нибудь душевное.* "Play something lyrical." ●**Лаба́ть/слаба́ть музо́н**, *idiom, youth.* To play (on a musical instrument). ◆*Ты умеешь лабать музон?* "Can you play?"

ЛАБУДА́, -ы́, *f., neg.* Nonsense, baloney, garbage. ◆*Не говори так, это всё лабуда.* "Don't talk like that — it's all nonsense." ●**В лабуду́,** *neg.* Extremely drunk. ◆*Ты вчера пришёл в лабуду, надо уметь пить.* "You were completely soused yesterday — you don't know how to hold your liquor."

ЛА́БУХ, -а, *m., youth.* A musician. ◆*Он в лабухи подался.* "He's become a musician."

ЛАБЭ́, n., *indecl., crim.* Money. ◆*Сколько лабэ он тебе должен?* "How much money does he owe you?"

ЛА́ВОЧКА: По пья́ной ла́вочке, *idiom, neg.* While drunk, because of intoxication. ◆*Они по пьяной лавочке кого-то там избили.* "They beat someone up while they were drunk."

ЛАДУ́РА, -ы, *f., crim.* A wedding. ◆*Ты идёшь на ладуру погулять?* "Are you going to the wedding? It'll be fun."

ЛАДЫ́, *adv.* Okay, agreed! (from ладно). ◆*Ну, лады, я принесу тебе книги.* "Okay, I'll bring you the books."

ЛА́ЖА, -и, *f.* Nonsense; misunderstanding. ◆*Всё, что он пишет, лажа.* "Everything he writes is garbled."

ЛАЖА́ТЬ/ЛАЖАНУ́ТЬ, *neg.* To deceive, cheat, break a promise. ◆*Ты опять нас лажанул, не привёз стройматериалы.* "You cheated us again by not bringing the construction materials."

ЛАЖА́ТЬСЯ/ЛАЖАНУ́ТЬСЯ, *neg.* To fail, fall short, lose out. ◆*Он лажанулся на экзаменах.* "He flunked his exams."

ЛАЖО́ВЫЙ, -ая, -ое, *neg.* Bad. ◆*Здоровье у меня стало совсем лажовым, ревматизм замучил.* "My health has become very bad; my rheumatism's been killing me."

ЛА́ЗИТЬ/СЛА́ЗИТЬ на ба́бу, *idiom, rude.* To have sex with (lit., to climb onto) a woman. ◆*Ты успел слазить на бабу до отъезда?* "Did you manage to get her to bed before you left?"

ЛА́ЙБА, -ы, *f., obs.* An old or poor vehicle (originally a bicycle). ◆*Садись на лайбу, гони в магазин за сигаретами.* "Get in the jalopy, and run over and buy some cigarettes."

ЛА́ЙКАТЬ/ЗАЛА́ЙКАТЬ, *youth.* To like (from Eng. "like"). ◆*Ты мясо лайкаешь?* "Do you like meat?"

ЛАЙФ, -а, *m., youth.* Life (from Eng. "life"). ◆*Лайф пошла крутая.* "Life has become harder." ●**Без ка́йфа не́ту ла́йфа,** see under **без.**

ЛА́КЕР, -а, *m., youth.* A lacquered jewelry box (from лак, "lacquer"). ◆*Почём на Арбате эти лакеры?* "How much are these lacquer boxes selling for on the Arbat?"

ЛАМПА́ДА, -ы, *f.* A light bulb, light (lit., an oil lamp, esp. for burning before icons). ◆*Зажги лампаду!* "Turn on the light!"

ЛАМПА́СНОЕ ПРА́ВО, *idiom, army.* The right of senior officers to give orders (lit., the right of the stripes). ◆*Лампасное право тут ни причём, мы командира уважаем и поэтому подчиняемся.* "We follow our commander because we respect him, not because he has rank and authority to give orders."

ЛА́МПОЧКА: До ла́мпочки, *idiom, neg.* It doesn't matter, it's all one. ◆*Мне до лампочки, что ты обо мне думаешь.* "I don't care what you think of me."

ЛА́ПА, -ы, *f.* Lit., paw. **1.** Pal, friend, dear, darling . ◆*Поставь, лапа, чайник.* "Put the kettle on, dear." **2.** *neg.* Corruption, protection. ◆*У него есть лапа в министерстве.* "He's got a connection in the ministry." ●**Дава́ть/дать на ла́пу,** see under **дава́ть. Мохна́тая ла́па,** see under **мохна́тая. Су́чья ла́па,** see under **су́чий.**

ЛА́ПАТЬ/ЗАЛА́ПАТЬ, *neg.* Cf. **ла́па.**

1. To soil something with dirty hands. ♦*Вы мне всю скатерть залапали.* "You've gone and dirtied my tablecloth with your filthy paws." **2.** To feel up, paw. ♦*Не лапай девушку, она не твоя.* "Don't paw her; she's not yours."

ЛА́ПКИ КВЕ́РХУ, *idiom.* Surrender (lit., paws up). ♦*Тебя чуть тронули, помяли, а ты и лапки кверху.* "They hardly touched you — just roughed you up a little — and you gave up!"

ЛА́ПОТНИК, -а, *m., crim.* One who takes bribes. ♦*Он лапотник, сидит за взятки.* "He's doing time for taking bribes."

ЛА́ПОТЬ, ла́птя, *m., neg.* **1.** A bungler, good-for-nothing, oaf (lit., a bast shoe worn by peasants). ♦*Опять, лапоть, ты не смог купить всё, что надо.* "You bungler, you never manage to buy everything you're told to." **2.** *pl.* Ugly shoes. ♦*Я эти лапти носить не буду.* "I wouldn't be caught dead in those clodhoppers." •**Ла́пти гну,** *idiom.* Lit., I'm bending лапти; a nonsense rhyme used in evasive reply to the urging ну, ну, "come on, tell me about it" (cf. **ну́кать**). ♦*Ну, ну, рассказывай! — Ну, ну! Лапти гну.* "Come on, tell me, already! — Come on, come on! Nothing doing, I'm not telling." **Отбра́сывать/отбро́сить ла́пти,** see under **отбра́сывать.**

ЛАПША́, -и́, *f., obs.* A cable-knit sweater (lit., noodle). ♦*Надень лапшу, она идёт к серьгам.* "Wear the cable-knit; it'll go with your earrings." •**Ве́шать/пове́сить лапшу́ на́ уши,** see under **ве́шать.**

ЛАПШИ́СТ, -а, *m.* A liar, an unreliable person, a person who should not be believed. See **ве́шать лапшу́.**

ЛА́СТА, -ы, *f., neg.* Hand, foot (lit., flipper). ♦*Убери ласты, не трогай, не тебе.* "Get your paws off! It's not for you, so don't touch it." •**Отки́нуть ла́сты,** see under **отки́нуть.**

ЛА́СТОЧКА, -и, *f.,* **1.** *army.* A truck (lit., a swallow). ♦*Грузи снаряды на ласточку!* "Load the ammunition onto the truck!" **2.** A method of immobilizing violent drunks by tying them face-down.

♦*Будешь шуметь, полежишь у нас ласточкой.* "One peep out of you and we'll give you a 'swallowtail'" **3.** A prostitute (lit., a swallow). ♦*Если надо бабу, войдёшь в кафе, ласточки сидят всегда справа.* "If you're looking for a call girl go into that cafe and you'll find the whole lot of them sitting at a table on the right." **4.** Any attractive woman. ♦*Не пойму, чего он от неё на сторону ходит, у него такая ласточка—загляденье!* "I can't figure out why he constantly runs around on her, she's such a looker!" **5.** *Army.* A special kind of torture used to bend a man's back by tying his legs and head from behind. **6.** A woman in a secret service. **7.** A soldier with a concussion caused by a mine (describing soldiers flying like birds after an explosion).

ЛАТИ́Н, -а, *m.* A Latin American. ♦*Ко мне один латин приходит, говорит, что в Уругвае переворот.* "So this Latin guy comes up to me and says there's a revolution going on in Uruguay."

ЛАФА́, -ы́, *f., pos.* A comfortable or luxurious life. ♦*У тебя не жизнь — лафа, всё у тебя есть: и дом, и машина!* "You're really on easy street with your house, your car, and everything!"

ЛАФЕ́ТНИЧЕК, лафе́тничка, *m., obs.* A vodka glass (originally of thick, greenish ribbed glass.) ♦*Давай по лафетничку дерябнем с мороза.* "Let's have a shot to warm up."

ЛАХМА́Н, -а, *m., crim.* The cancellation of a gambling debt. ♦*Тебе лахмана не будет.* "Your debt won't be forgiven."

ЛАХУ́ДРА, -ы, *f., neg.* **1.** A slovenly woman. ♦*Что ты ходишь как лахудра, приоденься немного.* "Why are you going around like such a frump? Put on some nice clothes." **2.** A whore. ♦*Ты опять к этой лахудре ходил?* "Did you visit that whore again?"

ЛДПР, *abbr.* Zhirinovsky's Liberal Democratic Party of Russia, deciphered as Люблю дурачить простых ребят, "I love making fools of simple people."

ЛЕБЕДЯ́НЬ, -и, *f., joc.* Any speech of Alexander Lebed, Governor of Krasnoyarsk and a prominent public figure (by wordplay on дрянь, "rubbish"). ♦*Лебедянь всем поднадоела.* "Everyone is sick of Lebed's speeches."

ЛЕБЕЗЯ́ТНИК, -а, *т., neg.* A fawning person, toady. ♦*У нас завёлся лебезятник.* "We've got an ass-licker among us."

ЛЕ́БЛЯДЬ, -и, *f.* A prostitute (a wordplay on лебедь, a swan, and блядь, a prostitute).

ЛЕВА́К, -а́, *т., obs.* From левый, "left side." **1.** The driver of a private car who moonlights by carrying passengers for a fee. ♦*Давай возьмём левака, здесь такси не поймаешь.* "Let's hire a 'lefty'; it's impossible to get a regular taxi here." **2.** A fence, dealer in stolen or resold goods. ♦*Надо купить кирпич у левака.* "We'll have to buy the bricks from a 'lefty.'"

ЛЕ́ВЫЙ, -ая, -ое, *youth, neg.* Unpleasant, bad (lit., left). ♦*Это всё левые приколы, я это не лайкаю.* "I don't like all this nasty nagging." ●**Ле́вая рабо́та,** *idiom.* Moonlighting, doing a supplementary job (lit., work on the left). ♦*Он всё время делает левую работу.* "He's always got some moonlighting job." **Ле́вой ного́й,** *idiom, neg.* Carelessly, any old way (lit., with one's left foot). ♦*Ты этот рисунок делал левой ногой.* "You made that drawing carelessly."

ЛЕГА́ВКА, -и, *f., neg.* A police station (cf. **лега́вый**). ♦*В легавку лучше не попадаться, сначала побьют, потом оштрафуют.* "Better not fall into the hands of the police; first they'll beat you, then they'll fine you."

ЛЕГА́ВЫЙ, -ого, *т., neg.* A police officer (from легавая собака, a hunting dog). ♦*Легавые идут, сматываемся.* "Here comes the law. Let's cut bait."

ЛЕГА́Ш, -а, *т., neg.* See **лега́вый**.

ЛЕ́ГЧЕ ДАТЬ, ЧЕМ ОБЪЯСНИ́ТЬ, *idiom, joc.* Lit., "It's easier to give (you what you want, i.e., to go to bed with you) than to explain." Used to express exasperation with someone's failure to understand.

ЛЁД, льда, *т., crim.* Lump sugar (lit.,

ice). ♦*Сколько у нас льда осталось, больше килограмма?* "How much sugar is left? Is there more than a kilogram?"

ЛЕЖА́К, -а́, *т.* An apartment (lit., a deck chair). ♦*А где у тебя лежак, на метро или пешком пойдём?* "Where's your pad, do we need to take the metro or can we walk?"

ЛЕЖА́ТЬ/ЛЕЧЬ, *youth.* To be amazed (lit., to lie down). ♦*Я так и легла, когда узнала, что он уехал за бугор.* "I practically fainted when I heard he had gone abroad!"

ЛЕЖА́ЧИЙ: Не бей лежа́чего, see under **не.**

ЛЁЖКА: В лёжку, *idiom, neg.* Very drunk. ♦*Они там в лёжку перепились.* "They've drunk themselves under the table over there."

ЛЕЗТЬ в буты́лку, *idiom.* To lose control of oneself, become aggressive (lit., to crawl into the bottle). ♦*Успокойся, не лезь в бутылку.* "Calm down; don't get all hot under the collar."

ЛЕЙТЁХА, -и, *т., army, joc.* A lieutenant. ♦*А наш лейтёха совсем зелёный.* "Our lieutenant is completely inexperienced."

ЛЕКА́ЛИТЬ/ПОЛЕКА́ЛИТЬ, *youth.* To engage in oral sex (from лекало, a guide for drawing curves). ♦*Они там в соседней комнате лекалят.* "They're 'making curves' over there in the other room."

ЛЕКА́ЛЬЩИЦА, -ы, *f., rude.* A girl who engages in oral sex (from лекальщик, a skilled metal turner). ♦*Она известная лекальщица.* "Everyone knows she gives blow jobs."

ЛЕКА́РСТВО, -а, *п., joc.* Liquor, esp. when drunk as a supposed remedy for a hangover (lit., medicine). ♦*Лекарство есть, полечиться надо.* "Is there anything to drink? I need a cure."

ЛЕКА́РСТВО ОТ ЛЮБВИ́, *idiom, army, joc.* Two years of army service (lit., a cure for love, meaning that girlfriends rarely wait for soldiers to come home).

ЛЕ́МОН, -а, *т.* A lemon (distorted from лимон, imitating the English pronunciation). ♦*Чай с лемоном будем пить или так?* "Shall we have our tea plain or with lemon?"

ЛЕ́НА, РАЗДВИ́НЬ КОЛЕ́НА, *idiom, rude.* A rhyming chant used to tease girls named Lena. ♦*Почему ты не дала списать задачу, Лена, раздвинь колена.* "Why didn't you let me copy your math problem, Lena-spread-your-knees?"

ЛЕНИ́ВЫЙ РЫ́НОК, *idiom, business.* Absense of trade in the market or exchange (lit., lazy market). ♦*Сегодня как никогда ленивый рынок, никто не хочет рисковать.* "The market is slower than ever these days. No one is willing to take any risks."

ЛЕ́НКА-ПЕ́НКА, *idiom.* A rhyming phrase used to tease girls named Lena (lit., Lena is scum).

ЛЕПИЗДРИ́ЧЕСКИЙ, -ая, -ое, *joc.* Electric (by wordplay on **пизда́** and **электри́ческий,** "electrical"). ♦*У тебя есть лепиздрический паяльник?* "Have you got an electric soldering iron?"

ЛЕПИЗДРИ́ЧЕСТВО, -а, *n., joc.* Electricity (cf. **лепиздри́ческий**). ♦*У нас вчера лепиздричество вырубилось, а у вас?* "We had a power outage yesterday. Did you?"

ЛЕПИ́ЛА, -ы, *m. & f., youth.* A liar, hoaxer. ♦*Пойдём послушаем, что там лепила говорит.* "Let's go hear what that hogwash artist is saying."

ЛЕПИ́ЛОВО, -а, *n., youth.* Lying, a pack of lies (cf. **лепи́ла**).

ЛЕПИ́ТЬ/ЗАЛЕПИ́ТЬ: Лепи́ть/залепи́ть горба́того, *idiom, crim.* **1.** To put down an improper card in card games (lit., to paste on a deformed one). ♦*Ты лепишь горбатого, нужны пики.* "You've put down the wrong card — you need a spade." **2.** To lie. ♦*Что ты лепишь горбатого, мы там не были.* "Why are you lying? We weren't there at all." **Лепи́ть/залепи́ть скок,** *idiom, crim.* To rob an apartment. ♦*Они вдвоём залепили скок, неплохо поработали.* "The two of them did an apartment robbery; they made out pretty well."

ЛЕПОТА́, -ы́, *f.* Something beautiful. ♦*Погода сегодня—лепота.* "The weather today is beautiful."

ЛЕ́СБА, -ы, *f.* A lesbian. ♦*Она что, лесба?* "Is she a lesbian or what?"

ЛЕСНИ́К, -а́, *m., army, neg.* A general (lit., a forest ranger, with reference to the fancy uniform). ♦*Ну, вот лесник приехал, сейчас поведут на учения.* "Here comes the general — time for maneuvers."

ЛЕ́ТЕРГ, -а, *m., crim.* A police lieutenant. ♦*Кто тебя допрашивал, летерг вон тот или другой?* "Who interrogated you? Was it that lieutenant over there or someone else?"

ЛЕТЕ́ТЬ/ПОЛЕТЕ́ТЬ. To be out of order, to be broken (lit., to fly). ♦*У меня генератор полетел, надо перебрать.* "My generator has been broken, it's got to be dismantled and repaired."

ЛЕТУ́ЧКА, -и, *f.* A briefing (from **лететь,** to fly). ♦*Летучка через час, надо успеть перекусить.* "The pre-flight brief starts in an hour, let's grab some chow beforehand."

ЛЕЧИ́ТЬ/ПОЛЕЧИ́ТЬ, *neg.* Lit., to cure. **1.** To scold, punish. ♦*Приготовься, сейчас родители лечить будут.* "Get ready; your parents are really going to give it to you now." **2.** To insist, try to persuade. ♦*Не надо меня лечить, я всё равно сделаю по-своему.* "Don't bother trying to convince me; I'm going to do it my own way anyhow."

ЛЕША́К, -а́, *m., neg.* A forest ranger. ♦*Зайти к лешаку, что ли? Он неподалёку живёт.* "Would you run over to the forest ranger's? It's not far."

ЛЕЩ, -а́, *m.* A spanking, a smack on the butt with the palm of one's hand. See **дава́ть/дать леща́.**

ЛИ́ВЕР, -а, *m., joc.* A fat man. ♦*Этого ливера не накормишь, жрёт за двоих.* "That fatso will eat you out of house and home."

ЛИЗА́ТЬСЯ/ПОЛИЗА́ТЬСЯ, *joc.* To kiss. ♦*Хватит лизаться, пора и делами заняться.* "Enogh smooching! It's time to get down to business."

ЛИКВИДА́ТОР, -а, *m.* **1.** A reservist who participated in cleaning up debris after the Chernobyl catastrophe (lit., a liquidator). ◆*Он был ликвидатором, сейчас инвалид, схватил дозу.* "He helped clean up after Chernobyl. He is disabled now, for he got radiation poisoning." **2.** Anyone working for the Ministry of Extreme Situations (МЧС, Министерство по Чрезвычайным Ситуациям).

ЛИКЁР «ШАССИ́», *idiom, army, joc.* An alcoholic drink made by flavoring pure spirits (lit., chassis liquor). ◆*Разливай ликёр «шасси», пора расслабиться.* "Pour us some crankcase oil; it's time for a break."

ЛИМА́Н: На лима́не, *idiom, crim.* In hiding from the police (lit., in the marshes). ◆*Он уже месяц на лимане.* "He's been in hiding for a month."

ЛИМИТА́, -ы́, *f., collect., neg.* Temporary workers who don't have regular authorization to live permanently in the city where they are working. ◆*В этом доме живёт одна лимита.* "The people who live in that building are all transients."

ЛИМИ́ТЧИК, -а, *m., neg.* An individual of the **лимита́**.

ЛИМО́Н, -а, *m., youth.* A million rubles (lit., a lemon; from the yellow color of the one-million-ruble bill of the 1920's). ◆*Он весит лимон.* "He's worth a million." •**Большо́й лимо́н**, *idiom.* A billion rubles (lit., a big lemon; cf. **арбу́з**).

ЛИМОНА́Д, -а, *m., youth, neg.* A millionaire. ◆*Туда не пойдём, этот кабак для лимонадов.* "Let's not go there — that restaurant is strictly for millionaires."

ЛИМО́НКА, -и, *f., crim.* A woman who engages in perverse sexual practices. ◆*Эта лимонка на всё готова.* "That 'lemon' is willing to do anything."

ЛИ́НЗА, -ы, *f., crim.* A shop window, display window (lit., a lens). ◆*Если эту линзу разбить, то можно много взять в магазине.* "If we can break that window, there's a lot we can loot in that store."

ЛИНЯ́ТЬ/ПОЛИНЯ́ТЬ, *business.* To suffer losses (lit., to fade, to bleed). ◆*Осенью все полиняли и намного.* "This autumn everyone suffered great losses."

ЛИНЯ́ТЬ/СЛИНЯ́ТЬ, *joc.* To slip away,

leave unnoticed (lit., to bleach out, fade away). ◆*Когда это он слинял, никто не заметил?* "When did he manage to slip away without anyone noticing?" •**Линя́ть/слиня́ть в нору́**, *idiom, youth.* To leave, go home (lit., to slip into one's burrow). ◆*Я линяю в нору в 12 часов.* "I'm going home at 12 o'clock."

ЛИ́ПА, -ы, *f.* Forgery, fakery (lit., linden wood). ◆*У него документы — липа.* "His papers are phony."

ЛИПУ́ЧКА, -и, *f., crim.* A stick with a gummy or gluey end for stealing money from a counter at a store (lit., flypaper). ◆*Она деньги держит в ящике под прилавком, здесь нужна липучка.* "She keeps the money in a box under the counter. We'll need a sticky-stick." •**На липу́чках**, *idiom.* By means of Velcro, with Velcro fastenings. ◆*У него куртка на липучках.* "His coat fastens with Velcro."

ЛИСТ, -а́, *m., youth.* A packet of pills, a sheet or card of pills (narcotics). ◆*У меня ещё лист остался, возьми в ящике.* "I still have another sheet of pills — get it out of the drawer."

ЛИТА́ВРЫ, лита́вр, *pl., crim. & youth.* Breasts (lit., cymbals). ◆*Литавры у неё — что надо.* "She's got quite a pair of knockers."

ЛИТЕРИ́ТЬ/ЗАЛИТЕРИ́ТЬ, *crim.* To be obsequious, servile; to fawn on someone (cf. **шестери́ть**). ◆*Кто у него литерит сейчас?* "Who's dancing attendance on him these days?"

ЛИ́ТЕРКА, -и, *f., crim., neg.* A toady, ass-licker. ◆*Ты в литерки записался, всем угождаешь?* "How come you're toadying to everyone like that?"

ЛИТРБО́Л: Ма́стер спо́рта по литрбо́лу, see under **ма́стер**.

ЛИТЬ/ВЫ́ЛИТЬ КИСЕ́ЛЬ НА НО́ГИ, *idiom.* To tease, to pester, to challenge (lit., to pour кисель, a Russian drink made from boiled fruit and starch). ◆*Не надо лить кисель на ноги, давай спокойно всё обговорим.* "If you quit pestering me there's a possibility we can work this out calmly, OK?"

ЛИТЬ/ОТЛИ́ТЬ, *rude.* To urinate. ♦*Надо бы отлить, где здесь толчок?* "I need to take a leak. Where's the can around here?"

ЛИХОРА́ДКА, -и, *f., crim.* A trial, court process (lit., a fever). ♦*Когда у него лихорадка?* "When's his trial?"

ЛИЦО́ КАВКА́ЗСКОЙ НАЦИОНА́ЛЬ-НОСТИ, *idiom.* A "person of the Caucasian nationality," a Caucasian. ♦*В Москве милиция не даёт проходу лицам кавказской национальности, то штрафует, то проверяет документы.* "In Moscow the police are harassing Caucasians by fining them and checking their id's."

ЛИ́ЧКА, *f., army.* A personal bodyguard (from <u>личная</u> охрана). ♦*Ему не положена личка, не тот уровень.* "He's not important enough to have a personal body guard."

ЛИ́ШКУ: Вы́пить ли́шку, see under **пить.**

ЛОБ: Здоро́вый лоб, see under **здоро́вый.**

ЛОБЕ́ШНИК, -а, *m., joc.* A forehead, brow (from лоб). ♦*Сейчас получишь в лобешник.* "Now you're going to get it right to the head."

ЛОВИ́ТЬ, *imperf. only, youth.* To succeed in getting, acquiring (lit., to catch). ♦*Здесь ловить нечего, в магазине пива нет.* "We won't be able to pick up anything here; there's no beer in the store." **Не лови́ть мыше́й,** *idiom, neg.* Not to do one's duty or carry out one's assignment (lit., not to catch mice). ♦*Ему поручили купить книги в библиотеку, а он мышей не ловит.* "They commissioned him to buy books for the library, but he's not catching any mice."

ЛОВИ́ТЬ/ПОЙМА́ТЬ, СЛОВИ́ТЬ кайф, *idiom.* To get drunk, get a thrill. ♦*От стакана я сразу поймал кайф.* "I got really high just from that one glass."

ЛО́ВКОСТЬ РУК, И НИКАКО́ГО МОШЕ́НСТВА, *idiom.* "It's skill, not fraud"; used in ironic explanation of unexpected success. ♦*Как тебе удалось достать шампанское на Новый год? — Ловкость рук, и никакого мошен-* ства. "How did you manage to get champagne for New Year's? — Believe me, it was skill, not fraud."

ЛО́ГОВО, -а, *n.* Home, abode ♦*Он сидит в своём логове на даче, никуда не ходит.* "He just sits home at his dacha and doesn't go anywhere."

ЛО́ЖИТЬ, *imperf., army.* To eat greedily (from ложка, a spoon). ♦*Так ложить, без ложек и вилок, что любой аппетит пропадёт.* "The way you shovel food down your throat spoils everybody's appetite. You don't even bother to use forks and knives!"

ЛОЖИ́ТЬСЯ/ЛЕЧЬ на дно, *idiom.* To be in hiding, keep out of sight (lit., to lie on the bottom, as of a submarine). ♦*О наших делах знает слишком много народа, надо лечь на дно.* "There are too many people who know about our affairs; we'd better lie low for a while." •**Ложи́тся/лечь на у́хо,** *idiom.* To stick in one's memory. ♦*Эта музыка сразу легла на ухо.* "That tune stuck in my head the minute I heard it."

ЛОКА́ТОР, -а, *m.* An ear (lit., radar set). ♦*Не настраивай локаторы, не про тебя разговор.* "Don't tune in on this, it's not for your ears."

ЛОКШ, -а, *m., crim.* Bad luck, misfortune. ♦*У него локши, его арестовали.* "He had a piece of bad luck — he got arrested."

ЛОКША́, -ы́, *f., crim.* Poor-quality clothes. ♦*Не могу носить эту локшу.* "I wouldn't be caught dead in those rags."

ЛОМ: Не в лом, *idiom, youth, neg.* Against one's will. ♦*Читать эти учебники мне не в лом.* "I don't want to read these textbooks at all." **В лом,** *idiom.* Completely, utterly. ♦*Он нажрался в лом.* "He drank himself into unconsciousness." **Про́тив ло́ма нет приёма (, окромя́ друго́го ло́ма),** see under **про́тив.**

ЛОМАНУ́ТЬСЯ, *perf. only, youth.* To try, make a strong effort. ♦*Ломанёмся в кабак?* "Shall we have a go at getting into the restaurant?"

ЛОМА́ТЬ¹, *imperf. only.* To dicker with,

haggle with, bargain with someone. ♦*Их ещё ломать надо, они не хотят скинуть цену.* "We'll have to dicker with them some more; so far they're unwilling to give a discount."

ЛОМÁТЬ²/ОБЛОМÁТЬ рогá кому́-л., *idiom, neg.* To beat up (lit., to tear out someone's horns). ♦*Я тебе рога обломаю за всё.* "I'll tear you limb from limb for what you did."

ЛОМÁТЬ³/ПОЛОМÁТЬ буты́лку, *idiom.* To drink a bottle of liquor, usually with another person (lit., to break a bottle). ♦*Не много ли будет? — Что мы, не можем поломать бутылку?* "Isn't that a lot to drink? —Are you kidding? We can certainly break a bottle between us."

ЛОМÁТЬ⁴/СЛОМÁТЬ кайф, *idiom.* To spoil the fun, ruin the enjoyment of an occasion. ♦*Ты нам весь кайф сломал шуточками.* "You've spoiled the fun with your tricks." •**Ломáть/сломáть чéрез колéно,** *idiom, neg.* To do something quickly and violently (lit., to break over one's knee). ♦*Нельзя же всю страну ломать через колено, — сегодня строим коммунизм, завтра капитализм.* "You can't just turn the whole country upside-down like that, building communism one day and capitalism the next!"

ЛОМÁТЬСЯ/СЛОМÁТЬСЯ. 1. To drink oneself unconscious. ♦*Ты, я вижу, сломался, тебе хватит.* "I see you've drunk yourself into a stupor — enough, already!" **2.** To be tired, exhausted. ♦*Всё, пора отдыхать, я сломался.* "Enough! Time for a rest. I'm knocked out."

ЛОМИ́НА, -ы, *f., youth, neg.* A strong man (from лом). *Что же ты, такой ломина, а работать не хочешь.* "What's wrong with you? A big fellow like you, and you won't work?" •**В ломи́ну,** *idiom, youth.* Much, a lot (said of drinking). ♦*Где это вы успели надраться в ломину?* "Where did you manage to get so loaded?"

ЛОМОВÓЙ, -áя, -óе, *youth.* **1.** Good, fine, excellent. ♦*У нас будет ломовая поездка.* "We're going to have a great trip." **2.** Expensive, high (of prices). ♦*Цены сегодня ломовые.* "Prices are high today."

ЛОНГÓВЫЙ, -ая, -ое, *youth.* Tall, long (from Eng. "long"). ♦*Эти трузера лонговые будут.* "These pants are too long."

ЛОПÁТА, -ы, *f., crim.* A wallet, purse (lit., a spade). ♦*Доставай лопату, платить пора.* "Where's your wallet? It's time to pay up."

ЛÓПАТЬ/СЛÓПАТЬ, *neg.* To eat ravenously, greedily. ♦*Когда это вы слопали всё мясо?* "When did you wolf down all that meat?"

ЛÓПНУТЬ: Чтоб мне лóпнуть, see under **чтоб.**

ЛОПУ́Х, -á, *m., neg.* A fool, idiot, simpleton (lit., burdock). ♦*Тебя, лопуха, нетрудно обмануть.* "It's not hard to fool you, you idiot."

ЛОПУХÁТЬСЯ/ЛОПУХНУ́ТЬСЯ, *neg.* To be deceived, cheated, fooled. ♦*Знаешь, как мы вчера лопухнулись, купили костюм, а он не того размера.* "You know how we got fooled yesterday? They sold us a suit, but it was the wrong size."

ЛОХ, -а, *m., youth, neg.* A country bumpkin, provincial person. ♦*Он Москву совсем не знает, лох он и есть лох.* "He doesn't know Moscow at all; he's a complete hick."

ЛОХÁНКА, -и, *f., neg.* A mouth (lit., a wooden tub). ♦*Закрой лоханку, ругань надоело слушать.* "Shut your trap. I'm tired of your scolding."

ЛОХМÁТАЯ КРÁЖА, *idiom, crim.* Rape (lit., hairy theft). ♦*За что сидишь, не за лохматую кражу, случайно?* "What are you doing time for? Not rape, by any chance?"

ЛОХМÁТЫЙ, -ая, -ое, *adj.* **1.** Unkempt, ratty (referring especially to hair). **2.** *youth, pos.* Fashionable. ♦*У тебя очень лохматые очки.* "Those are really fashionable glasses you're wearing."

ЛÓХМЫ, *pl.* Hair, especially when shaggy or unkempt. ♦*Отрастил себе лохмы, пора стричься.* "My mop has grown really long. It's time for a haircut."

ЛОХУ́ШКА, -и, *f., youth, neg.* An unattractive girl. ♦*Ты в этом платье стопроцентная лохушка.* "You really look like a dog in that dress."

ЛО́ШАДИ, -ей, *pl.* Horsepower (lit., horses). ♦*Сколько лошадей в этих "Жигулях"?* "How much horsepower do those Zhigulis have?" •*«Эй», — зову́т* **лошаде́й,** see under **эй.**

ЛОШАДИ́НАЯ ДО́ЗА, *idiom.* A large amount (lit., a horse's dose). ♦*Не наливай такие лошадиные дозы, давай потихоньку, не гони коней.* "Don't pour such enormous drinks. Take it easy — don't be in such a hurry."

ЛУДИ́ТЬ/ЗАЛУДИ́ТЬ. 1. To beat up (lit., to tin). ♦*Ты нас не заводи, лудить будем, мало не покажется.* "Don't piss us off or we'll beat you to a pulp." **2.** To build, to construct, to work hard. ♦*Мы с тобой уже залудили половину словаря.* "We've slaved and finished half of the dictionary."

ЛУ́ЖА, -и, *f., Moscow.* A sports center in Moscow where a clothing market is held (Лужники). ♦*Ты сегодня пойдёшь в Лужу?* "Are you going to the Luzha today?"

ЛУ́КАТЬ/ПОЛУ́КАТЬ, ЛУКНУ́ТЬ, *youth.* **1.** To look (from Eng. "look"). ♦*Лукни, кто пришёл.* "Look who's here!" **2.** To listen, be attentive. ♦*Лукай сюда, что тебе говорят.* "Pay attention to what you're being told."

ЛУКИ́Ч, -а, *m., youth.* Lenin. ♦*Встретимся возле Лукича на Октябрьской.* "Let's meet at the Lenin monument at October Square."

ЛУНА́ТИК, -а, *m., crim.* A night robber (lit., a sleepwalker). ♦*Сейчас опасно на улицах, можешь встретиться с лунатиком.* "It's dangerous in the streets at this hour; there are night robbers out there."

ЛУПА́РА, -ы, *f.* A sawed-off shotgun. ♦*Бери свою лупару, идём охотиться.* "Bring your gun and let's go hunting."

ЛУПЕ́ТКИ, лупе́ток, *pl., youth, rude.* Eyes (from лупиться, "to stare"). ♦*Убери лупетки, ничего интересного в этом нет.* "Turn your eyes away; there's nothing to look at here."

ЛУ́ПИЛКИ, лупилок, *pl.* See **лупе́тки.**

ЛУПИ́ТЬ/ОТЛУПИ́ТЬ. To beat up. ♦*Делай, что тебе говорят, пока не отлупили.* "Do what you're told, or you'll get a beating."

ЛУПИ́ТЬ/СЛУПИ́ТЬ, *joc.* To eat very quickly (lit., to beat, punish). ♦*Вы уже слупили всё мороженое, ничего не оставили.* "You've already wolfed down the ice cream and you didn't leave any for me!"

ЛУПЦЕВА́ТЬ/ОТЛУПЦЕВА́ТЬ. To hit, to beat up. ♦*Родители его лупцуют каждую неделю.* "His parents beat him every week."

ЛУ́ЧШЕ ПЕРЕБЗДЕ́ТЬ, ЧЕМ НЕДО-БЗДЕ́ТЬ, *idiom, rude.* It's better to be overcautious than to take unnecessary risks (lit., "Better to overfart than to fart incompletely"). ♦*Зачем закрывать дверь на все замки, одного хватит. — Лучше перебздеть, чем недобздеть.* "Why bother locking all the locks on this door? One's enough. — Better safe than sorry."

ЛУ́ЧШЕ ПО́ЗДНО, ЧЕМ НИКОМУ́ (ДАТЬ), *idiom, joc.* Lit., "Better late than to no one," an off-color twist on "Better late than never."

ЛУ́ЧШЕ СТУЧА́ТЬ, ЧЕМ ПЕРЕСТУ́-КИВАТЬСЯ, *idiom.* It's better to inform on someone than to go to jail yourself." Cf. **стуча́ть.**

ЛУ́ЧШЕ ЧЕ́СТНО ПЁРДНУТЬ, ЧЕМ ПО-ШПИО́НСКИ БЗДНУТЬ, *idiom, rude.* "Better to fart honestly than secretly like a spy." ♦*Не скрывай от нас, всё равно узнаем. Лучше честно пёрднуть, чем по-шпионски бзднуть.* "Don't hide it from us, we'll find out anyway. It's better to fart honestly than secretly like a spy."

ЛУ́ЧШИЕ НО́ЖКИ ФРА́НЦИИ, Е́СЛИ ПОБРИ́ТЬ И ВЫ́ПРЯМИТЬ, *idiom, joc.* Lit., "The best legs in France, if you just shave them and straighten them out"; used to describe an unattractive woman.

ЛУШПА́ЙКА, -и, *f., crim., neg.* A slovenly woman (from Ukr., husk of a sunflower seed). ♦*Кто эта лушпайка, ну и страшна.* "Who's that hag? She's really awful."

ЛЫ́БИТЬСЯ/ЗАЛЫ́БИТЬСЯ, *neg.* To grin. ♦*Что ты лыбишься, это не смешно.* "What are you smirking at? This isn't funny!"

ЛЫСА́К, -а, *m., joc.* A bald man. **Бы́ли рысака́ми, ста́ли лысака́ми,** *idiom.* A rhyming phrase used of aging people: "Formerly trotters, now baldies."

ЛЫ́СИК, -а, *m., joc.* A bald man. ♦*Ты у меня совсем лысик.* "You've gone completely bald."

ЛЫ́СИНА, -ы, *f., rude.* A penis (lit., bald spot). ♦*У меня лысина покраснела, надо лечить.* "There's a red mark on my dick. I'll have to see a doctor."

ЛЫ́СЫЙ¹, -ая, -ое. Bald. •**Чёрт лы́сый,** see under **чёрт.** **(А чёрта) лы́сого не хо́чешь?,** see under **чёрт.**

ЛЫ́СЫЙ², -ого, *m., joc., obs.* **1.** A ruble coin with a portrait of Lenin. ♦*У меня ещё один лысый есть.* "I've got one 'baldie' left." **2.** A bald tire. ♦*У меня все шины лысые, пора их менять.* "All my tires are bald; it's time to change them."

ЛЫ́ЧКА: Ве́шать/пове́сить лы́чки, see under **ве́шать.**

ЛЮ́БА, СЛЕЗА́Й С ДУ́БА, *idiom, joc.* Rhyming phrase for teasing girls named Lyuba. ♦*Люба, слезай с дуба, мы с тобой не играем.* "Lyuba-come-down-from-the-oak-tree, we won't play with you."

ЛЮ́БЕР, -а, *m.* A member of the Lyubertsy youth group, which arose under Gorbachev as an anti-Western, military-flavored gang and ultimately became associated with organized crime. ♦*Люберы контролируют всю торговлю в своём городе.* "The Lyubers control all commercial activity in their city."

ЛЮБИ́ТЬ: Вы не люби́ли, вам не поня́ть, see under **вы.**

ЛЮБО́ВЬ: Крути́ть любо́вь, see under **крути́ть. Прошла́ любо́вь, завя́ли помидо́ры,** see under **прошла́.**

ЛЮ́ДИ: Каки́е лю́ди — и без охра́ны! see under **каки́е. Будь про́ще, и к тебе́ потя́нутся лю́ди,** see under **будь.**

ЛЮ́ДИ НА БОЛО́ТЕ, *idiom, army.* Dishwashers (lit., men in a swamp). ♦*Скоро ужин, а люди на болоте еще и не начинали мыть посуду.* "It's almost time for lunch but the mess men haven't even started washing the dirty dishes."

ЛЮКСО́ВЫЙ, -ая, -ое, *youth.* Good, excellent. ♦*Это люксовая музыка.* "This is wonderful music."

ЛЭЙБЛ, -а, *m., youth.* A label, make (from Eng. "label"). ♦*Лэйбл не тот, я эти трузера не беру.* "I'm not going to buy these slacks — they're not the right make."

ЛЯГУША́ТНИК, -а, *m., neg.* A Frenchman (lit., a frogger). ♦*Лягушатники не пьют водку, они пьют вино.* "Those frogs drink wine instead of vodka."

ЛЯГУ́ШКА, -и, *f., crim.* A sexual position (lit., frog). ♦*Сделай лягушку, давно так не пробовали.* "Make the frog — we haven't tried it that way in a long time."

ЛЯД: Ну кого́-л. к ля́ду! *idiom., rude.* The hell with (somebody). ♦*Ну его к ляду, не хочу его видеть.* "The hell with him! I don't want to see him."

ЛЯ́ЛЬКА, -и, *f., students.* A girl (lit., doll). ♦*А не позвать ли нам пару лялек потанцевать?* "Why don't we ask a couple of dolls out dancing?"

ЛЯ-ЛЯ́: Не на́до ля-ля́ (на́шим ребя́там), see under **не.**

ЛЯЛЯ́КАТЬ/ПОЛЯЛЯ́КАТЬ, *neg.* To chitchat. ♦*Некогда мне с вами ляля-кать.* "I have no time to yak with you guys."

ЛЯМУ́Р, -а, *m., joc.* Love, a love affair (from Fr. "l'amour"). ♦*У них давно лямур?* "Have they been in love for a long time?"

ЛЯ́ПАТЬ/ЛЯ́ПНУТЬ, *neg.* To speak unguardedly. ♦*А он возьми и ляпни об этом.* "He up and spilled the beans about it."

ЛЯ́РВА, -ы, *f., rude.* **1.** A promiscuous

woman. ♦*Да она же самая настоящая лярва.* "She's a real whore." **2.** An unattractive, ill-tempered woman. ♦*Этой лярве обругать человека ничего не стоит.* "That shrew thinks nothing of bawling people out."

ЛЯ́СЫ-БАЛЯ́СЫ, *rhyming phrase, neg.*

Empty chatter (from лясы, wooden forms for making spoons, a winter evening activity accompanied by lots of chatting). ♦*У вас всё лясы-балясы о политике, а дела нет.* "You babble about politics all the time, but you never do anything."

МАГАРЫ́Ч, -а, *m.* A drink offered as a kind of payment for help. ♦*Мы тебе помогали, ставь магарыч.* "We helped you, so stand us a drink."

МАДЕ́ЙРА, -ы, *f., army, joc.* Diluted spirits. ♦*Ты как раз вовремя, угощайся, мадейра — первый сорт!* "You're just in time. Help yourself to some 'Madeira' — it's top quality!"

МАЖО́Р, -а, *m., youth, neg.* **1.** A child of high-ranking parents. ♦*Этому мажору жить легко, всегда родители помогут.* "That silver-spoon has it easy; his parents always help him out." **2.** *crim.* A homosexual. ♦*Этот мажор к тебе не приставал?* "Did that fairy come on to you?"

МА́ЗА, -ы, *f., youth.* **1.** An influential connection, useful acquaintance. ♦*У него есть маза на самом верху.* "He's got a friend at the top." **2.** Advantage, benefit. ♦*Нет мазы это делать.* "There's no advantage in doing that." •**Без ма́зы,** *idiom, youth.* Uninteresting, profitless, without advantage. ♦*Мне это делать без мазы.* "There's nothing in it for me." **Держа́ть ма́зу,** see under **держа́ть.**

МА́ЗАТЬ¹/ЗАМА́ЗАТЬ, *youth.* To bet, stake money. ♦*Мажу на сто рублей, что ты этого не сделаешь.* "I bet you a hundred rubles you won't do it."

МА́ЗАТЬ²/ПРОМА́ЗАТЬ. 1. To miss (a target). ♦*Ты всё время мажешь, дай я покажу, как надо стрелять.* "You keep missing — let me show you how to aim." **2.** To pass by (mistakenly), overshoot one's goal. ♦*Кажется, я промазал мимо поворота, надо возвращаться.* "I seem to have missed my turn. I'll have to go back."

МАЗИ́ЛА, -ы, *m., neg.* **1.** A bad soccer player. ♦*Этот мазила с двух метров попасть в ворота не может.* "That klutz couldn't get a goal from two meters away." **2.** A bad artist.

МАЗНЯ́, -й, *f., neg.* A bad drawing or picture. ♦*За эту мазню я и рубля не дам.* "I wouldn't pay a single ruble for that junk."

МАЗУ́РИК, -а, *m.* **1.** A petty thief. **2.** A dead body. ♦*Там один мазурик валяется, не беспокой медицину, он не наш.* "That's one of theirs, don't bother the medics with that piece of meat."

МАЗУ́Т, -а, *m., army, joc.* **1.** An officer of a tank division (lit., grease, with reference to grimy appearance). ♦*Он мазут уже 10 лет и всего лишь старший лейтенант.* "He's been a tank officer for 10 years and he's still only a lieutenant." **2.** A soldier from the artillery or tank corps (wearing black epaulets). ♦*К нам в гости приедут мазуты.* "The artillery guys are coming to visit."

МАЙ: Не май ме́сяц, see under **не.**

МАЙДА́Н, -а, *m., crim.* A railroad train. ♦*Это наш майдан?* "Is that our train?"

МАЙДА́ННИК, -а, *m., crim.* A thief who specializes in robbing passengers in railroad trains. ♦*На этой линии майданников полно.* "This line is full of train thieves."

МАКА́КА, -и, *f., neg.* An ugly person (lit., macaque). ♦*Ну и рожа у него, чистая макака!* "What a mug! A real monkey!"

МАКА́Р, -а, *m., army.* A Makarov gun. ♦*Без макара я на улицу не выхожу ночью.* "I never go out at night without a gun."

МАКАРО́НИНА, -ы, *f.* A thin person (from макароны, "macaroni"). ♦*На этой макаронине всё висит, как на вешалке.* "That scarecrow's clothes hang on him like on a pole."

МАКАРО́ННИК, -а, *m., neg.* An Italian. ♦*Макаронники никогда не умели воевать.* "Those wops have never known how to fight."

МАКАРО́НЫ ПО-СКО́ТСКИ, *idiom, army.* Said about any badly cooked food (lit., macaroni cooked for animals, in a "beastly" way, from макароны по-флотски, macaroni in a naval way, usually macaroni cooked with minced meat). ♦*Нам дают есть всякую дрянь, прямо макароны по-скотски.* "This stuff they give us to eat is horrible, shit on a shingle."

МАКА́ТЬ/МАКНУ́ТЬ, *youth, neg.* To scold, blame (lit., to dip). ♦*Хватит меня макать, раз ошибся, вы всю жизнь вспоминать будете.* "Okay, stop rubbing my nose in it. I make one mistake and you never let me forget it."

МАКАШИ́, -е́й, *pl., neg.* Rightist, followers of former general A. Makashov (by wordplay on **алка́ш**). ♦*У макашей враг один — евреи!* "Makashov's people recognize only one enemy — the Jews."

МАКИЯ́Ж, -а, *m.* Makeup, cosmetics. ♦*Не много ли на тебе макияжа?* "Aren't you wearing a little too much makeup?" •**Наводи́ть/навести́ макия́ж**, see under **наводи́ть**.

МА́КОВКА, -и, *f.* A head, a crown, a cupola. ♦*По маковке настучать недолго, так что не выступай.* "You'd better keep a low profile or you'll get it straight in the head."

МАЛИ́НА, -ы, *f.* Lit., raspberries, berry patch; with reference to sweetness. **1.** *crim.* A thieves' den. ♦*Сегодня собираемся на малине у Витьки.* "Today we're getting together at Vic's place." **2.** A gathering place, hangout. ♦*Там у них настоящая малина, не знаю, куда родители смотрят.* "They're running a regular hangout there — I don't know why their parents don't seem to notice."

МАЛИ́ННИК, -а, *m., joc.* A group of women among whom there is only one man (from **мали́на**). ♦*Смотри, в какой малинник ты попал.* "Look what a berry patch of women you've fallen into!"

МА́ЛО НЕ ПОКА́ЖЕТСЯ, *idiom.* A threat or warning of disaster (lit., It won't seem like too little). ♦*Если все шахтёры выйдут на рельсы, мало не покажется.* "If the miners block the railways, there'll be hell to pay."

МА́ЛОЙ КРО́ВЬЮ. See under **кровь**.

МАЛОФЬЯ́, -и́, *f., rude.* Semen. ♦*У тебя штаны в малофье.* "You've got come on your pants."

МАЛОХО́ЛЬНЫЙ, -ая, -ое, *neg.*

Depressed, stuporous. ♦*Что ты сидишь такой малохольный?* "Why are you sitting around with such a long face."

МА́ЛЫЙ: Ма́лый не дура́к, *idiom, pos.* A clever guy. ♦*Значит, ты решил на ней жениться? Ты малый не дурак, она богатая невеста.* "So you've decided to marry her? How clever of you! She's real rich." **Ма́лый не дура́к и дура́к не ма́лый**, *idiom, neg.* A fool, no small fool. (By wordplay on малый, "guy," and немалый, "small"). ♦*Значит, ты решил на ней жениться? Ты малый не дурак и дурак не малый, она уже была три раза замужем.* "You think you're awfully clever to marry her, but in fact you're quite a fool — she's been through three marriages already."

МА́ЛЬЧИК, -а, *m., crim.* A key (lit., a boy). ♦*Доставай мальчика, я свой забыл.* "Get the key; I've forgotten mine." •**Как ма́льчик Юнь Су**, see under **как**.

МА́МА-ПА́ПА, -ы, *m.* An electric outlet (lit., mom and dad connection). ♦*Если у тебя найдётся мама, у меня папа, сейчас соединим провод и телик заработает.* "I have a male. If you have a female, we can get this cable TV working."

МАМЕ́Д, -а, *m.* A Central Asian (from a popular name). ♦*Мамеды свинину не едят.* "Mameds don't eat pork."

МА́МКА, -и, *f.* The motherboard of a computer. ♦*Мамка должно быть вылетела, машина не пашет.* "My motherboard must be gone. My machine is not working."

МАМЛЮ́К, -а, *m., neg.* A Central Asian, implying aggressive, wild character (from мамелюк, "Mameluke"). ♦*У мамлюков самый доходный бизнес — торговля людьми.* "Those Asians have found the most profitable business — the slave-trade."

МА́МОНТ, -а, *m., joc.* A big, heavy man. ♦*Пусть этот мамонт сядет на диван, а то он стул раздавит.* "That giant had better sit on the sofa, a chair won't survive him."

МАНА́ТКИ, мана́ток, *pl., neg.* Things,

possessions. ♦*Собирай свои манатки и убирайся!* "Take your things and get out of here!"

МАНДА́, -ы́, *f., rude.* Female genitals. ♦*Иди в манду.* "Go to hell."

МАНДАВО́ШКА, -и, *f., rude.* **1.** Pubic lice, crabs. ♦*У меня мандавошки завелись.* "I've got crabs." **2.** A worthless person, scoundrel. ♦*Кто привёл эту мандавошку, она же воровка.* "Who brought that nasty woman here? She's a thief."

МАНДЁЖ, -а, *m., rude.* Nonsense, twaddle. ♦*Этот мандёж о ценах мне надоел.* "I'm sick of this nonsense about prices."

МАНДЕ́НЬ, -и, *f., neg., rude.* **1.** Large female genitals. ♦*Ну у неё и мандень!* "What a cunt she's got!" **2.** Trash, garbage. ♦*Я эту мандень есть не буду.* "I'm not going to eat that garbage." •**Мандень че́шется у кого́-л.,** *idiom, rude.* Someone is sexually excited (lit., her cunt itches). ♦*У тебя что, мандень чешется?* "What's with you, an itch in your panties?"

МАНДРОВА́ТЬ/ПОМАНДРОВА́ТЬ, *joc.* To go (from Ukr. мандровать, "to travel," "to go"). ♦*Помандровали, что ли?* "Shall we go?"

МАНДУ́ЛА, -ы, *f.* A bid unwieldy object. ♦*Купили пианино, а как эту мандулу затащить на пятый этаж, не знаем.* "We've bought a piano, but now we don't know how to get that mama up to the fifth floor."

МАНТУ́ЛИТЬ/ПРИМАНТУ́ЛИТЬ. 1. To fix, to attach. ♦*Дверь скоро упадёт, пора её примантулить.* "The door's falling off its hinges. It's time to fix it." **2.** To please, to flatter (lit., to work as a lackey, a waiter). **3.** To work hard. ♦*Здесь мантулить недели на две, а ты говоришь, три дня.* "This isn't a three-day job. To finish it we'll have to work like slaves for two weeks." **4.** To beat up. ♦*Ещё раз придёшь в таком виде на смотр, тебя отмантулят как надо.* "If you show up for inspection looking like that they'll beat you up."

МАНЬЯ́ЧИТЬ, *imperf., student.* To like, to be fond of (from маньяк, "maniac"). ♦*Я давно не маньячу на видео.* "I've lost my taste for videos."

МА́РА, -ы, *f., crim. & youth, rude.* A girl, girlfriend; a prostitute. ♦*У него мара есть?* "Has he got a girl?"

МАРАЗМИ́РОВАТЬ/ЗАМАРАЗМИ́РОВАТЬ. (From маразм, "senility"). **1.** To be preoccupied with trivial things. ♦*Сколько можно маразмировать с этими компьютерными игрушками?* "You're wasting too much time playing these stupid computer games!" **2.** To blike, to be fond of. ♦*Она совсем замаразмировала на астрологических прогнозах.* "She's gone wild over astrological charts."

МАРАКЕ́Ш, -а, *m., youth, neg.* Obscurity, darkness, a bad situation (by wordplay on мрак, "darkness," and Маракеш, the city Marrakesh). ♦*В науке сейчас маракеш, никто не знает, что делать дальше.* "The situation in science is foggy right now; no one knows what to do next."

МАРАКОВА́ТЬ/ПОМАРАКОВА́ТЬ, *joc.* To think. ♦*Дай помараковать немного, потом решим.* "Let's mull it over a bit before we decide."

МАРА́Л: Ора́ть как мара́л, see under **ора́ть.**

МАРАФЕ́Т, -а, *m., crim.* A cocaine-type drug. •**Наводи́ть/навести́ марафе́т,** see under **наводи́ть.**

МАРАФЕ́ТИТЬСЯ/НАМАРАФЕ́ТИТЬСЯ. See **наводи́ть/навести́ марафе́т.**

МАРИНОВА́ТЬ/ПРОМАРИНОВА́ТЬ. To keep someone waiting (lit., to marinate). ♦*Ты нас маринуешь уже час, ни да ни нет не говоришь.* "You've kept us waiting for an hour without saying either yes or no."

МА́РОЧКА, -и, *f., crim.* A handkerchief. ♦*Дай марочку вытереть руки.* "Let me have a hankie to wipe my hands."

МАРУ́СЬКА, -и, *f., youth.* Marijuana (diminutive of the name Мария). ♦*Садись покурим, маруськи хватит на двоих.* "Let's sit down and have a smoke. There's enouth 'Marianna' for both of us."

МАРУ́ХА, -и, *f., crim.* **1.** A prostitute. ♦*Там одни марухи стоят.* "Those women standing over there are all prostitutes." **2.** A girlfriend. ♦*Это Ленькина маруха.* "That's Leonid's girl."

МАРЦЕФА́ЛЬ, -я, *m., youth.* Narcotics, drugs. ♦*У меня марцефаль кончился.* "I'm out of dope."

МАРШРУ́ТКА, -и, *f.* A fixed-route taxi-van. ♦*Садись на маршрутку, туда минут двадцать езды.* "Take a route taxi; it'll take twenty minutes to get there."

МАРЬЯ́ЖИТЬ/ПОМАРЬЯ́ЖИТЬ. 1. To beat around the bush, be evasive. ♦*Не марьяжь меня, говори сразу, что тебе надо.* "Don't beat around the bush with me; tell me straight out what you want." **2.** To distract someone in order to cheat him. ♦*Не надо меня марьяжить, я вас вижу насквозь.* "Don't try to pull the wool over my eyes — I see right through you."

МАРЬЯ́НА, -ы, *f., crim.* A woman. ♦*А сколько там марьян будет?* "How many women will be there?"

МАСЛИ́НА, -ы, *f., crim.* A bullet (lit., an olive). ♦*Хочешь маслину получить?* "Are you trying to get shot?"

МАСО́Н, -а, *m., neg.* A Jew. ♦*Опять масоны пачками едут за границу.* "Again the 'Masons' are going abroad in packs."

МА́ССА: Дави́ть на ма́ссу, see under **дави́ть.**

МА́СТЕР МАШИ́ННОГО ДОЕ́НИЯ, *idiom.* A corrupted traffic policeman (lit., an expert in machine milking).

МА́СТЕР СПО́РТА ПО ЛИТРБО́ЛУ, *idiom, joc.* A heavy-drinking, unathletic person (lit., master of the sport of liter-ball). ♦*Куда ему участвовать в соревновании, он мастер спорта по литрболу.* "How could he be in the play-offs? His only sport is literball."

МАСТЫ́РИТЬ/ЗАМАСТЫ́РИТЬ. To make, construct (distorted form from мастер). ♦*Посмотри, какую я дачу за-*

мастырил. "Look at the dacha I built."

МАСТЫ́РКА, -и, *f., crim.* A faked illness or wound (cf. **мастырить**). ♦*У меня мастырка, видишь, рану расковырял, хочу получить освобождение от работы.* "Look at my 'construction' — I opened that wound in order to get out of working."

МАСТЬ, -и, *f., crim.* Narcotics for smoking. ♦*Масть принёс?* "Did you bring the dope?" •**В масть,** *idiom.* Excellent, appropriate (lit., matching the suit, as at cards). ♦*То, что ты предлагаешь, прямо в масть, я сам это собирался сделать.* "What you're suggesting is exactly right — it's what I myself was going to do."

МАТ, -а, *m.* Obscene or abusive speech, a swearword, an abusive expression. •**Гнуть/загну́ть (крыть/покры́ть, обкла́дывать/обложи́ть) ма́том,** see under **гнуть.**

МАТА́Н, -а, *m., youth.* Mathematical analysis (a school subject). ♦*Ты сделал матан?* "Have you taken math-an?"

МАТЕРИ́ТЬ/ИЗМАТЕРИ́ТЬ, ОТМАТЕРИ́ТЬ, *neg.* To scold with swear-words, swear at, curse. ♦*Он её всю изматерил за это.* "He swore at her for that."

МАТЕРЩИ́ННИК, -а, *m., neg.* Someone who uses foul or abusive language. ♦*Он матерщинник, каких свет не видел.* "He can outswear anyone."

МА́ТКА ВЫ́ВАЛИТСЯ!, *idiom, rude, army.* Stand at attention! (lit., you'll drop your womb!) ♦*Сомкнуть пятки (в строю)! Как стоишь, матка вывалится!* "Stand at attention, soldier! You're spilling your guts (womb)!"

МА́ТКА ОПУСКА́ЕТСЯ у кого́-л., *idiom, rude.* Said of feelings of fright or anxiety (lit., someone's womb drops). ♦*У меня матка опускается, когда я вижу, как дети перебегают улицу, а там движение страшное.* "My womb drops when I see the children running across the street with all that traffic."

МА́ТКУ ЗАСТУ́ДИШЬ!, *idiom, army, rude.* Stand at attention! (lit., your womb will catch cold). See **Ма́тка вы́валится!**

МАТ-ПЕРЕМА́Т, ма́та-перема́та, *т.* Much or intense swearing, bad language. *Что у вас здесь мат-перемат, укоротите языки.* "Why are you swearing like that? Watch your language!"

МАТРА́Ц: Раз-ра́з и на матра́ц, see under **раз-ра́з.**

МАТРО́С: У матро́сов нет вопро́сов, see under **у.**

МАТРО́СИТЬ/ПОМАТРО́СИТЬ, *neg.* To have a casual sex with a woman (from матрос, "sailor"). ♦*С ним будь поосторожней, поматросит и бросит.* "Be careful with him, he'll just use you and cast you off."

МАТЬ: •**Мать ва́шу за́ ногу,** *idiom, euph.* Damn it! (lit., your mother by the foot). •**Мать моя́ же́нщина!** *idiom, rude.* Damn it! ♦*Мать моя женщина! Ну и цены стали, ничего купить нельзя.* "Damn it! With these prices, you just can't afford to buy a thing." **Япо́на мать!,** see under **япо́на.**

МАТЮГА́ЛЬНИК, -а, *т., joc.* A megaphone. ♦*Возьми матюгальник, скажи людям, куда надо идти.* "Take a megaphone and tell the people where to go."

МАТЮГА́ТЬ(СЯ)/ЗАМАТЮГА́ТЬ(СЯ), *neg.* To use curse words, to abuse with foul language (cf. **мат**). ♦*Хватит матюгаться!* "Stop cursing!"

МАТЮГИ́, -о́в, *pl., neg.* Curse words, swearing. ♦*От него только матюги и слышишь.* "The only thing you ever hear from him is cuss words." •**Крыть/покры́ть матюга́ми,** see under **крыть.**

МАФИО́ЗИ, *sg. & pl.* Mafioso, mafiosi. ♦*На рынке орудуют мафиози.* "Mafiosi are operating in the market."

МАХ: Дава́ть/дать ма́ху and **Дава́ть/дать Ма́ху и Фейерба́ху,** see under **дава́ть.**

МАХА́ЛОВКА, -и, *f.* A fistfight. ♦*Уходим, сейчас начнётся махаловка.* "Let's get out of here — there's going to be a fight."

МАХА́ТЬСЯ/МАХНУ́ТЬСЯ. To exchange. ♦*Давай махнёмся куртками.* "Let's exchange coats."

МАХНУ́ТЫЙ -ая, -ое, *youth, neg.* Odd, peculiar (euphemism for **ебану́тый**). ♦*Он всегда такой махнутый?* "Is he always such a weirdo?"

МАХРА́, -ы́, *f., neg.* Interior tobacco, low-quality cigarettes.

МА́ЦАТЬ/ПОМА́ЦАТЬ, *south, neg.* To touch. ♦*Не мацай яблоки грязными руками!* "Don't touch those apples with your dirty hands!"

МА́ША-ПРОСТОКВА́ША. A rhyming chant used to tease girls named Maria (lit., Masha sour-milk).

МА́ША-РАСТЕРЯ́ША. An absent-minded person. ♦*Какой ты Маша-растеряша, никогда не помнишь, куда ты задевал свои инструменты.* "You're so absent-minded, you never remember where you put your tools."

МАЯ́ЧИТЬ/ЗАМАЯ́ЧИТЬ. 1. To be visible, in view. ♦*Прекрати маячить перед глазами!* "Stop standing in front of me!" **2.** To have an erection. ♦*У него давно уже не маячит.* "He hasn't had an erection for quite a while."

МЕ́БЕЛЬ: Для ме́бели, *idiom, neg.* To no purpose (lit., for furniture). ♦*Ты сюда пришёл для мебели, почему не помогаешь?* "Did you come here just as furniture? Why don't you help out?"

МЕДВЕ́ДЬ: •**Медве́дь в берло́ге сдох,** *idiom, joc.* Lit., a bear died in his den; with reference to a rare or unusual event. ♦*Что это ты решил матери помочь, медведь в берлоге сдох, что ли?* "How come you suddenly decided to help your mother? Did a bear die in his den?" **Бе́лый медве́дь,** see under **бе́лый.**

МЕДВЕЖА́ТНИК, -а, *т.* A specialist in breaking into safes (lit., a bear hunter, with reference to danger and skill). ♦*Сейчас медвежатников очень мало.* "These days there aren't many safe-crackers."

МЕДВЕЖО́НОК, медвежо́нка, *т., crim.* A small, fireproof safe. ♦*Ты этот медвежонок открыть сможешь?* "Will you be able to open this safe?"

МЕДЛЯ́К, -а́, *т.* Something slow, esp. music. ♦*Поставь медляк, надоело трястись.* "Play something slow; we've had enough fast dances."

МЕДЯ́К, -á, *m., obs.* Small change (lit., copper). ♦*В кармане одни медяки.* "All I've got in my pocket is some small change."

МЕДЯ́ШКА, -и, *f.* See **медя́к.**

МЕ́ЖДУ НА́МИ, ДЕ́ВОЧКАМИ (, говоря́), *idiom, joc.* Frankly speaking (lit., just between us girls). ♦*Между нами, девочками, говоря, это — наглость.* "Just between you and me, he's out of line."

МЕЖДУСОБО́ЙЧИК, -а, *m.* A friendly drink, an intimate conversation (lit., between fellow warriors). ♦*У нас здесь междусобойчик, закрой дверь.* "Shut the door — we're having a heart-to heart here."

МЕ́ЛКИЙ, -ого, *m.* A short man. ♦*А кто это там мелкий стоит?* "Who's that shorty standing over there?"

МЕ́ЛОН, -а, *m., business.* A large extra dividend (often in the form of free shares) (from Eng. "melon"). ♦*Никто такой мелон не ожидал, вот повезло-то!* "No one expected such a bonanza! What great luck!"

МЕЛОЧЁВКА, -и, *f.* Details, trivialities, little things. ♦*Все дела на сегодня я сделал, осталась мелочёвка — поставить подписи.* "I've finished all the real work for today — now there are just some little things, like signing letters."

МЕ́ЛОЧЬ ПУЗА́ТАЯ, *idiom, joc.* Children, young people (lit., little things with bellies). ♦*А ну, мелочь пузатая, не спорить со старшими.* "Come on, kids, don't argue with your elders."

МЕЛЬТЕШИ́ТЬ/ЗАМЕЛЬТЕШИ́ТЬ, *neg.* To make a fuss, to bustle around. ♦*Не мельтеши перед глазами.* "Don't go fussing around like that."

МЕЛЬЧИ́ТЬ/ЗАМЕЛЬЧИ́ТЬ, *neg.* To squabble over trifles. ♦*Не будем мельчить, поговорим о главном.* "Let's stop splitting hairs and get to the point."

МЕНЗУ́РКА, -и, *f.* A glass (lit., a laboratory measuring glass). ♦*Где ещё мензурка, некуда ему налить.* "Is there another glass? I have nothing to pour him

a drink in."

МЕНС, -а, *m.* Menstrual period. ♦*Кажется, менс начинается.* "I think, my period is starting."

МЕНТ, -á, *m., neg.* A police officer. ♦*Я в менты не пойду.* "I'm not going to join the police." •**Менты́ не кенты́,** *idiom, youth.* The cops are no friends of ours; we don't want to have anything to do with the police (cf. **кент**). ♦*Нам менты не кенты, уходим.* "Here come the cops! Let's get out of here."

МЕНТИ́ТЬ/ЗАМЕНТИ́ТЬ. To arrest (cf. **мент**). ♦*Без документов не ходи по Москве, сразу заментят.* "Don't go around Moscow without identification, or you'll be areasted."

МЕНТО́ВКА, -и, *f.* A police vehicle. ♦*Ментовка его забрала.* "They took him away in a police car."

МЕНТОВО́З, -а, *m.* See **менто́вка.**

МЕНТО́ВСКИЙ, -ая, -ое. Of or pertaining to the police. ♦*Это машина с ментовскими номерами.* "That car has police license plates."

МЕНТУ́РА, -ы, *f., neg.* The police, a police station. ♦*Их забрали в ментуру.* "They took them in to the police station."

МЕНЬЖЕВА́ТЬСЯ/ЗАМЕНЬЖЕ-ВА́ТЬСЯ, *neg.* To waver, hesitate, be indecisive. ♦*Меньжеваться сейчас не время, надо действовать.* "This is no time for shilly-shallying; we've got to take action."

МЕНЬШЕВИ́К, -á, *m.* A member of a sexual minority. ♦*Сейчас голубых меньшевиками зовут.* "Now they're calling fags 'mensheviks'."

МЁРЗНУТЬ/ЗАМЁРЗНУТЬ как цу́цик, *idiom, joc.* To be freezing cold, to freeze (lit., to freeze like a puppy). ♦*Дай чаю, а то мы замёрзли как цуцики.* "Let's have some tea before we freeze like puppies."

МЕ́РИН, -а, *m.* Mercedes-Benz (lit., a gelding, a type of stallion). See **мерс.**

МЕРКАНЧИ́НА, -ы, *m., joc.* An American (distorted from Америка). ♦*Что эти мерканчины могут понять в нашей жизни?* "What can those

Americans possibly understand about our life?"

МЕРС, -а, *m.* A Mercedes-Benz car, as a sign of wealth and success. ♦*Учился хуже всех, а сейчас на мерсе ездит.* "He was a failure in school, and now he's driving around in a Mercedes."

МЁРТВЫЕ НЕ ПОТЕ́ЮТ, *idiom.* Said of difficult exercise, work or debilitating illness (lit., the dead never sweat). ♦*На марш-броске потеешь как собака, но ничего, только мёртвые не потеют.* "Yes, true, we're sweating buckets on this forced march, but remember that only the dead don't sweat."

МЁРТВЫЙ: Как мёртвому примо́чки, see under **как. Ты и мёртвого изнаси́луешь (подни́мешь),** see under **ты.**

МЁРТВЫЙ ТОВА́Р, *idiom, business.* Slow-moving merchandise. ♦*Виски сейчас мёртвый товар, не по карману.* "Whisky is selling poorly, people just can't afford it."

МЕРТВЯ́К, -а́, *m., neg.* A corpse; a listless, spiritless person. ♦*Что ты ходишь как мертвяк?* "Why are you dragging yourself around like a corpse?"

МЕСИ́ЛОВКА, -и, *f., neg.* A fistfight (cf. **меси́ть**). ♦*У них каждый день месиловка.* "Those guys have a fistfight every day."

МЕСИ́ТЬ/ЗАМЕСИ́ТЬ, *youth, neg.* To beat, beat up (lit., to knead). ♦*Не приставай к ней, а то замесят.* "Don't touch that woman or you'll get beaten up."

МЕСТИ́/ЗАМЕСТИ́. To arrest (lit., to sweep up). ♦*Вчера всех наших замели.* "Yesterday they arrested our whole gang."

МЕ́СТНОСТЬ: Сойдёт для се́льской ме́стности, see under **сойти́.**

МЕ́СТНЫЙ РОЗЛИ́В, *idiom, joc.* Of poor quality, provincial, not up to high standards (lit., local bottling). ♦*Это поэт местного розлива.* "He's a home-spun poet."

МЕ́СТО: Места́ знать на́до, *idiom, joc.* Lit., one has to know the right places; used to avoid answering the question "Where?" ♦*Где ты взял эту книгу? — Где? Места знать надо.* "Where did you get that book? — Oh, you have to know the right places." **Занима́йте места́ согла́сно ку́пленным биле́там,** see under **занима́йте. Иди́ в одно́ ме́сто,** see under **идти́. Мя́гкое ме́сто,** see under **мя́гкое.**

МЕТА́ЛЛ, -а, *m., youth.* Hard rock (music). ♦*Он слушает только металл.* "Hard rock is all he listens to."

МЕТАЛЛИ́СТ, -а, *m., youth.* A fan of hard rock; one who wears a lot of metal ornaments. ♦*Ты стал металлистом, смотри, сколько на тебе колец, цепей?* "What are you, a 'metallist,' wearing all those rings and chains?"

МЕТА́ТЬ/ЗАМЕТА́ТЬ: Мета́ть/замета́ть икру́, *idiom, joc.* To be excited, be nervous (lit., to throw off roe, used of fish spawning). ♦*Успокойся, что ты икру мечешь, всё будет хорошо.* "Calm down. Don't get all lathered up. Everything will be all right." **Мета́ть харчи́,** *idiom.* To eat a lot and quickly. ♦*Смотри, харчи мечет, как будто неделю не ел.* "He's wolfing down that food as if he hasn't eaten in a week."

МЕТЕ́ЛИТЬ/ОТМЕТЕ́ЛИТЬ, ИЗМЕТЕ́ЛИТЬ. To beat, hit. ♦*Кто это тебя так отметелил, фонарь под глазом с кулак?* "Who beat you up like that? You've got a black eye the size of a fist!"

МЕТЛА́, -ы́, *f.* Tongue (lit., broom). ♦*Метла у тебя работает день и ночь.* "You never give your tongue a rest."

МЕ́ТОД ТЫ́КА, *idiom, joc.* At random, without checking (from тыкать, "to jab, poke"). ♦*Я не буду действовать методом тыка, дело слишком серьёзное.* "I'm not going to go into this blind; it's too serious a matter."

МЕТР С КЕ́ПКОЙ НА КОНЬКА́Х, *idiom.* Said about a short person, a shrimp (lit., a meter with a cap on skates). Cf. "five foot two in high heels."

МЕ́ЧЕНЫЙ, -ого, *m., neg.* M. S. Gorbachev (lit., the marked one, alluding to the prominent birthmark on his forehead as a mark of the devil). ♦*А что сейчас меченый делает?* "What's that devil's spawn up to these days?"

МЕШО́К С ГОВНО́М (ДЕРЬМО́М). See under **говно́**.

МИГА́ЛКА, -и, *f.* A police car or ambulance (from мигать, "to flash"). ♦*Сзади мигалка, освободи дорогу.* "There's a flasher behind us, you'd better pull over."

МИКРО́ХА, -и, *f.* A microelectronic circuit (a wordplay on micro and кроха, something tiny or small).

МИКСТУ́РА, -ы, *f., joc.* An alcoholic drink, esp. as a remedy for a hangover. ♦*Прими сто грамм микстуры, сразу легче станет.* "Take a hundred grams of brew; you'll feel better right away."

МИЛА́ХА, -и, *f.* Dear, darling. ♦*А ты, милаха, с нами едешь или нет?* "What about you, dear? Are you coming with us?"

МИМО́ЗА, -ы, *m. and f., joc.* A weak, delicate person. ♦*А ты, наш мимоза, уже замёрз!* "What a tender bud you are! You're already shivering with cold!"

МИМО́ЗНИК, -а, *Moscow.* A student at МИМО (Московский институт международных отношений, Moscow Institute of International Relations).

МИНЕРА́ЛЬНЫЙ СЕКРЕТА́РЬ, *idiom.* A nickname of M. Gorbachev (lit., mineral secretary, by wordplay on генеральный секретарь, "general secretary," and минеральная вода, "mineral water," alluding to his tee-totaling).

МИНЕ́Т, -а, *m.* Oral sex, an oral sex act. ♦*Я минетом не занимаюсь.* "I don't do blow jobs."

МИНЕ́ТЧИЦА, -ы, *f., rude.* A woman who practices oral sex. ♦*Ты с ней можешь делать что хочешь, она минетчица.* "You can do anything you want with her — she gives blow jobs."

МИ́ТИНГ, -а, *m.* Meeting (from Eng. "meeting"). ♦*Когда у нас митинг?* "When is our meeting?" •**Забива́ть/ заби́ть ми́тинг,** see under **забива́ть**.

МНО́ГО БУ́ДЕШЬ ЗНАТЬ, ПЛО́ХО БУ́ДЕШЬ СПАТЬ, *a rhyming phrase, joc.* It's none of your business, I won't tell you (lit., If you know a lot, you'll sleep badly).

МОБИ́ЛА, -ы, *f.* A mobile phone (cellular telephone). ♦*Сейчас мобилы делают с фотокамерами и музыкой.* "Nowadays cell phones are made with internal cameras and music."

МОБИ́ЛЬНИК, -а, *m.* See **моби́ла**. A cell phone.

МОЗГА́ ЗА МОЗГУ́ ЗАХО́ДИТ, *idiom, joc.* To be mentally exhausted, unable to think (lit., one brain goes behind the other). ♦*У меня мозга за мозгу заходит, надо отдохнуть.* "My brains have had it; I need to take a rest."

МОЗГИ́, -о́в, *pl.* Brains. •**МОЗГИ́** *(nom.)*: **Мозги́ пое́хали,** *idiom, neg.* To be shocked, lose one's mind. ♦*У него от этой новости мозги поехали.* "His brains have taken off as a result of this news." **Мозги́ со́хнут,** *idiom.* To be tired of thinking (lit., one's brains are dried up). ♦*Не знаю, что делать, покупать или не покупать машину, мозги сохнут.* "I just don't know whether to buy the car or not; my brains are addled from thinking about it." **У тебя́ мозги́ есть?** Are you in your right mind? ♦*Зачем ты это сделал, у тебя мозги есть?* "Why did you do that? Are you in your right mind?" **МОЗГИ́** *(acc.)*: **Вправля́ть/ впра́вить мозги́,** see under **вправля́ть**. **Забива́ть/заби́ть мозги́,** see under **забива́ть**. **Па́рить мозги́,** see under **па́рить**. **Пу́дрить/запу́дрить мозги́,** see under **пу́дрить**. **Ка́пать на мозги́,** see under **ка́пать**. **МОЗГА́М** *(dat.)*: **Дава́ть/дать по мозга́м,** see under **дава́ть**. **Бить по мозга́м,** see under **бить**. **МОЗГА́МИ** *(instr.)*: **С мозга́ми,** *idiom.* Clever. ♦*Он — единственный мужик с мозгами во всей компании.* "He's the only one with brains in the whole group." **Раски́нуть мозга́ми,** see under **раски́нуть**. **Шевели́ть/ пошевели́ть мозга́ми,** see under **шевели́ть**.

МОЗГОВА́ТЬ/ОБМОЗГОВА́ТЬ. To think over, consider carefully (cf. мозг). ♦*Это дело надо обмозговать.* "That needs to be carefully thought out."

МОЗГОЁБ, -а, *m., neg., rude.* A pest, annoyingly insistent or pedantic person (lit., brain-fucker, from мозг and **ёб-**). ♦*Сейчас этот мозгоёб опять со своей политикой приставать будет.* "Here comes that pest again with his relentless political talk."

МОЗО́ЛИТЬ/НАМОЗО́ЛИТЬ ГЛАЗА́, *idiom.* To be an eyesore. ♦*Уйди отсюда, не мозоль мне глаза!* "Get out of here, I can't stand looking at you!"

МОЗО́ЛЬ, -я, *m., joc.* Belly. ♦*Хороший мозоль ты успел себе наесть за год.* "That's quite a belly you've managed to put on in one years."

МО́ЗЯ, *idiom, joc.* One may, it's okay (a distorted form of можно). ♦*К вам мозя или вы спите?* "May I come in, or you are still sleeping?"

МОКРЕ́ТЬ, -и, *f.* Wet weather, rain. ♦*На улице мокреть, надень резиновые сапоги.* "It's wet outside. Put on rubber boots."

МО́КРОЕ ДЕ́ЛО, *idiom, crim.* Murder (lit., wet business). ♦*Он специалист по мокрым делам.* "He specializes in murder."

МОКРОХВО́СТКА, -и, *f., rude.* A young, inexperienced girl (lit., one with a wet tail). ♦*Тебя, мокрохвостку, никто слушать не будет.* "No one's going to listen to you, little girl."

МОКРОЩЁЛКА, -и, *f., rude.* See **мокрохвостка.**

МОКРУ́ХА, -и, *f., crim.* Murder (cf. **мо́крое де́ло**). ♦*Я на мокруху не пойду.* "I'm not going to participate in a murder."

МОКРУ́ШНИК, -а, *m., crim.* One convicted for murder (cf. **мокру́ха**). ♦*Этот мокрушник давно сидит.* "That murderer has been in jail a long time."

МОЛЛЮ́СК, -а, *m., joc.* A young person, teenager (lit., a mollusk). ♦*Что вы собираетесь делать, моллюски?* "What are you planning to do, kids?"

МОЛОДЕ́Ц КАК СОЛЁНЫЙ ОГУ-РЕ́Ц, *idiom.* A rhyming phrase of approval: "Good for you!" (lit., you're as good as a pickled cucumber).

МОЛОДНЯ́К, -а́, *m., collect.* Youth, young people. ♦*Молодняк гуляет, шумит.* "The young people are having fun and making noise."

МОЛОДО́Й, -о́го, *m., army, joc.* A new recruit. ♦*Эй ты, молодой, принеси воды!* "Hey, young one, bring us some water!"

МО́ЛОДОСТЬ: Проща́й-мо́лодость, see under **проща́й.**

МОЛОКО́, -а́, *n., army.* A total miss (lit., milk, meaning a complete miss of the blackened center of the target). ♦*Попал или молоко?* "Did I hit anything or was that a 'milk' shot?"

МОЛОТИ́ЛА, -ы, *m. and f., youth.* A first-fighter.

МОЛОТИ́ЛКА, -и, *m., neg.* Lit., a threshing machine. **1.** A chatterbox, one who is constantly talking. ♦*Ты когда-нибудь замолчишь, молотилка несчастный?* "Can't you shut up, you wretched chatterbox?" **2.** One who eats very quickly. ♦*И ты всё это съел? Ну ты и молотилка!* "You already ate all that? What a 'thresher' you are!"

МОЛОТИ́ТЬ¹/ЗАМОЛОТИ́ТЬ, *joc.* To speak very quickly (cf. **молоти́лка 1**). ♦*Не молоти так быстро, расскажи всё по порядку.* "Don't talk in such a rush! Tell everything in order."

МОЛОТИ́ТЬ²/СМОЛОТИ́ТЬ, *joc.* To eat very quickly (cf. **молоти́лка 2**). ♦*Вы уже всё мясо успели смолотить?* "You've already managed to wolf down all that meat?!"

МОЛОТО́К, молотка́, *m.* A champion, hero (lit., a hammer, by wordplay on молодец). ♦*Ты у нас молоток!* "You're our hero!"

МО́ЛЧА, *participle.* Don't ask questions, just do it (lit., silently). ♦*Как мы туда доедем? — Молча.* "How are we going to get there? — Shut up. Let's just go."

МОЛЧА́НКА, -и, *f., neg.* Silence. ♦*Я их спрашиваю, а в ответ — молчанка.* "I ask them a question, and in reply they give me the silent treatment." ●**Игра́ть в молча́нку,** see under **игра́ть.**

МОЛЧА́ТЬ/ЗАМОЛЧА́ТЬ в тря́почку,

idiom. **1.** To be silent out of cowardice (lit., to be silent into one's hankie). ♦*Когда его выгоняли, все вы молчали в тряпочку, а теперь все стали друзьями, когда ситуация переменилась.* "When they kicked him out, not one of you had the balls to say a word; now that the situation has changed, you're all suddenly his friends." **2.** To be silent. ♦*Сиди уж, молчи в тряпочку, тебя не спрашивают.* "Sit down and hold your tongue. No one asked your opinion." •**Молча́ть как партиза́н (на допро́се),** *idiom, joc.* To keep mum, keep secret, refuse to answer questions (lit., to keep quiet as a partisan [under questioning]). ♦*Что ты молчишь как партизан на допросе, ты знаешь или не знаешь, где он?* "Why are you being so close-mouthed with the investigator? Do you know or not?" •**Молча́ть, пока́ зу́бы торча́т,** *rhyming phrase, rude.* A threat to hit in the mouth ("Shut up while you still have your teeth!") •**Молчи́ погро́мче!** *idiom, joc.* Keep quiet, shut up (lit., be quiet a little louder). ♦*Молчи погромче, тебя не спрашивают.* "Shut up! No one's asking your opinion."

МО́НСТРА, -ы, *f., youth, neg.* An ugly person. ♦*Смотри, какая монстра идёт навстречу.* "Look at that monster coming towards us."

МОРГА́ЛЫ, морга́л, *pl., rude.* Eyes (from моргать, "to blink"). ♦*Отверни свои моргалы.* "Don't stare at me."

МО́РДА, -ы, *f., rude.* **1.** Face (lit., animal's muzzle). ♦*Ну и морду он себе отъел!* "His face sure has gotten fatter." **2.** A site interface in a computer. •**Мо́рда лица́,** *idiom, joc.* Face (lit., muzzle face). ♦*Что у тебя такая морда лица, ты расстроен чем-то?* "What's with the long face? Is something eating you?" **Вози́ть/повози́ть мо́рдой об асфа́льт (об стол),** see under **вози́ть.** **Мо́рда кирпича́ про́сит,** see **ро́жа кирпича́ про́сит** under **ро́жа. Мо́рда тре́снет,** see **ро́жа тре́снет** under **ро́жа.**

МОРДАВИ́НД, -а, *m., army.* A head wind (from морда, face, animal's muzzle, and винд, Engl. wind). ♦*Мордавинд силь-* ный, трудно плыть против ветра. "We can't make headway against this wind, it's blowing right up our noses."

МОРДА́НТ -а, *m., neg.* A man with a fat face (see **мо́рда**).

МОРДАТЫ́К, -а, *m.* From морда, face, and тык, a punch, a stroke. "This wind we're up against is like a punch in the nose." See **мордави́нд.**

МОРДЕ́НЬ, -и, *f., neg.* Face. ♦*Наел ты себе мордень.* "You've put some flesh on your face."

МОРДОВОРО́Т, -а, *m., neg.* A thuggish, dangerous-looking man (lit., a face-disfigurer). ♦*Что там за мордоворот сидит?* "Who's that thug sitting over there?"

МО́РЕ РАЗЛИВА́ННОЕ, *idiom.* A lot of alcoholic liquor (lit., an overflowing sea). ♦*Приходим вчера к Николаю, а там спирту — море разливанное.* "So we went over to Nick's yesterday, and we had a regular ocean of drink."

МОРЕМА́Н -а, *m.* A sailor (from море, sea, and ман, a man). ♦*Он бывший мореман, служил во флоте на Балтике.* "He's a former seaman, he served in the Navy in the Baltic."

МОРЖ, -а, *m., abbr., rude.* A Jew (from морда жидовская. ♦*Все моржи, кто хотел, уже уехали в свой Израиль.* "All the Jew-faces who wanted to leave for their dear Israel, already left."

МОРКО́ВКА, -и, *f., joc.* A penis (lit., carrot). ♦*Что ты всё время свою морковку трогаешь, болит, что ли?* "How come you keep touching your 'carrot' — does it hurt?" •**Во́вка-морко́вка,** see under **Во́вка.**

МОРО́ЗКО, -а, *n., youth, neg.* A dull, boring person. ♦*Ну и друг у тебя — морозко. Сидит, всё время молчит, скучно с ним.* "What a cold fish your friend is, sitting there without a word."

МОРО́КА: Разводи́ть/развести́ моро́ку, see under **разводи́ть.**

МОРО́ЧИТЬ/ЗАМОРО́ЧИТЬ я́йца. See under **яйцо́.**

МОРПЕ́Х, -а, *m.* A marine or member of naval infantry (from море, sea, and пехота, infantry).

МÓРЩИТЬ/НАМÓРЩИТЬ ЖÓПУ, *idiom, rude.* **1.** To think hard (lit., to wrinkle one's ass). ♦*Не твоя проблема, не стоит и жопу морщить.* "Don't wrinkle your ass about that, it's not your problem." **2.** To worry. ♦*Не буду я морщить жопу, что там будет после армии.* "I'm not going to wrinkle my ass about what's going to happen when I get out of the army."

МÓРЩИТЬ/НАМÓРЩИТЬ РÉПУ, *idiom.* **1.** To frown, to express displeasure (lit., to wrinkle one's turnip). See **репа**. ♦*Не морщи репу, завтра всё будет как надо.* Wipe that frown off your 'turnip,' life will look better tomorrow." **2.** To think. ♦*Тут долго морщить репу некогда, ты покупаешь машину или нет?* "No need to wrinkle your turnip about it, either buy the car or don't."

МОРЯ́К — С ПÉЧКИ БРЯК, *idiom.* A rhyming phrase describing an inexperienced sailor. ♦*Какой он моряк? — Моряк — с печки бряк.* "What sort of a sailor is he?" — "A good-for-nothing sailor."

МОСЁЛ, мосла́, *т.* A leg or an arm (lit., a bone). ♦*Мослы у тебя больно худые.* "Your legs are awfully skinny."

МОСКА́ЛЬ, -я́, *т., neg.* A Muscovite; a Russian (from the point of view of non-Russians, esp. Ukrainians). ♦*Наш президент продался москалям.* "Our president has sold out to Moscow."

МОТА́ТЬ срок, *idiom, crim.* To serve time, serve a prison sentence (lit., to wind [as thread] one's term). ♦*Он давно срок мотает?* "Has he been in prison long?"

МОТА́ТЬСЯ/МОТАНУ́ТЬСЯ. To go quickly (lit., to flap). ♦*Мотанись в магазин, купи хлеба.* "Run into the store and buy some bread."

МОТÓР, -а, *т.* A car, taxi. ♦*Надо мотор брать, а не то опоздаем.* "We'd better take the car or we'll be late."

МОТÓРНЫЙ, -ая, -ое. Active, businesslike, efficient. ♦*Он парень моторный, сделает что надо в срок.* "He's an efficient fellow; he'll do it right and on

time."

МОХНА́ТАЯ ЛА́ПА, *idiom, neg.* An influential friend, connection (lit., hairy paw). ♦*У него, кажется, мохнатая лапа в банке.* "Apparently he's got a connection at the bank."

МОХНА́ТКА, -и, *f., crim., rude.* Female genitals (lit., hairy one). ♦*Ты только о мохнатке и думаешь.* "All you ever think about is getting some pussy."

МОЧА́ В ГÓЛОВУ УДА́РИЛА/ УДА́РИТ, *idiom, rude.* Lit., someone's urine goes to his head; used of bizarre or unpredictable behavior. ♦*Никто не знает, когда ему моча в голову ударит, и он все планы изменит.* "No one knows when he'll suddenly get a bee in his bonnet and change all the plans."

МОЧА́ЛИТЬ/НАМОЧА́ЛИТЬ, *idiom.* To punish, to scold (lit., to sponge someone's neck). ♦*Тебе шеф намочалит шею, если будешь опаздывать.* "The boss will punish you if you keep coming late."

МОЧА́ЛКА, -и, *f., neg.* An unattractive or promiscuous woman (lit., a piece of bast). ♦*Опять эта мочалка в гости придёт?* "Is that fright of a floozy coming to visit again?"

МОЧЕВÓЙ ПУЗЫ́РЬ, *idiom, army.* Rainy weather not fit for flying (lit., bladder). ♦*Опять мочевой пузырь, летать нельзя, тучи и дождь как из ведра.* "There's a bag of rain out there. We can't fly today, clouds and rain—like from a bucket."

МОЧЁНЫЙ, -ая, -ое, *youth.* Very good. ♦*Мне бы эту мочёную тачку.* "I'd sure like to have that great car."

МОЧИ́ЛОВО, -а, *n., youth, neg.* A scuffle, fight (cf. **мочить**). ♦*Мне мочилово здесь не надо.* "I don't want any fighting here."

МОЧИ́ТЬ/ЗАМОЧИ́ТЬ, *crim. & youth.* **1.** To kill (lit., to wet). ♦*Сейчас в Москве мочат банкиров.* "These days they're murdering bankers in Moscow." **2.** To hit, beat. ♦*Сейчас мы вас мочить будем.* "Now we're going to beat you up."

●**Замочи́ть жа́ло,** *idiom, rude.* To have

sex with a woman (lit., to wet one's stinger). ◆*С кем бы жало замочить?* "Which woman should I go to bed with?" **Замочи́ть рога́,** *idiom, crim.* To get into an unpleasant situation, get into trouble (lit., to wet one's horns). ◆*Мы в квартиру через окно, а там собака, замочили рога и бежать.* "We entered the apartment through a window, but there was a dog inside, so we were in hot water and had to run for it."

МОЧКОВА́ТЬСЯ/ЗАМОЧКОВА́ТЬ-СЯ, *youth, neg.* To be frightened, show cowardice. ◆*Не мочкуйся, они нас не тронут.* "Don't be scared; they won't hurt us."

МОЧКО́ВЫЙ, -ая, -ое, *youth.* Cowardly (cf. **мочи́ть**").

МОЧО́К, мочка́, *m., youth, neg.* A coward. ◆*С мочками дел не имею.* "I won't have anything to do with cowards."

МОЯ́ ТВОЯ́ НЕ ПОНИМА́Й, *idiom, joc.* I don't understand what you're saying (imitation of broken Russian).

МРАК, *pred., neg.* Awful, terrible (lit., gloom, darkness). ◆*Погода — мрак, холод собачий!* "This weather is awful, cold as hell!"

МРАЧИ́ЛОВО, -а, *n.* A bad mood, depression, misery (from мрак, darkness). ◆*Что-то мрачилово не проходит, жить не хочется.* "I'm in a dark mood, I feel like killing myself."

МУДА́К, -а́, *m., neg.* A fool, idiot (cf. **муде́**). ◆*Мудаком был, мудаком и остался.* "He always was a fool and he still is."

МУДАШВИ́ЛИ, *m., indecl., joc.* A fool, an idiot (from **муда́к** and the typical Georgian surname formative -швили). ◆*Что хочет этот мудашвили?* "What does that idiot want?"

МУДЕ́, -я́, *n., rude.* Male genitals. ◆*Зачеса́лося в муд́ях, бу́дет переме́на пого́ды на днях,* *idiom, rude.* "An itch in the crotch means the weather will change soon." **Звене́ть/зазвене́ть муд́ями,** see under **звене́ть.**

МУДЁЖ, -а́, *m., neg., rude.* Stupidity, foolishness, nonsense (cf. **муда́к**). ◆*Это*

не статья, а муд́еж. "This isn't an article — it's just nonsense."

МУДИ́СТИКА, -и, *f., rude.* A boring subject (cf. **муда́к**). ◆*Как ты эту мудистику можешь изучать?* "How can you stand studying that boring stuff?"

МУДИ́ТЬ/НАМУДИ́ТЬ, *rude.* To spoil, break (cf. **муда́к**). ◆*Что вы намудили тут с телевизором?* "How did you break the television?"

МУ́ДО, -а, *n., rude.* A fool, idiot (by wordplay on чудо, "miracle," and **муда́к**). ◆*Ну ты и мудо, ходишь зимой без пальто.* "You're a choice idiot, going around without a coat in the middle of winter!"

МУДО́ВЫЙ, -ая, -ое, *rude.* Foolish, idiotic, unpleasant (cf. **муда́к**). ◆*Мне надоела эта мудовая погода, всё время дождь и дождь.* "I'm sick of this disgusting weather; it just rains and rains." **Муд́овые рыда́нья,** *idiom, neg.* Nonsense, empty babble. ◆*Что-нибудь было интересное на конференции? — Нет, одни мудовые рыданья.* "So, did anything interesting happen at the conference? — No, just a lot of babble."

МУ́ДОМ МА́ЯТЬСЯ, *idiom, rude.* See **ду́рью ма́яться.**

МУДОЗВО́Н, -а, *m., rude.* A fool, idler, foolish chatterer (lit., one who rings his balls; from **муде́** and звонить). ◆*Ничего умного этот мудозвон не скажет.* "You won't hear anything intelligent from that idiot."

МУДО́ХАТЬ/ОТМУДО́ХАТЬ, *rude.* To beat up, beat severely (cf. **муда́к**). ◆*Тебя мало отмудохали в прошлый раз, ещё хочешь?* "What's the matter, you didn't get enough of a beating last time?"

МУДО́ХАТЬСЯ/ЗАМУДО́ХАТЬСЯ, *rude.* To do something with difficulty, wear oneself out with effort (cf. **муда́к**). ◆*Мы совсем замудохались с этим мотором, ничего не получается.* "We've completely exhausted ourselves over this motor and we still can't get it to work."

МУДОШЛЁП, -а, *m., neg. rude.* A good-for-nothing, incompetent person (by wordplay on губошлёп, "lip smacker," i.e., baby, and **муда́к**). ♦*Ты опять, мудошлёп, прозевал свою очередь.* "You big baby, you've missed your turn again."

МУДЯ́НКА, -и, *f., neg., rude.* Something boring (cf. **муда́к**). ♦*В парламенте мудянку разводят, речи говорят, а народу жрать нечего.* "In Parliament they drone on with their speeches, while the people have nothing to eat."

МУЖ: Муж объе́лся груш, *rhyming phrase, joc.* Lit., someone's husband ate too many pears; an absurd rhyming phrase used of an incompetent or disappointing husband. ♦*Мой муж, муж объелся груш, даже гвоздь забить не умеет.* "My husband ate too many pears — he can't even hammer a nail." **Не говори́, у само́й муж пья́ница,** see under **не.**

МУЖСКА́Я ЛО́ГИКА, *idiom, joc.* Lit., male logic; used to characterize typical male prejudices. The prime example is ♦*Что такое мужская логика? Это когда мужчина говорит о женщине: — Дала. Вот блядь! — Не дала. Вот блядь!* "What is male logic? It's when a man calls a woman a bitch both for going to bed with him and for refusing to go to bed with him."

МУЖЧИ́НА, КАК ЗАГА́Р, СНАЧА́ЛА ПРИСТАЁТ К ЖЕ́НЩИНЕ, ПОТО́М СМЫВА́ЕТСЯ, *idiom, joc.* Men can't be trusted; lit., "A man is like a suntan: at first he sticks to a woman, but then he fades away." ♦*Значит, он к ней уже не ходит, ну что ж, мужчина, как загар. . . .* "So he's broken up with her? Well, a man is like a suntan. . . ."

МУЗО́Н, -a, *m., youth.* Music. ♦*Заведи музон.* "Play some music."

МУ́ЛЬКА, -и, *f., youth.* Narcotics, dope. ♦*У меня осталась мулька, угощайся.* "I still have some dope — help yourself!"

МУЛЯ́КА, -и, *f., south.* **1.** Muddy water. ♦*В колодце одна муляка, пить нельзя.* "That stuff in the well is mud, we can't drink it." **2.** Young wine.

МУМУ́: Не на́до муму́, see under **не.**

МУР-МУ́Р, -a, *m.* Love (lit., the sound of a

cat purring). ♦*Как там у них мур-мур, к свадьбе дело идёт?* "Is it still all kisses and purring between them? Are they going to get married?"

МУРА́, -ы́, *f., neg.* Nonsense. ♦*Зачем ты пишешь эту муру?* "Why do you write such nonsense?"

МУРАВЬЁВ ТЕБЕ́ В ШТАНЫ́, *idiom, neg.* May you be punished (lit., [may you have] ants in your pants). ♦*За эти слова муравьёв тебе в штаны.* "May you fry in hell for saying that."

МУРЛО́, -á, *n., rude.* **1.** A face. ♦*Отверни мурло!* "Get your face out of my sight!" **2.** A dull, ignorant person. ♦*Это мурло ко всем пристаёт с указаниями.* "That ignoramus is always bossing everyone around."

МУРМУДО́Н, -a, *m., neg.* An idiot, a fool. ♦*Какой мурмудон это сделал?* "Who's the jerk that did this?"

МУРЫ́ЖИТЬ/ПРОМУРЫ́ЖИТЬ, *neg.* To keep someone waiting, make someone wait. ♦*Он меня в коридоре промурыжил почти час.* "He kept me waiting in the corridor almost an hour."

МУСЁЛ, мусла́, *m., army, neg.* A Muslim militant (from мусульманин, a Muslim, and осёл, a donkey). ♦*В город не ходи, там за каждой дверью мусёл с Калашом.* «Don't go into town, there's a rag-head with a Kalashnikov behind every door."

МУСКУЛА́НТ, -a, *m., youth, joc.* A muscular person, a bodybuilder. ♦*Каким ты мускулантом стал.* "What a Mr. Muscles you've become!"

МУ́СКУЛЫ: Кача́ть/накача́ть му́скулы, see under **кача́ть.**

МУСО́ЛИТЬ/ЗАМУСО́ЛИТЬ, *neg.* **1.** To soil, stain. ♦*Ты мне всю книгу замусолил.* "You've smudged up my whole book." **2.** To discuss at length, to go over and over something. ♦*Сколько можно мусолить этот вопрос?* "There's a limit to how long we can keep discussing this question."

МУ́СОР, -a, *m., neg.* A police officer (lit., rubbish). ♦*Этот мусор у них самый активный.* "That cop is the most active one among them."

МУ́СОРНИК, -а, *m., crim., neg.* A police station (cf. **му́сор**).

МУСОРОВО́З, -а, *m., neg.* A police car (lit., garbage truck).

МУСТА́НГ, -а, *m., youth, joc.* A louse (lit., a mustang). ♦*У вас мустанги в общаге есть?* "Are there mustangs in your dorm?"

МУСТАША́, -ей, *pl., youth.* Mustaches (from Eng. "mustache"). ♦*Надо мусташа себе завести.* "I think I'll grow a mustache."

МУТИ́ТЬ/ЗАМУТИ́ТЬ, *youth.* To dilute narcotics for injecting (lit., to muddy). ♦*Замутил, коли скорей, не могу ждать.* "If you've got it diluted, give me a shot quickly — I can't wait any longer."

МУТИ́ТЬСЯ/ЗАМУТИ́ТЬСЯ, *crim. & youth.* To get high on drugs (lit., to get muddy). ♦*Они там сидят за домом, мутятся травкой.* "They're sitting behind the house getting high on grass."

МУ́ТНЫЙ, -ая, -ое, *neg.* Drunk, high (cf. **мути́ться**). ♦*Не давай ему больше пить, он уже мутный.* "Don't let him drink any more, he's drunk already." •**Му́тный глаз,** *joc.* A bar, tavern (lit., muddy eye). ♦*Сходим в мутный глаз, выпьем.* "Let's drop into the 'muddy eye' and have a drink."

МУТОТА́, -ы́, *f., neg.* Something dull, tedious, boring. ♦*Он пишет всякую мутоту, читать невозможно.* "He writes such boring stuff that you just can't read it."

МУТУ́ЗИТЬ/ОТМУТУ́ЗИТЬ. To beat up. ♦*Кого они там вдвоём мутузят?* "Who's that the two of them are beating up over there?"

МУТЬ, -и, *f., neg.* Nonsense, rubbish. ♦*Всё это муть, не верь этим слухам.* "That's all nonsense! Don't believe those rumors."

МУФЛО́Н, -а, *m., neg.* An idiot. ♦*Такому муфлону ничего не объяснишь.* "There's no use trying to explain anything to an idiot like that."

МУ́ХА: Кака́я му́ха це-це́ укуси́ла за яйцё? see under **яйцо́. Под му́хой,**

idiom, joc. Drunk (lit., under a fly). ♦*Он пришёл слегка под мухой.* "He arrived slightly under the influence." **До́хнуть как му́хи,** see under **до́хнуть.**

МУХОМО́Р, -а, *m., joc.* An old man (lit., fly agaric). ♦*Этот мухомор твой дед?* "Is that old geezer your grandfather?"

МЫ ПАХА́ЛИ, *idiom, joc.* Don't exaggerate, don't boast (used in reaction to someone's boasting; lit., we plowed). ♦*Ты знаешь, мы вдвоём за день вскопали весь огород. — Ну да, мы пахали.* "The two of us managed to hoe the whole garden in one day. — Big deal."

МЫ́ЛИТЬСЯ: Не мы́лься, бри́ться не бу́дешь, see under **не.**

МЫ́ЛО, -а, *n.* **1.** A soap opera or cheesy TV serial (lit., soap). ♦*Я это мыло не переношу.* "I can't stand soaps." **2.** E-mail. ♦*Пришли мне по мылу фотки.* "Send me some pics over the e-mail."

МЫ́ЛО: Без мы́ла (в)лезть в жо́пу (в зад), see under **жо́па.**

МЫ́ЛЬНИЦА, -ы, *f., joc., neg.* Cheap, esp. plastic things (lit., soapbox). ♦*Такой мыльницей хороших снимков не сделаешь.* "You can't get good snapshots from that cheap camera."

МЫ́МРА, -ы, *f., neg.* An unattractive woman. ♦*Где он себе эту мымру нашёл?* "Where did he find himself that hag?"

МЫ́МРИК, -а, *m., joc.* A nickname of Communist Party leader G. Zyuganov (by wordplay on Мымрино, the village where he was born, and мымра (*obs.*), "a gloomy, dull person").

МЫ́РДА, -ы, *f.* Морда, лицо; a muzzle, a face. ♦*Вот уж мырда так мырда, смотреть противно.* "That is the ugliest mug I have ever seen."

МЫСЛИ́ТЕЛЬНАЯ ЧАСТЬ, *idiom.* A behind (lit., a thinking part). Standard Russian has words for a thinking mind (ум) and a "back mind" (задний ум) which sounds the same as the word for buttocks (зад). Мыслительная часть means literally the buttocks. ♦*Поднимай свою мыслительную часть, пора работать.* "Stop sitting on your mind and get to work." See **ду́мать за́дницей.**

МЫЧА́ТЬ: Не мычи́т, не те́лится, see under **не.**

МЫШИ́НЫЙ ГЛАЗ, *idiom, pos., rude.* Small female sexual organs (lit., a mouse's eye). ♦*Все знают, у неё мышиный глаз, хорошо бы попробовать.* "Everyone knows she's got a mouse's eye — I sure would like to try it."

МЫ́ШКА-НОРУ́ШКА, *idiom.* Lit., mouse hole, from the name of a fairy-tale heroine. **1.** Surveillance. ♦*Надо проверить, нет ли где мышки-норушки.* "We've got to check whether this place is under surveillance." **2.** A detective, a spy. ♦*Вон там в углу сидит мышка-норушка.* "There's an undercover agent sitting in the corner."

МЫШЬ: Не лови́ть мыше́й, see under **лови́ть.**

МЭ, *n., indecl.* A men's bathroom (abbreviation for мужской, "men's"). ♦*Где здесь мэ?* "Is there a men's room around here?"

МЭН, -а, *m., youth.* A man, especially a good-looking one (from Eng. "man"). ♦*Познакомь меня с этим мэном.* "Introduce me to that fellow."

МЭ́НОВЫЙ, -ая, -ое, *youth.* Men's, of men (cf. **мэн**). ♦*Где здесь мэновый прикид?* "Where's the men's clothing department?"

МЭ́НША, -и, *f., youth.* A woman, girl (from Eng. "man" with a feminine suffix). ♦*Эта мэнша танцует?* "Does that girl dance?"

МЯ́ГКОЕ МЕ́СТО, *idiom, joc.* Buttocks. ♦*Ты не отсидел себе мягкое место?* "Haven't you worn out your 'soft spot,' sitting for so long?"

МЯ́ЛКА, -и, *f., neg.* A mouth (cf. **мять**). ♦*Чего-то забросить в мялку приготовила?* "Have you made anything to eat?"

МЯ́МЛЯ, -и, *f., neg.* An indecisive person. ♦*С этим мямлей тебе будет непросто.* "You're in for a hard time with that wishy-washy fellow."

МЯТЬ/УМЯ́ТЬ. To eat (lit., to crumple). ♦*Хорошо бы молодой картошечки умять с маслом!* "It would be nice to have some buttered new potatoes!"

МЯТЬ ха́рю, *idiom, rude.* To sleep (lit., to crumple one's face). ♦*Я пошёл харю мять.* "I'm going to take a nap."

НА БАБЦА́ И ЗВЕРЬ БЕЖИ́Т, *idiom, joc.* A woman always attracts men (punning on the proverb На ловца и зверь бежит, "The game actually runs into the hunter's net"; lit., "the game actually runs into the woman's net").

НА БЕЗРЫ́БЬЕ САМА́ РА́КОМ СТА́НЕШЬ, *idiom, rude.* When there is a shortage of men, you can't be too choosy (lit., "when there are no fish, you have to assume the crab's position." This expression is a conflation of two idioms: На безрыбье и рак рыба, "When there are no fish, even a crab counts as a fish," and **станови́ться/стать ра́ком**). ♦*А что делать, приходится с ним спать. — На безрыбье сама раком станешь.* "I'm not so crazy about him, but I'm reduced to sleeping with him. — Well, when there are no fish, you have to present your own ass."

НА ВСЯ́КИЙ ПОЖА́РНЫЙ СЛУ́ЧАЙ, *idiom.* Just in case, in case of emergency (lit., in case of fire). ♦*На всякий пожарный случай возьми тёплую одежду, вдруг похолодает.* "Take some warm clothes just in case it gets cold."

НА ГОЛУБО́М ГЛАЗУ́, *idiom.* Outright, blazenly (lit., on a blue eye). ♦*Он уверял меня на голубом глазу, а оказалось всё враньё.* "He assured me of this to my face, but it turned out to be a pack of lies."

НА ЗАРЕ́ ТУМА́ННОЙ Ю́НОСТИ, *idiom, joc.* Long ago (lit., at the dawn of misty youth). ♦*Читали и мы поэзию на заре туманной юности.* "We too used to read poetry back in the days of our youth."

НА КАРА́ЧКАХ, *idiom.* On all fours. ♦*Где ты так напился? На карачках домой приполз!* "Where did you get so drunk? You came crawling home on all fours."

НА КУДЫ́КИНУ ГО́РУ (ворова́ть поми́дры), *rhyming phrase, joc.* Used in answer to the question "Where are you going?" in the sense of "none of your business," "never mind" (lit., to the mountain over there [to steal tomatoes]; by a nonsense rhyme). ♦*Ты куда? — На кудыкину гору воровать помидоры.* "Where are you going? — None of your business."

НА ЛЁГКОМ КА́ТЕРЕ К ЕДРЁНОЙ МА́ТЕРИ, *rhyming phrase, rude.* (Worthless! No way! (Lit., on a light launch to a fucking mother). ♦*Хорошо бы твою статью — на лёгком катере...* "Your article is a piece of junk."

НА РАЗ ПОССА́ТЬ, *idiom, rude.* A dismissive remark about a small penis (lit, good for only one piss).

НА ХАЛЯ́ВУ И У́КСУС СЛА́ДКИЙ, *idiom, joc.* Lit., even vinegar is sweet when it's free. ♦*Мне понравился санаторий, всё бесплатно, за всё платит профсоюз. — На халяву и уксус сладкий.* "I had a great vacation — everything was free, the union paid for it all. — Yes, even vinegar is sweet when it's free."

НА ХЕРА́ ТА ХА́ТА?, *idiom, neg.* It's useless, there's no point. (Imitating the sound of Japanese). ♦*Будем покупать зимние шины? — На хера та хата?* "Should we buy snow tires?" — "What the hell for?"

НА ХУ́ТОР БА́БОЧЕК ЛОВИ́ТЬ, *idiom, rude.* Lit., to the village to catch butterflies; used as an evasion of the question "Where are you going?" ♦*Ты куда идёшь? — На хутор бабочек ловить.* "Where are you going? — None of your business."

НАБИВА́ТЬ/НАБИ́ТЬ (текст), *idiom.* To type some text on the computer. ♦*Набей мне пару страниц.* "Type me a couple pages."

НАБИВА́ТЬ/НАБИ́ТЬ жа́ло, *idiom.* To eat (lit., to stuff one's mouth); cf. **жа́ло.** ♦*Пора бы и жало набить.* "It's time to eat."

НАБИРА́ТЬСЯ/НАБРА́ТЬСЯ, *neg.* To get drunk (lit., to fill oneself). ♦*Где ты уже успел набраться?* "Where did you manage to get so drunk already?"

НАБЛАТЫ́КИВАТЬСЯ/НАБЛАТЫ́-КАТЬСЯ, *crim. & youth.* **1.** To adopt criminal manners. ♦*Я вижу, ты наблатыкался, куришь, ругаешься матом.* "I see you've become quite a hood, smoking and swearing like that." **2.** To acquire a skill. ♦*Где ты так наблатыкался в английском?* "Where did you manage to get so good at speaking English?"

НАБОДА́ТЬСЯ, *perf.* To get drunk (from бодаться, to butt heads). ♦*Когда же вы успели так набодаться, идти не можете.* "When did you have time to get so wasted? You can't even walk."

НАБРА́СЫВАТЬ/НАБРО́СИТЬ. To add onto a sum (lit., to throw on). ♦*Набрось ещё тысячу, тогда продам этот арбуз.* "Throw in another thousand and the watermelon is yours."

НАБРОСА́ТЬ понты́, *idiom, neg.* To tell lies. ♦*Тебе ничего не стоит набросать понты.* "You think nothing of lying."

НАВА́ЛИВАТЬ/НАВАЛИ́ТЬ (ку́чу), *rude.* To soil, to make a mess (lit., to make a heap). ♦*Не ходи, там кто-то навалил кучу.* "Watch your step. Someone left a pile over there."

НАВА́ЛОМ, *adv.* A lot (lit., in bulk, in heaps). ♦*У него денег навалом.* "He's got heaps of money."

НАВА́Р, -а, *m.* Profit, advantage (lit., a thick meat broth). ♦*А мне какой навар от этого будет?* "What profit will I get from it?"

НАВА́РИВАТЬ/НАВАРИ́ТЬ. To make money (lit., to boil broth; cf. **нава́р**). ♦*Он на продаже джинсов наварил приличную сумму.* "He made quite a sum of money selling jeans." •**Навари́ть ча́йник,** *idiom, crim.* To become infected with gonorrhea. ♦*Будешь у девок, не навари чайник, среди них есть заразные.* "Be careful not to get the clap if you're going to be with the girls — a lot of them have it."

НАВЕРНУ́ТЬ, *perf. only.* To strike, hit. ♦*Ты видел, как она его навернула тарелкой?* "Did you see the way she hit him with that plate?"

НАВЕ́ШАННЫЙ, -ая, -ое, *youth.* Fashionable dressed.

НАВЕ́ШИВАТЬ/НАВЕ́СИТЬ пилюле́й, *idiom, joc.* To beat, hit. ♦*Ему вчера здорово навесили пилюлей.* "They gave him quite a beating yesterday." **Навеши-вать/наве́сить пиздюле́й,** see under **дава́ть.**

НАВИСА́ТЬ/НАВИ́СНУТЬ, *neg.* To interfere or get in the way by hovering about, standing over someone's shoulder. ♦*Не нависай, дай закончить письмо.* "Don't keep fluttering around me like that! Let me finish my letter!"

НАВОДИ́ТЬ/НАВЕСТИ́. To inform, put in the know. ♦*Кто вас навёл на этих мафиози?* "Who put you on to those mafiosi?" •**Наводи́ть/навести́ макия́ж,** *idiom.* To put on makeup, make oneself up. ♦*Сейчас наведу макияж и я готова ехать на концерт.* "I'll just put on some makeup and I'll be ready to go the concert." **Наводи́ть/навести́ мара-фе́т,** *idiom.* To dress up, spruce up, deck oneself out. ♦*Ты навёл такой марафет, куда идёшь?* "Where are you going all dressed up like that?" **Наводи́ть/навести́ шо́рох,** *idiom.* To make a row, raise confusion. ♦*Мы на танцах навели шорох, долго помнить будут.* "We kicked up such a row at the dance, it won't be forgotten." **Наводи́ть/навести́ шмон,** *idiom.* To make a scene, brawl, raise a ruckus. ♦*Пора уходить, а то мать такой шмон наведёт.* "We'd better get out of here before your mother kicks up a fuss."

НАВО́ДКА, -и, *f.* Instruction, direction. ♦*Так будет какая-нибудь наводка, что делать дальше, или нет?* "So will there be any instructions about what to do next, or not?"

НАВО́ДЧИК, -а, *m., neg.* A traitor, betrayer. ♦*Так вот кто наводчик, это ты нас предал!* "So you're the traitor who gave us away!"

НАВОРА́ЧИВАТЬ/НАВЕРНУ́ТЬ, *joc.* To eat much and quickly (lit., to heap up, pile on). ♦*Хорошо мы навернули борща.* "We really pigged out on borscht."

НАВОРО́Т, -а, *m., youth.* **1.** Decorations,

costume jewelry. ♦*Сколько у тебя на-
воротов, и это все твои?* "Are all those
bangles you're wearing yours?" **2.** *pl.
only, neg.* Complications, difficulties. ♦*Я
в такие навороты не въезжаю.* "I'm
not going to get involved in those complications."

НАВОРО́ЧЕННЫЙ, -ая, -ое, *youth.*
Fashionably and expensively dressed.
♦*Он всегда такой навороченный!*
"He's always such a clotheshorse."

НАГА́Р, -а, *m.* Profit, advantage (lit., burnt
wick of a candle). ♦*А мне какой нагар
светит?* "What's in it for me?"

НА́ГЛОСТЬ — ВТОРО́Е СЧА́СТЬЕ,
idiom, neg. Lit., selfishness is a second
happiness; used in reproach of selfish or
pushy people. ♦*Смотри, он уже без
очереди влез, наглость — второе счастье.* "Look at that guy cutting ahead in
line there! Well, selfishness is a second
happiness."

НАГЛОТА́ТЬСЯ, *perf.* To overeat. ♦*Так
наглотался, спать захотелось.* ""I ate
so much that I got sleepy."

НА́ГЛУХО, *adv.* Entirely, completely (lit.,
to deafness). ♦*Я наглухо забыл, о чём
мы договорились.* "I completely forgot
what we agreed on."

НА́ГЛЫЙ КАК ТАНК, *idiom, neg.*
Pushy, aggressive. ♦*Он всё равно всё
возьмёт без очереди, он наглый как
танк.* "He gets everything he wants
without waiting in line — he's pushy as a
tank."

НАГОВНЯ́ТЬ, *perf., neg.* To spoil, to
harm (from **говно́**). ♦*Ты чинил мотор
и всё наговнял.* "You ruined the motor
when you tried to fix it."

**НАГОРЕ́ТЬ: Кому́-л. нагори́т (наго-
ре́ло) за что-л.,** *idiom.* Someone will be
(was) punished for something. ♦*Тебе
ещё нагорит за потерю денег.*
"You're going to be in hot water for losing the money."

НАГРАЖДА́ТЬ/НАГРАДИ́ТЬ доско́й,
idiom. To reward for good work (at
school, a factory, etc.) by hanging someone's photo on a board of honor (lit., to
reward with a board). ♦*Тебя наградили*

доской или дали премию? "Did you get
a bonus or did they just reward you with a
board?"

НАГРЕ́ТЬ, *perf. only, neg.* To cheat; to
win from someone (lit., to heat). ♦*На
сколько они тебя нагрели в карты?*
"How much did they take you for in the
card game?" •**Нагре́ть ру́ки,** *idiom.* To
make money (lit., to warm one's hands).
♦*Он на бананах нагрел руки.* "He
made a bundle trading in bananas."

НАДЕВА́ТЬ/НАДЕ́ТЬ   намо́рдник,
idiom. To supress, to silence (lit., to
muzzle). ♦*Кто же наденет намордник
на прессу?* "Who can muzzle the press?"

НАДИРА́ТЬСЯ/НАДРА́ТЬСЯ, *joc.* To
get very drunk. ♦*Ты опять надрался с
друзьями?* "So you got blotto with your
friends again?"

НАДРОЧИ́ТЬСЯ, *perf. only, rude.* To
learn to do something very well (cf. **дро-
чи́ть**). ♦*Знаешь, как он надрочился
шить брюки, делает как фирменные.*
"He's become an expert at sewing slacks
— the ones he makes are just like those
from a commercial firm."

НАДРЫВА́ТЬ/НАДОРВА́ТЬ пуп, *idiom,
neg.* To work very hard (lit., to split one's
navel, i.e., get a hernia). ♦*Я больше пуп
надрывать не собираюсь.* "I'm not
going to knock myself out anymore."

НАДУВА́ТЬСЯ/НАДУ́ТЬСЯ, *business.*
To spend all one's money on something
(lit., to blow oneself up). ♦*Вся семья
надулась, мы, наконец, купили компьютер.* "Our whole family blew all our
money on a computer."

НАДУВНО́Й МАТРА́С, *idiom, joc.* A
cultured, educated person (lit., unflatable
mattress). ♦*Ты у нас один надувной
матрас, на все вопросы знаешь
ответы.* "You're the only egghead
among us; you know all the answers."

НАДУ́ЛО, *idiom, joc.* Of unknown paternity (lit., it blew in; an evasive answer to
the question of a child's paternity). ♦*От
кого у неё сын? — Не знаю, надуло.*
"Who's the father of her child? — I don't
know. It just came along like a puff of
wind."

НАДЫ́БАТЬ, *perf. only.* To find, come upon. ♦ *Я надыбал интересную книгу.* "I've come upon an interesting book."

НАЁБ, -а, *m., rude.* Cheating, deceit (cf. **ёб-**). ♦ *Мне твой постоянный наёб осточертал.* "I'm sick and tired of your constant cheating." ●**Наёб трудово́го наро́да,** *idiom, rude.* Widespread deception, fooling a lot of people (lit., deception of the working people). ♦ *Опять с зарплатой — наёб трудового народа.* "Again they've ripped off the working people with these salaries."

НАЕБА́ЛОВКА, -и, *f., rude.* Deceit, trickery, scam (cf. **наёб**). ♦ *С ценами происходит сплошная наебаловка.* "Prices now are a complete rip-off."

НАЕБНУ́ТЬ, *perf. only, rude.* Cf. **наёб**. **1.** To hit, beat. ♦ *Наебни его чем-нибудь, чтобы выключил радио.* "Hit him with something so he'll turn off the radio." **2.** To eat something quickly. ♦ *Давай наебнём суп.* "Let's knock down a bowl of soup."

НАЁБЫВАТЬ/НАЕБА́ТЬ, *rude.* To deceive, cheat (cf. **наёб**). ♦ *Меня крупно наебали на рынке.* "They really ripped me off at the market."

НАЁБЫВАТЬСЯ/НАЕБНУ́ТЬСЯ, *rude.* Cf. **наёб**. **1.** To fall. ♦ *Здесь лёд, не наебнись.* "Don't fall on the ice here." **2.** To be mistaken, to come to nothing, to fall through. *Наша с ним сделка наебнулась.* "Our deal with him fell through." ●**Наебну́ться ме́дным та́зом,** *idiom, rude.* To have something come to nothing, to have one's hopes frustrated (lit., to be covered by a copper pot). ♦ *Моя подруга наебнулась медным тазом с поездкой в Штаты.* "My girlfriend's plan to go to the States came to nothing."

НАЕЗЖА́ТЬ/НАЕ́ХАТЬ, *youth, neg.* To demand, insist, exert pressure. ♦ *Не наезжай, всё равно не скажу, где взял деньги.* "It's no use pressuring me. I'm not going to tell you where I got the money."

НАЖИРА́ТЬСЯ/НАЖРА́ТЬСЯ, *neg.* To get very drunk. ♦ *Стоит ли так нажираться?* "What's the use of getting

that drunk?" ●**Нажира́ться /нажра́ться в дыми́ну,** *idiom.* To drink oneself "into a fog." ♦ *Что же ты нажрался в дымину, даже идти не можешь?* "Look at you — you've drunk yourself into such a fog that you can't even walk." **Нажира́ться/ нажра́ться в жо́пу,** see under **жо́па**. **Нажира́ться/нажра́ться до порося́чьего ви́зга,** *idiom, neg.* To get drunk "to a pig's squeal." ♦ *Ты с ним всегда нажираешься до поросячьего визга.* "You always get squealing drunk with him." **Нажира́ться/нажра́ться до уса́чки,** *idiom, rude.* To get "shitting drunk." ♦ *Вы смотрите, не нажритесь до усрачки на рыбалке, знаю я вас.* "See to it that you don't get shitting drunk on your fishing trip." **Нажира́ться/на-жра́ться как свинья́,** *idiom, neg.* To get drunk to the point of sickness (lit., drunk as a pig). ♦ *Каждый раз ты нажираешься как свинья!* "You always get drunk as a pig!"

НАЖО́ПИТЬ, *perf.* To spank (cf. **жо́па**). ♦ *За разбитую чашку нажопить тебя надо!* "You're going to get a spanking for breaking that cup!"

НАЖО́Р: В нажо́ре, *idiom, neg.* In a state of extreme drunkenness. ♦ *Он со вчерашнего вечера в нажоре.* "He's been blotto since last night's party."

НАЖО́РИСТЫЙ, -ая, -ое, *youth.* Highly intoxicating. ♦ *Надо всё время этот портвейн брать, он нажористый.* "This wine is the thing to drink — it's very strong."

НАИВНЯ́К, -а́, *m., joc.* A sucker, naive person. ♦ *И ты, наивняк, ему поверил?* "So you were enough of a sucker to believe him?"

НАЙТ, -а, *m., youth.* Night (from Eng. "night"). ♦ *С кем ты сегодня найт проводишь?* "Who are you spending the night with tonight?"

НАЙТА́ТЬ/ПЕРЕНАЙТА́ТЬ, *youth.* To spend the night (cf. **найт**). ♦ *Где ты сегодня найтаешь?* "Where are you going to spend the night?"

НАКА́ЛЫВАТЬ/НАКОЛО́ТЬ, *neg.* To deceive, cheat (lit., to impale). ♦ *Что же ты меня наколол, обещал, а не сде-*

лал? "How come you tricked me and didn't do what you promised?"

НАКА́ЛЫВАТЬСЯ/НАКОЛО́ТЬСЯ, *neg.* To be tricked, deceived. ♦*На этом деле я уже раз накололся, хватит.* "I was ripped off that way once, but never again."

НАКАТИ́ТЬ В РЕ́ПУ, *idiom.* To hit, to beat up (lit., to roll in the turnips). ♦*Слова вы не понимаете, остается накатить вам в репу раз и навсегда.* "If you won't listen, I'll just have to beat you up."

НАКА́ТЫВАТЬ/НАКАТИ́ТЬ. To drink (lit., to roll on). ♦*Ну, давай накатим по сто грамм.* "Come on, let's have a shot."

НАКА́ЧЕННЫЙ, -ая, -ое. Strong, muscular (lit., pumped; cf. **качо́к**). ♦*Какой сын у тебя накаченный!* "What an ironman your son is!"

НАКА́ЧИВАТЬ/НАКАЧА́ТЬ, *rude.* To impregnate (lit., to pump). ♦*Он её давно накачал, видишь, уже живот большой.* "He knocked her up a long time ago. You can see her pregnancy is pretty far along."

НАКА́ЧИВАТЬСЯ/НАКАЧА́ТЬСЯ. Lit., to pump oneself up. **1.** To practice bodybuilding (cf. "pumping iron"). ♦*Смотри, как ты накачался за лето.* "Look how much you've built up your body this summer." **2.** *neg.* To drink a lot, get drunk. ♦*Когда вы успели накачаться?* "When did you manage to tank up like that?"

НАКА́ЧКА, -и, *f.* A reprimand, punishment (lit., pumping). ♦*Сейчас будет у начальства накачка за прошлые проколы.* "Now the management is going to get into trouble for their past mistakes."

НАКЛА́ДЫВАТЬ/НАКЛА́СТЬ В КИ́СУ, *idiom.* To beat up (lit., to put in a pocket, *dated*). ♦*Накласть в кису не помешает, слишком нос начал задирать.* "He's got a piss-poor attitude. Beating his face in wouldn't be a bad idea."

НАКЛО́КИВАТЬ/НАКЛО́КАТЬ. Said of time (from Engl. clock). See **ти́кать.** ♦*Сколько там наклокало?* "What time is it?"

НАКЛЮ́КАТЬСЯ, *perf.* To get drunk.

НАКО́ЛКА, -и, *f.* Lit., a sting, prick. **1.** A trick, joke ♦*Это что, наколка? А мы поверили.* "What is this, a joke? And we believed it!" **2.** A tattoo. ♦*Смотри, он весь в наколках.* "Look at that guy — he's completely covered with tattoos." **3.** An intelligence tip received by an unofficial source (from наколоть карты, to cheat by marking playing cards with a needle). ♦*У наших разведчиков есть наколка, духи устроят засаду у реки.* "Our mobile recon team received a tip that Chechen guerrillas will be setting up an ambush near the river."

НАКО́ЛЬЩИК, -а, *m.* A practical joker, a cheater. ♦*Не верь ему, он известный накольщик.* "Don't believe him, everyone knows he's a practical joker."

НАКОПЫ́ТИТЬ, *perf.* To procure, to get (money). ♦*Где бы нам накопытить пару сотен?* "Where can we get a couple of hundred?"

НАКОРОТКЕ́, *adv.* Quickly, briefly. ♦*Встретимся накоротке завтра.* "Let's meet briefly tomorrow."

НАКОСТЫЛЯ́ТЬ, *perf.* To beat up, to punish (from костыль, "crutch"). ♦*Тебя уже раз накостыляли, тебе мало?* "You've already been beaten up once, isn't that enough for you?"

НАКРУ́ТКА, -и, *f.* A false document, faked account. ♦*На этой стройке одни накрутки, поэтому все зарабатывают неплохо.* "The accounts on this construction job are all faked; that's why everyone's earning so much."

НАКРУ́ЧИВАТЬ/НАКРУТИ́ТЬ. 1. To influence somebody (lit., to twist, to wind). ♦*Он сильно изменился, она его давно накрутила против друзей.* "He's completely brainwashed. She's successfully turned him against his friends." **2.** To complicate, to aggravate, to make things more difficult. ♦*Не надо ничего усложнять в плане, как только засвистят пули, всё зависит от простоты и инстинктов.* "Don't overcomplicate your plan. Once bullets start flying it's all about simplicity and instinct."

НАКРЫВА́ТЬ/НАКРЫ́ТЬ, *army.* **1.** To be killed during a bombing or shelling (lit., to cover). ♦*Троих накрыло бомбой прошлой ночью, даже медальонов не нашли.* "Three soldiers were taken out by last night's bombing raid, not even their dog tags were found." **2.** To catch. See **засека́ться.**

НАКРЫВА́ТЬСЯ/НАКРЫ́ТЬСЯ. To come to nothing, not to work out. ♦*Моя поездка на юг накрылась.* "My trip south didn't come off." •**Накрыва́ться/накры́ться ме́дным та́зом,** *idiom, joc.* To be all over, all gone, all lost (lit., to be covered by a brass tub). ♦*Моя работа накрылась медным тазом.* "I've lost my job."

НАЛИЧМА́Н, -а, *m., youth.* Cash (from наличность). ♦*Сколько у тебя наличманом?* "How much do you have on you in cash?"

НАЛОВИ́ТЬ гра́дуса, *idiom.* To get drunk (lit., to catch a degree). ♦*Как наловишь градуса — сразу драться.* "As soon as you get drunk, you get into a fight."

НАЛОЖИ́ТЬ в штаны́, *idiom, rude.* To be frightened (lit., to shit in one's pants). ♦*Никто тебя пальцем не тронул, а ты уже наложил в штаны.* "No one's even laid a finger on you and you're already shitting in your pants."

НАМ НЕ СТРА́ШЕН СЕ́РЫЙ ВОЛК, НАС У МА́МЫ ЦЕ́ЛЫЙ ПОЛК, *idiom, joc.* A rhyming phrase used of a family with many children (lit., We're not afraid of the grey wolf, our mama's got a whole regiment).

НАМА́ТЫВАТЬ/НАМОТА́ТЬ на винт, *idiom.* **1.** To look down on, be contemptuous of. ♦*Я твои слова на винт намотал.* "I spit on your words." **2.** To contract a venereal disease. ♦*Смотри, не намотай на винт у этих баб.* "Be careful not to get the clap if you go with those dames."

НАМУХОМО́РИТЬСЯ, *perf.* To get drunk. ♦*Как можно так с утра пораньше намухомориться?* "How can you get drunk like that first thing in the morning?"

НАМЫВА́ТЬ/НАМЫ́ТЬ, *youth.* To get (money) (lit., to wash gold dust). ♦*Намой где-нибудь денег.* "Get some money someplace."

НАМЫ́ЛИВАТЬ/НАМЫ́ЛИТЬ табло́ кому́-л., *youth, rude, neg.* To beat someone up (lit., to wash someone's face). ♦*Мой брат ему намылит табло, тогда он не будет больше приставать к тебе.* "My brother will wash his face for him so that he'll stop bothering you."

НАМЫ́ЛИВАТЬСЯ/НАМЫ́ЛИТЬСЯ, *joc.* To get ready to go somewhere (lit., to lather up). ♦*Куда это ты намылился?* "Where are you off to?"

НАНА́ЙСКИЙ, -ая, -ое. Strange, alien, bad (from нанаец, a member of a Nothern people). ♦*Что за нанайский мотор, никак не заводится!* ""The damned motor won't start!"

НАПА́РЫВАТЬСЯ/НАПОРО́ТЬСЯ, *neg.* To encounter, run into. ♦*Они напоролись на патруль без увольнительных.* "They ran into a police squad when they weren't carrying any papers."

НАПЁРСТОК, напёрстка, *m.* A game in which one bets on guessing under which of three covers ("thimbles") a ball or other object is hidden (lit., thimble). ♦*Не смей играть в напёрсток, проиграешь все деньги.* "Don't you dare to go playing 'thimbles!' You'll lose all your money."

НАПЁРСТОЧНИК, -а, *m., neg.* An organizer of games of "thimbles" (see **напёрсток**). ♦*На рынке развелось много напёрсточников.* "Lots of 'thimbles' con-artists have appeared in the market."

НАПИ́ЗДИТЬ, *perf. only, rude.* To steal a large quantity (cf. **спи́здить**). ♦*Мы напиздили из ресторана стаканы, хватит для всех.* "We stole a supply of glasses from the restaurant. There's enough for everybody."

НАПИЗДЯ́КИВАТЬСЯ/НАПИЗДЯ́-КАТЬСЯ, *rude.* To drink too much. ♦*Где вы успели так напиздякаться?* "Where did you guys manage to get so drunk?"

НАПРЯ́Г, -а, *m., joc.* Pressure, tension

(from напряжение, "tension"). ◆*У меня со временем напряг, только полчаса и бежать.* "I'm under some time pressure — I'll just stay half an hour and I'm off."

НАПРЯГА́ЛОВО, -а, *n., youth.* See **напря́г.**

НАПРЯГА́ТЬ/НАПРЯ́ЧЬ. To force, pressure (cf. **напря́г**). ◆*Не напрягай меня, я это делать не буду.* "Don't pressure me. I won't do it."

НАПРЯЖЁНКА, -и, *f.* Difficulties, problems. ◆*У меня со временем напряжёнка.* "'I'm pressed for time."

НАПРЯ́ЖНО, *adv., youth, neg.* Tense, unpleasant, dangerous (cf. **напря́г**). ◆*На Кавказе сейчас очень напряжно.* "Things are very tense in the Caucasus these days."

НАПРЯ́ЖНЫЙ, -ая, -ое, *youth, neg.* Annoying, unpleasant (cf. **напря́г**). ◆*Он очень напряжный, я с ним не поеду на юг.* "He's awfully unpleasant; I don't want to travel to the south with him."

НАРЕЗА́ТЬ/НАРЕ́ЗАТЬ ВИНТА́, *idiom, army.* To run away, to bolt (lit., to rethread a stripped bolt). See **винти́ть.**

НАРЕЗНО́Й, -о́го (-а́я, -о́й), *m. (f.), neg.* A toady, apple-polisher. ◆*Нарезной опять в гору пошёл, начальство его любит.* "That toady has taken another step up the career ladder. The management loves him."

НАРИСОВА́ТЬСЯ, *perf. only.* To appear, show up. ◆*Когда ты у нас нарисуешься?* "So when will you show up at our place?"

НАРКО́МАН, -а, *m., joc.* A drug addict (by wordplay on нарко-, "drug," and нарком, abbr. of народный комиссар, "people's commissar"). ◆*Один наркоман и говорит: «Есть план по лимону».* "So this druggie comes up and says, 'I can get you some for one million rubles.'"

НАРКОТА́, -ы́, *f., collect., neg.* Drug addicts. ◆*Опять возле тебя всякая наркота крутится.* "Again you've been hanging around with all sorts of druggies."

НАРО́ДА БО́ЛЬШЕ, ЧЕМ ЛЮДЕ́Й, *idiom, joc.* A crowd (lit., more people than people; by wordplay as if народ, "people," were different from люди, "people"). ◆*В магазине народа больше, чем людей, туда не пойдём.* "There's a huge crowd in the store; let's not go there."

НА́РЫ, нар, *pl.* A bed (lit., a plank bed). ◆*Кто это спит на моих нарах?* "Who's that sleeping in my bed?" ●**Ша, по нарам!** *idiom, joc.* Hush! Quiet! (lit., "Quiet in the plank beds!"). ◆*Ша, по нарам, училка идёт.* "Quiet! Here comes the teacher." **Гну́ться под на́ры,** see under **гну́ться.**

НАРЫВА́ТЬСЯ/НАРВА́ТЬСЯ, *neg.* To act aggressive. ◆*Ты всё время нарываешься, смотри, получишь.* "If you go around acting so tough all the time you're going to get it."

НАСА́ЖИВАТЬ/НАСАДИ́ТЬ на ка́нцур (на каркалы́к), *idiom, rude.* To have sex with a woman (from насаживать/насадить на крючок, lit., to bait a fishhook; cf. **ка́нцур, каркалы́к**). ◆*Я её не прочь насадить на канцур.* "I wouldn't mind screwing that girl."

НАСКРО́ЗЬ, *adv., joc.* Through and through, completely (distorted from насквозь). ◆*Дождь лупит, все наскрозь промокли.* "It's pouring rain. Everyone's soaked to the bone."

НАСТРА́ИВАТЬ/НАСТРО́ИТЬ РАДА́РЫ, *idiom, army.* To look closely (lit., to tune radars). ◆*Будешь на посту, настрой свои радары на бункер. Увидишь что, сразу докладывай.* "During your watch, don't take your eyes off of that bunker. If you see any movement, notify me immediately."

НАСТРУГА́ТЬ, *perf., joc.* To produce in abundance. ◆*Ты знаешь, сколько книг он настругал за год?* "Do you know how many books he's cranked out this year?"

НАСТУЧА́ТЬ РО́ЖУ (ха́рю), *idiom.* To beat up (lit., to knock on a mug). ◆*Неплохо бы ему настучать смазливую рожу, тогда не будет задирать нос.* "I'd like to whale on that pretty boy's face, maybe then he wouldn't think he was so special."

НАСТУЧА́ТЬ ПО ТЫ́КВЕ, *idiom.* See **дава́ть по ты́кве** and **настуча́ть ро́жу.**

НАСТУЧА́ТЬ ЧАН, *idiom.* To beat up (lit., to knock on someone's tub). ♦ *Это такая сволочь, так и хочется настучать чан.* "He's an sob. I'd like to beat his head in."

НАСЫПА́ТЬ/НАСЫ́ПАТЬ со́ли под хвост, *idiom.* To get someone into trouble; to get vengeance against someone (lit., to sprinkle salt under someone's tail). ♦ *Министрам насыпали соли под хвост в парламенте, их ругали за социальную политику.* "They got the ministers into hot water in Parliament by criticizing them for their social policy."

НАТРЕ́СКИВАТЬСЯ/НАТРЕ́СКАТЬ-СЯ. To get drunk (from трескать, to eat). See **нажира́ться.**

НАТУ́РА: В нату́ре, *crim. & youth.* Really, actually. ♦ *Он в натуре ничего не понимает.* "He actually doesn't understand a thing." •**Ты что, в нату́ре?** *idiom.* Are you serious? Are you out of your mind? (banteringly answered with **Соси́ хуй в прокурату́ре**; cf. under **хуй**). **Плати́ть/заплати́ть нату́рой**, see under **плати́ть.**

НАТЯ́Г, -а, *m., youth.* An unpleasant, tense situation. ♦ *У меня в семье натяг сейчас, мне нельзя задерживаться.* "I've got a family problem right now so I can't stay long."

НАТЯ́ГИВАТЬ/НАТЯНУ́ТЬ, *rude.* To have sex with a woman (lit., to pull on, as a sock). ♦ *Ты её хоть натянул?* "Well, did you have any success with her?"

НАУ́СЬКИВАТЬ/НАУ́СЬКАТЬ, *neg.* To make hostile, to set against. ♦ *Любишь ты науськивать всех против всех.* "You always get everyone angry with each other."

НАУ́ХАТЬСЯ, *perf.* **1.** To get drunk. **2.** To get tired. ♦ *Наухался за целый день, падаю с ног.* "I'm falling off my feet with exhaustion from today's work."

НАФАРШИРО́ВАННЫЙ, -ая, -ое, *joc.* Well-dressed (from фарш, "forcemeat"). ♦ *Друг у тебя нафаршированный от и*

до. "Your friend is well turned out from head to toe."

НАХА́ЛКА, -и, *f., neg.* A pushy woman. ♦ *Ты думаешь, нахалка, платить за квартиру?* "Well, you shrew, are you planning to pay the rent or not?" •**По наха́лке,** *idiom, neg.* Pushily, selfishly. ♦ *Он без очереди по нахалке оторвал себе сапоги.* "He selfishly grabbed himself a pair of boots without waiting in line."

НАХЛЕБА́ТЬСЯ СОПЛЕ́Й-ВАФЛЕ́Й, *a rhyming phrase.* To be beaten to a pulp (lit., to swallow his snot and waffles). ♦ *Он ещё нахлебается соплей-вафлей за всё, что натворил.* "He ought to get beaten to a pulp for what he did."

НАХРЮ́КАТЬСЯ, *perf.* To get very drunk (lit., to grunt).

НАХУЯ́РИВАТЬ/НАХУЯ́РИТЬ, *rude.* To do a lot of something, do something to a great extent. ♦ *Когда ты успела нахуярить столько писем?* "When did you manage to write such a heap of letters?"

НАХУЯ́РИВАТЬСЯ/НАХУЯ́РИТЬСЯ, *rude.* To drink too much. ♦ *Голова болит, вчера нахуярились на дне рождения.* "I've got a headache from drinking too much at the birthday party."

НАЦМЕ́Н, -а, *m., neg.* A non-Russian, a member of a non-Russian nationality (lit., an abbreviated form of национальное меньшинство, "national minority"). ♦ *Её муж слишком черноволосый, он что, нацмен?* "Her husband is awfully dark-haired. Is he a non-Russian?"

НАЧИ́СТИТЬ мо́рду, *idiom, rude.* To beat up (lit., to clean up someone's face). ♦ *Тебе когда-нибудь морду начистят за наглость.* "You're going to get beaten up one of these days for your pushiness."

НАЧИСТЯ́К, *adv., crim.* Completely, altogether. ♦ *Он его с одного удара завалил начистяк.* "He knocked him out completely with one blow."

НАШ ВЕЛИ́КИЙ И МОГУ́ЧИЙ, *idiom, joc.* Swearing or obscenity (lit., "Our great and mighty [language]," a phrase from Turgenev's praise of the Russian language). ♦*Опять наш великий и могучий, слова без мата сказать не могут.* "There he goes again with 'our great and mighty one' — he can't even open his mouth without using swearwords."

НАШ ДОМ — ГАЗПРО́М, *idiom, joc.* A rhyming distortion of the name of the political party "Наш дом — Россия," "Our home is Russia," alluding to the fact that its leader, Victor Chernomyrdin, is closely connected with the interests of the gas company Газпром.

НАШАРА́ШИВАТЬ/НАШАРА́ШИТЬ. To do or produce something quickly. ♦*Сколько страниц словаря вы нашарашили сегодня?* "How many pages of your dictionary did you guys manage to churn out today?"

НА́ШИ ЧАСЫ́ СА́МЫЕ БЫ́СТРЫЕ В МИ́РЕ, *idiom, joc.* Lit., Our watches are the fastest in the world — a sardonic comment on the poor quality of domestic Russian goods.

НАЯ́БЫВАЙ СО́ПЛИ В РОТ, *idiom, rude.* Mind your own business (lit., take your snot into your mouth). ♦*Не лезь со своими советами, наябывай сопли в рот.* "Don't butt in with your advice! Mind your own business."

НЕ БЕЙ ЛЕЖА́ЧЕГО, *idiom, joc.* Very easy. ♦*У тебя работа — не бей лежачего.* "Your job is a piece of cake."

НЕ БЕРИ́ В ГО́ЛОВУ, *idiom, joc.* Don't worry about it, don't take it to heart. ♦*Не бери в голову эти цены, заработаем.* "Don't be discouraged by these prices; we'll earn the money." **Не бери́ в го́лову, бери́ в рот,** *idiom, rude, joc.* Don't worry, don't take it to heart (lit., "Don't take it into your head, take it into your mouth," alluding to fellatio). ♦*Мне не по себе: опять они не отдают долг. — Не бери в голову, бери в рот.* "This is driving me crazy. They still haven't paid me what they owe. — Don't worry about it."

НЕ БУДЬ, ЧЕМ ЩИ НАЛИВА́ЮТ, *neg.* Don't be a fool (lit., don't be a soup ladle). ♦*Я эти деньги не возьму. — Бери, не будь, чем щи наливают.* "I

wouldn't take that money. — Go ahead and take it! Don't be a fool!"

НЕ В ДЕНЬГА́Х СЧА́СТЬЕ, А В ИХ КОЛИ́ЧЕСТВЕ, *idiom, joc.* Used in mock-disparaging answer to claims that money has no importance (lit., "Happiness isn't to be found in money, but in a lot of money"). ♦*У меня нет денег, зато и нет проблем с покупками. — Да, не в деньгах счастье, а в их количестве.* "I have no money, but to make up for that, I don't have to worry about the security of my possessions. — Sure, it's not money that brings happiness, but a lot of money."

НЕ ВСКЛАД, НЕВПОПА́Д, ПОЦЕЛУ́Й КОБЫ́ЛУ В ЗАД, *idiom, rude.* A rhyming phrase used to criticize bad writing or speech (lit., Out of place, badly rhymed, kiss a mare's ass).

НЕ ГОВОРИ́, У САМО́Й МУЖ ПЬЯ́НИЦА, *idiom, joc.* Lit., "No need to explain, my husband is a drunk, too"; used to express the idea of sharing someone else's problems. ♦*Ты знаешь, меня дети совсем не слушают, весь день где-то гуляют, не учатся. — Не говори, у меня самой муж пьяница.* "My children don't listen to me at all. They run around all day and don't study. — I've got the same problem."

НЕ ДЛЯ СРЕ́ДНЕГО УМА́ (НЕ ДЛЯ СРЕ́ДНИХ УМО́В), *idiom, joc.* You wouldn't understand (lit., it's not for the average mind). ♦*Что-то я не понимаю, что это за закон новый? — Это не для средних умов.* "Somehow I don't get it. What sort of new law is this? — It's not for the average mind."

НЕ КА́ШЕЛЬ, НЕ ПЕРДЁЖ, НИЧЕГО́ НЕ РАЗБЕРЁШЬ, *neg., rude.* A rhyming phrase used to criticize incomprehensible speech (lit., It's not a cough, it's not a fart, you can't make anything of it).

НЕ КОМА́Р ЧИХНУ́Л, *idiom, joc.* Lit., It's not a mosquito's sneeze. See **Не му́ха нага́дила.**

НЕ МАЙ МЕ́СЯЦ, *idiom.* It's cold (lit., it's not the month of May; used in criticism of someone who isn't dressed warmly enough for winter weather). ♦*Наде́нь ша́пку, не май ме́сяц.* "Put on a hat! It's not the month of May."

НЕ МУ́ХА НАГА́ДИЛА, *idiom.* It's in earnest, it's serious business (lit., It's not fly-shit). ♦*Там не́фти на миллиа́рды, э́то тебе́ не му́ха нагади́ла.* "These oil deposits cost billions of dollars, it's nothing to sneeze at."

НЕ МЫ́ЛЬСЯ, БРИ́ТЬСЯ НЕ БУ́-ДЕШЬ, *idiom, neg.* Don't get your hopes up (lit., no use lathering your face — you're not going to have a shave). ♦*Не мы́лься, бри́ться не бу́дешь, никто́ тебя́ не собира́ется приглаша́ть в го́сти.* "Don't get your hopes up. No one's about to invite you to dinner."

НЕ МЫЧИ́Т, НЕ ТЕ́ЛИТСЯ, *idiom, neg.* Lit., someone "neither moos nor calves"; used to describe someone inert, passive, unproductive. ♦*Тебе́ пора́ устра́иваться на рабо́ту, а ты не мычи́шь, не те́лишься.* "It's high time you got yourself a job, but you neither moo nor calve."

НЕ НА́ДО ЛЯ-ЛЯ́ (на́шим ребя́там), *idiom, neg.* Don't lie, tell tales, gossip. ♦*Не на́до ля-ля́, не брал я твой маг-нитофо́н.* "Don't tell lies! I didn't take your tape recorder."

НЕ НА́ДО МУМУ́, *joc.* This expression derives from Turgenev's story "Mumu," in which the dumb peasant Gerasim is attached to a puppy called Mumu. **1.** Don't be silent. ♦*Говори́, не на́до муму́.* "Speak up! Cat got your tongue?" **2.** Don't try to fool me, don't take me for a sucker. ♦*Не на́до муму́, я зна́ю, что ты хо́чешь.* "Don't try to fool me. I know what you're up to."

НЕ НА́ДО ПЕ́СЕН, *idiom, neg.* Don't lie, don't be evasive (lit., there's no need of songs). ♦*То́лько не на́до пе́сен, ты где был?* "Tell me straight out — where have you been?"

НЕ НУ́КАЙ, НЕ ЗАПРЯ́Г! "Don't keep saying 'Come on!' to me. I'm not a horse (lit., you haven't harnessed me)."

НЕ ОТКЛА́ДЫВАЙ НА ЗА́ВТРА ТО, ЧТО МО́ЖНО СЪЕСТЬ СЕГО́ДНЯ, *idiom, joc.* Lit., Don't put for tomorrow what you can eat today. A twisted form of Не откла́дывай на за́втра то, что мо́жно сде́лать сего́дня, "Don't put off for tomorrow what you can do today."

НЕ ПА́ДАТЬ У́ХОМ, *idiom.* Not to despair (a wordplay on па́дать ду́хом, to despair, and па́дать у́хом, to fall on one's ear). ♦*Не па́дай у́хом, всё бу́дет как на́до.* "Don't despair, everything will be okay."

НЕ ПЕ́РВЫЙ ГОД ЗА́МУЖЕМ, *idiom.* I know how to handle it, I wasn't born yesterday (lit., I'm not in my first year of marriage). ♦*Я зна́ю, что де́лать в таки́х слу́чаях, не пе́рвый год заму́-жем.* "I know what to do in such cases — I wasn't born yesterday, you know."

НЕ ПО УМУ́, *idiom, neg.* Wrong, thoughtless, unreasonable. ♦*Вся э́та рефо́рма сде́лана не по уму́. Пострада́ли опя́ть бе́дные, а не бога́тые.* "This whole reform has been done stupidly. Again it's the poor who are suffering, not the rich."

НЕ ПОЙМИ́ТЕ МЕНЯ́ ПРА́ВИЛЬНО, *idiom, joc.* I'm only joking, don't take me seriously (lit., Don't understand me correctly, playing on Не пойми́те меня́ непра́вильно, "Don't misunderstand me").

НЕ ПРОТЯ́ГИВАЙ РУ́КИ, А ТО ПРОТЯ́НЕШЬ НО́ГИ, *idiom.* A warning not to touch something (lit., Don't reach with your hands or you'll reach with your legs).

НЕ ПЬЁТ ТО́ЛЬКО СОВА́: она́ днём спит, а но́чью магази́ны закры́ты, *idiom, joc.* A proverbial expression used to assert, in response to the question whether someone drinks, that, of course, everyone drinks (lit., "The owl is the only creature that doesn't drink, because in the daytime she's asleep, and at night the stores are closed"). ♦*Вы́пьешь с на́ми? — Не пьёт то́лько сова́....* "Will you have a drink with us? — Of course! After all, the only creature that doesn't drink is the owl...."

НЕ ПЬЁТ ТО́ЛЬКО ТЕЛЕГРА́ФНЫЙ СТОЛБ (, у него́ ча́шки вниз), *idiom, joc.* Most people drink, it's the usual thing for people to drink (cf. preceding entry; lit., "Only a telephone pole doesn't drink [; it's got its cups, i.e., resistors, upside down]"). ◆*А разве он пьёт? — Не пьёт только телеграфный столб...."* "So you mean he drinks? — Well, after all, who but a telephone pole doesn't drink?"

НЕ РАЗБЕЖИ́ШЬСЯ, *idiom.* You can't expect to get much; you'll have to be thrifty. ◆*На эти деньги в ресторане не разбежишься.* "You can't expect to get much for that money in a restaurant."

НЕ СПИ, ЗАМЁРЗНЕШЬ, *idiom, joc.* Pay attention, don't let your mind wander (lit., don't sleep — you'll freeze to death). ◆*Ты что замолчал? Не спи, замёрзнешь.* "How come you have nothing to say? Pay attention!"

НЕ ССЫ (, прорвёмся)! *idiom, rude.* Don't be scared (, we'll come through all right) (cf. **ссать**). ◆*Не знаю, как мы доживём до получки, денег нет совсем. — Не ссы, прорвёмся!* "I don't see how we're going to survive till payday. We have no money at all. — Don't worry. We'll come through all right."

НЕ СУЕТИ́СЬ ПОД КЛИЕ́НТОМ, *idiom, joc.* Relax, calm down (lit., "don't fidget under the client," where the client is a prostitute's). ◆*Посиди немного, не суетись под клиентом.* "Sit down and relax! Don't fidget under the client."

НЕ СЫПЬ МНЕ СОЛЬ НА РА́НЫ, *idiom.* Don't irritate me, don't pain me (lit., Don't pour salt on my wounds). ◆*Не сыпь мне соль на раны, не говори мне о банках, там сгорели все мои сбережения.* "Your talk about banks just pours salt on my wounds; I lost all my savings there."

НЕ ТЯНИ́ КОТА́ ЗА ХВОСТ, *idiom.* Speak out, out with it, don't hem and haw (lit., don't drag the cat by its tail). ◆*Ну, так что у тебя произошло, говори прямо, не тяни кота за хвост.* "Tell me exactly what happened to you. Don't beat around the bush."

НЕ У ПРО́НЬКИНЫХ, *idiom.* We're not such fools as you think (lit., "You're not dealing with the Pronkins" [family name

of simple people]). ◆*Ты не у Пронькиных, никто джинсы за такую сумму не купит.* "What kind of fool do you take me for? No one pays such a price for jeans."

НЕ УЧИ́ МЕНЯ́ ЖИТЬ (, лу́чше помоги́ материа́льно)!, *idiom, youth, joc.* I don't need your advice (lit., Don't teach me how to live [; it would be better to give me some financial help]). ◆*Тебе не надо бы бросать институт. — Не учи меня жить, лучше помоги материально.* "You shouldn't quit school. — I don't need your advice, just your money!"

НЕ УЧИ́ УЧЁНОГО, ПОЕ́ШЬ ГОВНА́ ПЕЧЁНОГО! *idiom, rude.* Don't tell me what to do, don't nag me with your advice (lit., "Don't teach one who already knows; eat some baked shit!"; a rhyming phrase).

НЕ ФОНТА́Н, *idiom.* Bad, unsatisfactory (lit., not a fountain). ◆*Эта сделка не фонтан.* "That's a bad deal."

НЕ ФУНТ ИЗЮ́МУ, *idiom.* It's no joke, it's not a laughing matter (lit., it's not a pound of raisins). ◆*Это серьёзное дело, не фунт изюму.* "This is something serious; it's not a laughing matter."

НЕ ХУХРЫ́-МУХРЫ́, a nonsense rhyming phrase. It's not that simple, it's difficult. ◆*Это тебе не хухры-мухры без сна идти трое суток.* "It's not that easy to go three days without sleep."

НЕВПРОТЫ́К, *adv.* Hardly, with difficulty. ◆*Жить стало невпротык при новых ценах.* "Life has become difficult with the new prices."

НЕВПРОТЫ́ЧНЫЙ, -ая, -ое. Impossible, insoluble. Cf. **невпротык**.

НЕВРУБО́Н, -а, *m.* Lack of understanding. ◆*У меня неврубон на компьютер.* "The computer is beyond my comprehension."

НЕВЫЕЗДНО́Й, -ого, *m., obs., Soviet.* A Soviet citizen denied the right to travel abroad (hence, a Soviet citizen officially marked as of questionable loyalty; cf. **выездно́й**).

НЕГАТИ́В, -а, *m., neg.* **1.** An African, a

black person. ♦*Здесь учится много негативов.* "A lot of blacks study here." **2.** The negative or dark side of things. ♦*В его романе один негатив.* "His novel only shows the dark side of things." **3.** Compromising information. ♦*У них на меня негатив.* "They have some dirt on me."

НЕГР: (Темно́) как у не́гра в жо́пе, see under **жо́па.**

НЕГРИТО́С, -а, *m., neg.* A Negro. ♦*В оркестре у него одни негритосы.* "His orchestra is made up entirely of blacks."

НЕГРИТО́СИЯ, -ии, *f., neg.* Any African country. ♦*Он уехал послом в какую-то Негритосию.* "He went as an ambassador to some Darkland or other."

НЕДЕРЖА́НИЕ РЕ́ЧИ, *idiom, neg.* Overtalkativeness (playing on недержа-ние мочи, "incontinence"). ♦*Он помолчать не может и минуты, недержание речи какое-то.* "He can't keep quiet for a single minute, he's got such a case of speech incontinence."

НЕДОДЕ́ЛАННЫЙ, -ая, -ое, *neg.* Idiotic, stupid (lit., defectively made). ♦*Какой-то ты недоделанный, всё делаешь не как люди.* "How can you be so stupid! You don't do anything like a normal person."

НЕДОЁБАННЫЙ, -ая, -ое, *rude.* Out of sorts, in a bad mood. ♦*Что с ним, сегодня он какой-то недоёбанный.* "What's with him today? He seems to be in a bad mood."

НЕДОПЕРЕПИВА́ТЬ/НЕДОПЕРЕ-ПИ́ТЬ. Paradoxical word from недо, lit., less, and пере, lit., more. ♦*Он злой, как чёрт, явно недоперепил вчера.* "He's mad as hell, it's obvious that he didn't drink as much as he should yesterday."

НЕДО́ПИЛ, -а, *m.* Not enough to drink. ♦*Это будет недопил, надо ещё бутылку купить.* "This won't be enough to drink, we'll have to buy another bottle."

НЕДОТЫ́КОМКА, -и, *m. & f., neg.* An idiot, fool (lit., not fully penetrated, incomplete or defective in the manner of generation). ♦*Какая ты недотыком-*

ка, никак не хочешь понять, что тебе надо говорить, когда спросят. "What an idiot you are! Can't you understand that you have to answer when you're asked a question?"

НЕДОУ́МОК, недоу́мка, *m., neg.* An idiot, fool. ♦*Как можно с таким недоумком дружить?* "How can you be friends with such an idiot?"

НЕЗАВЕРШЁНКА, -и, *f.* Incomplete work, work left undone (esp. construction work). ♦*У нас в городе незавершёнки хватает.* "In our city there are a lot of abandoned construction jobs."

НЕЗВА́НЫЙ ГОСТЬ ЛУ́ЧШЕ ТАТА́-РИНА, *idiom, joc.* Lit., An unexpected guest is better than a Tartar (by comic distortion of the saying "Незваный гость хуже татарина,", "An uninvited guest is worse than a Tartar").

НЕКАЙФЫ́, -о́в, *pl., youth, neg.* Unpleasantness, difficulties (cf. **кайф**). ♦*От этой герлы одни некайфы.* "There's never anything but trouble with this girl."

НЕКИ́СЛЫЙ, -ая, -ое, *pos.* Good (lit., not sour). ♦*У него некислая зарплата.* "He's making a good salary."

НЕНАВЯ́ЗЧИВЫЙ СЕ́РВИС, *idiom, joc.* Poor, inattentive service (lit., service that is not too insistent). ♦*Здесь в ресторане ненавязчивый сервис, час сидим, а ещё заказ не приняли.* "The service in this restaurant is not very insistent — we've been sitting here an hour already and no one has taken our order yet."

НЕНАЁБА, -ы, *m. & f., rude.* A sexually tireless or insatiable person. ♦*Ему мало двух баб, вот ненаёба.* "Two women aren't enough for that stud."

НЕПРОХОДНЯ́К, -а́, *m.* A hopeless business, a doomed enterprise. ♦*То, что ты предлагаешь, — непроходняк.* "Your proposal hasn't got a chance."

НЕПРОХОНЖА́, *indecl., pred.* Nothing doing. ♦*В его банк устроиться — непрохонжа.* "It's impossible to get a job in his bank."

НЕПРУ́ХА, -и, *f.* Bad luck, failure. ♦*Что-то мне во всём непруха сегод-*

ня. "Somehow everything's going wrong for me today."

НЕРВА́, -ы́, *f.* The state of one's nerves. ♦*Что-то нерва слаба стала, плохо сплю, думаю, что дальше будет.* "I've been nervous, sleeping poorly, and constantly thinking about what's going to happen." •**Нерва́ сдаёт у кого́-л.,** *idiom.* To lose one's nerve. ♦*У него нерва сдала, он не пошёл сдавать экзамен.* "He lost his nerve and didn't even take the examination."

НЕРВОТРЁПКА, -и, *f., neg.* A tense, nervous situation. ♦*Я эту нервотрёпку больше выносить не могу.* "I can't stand this tension any more." •**Устра́ивать/устро́ить нервотрёпку,** see under **устра́ивать.**

НЕ́РВЫ: Без не́рвов, *idiom.* Calmly, coolly. ♦*Надо всё спокойно обдумать и только без нервов.* "We've got to think it over calmly and collectedly." **На не́рвах,** *idiom.* On edge, in a state of tension. ♦*В последнее время все живут на нервах.* "Everyone's been living in a state of tension recently." **Не́рвы подкача́ли,** *idiom.* To lose one's self-possession. ♦*Не выдержал я, нервы подкачали, я ему в зубы и врезал.* "I couldn't restrain myself. I lost my cool and socked him in the mouth." **Не́рвы не выде́рживают,** *idiom.* To be unable to endure something. ♦*Больше так жить, нервы не выдерживают.* "I can't stand living like this any longer." **Не́рвов не хвата́ет,** *idiom.* To be unable to endure something. ♦*У меня никаких нервов не хватает с ним работать.* "I absolutely can't stand working with him."

НЕРУ́ССКИЙ, -ая, -ое. Bad, strange (lit., non-Russian). ♦*Это какой-то нерусский телевизор, ничего не показывает.* "This is a strange sort of television — the screen is blank."

НЕСКЛАДУ́ХА, -и, *joc.* **1.** *m. & f.* A slow, clumsy person. ♦*Он у меня такой нескладуха.* "That fellow is all thumbs." **2.** *f.* Absurdity, unreasonableness. ♦*Какая-то в этих чертежах нескладуха, ничего не поймёшь.* "Something's screwed up in these designs — they're

unintelligible."

НЕСЛАБО́, *adv.* Well. ♦*Неслабо мы вчера погуляли.* "We had a real good time yesterday."

НЕСЛА́БЫЙ, -ая, -ое, *youth, pos.* Good (lit., not weak). ♦*Это неслабый фотоаппарат.* "This is a good camera."

НЕСТИ́/ПОНЕСТИ́: Нести́/понести́ чепуху́, *idiom.* To talk nonsense. ♦*Ты несёшь чепуху, никто тебя не собирается обидеть.* "You're talking nonsense. No one is trying to insult you." **Нести́ как из помо́йки,** *idiom, neg.* Something smells bad (lit., as if from the garbage). ♦*Почисти зубы, изо рта несёт как из помойки.* "Brush your teeth. Your mouth smells terrible."

НЕСТОЯ́НИЕ, -я, *n.* Impotence. ♦*У меня состояние нестояния.* "I'm not sexually aroused."

НЕСУ́Н, -а́, *m., neg.* A petty thief who steals from plants or industries. ♦*У несунов всё можно достать — и мясо и запчасти.* "You can buy anything from those factory thieves, from meat to spare parts."

НЕТЛЕ́НКА, -и, *f., prof., joc.* A work of art (from тлен, "decay"). ♦*Он творит очередную нетленку.* "He's working on his next 'immortal' job."

НЕУВЯ́ЗОК, -ка, *m., army, neg.* A blunderer. ♦*Ты когда научишься стрелять, неувязок чёртов?* "When are you going to learn to shoot straight, you shlump!"

НЕ́УВЯЗЬ, -и, *m., army, neg.* See **неувя́зок.**

НЕУДО́БНО ШТАНЫ́ ЧЕ́РЕЗ ГО́ЛОВУ НАДЕВА́ТЬ, *idiom, neg.* Lit., it's awkward to put on your pants over your head; used in dismissal of claims that something is awkward or unpleasant. ♦*Мне неудобно просить его об этом. — Брось ты, неудобно штаны через голову надевать.* "It's uncomfortable for me to ask him about that. — Oh, go on! What's uncomfortable is to put your pants on over your head."

НЕФОРМА́Л, -а, *m., obs.* A member of an unauthorized (i.e., non-Party) organization. ♦*Неформалы собираются завтра на митинг.* "The 'informals' are having a meeting tomorrow."

НЕШУ́ТОЧНЫЙ, -ая, -ое, *youth, pos.* Well-off, prosperous (lit., not in play, i.e., for real). ♦*Ты у нас нешуточный, и машина у тебя, и дача.* "You're the prosperous one among us; you've got both a car and a dacha."

НИ БЗДНУ́ТЬ, НИ ПЁРДНУТЬ, *idiom, rude.* Crowded on all sides, in a tight spot, packed like sardines (lit., without enough room to fart). ♦*В машине нас ехало шесть человек: ни бзднуть, ни пёрднуть.* "There were six of us packed in the car — there wasn't even room to fart."

НИ БУМ-БУ́М, *idiom, joc.* To understand nothing (from the sound of striking a hollow object; sometimes accompanied by a gesture of tapping the forehead or head). ♦*Он по-русски ни бум-бум.* "He doesn't understand a word of Russian."

НИ БЭ, НИ МЭ, НИ КУКАРЕ́КУ, *idiom, neg.* Lit., "neither *b* nor *m* nor cock-a-doodle-doo." Used of a dull-witted person, especially one who can barely express himself. ♦*Он по-русски ни бэ, ни мэ, ни кукареку.* "He can't speak a word of Russian."

НИ ДАТЬ НИ ВЗЯТЬ, *pl., indecl., joc.* Pantyhose (lit., "neither give nor take," alluding to their being inconvenient for sex). *Ты опять надела ни дать ни взять.* "Too bad you're wearing these barrier-hose again."

НИ КО́ЖИ НИ РО́ЖИ, *rhyming phrase, neg.* A thin, ugly person (lit., neither skin nor face). ♦*Она мне не нравится, ни кожи ни рожи.* "I don't find her attractive — she's all skin and bones."

НИ ТПРУ НИ НУ, *idiom, joc.* An impasse, a standstill, a dead end (lit., neither stop nor go; from the commands given to horses). ♦*Уже было договорились, как поправить конфликтную ситуацию, а потом ни тпру ни ну, все переговоры застопорились.* "In theory they came to an agreement about how to resolve the conflict, but then in practice everything came to a standstill." **Ни**

тпру, ни ну, ни кукаре́ку, *idiom, joc.* Nothing doing, no answer, no reaction. ♦*Мы его уже месяц об этом просим, а он ни тпру, ни ну, ни кукареку.* "We've been asking him about it for a month already, but on his side there's been no response at all."

НИ У́ХА НИ РЫ́ЛА, *idiom, neg.* Ignorant, at a loss (lit., neither ear nor snout). ♦*Он ни уха ни рыла в технике.* "He doesn't know a thing about anything technical."

НИ́ЖНИЙ ЭТА́Ж, *idiom.* Said of female genitals (lit., the ground floor).

НИЗЯ́, *adv., joc.* It's not permitted, it's forbidden (distorted from нельзя). ♦*Туда низя, сюда низя! Куда можно?* "We're forbidden to go here, we're forbidden to go there, where *can* we go?"

НИКАКО́Й, -а́я. Drunk to unconsciousness. ♦*Он выпьет стакан и сразу никакой.* "He gets drunk out of his mind on just a single glass."

НИ́НДЗЯ, -и, *m., army.* A commando (lit., a ninja). ♦*Пусть ниндзи штурмуют самолёт с заложниками, это их дело.* "Let the commandos storm the airplane and rescue the hostages. It's what they do."

НИТРА́ТНЫЙ, -ая, -ое, *joc.* Oversized, extra-large (lit., nitrate). ♦*У них все дети нитратные.* "All their children are extra-large."

НИЧЕ́ЙКА, -и, *f., army.* No man's land (from ничей, no one's). ♦*Когда перейдём ничейку, там дальше уже граница с Афганом.* "When we finally make it across this no man's land we'll reach the Afghan border."

НИШТЯ́К, *pred. use, youth, pos.* **1.** Good, not bad. ♦*У тебя костюм — ништяк!* "That suit you're wearing is not bad!" **2.** Nothing to worry about, no problem. ♦*Ништяк — прорвёмся!* "Don't worry, we'll have a breakthrough!"

НО́ВЫЕ НЕРУ́ССКИЕ, *idiom, neg.* The Russian nouveaux riches (lit., new non-Russians, from **но́вые ру́сские**). ♦*Почему все говорят: "Новые русские, новые русские"? Это новые нерусские.* "Why are they called 'new Russians'? People like that are non-Russian."

НО́ВЫЕ РУ́ССКИЕ, но́вых ру́сских, *pl., neg.* Russians who have become rich, materialistic, and showy in postcommunist conditions; the post-Soviet nouveaux riches (lit., the new Russians). ♦*Но́вые русские делают деньги, на остальное им наплевать.* "The New Russians are busy making money; they don't give a damn for anything else."

НО́ВЫЙ: По но́вой, *idiom.* Again. ♦*Ставь эту музыку по новой.* "Play that piece again."

НОВЬЁ, -я́, *n.* A brand-new possession. ♦*Эта машина — новьё.* "That car is brand-new."

НО́ГИ, ног, *pl., crim.* A pass, an official authorization to leave work (lit., feet). ♦*Я получил ноги, могу уходить в город.* "I've received a pass to go into town." •**Но́ги, как у ца́пли,** *idiom, neg.* Skinny, unattractive legs. ♦*Ноги у неё как у цапли, а ещё считается королевой красоты.* "She's got legs like a heron, but she's still considered a beauty queen." **Но́ги ци́ркулем у кого́-л.,** *idiom, neg.* Lit., someone's legs are like a pair of compasses; used to describe a skinny woman. **Но́ги из-под мы́шек расту́т у кого́-л.,** *idiom, joc.* Lit., someone's legs grow from his armpits; used to describe a long-legged person. **Все но́ги отдави́ли,** *idiom, neg.* Lit., "everyone crushed my feet"; used to describe a dense crowd or a long line of people. ♦*Стояла два часа за сахаром, все ноги отдавили.* "I stood in line for sugar for two hours; everyone crushed my toes." **Но́ги оторву́,** *idiom, rude.* I'll beat you up (lit., I'll tear off your legs). ♦*За такие дела я тебе ноги оторву!* "I'm going to kill you for this!" **Брать/взять но́ги в зу́бы,** see under **брать.** **Де́лать/сде́лать но́ги,** see under **де́лать. Приде́лывать/приде́лать но́ги,** see under **приде́лывать.**

НО́ГОТЬ: К но́гтю, *idiom, neg.* To punish, destroy (lit., [to crush] against one's fingernail). ♦*Их надо к ногтю за такие дела.* "We'll have to snuff them

out for this."

НО́ЖКИ: Но́жки Бу́ша, *idiom, joc.* Chicken legs imported from the United States (lit., Bush's legs; so called because their import began under the Bush administration, partly subsidized at first as humanitarian aid; prior to that time separate chicken parts were unknown in Russian markets). ♦*Ножки Буша сильно подорожали в октябре.* "The price of Bush's legs rose steeply in October." **Лу́чшие но́жки Фра́нции, е́сли побри́ть и вы́прямить,** see under **лу́чшие.**

НОЛЁВКА, -и, *f., army.* Said of a very close haircut (from ноль, zero, nothing). ♦*А где сержант? Он в парикмахерской, делает себе нолёвку.* "Where is the sergeant? He is at the barber shop getting a 'buzz'."

НОЛЬ: В ноль, *idiom.* Extremely, intensely (of drunkenness). ♦*Хочется надраться в ноль.* "I feel like getting completely plastered." **Два ноля́,** *idiom.* A toilet (lit., two zeros). ♦*Где здесь два ноля?* "Where's the bathroom around here?"

НОЛЬ ДВА́ДЦАТЬ ПЕ́РВЫЙ, *idiom, army.* A dead body. See **груз 200.**

НОЛЬ НА ВЫ́ХОДЕ, *idiom, army.* Lack of knowledge (lit., zero voltage in an electric wire). ♦*Физически этот боец подготовлен ко всему, но знание техники—ноль на выходе.* "That soldier is physically capable of almost anything, but when it comes to technical knowledge he's clueless."

НОРА́, -ы́, *f.* Home (lit., burrow). ♦*Хочу добраться до норы и спать, спать.* "I want to go home and sleep and sleep."

НОРМАЛЁК, *adv., joc.* All right, okay. ♦*Как дела? Нормалёк!* "How are things? — Okay."

НОСА́Н, -а, *m., joc.* A Jew (from нос, "nose"). ♦*Посмотри, кто у нас в правительстве — все носаны как один.* "Look at our government! It's a pack of Jews!"

НОСО́К, носка́, *m., student.* A middle-aged man (lit., a sock). ♦*Носков на вечер не приглашать, ни к чему они *нам.* "Don't invite any oldsters to the party. What would we do with them?"

НОСОПЫ́РКА, -и, *f., joc.* A nose. ♦ *Вытри носопырку, платок есть?* "Do you have a handkerchief? Wipe your nose!"

НОЧНÁЯ БÁБОЧКА, *idiom.* A prostitute (lit., a moth). ♦ *Где сейчас сбор ночных бабочек?* "Where are the prostitutes hanging out these days?"

НОЧНÓЕ, -óго, *n., student.* Late-night studying, as before exams. ♦ *Купи побольше кофе, мы сегодня в ночном.* "Get some more coffee, we're going to pull an all-nighter."

НРÁВИТЬСЯ, НЕ НРÁВИТЬСЯ, ЕШЬ, МОЯ́ КРАСÁВИЦА! *rhyming phrase, joc., rude.* Lit., "Whether you like it or not, eat it, my beauty!" Used in response to complaints about food. It's the punch line of a popular rhyme that begins Как-то раз Анжела Девис проглотила чей-то пенис, "Once upon a time, Angela Davis swallowed someone's penis."

НУ И ПИРОГИ́! *idiom.* An exclamation of annoyance or incredulity: Incredible! Is it possible? ♦ *Ну и пироги, опять она не пришла.* "Well, here's a fine kettle of fish — she's stood me up again!"

НУ ТЫ ДАЁШЬ! An expression of amazement, admiration. ♦ *Ты столько цветов купил, ну ты даёшь!* "Wow, look at all the flowers you bought!"

НУДИ́ТЬ/ЗАНУДИ́ТЬ, *neg.* To whine, nag, be a nudnick. ♦ *Не нуди, всё равно я не куплю тебе мороженое.* "Stop your whining. I'm not going to get you an ice cream."

НУЖНИ́К, -á, *m., obs.* An outhouse, outdoor toilet. ♦ *У него на даче нужник во дворе.* "He's got an outhouse in the yard at his dacha."

НУ́КАТЬ/ЗАНУ́КАТЬ. To hurry or pressure someone by repeating ну, ну ("well, come on"). •**Не ну́кай, не запря́г!,** see under **не.**

НУЛЬ: По нуля́м, *idiom.* A draw, an even score. ♦ *Как ты сыграл в карты?* — *По нулям.* "How did you make out in the card game? — It was a draw." **Сиде́ть на нуле́/сесть на нуль,** see under **сиде́ть.**

НУЛЬСÓН В СМÁЗКЕ, *idiom, army.* An inexperienced first-year soldier or marine.

НУТРÓ: Нутрó гори́т, *idiom.* Lit., someone's insides are burning; used to describe a hangover. ♦ *Надо бы хоть пива выпить, нутро горит.* "My insides are on fire. I need a beer or something." **Не по нутру́ кому́-л.,** *idiom.* Not to someone's taste, disagreeable. ♦ *Мне не по нутру, что ты хочешь сделать.* "I don't like what you want to do." **Гнилóе нутрó у когó-л.,** see under **гнилóй.**

НЬЮС, *pl., youth.* News (from Eng. "news"). ♦ *Ну, какие ньюс?* "Well, what's the news?"

НЫ́ЧКА, -и, *f.* A secret place to hide something (from заныкивать, to hide). ♦ *Доставай из нычки бутылку, выпить охота.* "Do you have any vodka left in your stash? I need a drink!"

НЮ́НИ, нюнь, *pl., neg.* Tears, crying. ♦ *Опять нюни, сколько можно?* "Are you crying again? Enough with the tears, already!" •**Распускáть/распусти́ть ню́ни,** see under **распускáть.**

НЮХ: Давáть/дать в нюх, see under **давáть.**

НЮ́ХА, -и, *f., neg.* A promiscuous woman, prostitute. ♦ *Что это ты за нюху притащил?* "Where did you drag in that slut from?"

НЮ́ХАЛКА, -и, *f., joc.* A nose (from нюхать, "to smell"). ♦ *Моя нюхалка не обманывает — здесь шашлыки готовят.* "My sniffer tells me someone's cooking shashlik here."

НЮ́ХАЛО, -a, *n., neg.* A nose (see **ню́халка**).

НЮ́ХАТЬ/ВЫ́НЮХАТЬ. To find out, to get to know (lit, to sniff). ♦ *Ты нюхал, какой курс доллара будет завтра?* "Have you found out what the exchange rate on the dollar will be tomorrow?"

НЮХÁЧ, -á, *m., youth.* A drug addict. ♦ *Нюхачи без кокаина и дня прожить* *не могут.* "Addicts can't get through a single day without their cocaine."

НЮ́ШКА, -и, *f., neg.* A promiscuous woman; an untidy, slovenly woman. ♦ *И эта нюшка у нас будет работать?* "You mean that slut is going to be working here?"

◆ О ◆

ОБАЛДЕВА́ТЬ/ОБАЛДЕ́ТЬ, *neg.* To be tired, worn out (from **балда́**). ♦*Я обалде́л от шу́ма.* "I'm exhausted from the noise."

ОБАЛДЕМО́Н, **-а**, *m.* Something outstanding, excellent. ♦*Сего́дня пи́во — по́лный обалдемо́н!* "We've got some terrific beer today."

ОБАЛДЕ́НИЕ, **-я**, *n., neg.* Exhaustion (cf. **обалдева́ть**). ♦*Вчера́ занима́лись матема́тикой до обалде́ния.* "Yesterday we worked on the math homework to the point of stupefaction."

ОБАЛДЕ́ННЫЙ, **-ая**, **-ое.** Excellent, first-rate. ♦*На у́лице обалде́нная пого́да.* "The weather is gorgeous today."

ОБВЕ́ШИВАТЬ/ОБВЕ́ШАТЬ ху́ями. See under **ху́й**.

ОБГОВНЯ́ТЬСЯ, *perf., rude.* To be taken in, to make a stupid mistate, to fail (from **говно́**). ♦*На́ши в хокке́й совсе́м обговня́лись.* "Our hockey team messed up completely."

ОБГРЫЗА́ТЬ/ОБГРЫ́ЗТЬ, *youth.* To steal (from **грызть**, "to gnaw"). ♦*Вчера́ обгры́зли маши́ну, вы́нули магнито́фон.* "Yesterday they stole the tape deck from the car."

ОБДА́ЛБЫВАТЬСЯ/ОБДОЛБА́ТЬСЯ, *youth.* To take drugs, to be under the influence of narcotics. ♦*Он уже́ обдолба́лся, ничего́ не сообража́ет.* "He's so high he doesn't understand a thing."

ОБДОЛБА́НИЕ, **-я**, *n., youth.* 1. Intoxication. 2. Depression. ♦*Тебе́ на́до выбира́ться из обдолба́ния, дела́ все стоя́т.* "You've got to pull yourself out of your depression, there's work to be done."

ОБДО́ЛБАННЫЙ, **-ая**, **-ое.** Stoned, highly intoxicated with narcotics (see **обдолба́ться**).

ОБДОНАЕ́СТЬ, *perf.* To annoy, to irritate. ♦*Ты мне за э́ти два дня обдонае́л.* "You've driven me up the wall these last couple of days."

ОБДРИСТА́ТЬСЯ, *perf. only, rude.* 1. To defecate in one's pants, to soil oneself. ♦*Е́ле до угла́ добежа́л, чуть не обдриста́лся.* "I barely made it to the can without going in my pants." 2. To fail, mess up, come to nothing. ♦*Они́ со свои́м пла́ном экономи́ческого подъёма обдриста́лись.* "They really struck out with their plan for economic development."

ОБЕЗЬЯ́ННИК, **-а**, *m.* A detention ward in a police station (lit., monkey-house). ♦*Вчера́ морема́ны с мазута́ми передра́лись на та́нцах, сидя́т тепе́рь в обезья́ннике.* "There was a big brawl at the disco last night that landed a group of sailors in the brig."

ОБЖИМА́ТЬ/ОБЖА́ТЬ, *neg.* To cheat, deceive (from **жать**, "to squeeze"). ♦*Ка́жется, меня́ обжа́ли на ты́сячу.* "They seem to have cheated me out of a thousand rubles."

ОБИ́ДНО, ДОСА́ДНО, ДА ТЬФУ, ДА НУ, ДА ЛА́ДНО, *idiom, joc.* A rhyming phrase expressing contempt for difficulties: "It's offensive, it's annoying, but never mind!"

ОБКЛА́ДЫВАТЬ/ОБЛОЖИ́ТЬ ма́том. See **гнуть/загну́ть ма́том**.

ОБЛА́МЫВАТЬ/ОБЛОМА́ТЬ, *neg.* Lit., to break, prune. 1. To humble, bring down in spirit. ♦*Тебя́ ещё жизнь облома́ет.* "Life will humble you yet." 2. *youth.* To distress, put someone in a bad mood. ♦*Ты меня́ облома́л э́той но́востью.* "You've really bummed me out with this news." ●**Обла́мывать/облома́ть ве́тки**, *idiom, neg.* To punish, to beat up (lit., "to break branches"). ♦*Э́ти лю́ди тя́нут ру́ки к на́шему магази́ну, хорошо́ бы им ве́тки облома́ть.* "Those guys are threatening our store. We'd better give them a beating." ●**Обла́мывать/облома́ть рога́**, *idiom, neg.* To punish, put down, put in one's place. ♦*Сли́шком он вольно́ себя́ чу́вствует, на́до бы ему́ облома́ть рога́.* "He's feeling a little too free around here. We'll have to take him down a peg."

ОБЛА́МЫВАТЬСЯ¹/ОБЛОМА́ТЬСЯ, *youth, neg.* **1.** To be distressed. ♦*Не стоит так обламываться.* "It's not worth getting so upset about." **2.** To be averse to doing something. ♦*Я обломался идти в город.* "I don't feel like going into town."

ОБЛА́МЫВАТЬСЯ²/ОБЛОМИ́ТЬСЯ кому́-л. To be advantageous or profitable to someone. ♦*Сколько ты с этого дела поимел? — Штука обломилась.* "How much did you make on that deal? — My profit was a thousand."

ОБЛАПО́ШИВАТЬ/ОБЛАПО́ШИТЬ, *joc.* To cheat, take advantage of someone (from лапа, "paw"). ♦*Эти пройдохи нас точно облапошат.* "You can be sure those rascals are cheating us."

ОБЛЕГЧА́ТЬСЯ/ОБЛЕГЧИ́ТЬСЯ, *joc.* To urinate (or defecate) (lit., to relieve oneself). ♦*Надо бы облегчиться, останови машину.* "Stop the car. I've got to take a leak."

ОБЛОКОТИ́ТЬСЯ, *perf. only, youth, neg.* To consider worthless, not give a damn about, have contempt for (lit., to lean one's elbows on). ♦*Я давно облокотился на твои замечания.* "It's been ages since I stopped giving a damn about your remarks."

ОБЛО́М, -а, *m., youth, neg.* **1.** A misfortune, failure. ♦*С квартирой у меня облом.* "I'm not having any luck with finding an apartment." **2.** An aversion to doing something. ♦*Мне облом обед готовить.* "I don't feel like making dinner." •**Обло́м вы́шел,** *idiom, youth, neg.* A misfortune took place, something bad happened. ♦*С деньгами облом вышел.* "I had a financial calamity." **В обло́ме,** *idiom, youth, neg.* In a bad mood. ♦*Не трогай его, он в обломе.* "Don't bother him. He's in a lousy mood."

ОБЛОМИ́ТЬСЯ, *perf.* To appear suddenly. ♦*Откуда ты обломился, давно не виделись.* "Where did you show up from?! I haven't seen you for ages!"

ОБЛО́МОВ, -а, *m., youth, neg.* A person who gets on one's nerves, who annoys others (from Oblomov, the hero of Gon-

charov's novel.) ♦*Мне этот Обломов надоел.* "I'm sick and tired of that Oblomov."

ОБЛО́МОВЩИНА, -ы, *f., youth.* Bad luck, trouble, failure (from облом and Oblomov, the hero of Goncharov's novel). ♦*Обломовщина скоро кончится, всё будет в порядке.* "All this trouble will be over soon, and things will get back to normal."

ОБЛО́МЩИК, -а, *m., youth, neg.* See **сачо́к.**

ОБЛО́ПЫВАТЬСЯ/ОБЛО́ПАТЬСЯ. To overeat (cf. **ло́пать**). ♦*Не облопайся груш, плохо будет!* "Don't eat too many pears or you'll make yourself sick."

ОБМАНУ́ЛИ ДУРАКА́ НА ЧЕТЫ́РЕ КУЛАКА́, *rhyming phrase, joc.* It was your own fault you were cheated or deceived; be more careful next time (used as a taunt in children's speech; lit., they deceived a fool in the hand-counting game).

ОБМИШУ́РИВАТЬСЯ/ОБМИШУ́-РИТЬСЯ, *joc.* To be mistaken, be taken in, be cheated (from мишура, "tinsel"). ♦*Как же ты так обмишурился?* "How did you manage to get taken in like that?"

ОБМЫВА́ТЬ/ОБМЫ́ТЬ. To drink in honor of (a success or a new purchase; lit., to wash). ♦*Давай обмоем мой новый костюм, а то носиться не будет.* "Let's drink to my new suit so that it will wear well."

ОБМЫ́ЛОК, обмы́лка, *m., rude.* Lit., a remnant of a soap case. **1.** A short man. ♦*Казалось бы обмылок, а сила есть.* "He looks puny, but he's strong." **2.** A small penis.

ОБНАЖА́НС, -а, *m., joc.* A striptease, stripping (from обнажать, "to strip"). ♦*Они думают, если на сцене всё время обнажанс, то это и есть современный театр.* "They think contemporary theater is nothing but a perpetual striptease."

ОБНАКОВЕ́ННО, *joc.* All right, okay, as usual (distorted from обыкновенно). ♦*Как поживаешь? — Обнаковенно.* "How are you? — Okay."

ОБНОСИ́ТЬ/ОБНЕСТИ́. To rob (from носить, "to carry"). ♦*Вчера квартиру соседей обнесли начисто.* "Yesterday our neighbors' flat was robbed clean."

ОБОЗНА́ТУШКИ, *idiom, joc.* You're mistaken, I'm not who you think I am (from обознаться, "to take someone for someone else"). ♦*Вы Павел? — Обознатушки.* "Paul? — No, you're mistaken."

ОБО́ЛТУС, -а, *m., neg., rude.* An idiot, fool. ♦*Когда же этот оболтус из школы придёт?* "When does that idiot get home from school?"

ОБОРЗЕ́ЛЫЙ, -ая, -ое, *neg.* Pushy, aggressive (from борзой, "wolfhound").

ОБОРМО́Т, -а, *neg., joc.* A fool, blockhead. ♦*С таким обормотом, как ты, трудно о чём-то договориться, слушаешь только себя.* "How can I make a deal with a blockhead like you? You only listen to yourself."

О́БОРОТЕНЬ, о́боротня, *m.* A policeman mixed up in crime, a dirty cop (lit., a werewolf). ♦*Сейчас не поймёшь, кто оборотень, а кто честный мент.* "Now I can't figure out who's a dirty cop and who's honest."

ОБОСРА́ЛИ, ОБТЕКА́Ю, *idiom, rude.* I've been hurt, but I'll get over it (lit., "I've been shat on, but it's coming off"). ♦*Ну, как ты? Сильно ругали? — Да, обосрали, обтекаю.* "How are you feeling after that dressing-down they gave you? — They really dumped on me, but it's washing away now."

ОБОССА́ТЬ, *perf. only, rude.* To urinate on (cf. ссать). ♦*Ты что же всю постель обоссал?* "How come you pissed all over the bed?" •**Как два па́льца обосса́ть,** see under **как.**

ОБОССА́ТЬСЯ И НЕ ЖИТЬ, *idiom, rude.* Incredible, amazing (lit., [one could] piss in one's pants and drop dead). ♦*Неужели он так и сказал, обоссаться и не жить!* "Did he really say that? I'm astounded!"

ОБРЕ́ЗКИ, -ов, *pl., joc.* Hands or feet (lit., ends). ♦*Снимай обувь, грей свои обрезки у огня.* "Take off your shoes and warm your feet by the fire."

ОБРЫВА́ТЬ/ОБОРВА́ТЬ КРЫ́ЛЫШ - КИ. To disgrace, to beat up (lit., to tear off someone's wings). ♦*Пора ему оборвать крылышки, слишком зазнался.* "We need to put him in his place, he acts like he's better than the rest of us."

ОБСЕРА́ТЬ/ОБОСРА́ТЬ, *rude.* To insult, humiliate (lit., to defecate on; cf. **срать**). ♦*Хватит вам обсерать друг друга.* "Stop badmouthing each other." •**Обосра́ть и на моро́з,** *idiom, rude.* To ridicule, humiliate. ♦*Какие вы, обосрали и на мороз, хватит шутить.* "What sort of people are you, humiliating him like that? Stop playing those games."

ОБСТРУ́ГИВАТЬ/ОБСТРУГА́ТЬ. Lit., to shave wood. **1.** To scold. ♦*Целый день меня родители обстругивали, теперь ещё и ты туда же.* "First my parents bawl me out all day, and now you too!" **2.** To give a haircut. ♦*Где это тебя так обстругали коротко.* "Who cut your hair so short?!"

ОБСУЖДА́ЛОВО, -а, *n., youth, neg.* A pointless discussion (from обсуждать, "to discuss"). ♦*В Думе обсуждалово без конца, от скуки умереть можно.* "The way they babble on in the Duma, you could die of boredom."

ОБТА́ЧИВАТЬ/ОБТОЧИ́ТЬ сапоги, *army.* To prepare for demobilization (lit., to file down one's boots, i.e., to remove the protruding welts that distinguish army boots from civilian ones). ♦*Я уже обточил сапоги, скоро домой.* "I've already filed down my boots, and I'm on my way home."

ОБТРЯ́СЫВАТЬ/ОБТРЯСТИ́. To rob (lit., to shake). ♦*На этой улице и обтрясти могут.* "You could be robbed on this street."

ОБУВА́ТЬ/ОБУ́ТЬ, *joc.* **1.** To cheat (lit., to shoe, put shoes on someone). ♦*Тебя обули минимум на пару тысяч, эти джинсы столько не стоят.* "They cheated you out of at least a couple of thousand rubles on those jeans." **2.** To change tires. ♦*Пора обуть на зиму нашу машину.* "It's time to change our tires for the winter."

ОБУ́ВКА, -и, *f.* Footwear. ♦ *Зимнюю обувку когда покупать будем?* "When are we going to buy winter shoes?"

ОБУРЕ́ТЬ, *perf. only, neg.* To be insolent, impudent (from бур, "drill"). ♦ *Он что, совсем обурел, такую дрянь продавать за такие деньги.* "The nerve of him — selling trash like that at such high prices!"

ОБХАЙРА́ТЬ, *perf., youth.* To cut someone's hair. ♦ *В армии тебя быстро под ноль обхайрают.* "In the army they'll shear you bald."

ОБХЕ́ЗЫВАТЬ/ОБХЕ́ЗАТЬ, *rude.* **1.** To soil, to shit on. ♦ *Кто весь унитаз обхезал?* "Who got shit all over the toilet?" **2.** To slander, speak ill of. ♦ *Твои друзья тебя же и обхезали.* "Your friends have been spreading dirt about you."

ОБХОДИ́ТЬСЯ/ОБОЙТИ́СЬ без соплИ́вых, *idiom, neg.* Not to need someone's advice, especially the advice of the young (lit., to get along without runny-nose kids). ♦ *Лучше бы тебе, мать, не покупать сейчас машину. — Молчи, обойдёмся без сопливых.* "It would be better for you not to buy a car right now, Mom. — No one asked your advice. We can manage without runny-nose kids."

ОБША́РПАННЫЙ, -ая, -ое, *youth, joc.* Owning Sharp-brand of audio or video equipment (by wordplay on обшарпанный, "shabby").

ОБЩА́ГА, -и, *f., youth.* A dormitory. ♦ *В общаге они живут вдвоём в комнате.* "In their dorm they live two in a room."

ОБЩА́К, -а́, *m., crim.* A general fund for supporting imprisoned criminals and their families. ♦ *Пора сдавать деньги в общак.* "It's time to make a contribution to the general fund."

ОБЪЁБЫВАТЬ/ОБЪЕБА́ТЬ, *rude.* To cheat, deceive (cf. **ёб-**). ♦ *Хватит меня объёбывать, я знаю, где ты был.* "Stop trying to fool me. I know where you've been."

ОБЪЯ́ВА, -ы, *f., youth.* A manufacturer's label on clothing or other merchandise. ♦ *Рубашечка хорошая, покажи объяву.* "That's a nice shirt. Let me see the label."

ОВЁС, овса́, *m.* Lit., oats. **1.** Money. ♦ *Овса, как всегда, маловато, но на сегодня хватит.* "As usual, I'm short of money, but at least there's enough for today." **2.** Food. ♦ *Задай им овса, видишь — голодные.* "Give them some chow, can't you see they're hungry?!"

О́ВОЩ, -а, *m.* A helpless or senile person. ♦ *После инсульта он уже овощ.* "He's been a vegetable since his stroke."

ОГЛО́БЛЯ, -и, *f., joc.* A tall person (lit., shaft). ♦ *У них в центре такая оглобля играет, больше двух метров.* "The guy they've got playing center is over two meters tall."

ОГЛОЁБ, -а, *m., rude.* An idiot, good-for-nothing, clumsy person (by wordplay on **охламо́н,** "clumsy person," and **ёб-**). ♦ *Какой оглоёб разбил тарелку?* "Where's the bumbler who broke this plate?"

ОГЛОЕ́Д, -а, *m., neg.* **1.** A pushy, selfish person. ♦ *Эти оглоеды всем надоели, только и делают, что чего-то требуют.* "Everyone's sick of those pushy fellows — all they ever do is make demands." **2.** One who eats on someone else's account. ♦ *Сколько можно бесплатно кормить этих оглоедов?* "How long can I go on feeding those moochers for free?"

ОГЛОУ́ШИВАТЬ/ОГЛОУ́ШИТЬ, *neg.* To drink a large quantity of liquor. ♦ *Когда вы всё это успели оглоушить?* "When did you guys manage to drink all this wine?"

ОГНЕТУШИ́ТЕЛЬ, -я, *m.* A liquor bottle containing three-fourths of a liter (lit., a fire extinguisher). ♦ *Там продают огнетушители, сколько брать?* "They sell those big bottles there — how many should I buy?"

ОГОРЧЕ́НЬЕ: Быва́ют в жи́зни огорче́нья, вме́сто хле́ба ку́шаешь пече́нье, see under **быва́ют.**

ОГРЕБА́ТЬ/ОГРЕСТИ́ (встря́ску, пиздюле́й). To be punished, to be beaten up (from грести, "to grab"). ♦*Сейчас огре-бёшь.* "Now you're going to get it."

ОГРЕБА́ТЬ/ОГРЕ́СТИ ПОЛУ́НДРУ, *idiom, army.* To serve in the navy (lit., to possess "полундра." See **полу́ндра**). ♦*Я всю полундру огреб, от звонка и до звонка,—три года на Балтике.* "I served my full time in the navy—three long years in the Baltic Fleet."

ОГРЕ́ТЬ, *perf. only, neg.* To hit. ♦*Он домой пришёл без получки, пропил всё, а жена его как огреет тарелкой.* "He came home without his pay — spent it all on drink — and his wife hit him with a plate."

ОГРЫ́ЗОК, огры́зка, *m., neg.* A short man (lit., a bitten-off piece).

ОГУРЕ́Ц, -рца́, *m., army.* **1.** A soldier in his first six months of service (lit., a cucumber, refers to the color green, which signifies inexperience). ♦*Какие у нас работы на сегодня, всех огурцов послать на кухню.* "I want all the new recruits in the kitchen peeling potatoes." **2.** A young officer.

ОГУРЕ́Ц: Раз пошла́ така́я пья́нка, режь после́дний огуре́ц, see under **раз.**

ОГУРЦО́М, *indecl.* Good for you! (lit., like a cucumber). ♦*А ты — огурцом! Не испугался.* "You were great! You didn't get frightened at all!"

ОДНОВА́, *adv.* It doesn't matter, it's all the same. ♦*Мне однова, что туда ехать, что сюда.* "I don't care whether we go there or not."

ОДНОМАНДА́ТНИК, -а, *m., joc., rude.* A faithful husband (by wordplay on мандат, "mandate," and **манда́**). ♦*Наш одномандатник на сторону не ходит.* "Our monogamist friend never leaves the straight path."

ОДНОХУ́ЙСТВЕННО, *adv., rude.* It doesn't matter, it's all the same (lit., it's all one prick to me; cf. **хуй**). ♦*Мне одно-хуйственно, куда идти — на пляж или в кафе.* "I don't care whether we go to the beach or to the café."

ОДУВА́НЧИК, -а, *m., army.* **1.** An anti-aircraft shell burst (lit., a dandelion). ♦*Дальше не полетим, уходим, всё*

небо в одуванчиках. "It's too dangerous to advance now, we have to take cover, there are dandelions all over the sky." **2.** A parachute.

ОДЫ́БАТЬСЯ, *perf. only, neg.* To recuperate, recover from illness. ♦*Он еле одыбался после гриппа, было осложнение на лёгкие.* "He had barely gotten over the flu when he turned out to have some complication in his lungs."

ОЗАБО́ЧЕННЫЙ, -ая, -ое, *neg.* Obsessed with sex (lit., preoccupied, anxious). ♦*Ты что озабоченный, ко всем девушкам пристаёшь?* "What are you, sex-starved or something, the way you keep after all the girls?"

ОЗАДА́ЧИВАТЬ/ОЗАДА́ЧИТЬ. To commission, to assign. ♦*Озадачь брата насчёт билетов в театр.* "Get your brother to buy the theater tickets."

ОЗЕЛЕНЕ́НИЕ, -я, *n., youth.* The purchase of dollars (lit., the planting of greenery). ♦*Надо заняться озеленением, пока рубли есть.* "I should do a little green-gardening now while I've got the rubles."

ОКЛЕМА́ТЬСЯ, *perf. only.* To recover from illness. ♦*Я после болезни еле оклемался.* "I had barely recovered from my illness."

ОКОВА́ЛОК, -лка, *m., neg.* A short, fat man (from оковалок, a large joint of beef). ♦*Куда ты столько свинины ешь, и так уже оковалком стал.* "What are you eating all that pork for? You've already turned into a fatso!"

ОКОЛЬЦО́ВЫВАТЬ/ОКОЛЬЦЕ-ВА́ТЬСЯ, *joc.* To get married (lit., to be ringed). ♦*Когда вы успели окольце-ваться?* "When did you manage to tie the knot?"

ОКОРА́ЧИВАТЬ/ОКОРОТИ́ТЬ, *neg.* To humble someone, put someone in his place (from короткий). ♦*Он обнаглел, надо его окоротить.* "He's been so insolent, we'll have to pull him down a peg."

ОКОРОКА́, -о́в, *pl., neg.* Fat thighs. ♦*Ну и окорока же у неё.* "Look at the fat thighs on her!"

ОКУ́ЧИВАТЬ/ОКУ́ЧИТЬ. Lit., to heap up earth around potato plants (from куча, "heap"). **1.** To work fast, do something efficiently. ♦*Не зевай, успевай окучивать, а то не успеем.* "Don't slack off. We need to forge ahead if we're going to finish." **2.** To hit, beat. ♦*Их было человек десять, ну мы их давай окучивать.* "There were ten of them, and we beat them up."

ОЛДО́ВЫЙ, -ая, -ое, *youth.* Old (from Eng. "old"). ♦*Это олдовый шуз.* "This is an old pair of shoes."

ОЛИГА́РХ, -а, *m.* A rich and influential banker or businessman (lit., oligarch). ♦*У наших олигархов новая мода — не платить налоги.* "It's the fashion with our rich New Russians not to pay any taxes."

ОМУМЫ́ЛИВАТЬ/ОМУМЫ́ЛИТЬ. 1. To beat up. **2.** To finish, to consume. ♦*Кто это всё мясо омумылил?* "Who ate up all the meat?"

ОМЫ́ЛОК, омы́лка, *m., neg.* See **обмы́лок.**

ОН ПА́РЕНЬ НЕПЛОХО́Й, ТО́ЛЬКО ССЫ́ТСЯ И ГЛУХО́Й, *idiom, rude.* Said about a bad guy (lit., he's not a bad guy but he's pissing into his pants and he's deaf).

ОНДА́ТРА, -ы, *f., neg.* A bureaucrat (lit., muskrat, alluding to their fashion of wearing expensive fur hats). ♦*Где эта ондатра служит?* "Where does that official work?"

ОНО́, *pron., crim.* A lesbian (lit., an "it"). ♦*Она давно уже оно.* "She's been a lesbian for a long time."

ОПИЗДЕНЕВА́ТЬ, *imperf. only, rude.* To feel bad, be in a bad mood (cf. **пизда́**). ♦*Я опизденеваю от жары.* "This heat is making me feel rotten."

ОПИЗДЕНЕ́ЛЫЙ, -ая, -ое, *rude.* Dull, worn-out, tired (cf. **пизда́**). ♦*Ты какой-то опизденелый сегодня, плохо спал, что ли?* "You seem tired today. Didn't you get enough sleep last night?"

ОПИЗДЕНЕ́ТЬ, *perf. only, rude.* To bore, weary, wear out (cf. **пизда́**). ♦*Не ной, опизденел.* "Stop your nagging, I'm sick of it."

ОПИРА́ТЬСЯ/ОПЕРЕ́ТЬСЯ, *youth.* To ignore, to neglect (lit., to lean on). See **облокоти́ться.**

ОПОРОСИ́ТЬСЯ, *perf., joc.* To produce something after lengthy efforts (lit., to farrow). ♦*Он уже опоросился, написал свой словарь?* "Has he finished cranking out that dictionary of his yet?"

О́ППАНЬКИ!, *interj.* Wow! Amazing! ♦*Оппаньки! Откуда ты взялся?* "Wow! Where did you come from?"

ОПРА́ВДЫВАТЬСЯ БУ́ДЕШЬ ПЕ́РЕД ПРОКУРО́РОМ, *idiom, joc.* Don't make excuses (lit., you can defend yourself to the prosecutor). ♦*Оправдываться будешь перед прокурором, а сейчас расскажи по порядку, что случилось.* "Save your excuses for the prosecutor. As for me, just tell me straight out what happened."

ОПРАВЛЯ́ТЬСЯ/ОПРА́ВИТЬСЯ. To defecate (lit., to put oneself in order). ♦*Где здесь можно оправиться?* "Where can a person take a shit around here?"

ОПРЕДЕЛЯ́ТЬ/ОПРЕДЕЛИ́ТЬ, *army.* To destroy, to kill (lit., to fix, to determine). ♦*Видишь, там пулемёт, его надо определить в первую очередь перед атакой на высоту.* "That machine gun position has to be taken out before we advance on the hill."

ОПРИХО́ДОВАТЬ, *perf.* To beat up, to hit (lit., to register). ♦*Хорошо ты его справа оприходовал.* "That's a good right hook you have him."

ОПУПЕ́Й, -я, *m.* **1.** A dull, unpleasant situation or state of mind (from опупеть, to feel silly, to get tired). ♦*После трёх ночных дежурств, у меня полный опупей, от усталости не могу даже спать.* "After three straight days on night duty I was completely zoned out, I was too tired to sleep and couldn't make sense of anything." **2.** An unpleasant, stupid person. ♦*Он такой опупей, к нему в гости лучше не ходить, через пять минут засыпаешь от скуки.* "Please tell me that you don't want to go to his party. He's so incredibly dull that after five minutes with him all you want to do is sleep."

ОПУСКА́ТЬ/ОПУСТИ́ТЬ, *youth, neg.* To degrade, humiliate (lit., to lower). ♦ *Вы меня не сможете опустить своими шутками.* "Your tricks can't humiliate me." •**Опуска́ть/опусти́ть по́чки,** *idiom, neg.* To beat severely (lit., to drop someone's kidneys). ♦ *Этому стукачу наконец опустили почки.* "They finally beat the hell out of that informer."

ОПУХА́ЛОВО, -а, *n., youth.* Tiredness, boredom (from опухать, "to swell"). ♦ *От телика у меня уже опухалово.* "I'm sick and tired of watching TV."

ОПУХА́ТЬ/ОПУ́ХНУТЬ, *neg.* Lit., to swell up. **1.** To be tired of or bored by something. ♦ *Я опух от его анекдотов.* "I'm sick of his jokes." **2.** To act strange. ♦ *Он совсем опух, бросил есть мясо.* "He's become quite eccentric — given up meat entirely."

ОПЯ́ТЬ ДВА́ДЦАТЬ ПЯТЬ, ЗА РУБЛЬ ДЕ́НЬГИ, *idiom.* An expression of annoyance at repeated requests. ♦ *Опять двадцать пять... Не пойду в кино, сто раз сказал!* "Don't keep pestering me, I've told you a hundred times that I'm not going to the movies."

ОРА́НЖЕВАЯ РЕВОЛЮ́ЦИЯ, *idiom.* The change of political power in Ukraine in December 2004. The orange color was the symbol chosen by the proponents of the new authorities.

ОРА́ТЬ/ЗАОРА́ТЬ как мара́л, *idiom, neg.* To yell, howl (lit., to howl like a stag). ♦ *Что ты орёшь как марал?* "Why are you howling like a stag?"

ОРГАНО́Н, -а, *m., joc.* A body (from орган, "bodily organ"). ♦ *У меня, наверное, грипп, весь органон болит.* "I must have caught a flu, my whole body aches."

О́РГИ, -ов, pl. Corrective measures (from организационные мероприятия).

ОРЁЛ, орла́, *m., army.* Said to describe a paratrooper after his parachute has opened (lit.. an eagle). ♦ *Самое при-*

ятное в прыжках, когда ты орёл, парашют раскрылся и всё в порядке. "The best part of a jump is after your chute opens and you're flying safe and free like an eagle."

ОРЁЛИК КО́МНАТНЫЙ, *idiom, army.* A presumptuous, high-handed soldier (lit., a pet eagle). ♦ *Мы тебе, орёлик комнатный, быстро крылья обрежем.* "We'll clip your wings for you, little eaglet!"

ОРЕ́Х, -а, *m., joc.* A head (lit., nut). ♦ *У тебя орех на что?* "Why don't you use your head?"

ОСА́ДОК: В оса́дке, *idiom, neg.* Exhausted, without strength (lit., in the sediment). ♦ *К вечеру я уже в полном осадке.* "By evening I'm completely wiped out." **Выпада́ть/вы́пасть в оса́док,** see under **выпада́ть.**

ОСКОРБЛЯ́ТЬ/ОСКОРБИ́ТЬ, *joc.* To present as a gift (lit., to offend). ♦ *Оскорби меня ещё цветами.* "Give me some more flowers."

ОСНОВНЯ́К, -а, *m.* **1.** The bulk of one's savings. ♦ *Не знаешь, где он основняк прячет?* "Do you know where he keeps his savings?" **2.** An important person, bigwig.

ОСТАКА́НИВАТЬСЯ/ОСТАКА́НИТЬСЯ, *joc.* To drink as a remedy for a hangover (from стакан, "glass"). ♦ *Вот остаканились, сразу легче стало.* "As soon as they had a glass they felt better."

ОСТЕПЕНЁННЫЙ, -ая. Having an advanced degree (by wordplay on степень, "degree," and степенный, "sedate"). ♦ *В семье у них все остепенённые.* "Everyone in their family has an advanced degree."

ОСТЕПЕНИ́ТЬСЯ, *perf. only.* **1.** To defend a dissertation, receive an advanced degree (from степень, "degree"). ♦ *Он остепенился в марте.* "He got his degree in March." **2.** To receive a disbursement of a fellowship, stipend. ♦ *Иди остепенись, сегодня деньги дают.* "Go get your money, they're distributing the stipends today."

ОСТОГРА́ММИТЬСЯ, *perf. only, joc.*

To drink 100 grams of vodka as a remedy for a hangover (from сто грамм, "100 grams"). ♦*Пора нам остограммиться.* "It's time for us to drink 100 grams."

ОСТОЕБÉНИВАТЬ/ОСТОЕБÉНИТЬ, *rude.* To be boring, wearisome (cf. **ёб-**). ♦*Выключи радио, остоебенило.* "Turn off the radio. I'm tired of it."

ОСТОНАДОЕДÁТЬ/ОСТОНАДО-ÉСТЬ, *euph., neg.* To be annoying. ♦*Ты мне остонадоел своими жалобами.* "I'm sick and tired of your complaints."

ОСТОПИЗДЕНИВÁТЬ/ОСТОПÍЗ-ДЕТЬ, *rude.* To be boring, wearisome (cf. **пиздá**). ♦*Мне тяжёлый рок осто-пиздел.* "I'm sick of hard rock music."

ОСТОХУЕВÁТЬ/ОСТОХУÉТЬ. See **остопизденивáть**.

ОТ ДÓХЛОГО ОСЛÁ ÚШИ, *idiom.* No way, no chance (lit., a dead donkey's ears). ♦*От дохлого осла уши ему, а не премию!* "He sure isn't going to get a bonus."

ОТБИВÁТЬ/ОТБÍТЬ бáбки, *idiom, youth.* To return money. ♦*Алекс, когда ты отобьёшь бабки?* "When are you going to give me back my money, Alex?"

ОТБИВНÚХА, -и, *f.* A pork chop (from отбивная котлета). ♦*Сейчас бы па-рочку, троечку отбивнух и поспать.* "What I want right now is to eat a few pork chops and take a nap."

ОТБРÁСЫВАТЬ/ОТБРÓСИТЬ лáпти, *idiom.* To die (lit., to throw out one's bast shoes; cf. **лáпти**). ♦*Скоро лапти от-брошу, тогда делайте, что хотите.* "Soon I'll kick the bucket, and then you can do whatever you want."

ОТВÁЛ (ПЕТРÓВИЧ)!, *idiom, joc.* (Go away, get out of here. ♦*Ну всё! Отвал Петрович, спать пора.* "Enough! Buzz off now, I've got to get to sleep."

ОТВÁЛИВАТЬ/ОТВАЛÍТЬ. To leave, pull out (lit., to cast off, of a ship). ♦*Давай отваливай отсюда!* "Get out of here!"

ОТВÁЛИВАТЬСЯ/ОТВАЛÍТЬСЯ, *youth.* To admire, to be amazed (lit., to fall off). ♦*Я отваливаюсь, какая у тебя причёска.* "I adore your haircut!"

ОТВÁЛЬНЫЙ, -ая, -ое, *youth.* Wonderful, astonishing. See **отвáливаться**.

ОТВÁЛЬНАЯ, -ой, *f.* A farewell party (from отваливать, "to leave"). ♦*Ника-ких отвальных я не собираюсь делать.* ""I'm not planning to have any farewell parties."

ОТВÉТКА, -и, *f., army.* **1.** Resistance against the superiority and authority of experienced soldiers. ♦*На твоём месте я бы не гнал ответку, деды этого не потерпят.* "If I were you I wouldn't try to challenge the old timers, they won't tolerate it." **2.** A counterattack. ♦*Через час надо идти в ответку, проверьте оружие и снаряжение.* "We'll start the counterattack within the hour, get your weapons ready and check each other's gear."

ОТВЁРТКА, -и, *f.* A cocktail made with Fanta and vodka (lit., a screwdriver). The carbonation in the Fanta absorbs the vodka quicker and makes it easier to get drunk.

ОТВÉШИВАТЬ/ОТВÉСИТЬ пиздю-лéй. See under **давáть**.

ОТВИНТÓВЫЙ, -ая, -ое. Said of a person who seems detached from reality, isn't affected by anything, or has a strange mindset and way of life. ♦*С ним поосторожней, на войне он стал совсем отвинтовым.* "Be careful around that guy. He's got a screw loose. He completely lost it during the war."

ОТВÍНЧИВАТЬ/ОТВИНТÍТЬ Úши, *idiom, neg.* To beat up (lit., to unscrew someone's ears). ♦*Я тебе уши отвин-чу, если возьмёшь мой магнитофон.* "I'll twist your ears off if you take my tape recorder."

ОТВЯ́ЗАННЫЙ, -ая, -ое, *youth, pos.* **1.** Relaxed, at ease. ♦*Он всегда и везде отвязанный.* "He's always at ease." **2.** Independent. ♦*Они тебя не будут слушать, они отвязанные.* "They're independent people; they'll never listen to you." **3.** Out of control, wild.

ОТВЯ́ЗКА, -и, *f., youth.* Entertainment, relaxing distraction, dancing. ♦*Устал я, надо бы отвязку устроить.* "I'm worn out; let's do something entertaining."

ОТВЯ́ЗЫВАТЬСЯ/ОТВЯЗА́ТЬСЯ, *youth.* To relax, have a good time. ♦*Вчера мы неплохо отвязались, потанцевали, поорали песни.* "We had a pretty good time yesterday dancing and singing."

ОТВЯ́НУТЬ, *perf. only, youth, neg.* To leave alone, stop bothering (lit., to fade out). ♦*Отвянь, не хочу я идти в кино.* "Leave me alone, I don't want to go to the movies."

ОТГЛЯНЦЕВА́ТЬ, *perf.* To drink some beer or wine after vodka (lit., to gloss a photo print). ♦*Хорошо бы ещё и отглянцевать, а потом по домам.* "Let's give ourselves a little gloss before everyone goes home."

ОТГРО́ХИВАТЬ/ОТГРО́ХАТЬ. To build something huge (from грохотать, "to thunder"). ♦*Он себе такую дачу отгрохал — целый дворец.* "He built himself an enormous country house, a regular palace."

ОТДАВА́ТЬ/ОТДА́ТЬ концы́, *idiom, joc.* To die (lit., to untie the guy ropes). ♦*Без воды быстро отдашь концы.* "Without water you'll kick the bucket fast."

ОТДА́ЧА, -и, *f., joc.* Breath smelling of liquor (lit., recoil). ♦*У тебя такая отдача, за километр несёт.* "Your breath stinks of booze from a mile away."

ОТДУПЛИ́ТЬСЯ, *perf.* To finish, complete (from дуплиться, a term in dominoes). ♦*Ты уже отдуплился на работе, заходи в гости.* "If you're done working, drop by at my place."

ОТЗЫ́НУТЬ, *perf. only, youth, neg.* To leave, go away. ♦*Тебе сказали, отзынь!* "How many times do I have to tell you? Get lost!"

ОТКА́ЗНИК, -а, *m.* A "refusenik," someone who has been refused an emigration visa to leave the country (from отказать; cf. **рефью́зник**).

ОТКА́ЛЫВАТЬ/ОТКОЛО́ТЬ хо́хму, *idiom.* To play a trick, play a practical joke (cf. **хо́хма**). ♦*Знаешь, какую они хохму отмочили, поменяли все номера*

машин во дворе. "Did you hear about the trick they played? They switched around the license plates of all the cars in the driveway!"

ОТКА́Т, -а, *m.,* **1.** *youth.* Something wonderful, terrific. ♦*Сейчас мы смотрели видик — откат!* "The film we just saw is something fantastic!" **2.** A bribe for receiving credit or a contract, work (lit., recoil). ♦*Этому откат пять процентов, тому откат—десять, не хватит денег для выполнения работ.* "That guy gets a five percent kickback, that one ten, and then you end up without enough money to do the work that was contracted."

ОТКА́ТНЫЙ, -ая, -ое, *youth.* Wonderful, terrific (cf. **отка́т**). ♦*Где ты достал такой откатный плейер?* "Where did you get that terrific tape player?"

ОТКИ́ДЫВАТЬ/ОТКИ́НУТЬ ХВОСТ, *idiom.* To die (lit., to kick a tail away). ♦*Пусть кто-нибудь тебя прикрывает, откинуть хвост здесь недолго, вот выжить—это задача.* "Make sure you've got someone covering you at all times. It's a lot easier to die here than it is to survive."

ОТКИ́ДЫВАТЬСЯ/ОТКИ́НУТЬСЯ, *crim.* To complete a prison sentence, to be released. ♦*Я своё отсидел, скоро откинусь.* "I've served my term, I'll be out soon."

ОТКИ́НУТЬ копы́та, *idiom.* To die (lit., to throw one's hooves outwards). ♦*Из-за чего он копыта откинул?* "What did he die of?"

ОТКЛЕ́ИВАТЬСЯ/ОТКЛЕ́ИТЬСЯ, *neg.* To leave alone, stop bothering (lit., to come unstuck). ♦*Слушай, отклейся, не хочу тебя видеть.* "Leave me alone! Get out of my sight."

ОТКЛОНЕ́НИЕ, -я, *n.* An eccentricity, a strange feature (lit., deviation). ♦*У него отклонение на женщин, он их терпеть не может.* "He has a thing about women — he just can't stand them."

ОТКЛЮЧА́ТЬСЯ/ОТКЛЮЧИ́ТЬСЯ. **1.** To fall asleep (lit., to be disconnected). ♦*После ужина мы сразу отключи-*

лись, все очень устали. "We were all so tired that after dinner we conked out." **2.** To faint, lose consciousness. ◆ *На работе он вдруг отключился, вызвали скорую.* "He suddenly fainted at work; they had to call an ambulance."

ОТКЛЮ́ЧКА: В (по́лной) отклю́чке, *idiom, neg.* In a drunken stupor, out cold from intoxication. ◆ *Не разговаривай ты с ним, видишь, он в полной отключке.* "Don't try to talk with him — he's out cold."

ОТКЛЮ́ЧНЫЙ, -ая, -ое, *youth.* Excellent, of high quality. ◆ *У неё отключная шуба!* "She's got a terrific fur coat."

ОТКРЫВА́ТЬ/ОТКРЫ́ТЬ ЖА́ЛО, *idiom.* To speak, to talk (lit., to open someone's stinger). ◆ *Правило простое—жало поменьше открывай, подольше жить будешь.* "It's a simple rule: the less you talk the longer you live."

ОТЛИВА́ТЬ/ОТЛИ́ТЬ, *rude.* To urinate. ◆ *Отлить хочется, умираю.* "I need to take a leak really badly."

ОТЛУ́П, -а, *m.* Refusal (from отлупить, to dispel, to dismiss). ◆ *Даже и не проси его, отлуп тебе гарантирован.* "Don't waste your breath asking him. He'll turn you down."

ОТМА́ЗКА, -и, *f.* An excuse, an escape from a duty or responsibility. See **отма́зываться.**

ОТМА́ЗЫВАТЬ/ОТМА́ЗАТЬ. To make excuses for someone, protect someone with a pretext. ◆ *Я не пойду сегодня на работу, а вы меня отмажьте.* "I'm not going to work today. You make up some excuse for me."

ОТМА́ЗЫВАТЬСЯ/ОТМА́ЗАТЬСЯ. 1. To beg off, make excuses for escaping a duty. ◆ *Отмазывайся на работе и поехали на рыбалку.* "Make some excuse to get out of work, and let's go fishing." **2.** To justify oneself, escape responsibility. ◆ *Ему теперь не отмазаться за это дело, сядет в тюрьму.* "He can't get out of it now. He's going to land in prison."

ОТМАНТУ́ЛИТЬ, *perf.* To beat up.

◆ *Тебя уже раз отмантулили, всё мало?* "You've already been beaten up once, isn't that enough for you?"

ОТМА́ЧИВАТЬ/ОТМОЧИ́ТЬ, *neg.* To do or say something wrong, bad, disappointing, shocking. ◆ *Знаешь, что он опять отмочил? Продал все украшения жены.* "Have you heard about his latest stunt? He sold off all his wife's jewelry!"

ОТМОРО́ЖЕННЫЙ, -ая, -ое. Lit., frostbitten. **1.** Unscrupulous, hardhearted, without conscience. ◆ *Он у них самый отмороженный, убьёт, не задумываясь.* "He's the most hardened of the lot — he'll kill without a second thought." **2.** Passive, depressed, dull. ◆ *Случилось что? Сидите какие-то отмороженные.* "Is something wrong? Why are you sitting around so glumly?"

ОТМОРО́ЗОК, -зка, *m., neg.* A hardhearted, remorseless person. See **отморо́женный.**

ОТМОТА́ТЬСЯ, *perf. only.* To get out of doing something, beg off (lit., to unwind one's reel). ◆ *Отмотайся от поездки, там будет скучно.* "Beg off that trip! It'll be a bore."

ОТМЫВА́ТЬ ДЕ́НЬГИ, *idiom, business.* See **отсти́рывать де́ньги.**

ОТМЫВА́ТЬСЯ/ОТМЫ́ТЬСЯ, *neg.* To clear oneself, vindicate oneself (lit., wash oneself off). ◆ *Я не буду это делать, потом всю жизнь не отмоешься.* "I wouldn't do that. It's the sort of thing you'd never be able to clear yourself of afterwards."

ОТОВА́РИВАТЬ/ОТОВА́РИТЬ. To beat, hit (lit., to deliver the merchandise). ◆ *Хорошо, что ты не пошёл на танцы, нас там сильно отоварили.* "It's a good thing you didn't come to the dance with us — they really gave it to us there."

ОТОВА́РИВАТЬСЯ/ОТОВА́РИТЬСЯ. To do one's shopping (lit., to trade). ◆ *Я уже отоварился, иду домой.* "I've finished my shopping, and I'm on my way home."

ОТОВА́РКА, -и, *f.* A first fight (cf. **отова́ривать**).

ОТÓРВА, -ы, *m. & f., neg.* A reckless person (from оторванный, "torn off"). ♦ *Этот оторва не пропадёт, за него беспокоиться не стоит.* "That reckless fellow always lands on his feet; don't worry about him."

ОТПÁД, -а, *m., youth.* Something wonderful, terrific (lit., a fainting fit). ♦ *Этот концерт — отпад!* "That concert was wonderful!"

ОТПАДÁТЬ/ОТПÁСТЬ. To be amazed (lit., to faint; cf. **отпáд**). ♦ *Они мою шубу увидели, сразу отпали.* "When they saw my fur coat they practically passed out."

ОТПÁДНЫЙ, -ая, -ое. Excellent, outstanding (cf. **отпáд**). ♦ *Такого отпадного моря давно не было.* "The sea hasn't been so perfect for a long time."

ОТПИ́ЗДИТЬ, *perf. only, rude.* To beat up (cf. **пизда́**). ♦ *Ты хочешь, чтобы отпиздили за воровство?* "Are you looking to get beaten up for robbery?"

ОТРАЖÁТЬ/ОТРАЗИ́ТЬ. Lit., to repel, to reflect. **1.** To refuse. ♦ *Все наши просьбы он отразил.* "He turned down all our requests." **2.** To give an unsatisfactory mark on an examination. ♦ *Меня уже два раза отразили.* "They've already failed me twice."

ОТРИХТÓВЫВАТЬ/ОТРИХТОВÁТЬ. To beat up (lit., to even a surface). ♦ *Сильно ему рожу отрихтовали, сплошной синяк.* "Somebody beat his face in good, it's nothing but one big black and blue mark."

ОТРУ́Б, -а, *m., neg.* Drunkenness, a state of drunkenness. ♦ *Он уже три дня в отрубе.* "He's been on a binge for three days."

ОТРУБÁТЬСЯ/ОТРУБИ́ТЬСЯ. To faint, to lose consciousness (lit., to be cut off). See **отключáться**.

ОТРЫВÁТЬ/ОТОРВÁТЬ. To buy. ♦ *Где это ты себе такое платье оторвала?* "Where did you buy that dress?" •**Отрывáть/оторвáть бóшку,** *idiom.* To punish (lit., to tear someone's head off). ♦ *Я тебе бошку оторву, если ещё раз увижу тебя с ней.* "I'll kill you if I catch you with her again." •**Отрывáть/оторвáть пýговицу с мя́сом,** *idiom.* To get a button pulled off with a piece of the fabric (lit., to tear off a button with its flesh). •**Отрывáть/оторвáть с рукáми (и ногáми),** *idiom.* To be glad to buy something that is in great demand. ♦ *Не знаю, возьмут ли эту шапку за 50000. — Да ты что, с руками и ногами оторвут.* "I don't know if this hat will sell for 50000 rubles. — Are you kidding? They'll eat it up!" •**Отрывáть/оторвáть фáзу,** *idiom.* To go mad (lit., to tear a phase off). ♦ *Чувствую, фазу оторвёт, если ещё будут проверки на неделе.* "I swear I'll lose my mind if we have anymore pop-inspections this week." **Отрывáть/оторвáть я́йца,** see under **яйцó**.

ОТРЫВÁТЬСЯ/ОТОРВÁТЬСЯ. To relax, enjoy leisure activities. ♦ *Хочу в воскресенье оторваться, поиграть в теннис.* "I want to have some relaxation on Sunday — maybe a nice game of tennis."

ОТРЫ́ЖКА ПЬЯ́НОГО ИНДУ́СА, *idiom, neg.* Bad-tasting food of poor quality (lit., the burp of a drunken Indian). ♦ *Ну, как салат? — Отрыжка пьяного индуса.* "How's the salad? — Ugh. It's the burp of a drunken Indian."

ОТСКÓК, -а, *m., youth.* Departure (lit., a jump-off). ♦ *Мне пора отскок делать.* "Well, it's time for me to get out of here."

ОТСЛЮ́НИВАТЬ/ОТСЛЮНИ́ТЬ, *joc.* To count out (money, bills) in payment (from слюна, "saliva," with reference to moistening one's fingers in the process of counting). ♦ *Сколько тебе отслюнить на сегодня?* "How much do I owe you for today?"

ОТСÓС, -а, *m., rude.* **1.** Oral sex, fellatio. ♦ *Она отсосом занимается?* "Does she do blow jobs?" **2.** Used as a rude dismissal or negation: certainly not, no way. ♦ *Я туда не пойду, отсос.* "I wouldn't go there. No way." **3.** A lazy person (from отсасывать, to suck, meaning to live at someone else's expense). See **сачóк**. **4.** Mooch. ♦ *Ну ты и отсос, ты хоть раз расплатился за что-нибудь?* "You are such a mooch! You have never paid a single cent for anything."

ОТСТЁБЫВАТЬ/ОТСТЕБА́ТЬ. To ridicule, to make fun of (cf. **стёб**). ♦*Хорош его отстёбывать, надоело.* "Enough making fun of him already! It's getting boring."

ОТСТЁГИВАТЬ/ОТСТЕГНУ́ТЬ, *joc.* To pay, to count out money (lit., to unbutton). ♦*Мне надоело отстёгивать деньги каждую неделю на ерунду.* "I'm sick of making weekly payments for this junk."

ОТСТЁГИВАТЬСЯ/ОТСТЕГ- НУ́ТЬСЯ, *youth.* To decline, to refuse (lit., to be unbuttoned). ♦*Я отстёгиваюсь от прогулки, устал.* "I'm tired, I don't want to go for a walk."

ОТСТИ́РЫВАТЬ ДЕ́НЬГИ, *idiom, business.* To launder money. ♦*Как они отстирывают деньги за наркотики?* "How do they launder the drug money?"

ОТСТРЕЛЯ́ТЬСЯ, *perf.* To finish, to compelte (from стрелять, "to shoot").

ОТТЯ́Г, -а, *m., youth, pos.* A vacation, rest, break (cf. **оття́гиваться**). ♦*Летом будет тебе оттяг.* "You'll get a vacation in the summer."

ОТТЯ́ГИВАТЬ/ОТТЯНУ́ТЬ, *joc.* To give relief as a remedy for a hangover (lit., to draw off, with reference to the bad effects of the previous night's drinking). ♦*Пиво хорошо оттягивает.* "Beer works well as a hangover remedy."

ОТТЯ́ГИВАТЬСЯ/ОТТЯНУ́ТЬСЯ, *youth, pos.* To rest, relax (cf. **оття́г**). ♦*Пора нам оттянуться.* "It's time for us to take a break."

ОТТЯ́ЖНИК, -а, *m., youth.* A playboy (cf. **оття́гиваться**).

ОТТЯ́ПЫВАТЬ/ОТТЯ́ПАТЬ. To grab, to take (from тяпать, "to chop"). ♦*Все родительские деньги брат себе оттяпал.* "My brother took all our parent's money."

ОТФЕ́ЙСИТЬ, *perf., youth.* To hit, to beat (from Eng. "face"). ♦*Кто кого там отфейсил, не помню.* "I can't remember who hit who."

ОТХВА́ТЫВАТЬ/ОТХВАТИ́ТЬ. To buy, to get (lit., to snap off). ♦*Смотри, какой я себе костюм отхватил.* "Look at this suit I bought for myself."

ОТХОДНЯ́К, -á, *m., youth.* A hangover (from отходить после болезни, "to recover from an illness"). ♦*Что ты лежишь, на работу не пойдёшь? — Нет, у меня сегодня отходняк.* "Why are you still in bed? Aren't you going to work today? — No, I've got a hangover."

ОТХУЯ́РИВАТЬ/ОТХУЯ́РИТЬ, *rude.* Cf. **хуй**. **1.** To go a long distance. ♦*Мы отхуярили уже 10 километров, а деревни всё нет.* "We've already covered ten kilometers, and there's still no sign of a village." **2.** To beat up. ♦*Тебя старший брат отхуярит за порванные джинсы.* "Your older brother is going to beat you up for ripping his jeans." **3.** To work a long time. ♦*Ещё отхуярим пару часов и конец смены.* "We have to slog through another couple of hours and then it'll be the end of our shift."

ОТЧА́ЛИВАТЬ/ОТЧА́ЛИТЬ. To leave, depart (cf. **отва́ливать**). ♦*Нам пора отчаливать.* "It's time for us to get going."

ОТЧЕБУ́ЧИВАТЬ/ОТЧЕБУ́ЧИТЬ. See **отма́чивать**.

ОТШИБА́ТЬ/ОТШИБИ́ТЬ рога́, *idiom, neg.* To beat up, punish (lit., to knock someone's horns off). ♦*Я тебе рога отшибу за твои штучки!* "I'm going to knock your block off for those tricks of yours!"

ОТШИВА́ТЬ/ОТШИ́ТЬ, *neg.* **1.** To reject, break off relations with someone. ♦*Он предлагал ей выйти за него замуж, она его отшила.* "When he asked her to marry him, she broke off with him completely." **2.** To chase away, force to leave. ♦*Отшей его, я не хочу, чтобы он оставался.* "Get rid of him. I don't want him to stay."

ОТЪЁБЫВАТЬСЯ/ОТЪЕБА́ТЬСЯ, *rude.* To cease, stop (cf. **ёб-**). ♦*Отъебись со своими расспросами.* "That's enough of your requests."

ОТЪЕЗЖА́ТЬ/ОТЪЕ́ХАТЬ. To die. ♦*Да она уже года два назад как* *отъехала.* "Oh, she died about a year or two ago."

ОТЪÉХАВШИЙ, -ая, -ее, *youth, neg.* Lit., gone, departed. **1.** Eccentric, abnormal. ♦ *Ты у нас отъехавший совсем, даже не знаешь, когда экзамены.* "You're completely out of it! You don't even know when our exams are going to be!" **2.** Drunk. ♦ *Пусть поспит, он уже отъехавший.* "Let him sleep — he's dead drunk."

ОФИГЕНИВÁТЬ/ОФИГÉТЬ, *joc.* **1.** To become exhausted. ♦ *Я офигел от твоих разговоров.* "I've had it up to here with your talk." **2.** To go crazy. ♦ *Ты что, офигел?* "What are you, crazy?"

ОФИГÉНИЕ, -я, n., joc. Exhaustion, stupor. ♦ *Вчера мы сидели над рукописью до офигения.* "Yesterday we worked on the manuscript to the point of exhaustion."

ОФИГÍТЕЛЬНЫЙ, -ая, -ое. Outstanding, excellent. ♦ *Я вчера попал на офигительный концерт.* "I went to a terrific concert yesterday."

ОФИЦИÓЗ, -а, m., neg. An official function, formal or ceremonial occasion. ♦ *Я на этот официоз не пойду, у меня нет галстука.* "I haven't got a tie so I'm not going to the official do." •**Разводѝть/развестѝ официóз,** see under **разводѝть.**

ОФОНАРÉНИЕ, n., neg. Stupor, stupidity (from фонарь, "streetlight"). ♦ *Сейчас у всех офонарение от жары.* "Everyone's stupefied by this terrible heatwave."

ОФОНАРÉТЬ, *perf.* **1.** To be surprised, shocked. ♦ *Я офонарел совсем, когда узнал, каким боссом он заделался.* "I was amazed to find out what a big boss he's become." **2.** To be exhausted. ♦ *Мы совсем офонарели от словаря, сидим день и ночь.* "We worked on the dictionary day and night until we dropped."

ОФОРМЛЯ́ТЬ/ОФÓРМИТЬ. To have sex with someone (lit., to formalize). ♦ *Ты же, я знаю, двоих успел оформить.* "I realize you've managed to sleep

with both of them."

ОХВÁТЫВАТЬ/ОХВАТИ́ТЬ, *joc.* To commission, give someone a job or duty. ♦ *Тебя ещё не охватили, иди на кухню, помоги готовить.* "You haven't been assigned a job yet. Go into the kitchen and help with the cooking."

ОХЛАМÓН, -а, m., neg. A clumsy person. ♦ *Этот охламон ничего не умеет делать.* "He's so clumsy he can't do anything right."

ОХЛЯ́ТЬ, *perf. only, neg.* To be emaciated, worn down. ♦ *Ты совсем охлял, тебе надо отдохнуть.* "You're completely worn out — you need a vacation."

ОХМУРЯ́ТЬ/ОХМУРИ́ТЬ, *neg.* To deceive, cheat (lit., to cast a shadow on; from хмурь, "gloom"). ♦ *Они пытались меня охмурить, но я отказался возить их на дачу.* "They tried to pull one over on me, but I simply refused to take them to the dacha."

ОХНÁРИК, -а, m. A partially smoked cigarette. See **бычóк.**

ОХРЕНЕВÁТЬ/ОХРЕНÉТЬ, *rude.* To lose one's patience, become worn out (cf. **хрен**). ♦ *Я совсем здесь от скуки охренел, пока вас ждал.* "I've been bored to tears waiting for you."

ОХУЕВÁТЕЛЬСКИЙ, -ая, -ое, *rude.* Excellent, splendid (cf. **хуй**). ♦ *Там играет охуевательский оркестр.* "The orchestra that's playing there is fantastic."

ОХУЕВÁТЬ/ОХУÉТЬ, *rude.* To be tired of, worn out by something (cf. **хуй**). ♦ *Ты ещё от телевизора не охуел?* "Aren't you sick of watching television?"

ОХУÉНИЕ, -я, n., rude. Dullness, weariness (cf. **хуй**). ♦ *Мы накурились до охуения.* "We smoked ourselves into a stupor."

ОХУИ́ТЕЛЬНЫЙ, -ая, -ое, *rude.* Excellent, wonderful (cf. **хуй**). ♦ *Надо пройтись, охуительный вечер.* "Let's go for a walk — the weather's wonderful."

ОЧКÓ, -á, n. **1.** Blackjack (the card game). ♦ *Давай сыграем в очко.* "Let's have a game of blackjack." **2.** Rectum. ♦ *Готовь очко, сейчас поставлю клизму.*

"Okay, get your asshole ready for an enema." •**У кого́-л. очко́ игра́ет,** *idiom, rude.* To be afraid. ♦*У тебя что, очко играет подраться с ним?* "What's the matter, are you scared to fight him?" **3.** Toilet hole in an outhouse. ♦*Ты уже сделал очко в уборной?* "Have you dug the hole for the outhouse yet?" •**Сиде́ть на очке́,** see under **сиде́ть.**

ОЧУМÉВАТЬ/ОЧУМÉТЬ, *neg.* To be bored, worn out (from чума, "plague"). ♦*Мы на лекции чуть не очумели от скуки.* "We practically died of boredom at that lecture."

ОЧУ́ХИВАТЬСЯ/ОЧУ́ХАТЬСЯ, *joc.* To come to one's senses, recover oneself (lit., to scratch oneself). ♦*Я еле очухался от этой новости.* "The news shocked me so much I had to pinch myself to recover from it."

ОШАРÁШИВАТЬ/ОШАРÁШИТЬ, *neg.* To astound, upset, startle (lit., to shake). ♦*Меня эти цены ошарашили.* "I'm overwhelmed by these prices."

ОШИВÁТЬСЯ, *imperf. only, neg.* To hang around, spend time. ♦*Они всегда ошиваются возле магазина.* "They're always hanging around near the store."

ПА́ДАТЬ, *imperf., business.* To be determined. ◆*Ты падаешь на это дело или нет?* "Are you determinded to go through with this business or not?" •**Я па́даю**, see under **я**.

ПА́ДАТЬ/УПА́СТЬ, *army.* To be assigned a duty. ◆*Кто у нас сегодня падает на кухню?* "Who's on kitchen duty today?" •**Па́дать/упа́сть в строй**, *idiom, army.* To take one's place in formation (lit., to fall into formation). ◆*Падай в строй и больше никаких опозданий у меня!* "Fall in and don't let me catch you being late again!" •**Па́дать/упа́сть на хвост кому́-л.**, *idiom, youth, neg.* Lit., to fall onto someone's tail. **1.** To drink at someone else's expense. ◆*Если ты хочешь упасть нам на хвост, ничего не выйдет, слишком мало.* "If you're hoping to drink our liquor — nothing doing! We haven't got enough for us." **2.** To be unwanted company, to hang around someone against that person's will. ◆*Не знаю, что с ним делать, упал на хвост и весь вечер покою не даёт.* "I just don't know what to do with him — he's attached himself to me and hasn't given me a moment's peace all evening." •**Я па́даю**, see under **я**.

ПА́ДЛА, -ы, *f., rude.* A worthless person, scoundrel (from падаль, "corpse of an animal"). ◆*Он поступил, как последняя падла.* "He behaved like an absolute scoundrel."

ПА́КУР, -а, *m., army.* From покурить. **1.** A smoking break. ◆*Пока нам пакур устроить.* "Let's take a smoking break." **2.** Tobacco, cigarettes. ◆*Пакур есть?* "Is there anything to smoke?"

ПА́ЛА, -ы, *f., rude.* A worthless or bad woman (cf. **па́дла**). ◆*Опять эта пала нас наколола.* "That bitch cheated us again."

ПА́ЛЕВО, -а, *n., youth, neg.* A risky venture, a dangerous business (from палить, "to burn to ashes"). ◆*На это палево меня не заманишь.* "You won't get me into that risky venture."

ПА́ЛЕЦ: Па́льцем де́ланный, *idiom, rude.* A fool, idiot (lit., made with a finger). ◆*Он не пальцем деланный, всё сделает что нужно.* "He's no fool; he'll do everything just right." **Два́дцать пе́рвый па́лец**, see under **два́дцать**. **Как два па́льца обосса́ть**, see under **как**.

ПА́ЛКА: Броса́ть/бро́сить па́лку, see under **броса́ть**. **Ядрёна па́лка**, see under **ядрёна**.

ПА́ЛКИ-МОТА́ЛКИ, *idiom, rude.* Damn it! ◆*Ты когда-нибудь заткнёшься, палки-моталки?* "Can't you shut up, damn it!"

ПАЛЬ, -и, *f., crim. & youth.* Narcotics for smoking (cf. **па́лево**). ◆*Вот пали немного, угощайся!* "Here's some dope — help yourself!"

ПА́ЛЬЦЕМ ДЕ́ЛАННЫЙ. See under **па́лец**.

ПА́ЛЬЦЫ ВЕ́ЕРОМ, *idiom.* A characteristic gesture of bandits, gang symbols, usually threatening in nature (lit., fingers as a fan). See **гнуть па́льцы**.

ПАМПУ́ШКА, -и, *f., joc.* A plump, pink-cheeked girl (lit., a bun). ◆*Тебе всегда пампушки достаются, а у меня сплошные скелеты.* "You always manage to get hooked up with those kewpie-dolls, and I get all the scarecrows."

ПА́МЯТНИК, -а, *m.* A member of the supernationalistic Pamyat organization (lit., a monument). ◆*Памятники хотят построить великую Россию, читай, Советский Союз.* "Those 'monuments' want to rebuild Greater Russia, that is, the Soviet Union."

ПА́МЯТЬ: Де́вичья па́мять (кому́ дала́, не по́мню), see under **де́вичья**.

ПАНКАТУ́РА, -ы, *f., youth.* **1.** *collect.* Punks. ◆*Я слышал, в этом кафе панкатура собирается.* "I've heard that the punks hang out in this cafe." **2.** A punk hairdo. ◆*Смотри, какая у него на голове панкатура.* "Look at the punk hairdo on that fellow!"

ПАНКОВА́ТЬ/ЗАПАНКОВА́ТЬ, *youth.* **1.** To be or become a punk. ♦*Твой сын, вижу, панкует, причёску себе сделал гребешком, весь в коже.* "I see your son is turning into a punk — he wears his hair like a cock's comb and dresses all in leather." **2.** To act extravagant, to dress strangely. ♦*Ты что панкуешь, ишь как вырядился?* "What's that punky outfit you've got yourself rigged up in?"

ПА́ПА, -ы, *m., army.* A commander. ♦*Папа приказал убрать снег.* "The commander ordered us to clear the snow." •**Как па́па Ка́рло,** see under **как.**

ПА́ПА ЗЮ, *idiom.* A nickname for Zyuganov, the leader of the Communist Party of Russia (playing on Папа Док, the former Dictator of Haiti).

ПАПА́Н, -а, *m.* Father. ♦*Папан, ты не знаешь, где мои перчатки?* "Dad, do you know where my gloves are?"

ПАПА́ХЕН, -а, *m., joc.* See **папа́н.**

ПА́ПИК, -а, *m., youth, neg.* An old man. ♦*Папик, не приставай к девушке.* "Hey, old man, don't bother the girl."

ПАРАДНЯ́К, -á, *m., army.* A parade uniform. ♦*Надо погладить парадняк.* "I've got to iron my parade uniform."

ПАРАЛЛЕ́ЛЬНО, *adv.* It's all the same, it doesn't matter (lit., parallel). ♦*Кому параллельно, а кому и нет, что у нас сейчас делается в стране.* "To some it doesn't matter, to others it does, what is happening now in our country."

ПАРА́ША, -и, *m., crim.* **1.** A slop bucket, can. ♦*Там параша стоит, брось туда мусор.* "There's the slop bucket. Throw out the garbage." **2.** Garbage, slops. ♦*Я эту парашу есть не буду.* "I'm not going to eat this garbage." **3.** A lie. ♦*Всё это параша, не верь ему.* "That's all a lie. Don't believe him."

ПАРА́ШЛИВЫЙ, -ая, -ое, *neg.* Bad, disgusting, dirty. ♦*Что у тебя вид такой парашливый?* "How come you look so sloppy?"

ПАРАШЮТИ́СТ, -а, *m., obs. (Brezhnev era), neg., joc.* People coming to Moscow from the suburbs to buy food not available in their home towns (lit., paratroopers, from their appearance, bedecked with knapsacks for hauling off their purchases, and from Muscovites' regarding them as invaders). ♦*Везде парашютисты, ничего нельзя купить без очереди.* "With those paratroopers swarming all over the place, we have to wait in long lines to buy anything."

ПА́РЕНЬ ИЗ ДЕРЕ́ВНИ ВО́ДКИНО, *idiom, joc.* A drunk (lit., a guy from Vodkaville).

ПА́РИТЬ/ЗАПА́РИТЬ, *youth, neg.* To bore, irritate (lit., to steam). ♦*Запарил ты всех своими жалобами.* "You've worn everybody out with your complaints." •**Па́рить мозги́,** *idiom, neg.* To tire, wear out (lit., to steam someone's brains). ♦*Он уже целый час парит всем мозги о бизнесе.* "He's been boring everyone about business for a whole hour."

ПАРНИ́ША, -и, *m., joc.* A fellow, guy (from парень, "guy"). ♦*Шёл бы ты, парниша, куда подальше.* "Buzz off, mister."

ПАРНО́С, -а, *m., youth.* Income, profit (from Heb. "parnasa"). ♦*Какой парнос я с этого дела иметь буду?* "What's the profit for me in this business?"

ПАРТАЙГЕНО́ССЕ, *m., indecl., obs., joc., neg.* A member of the Communist Party of the Soviet Union (Ger.; alluding to a similarity with Nazi Party membership). ♦*Он бывший партайгеноссе.* "He's a former Party member."

ПА́РФА, -ы, *f., youth & crim.* Poor-quality narcotics made from perfume. ♦*Дай хоть парфы, лом начинается.* "Let me at least have some 'perfume' — I'm feeling bad."

ПАРХА́ТЫЙ ЖИД, *idiom, neg.* A Jew, a real or thorough Jew (lit., scrofulous Jew). ♦*Хоть бы они все, жиды пархатые, убрались в свой Израиль.* "I wish they'd send all the filthy Jews packing to their dear Israel!"

ПАС, *indecl.* That's all, that's the end, no more (from Eng. "pass," as at cards). ♦*Я* *туда больше не пойду, пас.* "I'm not going there any more — I've had enough."

ПАСКУ́ДА, -ы, *m. & f., rude.* **1.** A scoundrel, bastard. ♦*Ты паскудой был, паскудой и остался.* "You always were a bastard and you still are." **2.** A prostitute. ♦*Эта паскуда спит со всей улицей.* "That whore sleeps with everyone on the block."

ПАССИ́В, -а, *m.* A passive homosexual.♦*Он актив или пассив?* "Is he the active partner or the passive one?"

ПА́ССИЯ, -ии, *f.* Girlfriend, lover. ♦*Вон та чёрненькая его пассия?* "Is that brunette over there his flame?"

ПАСТИ́/ПОПАСТИ́. To follow, keep under surveillance (lit., to pasture). ♦*Милиция его пасёт уже неделю.* "The police have been following him for a week."

ПАСТЬ, -и, *f., rude.* A mouth, maw. ♦*Посмотри, какая у неё пасть!* "Look at the big maw on her." ♦*Закрой пасть!* "Shut your mouth." •**Замкну́ть пасть,** see under **замкну́ть. Порва́ть пасть,** see under **порва́ть. Разева́ть/рази́нуть пасть,** see under **разева́ть.**

ПА́ТИ, *f., indecl., youth.* A party (from Eng. "party"). ♦*Ты идёшь к ней на пати?* "Are you going to her party?"

ПА́ТЛЫ, патл, *pl., neg.* Long, unkempt hair. ♦*Отрастил себе патлы, думаешь, красиво?* "Do you think that mop of yours is attractive."

ПА́УЗА: Держа́ть па́узу, see under **держа́ть.**

ПАХА́Н, -а́, *m.* **1.** The head of a group. ♦*Кто у них пахан?* "Who's their chief?" **2.** A father. ♦*Мой пахан не любит, когда я курю.* "My father doesn't like it when I smoke."

ПАХА́НКА, -и, *f., crim. & youth.* A mother. ♦*Чего паханка на тебя ругалась?* "What was your mother scolding you for?"

ПА́ХАРЬ, -я, *m.* A good worker. ♦*Какой же он пахарь, за год четыре книги написал!* "What a workhorse! He's

written four books in one year!"

ПАХА́ТЬ/НАПАХА́ТЬ. To work hard, to serve (lit., to plough). ♦*Я всю жизнь на вас пашу.* "I've been slaving for you all my life."

ПАХА́ТЬ: Мы паха́ли, see under **мы.**

ПАЦА́Н, -а́, *m.* A teenager. ♦*Он же ещё пацан, жизни не знает.* "He's still a teenager, he doesn't know life at all."

ПА́ЧКА, -и, *f., neg.* A big face (lit., a pack). ♦*Я ему дал по пачке, он с копыт.* "I punched him in the face, and he fell down." •**Вали́ть/повали́ть па́чками,** see under **вали́ть**[1]. **Дать в па́чку,** see under **дава́ть. Получи́ть па́чку,** see under **получи́ть.**

ПАЯ́ЛЬНИК, -а, *m., joc.* A nose (lit., soldering iron). ♦*Убери свой паяльник, это тебе не надо знать.* "Get your nose out of this! It's none of your business."

ПЕД, -а, *m., neg.* A homosexual, pederast. ♦*Где этот пед живёт?* "Where does that bugger live?"

ПЕДА́ЛИ: Крути́ педа́ли, пока́ не да́ли, see under **крути́ть**[1].

ПЕДА́ЛЬ, -и, *f.* **1.** A foot (lit., pedal). ♦*Педали вытирай, когда в дом входишь.* "Wipe your feet when you come in the house!" **2.** *f.* A slow-thinking person.

ПЕДЕРЯ́ГА, -и, *m., youth, neg.* A pederast. ♦*Знать этого педерягу не хочу.* "I don't want to have anything to do with that bugger."

ПЕЙДЖЕРИ́ТЬ/ЗАПЕЙДЖЕРИ́ТЬ. To page, to send a message to a pager. ♦*Запейджери ему наш номер, пусть срочно позвонит.* "Page our number to him so he can call us immediately."

ПЕЙС, -а, *m., neg.* A Jew (from пейсы, "forelocks"). ♦*Если он пейс, то на русской не женится.* "If he's a Jew, he won't marry a Russian woman."

ПЕЛЬМЕ́НЬ, -я, *m.* A simpleton, a country bumpkin (lit., pelmeni, Siberian meat dumplings). ♦*Зря мы с этим пельменем связались, ничего он не рубит в компьютерах.* "It's our fault for connecting with this simpleton, he doesn't know the first thing about computers."

ПЕ́НА, -ы, *f., neg.* Nonsense, trash (lit., foam). ♦*Не обращай внимания, всё это — пена.* "Pay no attention — that's all nonsense."

ПЕ́НДЕЛЬ, -я, *m., joc.* A kick in the leg. ♦*Ты что, пенделя хочешь?* "You want a kick in the leg?"

ПЕНЖИ́ЛОВКА, -и, *f., students, neg.* **1.** Humiliation. ♦*Никогда не забуду эту пенжиловку в армии.* "I'll never forget how they humiliated me in the army. **2.** Defeat. ♦*Наши вчера устроили пенжиловку шведам.* "Our team was creamed by the Swedes in yesterday's match."

ПЕ́НЖИТЬ, *imperf., youth, neg.* **1.** To humiliate. **2.** To be victorious in an athletic contest. ♦*Кто кого пенжит?* "Who's winning?"

ПЕ́НКА, -и, *f.* A joke, a witticism (lit., the skin of boiled milk). ♦*У него что ни слово, то пенка.* "Every word out of his mouth is another joke."

ПЕНТАГО́Н, -а, *m.* The Russian Defense Ministry (lit., Pentagon). ♦*Ты знаешь, где в Москве Пентагон?* "Do you know where in Moscow the Pentagon is located?"

ПЕНЬ С УША́МИ, *idiom, joc.* A fool, idiot (lit., a stump with ears). ♦*Ну когда ты, пень с ушами, поймёшь, что этого нельзя делать?* "You idiot! Can't you understand that you mustn't do that?"

ПЁР, -а, *m.* Good luck. Cf. **переть/попере́ть.**

ПЕРДЕ́ТЬ/ПЁРДНУТЬ, *rude.* To fart. ♦*Ну и дух у вас, кто-то пердит, что ли?* "There's a smell here as if someone's been farting." •**Лу́чше че́стно пёрднуть, чем по-шпио́нски бздну́ть,** see under **лу́чше.**

ПЕРДИ́ЛЬНИК, -а, *m., rude.* Buttocks, rear end. ♦*Убери пердильник, некуда вещи положить.* "Move your ass. There's no room to put the things down."

ПЕРДУ́Н, -а́, *rude.* An old man. ♦*Зачем этому старому пердуну власть?* "How come that old fart is in power?"

ПЕРЕБИРА́ТЬ/ПЕРЕБРА́ТЬ. To drink too much (lit., to draw too high a card, as in blackjack). ♦*Чувствую, что переберу, не наливай!* "I feel I've had too much; don't pour me any more."

ПЕРЕБО́Р, -а, *m.* **1.** A mistake. ♦*Это явный перебор, нельзя было так с ним поступать.* "It was a big mistake to act like that with him." **2.** Too much to drink. ♦*Не надо было пить последний бокал, это был перебор.* "I shouldn't have had that last drink. It put me over the edge."

ПЕРЕВА́РИВАТЬ/ПЕРЕВАРИ́ТЬ. **1.** To understand (lit., to digest). **2.** To tolerate. ♦*Я его не перевариваю со студенческих времён.* "I haven't been able to stand him since our student days."

ПЕРЕВЕРНУ́ТЬСЯ, *perf.* To die (lit., to turn over). ♦*Жена сразу же после мужа перевернулась.* "She died right after her husband."

ПЕРЕВОДИ́ТЬ/ПЕРЕВЕСТИ́ проду́кт, *idiom, neg.* To vomit (lit., to waste nourishment). ♦*Ты только продукт переводишь, выпьешь — и в туалет блевать.* "You're just wasting good nourishment — you have a drink and then you bring everything up."

ПЕРЕГРЕ́ТЬСЯ, *perf. only, neg.* To go crazy (lit., to get sunburned). ♦*Зачем ты меня ударил, перегрелся?* "Why did you hit me? Have you gone out of your mind?"

ПЕРЕДОЗНЯ́К, -а́, *m., youth.* An overdose of drugs. ♦*От передозняка можно концы отдать.* "You can die from an overdose."

ПЕРЕДО́К, передка́, *m., rude.* The female genitals. ♦*Посмотри, что у меня на передке, болит.* "Can you see what's wrong with my pussy? Something hurts there." •**Слаба́ на передо́к,** see under **слаба́.**

ПЕРЕКИ́НУТЬСЯ, *perf.* To die. See **перевернуться.**

ПЕРЕКРЫВА́ТЬ ЕНИСЕ́Й, *idiom, joc.* To do something futile or useless (lit., to dam the Yenisei River, the biggest river in Siberia. The phrase echoes a song by

Galich, popular in the 1960s, about crazily grandiose Soviet projects: . . . перекрываем Енисей, / А также в области балета / Мы впереди планеты всей, ". . . we're going to dam the Yenisei / and also in the field of ballet / we're leading the planet in every way"). ♦*Вместо того, чтобы рубашки шить людям, мы всё перекрываем Енисей.* "Instead of doing something useful, like sewing shirts for people, we're always busy damming the Yenisei."

ПЕРЕКРЫВÁТЬ/ПЕРЕКРЫ́ТЬ кисло-рóд кому́-л., *idiom.* To prevent or stop somebody (lit., to block someone's airhose). ♦*Он будет президентом, если ему не перекроют кислород.* "He'll become president, if someone doesn't stop him."

ПЕРЕКУ́ШИВАТЬ/ПЕРЕКУ́ШАТЬ, *joc.* To drink too much. ♦*Вчера в гостях мы сильно перекушали.* "We drank far too much at the dinner party yesterday."

ПЕРЕЛÁЗИТЬ/ПЕРЕЛÉЗТЬ чéрез за-бóр, *idiom, business.* To export raw materials under falsified documents (lit., to climb over the fence). ♦*А кто ещё перелазит через забор с медью?* "So who else is smuggling out copper?"

ПЕРЕМÁРГИВАТЬ/ПЕРЕМОРГÁТЬ, *joc.* To endure punishment or criticism, to tough it out (from моргать, "to blink"). ♦*Я его ругань не могу больше терпеть. — Ничего, переморгаешь.* "I just can't take any more of his scolding. — Never mind. You'll just tough it out."

ПЕРЕОБУВÁТЬ/ПЕРЕОБУ́ТЬ. To change tires. ♦*Хорошо бы на зиму переобуть машину.* "I'd better change my tires for the winter."

ПЕРЕПИЗДÉТЬ, *perf. only, rude.* To have a chat (cf. **пизда́**). ♦*Выйдем, перепиздеть надо.* "Come on! We need to have a chat."

ПЕРЕПИ́ХИВАТЬСЯ/ПЕРЕПИХ-НУ́ТЬСЯ, *rude.* To have sex (from пихать, "to push"). ♦*Перепихнуться она никогда не прочь.* "She's always ready for a roll in the hay."

ПЕРЕСЕКÁТЬСЯ/ПЕРЕСÉЧЬСЯ. To meet, to become acquainted (lit., to intersect). ♦*Мы с вами где-то пересекались.* "Haven't you and I crossed paths somewhere before?"

ПЕРЕСТÁРКА, -и, *f., neg.* A woman inappropriately older than her companions. ♦*Не приглашай эту перестарку, она нам не компания.* "Don't invite that old woman. She's no fun for us to be with."

ПЕРЕТИРÁТЬ/ПЕРЕТЕРÉТЬ. To resolve a problem, to discuss questions (lit., to grind). ♦*Надо эти дела перетереть, а то драка будет.* "We'd better find a resolution to this issue or there's going to be a fistfight."

ПЕРЕТОПТÁТЬСЯ, *perf. only, neg.* To get along without something, manage without. ♦*Дай взайми 1000 рублей. — Перетопчешься.* "Loan me 1000 rubles, would you? — Sorry. You'll have to manage without."

ПЕРÉТЬ/ПОПЕРÉТЬ, *neg.* To act aggressive or provocative (lit., to push). ♦*Что ты на меня-то прёшь, я ни в чём не виноват.* "Why are you leaning on me as if I had done something wrong?"

ПЕРÉТЬСЯ, *perf., neg.* To push through a crowd, to break into a line. ♦*Куда ты прёшься, все сейчас выходят.* "Don't push, everyone's getting off at the next stop!"

ПЕРЕТЯНУ́ТЬ, *perf.* To strike on the back with a belt or stick. ♦*Перетяни его ещё раз, чтоб знал, на кого руку поднимать.* "Hit him again so he'll remember who to threaten!"

ПÉРЕЦ, пéрца, *m.* A penis (esp. a child's; lit., pepper). ♦*Надень что-нибудь тёплое, а то перец отмёрзнет.* "Put on some warm clothes or your pepper will freeze."

ПЕРНÁТЫЙ, -ая, -ое. Having a surname derived from the name of a bird. ♦*Когда этот пернатый, Сорокин придёт?* "When will that what's-his-bird-name get here? — You know, Sorokin."

ПЕРÓ, -á, *n., crim.* A knife (lit., pen).

◆*Осторожно, у него перо!* "Watch out, he's got a knife!"

ПЕ́РСИК, -а, *m., joc.* A Persian, Iranian (from персик, "peach").

ПЕРСОНА́ЛКА, -и, *f.* **1.** An office car for VIP's. **2.** A personal computer. **3.** *(obs)* A personal file recording an investigation into a violation of party discipline.

ПЕРФО́РМАНС, -а, *m.* An event, happening (from Eng. "performance"). ◆*Из дня рождения устроили целый перформанс — и артисты, и певцы, и политики — все поучаствовали.* "They put together quite an event for his birthday — celebrities, singers, politicians."

ПЁРЩИК, -а, *m.* A lucky person. ◆*С этим пёрщиком в карты не садись, бесполезно.* "There's no point in playing cards with him, he always lucks out."

ПЁС, пса, *m., crim., neg.* A prison warden (lit., a dog). ◆*Тише, псы идут.* "Shush. Here come the wardens."

ПЁСИЙ, пёсья, пёсье, *neg.* Bad (lit., "dog's"). ◆*Что за пёсья погода!* "What crappy weather!"

ПЕСКОСТРУ́ЙЩИК, -а, *m., joc.* A decrepit old man (lit., someone who is losing his sand). ◆*Что ты жалуешься на здоровье, как пескоструйщик?* "Why are you whining about your health like a decrepit old man?"

ПЕ́СНЯ: Не на́до пе́сен, see under **не.**

ПЕСО́К СЫ́П(Л)ЕТСЯ из кого́-л., *idiom.* Someone is old and decrepit (lit., the sand is spilling out of someone). ◆*Из тебя песок сыплется, а ты за девчонками бегаешь.* "You're already losing your stuffing, but you're still running after the girls."

ПЁТР ИВА́НОВИЧ, -а, *m.* A nickname for the Moscow Detective Department at 38 Petrovka Street. ◆*Кажется, нами заинтересовался Пётр Иванович!* "It looks like the police have got curious about us."

ПЕ́ТРИТЬ, *imperf.* To understand, to catch on. ◆*Она ничего не петрит в математике.* "She doesn't get a thing in mathematics."

ПЕТРУ́ШКА, -и, *f., youth.* A girl, a young woman (lit., parsley). ◆*Кто привёл эту петрушку. пусть и домой провожает.* "Whoever brought that gal should take her home."

ПЕТУ́Х, -а́, *m., crim., neg.* A passive homosexual (lit., a rooster). ◆*Он в колонии был петухом.* "In the labor camp he was buggered by everyone." ●**Держа́ть петуха́** or **ударя́ть/уда́рить по петуха́м,** see under **держа́ть.**

ПЕТУШИ́ТЬ/РАСПЕТУШИ́ТЬ. To scold, to critisize. ◆*Хорошо его распетушили в газетах за коррупцию.* "He was harshly critized in the papers for corruption."

ПЕ́ХОМ, *adv., joc.* On foot. ◆*Сколько ещё пёхом осталось?* "How much farther is it to walk?"

ПЕШКОДРА́ЛОМ, *adv.* On foot. ◆*Туда метро не ходит, придётся добираться пешкодралом.* "There's no subway station there, we'll have to go on foot."

ПЕШКО́М: Стоя́ть/постоя́ть пешко́м, see under **стоя́ть.**

ПИА́РИТЬ/ПРОПИА́РИТЬ, *neg.* To advertise a political figure or goods using slanted, partial, skewed information in order to manipulate the public. ◆*Пиарили, пиарили, а ничего у них на Украине не вышло, народ всё труднее обмануть.* "They tried and tried to manipulate the public in Ukraine with dirty campaigning but didn't achieve their political goals; it's tough to fool the people." (Note: In Russian, Public Relations or PR always has a negative connotation and refers to manipulation of the public.)

ПИ́ВО: Ударя́ть/уда́рить по пи́ву, see under **ударя́ть.**

ПИ́ДОВСКИЙ, -ая, -ое, *neg.* Homosexual, pederastic. ◆*Прекрати свои пидовские штучки, убери руки.* "Get your fairy hands off me." ●**По-пи́довски,** *adv., neg.* In an effeminate way, like a homosexual. ◆*Он ведёт себя по-пидовски, он голубой?* "Is he gay? He acts like a fairy."

ПИ́ДОР, -а, *m., rude.* A homosexual.

•**Пи́дор гно́йный,** *idiom, rude.* A scoundrel, bastard. ♦*Ты, пидор гнойный, опять угробил машину.* "You dirty bastard — you've gone and wrecked the car again."

ПИЗДА́, -ы́, *f., rude.* Cunt. •**ПИЗДА́** *(nom.):* **Пизда́ воню́чая,** *idiom, rude.* A worthless person, bastard, scoundrel. ♦*Пусть замолчит, пизда вонючая.* "That stinking bitch should shut up." **Пизда́ рва́ная,** *idiom, rude.* A whore, good-for-nothing (lit., a torn-up cunt). ♦*С кем ты опять гуляешь, пизда рваная?* "Who are you going around with now, you whore?" **Пизда́ ста́рая,** *idiom, rude.* An old woman. ♦*Не слушай эту пизду старую. Что она понимает?* "Don't listen to that old cunt — she doesn't understand a thing." **Пизда́ с уша́ми,** *idiom, rude.* Someone or something ridiculous, out of place, strange (lit., a cunt with ears). ♦*Ты, пизда с ушами, что ты несёшь?* "What are you talking about, you cockamamie fool!" **Пизда́ тебя́ родила́,** *idiom, rude.* A general phrase of abuse (lit., a cunt gave birth to you). ♦*Даже кофе сварить не можешь, пизда тебя родила.* "You can't even boil the water for coffee, you idiot." **Глаз не пизда́, проморга́ет,** *idiom, rude.* The damage isn't permanent; it will pass (lit., an eye isn't a cunt, it blinks itself clean). **Нет лу́чше зе́лья, чем пизда́ на похме́лье,** *idiom, rude.* Lit., There's no better potion for a hangover than a cunt. **Пизда́-засра́нец, пизды́-засра́нца,** *m., rude.* A worthless person (cf. **засра́нец**). ♦*От этого пизды-засранца помощи не жди.* "Don't expect any help from that bastard." **Йли хуй попола́м, и́ли пизда́ вдре́безги,** see under **хуй. Хуй и пизда́ из одного́ гнезда́,** see under **хуй. ПИЗДУ́** *(acc.):* **Смеши́ть пизду́,** *idiom, rude.* To joke around, talk nonsense, be kidding. ♦*Не смеши пизду, никто туда так поздно не пойдёт.* "Don't talk nonsense. No one would go there so late at night." **Не смеши́ пизду́, она́ и так смешна́я,** *idiom, rude.* What you're saying is ridiculous (lit., "Don't make the

cunt laugh; it's funny enough already"). **Иди́ в пизду́ на перепла́вку,** *idiom, rude.* Go to hell, get out of here, go to the devil (cf. **переплавка,** "smelting"). ♦*Иди в пизду на переплавку со своими шуточками.* "Go to hell with your tricks." **Про пизду́ глу́пости,** *idiom, rude.* A chatterbox, idle chatterer. ♦*Ты опять про пизду глупости, а нам надо серьёзно поговорить.* "There you go chattering again when we need to have a serious talk." **ПИЗДЫ́** *(gen.):* **Дава́ть/дать пизды́,** *idiom, rude.* To scold, punish. ♦*Мне пора домой, а то жена даст пизды.* "I've got to go home now or my wife will really give it to me." **До пизды́ кому́-л.,** *idiom, rude.* It doesn't matter, it's of no concern. ♦*Что он говорит обо мне, мне до пизды.* "I don't care what he says about me." **Свали́ться из пизды́,** *idiom, rude.* To be oblivious, out of touch; to be like a creature from Mars (lit., to fall from a cunt). ♦*Ты как из пизды свалился, разве ты не слышал о перевороте?* "How can you be so out of it! You really haven't heard about the coup?" **ПИЗДЕ́** *(dat.):* **Не пришей пизде́ рука́в,** *idiom, rude.* Unwanted, out of place (lit., don't sew a sleeve onto a cunt). ♦*Сейчас поздно, этот кофе не пришей пизде рукав.* "It's late already; we need this coffee like a hole in the head." **Ну́жно как пизде́ две́рцы (как до пизды́ две́рца),** *idiom, rude.* Unwanted, superfluous, in the way (lit., needed like doors on a cunt). ♦*Мне твои советы нужны как пизде дверцы.* "I need your advice like a hole in the head." **ПИЗДЕ́** *(prep.):* **В ка́ждой пизде́ заты́чка,** *idiom, rude.* A busybody, a meddler (lit., a tampon in every cunt). ♦*Не будь в каждой пизде затычкой, тебя никто не просил ей помогать.* "Don't be such a buttinsky. No one asked you to help her." **Не повезёт, так в пизде́ на гвоздь наткнёшься,** *idiom, rude.* "Unless you're in luck, you could always get snagged on a nail in a cunt."

ПИЗДАНУ́ТЬСЯ, *perf. only, rude.* Cf. **пизда́. 1.** To go crazy. ♦*Ты там от скуки не пизданулся?* "Didn't you go crazy from boredom there?" **2.** To fall. ♦*Вчера я пизданулся на улице.* "Yesterday I fell down in the street."

ПИЗДА́СТЫЙ, -ая, -ое, *rude.* Huge, enormous (cf. **пизда́**). ♦*Зачем ты купил такой пиздастый чемодан?* "Why did you buy such a huge suitcase?"

ПИЗДА́ТО, *adv., rude.* Wonderfully well (cf. **пизда́**). ♦*Я выкурил первую сигарету за день и мне пиздато!* "I just smoked my first cigarette of the day and I feel terrific!"

ПИЗДА́ТЫЙ, -ая, -ое, *rude.* Excellent, extraordinary (cf. **пизда́**). ♦*Где ты достал такие пиздатые кроссовки?* "Where did you manage to get those great running shoes?"

ПИЗДЁЖ, -а́, m., rude. Chatter, twaddle, nonsense (cf. **пизда́**). ♦*Кончай пиздёж.* "Cut the crap." •**Разводи́ть/развести́ пиздёж,** see under **разводи́ть.**

ПИЗДЁНЫШ, -а, m., rude. A little, weak fellow (esp. one with pretensions to power; cf. **пизда́**). ♦*Каждый пиздёныш будет мне указывать, что делать.* "Guys who are still wet behind the ears are trying to tell me what to do."

ПИЗДЕ́НЬ, -и, f., rude. Large female genitals (cf. **пизда**). ♦*Пиздень у неё — все поместятся.* "There's room for everyone in her big cunt."

ПИЗДЕ́ТЬ/СПИЗДЕ́ТЬ, *rude.* To lie, tell stories (cf. **пизда́**). ♦*Ты спиздел о его приезде?* "Were you kidding about his arrival?"

ПИЗДЕ́Ц, -а́, m., rude. Cf. **пизда́. 1.** Enough, time to stop. ♦*Ну, пиздец, пора кончать пить.* "That's enough. Time to stop drinking." **2.** A danger, a threat. ♦*Мне пиздец, они меня убьют.* "It's all over with me — they're going to kill me." •**Пизде́ц подкра́лся незаме́тно,** *idiom, rude.* Something unexpectedly unpleasant happened (lit., crept in unnoticed). ♦*Ты слышал о денежной реформе? Пиздец подкрался незаметно.* "Have you heard about the monetary reform? That nasty trick snuck up on us unnoticed."

ПИ́ЗДИТЬ¹/ПИЗДАНУ́ТЬ, *rude.* To hit,

beat (cf. **пизда́**). ♦*Как пиздану, не будешь больше воровать.* "The way I'm going to beat you up, you won't be doing any more robberies."

ПИ́ЗДИТЬ²/СПИ́ЗДИТЬ, *rude.* To steal (cf. **пизда́**). ♦*Ты не можешь спиздить немного сигарет у отца?* "Can't you swipe a few cigarettes from your father?"

ПИЗДОБО́Л, -а, m., rude. An idle chatterer (cf. **пизда́**). ♦*Сколько можно слушать этого пиздобола?* "How long can you listen to that blabbermouth?"

ПИЗДОБО́ЛИТЬ/ПОПИЗДОБО́-ЛИТЬ, *rude.* To tell tales, chatter idly, be kidding, lie (cf. **пизда́**). ♦*Любишь ты пиздоболить, на самом деле всё было не так.* "You're just kidding. It wasn't really like that at all."

ПИЗДОБРА́ТИЯ, -и, f., rude. A group of people, set, company (cf. **пизда́**). ♦*Это что за пиздобратия там собралась?* "What sort of group is that over there?"

ПИЗДОВОНЮ́ЧКА, -и, f., rude. A worthless or bad woman (cf. **пизда́**). ♦*Не приводи в дом эту пиздовонючку.* "Don't bring that bitch into this house."

ПИЗДОПРОТИ́ВНЫЙ, -ая, -ое, *rude.* Offensive, repulsive (cf. **пизда́**). ♦*Сегодня пиздопротивная погода.* "What disgusting weather today."

ПИЗДОРВА́НЕЦ, пиздорва́нца, m., rude. A worthless or bad person (lit., a torn-up cunt; cf. **пизда́**). ♦*Когда ты научишься дверь за собой закрывать, пиздорванец, холодно.* "When will you ever learn to shut the door after you, you idiot! It's cold!"

ПИЗДОРВА́НКА, -и, f. See **пиздорва́нец.**

ПИЗДО́С, -а, m., rude. An idiot, bastard (cf. **пизда́**). ♦*Что ещё натворил этот пиздос?* "What mischief has that bastard been up to this time?"

ПИЗДОСТРАДА́ТЕЛЬ, -я, m., rude. A romantic, sentimental person (lit., a cunt-sufferer; cf. **пизда́**). ♦*Он ей всё время стихи пишет, пиздострадатель.* "That lovesick fellow is always writing poetry to her."

ПИЗДОСТРАДА́ТЕЛЬНЫЙ, -ая, -ое,

rude. Sentimental, lovesick (cf. **пиздо-страда́тель**). ♦*Сейчас он поёт только пиздострадательные песни.* "These days he sings only sentimental stuff."

ПИЗДО́СЯ, -и, *m. & f., rude*. An absent-minded person (cf. **пизда́**). ♦*Ты забыл принести закуски, пиздося.* "You forgot to bring the hors d'oeuvres, you scatterbrain."

ПИЗДО́ШИТЬ/ИСПИЗДО́ШИТЬ. See **пиздя́чить**.

ПИЗДЮЛИ́, -е́й, *pl., rude*. A beating, blows (cf. **пизда́**). ♦Дава́ть/дать (наве́шивать/наве́сить, отве́шивать/отве́сить) пиздюле́й, see under **дава́ть**.

ПИЗДЮ́ЛИНА, -ы, *f., rude*. A thingamajig, gizmo, whatchamacallit (cf. **пизда́**). ♦*А где здесь была такая металлическая пиздюлина?* "Where's that little metal gizmo?"

ПИЗДЯ́КНУТЬСЯ, *perf. only*. See **пиздану́ться**.

ПИЗДЯ́ТИНА, -ы, *f., rude*. Cf. **пизда́**. **1.** Disgusting food. ♦*Это не жаркое, а пиздятина какая-то.* "This isn't meat. It's something disgusting." **2.** An unpleasant smell. ♦*Открой форточку, пиздятиной пахнет.* "Open the window. It stinks in here."

ПИЗДЯ́ЧИТЬ¹/ЗАПИЗДЯ́ЧИТЬ, *rude*. To hit, beat (cf. **пизда́**). ♦*Его запиздячили бутылкой по голове.* "They hit him over the head with a bottle."

ПИЗДЯ́ЧИТЬ²/ОТПИЗДЯ́ЧИТЬ, *rude*. Cf. **пизда́**. **1.** To work hard. ♦*Он отпиздячил на стройке 10 лет.* "He slaved as a construction worker for 10 years." **2.** To beat up. ♦*Кто это тебя отпиздячил?* "Who beat you up like that?"

ПИ́КА, -и, *f., crim*. A file sharpened for use as a weapon (lit., a spear). ♦*Нам бы пику сделать, опасно тут.* "We'd better make ourselves a 'spear' — it's dangerous here."

ПИ́КАТЬ/ПИ́КНУТЬ. To tell, reveal. ♦*Ты только пикни о том, что было, и тебе конец.* "If you make one peep about what happened, it'll be all over with you."

ПИ́ЛЕННЫЙ/ПОПИ́ЛЕННЫЙ, -ая, -ое, *youth*. **1.** Cut up, scarred up. ♦*У неё мужик — весь пиленный.* "Her boyfriend is all cut up." ♦*У май лавера в мозгу — нот а сингл извилины; Джаст а хип впадёт в тоску — все хенды попилены"* (from a popular song: "My boyfriend hasn't got any gray matter at all; he's just a hippie, and when he's down, all his veins are cut"). **2.** Worn out, worn-looking (as a mark of high fashion). ♦*У него прикид пиленный.* "His clothes are all worn out."

ПИЛИ́ТЬ¹, *rude*. To have sex with a woman. ♦*Ты знаешь, кто её пилит?* "Do you know who's sleeping with her?"

ПИЛИ́ТЬ²/ЗАПИЛИ́ТЬ, *neg*. To scold, abuse verbally (lit., to saw). ♦*Ты его совсем запилил.* "You gave him quite a bawling out."

ПИЛИ́ТЬ³/ПОПИЛИ́ТЬ. 1. *joc*. To go, walk. ♦*Долго ещё пилить?* "Is it still far to go?" **2.** *youth*. **1.** To cut one's veins (lit., to saw). ♦*Он себя попилил.* "He cut his wrists." **3.** To age clothing so that it will look worn. ♦*Когда ты успел джинсы попилить?* "When did you manage to age your jeans?"

ПИЛОТА́Ж: Вы́сший пилота́ж!, see under **вы́сший**.

ПИЛЮЛЯ: Наве́шивать/наве́сить пилю́лей, see under **наве́шивать**.

ПИНГВИ́НЫ, -ов, *pl., joc*. Busts of Communist Party leaders at the Kremlin Wall (lit., penguins). ♦*Когда уже всех этих пингвинов уберут с Красной площади, не площадь, а кладбище.* "I wonder when they're going to get rid of all those busts on Red Square. It looks more like a cemetery than a square."

ПИНЦЕ́Т, -а, *m., euph., student*. See **пизде́ц**. **1.** The end, ruin, "curtains." **2.** Something very good or very bad. ♦*Эта группа — пинцет. Все тащатся.* "This rock-group is awesome, everybody's crazy about it."

ПИПИ́РКА, -и, *f., joc*. A penis, esp. of small size. ♦*Надень тёплое бельё, а то пипирка отмёрзнет.* "Put on some warm underwear or your little tool will freeze off."

ПИ́ПКА, -и. See **пипи́рка.**

ПИПЛ, -а (*pl.* **пиплс, -о́в**), *youth.* People (from Eng. "people"). ◆*Пипл, что будем делать?* "Well, folks, what are we going to do now?"

ПИР ВО ВРЕ́МЯ ЧЕЧНИ́, *idiom.* A celebration or festivities at a time of troubles or crisis (from the title of Pushkin's play "Пир во время чумы," *A Feast During the Plague*). The idiom refers to the Chechnya war.

ПИРО́Г: Таки́е пироги́!, see under **таки́е. Ну и пироги́!,** see under **ну.**

ПИРОЖО́К: Возьми́ с по́лки пирожо́к, see under **брать.**

ПИСА́ТЕЛЬ, -я, *m., youth.* A drunk (lit., writer, from the saying "Идёт как пишет: одной пишет, другой зачёркивает" — "He walks as if he's writing with one hand and erasing with the other"). ◆*Ещё один писатель идёт, где-то Новый год справлял.* "Here's another drunk stumbling home from a New Year's party."

ПИ́САТЬ кипятко́м, *idiom, joc.* To be in ecstasy; to be extremely enthusiastic (lit., to pee boiling water). ◆*Все от его стихов писают кипятком, а мне не нравятся.* "Everyone's peeing in their pants over his poetry, but I don't like it."

ПИСА́ТЬСЯ, *imperf., youth.* To protect, to patronize. ◆*Его трогать нельзя, за него сам президент пишется.* "He's prosecution-proof, he's under the protection of the President himself."

ПИСДО́М, -а, *m., prof., joc.* A building for writers. ◆*Она живёт в писдоме сразу возле метро.* "She lives in the writers' building right next to the metro station."

ПИСЕ́Ц, *ejaculation, rude.* Damn it! Hell! (cf. **пизде́ц** and песец, "Arctic fox").

ПИСТО́Н, -а, *m.* **1.** A pocket in pants for carrying a pocket watch. ◆*Зачем сейчас делают пистоны, никто уже в брюках часы не носит.* "Why do they still make watch pockets in pants when no one carries a pocket watch any more?" **2.** *rude.* Sex, a sex act (lit., a percussion cap). ◆*Ну как тебе понравился пистон?* "Well, how did you like it? Was I

good?" ●**Ста́вить/поста́вить (гнило́й) писто́н,** see under **ста́вить.**

ПИСЮ́К, -а, *m.* A personal computer.

ПИТИЕ́ ОПРЕДЕЛЯ́ЕТ СОЗНА́НИЕ, *idiom, joc.* Drinking is the main thing (lit., drinking determines consciousness) (by wordplay on Marx's phrase бытие определяет сознание, "being determines consciousness").

ПИТЬ/ВЫ́ПИТЬ: Пить/вы́пить чайко́вского, *idiom, joc.* To drink tea (playing on чай, "tea," and Чайковский, the composer). ◆*Давай чайковского.* "Let's have some tea." **Пить как ло́шадь,** *idiom, neg.* To drink very heavily (lit., to drink like a horse.) ◆*Ты ела что-то солёное, что пьёшь как лошадь?* "How come you're drinking like a horse? Did you eat a lot of herring?" **Вы́пить ли́шку,** *idiom.* To drink too much. ◆*Голова трещит, вчера выпил лишку.* "I've got a splitting headache — I drank too much yesterday." **(Пить/вы́пить) из го́рла,** see under **го́рло.**

ПИЩА́ТЬ, *imperf.* To want badly, to desire intensely (lit., to peep). ◆*Он так хочет новую квартиру, аж пищит.* "He's bursting with desire for that new apartment."

ПИЩА́ТЬ/ПИ́КНУТЬ, *neg.* To say, to dare to say. ◆*Об этом никто пикнуть не посмеет.* "No one will dare to mention it."

ПЛАВНИ́К, -а, *m.* An arm, a hand (lit., fin). ◆*Быстро мыть плавники и за стол.* "Wash your hands quickly and come right to the table."

ПЛА́МЯ: Гори́ (всё) си́ним пла́менем, see under **гори́.**

ПЛАНОВО́Й, -ая, -ое. Smoking marijuana regularly. ◆*Его друзья все до одного плановые.* "All his friends are potheads."

ПЛАСТИЛИ́Н, -а, *m., youth.* A cannabis-derived drug (lit., children's modeling clay).

ПЛАТИ́ТЬ/ЗАПЛАТИ́ТЬ нату́рой, *idiom.* To pay in kind, barter. ◆*Деньги когда отдашь? — Я заплачу натурой.* "When are you going to pay me back? —

I'll pay you in kind."

ПЛЕВО́К, плевка́, -а, *m., neg.* An unattractive, short man.

ПЛЁВЫЙ, -ая, -ое. Easy, not difficult (from плевать, "to spit"). ♦ *Это плёвое дело, сделаю за пять минут.* "It's a cinch, I'll get it done in five minutes."

ПЛЕМЯ́Ш, -á, *m.,* A nephew (cf. племянник). ♦ *Сегодня должен племяш из Москвы приехать, надо его встретить.* "My nephew from Moscow is arriving today — I have to go meet him."

ПЛЕЧО́, -á, *n.* Distance, length of a trip. ♦ *Пора ехать, у нас сегодня плечо 500 километров.* "Let's get moving. We've got to cover a distance of 500 kilometers today."

ПЛЕ́ШКА, -и, *f., joc.* A square, plaza (from плешь, "bald spot"). ♦ *Встретимся на плешке у метро.* "Let's meet at the square by the metro station."

ПЛЕШЬ: Проесть плешь кому́-л., see under **проесть.**

ПЛОСКОДО́НКА, -и, *f., rude, neg.* A flat-chested or skinny woman (lit., a type of flat-bottomed boat). ♦ *Что ты себе такую плоскодонку откопал?* "Where did you manage to dig up such a bag of bones?"

ПЛОХО́Й, -áя, -óе, *joc.* Lit., bad. **1.** Drunk. ♦ *Не пей, ты уже плохой.* "Don't drink any more — you're already drunk." **2.** Stupid. ♦ *Что-то ты совсем плохой стал, не поймёшь, в чём твоя выгода.* "You've somehow turned into such an idiot that you can't even figure out where your own interests lie."

ПЛУГ ПЛА́ЧЕТ по кому́-л., *joc.* Used as an accusation of laziness against someone who is not working (lit., the plow is crying for someone). ♦ *По тебе плуг плачет, а ты говоришь, что тебе нездоровится.* "The plow is crying for you, and you claim to be sick!"

ПЛЫТЬ/ПОПЛЫ́ТЬ, *joc.* **1.** To be unconscious (lit., to float). ♦ *Ты сильно ушибся, я вижу, ты плывёшь.* "You must have taken a hard blow — you seem to be all at sea." **2.** To be drunk. ♦ *Ты с одного стакана поплыл.* "You're

drunk after just one glass!"

ПЛЮ́НУТЬ НЕ́ГДЕ, *idiom, neg.* It's too crowded (lit., there's nowhere to spit). ♦ *Пошли в зал, послушаем лекцию. — Нет, там плюнуть негде.* "Let's go into the auditorium to hear the lecture. — No, it's too crowded in there."

ПЛЮ́ХА, -и, *f., sports.* A hit, a goal. ♦ *А ты помнишь, как он забил плюху «Спартаку»?* "Do you remember how he made that goal against the Spartak team?" ♦ **Дава́ть/дать плю́ху,** see under **дава́ть. Заса́живать/засади́ть плю́ху,** see under **заса́живать.**

ПЛЮЩ, -а, *m., joc.* Hair on the chest (lit., ivy). ♦ *Застегни рубашку, весь плющ наружу.* "Button your shirt, your chest hair is showing.'

ПЛЮ́ЩИТЬ/ЗАПЛЮ́ЩИТЬ. To be in a depressed mood, in low spirits, or to suffer from a hangover (lit., to flatten). ♦ *Как тебя плющит, выпей пива, легче станет.* "You are hanging hard, drink a beer, it'll make you feel better."

ПО ЖИ́ЗНИ, *idiom.* In reality. ♦ *С первого взгляда он слишком строг, а по жизни добрее человека не найти.* "At first glance he seems awfully strict, but in reality you couldn't find a nicer fellow."

ПО ОПРЕДЕЛЕ́НИЮ, *idiom.* Obviously (lit., by definition). ♦ *Не будет оз это делать по определению.* "He's obviously not going to do it."

ПО ХЛОПКУ́ — СМЕ́НА ПАРТНЁ-РОВ, *idiom, joc.* Lit., "At the signal, a change of partners"; used as a disparaging comment on sexual infidelity. ♦ *Они, кажется, давно любят друг друга. — Ну да, любят, по хлопку — смена партнёров.* "It seems they've been in love for a long time. — Oh, sure! At the signal, a change of partners!"

ПОВЁРНУТЫЙ, -ая, -ое, *neg.* Strange, showing strange behavior (lit., twisted). ♦ *Муж у неё какой-то повёрнутый, ничем ей не помогает.* "Her husband is a little peculiar; he doesn't help her out at all."

ПОВЕСТИ́СЬ: С кем поведёшься, от

тогó и залетúшь, see under с.

ПОВОЛОКЛÓ ПО КÓЧКАМ кого-л., *idiom, neg.* Things are going badly for someone (lit., someone is being dragged along over bumps). ◆*И поволоклó меня по кóчкам, что ни день, то подáрок: то нóгу сломáл, то на рабóте проблéмы.* "I'm being raked over the coals. Every day it's something else — first I break my leg, then I have problems at work."

ПОВЫШÁТЬ/ПОВЫ́СИТЬ ВОКÁЛ, *idiom.* To cry out, shout, to raise one's voice. ◆*Ты вокáл не повышáй, я хорошó слы́шу.* "Don't raise your voice, I can hear you just fine."

ПОВЯ́ЗАННЫЙ, -ая, -ое. Mutually dependent, involved in the same thing. ◆*Мы нáчали вмéсте рабóтать над кнúгой, поэ́тому мы надóлго повя́заны.* "We started co-authoring a book, so we're in for the long haul together."

ПОГÓДА ШÉПЧЕТ, *idiom, joc.* Lit., the weather is whispering. **1.** An allusion to a desire to play hooky or take time off from work. ◆*Ты всё смóтришь в окнó, погóда шéпчет?* "Why do you keep looking out the window? Is the weather whispering to you?" **2.** An allusion to a desire to get drunk. *Что мы сидúм? Погóда шéпчет, нáдо вы́пить.* "Why are we just sitting here? The weather is whispering — let's have a drink."

ПОГРЕМÚХА, -и, f., youth. A nickname (lit., a rattle). ◆*Забы́л твою́ погремýху, скажú ещё раз.* "I've forgotten your nickname — tell me again."

ПОД НОГТЯ́МИ ЧЕРНОЗЁМ, Э́ТО ЗНÁЧИТ АГРОНÓМ, *rhyming phrase, joc.* Lit., "Soil under the fingernails means you're an agronomist"; used as a reproach to children for dirty nails.

ПОДВИГÁТЬСЯ/ПОДВИ́НУТЬСЯ, *business.* To reduce the price (lit., to move). ◆*На скóлько онú подвúнулись? На лимóн, бóльше?* "How much is the discount? A million? More?"

ПОДГÁДИТЬ, *perf. only, neg.* To spoil, harm. ◆*Её мёдом не кормú, дай тóлько подгáдить блúжнему.* "All she really

likes is to spoil things for other people."

ПОДГРЕБÁТЬ/ПОДГРЕСТÚ, *joc.* To come, arrive (lit., to row in). ◆*Подгребáй к шестú часáм.* "Come over by six o'clock."

ПОДДАВÁЛА, -ы, m., neg. A drunk. ◆*Он извéстный поддавáла.* "Everyone knows he's a drunk."

ПОДДАВÁТЬ/ПОДДÁТЬ. To drink. ◆*Он поддáть не дурáк.* "He's quite a drinker." ●**Чтó-то стáло холодáть, не порá ли нам поддáть?,** see under **чтó-то.**

ПОДДУВÁЛО, -а, n., neg. A mouth (lit., flue). ◆*Закрóй поддувáло!* "Shut your trap!"

ПОДЖЕНÚТЬСЯ, *perf. only, rude.* To have sex with a woman. ◆*Ты тóлько и дýмаешь, с кем бы поженúться.* "All you ever think about is who to sleep with."

ПОДКÁЛЫВАТЬ/ПОДКОЛÓТЬ. To deflate, give someone a dressing down (lit., to prick). ◆*Ты егó хорошó подколóл насчёт егó жáдности.* "You gave him a good needling about his greed."

ПОДКАЧÁТЬ, *perf. only.* To fail, slip up. ◆*Смотрú, не подкачáй! Ты дóлжен вы́играть сегóдня в тéннис.* "Make sure you don't slip up. You've got to win the tennis game today."

ПОДКОВÁТЬ, *perf., sport.* To hit someone in the feet or legs (lit., to shoe [a horse]). ◆*Нáдо егó подковáть, слúшком бы́стро бéгает.* "We have to hit him, he runs too fast."

ПОДКÓЖНЫЕ, -ых, *pl., joc.* A hidden supply of money. ◆*Вот ещё есть подкóжные.* "I've got some more in my private stash."

ПОДКÓЛКА, -и, f. A trick, joke (from колóть, "to prick"). ◆*Ещё однá подкóлка, и ты у меня́ дождёшься.* "One more of those tricks and you're really going to get it from me."

ПОДЛÁВЛИВАТЬ/ПОДЛОВÚТЬ. To track down and beat up (from ловúть, "to catch"). ◆*Я тебя́ ещё подловлю́, ты у меня́ дождёшься!* "Just you wait, I'll catch you and give you a hiding!"

ПОДЛЯ́НКА, -и, f., neg. A malicious act

(from подлость). ♦*Он на любую под-лянку пойдёт.* "He'd stoop to any nasty deed." •**Бро́сить/подбро́сить подля́н-ку,** see under **бро́сить.**

ПОДМА́ХИВАТЬ/ПОДМАХНУ́ТЬ, *rude.* To have sex, with reference to moving about during sexual activity. ♦*Она хорошо подмахивает?* "Is she good in bed?"

ПОДМЫ́ШКА, -и, *f.* A mouse pad for a computer (lit., under a mouse or an armpit).

ПОДНАСИРА́ТЬ/ПОДНАСРА́ТЬ, *rude.* To treat badly (lit., to shit on). ♦*Кто же тебе так поднасрал, обвинил в чужих грехах?* "Who dumped on you like that, blaming you for what the others did?"

ПОДНА́ЧИВАТЬ/ПОДНА́ЧИТЬ, *joc.* To tease, jeer at. ♦*Хватит его подначивать, он уже звереет.* "Stop teasing him. He's already in a rage."

ПОДНА́ЧКА, -и, *f., neg.* Jeering, ridicule. ♦*Мне твои подначки надоели.* "I'm sick of you making fun of me."

ПОДНИМА́ТЬ/ПОДНЯ́ТЬ. To be able to afford something, have the money to buy something (lit., to lift). ♦*Сейчас ма-шину не подниму, через год, наверное.* "Right now I can't afford a car, but maybe in a year I'll have the money." •**Под-нима́ть/подня́ть ки́пеш,** *youth, neg.* To raise hell, make a scene. ♦*Кто здесь поднимает кипеш?* "Who's making all that hullabaloo?" •**Поднима́ть но́жку до аппе́ндикса,** *idiom, army, joc.* Said of a ceremonial high-kicking military step (lit., to lift one's leg to one's appendix, the word connoting a shapely female leg). ♦*Уже неделю поднимаем ножку до аппендикса, ноги болят.* "We've been practicing this kick-step for a week now. I have charley horses in both my dainty legs". **Поднима́ть/подня́ть стёб,** *idiom, youth.* To ridicule, mock (lit., to raise the whip). ♦*Что ты вечно стёб поднимаешь?* "How come you're always making fun of people?" **Под-нима́ть/подня́ть шара́п,** *idiom, neg.* To make noise, be tumultuous. ♦*Тише, тише, не поднимай шарап.* "Hush,

hush! Don't make such a racket." •**Поднима́ть/подня́ть шуми́ху,** *idiom.* To make a sensation, a scandal (lit., to raise a noise). ♦*Опять подняли шумиху о заказных убийствах.* "They've been making a stink again about killings on demand."

ПОДНИМА́ТЬСЯ/ПОДНЯ́ТЬСЯ, *crim.* **1.** To acquire and save money (lit., to rise). ♦*Ты уже поднялся на дачу?* "Have you saved up enough to buy a country house?" **2.** To get rich. ♦*Он так поднимается, не угонишься.* "He's getting so rich that nobody can keep up with him."

ПОДОГРЕ́В, -а, *m., crim.* Financial support. See **подогрева́ть.**

ПОДОГРЕВА́ТЬ/ПОДОГРЕ́ТЬ, *crim.* To support with money (lit., to warm up). ♦*А на эти деньги подогреешь наших.* "Here's a contribution for the support of our boys." **ПОДОГРЕ́ТЬ БРАТВУ́,** *idiom, crim.* To support imprisoned fellow criminals from a general fund. ♦*На то и есть общак — подогревать братву.* "That's why we keep a general fund, to support our brothers in prison."

ПОДПИСА́НТ, -а, *m., obs.* Someone who signs letters of protest against the actions of the Soviet Union or the Communist Party; a protester (lit., a signer, signatory). ♦*Этого подписанта мы не вы-пустим за границу.* "We won't give this protester permission to travel abroad."

ПОДПИ́СЫВАТЬ/ПОДПИСА́ТЬ, *youth.* To persuade, to talk into (lit., to sign up). ♦*Ты подписала его купить тебе шубу?* "Have you talked him into buying you a fur coat?"

ПО́ДПОЛ, -а, *m.* The rank of a lieutenant colonel (lit., a cellar). ♦*Ещё год, второй — получу подпола и в отставку.* "In another year or two I'll get my promotion and retire."

ПОДПО́ЛЬЩИК, -а, *m.* A closeted homosexual (lit., member of an underground organization). ♦*Что ты из себя подпольщика строишь, нас не обма-нешь.* "Why don't you come out? You're not fooling us anyhow."

ПОДРЕЗА́ТЬ/ПОДРÉЗАТЬ НОС, *idiom.* In driving, to pass a car too quickly, coming too close to it (lit., to trim someone's nose). ◆*Осторожно, сейчас он подрежет нос.* "Watch out! That guy's about to cut in on us."

ПОДРЫВА́ТЬ/ПОДОРВА́ТЬ, *crim.* To run away, leave quickly (lit., to burst). ◆*Кажется, сюда идут. Пора подрывать.* "It looks like they're coming this way — time to split!" •**Подрыва́ть/подорва́ть кран,** *idiom.* To urinate (lit., to burst one's tap). ◆*Не могу терпеть, а подорвать кран негде.* "Oh, I'm just bursting, but there's no place to take a leak around here!"

ПОДСА́ЖИВАТЬ/ПОДСАДИ́ТЬ (на джеф, на иглу́), *youth, neg.* To introduce someone to drug use, get someone started using drugs. ◆*Кто её подсадил на иглу?* "Who started her on drugs?" (Lit., "Who put her on the needle?")

ПОДСА́СЫВАТЬ, *imperf. only, youth.* To know something well, understand (lit., to apply the choke; cf. **подсóс**). ◆*Он в электронике подсасывает?* "Does he know electronics?"

ПОДСА́СЫВАТЬСЯ/ПОДСОСА́ТЬ- СЯ. To come to or to participate in another's activity (lit. to suckle). ◆*Подсасывайся к обеду, а там решим, что дальше делать.* "Come to lunch, then we'll decide what to do next."

ПОДСЕРА́ТЬ/ПОДОСРА́ТЬ, *rude.* To harm, mistreat. ◆*Не подсерай другим, тогда и тебя за человека считать будут.* "If you stop doing nasty things to others you'll be treated decently yourself."

ПОДСÉСТЬ, *perf. only, youth, neg.* To become addicted to drugs. ◆*Он подсел лет пять назад.* "He's been addicted for five years already."

ПОДСИРÓПИТЬ, *perf. only, neg.* To harm, mistreat. ◆*Ты мне подсиропил, подсунул помощника, а он ничего не умеет делать.* "You did me a nasty trick, palming that fellow off on me as an assistant. He doesn't know how to do anything."

ПОДСНÉЖНИК, -а, *m., joc.* A driver who takes his car off the road in the winter (lit., a snowdrop [spring flower]). ◆*Появились подснежники на дорогах, они совсем ездить разучились.* "The 'snowdrops' are on the road again, and they've completely forgotten how to drive."

ПОДСÓС, -а, *m.* The choke of an automobile. ◆*Убери подсос!* "Cut the choke."

ПОДСТАВЛЯ́ТЬ/ПОДСТА́ВИТЬ, *neg.* To blame or accuse falsely. ◆*Он не виноват, его дружки подставили.* "He didn't do it — his so-called friends framed him."

ПОДСУЕТИ́ТЬСЯ, *perf. only.* To rush to get something done. ◆*Я подсуетился и всё закупил на праздники заранее.* "I rushed about and got everything for the holiday ahead of time."

ПОДУ́ШКА, -и, *f., army.* A hovercraft (lit., a pillow). ◆*На эту подушку человек триста посадить можно.* "We can place three hundred men on this 'pillow.'"

ПОДХАЛИ́М, -а, *m.* A rotating fan (lit., a flatterer or yes-man, from the idea of bowing one's head to both left and right). ◆*Включи подхалим, дышать нечем.* "Turn on the fan — there's no air in here."

ПОДХАЛИМА́Ж, -а *m., neg.* Flattery, toadying. ◆*Мне их подхалимаж не нравится.* "I don't like their toadying."

ПОДЦЕПЛЯ́ТЬ/ПОДЦЕПИ́ТЬ, *neg.* **1.** To pick up a (venereal) disease. ◆*Смотри, не подцепи на юге какую-нибудь гадость.* "Be careful not to pick up a venereal disease down south." **2.** To make the casual acquaintance of a woman. ◆*Где ты подругу подцепил?* "Where did you pick up that gal?"

ПОДЪЕБА́ТЬСЯ/ПОДЪЕБНУ́ТЬСЯ, *rude.* To have sex (cf. **ёб-**). ◆*Хорошо бы подъебаться.* "It would be nice to get laid."

ПОДЪЁБКА, -и, *f., rude.* A joke, trick, practical joke, leg-pulling (cf. **ёб-**). ◆*Мне надоели твои вечные подъёбки.* "I'm sick of your constant jokes."

ПОДЪЁБЩИК, -а, *m., rude.* A joker, clown, buffoon (cf. **ёб-**). ♦*Нам ещё подъёбщиков не хватало, когда все на нервах.* "The last thing we need is some comedian, just when everyone's so tense."

ПОДЪЁБЫВАТЬ/ПОДЪЕБНУ́ТЬ, *rude.* To tease, annoy (cf. **ёб-**). ♦*Видишь, он уже злится, больше его не подъёбывай.* "You can see he's getting angry. Don't tease him any more."

ПОДЪЁМ, -а, *m., business.* Profit (lit., ascent). ♦*На какой подъём можно рассчитывать?* "How much of a profit can we count on?"

ПОДЫХÁТЬ/ПОДÓХНУТЬ. To die. ♦*Вот подохну, никто и не вспомнит.* "Nobody will remember me when I'm gone."

ПОЁБАНЫЙ, -ая, -ое, *rude.* Tired, depressed (cf. **ёб-**). •**Ходи́ть как поёбаный,** see under **ходи́ть.**

ПОЕБÓН, -а, *m., rude.* Sex, sex act (cf. **ёб**). ♦*Пора нам поебон устроить.* "It's about time we got laid."

ПОЕБÓТИНА, -ы, *f., rude.* Nonsense (cf. **ёб-**). ♦*Как ты можешь слушать по радио эту поеботину о любви?* "How can you listen to that nonsense about love on the radio?"

ПОЁБЫВАТЬ, *imperf. only, rude.* To sleep with someone occasionally (cf. **ёб**). ♦*Он её поёбывает время от времени.* "He sleeps with her from time to time."

ПОЖÁРНАЯ КОМÁНДА, *idiom.* Racketeers, gangsters (lit., fire brigade). ♦*Позвать пожарную команду или так отдать должок?* "Should we call in the brigade or just pay up?"

ПОЖУЁМ — УВИ́ДИМ, *idiom, joc.* It's too early to tell, let's wait and see, time will tell (distorted from the idiom поживём — увидим, "we'll live and see"). ♦*Он, наверное, станет хорошим спортсменом. — Пожуём — увидим.* "He'll probably be a very good athlete. — Let's wait and see."

ПОЗВОНÓК, позвонка́, *m.* A recipient of special favors, protection (lit., a phone call). ♦*Сколько студентов-позвонков у нас в институте?* "How many of our

students got in through connections?"

ПОЗВОНÓЧНЫЙ, -ого. A person with useful connections. See **позвонóк** and **телефóнное пра́во.**

ПÓЗДНО: Лу́чше пóздно, чем никому́ (дать), see under **лу́чше.**

ПОЗДНЯ́К МЕТÁТЬСЯ, *idiom.* It is too late (lit., it's too late to rush about). ♦*Я пенсионер, поздняк метаться, заниматься бизнесом не хочу.* "I am a pensioner, it's too late to rush about, I don't want to be involved in business anymore."

ПОЙМÁТЬ, *perf.* To be punished, to get what is coming to you. ♦*Ты сейчас поймаешь.* "You're going to catch it now!"

ПОЙТИ́ В МИ́НУС, *idiom, army.* To be killed (lit., to go to minus, from минусовать, to subtract).

ПОКÁ НЕ РОДИЛÁ, КАК РОЖУ́, ТАК СКАЖУ́, *rhyming phrase, joc.* Things are all right; nothing special is new (lit., "I haven't given birth yet; I'll tell you when I do"). Used in reply to "How are things with you?"

ПОКАЗУ́ХА, -и, *f., neg.* Something done for show or to make an impression; a merely outward appearance. ♦*Убрали Москву к праздникам, одна показуха, потом опять будет грязно.* "Moscow's been prettied up for the holiday but it's just camouflage; the dirt will come out again afterwards."

ПОКÁЗЫВАТЬ/ПОКАЗÁТЬ кóгти, *idiom, neg.* To show one's real character (lit., to show one's claws). ♦*А он не прост, показал когти, не хочет остаться без кресла.* "He's not such a simple fellow. He doesn't want to lose his position, and now he's showing his claws."

ПОКÁТ, -а, *m., pred. use, youth, pos.* Excellent, great (cf. **пока́тный**). ♦*Работа у них — покат, денежная и непыльная.* "They've got a great job — high pay and not much work."

ПОКÁТНЫЙ, -ая, -ое, *youth.* Funny, entertaining (from покати́ться [со смеху], "to roll [with laughter]"). ♦*Вчера*

*рассказали покатный анекдот, по-
слушай.* "Listen to this hilarious story I
heard yesterday."

ПОКÉДА! *idiom, joc.* So long! Be seeing
you! (distorted from пока and покуда).

ПОКУПÁТЬ/КУПИ́ТЬ. To deceive,
trick, cheat (lit., to buy). *♦Меня не купишь, я знаю, что эти сигареты плохие.* "You can't trick me — I know perfectly well those are lousy cigarettes."

ПО́ЛАК, -а, *m., neg.* A Pole. *♦Полаки
хотят вступить в НАТО, как тебе
это нравится?* "How do you like that!
Now those Polacks want to join NATO!"

**ПОЛБÁНКИ: Принимáть/принять
полбáнки,** see under **принимáть.**

ПО́ЛЕ ДУРАКÓВ, *idiom, army.* A parade
ground (lit., an idiot's field, evoking the
field of dreams where Pinocchio planted
his coins in the belief that they would
produce money plants). *♦Два часа были
на поле дураков, промокли и есть
охота.* "We spent two hours on a bloody
parade ground, we're all wet and hungry."

ПОЛЁТ: В полёте, *idiom.* Very drunk (lit.,
in flight). *♦Он каждый день в полёте.*
"He gets high as a kite every day."

ПОЛИВÁТЬ/ПОЛИ́ТЬ, *joc.* To scold,
verbally abuse (lit., to water, as with a
hose). *♦Он их давай поливать послед-
ними словами.* "He showered them with
the most extreme abuses."

ПОЛИ́ВКА, -и, *f.* **1.** A lie. *♦Не верь, это
поливка.* "Don't believe it, it's a lie." **2.**
A practical joke. *♦Он мастер на
поливки.* "He's an expert at practical
jokes."

ПОЛИ́НА ИВÁННА, *idiom, joc.* Furniture polish or other spirit solutions as
used for alcoholic drinks (lit., Paulina
Ivanovna, a woman's name formed after
политура or полировка, "polish"). *♦Да-
вай хоть Полины Иванны примем.*
"Let's have something to drink, even if
it's just 'Paulina Ivanovna.'"

ПОЛИРОВÁТЬ/ЗАПОЛИРОВÁТЬ,
joc. To drink wine after hard liquor (lit.,
to polish). *♦И всё это заполируем
домашним вином.* "Let's polish it off
with some homemade wine."

ПОЛКÁН, -а, *m., army.* A colonel (by
wordplay on Полкан, a common dog's
name, and полковник, "colonel"). *♦Сам
полкан будет проверку делать.* "The
colonel himself will be making
inspection."

**ПОЛ-ЛИ́ТРА: Без пол-ли́тра не разо-
брáться,** see under **без.**

ПОЛОВÓЙ РАЗБÓЙНИК, *idiom, joc.* A
man who changes sexual partners frequently (lit., a sexual bandit). *♦Опять
наш половой разбойник с новой деви-
цей.* "There's our sex fiend with a new
girl again."

ПОЛОВУ́ХА, -и, *f., youth, neg.* Sexual
subject matter (from половой, "sexual").
♦В этом фильме одна половуха. "The
whole film is just a bunch of bedroom
scenes."

ПОЛОЖИ́ТЬ С ПРИБÓРОМ, *idiom,
rude.* To despise, to consider beneath
attention. *♦Я положил с прибором на
твои угрозы.* "I don't give a damn for
your threats."

**ПОЛОСКÁТЬ/ПОПОЛОСКÁТЬ чьё-л.
и́мя,** *idiom, neg.* To gossip about someone (lit., to rinse someone's name). *♦Я
не хочу, чтобы его имя полоскали
кому не лень.* "I don't want everyone
who feels like it to go gossiping about
him."

ПОЛТИ́ННИК, -а, *m.* **1.** *obs.* A fifty-
kopeck coin. **2.** A fifty-ruble coin. **3.** Fifty
thousand rubles.*♦Сколько это стоит?
— Полтинник.* "How much is it? —
Fifty thousand rubles." **4.** *pl.* Eyes (lit.,
fifty-kopeck coins). *♦Что ты полтин-
ники выкатил, бабы никогда не
видел?* "Why are you bugging your eyes
out like that? Haven't you ever seen a
woman before?"

ПОЛУКРÓВКА, -и, *f.* A person whose
parents are of different nationalities (lit.,
half-blood). *♦Какой он русский, он
полукровка.* "He's no Russian, he's just
a half-breed."

ПОЛУМОТÓРНЫЙ, -ая, -ое, *south,
youth.* Silly, half-witted (lit., half-
motorized). *♦Соображай быстрей,
какой-то ты полумоторный сегодня.*

"Get on the ball! You're not cooking on all four burners today!"

ПОЛУ́НДРА!, *interj., army.* **1.** A warning of danger. **2.** In the navy and marines (but not the army) the phrase serves as a cheer.

ПОЛУФАБРИКА́Т, -а, *m.* See **полу-кро́вка.**

ПОЛУЧА́ТЬ/ПОЛУЧИ́ТЬ: Получа́ть/получи́ть бара́нку, *idiom, sports.* To receive a zero score, to lose. ♦ *Мы получи́ли бара́нку на после́дних соревнова́ниях.* "We got creamed in the last match." **Получи́ть па́чку,** *idiom.* To be beaten, hit. ♦ *Он получи́л па́ру па́чек и убежа́л.* "He was hit a couple of times, and he ran away."

ПОЛХУ́Я: Шу́тки шу́тками, а полху́я в желу́дке, see under **шу́тки.**

ПОЛШЕСТО́ГО: У кого́-л. на полшесто́го, *idiom, joc.* Someone doesn't have an erection (lit., "with him it's 5:30," referring to the hands of a clock). ♦ *А он непло́х в посте́ли? — Что ты, у него́ всё вре́мя на полшесто́го.* "So, is he pretty good in bed? — Are you kidding? Always half-past five!"

ПОЛШТУ́КИ, *f., indecl., obs.* Five hundred rubles. ♦ *Мне на́до полшту́ки на кни́ги.* "I need five hundred rubles for books."

ПОЛЯ́НА, -ы, *f., joc.* (Lit., a glade, a clearing). **1.** A bald spot. ♦ *Поля́на растёт всё бо́льше, ско́ро во́лос совсе́м не оста́нется.* "Your bald spot is getting bigger and bigger. Soon you won't have any hair left at all. **2.** A playground.

ПОЛЯ́НДИЯ, -ии, *f., joc.* Poland.

ПОМАЗО́К, помазка́, *m., army.* A soldier who has served more than one year and is therefore released from certain menial tasks (lit., a shaving brush). ♦ *Он уже́ помазо́к, он э́то де́лать не бу́дет.* "He's already a 'shaver'; he won't do that sort of work."

ПОМАТРО́СИТЬ И БРО́СИТЬ, *idiom, joc.* To break off a love affair, seduce and abandon (from матро́с, "sailor"). ♦ *Он тебя́ поматро́сил и бро́сил, а ты уже́ за́муж собра́лась.* "Well, so you've been seduced and abandoned — and you thought he was going to marry you!"

ПО́МЕСЬ НЕ́ГРА С МОТОЦИ́КЛОМ, *idiom, joc.* A strange combination. ♦ *Что э́то за дом? По́месь не́гра с мотоци́клом.* "What sort of a building is that? It looks like a cross between a Negro and a motorcycle."

ПОМЫ́ТЬ, *perf. only, crim.* To rob (lit., to wash). ♦ *Вчера́ помы́ли одного́ фра́ера, взя́ли па́ру лимо́нов.* "Yesterday they robbed some fellow of a couple of million."

ПОНАРО́ШКУ, *adv.* Not seriously, as a joke. ♦ *Не принима́й э́то бли́зко к се́рдцу, э́то всё понаро́шку.* "Don't take it too seriously, it's just a joke."

ПОНЕСЛИ́СЬ! *idiom.* Let's get going! Come on! (usually with reference to drinking). •**Понесли́сь! Душа́ в рай, а но́ги в мили́цию,** *idiom, joc.* Lit., "Let's have a drink! Our souls will be in heaven, even if we land at the police station."

ПОНЕСЛО́СЬ ДЕРЬМО́ ПО ТРУ́БАМ, *idiom, rude, neg.* Word got around fast, rumors or information spread quickly (lit., the shit rushed through the pipes). ♦ *Жена́ узна́ла, что он с ней спит, понесло́сь дерьмо́ по тру́бам.* "When his wife found out that he's sleeping with her, the shit hit the fan."

ПОНИЖА́ТЬ/ПОНИ́ЗИТЬ, *youth.* To rob (lit., to lower). ♦ *На ры́нке меня́ пони́зили на 100 ба́ксов.* "They shortened me by 100 bucks in the market."

ПОНИМА́Ю, КОГДА́ ВЫНИМА́Ю, *rhyming phrase, rude.* Yes, of course (used in answer to the question "Do you understand?"; lit., "I understand when I take it out," in allusion to the sex act). ♦ *Собира́емся в кино́ в семь часо́в, понима́ешь? — Понима́ю, когда́ вынима́ю.* "We'll meet at the cinema at seven, understand? — Of course!"

ПОНО́СНЫЙ, -ая, -ое, *neg.* Very bad (from поно́с, "diarrhea"). ♦ *Эту поно́сную кни́гу в ру́ки брать не хо́чется.* "I don't even want to touch that shitty book."

ПОНТ: Для по́нта, *idiom*. **1.** In jest, as a joke. ♦*Ты зачем обманул его? — А так, для понта.* "Why did you trick him? — Just for the fun of it." **2.** For looks, to make an impression. ♦*Давай нарядимся для понта.* "Let's get all dressed up to make an impression." **Брать/взять на понт,** see under **брать.**

ПОНТИ́ТЬСЯ/ЗАПОНТИ́ТЬСЯ. To boast (cf. **понт**). ♦*Понтиться все могут, а потом трусят.* "They all talk big, and then they get cold feet."

ПОНТО́ВЫЙ, -ая, -ое, *neg.* False, imaginary. ♦*Это понтовый разговор, а дела не будет.* "This is empty talk, nothing will come of it."

ПОНТЫ́, -о́в, *pl., youth, neg.* Lies, untruths. ♦*Это всё понты.* "That's all a bunch of lies." •**Наброса́ть понты́,** see under **наброса́ть.**

ПОНТЯ́РА, -ы, *f., neg.* A deception, trick. ♦*Это же понтяра чистой воды.* "This is an absolute fake."

ПО́ПА, -ы, *f.* Buttocks. ♦*Дай ему по попе, чтобы не капризничал.* "Smack him on the behind and he'll stop acting up."

ПОПАДА́ТЬ/ПОПА́СТЬ. To pay off (lit., to be trapped). ♦*Кажется, я попал на большие деньги.* "It seems I've fallen into a lot of debt." **Попада́ть/попа́сть в бидо́н,** *idiom.* To get into trouble (lit., to land in a milk can). ♦*Ну, попали в бидон, за нами менты идут.* "Well, it seems we've gotten into trouble and are going behind bars." **Попада́ть/попа́сть в очко́,** *idiom.* To guess correctly, be right (lit., to hit the bull's-eye). ♦*Хочешь, угадаю, что ты принёс? Ты купил торт. — Точно, попал в очко.* "Should I guess what you brought? A cake. — You're exactly right." **Попада́ть/попа́сть под трамва́й,** *idiom, neg., rude.* To be made the object of gang rape (lit., to fall under the tram). ♦*Не ходи к этим ребятам, попадёшь под трамвай.* "Don't go around with those guys — they'll rape you."

ПОПАЛИ́ТЬ, *perf., army.* To betray, to report. ♦*Если узнаю, кто меня попалил, убью.* "If I find out who reported on me, I'll kill him."

ПОПЕНГА́ГЕН, -а, *m., joc.* Buttocks, behind (by wordplay on **попа** and Копенгаген, "Copenhagen"). ♦*Ну и попенгаген у неё!* "What an ass on her!"

ПОПЕРЁК СЕБЯ́ ШИ́РЕ, *idiom, joc.* Fat, obese (lit., wider than oneself in the girth). ♦*Тебе на диету пора сесть, ты поперёк себя шире.* "You should go on a diet — you've become broader than you are tall."

ПОПИСА́ТЬ, *crim.* To cut, wound, with a knife or razor. ♦*Его вчера пописали в подъезде.* "They cut him in the hall yesterday."

ПО́ПКА, -и, *m. & f., crim., neg.* A prison guard stationed in a guard tower (lit., a parrot, as in a cage). ♦*Попки в воскресенье сменяются в восемь.* "They change guards at eight o'clock on Sundays."

ПОПКА́РЬ, -я́, *crim., neg.* An informer (cf. **попка**). ♦*Замолчи, попкарь идёт.* "Quiet, here comes that stool pigeon."

ПОПЛЫ́ТЬ, *perf., youth.* To go crazy (lit., to go swimming). ♦*После экзаменов он сразу и поплыл.* "As soon as his exams were over, he lost his marbles."

ПОПОЛА́М (кому́-л.), *adv.* It's all the same, there is no difference, it doesn't matter (lit., in two, half and half). ♦*А мне пополам, что там обо мне говорят.* "It makes no difference to me that they talk about me." **В попола́ме,** *youth, neg.* Extremely drunk (lit., doubled over). ♦*Ну и муженёк у неё, всё время в пополаме домой приходит.* "Her husband is always coming home plastered."

ПОПРА́ВЬ ВОРОТНИ́К, ВРАТЬ МЕ-ША́ЕТ, *idiom, joc.* Stop lying; what you're saying isn't true (lit., "Fix your collar — it's cramping your lying"). ♦*Я скоро женюсь. — Ой, поправь воротник, врать мешает.* "I'm getting married soon. — Oh, straighten your collar; it's interfering with your lie."

ПОПСА́, -ы́, *f.* Low-quality pop music. ♦*Ничего хорошего на эстраде нет, одна попса.* "There's nothing good on the stage, it's all trashy pop music."

ПОПУХА́ТЬ/ПОПУ́ХНУТЬ. To be

caught red-handed (lit., to swell up). ♦*Они попухли на взятке.* "They were caught red-handed taking bribes."

ПОРВА́ТЬ пасть, *idiom, rude.* To hit, beat. ♦*Уйди с дороги, а то пасть порву.* "Get out of my way or I'll punch you in the mouth."

ПОРНУ́ХА, -и, *f., neg.* Pornography. ♦*В этом журнале одна порнуха.* "All there is in this magazine is pornography."

ПОРНУ́ШНИЧАТЬ/ЗАПОРНУ́ШНИ-ЧАТЬ, *youth, neg.* To act dishonestly, behave badly. ♦*Они с нами порнушничать стали, опять вещи не отдали.* "They've started acting dishonest toward us, refusing to return our things."

ПОРНЬ, -и, *f., youth, neg.* Pornography. ♦*Порнь есть новая посмотреть?* "Any new porn to look at?"

ПО́РОВНУ (кому́-л.), *adv.* It's all the same, it doesn't matter (lit., in equal parts). ♦*Если тебе это поровну, то мне— нет!* "It seems it's all the same to you, to me it's not!"

ПОРОЖНЯ́К, -а, *m.* Bad luck, a failure (from порожний, "empty"). ♦*Сегодня порожняк, и ста рублей не заработал.* "Today was a bummer, I didn't even make a hundred rubles."

ПОРОСЁНОК, поросёнка, *m., crim.* A wallet (lit., a piglet). ♦*Посмотри, там у клиента поросёнок что надо.* "Look at that guy — he's carrying quite a wallet."

ПОРО́ТЬ, *imperf., army.* To eat (lit., to rip). ♦*Надоело три раза в день кашу пороть.* "I'm sick of eating kasha three times a day."

ПОРТВА́ЙН, -а, *m., joc.* Cheap, strong wine (by wordplay on портвейн, "port," and Eng. "wine"). ♦*Ну и кто будет пить этот портвайн, это же дрянь.* "Who do you think would drink this rotgut?"

ПОРТВЕШИ́СТ, -а, *m.* Someone who drinks only wine (from **портвешо́к**). ♦*Он портвешист, он водку пить не будет.* "He's strictly a wino — doesn't drink vodka."

ПОРТВЕШО́К, портвешка́, *m., joc., neg.* See **портва́йн.**

ПОРТО́ВАЯ БЛЯДЬ, *idiom, rude.* A bitch, prostitute, nasty woman (lit., a port prostitute for sailors). ♦*Как ты можешь дружить с этой портовой блядью?* "How can you associate with that bitch?"

ПОРЦА́, -ы́, *f.* A portion, share. ♦*Дай ещё порцу мяса.* "Give me another helping of the meat."

ПОРЫБЕ́НЬ, -и, *f.* Nonsense, rubbish. ♦*Порыбень всё это, что тут говорить.* "Everything you are talking about is complete nonsense."

ПОРЫ́ТЬ, *perf. only, youth.* To go (lit., to dig). ♦*Ты не знаешь, куда он порыл?* "Do you know where he went?"

ПОРЯ́ДОК В ТА́НКОВЫХ ВОЙ-СКА́Х, *idiom, joc.* Everything's fine, everything's in order (lit., order in the tank divisions). ♦*Всё купили для праздника? Все в сборе? — Да. — Ну, тогда порядок в танковых войсках.* "Have you bought all the holiday things? Is everyone here? — Yes. — Well, then, everything's in order."

ПОСЛЕ́ДНЯЯ БЛЯДЬ, *idiom, rude.* A nothing, a cipher, a worthless person (lit., the last whore). ♦*Я не буду, как последняя блядь, просить у вас помощи.* "I won't be reduced to begging you for help as if I were the lowest of the low."

ПОСМЕ́ТЬ: Что посме́ешь, то и пожмёшь, see under **что.**

ПОТОМУ́, ЧТО КОНЧА́ЕТСЯ НА "У", *idiom, joc.* A rhyming phrase used as an evasive answer to the question Почему?, "Why?" (Lit., Because it ends with the letter "U"). ♦*Почему ты сидишь, ничего не делаешь. — Потому, что кончается на "у".* "Why are you just sitting there?" — "Just because."

ПО́ТРОХ ДЕШЁВЫЙ, *crim., rude.* A scoundrel, bastard (lit., cheap guts). ♦*Это ты у меня взял инструмент, потрох дешёвый!* "So it was you who took my tools, you bastard!"

ПОТРЯ́СНО, *pred. use, youth.* Wonderful, excellent. ♦*В Сочи летом — потрясно!* "It's terrific in Sochi in the summertime!"

ПОХЕРА́ЧИТЬ, *perf. only, rude.* To go, leave (cf. **хер**). ♦ *Куда они похерачили?* "Where did they go?"

ПО́ХОДЬ, -и, *f., youth, joc.* A woman's sexually attractive way of walking (play on походка, "gait" or "stride," and похоть, "desire"). ♦ *Походь у неё, изнасиловать хочется.* "That sexy strut of hers makes me want her."

ПОХУЍСТ, -а, *m., rude.* Someone who looks down on everything, someone who doesn't care (cf. **по́ хуй** under **хуй**). ♦ *Его это не волнует, он похуист.* "It doesn't bother him. He couldn't care less."

ПОЦ, -а, *m., neg.* 1. A guy, fellow. 2. A fool, a worthless or unplesant person. ♦ *Какой поц здесь так наследил на ковре?* "What creep dirtied the carpet?"

ПОШЁЛ ТЫ РА́КОМ ВДОЛЬ ЗАБО́РА! *idiom, rude.* Get out of here; go to hell (lit., "Walk crabwise along the fence!"). ♦ *Я тебе ещё раз говорю, она тебе не пара. — А пошёл ты раком вдоль забора.* "I'm telling you, she's not for you. — Go to hell."

ПОШЛО́-ПОЕ́ХАЛО, *idiom, neg.* There you go again, there it goes again (an expression of disapproval). ♦ *Ну, пошло-поехало, опять вы ругаетесь.* "There you go yelling at each other again."

ПОЯ́БЫВАТЬ, *imperf. only, rude.* To have sex with a woman (cf. **ёб-**). ♦ *Её кто-нибудь поябывает?* "Is anyone screwing her?"

ПО́ЯС: Всё пони́же по́яса, see under **всё.**

ППЖ, *abbr., neg.* A mistress, lover (from походно-полевая жена, "battlefield wife"). ♦ *Она его ППЖ.* "She's his mistress."

ПРАВА́: Кача́ть права́, see under **кача́ть.**

ПРАВИ́ЛКА, -и, *f., crim.* A trial held by criminals or soldiers, a "kangaroo court" (from править, to correct). ♦ *На правилки решено, надо ему врезать за то, что крысятничал у своих.* "Our honorable kangaroo court decided that the thief needed to have the shit kicked out of him."

ПРА́ВО: Телефо́нное пра́во, see under **телефо́нное.**

ПРАЙС, -а, *m., youth.* From Eng. "price". 1. Price, cost. ♦ *А какой сейчас прайс на джинсы?* "How much do jeans cost now?" 2. Money. ♦ *У тебя сколько прайса?* "How much money do you have?"

ПРАЙСОВА́ТЬ/ЗАПРАЙСОВА́ТЬ, *youth.* To pay, finance (cf. **прайс**). ♦ *Сколько ты нам запрайсуешь?* "How much can you give us?"

ПРАЙСО́ВЫЙ, -ая, -ое, *youth.* Rich, wealthy. ♦ *Он у тебя прайсовый мэн.* "Your boyfriend is always flush."

ПРА́ПОР, -а, *m., army.* A прапорщик ("praporshchik"; similar to an ensign; rank between soldiers and officers, usually held by enlisted men voluntarily serving an extra term in the infantry). ♦ *Её сын служит в армии? — Да, он прапор.* "Is her son in the army? — Yes, he's a 'praporshchik.'"

ПРА́ЧЕЧНИК, -а, *m., business.* A money launderer (lit., laundry). ♦ *Срочно находи прачечника, наличность накопилась.* "We've accumulated a lot of cash, it's high time to find a laundry for it."

ПРЕДЕ́Л, -а, *m., youth, neg.* Misfortune, end. ♦ *Если он узнает обо всём, мне — предел.* "If he finds out about all this it'll be curtains for me."

ПРЕ́ДОК, пре́дка, *m., joc.* A parent (lit., ancestor). ♦ *Твои предки дома?* "Are your parents home?"

ПРЕДЪЯ́ВА, -ы, *f., youth.* Conditions, demands. ♦ *За это дело какая у них предъява?* "How much are they asking to do the job?"

ПРЕСС, -а, *m., crim.* A roll of bills. ♦ *Ладно, не жмись, доставай свой пресс, плати.* "Don't be a tightwad — take out your bankroll and pay up."

ПРЕССОВА́ТЬ/ЗАПРЕССОВА́ТЬ, *crim.* To beat up, prosecute (lit., to press, as with an industrial metal press). ♦ *Наверху решили прессовать его до конца.* "Headquarters decided to beat him into shape."

ПРИБАБА́Х: С прибаба́хом, *idiom, neg.* Eccentric, exhibiting strange or unusual behavior. ♦*Его не поймёшь, он с прибаба́хом.* "You can't make head or tail of him — he's a bit strange."

ПРИБА́ЛТ, -а, *m.* A national of any of the Baltic republics of the former Soviet Union. ♦*Все прибалты теперь иностранцы.* "Now all the Balts have suddenly become foreigners."

ПРИБА́ЛТЫБАТЬ/ПРИБОЛТА́ТЬ. To talk into, to persuade (from болтать, "to chatter"). ♦*Не могу мужа приболтать пойти в кино уже год.* "For the last year I haven't been able to talk my husband into going to the movies."

ПРИБАМБА́СЫ, -ов, *pl.* **1.** Decorations, frills. ♦*У меня нет в машине никаких прибамбасов: ни магнитофона, ни телефона, ни радио.* "I've got a no-frills car — no tape deck, no telephone, no radio." **2.** Complications, difficulties.

ПРИБАРАХЛЯ́ТЬСЯ/ПРИБАРАХ-ЛИ́ТЬСЯ, *joc.* To get new clothes (from барахло, "clothing"). ♦*Нам всем не мешает прибарахлиться, обносились.* "It would be a good idea for us all to get some new clothes; our old things are worn out."

ПРИБОМБИ́ТЬ. To buy, acquire. ♦*Где ты такие туфли прибомбила?* "Where did you manage to get such nice shoes?"

ПРИВОЗИ́ТЬ/ПРИВЕЗТИ́, *business.* To cheat. ♦*Ну вот, привезли новеньких на лимон.* "Well, they cheated the newcomers out of a cool million."

ПРИГОВО́Р, -а, *m., joc.* A bill, check (lit., verdict). ♦*Шеф, неси приговор.* "Waiter, bring the check."

ПРИДЕ́ЛЫВАТЬ/ПРИДЕ́ЛАТЬ, *neg.* **1.** To hit, beat. ♦*Его так за баб приделали, сейчас в больнице лежит.* "They beat him up so badly for his philandering that he's actually in the hospital now." **2.** To put someone in an uncomfortable situation. ♦*Как его приделали, когда доказали, что он на руку не чист.* "What a fix they got him into when they proved that he was on the take!" •**Приде́-лывать/приде́лать но́ги,** *idiom.* Lit., to put feet on something. **1.** To steal. ♦*Я вижу, этим часам приделали ноги.* "Apparently somebody stole my watch." **2.** To forward a document. ♦*Надо ещё бумаге приделать ноги, чтобы дело двинулось.* "We'll have to send these documents on in order to make any progress in the matter."

ПРИДНЕСТРОФИ́К, -а, *m., joc., neg.* The currency of the Pridnestr Region (by wordplay on дистрофия, "dystrophy"). ♦*Я приднестрофики не возьму, давай зелёные.* "Give me greenbacks, I don't want any of this local currency."

ПРИДОЛБА́ТЬСЯ, *perf.* To irritate, annoy, pester (from долбить, to chisel). ♦*Ну что ты ко мне придолбился со своими рассказами, мне неинтересно.* "Why do you keep pecking away at me with your dumb stories? I'm not interested."

ПРИДУ́РОК, приду́рка, *m., neg.* **1.** A fool, idiot. ♦*Что нужно этому придурку?* "What does that idiot want?" **2.** *crim.* A prison-camp inmate who serves the prison authorities. ♦*Он в придурки не пойдёт, он вор в законе.* "He'd never be a stooge; he keeps the thieves' code of honor."

ПРИЁБИСТЫЙ, -ая, -ое, *rude.* Nagging, critical, picky (cf. **ёб-**). ♦*Это комиссия очень приёбистая, будь готов ко всякому.* "This auditing team is very picky; you've got to be prepared for anything with them."

ПРИЁБЫВАТЬСЯ/ПРИЕБА́ТЬСЯ, *rude.* Cf. **ёб-**. **1.** To be hypercritical. ♦*Что ни скажу, всё не так, ты к каждому слову приёбываешься.* "Whatever I say is always wrong; you find fault with every word." **2.** To nag, be persistent. ♦*Больше с этими вопросами ко мне не приёбывайся.* "Don't keep nagging me with those questions."

ПРИЖМУ́РИТЬСЯ, *perf. only, joc.* To die (lit., to squint; see **жмур, жму́рик**). ♦*Он прижмурился ещё неделю назад.* "He died a week ago."

ПРИЖО́ПЛИВАТЬ/ПРИЖО́ПИТЬ, *rude.* To apprehend, catch, expose (cf.

жо́па). ◆*Когда его за махинации, наконец, прижопят?* "When are they ever going to catch him at his scams?"

ПРИЖУ́ЧИВАТЬ/ПРИЖУ́ЧИТЬ. To squelch, to suppress, put s.o. in his place. ◆*Никто его не может прижучить, обнаглел вконец.* "He's so pushy, no one can put him in his place."

ПРИ́ЗВЕЗДЬ, -и, *f., youth, neg.* A craze, fad, eccentricity (euph. for **при́пиздь**). ◆*Это у него призвездь читать все газеты подряд.* "It's a craze of his to read all the papers one after the other."

ПРИК, -а, *m., youth, rude.* A penis (from Eng. "prick"). ◆*На прик тебе это надо!* "What the hell do you need *that* for?"

ПРИКА́ЛЫВАТЬСЯ/ПРИКОЛО́ТЬ-СЯ, *youth.* 1. To pay attention (lit., to pin oneself to something). ◆*Прикалываешься, что тебе говорят?* "Are you paying attention to what they're telling you?" 2. *neg.* To be persistent, stick to something or someone. ◆*Он всё время прикалывается ко мне, делает всякие замечания.* "He's constantly hanging around me and making all sorts of comments."

ПРИКИ́Д, -а, *m., youth.* Stylish clothing. ◆*У него всегда прикид что надо.* "He's always wearing some sort of stylish outfit."

ПРИКИ́ДЫВАТЬСЯ/ПРИКИ́НУТЬ-СЯ шла́нгом, *idiom, neg.* To play dumb, pretend not to understand. ◆*Я прикинулся шлангом, стоял, делал вид, что ничего не понимал.* "So I played dumb — just stood there as if I didn't understand a thing."

ПРИКЛА́ДЫВАТЬ/ПРИЛОЖИ́ТЬ мо́рдой об стол, *idiom, neg.* To deceive, cheat, trick. ◆*Меня приложили мордой об стол, обещали взять на юг и не взяли.* "They tricked me — they promised to take me on vacation with them, and then they didn't do it."

ПРИ́КОВЫЙ, -ая, -ое, *youth, rude.* Bad, trashy, defective. ◆*Надоела эта приковая погода.* "I'm sick of this rotten weather."

ПРИКОЗЛИ́ТЬ, *perf.* To cheat (from козёл, "goat"). ◆*Как ловко нас прикозлили с этой покупкой!* "How cleverly they gypped us on this purchase!"

ПРИКОЗЛИ́ТЬСЯ, *perf.* To make a silly mistake. ◆*Не могу понять, как мы могли так прикозлиться.* "I can't understand how we could have made such a silly mistake!"

ПРИКО́Л, -а, *m.* An anecdote, interesting event (lit., pinch, prick). ◆*Хочешь, расскажу тебе один прикол?* "Do you want me to tell you a funny anecdote?"

ПРИКОЛИ́СТ, -а, *m., youth.* An entertaining person, a person who plays practical jokes or otherwise fools people. ◆*Надо его позвать в гости, он такой приколист.* "Let's invite him over — he's such a joker."

ПРИКО́ЛЬНЫЙ, -ая, -ое. Funny, entertaining. ◆*Это сильно прикольный анекдот.* "That's a really funny anecdote."

ПРИКРЫВА́ТЬ/ПРИКРЫ́ТЬ. To hush something up, get someone off the hook. ◆*Если бы его не прикрыли сверху, он бы сгорел.* "If the higher-ups hadn't hushed it up for him, he would have been in hot water." •**Прикрыва́ть/прикры́ть жо́пу,** *idiom, rude.* To take precautions, cover one's retreat. ◆*Прежде чем это делать, надо бы жопу прикрыть.* "Before we do this we'd better make sure to cover our asses." **Прикрыва́ть/прикры́ть лицо́ поду́шкой,** *idiom, joc.* To have sex with an unattractive woman (lit., to cover her face with a pillow). ◆*Она человек ничего, только лицо надо было прикрывать подушкой.* "She's a nice enough person, but I had to hide her face under the pillow."

ПРИЛИПА́ЛА, -ы, *m. & f., neg.* A persistent, clinging person. ◆*От этого прилипалы так просто не отделаешься.* "Once he attaches himself to you it's not so easy to get rid of him."

ПРИМОЛО́ТЫ, -ов, *pl., youth.* See **прибамба́сы.**

ПРИМО́ЧКА, -и, *f.* A joke, anecdote. ◆*Иди послушай, он такие примочки* *рассказывает.* "Don't miss this — he tells such wonderful anecdotes."

ПРИНАДЛЕ́ЖНОСТИ, -ей, *pl., joc.* Genitals (lit., belongings). ♦*У меня что-то болят принадлежности.* "Something hurts in my private parts."

ПРИНИМА́ТЬ/ПРИНЯ́ТЬ полба́нки, *idiom.* To drink a half-liter bottle. ♦*Мы уже приняли полбанки, на троих надо бы ещё добавить.* "We've already finished the half-liter; we'll need a little more for the three of us."

ПРИНУДИ́ЛОВКА, -и, *f., neg.* A job forced on someone against his will (from принуждать). ♦*Кому охота делать эту принудиловку?* "No one would be willing to be drafted into this job."

ПРИНУДРАБО́ТЫ, принудрабо́т, *pl.* Forced labor, a prison term of hard labor (abbr. of принудительные работы). ♦*Ему дали пять лет принудработ.* "He was sentenced to five years of hard labor."

ПРИПА́ХИВАТЬ/ПРИПАХА́ТЬ, *neg.* **1.** To do heavy labor. ♦*Мы припахивали на уборке снега.* "We slaved away at shoveling the snow." **2.** To force someone to work. ♦*Меня припахали на целый день, я в кино не пойду.* "They've put me to work for the whole day, so I can't go to the movies."

ПРИПА́ШКА, -и, *f., neg.* Heavy labor. ♦*Не дождусь, когда эта припашка кончится?* "I can't wait until we finish this heavy work."

ПРИ́ПИЗДЬ, -и, *f., rude.* A whim, quirk, peculiarity (distorted from придурь; cf. **пизда́**). ♦*Он человек с припиздью.* "He's got a certain quirk."

ПРИПУ́ХШИЙ , -ая, -ое, *youth, neg.* **1.** Selfish, pushy. ♦*Ты совсем припухший, что ли? А то тебя успокоим.* "Don't act so high and mighty or we'll put you in your place." **2.** Crazy. ♦*Ты что припухший, пить столько водки?* "Are you crazy, drinking that much vodka?"

ПРИСОБА́ЧИВАТЬ/ПРИСОБА́ЧИТЬ. To attach, fasten, affix. ♦*Присобачь мне каблук, отвалился.* "Can you fix the heel of my shoe? It's come loose."

ПРИСО́СКА, -и, *f., joc.* A hand (lit., a suction cup). ♦*Не трогай меня своими присосками.* "Don't touch me with your paws."

ПРИСПИ́ЧИВАТЬ/ПРИСПИ́ЧИТЬ, *neg.* To want very intensely (from спичка, "match"). ♦*Что тебе так приспичило туда идти?* "How come you're so fired up about going there?"

ПРИСТАВА́ТЬ/ПРИСТА́ТЬ как репе́й, *idiom.* To pester, bother (lit., to stick to someone like a burr). ♦*Что ты ко мне пристал как репей?* "Why are you keeping after me like that?"

ПРИСТАВУ́НЧИКИ, -ов, *pl.* Endearments, kissing, sexual advances. ♦*Опять приставунчики начинаются, подожди, я устала.* "Can you hold off the nuzzlings for later? I'm tired."

ПРИСТАВУ́ЧИЙ, -ая, -ое, *neg.* Nagging, annoying, irritating. ♦*У тебя муж приставучий, всё время тебя расспрашивает, где ты была, что делала.* "Your husband's an awful nag, always pestering you about where you've been and what you've been doing."

ПРИСТЕБА́Й, -я, *m., euph.* Cf. **разъеба́й.** **1.** A hanger-on, parasite, moocher. ♦*Этот пристебай ничего не делает, а деньги получает.* "That drone doesn't do a stitch of work but he keeps pulling in a salary." **2.** An importunate, intrusive person. ♦*Ты меня достал, пристебай, когда ты наконец уйдёшь?* "I'm sick of you, you pest! When are you going to leave already!"

ПРИСТЁГИВАТЬ/ПРИСТЕГНУ́ТЬ, *army.* To steal (lit., to fasten, latch on to). ♦*Присматривай за оружием, а то его быстро пристегнут.* "Keep an eye on your firearm. Someone will glom onto it as soon as you look the other way."

ПРИСТУ́КИВАТЬ/ПРИСТУ́КНУТЬ, *neg.* To kill (from [c]тук, the sound of a blow). ♦*Он может и пристукнуть, если узнает об этом.* "He's capable of killing someone if he finds out about this."

ПРИСЫ́ПАТЬСЯ, *perf.* To irritate, to pester (lit., to put sand or dust, as on a wound). ♦*Что ты опять присыпался, не хочу о старом говорить, понял?* "I told you I don't want to talk about it. Why are you throwing salt on this old wound of mine?"

ПРИТА́ПЛИВАТЬ/ПРИТОПИ́ТЬ. To speed (lit., to submerge, i.e., to drown the accelerator pedal). ♦*Ну-ка притопи, посмотрим, на что твоя тачка способна.* "Put the pedal to the metal, let's see what this old jalopy can do."

ПРИТВОРЯ́ТЬСЯ/ПРИТВОРИ́ТЬСЯ пря́ником (ча́йником), *idiom, neg.* To pretend to be foolish, play the fool (пряник, a gingerbread cookie; **ча́йник**). ♦*Ты всё понимаешь, не притворяйся пряником.* "You understand perfectly well what's going on, so don't play dumb."

ПРИТОРМА́ЖИВАТЬ/ПРИТОРМО-ЗИ́ТЬ, *students, neg.* To have trouble thinking, to think slowly (lit., to brake). ♦*Ты не притормаживай, эту задачу надо решить сегодня.* "This is no time for sluggish thinking, we've got to solve this problem today!"

ПРИХВА́Т, -а, *m., youth.* A quirk, peculiarity of behavior. ♦*Это у него прихват такой — всех ругать.* "He has this little habit of bawling people out."

ПРИХВАТИЗА́ЦИЯ, -и, *f.* Corrupt exploitation of unstable policies on the privatization of plants, factories, and stores (punning on прихватить, "grab," and приватизация, "privatization"). ♦*Это не приватизация, а прихватизация, все начальники разбогатели.* "This so-called privatization just means that all the bosses are getting rich."

ПРИХВА́ТЫВАТЬ/ПРИХВАТИ́ТЬ. To arrest, apprehend. ♦*Там двоих воришек прихватили.* "They've caught two petty thieves."

ПРИХЕРА́ЧИВАТЬ/ПРИХЕРА́ЧИТЬ, *rude.* 1. To arrive, come. ♦*Вместо пяти человек прихерачило человек двадцать пять.* "Twenty-five people showed up when we were expecting only five." 2. To drag, bring. ♦*Мы еле прихерачили эти ящики, что в них?* "What's in these cartons? We barely managed to

drag them here." 3. To attach, affix. ♦*Прихерачь эту доску к полу.* "Nail this board to the floor."

ПРИХО́Д, -а, *m., pos.* Intoxication, drunkenness. ♦*Ты почувствовал приход?* "Did you get a high?"

ПРИХОДИ́ТЬ/ПРИЙТИ́ ДОМО́Й ПО-ТЁМНОМУ, *idiom, army.* To be killed in action (lit., to come home in the dark, i.e., in a coffin). ♦*Главное, не прийти домой по-чёрному, остальное — чепуха.* "The most important thing is not to come back in a box, the rest is rubbish."

ПРИХУЯ́РИВАТЬ/ПРИХУЯ́РИТЬ, *rude.* Cf. **хуй.** 1. To arrive, come. ♦*Кто их звал, зачем они прихуярили?* "No one invited them — why did they show up?" 2. To hit, beat. ♦*Его вчера ножом прихуярили насмерть.* "They made a deadly attack on him with a knife yesterday." 3. To attach, affix. ♦*Куда эту картину прихуярить?* "Where should I nail up this picture?"

ПРИХУЯ́ЧИВАТЬ/ПРИХУЯ́ЧИТЬ. See **прихуя́ривать.**

ПРИЦЕ́Л, -а, *m., youth, joc.* Eyeglasses (lit., gun-sight). ♦*Протри прицел, все в грязи.* "Wipe your glasses — they're all dirty."

ПРИЦЕ́П, -а, *m., joc.* An additional or supplementary alcoholic drink (lit., trailer). ♦*У нас есть водка с прицепом — ещё бутылка вина.* "We've got vodka and a bottle of wine as a chaser."

ПРИЧА(Е/И)НДА́ЛЫ, -ов, *pl.* 1. Thingamajig. ♦*Таких причандалов к компьютеры я ещё не видел.* "I've never seen such odd computer acessories." 2. Genitals (cf. **принадле́жности**).

ПРИЧАЩА́ТЬСЯ/ПРИЧАСТИ́ТЬСЯ, *joc.* To drink as a supposed remedy for a hangover (lit., to take communion). ♦*Где бы причаститься?* "Where can we get a little eye-opener?"

ПРИЧЁСКА: Причёска «я у ма́мы вме́сто шва́бры», *idiom, joc.* Shaggy, unkempt hair (lit., the "I'm-my-mother's-floor-mop" hairdo). Also **причёска «я**

упа́ла с самосва́ла, тормози́ла голо-
во́й» (the "I-fell-out-of-a-dump-truck-
that-braked-on-my-head" hairdo), and
причёска «не одна́ я в по́ле кувыр-
ка́лась» (the "I-wasn't-alone-when-I-
took-a-roll-in-the-hay" hairdo). ♦*Тебе
пора подстричься, у тебя причёска
«я у мамы вместо швабры».* "You
need to get that shaggy mop cut."

ПРИЧЕСО́Н, -а, *m., youth.* A hairdo. ♦*У
тебя новый причесон, я вижу?* "I see
you've got a new hairdo."

ПРИЧЁСЫВАТЬ/ПРИЧЕСА́ТЬ, *joc.*
To win a decisive victory over someone
(lit., to do someone's hair). ♦*Я думаю,
мы их причешем в футбол.* "I think
we're going to cream them in the soccer
match."

ПРИШИ́ТЬ, *perf. only.* To knife to death,
stab to death (lit., to sew on). ♦*Вчера
друга твоего пришили.* "They knifed
your pal yesterday." •**Приши́ть бо́роду,**
idiom, crim. To deceive, trick (lit., to sew
a beard on someone). ♦*Как мы ему пришили бороду, а он ничего и не понял.*
"We really pulled the wool over his eyes,
and he didn't notice a thing."

ПРИШМАНДО́ВКА, -и, *f., neg., rude.* A
prostitute, whore. ♦*Откуда взялась
эта пришмандовка?* "Where did that
whore come from?"

**ПРИШПАНДО́РИВАТЬ/ПРИШПАН-
ДО́РИТЬ,** *joc.* To attach in a slipshod
way. ♦*Как сюда картину пришпандо-
рить, не пойму?* "I don't see how I'm
going to get the picture hung here."

ПРОБЗДЕ́ТЬСЯ, *perf. only, rude.* To go
for a walk, take an airing (lit., to fart oneself out). ♦*Погода стоит хорошая,
пойдём прибздимся?* "The weather is
fine — let's go out for some air."

ПРОБИВА́ТЬ/ПРОБИ́ТЬ. 1. To acquire
something with difficulty. ♦*Он наконец
пробил себе квартиру.* "He finally managed to get an apartment." **2.** *youth.* To
sell. ♦*Я вчера пробил одного иност-
ранца на лакер.* "Yesterday I sold a lacquer box to a foreigner."

ПРО́БКА, -и, *f., neg.* A fool, idiot (lit., a
cork). ♦*Это пробка, каких поискать!*

"He's a star idiot."

ПРО́БУ НЕ́ГДЕ СТА́ВИТЬ, *idiom, neg.*
Lit., there's no room to put a stamp of
approval; used to mean "she's a promiscuous woman" or "she's a prostitute."
♦*Ты думаешь, она порядочная, да на
ней пробу негде ставить.* "You imagine she's a respectable woman, but in fact
she's a whore."

ПРОВА́ЛИВАТЬ, *imperf. only, neg.* To
leave, get out. ♦*Проваливай, пока не
поздно!* "Get out of here before it's too
late!"

ПРОВЕ́РКА НА ВШИ́ВОСТЬ, *idiom.* A
test, inspectkon (lit., a check for lice).
♦*Сейчас будет тебе проверка на вши-
вость, покажи, как ты умеешь
водить машину.* "Now we're going to
test how well you can drive."

ПРОВЕ́РКА СЛУ́ХА, *idiom.* A tele-
phone-conversation expression meaning
"I have nothing special to say," "I just
called to say hello" (lit., a hearing test).
♦*Что-нибудь случилось? — Да так,
проверка слуха.* "Has something happened? — Nothing at all. I just called to
say hello."

ПРОГИ́Б: Са́льто с проги́бом, see under
са́льто.

ПРОГИБА́ТЬ/ПРОГНУ́ТЬ. To compel,
persuade (lit., to bend). ♦*Он не хочет
праздновать день рождения, надо его
прогнуть.* "He doesn't want to celebrate
his birthday; we'll have to twist his arm."

ПРОГИБА́ТЬСЯ/ПРОГНУ́ТЬСЯ, *neg.*
To confess. ♦*Он в милиции сразу про-
гнулся.* "He confessed immediately at the
police station."

ПРОГЛОТИ́ТЬ АРБУ́З, *idiom.* To
become pregnant (lit., to swallow a
watermelon). ♦*Не прошло и года, она
опять арбуз проглотила.* "She got
pregnant again in less than a year."

ПРОГО́Н, -а, *m., youth, neg.* Lying, tale-
telling, rumor-mongering (cf. **гон**). ♦*Всё
это прогон, а ты поверил.* "That's all a
bunch of lies! How could you have
believed it?"

ПРОГО́НЫ, -ов, *pl., youth.* Thoughts,
ideas. ♦*Мне прогоны о здоровье покоя*

не дают. "I'm constantly thinking about my health."

ПРОГОНЯ́ТЬ/ПРОГНА́ТЬ ПЫЛЬ, *idiom, army.* To dust (lit., to kick out, scatter, or spread around the dust). ♦*Везде прогони пыль в казарме, потом свободен.* "Dust off the barracks, then you can take a break."

ПРОДАВА́ТЬ дро́жжи, *idiom, joc.* To tremble from cold, shiver (lit., to sell yeast; by wordplay on дрожать, "to tremble," and дрожжи, "yeast"). ♦*Не надел свитер, теперь дрожжи продаёшь.* "Why didn't you wear a sweater? No wonder you're shivering."

ПРОДА́ЖА: Выбра́сывать/вы́бросить (в прода́жу), see under **выбра́сывать.**

ПРОДВИ́НУТЫЙ, -ая, -ое, *youth, pos.* Knowledgeable, expert. ♦*Они очень продвинутые в йоге.* "They're real experts in yoga."

ПРО́ДЫХ: Без про́дыху, *idiom, neg.* Without a break, constantly. ♦*Они пьют без продыху уже неделю.* "They've been drinking for a week without any let-up."

ПРОЁБЫВАТЬ/ПРОЕБА́ТЬ, *rude.* Cf. **ёб-. 1.** To satisfy sexually. ♦*Он её никак проебать не может.* "He can't satisfy her at all." **2.** To scold, yell at. ♦*Ну что, тебя проебали за пьянку?* "Well, did they bawl you out for getting drunk?"

ПРОЕ́СТЬ ПЛЕШЬ кому́-л., *neg.* To weary, bore, wear out (lit., to gnaw through someone's bald spot). ♦*Ты своими капризами мне всю плешь проел.* "You've totally exasperated me with your constant whims."

ПРОЕ́ХАТЬ, *perf. only, joc.* To miss the point, fail to catch the gist (lit., to miss one's stop). ♦*О чём вы тут говорили? — Проехал.* "What were you saying? — You missed it, so forget it; we're not going to repeat it."

ПРОЕ́ХАТЬСЯ на ша́ру, *neg.* To get away with not paying. ♦*Ты любишь проехаться на шару, давай деньги на билет.* "Pay me for the ticket — I'm not going to let you freeload."

ПРОЖЕКТОРА́, -о́в, *pl., youth, joc.* Eyes (lit., searchlights). ♦*Отверни прожектора, не видел голых баб, что ли?* "What are you staring at? Haven't you ever seen a naked woman?"

ПРОЗЮЗЮ́КИВАТЬ/ПРОЗЮЗЮ́-КАТЬ. To miss, to fail to notice. ♦*Я прозюзюкал прогноз погоды.* "I missed the weather forecast."

ПРО́ЙДА, -ы, *m. & f., neg.* A clever, pushy, active person. ♦*Этот пройда всё может достать.* "That clever rascal can manage to get his hands on anything he wants."

ПРОКА́ЛЫВАТЬСЯ/ПРОКОЛО́ТЬ-СЯ. To make a mistake, do something improper. ♦*Он прокололся на работе, пришёл пьяным.* "He made a bad move at work, coming in drunk like that."

ПРОКА́ТЫВАТЬ¹/ПРОКАТА́ТЬ. To talk over, think over (lit., to roll). ♦*Эту мысль прокатать надо, а затем уже действовать.* "This is a matter that has to be mulled over before taking any action."

ПРОКА́ТЫВАТЬ²/ПРОКАТИ́ТЬ, *neg.* To deceive, trick, cheat. ♦*Меня вчера прокатили на сто долларов.* "I was cheated out of a hundred dollars yesterday."

ПРОКА́ЧИВАТЬ/ПРОКАЧА́ТЬ. To check out, scrutinize (lit., to pump). ♦*Ты не знаешь, как он попал в правительство, надо бы его биографию прокачать.* "Do you know how he got into the government? It would be a good idea to look into his biography."

ПРОКИ́ДЫВАТЬ/ПРОКИ́НУТЬ. 1. To accomplish something successfully. ♦*Хорошо мы это дело прокинули.* "We brought that off very well." **2.** To mention in an offhand way. ♦*Прокинь ему эту новость, посмотрим, как он среагирует.* "Mention the news to him so we can see his reaction."

ПРОКИСА́ТЬ/ПРОКИ́СНУТЬ, *youth, neg.* To go bad, turn out badly, go wrong (from киснуть, "to sour"). ♦*Чувствую, мои деньги прокисли, не отдаст он долг.* "I have the feeling that my money has gone down the drain — he's not going to return what he borrowed."

ПРОКО́Л, -а, *m.* A mistake (lit., a puncture). ♦*У них на работе прокол за проколом.* "Their work is just one fiasco after another."

ПРОКУ́ШЕННЫЙ ГОНДО́Н, *idiom, neg.* See **Гондо́н што́паный.**

ПРОЛЁТ, -а, *m.* Bad luck (cf. **пролета́ть ми́мо ка́ссы**). ♦*У меня целый день одни пролёты.* "I've been having bad luck all day today."

ПРОЛЕТА́ТЬ/ПРОЛЕТЕ́ТЬ как фане́ра над Пари́жем, *idiom, joc.* To fail, lose, come to nothing (lit., to fly like plywood over Paris). ♦*Ты успел купить мебель по старым ценам? — Нет, пролетел как фанера над Парижем.* "Did you manage to buy the furniture before the prices went up? — No, I completely missed my chance." **Пролета́ть/ пролете́ть ми́мо ка́ссы,** *idiom.* To miss out, lose out (lit., to fly past the cashier). ♦*Я опять пролетел мимо кассы, не смог выиграть в лотерею.* "I missed the boat again on that lottery."

ПРОМОКА́ШКА, -и, *f., school.* A bookish girl, bookworm (lit., blotting paper). ♦*Не будь такой промокашкой, хватит сидеть за книгами.* "Don't be such a bookworm! You've spent enough time at your books."

ПРОМОТА́ТЬ, *perf. only, joc.* To promote (by wordplay on Eng. "promote" and Russian промотать, "to spend"). ♦*Когда я был в Франции, они меня хорошо промотали, я продал все картины.* "When I was in France my work was so vigorously promoted that I sold all my paintings."

ПРОНИКА́ТЬСЯ/ПРОНИ́КНУТЬСЯ. To feel attracted (lit., to be penetrated). ♦*Я к ним проникся, хорошие ребята.* "I like them, they're good guys."

ПРО́НЬКИНЫ: Не у Про́нькиных, see under **не.**

ПРОПЕРДЕ́ТЬСЯ, *perf. only, rude.* To go on an outing, get some fresh air (cf. **про-бзде́ться**). ♦*Надо бы на рыбалку съездить, пропердеться.* "Let's go on a fishing trip to get some fresh air."

ПРОПЕРДО́Н: Устра́ивать/устро́ить пропердо́н, see under **устра́ивать.**

ПРОПИЗДО́Н, -а, *m., rude.* Scolding, tongue-lashing (cf. **пизда́**). ♦*У меня уже был сегодня пропиздон, хватит.* "Enough! I've already been bawled out once today."

ПРОРЕ́ЗЫВАТЬСЯ/ПРОРЕ́ЗАТЬСЯ. To show up, appear (lit., to cut through, come through, as teeth). ♦*Наконец-то ты прорезался, ты где пропадал?* "So you finally showed up. Where have you been?"

ПРОРЫ́В НА ХА́ВКУ, *idiom, youth.* Intense hunger. ♦*У меня прорыв на хавку, пойдём в ресторан.* "I'm starving! Let's go to a restaurant."

ПРОСЕ́КАТЬ/ПРОСЕ́ЧЬ. Lit., to cut through. **1.** To guess, figure out. ♦*Он просёк, что мы о нём говорили.* "He guessed what we were saying about him." **2.** To know. ♦*Он математику неплохо просекает.* "He knows mathematics pretty well."

ПРОСИРА́ТЬСЯ/ПРОСРА́ТЬСЯ, *rude.* To defecate, empty one's bowels. ♦*С утра не могу просраться.* "I haven't had a good shit all day." ●**Дава́ть/дать кому́-л. просра́ться,** see under **дава́ть.**

ПРОСТЯ́ЧКА, -и, *f., crim.* A prostitute (by wordplay on простой, "simple," and проститутка, "prostitute"). ♦*Если хочешь переспать с ней, то всегда пожалуйста. Она простячка.* "You can sleep with her whenever you want — she's a prostitute."

ПРОСЫХА́ТЬ/ПРОСО́ХНУТЬ, *neg.* To sober up (lit., to dry out). ♦*Ты ещё не просох?* "Haven't you sobered up yet?"

ПРО́ТИВ ЛО́МА НЕТ ПРИЁМА, *rhyming phrase, joc.* Whoever is stronger or better armed wins; you can't fight city hall. ♦*Наши боксёры проиграли Кубе, против лома нет приёма.* "Our boxers lost to the Cubans, of course. What do you expect? Their guys are simply better trained." **Про́тив ло́ма нет приёма, окромя́ друго́го ло́ма,** *idiom.* In order to win against a superior enemy, one has to take a leaf from the enemy's book; one has to use the opposition's methods in order to win (lit., against a jackhammer there's no resource except another jackhammer).

ПРОТОКÓЛЬНАЯ РÓЖА, *idiom, neg.* A disapproving facial expression. ♦ *Не делай протокольную рожу.* "Don't look so disapproving."

ПРОТУХÁТЬ/ПРОТÝХНУТЬ, *neg.* (Lit., to rot). **1.** To be embarrassed, to feel uneasy. ♦ *Что ты протух, шуток не понимаешь?* "Why are you so freaked out? Can't you see it was just a joke?" **2.** To be bored. ♦ *Мы уже протухли, тебя ждём целый день.* "We got bored waiting for you all day." **3.** To be broken, to be out of order. ♦ *Телевизор ещё вчера протух.* "The TV went on the fritz yesterday."

ПРОФÝКИВАТЬ/ПРОФÝКАТЬ. To lose sight of, miss (from фук, to "huff" in the game of checkers, i.e., to remove an opponent's piece from the board as a forfeit for neglecting to capture an opposing piece). ♦ *Как же это вы такую партию наркоты профукали?* "How could miss such a big drug shipment? You really blew it this time."

ПРОФÝРА, -ы, *m. & f., neg.* **1.** A clever, self-promoting person. ♦ *Что ты о ней заботишься, эта профура не пропадёт.* "Why are you worrying about her? She knows how to look after herself." **2.** A promiscuous woman. ♦ *Эта профура спит с каждым встречным.* "That floozy will sleep with anyone she picks up."

ПРОХЛÓПАТЬ, *perf. only, neg.* To overlook, fail to notice. ♦ *Как ты мог его прохлопать?* "How could you have missed him?"

ПРОХОДИ́ТЬ/ПРОЙТИ́. To be considered, regarded as. ♦ *Он у нас проходит грамотным инженером.* "Among us he's considered a competent engineer." •**Проходи́ть/пройти́ за сухаря́,** *crim.* To be imprisoned for someone else's crime. ♦ *За что сидишь? — Я прохожу за сухаря.* "What are you serving time for? — I'm in for someone else's crime."

ПРОЧЁСКА, -и, *f., army.* See **зачи́стка.**

ПРОЧУХÁНКА, -и, *f., joc.* A tonguelashing, scolding (lit., scratching). ♦ *Нас ждёт хорошая прочуханка.* "We're in for a severe scolding." •**Дава́ть/дать прочуха́нку,** see under **дава́ть.**

ПРОЧÝХИВАТЬСЯ/ПРОЧÝХАТЬСЯ, *rude.* To sober up, to recover from drunkenness or a hangover. ♦ *Ты начал соображать, прочухался?* "You're starting to talk sense — sobered up, have you?"

ПРОШВЫРНÝТЬСЯ, *perf. only, joc.* To take a walk. ♦ *Давай прошвырнёмся по свежему воздуху.* "Let's go for a walk in the fresh air."

ПРОШЛÁ ЛЮБÓВЬ, ЗАВЯ́ЛИ ПОМИДÓРЫ, *idiom, joc.* The love affair is over (lit., love is gone, the tomatoes have faded).

ПРОШЛЯ́ПИТЬ, *perf.* To be late for, to miss. ♦ *Прошляпил повышение, теперь сиди!* "You've missed your chance for promotion, now you'll have to stay where you are."

ПРОЩÁЙ-МОЛОДОСТЬ!, *idiom, joc.* Unfashionable footwear, thick shoes or boots (lit., "Farewell, youth!"). ♦ *Купила себе прощай-молодость, больше ничего в магазинах нет.* "I bought myself some old ladies' shoes — it was the only kind they had in the stores."

ПРУДÓНИТЬ/НАПРУДÓНИТЬ. To urinate (from пруд, "pond"). ♦ *Осторожно, здесь кот напрудонил.* "Look out, the cat peed on the floor!"

ПРЯМ, *idiom.* No, nothing doing. ♦ *Ты хочешь с ним помириться? — Прям!* "Are you willing to forgive him?" — "Never!"

ПСИХ, -а, *m., neg.* An idiot, lunatic. ♦ *Ты будешь последним психом, если сделаешь это.* "You'd be crazy to do that." •**Псих на во́ле ху́же динами́та,** *idiom, neg.* Lit., "an insane person at liberty is worse than dynamite." ♦ *Значит, он сжёг свою рукопись? Псих на воле хуже динамита.* "So he actually burned his manuscript? Give a lunatic some rope and he'll hang himself."

ПСИХ-САМОВЗВÓД, -а, *m.* A nervous, bad-tempered person (lit., "psycho-cross-blow"). ♦*Как ты с этим пихом-самовзводом ладишь, он же на людей кидается.* "How can you be on friendly terms with this psycho? He's on a hair-trigger, could go off any minute."

ПСИ́ХИКА: Дави́ть на пси́хику, see under **дави́ть.**

ПСИХО́ВАННЫЙ, -ая, -ое, *neg.* Irritable, nervous. ♦*Ты что такой психо-ванный сегодня?* "Why are you so nervous today?"

ПСИХУ́ШКА, -и, *f.* A mental hospital. ♦*Он попал в психушку, нервный срыв.* "He had a nervous breakdown and landed in the bughouse."

ПУ́БЛИКА, -и, *f., business.* Nonprofessional dealers or brokers at the exchange. ♦*Публика нам не конкурент, там мелкая рыбёшка.* "We won't have any competition from the public — they're just small fry."

ПУ́ДРИТЬ/ЗАПУ́ДРИТЬ мозги́, *idiom, neg.* Lit., to powder someone's brains. **1.** To bore. ♦*Он надоел всем, пудрил мозги рассказами об Африке.* "He bored everyone with his stories about Africa." **2.** To deceive. ♦*Ты мне мозги не пудри, говори сразу, в чём дело.* "Don't try to deceive me. Just tell me straight out what's the matter."

ПУЗА́НЧИК, -а, *m., joc.* A person with a big belly (from пузо, "paunch"). ♦*Ты знаешь этого пузанчика?* "Do you know that guy with the beer belly?"

ПУ́ЗО: От пу́за, *idiom.* One's fill, as much as one wants. ♦*Вчера ездили помогать убирать виноград, наелись от пуза.* "Yesterday we went to help with the grape harvest, so of course we ate grapes to our heart's content."

ПУЗЫ́РЬ, -я́, *m., joc.* A bottle of liquor (lit., a bubble). ♦*Ты купил пузырь на вечер?* "Did you buy a bottle for the party?" ●**Пуска́ть пузыри́,** see under **пуска́ть.**

ПУ́КАЛКА, -и, *f., army.* A revolver, gun (lit., a farter). ♦*С этой пукалкой в атаке делать нечего, бери автомат.* "This little pop-gun is useless in an assault, take a machine gun with you."

ПУЛЕМЁТ, -а, *m., crim.* Playing cards, a deck of cards (lit., a machine gun). ♦*У кого пулемёт есть? Сыграем?* "Who's got a deck? Let's have a game."

ПУ́ЛЯ: Банди́тская пу́ля доста́ла, see under **банди́тская.**

ПУЛЯ́ТЬ/ЗАПУЛЯ́ТЬ. To throw (from пуля, "bullet"). ♦*Кончай пулять снежки в окна!* "Stop throwing snowballs at the windows!"

ПУ́НКЕР, -а, *m., youth.* Punk (from Eng. "punk"). ♦*Мне эти пункера не нравятся.* "I don't like those punks."

ПУП: Надрыва́ть/надорва́ть пуп, see under **надрыва́ть.**

ПУПЕ́ТЬ/ОПУПЕ́ТЬ, *neg.* **1.** To become exhausted by something. ♦*Я от этой работы совсем опупел.* "I'm completely knocked out by this job." **2.** To go crazy, do something bizarre. ♦*Ты что, опупел, даёшь ребёнку вино?* "Have you gone crazy, giving wine to the baby?"

ПУПО́К, -пка́, *m., army.* A soldier in his first months of service (lit., a navel). See **запупы́рь.** "Hey, 'bellybutton,' come over here and shine my boots!"

ПУПО́К РАЗВЯ́ЖЕТСЯ, *idiom, joc.* To get a hernia (lit., to get one's navel torn). ♦*Ты донесёшь этот чемодан, пупок не развяжется?* "Can you carry that suitcase without getting a hernia?"

ПУРШИ́ТЬ/ЗАПУРШИ́ТЬ. To complain, whine (from пурхать, *dated,* to fiddle with, to get soiled). ♦*Только сразу договоримся, ты не будешь пуршить о здоровье.* "Let's make a deal, you won't complain about your health."

ПУСКА́ТЬ/ПУСТИ́ТЬ: Пуска́ть/пусти́ть нале́во, *idiom, crim.* To shoot (lit., to let someone go to the left). ♦*Вчера ещё двоих пустили налево.* "Yesterday they shot two more guys." **Пуска́ть/пусти́ть пузыри́,** *idiom, neg.* To complain, whine (lit., to emit bubbles). ♦*Слишком ты любишь пускать пузыри.* "Don't be such a complainer." **Пуска́ть/пусти́ть шептуна́,** *idiom, neg.* To fart (lit., to let out a whisper). ♦*Опять кто-то пускает шептуна.* "Someone's farting again."

ПУСТЬ РАБОТАЕТ ТРАКТОР — ОН ЖЕЛЕЗНЫЙ, *idiom, joc.* Lit., "Let the tractor do it — it's iron" (and therefore doesn't get tired); used to express unwillingness to do some job. ♦*Давай работать, хватит курить. — Пусть работает трактор — он железный.* "You've had your smoke, now get to work. — Let the tractor do it. It's iron."

ПУТА́НА, -ы, *f.* A hard-currency prostitute (from Italian "puttana"). ♦*Путан в барах развелось.* "The number of hard-currency prostitutes in the bars has increased."

ПУТА́НИТЬ, *imperf., youth.* To engage in prostitution. ♦*Она путанит с 12-ти лет.* "She's been a hooker since she was 12."

ПУ́ТАНКА, -и, *f., army.* Uncoiled barbed wire or razor wire, deployed as an antipersonnel barrier (from путать, to tangle).

ПУЧЕГЛА́ЗЕЦ, пучегла́зца, *m., joc.* A Jew (from пучеглазый, "goggle-eyed"). ♦*Все они там возле Ельцына — пучеглазцы.* "That whole crew of Yeltsin's is a bunch of Jews."

ПУ́ШКА, -и, *f., joc.* A pistol (lit., cannon). ♦*Брось пушку, тебе говорят.* "Throw away the gun, do you hear?"

ПУ́ШКИН, -а, *m., joc.* Someone or other; I don't know who. ♦*И кто испортил ковёр? — Пушкин.* "Who made this stain on the carpet? — Pushkin."

ПУШНИ́НА, -ы, *f.* Money (lit., furs). ♦*Как у нас с пушниной?* "How are we fixed for money?"

ПЧЕЛА́, -ы́, *f., youth.* A girl (lit., a bee). ♦*Чего эта пчела к нам липнет?* "Why is that chick hanging around with us?"

ПШЕНИ́ЦА, -и, *f.* Vodka made from wheat (lit., wheat). ♦*Это пшеница или из картошки?* "Is this wheat vodka, or is it made from potatoes?"

ПШИК, -а, *m.* Nothing, no result. ♦*Из всей затеи получился пшик.* "Nothing came of that scheme." •*Один пшик, idiom.* Useless, pointless. ♦*Всё это — один пшик.* "That's all futile."

ПЫЛИ́ТЬ¹/ЗАПЫЛИ́ТЬ, *neg.* To talk nonsense, babble. ♦*Помолчи, не пыли!* "Shut up! Stop babbling!"

ПЫЛИ́ТЬ²/ПОПЫЛИ́ТЬ, *joc.* To go, leave, walk (lit., to make dusty). ♦*Пыли отсюда!* "Get out of here!"

ПЫ́ХАТЬ/ПЫ́ХНУТЬ дрянь, *idiom, youth.* To smoke drugs (lit., to puff junk). ♦*Давай пыхнем дрянь, не против?* "Come on, let's smoke some dope."

ПЫХТЕ́ЛКА, -и, *f., joc.* A scold, an abusive woman. ♦*Не слушай ты эту старую пыхтелку.* "Don't listen to that old scold."

ПЬЯ́НКА, -и, *f.* A drinking party, drinking bout. ♦*У нас на прошлой неделе была пьянка за пьянкой, некогда работать.* "Last week was just one drinking bout after another; there was no time to get any work done." •*Раз пошла така́я пья́нка, режь после́дний огуре́ц,* see under **раз.**

ПЬЯ́НСТВОВАТЬ во́дку, *idiom, joc.* To drink vodka, be or get drunk on vodka. ♦*Вы ещё долго будете сегодня водку пьянствовать?* "How long are you guys going to go on drinking vodka today?"

ПЬЯ́НЫЙ: Пья́ный в дугу́, *idiom, neg.* Extremely drunk (bent-over drunk; lit., so as to take on the shape of an arch). ♦*Он на работу не пойдёт, лежит пьяный в дугу.* "He's not going to work today; he's bent-over drunk." **Пья́ный в си́ську,** *idiom.* Extremely drunk (lit., drunk to a nipple). ♦*Он опять пьяный в сиську, не волокёт совсем.* "He's drunk completely out of his mind again." **Пья́ный в соси́ску,** *idiom, neg.* Extremely drunk (lit., drunk as a hot dog, i.e. flaccid, floppy). ♦*Он пьяный в сосиску, слова выговорить не может.* "He's dead drunk — he can't even speak intelligibly." **Пья́ный в сте́льку,** *idiom, neg.* Very drunk (lit., drunk to one's insoles). ♦*Вчера он опять пришёл на работу пьяным в стельку.* "Yesterday he came to work dead drunk again." **В ду́пель пья́ный,** *idiom, neg.* Very drunk. ♦*Смотри, там твой сын пошёл в дупель пьяный.* "Look, there goes your son, roaring drunk." **Пья́ный ёжик,**

пья́ного ёжика, *idiom, youth, joc.* Lit., a drunken hedgehog. **1.** A young person acting provocative or disorderly, possibly under the influence of alcohol. ♦*О чём там спорит этот пьяный ёжик?* "What's that drunken hedgehog making a row about over there?" **2.** A punk hairdo. ♦*Когда это ты стал носить "пьяного ёжика"?* "When did you start wearing that drunken hedgehog?" **Пья́ный как грязь,** *idiom, neg.* Stuporously drunk. ♦*Вон там шофёр наш пьяный как грязь лежит.* "There's our driver — out cold in a drunken stupor."

ПЬЯНЬ: По пьяни́, *idiom.* While drunk, because of drunkenness. ♦*Я его ударил по пьяни, а так мы друзья.* "I hit him when I was under the influence, but we're actually friends."

ПЭ́РЭНТ, -а, *m., youth.* A parent (from Eng. "parent"). ♦*Пэрэнты дома?* "Are your parents at home?"

ПЯ́ЛИТЬСЯ/ВЫ́ПЯЛИТЬСЯ. To stare.

♦*Чего пялишься, пьяных не видел?* "What are you gaping at? Never seen a drunk before?"

ПЯТА́К, -а́, *m.* A snub nose (from пятак, "snout"). ♦*Носа у него совсем нет, так, пятак только.* "He's got no nose at all, just a button."

ПЯ́ТАЯ ТО́ЧКА, *idiom, joc.* Buttocks (lit., fifth point). ♦*Он приземлился на пятую точку.* "He landed on his behind."

ПЯ́ТИФОН, -а, *youth.* Five rubles, a five-ruble coin.

ПЯ́ТКА, -и, *f., youth.* A butt, the end of a marijuana cigarette. ♦*Дай пятку докурить.* "Let me smoke that roach."

ПЯТНА́ДЦАТЬ КА́ПЕЛЬ НА ДИА-ФРА́ГМУ, *idiom.* A glass of vodka (lit., fifteen drops on one's diaphragm).

ПЯТНА́ШКА, -и. 1. Fifteen kopecks. **2.** Fifteen rubles.

ПЯТЬ: Держа́ть пять, see **держа́ть петуха́** under **держа́ть.**

РАБО́ТА, -ы, *f., crim.* An apartment, viewed as a target for robbery (lit., a job). ♦*Там работа без хозяев стоит уже неделю.* "The owners have been away from that job for a week already." •**Рабо́та не пы́льная,** *idiom, joc.* Easy work, an easy job. ♦*Переходи к нам, у нас работа не пыльная.* "Why don't you come work with us? We've got an easy job." •**Рабо́та от борта́,** *idiom.* Unauthorized work-carrying passengers for pay. ♦*Вообще-то он преподаёт, но его кормит работа от борта.* "He's actually a teacher, but he makes his living as a cabbie on the side." **Вы́вернуть рабо́ту,** see under **вы́вернуть. Ле́вая рабо́та,** see under **ле́вый.**

РАБО́ТАТЬ/СРАБО́ТАТЬ под кого́-л., *idiom.* To impersonate, act as. ♦*Он работает под крутого парня, но он слабый человек.* "He acts like a tough guy, but actually he's quite a weak person." **Рабо́тать на изно́с,** *idiom.* To work hard (cf. изнашивать, "to wear out"). ♦*Мы здесь работаем на износ, а ты прохлаждаешься.* "We're slaving away here while you're cool as a cucumber."

РАБОТЯ́ГА, -и, *m.* **1.** A worker. ♦*Он кто, инженер или работяга?* "Is he an engineer or a worker?" **2.** An industrious, productive person. ♦*Этот учёный — большой работяга.* "That scholar is very productive."

РАДА́РЫ, -ов, *pl.* Eyes (lit., radars). ♦*Радары наведи на резкость, что там на хребте, есть движение?* "Focus your eyes on that ridge, do you see any movement there?"

РАЗ: На раз, *idiom.* Easily or quickly disposed of. ♦*Ему эту задачу решить — на раз.* "For him it's as easy as pie to solve that problem."

РАЗ ПЛЮ́НУТЬ, *idiom.* Easily, without difficulty (lit., [as easy as] spitting once). ♦*Тебе же раз плюнуть, убрать квартиру.* "It's easy as pie for you to clean up the apartment."

РАЗ ПОШЛА́ ТАКА́Я ПЬЯ́НКА,

РЕЖЬ ПОСЛЕ́ДНИЙ ОГУРЕ́Ц, *idiom, joc.* An expression of grandiose hospitality or liberality (lit., "for a drinking party like this, one shouldn't hesitate to slice the last cucumber"). ♦*Вот ещё бутылка с меня, раз пошла такая пьянка. . . .* "This one's on me! For a drinking-party like this. . . ."

РАЗБЕЖА́ТЬСЯ, *perf. only.* To dream of, expect, wish for (in vain). ♦*Я разбежался, думал купить такое пальто, а их все успели продать.* "I was dreaming of buying one of those dresses, but they were sold out." •**Не разбежи́шься,** see under **не.**

РАЗБИВА́ТЬ/РАЗБИ́ТЬ. 1. To make change, change money. ♦*Разбей штуку.* "Give me change for a thousand rubles." **2.** To persuade, win over. ♦*Разбей его на поездку в лес.* "Persuade him to come to the forest with us."

РАЗБИРА́ТЬСЯ/РАЗОБРА́ТЬСЯ, *neg.* To quarrel, fight, have it out with someone. ♦*Слышишь крики? Это наши разбираются с солдатами.* "Do you hear those shouts? That's our guys having it out with the soldiers."

РАЗБО́ЙНИК: Полово́й разбо́йник, see under **полово́й.**

РАЗБО́Р ПОЛЁТА (ПОЛЁТОВ), *idiom, joc.* An analysis, inquest, post-mortem (lit., an inquiry into flights, with reference to airplane crashes). ♦*После падения рубля у президента был разбор полётов.* "There was a presidential inquest after the fall of the ruble."

РАЗБО́РКА, -и, *f., neg.* A quarrel, fight. ♦*Мне надоели ваши бесконечные разборки.* "I'm sick of your constant quarreling."

РАЗВЕДЁНКА, -и, *f.* A divorced woman. ♦*У неё мужа нет, она разведёнка.* "She has no husband — she's divorced."

РАЗВОДИ́ТЬ/РАЗВЕСТИ́: Разводи́ть/ развести́ (устра́ивать/устро́ить) барда́к, *idiom, neg.* To mess up, put into disorder. ♦*Хватит танцев, развели здесь бардак.* "Enough dancing — you've

made a mess here." **Разводи́ть/раз-
вести́ бодя́гу,** *idiom, neg.* To talk nonsense, talk without results. ♦*Вы, как
всегда, развели бодягу, а решить
проблему надо побыстрее.* "You were
just babbling on as usual, but this is a
problem that has to be solved decisively."
Разводи́ть/развести́ моро́ку, *idiom,
neg.* To fuss, bustle around pointlessly.
♦*Вокруг простого дела развели моро-
ку.* "They made a mountain out of a
molehill." **Разводи́ть/развести́ на
ба́бки,** *idiom.* To cheat (from разводить,
to regulate, and бабки, money). **Раз-
води́ть/развести́ официо́з,** *idiom, neg.*
To do something in an official, ceremonial, or formal way (cf. **официо́з**). ♦*Не
надо разводить официоз, когда приедет министр, так он хочет.* "There's
no call to make a state occasion of it when
the minister comes; he himself prefers to
keep it informal." •**Разводи́ть/развести́
пиздёж,** *idiom, rude.* To chatter, kid
around. ♦*О делах не говорили, развели
обычный пиздёж о ценах, о политике.*
"They didn't talk business; they just chat-
tered as usual about prices and politics."
Разводи́ть/ развести́ сы́рость, *idiom,
neg., joc.* To weep, cry. ♦*Не разводи
сырость, и так тошно.* "Don't turn on
the waterworks! Things are bad enough
without that." **Разводи́ть/развести́
ти́ти-ми́ти,** *idiom, joc.* To be amorous,
sentimental. ♦*Кончай разводить
тити-мити, ближе к делу.* "Enough
with the lovey-dovey stuff. Let's get
down to business." **Же́нщина разво́дит
нога́ми, а мужчи́на рука́ми,** see under
же́нщина.

РАЗВО́ДКА, -и, *f.* A fraud, swindle (from
разводить, "to dilute"). ♦*Они на
разводку не клюнули — серьёзные
люди.* "They never even took the bait;
they're no fools."

РАЗГИЛЬДЯ́Й, -я, *m., neg.* An irresponsible, unreliable person. ♦*На этого раз-
гильдяя ни в чём нельзя положиться.*
"You can't count on that erratic fellow
for anything."

РАЗГО́Н, -а, *m.* A drinking bout (lit., a
taking-off or speeding-up). ♦*Он опять в*

разгоне. "He's on another drinking
bout." •**Для разго́ну,** *idiom, joc.* For
starters, as a beginning (usu. in connection with drinking). ♦*Выпьем по
рюмочке для разгону.* "Let's have a little glass for starters."

**РАЗДАВИ́ТЬ буты́лку (ба́нку, ба́ноч-
ку),** *idiom.* To drink a bottle of liquor
together, divvy up a bottle (lit., to crush a
bottle). ♦*Пойдём раздавим баночку
пополам.* "Let's go split a bottle between
us."

РАЗДА́ЧА СЛОНО́В, *idiom, joc.* A distribution of bonuses, awards (lit., distribution of elephants, with ironic allusion to
the disappointing smallness of the much-
touted bonuses). ♦*Завтра будет раз-
дача слонов, премии всем дадут.*
"There's going to be a distribution of elephants tomorrow — everyone will get a
bonus."

РАЗДЕВА́ТЬ/РАЗДЕ́ТЬ. To win, beat at
cards (lit., to strip). ♦*Ты с ними в пре-
феранс не играй, они профессионалы
— разденут.* "Don't get into a game
with them. They're professionals —
they'll fleece you." •**Раздева́ть/разде́ть
маши́ну,** *idiom.* To dismantle, strip a car
for parts. ♦*Вчера на стоянке раздели
соседскую машину, сняли колеса.*
"Yesterday they stripped my neighbor's
car right in the parking lot — they took
his tires."

РАЗДО́ЛБ, -а, *m.* Ass chewing, counsel-
ing. See **втык.**

РАЗДОЛБА́Й, -я, *m., rude.* A bungler,
confused person. ♦*Этот раздолбай всё
перепутал, приехал на час позже.*
"That blunderhead got everything mixed
up and came an hour late."

РАЗДО́ЛБАННЫЙ, -ая, -ое. Worn-out,
broken-down (from долбать, "to strike").
♦*Мой раздолбанный пылесос отка-
зывается работать.* "This decrepit
vacuum cleaner of mine simply refuses to
work."

**РАЗЕВА́ТЬ/РАЗИ́НУТЬ, РАЗЯ́ВИТЬ
ва́режку,** *idiom.* **1.** To speak out of turn
or inappropriately. ♦*Тебя не спрашивают, варежку не разевай.* "No one's
asking your opinion, so don't go shooting

off your mouth." **2.** To gape in amazement. ♦*Мы все разинули варежки, когда увидели его новую машину.* "We all dropped our jaws when we saw his new car." **Разева́ть/рази́нуть пасть,** *idiom.* To long for, set one's heart on, covet. ♦*Она было разинула пасть на сапоги, но цена не по карману.* "She had her heart set on those boots, but they were too expensive." **Разе́вать/рази́нуть рот,** *idiom.* Lit., to open one's mouth wide. **1.** To talk. ♦*Когда не спрашивают, рот не разевай.* "Don't talk when you're not asked." **2.** To envy, begrudge. ♦*На чужое добро рот не разевай.* "Don't be envious of other people's good fortune." **3.** To be distracted, be oblivious. ♦*Будь внимательнее, а то рот разинешь — у тебя всё и стащат.* "Be more careful or you'll be robbed while you're not looking." **4.** To be amazed. ♦*Он как открыл сумку, мы рты так и разинули, — чего там только не было.* "When he opened the bag our jaws dropped at all the stuff in it."

РАЗЗЯ́ВИТЬ гло́тку, *idiom, neg.* To shout, scream (lit., to open one's throat wide). ♦*Что ты глотку раззявил, и так слышно.* "There's no need to shout. I can hear you just fine."

РАЗЛИ́В: Ме́стный разли́в, see under **ме́стный.**

РАЗЛИВА́ТЬ/РАЗЛИ́ТЬ по бу́лькам, *idiom.* To pour (liquor) in proper quantities by the sound of the bottle (lit., by the "glug-glugs"). ♦*Разливай по булькам, у всех разные стаканы.* "You'd better pour by sound, since we've all got different-shaped glasses."

РАЗМАЗНЯ́, -и, *f., neg.* A nobody (from каша-размазня, a type of gruel). ♦*Все друзья у тебя начальники, а ты, размазня, никто.* "All your friends have high posts, and you're such a loser."

РАЗМА́ЗЫВАТЬ/РАЗМА́ЗАТЬ, *neg.* To destroy, do in, kill (lit., to spread, smear). ♦*Его вчера на дирекции взяли и размазали, обвинили во взятках.* "They destroyed him at the meeting yesterday by accusing him of taking bribes."

•**Разма́зывать со́пли по забо́ру,** *idiom,*

neg. To break down in tears, to sob (lit., to smear snot along the fence; cf. **сопля́**). ♦*Все умеют сейчас размазывать сопли по забору, а что делать – никто не знает.* "Everyone can weep and moan about it, but no one knows what to do."

РАЗМОРДЕ́ТЬ, *perf. only, neg.* To gain a lot of weight, become fat (cf. **мо́рда**). ♦*Когда это она успела так размордеть?* "When did she put on all that weight?"

РА́ЗНИЦА: Без ра́зницы, *idiom.* Unimportant, indifferent, all the same. ♦*Мне без разницы, где работать.* "It doesn't matter to me where I work."

РАЗНЮ́НИТЬСЯ, *perf. only, neg.* To burst into tears (cf. **ню́ни**). ♦*Ну что ты разнюнился, не больно ведь совсем.* "What's with the tears? You're not hurt at all!"

РАЗ-РА́З И В ДА́МКИ, *idiom, neg.* Lit., "one-two and you're kinged," referring to the kinging of pieces in checkers. Used in disparagement of attempts at overhasty successes. ♦*Ты хотел быстро разбогатеть, раз-раз и в дамки, так не бывает.* "You'd like to get rich quick — one-two and you're kinged — but it doesn't happen that way."

РАЗ-РА́З И НА МАТРА́Ц, *idiom, joc.* Said of quick, decisive actions (lit., one-two and into bed). ♦*Я с этим делом возиться не буду, раз-раз и на матрац.* "I'm not going to waste time fussing over this business, just wham-bam-thank-you-ma'am."

РАЗРЯЖА́ТЬСЯ/РАЗРЯДИ́ТЬСЯ. To relax (lit., to unload, as a gun). ♦*Давай съездим в лес за грибами, надо разрядиться.* "Let's go mushroom hunting in the woods for a little relaxation."

РАЗУ́Й ГЛАЗА́, *idiom, rude.* Look where you're going, pay attention (lit., unshoe your eyes) ♦*Разуй глаза, чуть с ног не сбил!* "Look where you're going! You almost knocked me off my feet."

РАЗУКРА́ШИВАТЬ/РАЗУКРА́СИТЬ. To beat up (lit., to decorate). ♦*Кто тебя так разукрасил?* "Who decorated your face like that?"

РАЗЪЁБА, -ы, *m. & f.* See **разъеба́й.**

РАЗЪЕБА́Й, -я, *m.* (**разъеба́йка, -и,** *f.*), *rude.* An unreliable, careless, slipshod person (distorted from разгильдяй; cf. **ёб-**). ♦*Этот разъебай что-нибудь да перепутает.* "That good-for-nothing is bound to screw something up."

РАЗЪЕБА́ЙСТВО, -а, *n., rude.* Unreliability, irresponsibility. ♦*Это не разъебайство, это хуже, это наглость.* "This is worse than irresponsibility — this is downright brazenness."

РАЗЪЁБАННЫЙ, -ая, -ое, *rude.* Worn out, not working properly. ♦*Этот велосипед весь разъёбанный, на нём опасно ездить.* "This bicycle is an old wreck — it would be dangerous to ride it."

РАЗЪЁБКА, -и, *f., rude.* See **разъебо́н.**

РАЗЪЕБО́Н, -а, *m., rude.* A scolding, tongue-lashing. ♦*Сейчас нам устроят разъебон.* "Now they're going to bawl us out."

РАЗЪЁБЫВАТЬ/РАЗЪЕБА́ТЬ, *rude.* **1.** To break, smash up. ♦*Он вчера совсем разъебал машину.* "Yesterday he smashed up the car." **2.** To reprimand, criticize. ♦*Они разъебали его книгу.* "They blasted his book with criticism."

РАЙО́Н: Спа́льный райо́н, see under **спа́льный.**

РАК: Ра́ком, *rude.* Rear end up (lit., crabwise; esp. of position in sex act). ♦*А как ты меня хочешь? — Раком!* "How do you want me? — Crabwise." ●**На безры́бье сама́ ра́ком ста́нешь,** see under **на. Пошёл ты ра́ком вдоль забо́ра!,** see under **пошёл. Станови́ться/стать ра́ком,** see under **станови́ться. Стоя́ть ра́ком,** see under **стоя́ть.**

РАКЕ́ТЧИК, -а, *m.* A racketeer (lit., a rocket-artillery man). ♦*На вас ракетчики ещё не наезжали?* "You mean the 'rocketeers' haven't put the squeeze on you yet?"

РА́КОВЫЕ ВОЙСКА́, *idiom, army.* Strategic missile forces (lit., cancer forces, referring to the numerous cancerous diseases caused by radiation). ♦*В раковых войсках служить не мёд, вечно сидишь в какой-то дыре.* "Serv-ing in the strategic missile forces is no piece of cake, we're always stuck on a base in the middle of nowhere."

РАНЬЁ: С са́мого с ранья́, *idiom, joc., rude.* Early in the morning (playing on **раньё,** "early morning," and **срать,** "to shit"). ♦*Завтра с самого с ранья едем за грибами.* "Tomorrow we're going mushroom hunting shit-early in the morning."

РАСКАДРО́ВАННЫЙ, -ая, -ое, *youth.* Very good (cf. **кадр**). ♦*В такую раскадрованную погоду дома не сидят.* "You can't sit indoors in such fabulous weather."

РАСКА́ЛЫВАТЬ/РАСКОЛО́ТЬ. 1. To make someone tell the truth, make someone confess. ♦*Его трудно будет расколоть, ничего он не скажет.* "It's going to be hard to get him to own up; he'll try not to say anything." **2.** To pressure, force. ♦*Надо его бы расколоть на бутылку.* "We'll have to put the screws on him for a bottle."

РАСКА́ЛЫВАТЬСЯ/РАСКОЛО́ТЬСЯ. To confess. ♦*Он раскололся, мы знаем, где он прячет оружие.* "He cracked. Now we know where he's been hiding the guns."

РАСКА́ТЫВАТЬ/РАСКАТА́ТЬ губу́ (гу́бы), *idiom, joc.* To want something very much (lit., to roll one's lips). ♦*Не раскатывай губы, это торт детям.* "Don't start drooling; that cake is for the children."

РАСКВА́ШИВАТЬ/РАСКВА́СИТЬ. To smash (from квасить, "to pickle"). ♦*Уронила сумку на лестнице, все помидоры расквасила.* "I dropped the bag on the stairway and smashed all the tomatoes!"

РАСКИ́ДЫВАТЬ/РАСКИ́НУТЬ: Раски́дывать/раски́нуть черну́ху, *idiom, crim.* To tell lies, be misleading (lit., to spread trash). ♦*Я на следствии раскинул такую чернуху, что сам удивлялся.* "Under interrogation I told such lies that I myself was amazed." **Раски́нуть мозга́ми,** *idiom.* To think (lit., to spread out or unfold one's brains). ♦*Что же дальше делать, надо бы раски-*

нуть мозгами. "Now it'll take some thought to decide what to do next."

РАСКЛА́Д, -а, *m.* A situation, plan (lit., a hand at cards). ♦*Ну, какой расклад, мы едем в гости или нет?* "So, what's the plan? Are we going visiting or not?"

РАСКЛА́ДЫВАТЬСЯ/РАЗЛОЖИ́ТЬ-СЯ, *youth.* To quarrel, have it out with someone. ♦*Они раскладываются на кухне.* "They're having a quarrel in the kitchen."

РАСКЛЯ́ЧИТЬСЯ, *perf., neg.* To block someone's way (from кляча, "an old horse").

РАСКОРО́ВИТЬСЯ, *perf.* To become fat (from корова, "cow"). ♦*Тебе надо худеть, раскоровилась совсем.* "You'd better lose some weight, you've got much too fat."

РАСКОРЯ́КА, -и, *m. & f., neg.* **1.** A clumsy person, oaf. ♦*Что ты, раскоряка, наделал, разлил всё молоко!* "Look what you've done now, you clumsy oaf! You've gone and spilled all the milk!" **2.** A pair of crooked legs; a crooked-legged person. ♦*Такой раскоряке носить мини-юбку нельзя.* "A crooked-legged girl like that shouldn't wear a miniskirt."

РАСКОРЯ́ЧИВАТЬСЯ/РАСКОРЯ́-ЧИТЬСЯ, *neg.* **1.** To be uncertain what to do, to doubt, hesitate. ♦*Я совсем раскорячился, не знаю, куда идти, на вечер или в театр.* "I'm completely at a loss whether to go to the party or to the theater." **2.** To block someone's way, to be in the way. ♦*Что ты раскорячился у телефона, дай пройти.* "You're in the way with that telephone — let me by."

РАСКРУ́ТКА, -и, *f.* From раскручивать, "to unscrew." **1.** A drinking bout. ♦*Как ты после вчерашней раскрутки, голова не болит?* "How are you feeling after yesterday's spree? A little headachy?" **2.** The start-up of a business. ♦*На раскрутку торговли мы потратили две недели.* "We spent two weeks on the start-up phase of the business."

РАСКРУ́ЧИВАТЬ/РАСКРУТИ́ТЬ. 1. To get someone to talk through interroga-

tion. ♦*Делай, что хочешь, но расскрутить его надо.* "Use whatever measures you need in order to break him and make him talk." **2.** To manipulate, to use. ♦*Николай получил майора, надо его на ресторан раскрутить.* "You know, Nicholas made major, let's make him to take us out to dinner."

РАСПА́ХИВАТЬ/РАСПАХНУ́ТЬ ВА́РЕЖКУ, *idiom.* To drop one's jaw in surprise or amazement (lit., to open someone's mitten).

РАСПИЗДЕ́ТЬ, *perf. only, rude.* To speak too openly, spill secrets. ♦*Ты уже всем распиздел о нашей поездке.* "You already spilled the beans to everyone about our trip."

РАСПИЗДЕ́ТЬСЯ, *perf. only, rude.* To be noisy, have a quarrel. ♦*Чего он распизделся?* "What was he making such a scene about?"

РАСПИ́ЗДИТЬ, *perf. only, rude.* To steal gradually and completely (as employees stealing from a firm). ♦*Они уже весь завод распиздили.* "Over time they ripped off everything from the factory."

РАСПИЗДЯ́Й. See **разъеба́й.**

РАСПИЗДЯ́ЧИВАТЬ/РАСПИЗДЯ́-ЧИТЬ, *rude.* To break, smash. ♦*Вчера я распиздячил новые очки.* "Yesterday I smashed my brand new glasses."

РАСПОВСЮ́ДИТЬСЯ, *perf.* To spread, become known (from повсюду, everywhere). ♦*Слухи расповсюдились на корабле, говорят, что мы опаздываем в порт, точно?* "Rumors have already spread throughout the ship. So is it true that we are pulling into port late?"

РАСПРЯ́ГАТЬСЯ/РАСПРЯ́ЧЬСЯ, *youth.* To remove outer clothing (lit., to unharness). ♦*Ну что стоите, распрягайтесь!* "Don't just stand there, take off your coats!"

РАСПУЗЫ́РИВАТЬСЯ/РАСПУЗЫ́-РИТЬСЯ. 1. To say too much, reveal a secret (lit., to bubble). ♦*Ты забудь, я вчера распузырился, наболтал лишнего.* "Do me a favor and forget about what I said last night. I was babbling (bubbling) about things I shouldn't have." **2.**

To be upset. ♦*Что ты так распузырился, успокойся, всё будет как надо.* "What are you so down about? Don't worry about it, everything will be OK."

РАСПУСКА́ТЬ/РАСПУСТИ́ТЬ, *army.* To receive a higher status in the soldiers' barracks hierarchy, referring to the fact that enlisted men are granted the right to slightly loosen their belts after six months of service (lit., to loosen one's belt). **Распуска́ть/распусти́ть ню́ни,** *idiom, neg.* To cry (lit., to let out whimpers). ♦*Любишь ты распускать нюни по пустякам.* "You're always turning on the waterworks over trifles." **Распуска́ть/распусти́ть ру́ки,** *neg.* To let oneself get into a fight, let oneself hit someone. ♦*Ты руки не распускай, он же ещё ребёнок.* "Don't get into a fistfight with him — he's only a child."

РАССЕКА́ТЬ, *imperf., youth.* To drive an expensive car (lit., to slash). ♦*Как рассекали, так и будем рассекать на Мерсах, кризис не для нас.* "Crisis or no crisis, we'll keep driving our Mercedes as we've always done."

РАССЛА́БИТЬСЯ, *perf. only.* To relax, calm down. ♦*Расслабься, не вибрируй.* "Calm down. Don't be so tense."

РАССЛАБУ́ХА, -и, *f.* Leisure, vacation, carefree life. ♦*Каникулы начались, расслабуха полная.* "The holidays have started and I'm completely at leisure."

РАССУПО́НИВАТЬСЯ/РАССУПО́НИТЬСЯ. To take off one's outer clothing (lit., to get unharnessed). ♦*Рассупонивайся, здесь жарко.* "Take off your things. It's hot in here."

РАСТРЕПА́ТЬ(СЯ), *perf. only, neg.* To blurt something out, let out a secret. ♦*Он о нашем секрете всем растрепался.* "He blurted out our secret to everyone."

РАСТРЯСА́ТЬ/РАСТРЯСТИ́ жир, *idiom.* To move, act, do something (lit., to jolt one's fat). ♦*Пойди в магазин, растряси немного жир.* "Get off your ass and run down to the store."

РАСТУДЫ́ ТВОЮ́ МАТЬ, *idiom, euph.* See **Ёб твою́ мать.**

РАСХУЯ́КИВАТЬ/РАСХУЯ́КАТЬ,

rude. See **распизд́ячивать.**

РАСШИБЕ́Ц, *pred. use.* Good, fine. ♦*Сегодня погода — расшибец!* "The weather today is wonderful!"

РАХИ́Т, -а, *m., neg.* A skinny weakling (lit., rickets). ♦*На этом рахите вся одежда висит.* "That 90-pound weakling's clothes are always hanging loose on him."

РА́ШЕН-КВА́ШЕН, *idiom, indecl., neg.* Russian, Russian-style. ♦*Это рашен-квашен бизнес, товар продать, а деньги пропить.* "This is a Russian-style business — we sell the merchandise and drink up the money."

РВА́НЫЙ, -ого, *m., joc., obs.* A ruble (lit., a torn fellow). ♦*Вот возьми ещё рваный.* "Here, take another ruble."

РВА́ТЬ/РВАНУ́ТЬ. To go quickly and unexpectedly, to make an unplanned or spontaneous motion. ♦*Они рванули в кино.* "They suddenly took off for the movies." •**Рвать за́дницу,** *idiom, rude.* Lit., to tear one's behind. **1.** To fawn, be overeager to please. ♦*Что ты перед ним задницу рвёшь?* "Why are you always toadying to him?" **2.** To work very hard. ♦*На новой работе приходится рвать задницу.* "I'm breaking my ass on this new job." **Рвать ко́гти,** *idiom, youth.* To leave, go away (lit., to tear one's claws). ♦*Пора рвать когти.* "Well, it's time to be off."

РЕАНИМИ́РОВАТЬСЯ, *imperf. & perf., joc.* To recover from a hangover. ♦*Пойдём в пивбар реанимироваться.* "Let's go to the beer bar for a hangover remedy."

РЕГУЛЯ́РНО, *adv., joc.* As usual, regularly (used in reply to the question Как живёшь, "How are you doing?"; alluding to having a regular sex life). ♦*Ну, как живёшь? — Регулярно.* "How are you doing? — Fine."

РЕДИ́СКА, -и, *f., neg.* Lit., radish. **1.** A penis. ♦*Не трогай редиску грязными руками, будет болеть.* "Don't touch your radish with dirty hands — you'll make it sore." **2.** A bad or worthless person. ♦*Если обзываться будешь, ре-*

диска, я тебе рога обломаю. "You bastard — I'll beat you up if you call me names like that."

РЕЗА́К, -а́, *m.*, *army.* A bootlicker (lit., sharp one). ◆*А кто их любит резаков в частях!* "No one likes having a bootlicker in the unit."

РЕ́ЗАТЬ капу́сту, *idiom, joc.* To earn money (lit., to cut cabbage). ◆*Где ты режешь сейчас капусту?* "Where are you earning your money these days?"

РЕ́ЗАТЬСЯ в ка́рты, *idiom.* To be absorbed in playing cards, be involved in a card game. ◆*Ну хватит вам резаться в карты, займитесь делом.* "Enough of your card game! Let's get down to business."

РЕЗИ́НА: Тяну́ть/потяну́ть рези́ну, see under **тяну́ть.**

РЕЗИ́НКА, -и, *f.* 1. A condom. ◆*Резинки стали делать хуже некуда, всё время рвутся.* "The condoms they've been making lately are lousy — they keep tearing." 2. *Army.* A wet suit (lit., a rubber band or eraser). ◆*Под резинку свитер надень, там внизу холодно.* "Put a sweater on under your wet suit, it's cold down there."

РЕЗЬБА́: Сорва́ть резьбу́, see under **сорва́ть.**

РЕ́КОРД, -а, *m.*, *youth.* A record (from Eng. "record"). ◆*Зря я этот рекорд купил.* "It was a mistake to buy that record."

РЕ́ПА, -ы, *f.*, *youth, joc.* A head (lit., a turnip). ◆*Надень на репу что-нибудь, на улице мороз.* "Wear something on your head. It's cold out." •**Чеса́ть ре́пу,** see under **чеса́ть.**

РЕПЕ́Й: Пристава́ть/приста́ть как репе́й, see under **пристава́ть.**

РЕФЬЮ́ЗНИК, -а, *m.* A refusenik, someone who has been refused an emigration visa (usually on such grounds as having had access to state secrets or classified information — grounds widely understood, during Soviet times, to be manufactured). The original term was **отка́зник**; "refusenik" is the anglicized version. ◆*Он рефьюзник уже пять*

лет. "He's been a refusenik for five years already."

РЕЧУ́ГА, -и, *f.*, *neg.* A speech (from речь). ◆*Надоели мне речуги и старых и новых лидеров.* "I'm sick of all their speeches — the new leaders' as well as the old ones'." •**Толка́ть/толкну́ть речу́гу,** see under **толка́ть.**

РЖАТЬ/ПОРЖА́ТЬ, *neg.* To laugh loudly (lit., to neigh). ◆*Что вы всё время ржёте?* "Why do you keep guffawing like that?"

РИНГ, -а, *m.*, *youth.* 1. The ring of a telephone (from Eng. "ring"). ◆*Возьми трубку, не слышишь ринг?* "Pick up the phone — don't you hear it ringing?" 2. A telephone number. ◆*Какой у тебя ринг?* "What's your telephone number?" 3. A telephone. ◆*У тебя есть ринг?* "Do you have a phone?"

РИ́НГАТЬ/РИНГАНУ́ТЬ, *youth.* To phone, call by telephone (cf. **ринг**). ◆*Дай трубку, мне надо срочно ринга- нуть на работу.* "Give me the phone. I have to call the office immediately."

РИСК—БЛАГОРО́ДНОЕ ДЕ́ЛО, *idiom.*, *army.* Absence without official leave (lit., it's always noble to take a risk). ◆*Риск — благородное дело, но и цена за него приличная, если поймают.* "You may think it's noble to go AWOL but if you get caught it's your ass."

РИСКОВА́ТЬ: Кто не риску́ет, тот не пьёт шампа́нского, see under **кто.**

РИХТОВА́ТЬ/ОТРИХТОВА́ТЬ. To hit, to beat (lit., to smoothe a metal surface).

РОГ: На рога́х, *idiom, rude.* Very drunk (lit., on one's horns). ◆*Не давай ему больше водяры, он уже на рогах.* "Don't give him any more to drink; he's already falling-down drunk." **Дава́ть/ дать по рога́м,** see under **дава́ть. Обла́мывать/облома́ть рога́,** see under **обла́мывать. Отшиба́ть/отшиби́ть рога́,** see under **отшиба́ть. Рыть ро́гом зе́млю,** see under **рыть. Упира́ться/ упере́ться ро́гом,** see under **упира́ться.**

РОДНО́Й, -а́я, -о́е. 1. As a casual term of address: buddy, pal, dear (lit., kin, relative). ♦*Ну, родная, хочешь закусить с нами?* "Well, dear, would you like to grab a bite with us?" **2.** Original, never having been replaced (esp. of car parts). ♦*У тебя, я смотрю, резина почти лысая. — Так она у меня родная ещё, надо вообще-то уже менять.* "I see your tires are almost bald. — Yes, they're the ones that originally came with the car. It's really time to change them."

РО́ЖА: Ро́жа кирпича́ про́сит, *idiom, neg.* Lit., [someone's] face is asking for a brick; someone is just asking for trouble, punishment. ♦*Он такой наглый, у него рожа кирпича просит.* "That guy is so pushy, his face is just asking for a brick." **Ро́жа не тре́снет?** *idiom, neg.* An expression used in response to exorbitant demands; lit., "Won't your face split (from overindulgence)?" ♦*Ты мне за эту работу заплати сто долларов, тогда я это быстро сделаю. — А рожа не треснет?* "Pay me a hundred for the job and I'll get it done quickly. — That's far too much!"

РОЖА́ТЬ/РОДИ́ТЬ. To break silence, utter words (lit. to give birth). ♦*Ты долго молчать будешь? Рожай, где ты был две ночи?* "Cat got your tongue? Out with it — where have you been for the last two nights?" ●**(Что,) я тебе рожу́ (, что ли?)** *idiom, neg.* I don't have any, I can't do it (an expression of impatience). ♦*Откуда у меня деньги, я их тебе рожу, что ли?* "Where do you expect me to get the money? Do you think I can just give birth to it?" **Пока́ не родила́, как рожу́, так скажу́,** see under **пока́.**

РОЖА́ТЬ/РОДИ́ТЬ СЛОНА́, *idiom, joc.* To think hard (lit., to give birth to an elephant). ♦*Что ты так долго думаешь, слона рожаешь?* "What are you thinking about so hard?"

РОЗЕ́ТКА, -и, *f., youth, neg.* A prostitute (lit., an electrical outlet, socket). ♦*Брось ты эту розетку.* "You ought to break up with that whore."

РО́ЗОВАЯ, -ой, *f., youth.* A lesbian. ♦*С ней ничего не выйдет, она розовая.* "You have nothing to hope for from her — she's a lesbian."

РО́КЕР, -а, *m.* A member of a motorcycle gang. ♦*Мне эти рокеры по ночам спать не дают, гоняют под окнами.* "I can't get any sleep, the way those 'rockers' drive around at night right under my windows."

РОКЕРИ́ТЬ/ПОРОКЕРИ́ТЬ, *youth.* To hang around with a motorcycle crowd. ♦*Ты за своим сыном присмотри, он рокерить начал.* "You'd better watch that son of yours — he's begun hanging around with 'rockers.'"

РОСТ: В по́лный рост, see under **в.**

РОТ: В рот тебе́ парохо́д, see under **в. Закро́й рот, кишки́ просту́дишь,** see under **закро́й. Зубо́в боя́ться — в рот не дава́ть,** see under **зубо́в. Не бери́ в го́лову, бери́ в рот,** see under **брать.**

РО́ХЛЯ, -и, *f., neg.* A clumsy or sluggish person. ♦*Говорили тебе: не женись на рохле, ничего толком делать не умеет.* "We told you not to marry that slouch! She can't do anything right."

РУБА́ЛОВКА, -и, *f.* Food (cf. **руба́ть**). ♦*Сегодня рубаловка что надо.* "Today we're having a really good meal."

РУБА́НОК, руба́нка, *m.* A flatterer, yes-man (lit., a wood shaver, someone who tries to smooth out all rough edges). ♦*В рубанках никогда не был и не буду.* "I never was and I never will be a yes-man."

РУБА́ТЬ/ПОРУБА́ТЬ, *joc.* To eat (lit., to cut, chop). ♦*Дай чего-нибудь порубать.* "Let me have something to eat."

РУБИ́ЛЬНИК, -а, *m., neg.* A big nose (lit., a knife-switch). ♦*Сейчас получишь по рубильнику.* "I'm going to give it to you in the schnozzle."

РУБИ́ТЬ/ЗАРУБИ́ТЬ, *neg.* To forbid, ban (lit., to cut, slash). ♦*Они его книгу зарубили.* "They banned his book." ●**Руби́ть капу́сту,** see **ре́зать капу́сту.**

РУБИ́ТЬСЯ/ПОРУБИ́ТЬСЯ. To fight, to compete (from рубить, "to chop"). ♦*С кем они рубятся завтра, со Спартаком?* "What team are they plaing against tomorrow, is it Spartak?"

РУ́БКА ЛЕ́СА, *idiom.* A quarrel, a fight (lit., felling of trees). ♦*Что за рубка леса здесь происходит?* "What's the fight about?"

РУКÁ: Своя́ рукá, *idiom, neg.* Connections, protection. ♦*У него в министерстве своя рука, видишь, как идёт в гору.* "He's got connections in the ministry, that's why he's getting promoted so fast." **Рукá ру́ку мóет,** *idiom, neg.* Lit., one hand washes the other; used of corruption, nepotism. ♦*На работу устроили всех своих знакомых. — А что ты хочешь, рука руку моет.* "They've provided for all their friends at work. — Well, what do you expect? One hand washes the other." **Ру́ки как крю́ки,** *idiom, neg.* Clumsiness (lit., hands like hooks). ♦*Что у тебя руки как крюки, чай разлить не можешь, всю скатерть залил.* "You're all thumbs; you can't even pour the tea without getting it all over the tablecloth." **Ру́ки чéшутся,** *idiom, neg.* Lit., one's hands are itching; used to express intense desire to do something. ♦*Оставь в покое радиоприёмник, ты его сломаешь, у тебя что, руки чешутся?* "Leave that radio alone or you'll break it. What's wrong? Are your hands itching?" **По рукáм,** *idiom.* Agreed; it's a deal. ♦*Ну что, по рукам?* "So, is it a deal?" **Ру́ки в жóпе,** see under **жóпа. Ру́ки из жóпы (из одногó мéста) растýт,** see under **жóпа. Ру́ки под хуй затóчены,** see under **хуй. Дать по рукáм,** see under **давáть. Отрывáть/оторвáть с рукáми (и ногáми),** see under **отрывáть. Пойти́ по рукáм,** see under **ходи́ть.**

РУЛИ́ТЬ/ЗАРУЛИ́ТЬ. To go (lit., to steer). ♦*Рули к магазину.* "Go over to the store."

РУЛЬ, -я́, *m., neg.* A big nose (lit., a ship's rudder). ♦*Ну и руль у неё!* "Look at the beak on her!"

РУ́ЛЯ, -и, *m., army.* A driver (from руль, "steering wheel"). ♦*Наш руля не очень-то умеет водить.* "Our chauffeur isn't a very good driver."

РУ́ПИИ, -ий, *pl., joc.* Money (lit., rupees). ♦*Сколько у тебя рупий?* "How much money have you got on you?"

РУ́СИШ, -а, *m., joc.* The Russian language (from Ger. "Russisch"). ♦*Он русиш зна-*

ет? "Does he speak Russian?"

РУ́СИШЕ-КУЛЬТУ́РИШЕ, *idiom, joc.* An uncultured, rude person (from Germ. Russische, "Russian," and культура). ♦*Что от него можно ожидать, он же русише-культурише.* "Well, what can you expect from such an uncultured fellow?!"

РУ́ССКИЙ ЙÓГУРТ, *idiom, joc.* Vodka, sold in small plastic containers with foil caps, resembling yoghurt containers (lit., "Russian yoghurt). ♦*Сейчас на базарах запретили продавать русский йогурт.* "They're not allowed to sell 'Russian yoghurt' in the markets any more."

РУ́ХНУТЬ с дýба, *idiom., neg.* To go crazy, act strange (lit., to fall out of an oak tree). ♦*Ты что, рухнул с дуба, такие слова матери говоришь?* "Have you gone out of your mind, talking to your mother like that?"

РУ́ЧКА, -и, *f.* Stupid person (lit., emergency brake). See **ручнóй тóрмоз.**

РУЧНÁЯ СТИ́РКА, *idiom, youth, joc.* Masturbation (lit., hand laundry). ♦*Я скоро буду без баб ручной стиркой заниматься.* "If I go on without women for much longer I'm going to start masturbating."

РУЧНИ́К, -á, *m.* A hand brake. ♦*У меня ручник не работает.* "My hand brake isn't working." ●**На ручникé,** *idiom, youth, joc.* At a loss, oblivious (lit., having the brakes on). ♦*Ты ещё на ручнике, а надо быстро всё делать.* "You're standing there at a loss, but you have to act quickly."

РУЧНÓЙ ТОРМÓЗ, *idiom, neg.* An idiot, a fool (lit., handbrake).

РУЧÓНКИ ШАЛОВЛИ́ВЫЕ, *idiom, joc.* Lit., naughty hands. **1.** Clumsiness, destructiveness. ♦*Вот у тебя ручонки шаловливые, зачем трогал телевизор, всё испортил.* "You shouldn't have touched the TV with those naughty hands of yours. Look — you've gone and broken it." **2.** Sexual advances. ♦*Опять ты за своё, убери ручонки шаловливые.* "There you go, up to your old tricks again! Get your naughty hands off me!"

РЫ́БА, -ы, *f.* Lit., a fish. **1.** An outline, rough sketch. ♦ *Сделай рыбу отзыва на книгу, я доделаю.* "You make an outline for the book review, and I'll fill in the text." **2.** A sexless or sexually cold woman. ♦ *Она оказалась рыбой в постели.* "In bed she turned out to be completely frigid."

РЫГА́ЛОВКА, -и, *f., rude.* A poor-quality cafeteria (from рыгать, "to belch"). ♦ *Как ты можешь ходить в эту рыгаловку?* "How can you stand eating in that greasy-spoon?"

РЫДА́НЬЯ: Мудо́вые рыда́нья, see under **мудо́вый.**

РЫ́ЖИЙ, -ая, -ее. An exception, someone left out or excluded (lit., red-headed). ♦ *Что я, рыжий, все отдыхают, а я буду дежурить?* "What am I, some kind of black sheep, that I should be on duty while all the rest of you are free?"

РЫЖЬЁ, -я́, *n., crim.* Gold, things made of gold (cf. **рыжий**). ♦ *Взяли на той квартире не так много, рыжьё потянуло штук на сто.* "They didn't get very much from that apartment; the gold they took only brought in about 100,000 rubles."

РЫ́ЛО, -а, *n., neg.* A face, mug (lit., snout of a pig). ♦ *Ну и рыло у него!* "Look at the mug on that guy!" ♦**На рыло,** *idiom, rude.* Apiece, per head. ♦ *Сколько у нас еды на рыло?* "How much food do we have apiece?" **Вороти́ть/отвороти́ть рыло,** see under **вороти́ть. Ни у́ха ни рыла,** see under **ни.**

РЫ́ПАТЬСЯ/РЫ́ПНУТЬСЯ, *neg.* To thrash about, wriggle around. ♦ *Сиди и не рыпайся, ты ничем не поможешь.* "Sit down and don't thrash around; there's nothing you can do to help."

РЫТЬ ро́гом зе́млю, *idiom, joc.* To make great efforts, try very hard (lit., to dig up the ground with one's horn). ♦ *Он роет рогом землю, хочет купить дачу.* "He's making enormous efforts to raise the money to buy a dacha."

РЫ́ЧАГ, -а, *m.* An arm (lit., lever). ♦ *Убери свои рычаги, я сам сделаю.* "Take your arms away, I'll do this myself."

РЭ, *m., indecl.* A ruble (from the first letter of рубль). ♦ *Это тебе будет стоить пятьсот рэ.* "That'll cost you five hundred rubles."

РЭК, -а, *m., abbr.* A racketeer (from рэкетир).

РЭКЕТИ́Р, -а, *m.* A racketeer (from Eng.). ♦ *Вчера арестовали двух рэкетиров.* "Yesterday two racketeers were arrested."

РЮ́ХАТЬ¹, *imperf. only, youth.* **1.** To understand. ♦ *Он в этом ничего не рюхает.* "He doesn't understand a thing about it." **2.** To think, decide. ♦ *Рюхай скорей, ты идёшь с нами или нет?* "Make up your mind quickly — are you coming with us or not?"

РЮ́ХАТЬ²/ПОРЮ́ХАТЬ, *youth.* **1.** To hit, beat up. ♦ *Что, порюхать вас за эти штучки?* "You deserve a beating for those tricks of yours." **2.** To go, trot. ♦ *Рюхай отсюда!* "Get out of here!"

РЯ́БЧИК, -а, *m.* A ruble (lit., a grouse). ♦ *Где же все мои рябчики, улетели!* "All my pretty little rubles have flown the coop."

РЯ́ВКАТЬ/РЯ́ВКНУТЬ, *neg.* To yell, shout (lit., to roar). ♦ *Ты на меня не рявкай.* "Don't yell at me."

РЯ́ХА, -и, *f., rude.* A face. ♦ *Он себе ряху отъел.* "He put on a lot of weight" (lit., he fattened his face).

С КЕМ ПОВЕДЁШЬСЯ, ОТ ТОГО И ЗАЛЕТИ́ШЬ, *idiom, joc.* A remark about unintended pregnancies (lit. "Whomever you associate with, you get pregnant by," distorted from the saying С кем поведёшься, от того и наберёшься, "Whomever you associate with, you take on qualities similar to his").

С КОНЦА́ КА́ПАЕТ у кого́-л., *idiom, rude.* To have gonorrhea (lit., someone's prick is dripping). ◆*У него с конца ка-пает уже неделю, надо делать уколы.* "He's had the clap for a week — he'll have to get treatment."

С ПОДА́ЧИ, *idiom.* By the advice of, at the prompting of. ◆*С чьей это ты подачи снял деньги со счёта до краха?* "Who gave you the tip to close out your bank account before the crash?"

САДАНУ́ТЬ, *perf.* To deliver a blow, to strike, to hit. ◆*Кто-то меня саданул локтем в автобусе, до сих пор синяк.* "Somebody elbowed me on the bus during rush hour, I still have the bruise."

САДИ́ТЬСЯ/СЕСТЬ на́ уши, *idiom.* To bore with tedious or unwanted conversation (lit., to sit down on someone's ears). ◆*Не садись мне на уши со своим биз-несом, всё у уже слышал.* "Don't bore me with your business, I've already heard it all."

САЙГА́К, -а, *m., neg.* **1.** An idiot, blockhead. ◆*Вразумить такого сайга-ка нельзя.* "There's no talking sense into an idiot like that." **2.** A Central Asian.

САЙЗ, -а, *m., youth.* Size (from Eng. "size"). ◆*Мне этот батон не в сайз.* "This shirt isn't my size."

САЛАБО́Н, -а, *m., army, neg.* See **сала́га**.

САЛА́ГА, -и, *m.* **1.** An inexperienced first-year soldier or marine. **2.** Any young, inexperienced person. ◆*Что ты, сала-га, понимаешь в политике?* "You baby, what could you possibly understand about politics?!"

САЛА́ТНИК, -а, *m., joc.* Face (lit., salad-bowl). ◆*Салатник весь перепачкал клубникой, беги умойся.* "Go wash up,

you've got strawberry juice all over your face."

СА́ЛЬТО С ПРОГИ́БОМ, *idiom, indecl., youth.* A trick, strategem (lit., somersault ending in a standing position). ◆*Я эти сальто с прогибом знаю, он не раз так нас обманывал.* "I know those tricks; he's tricked us that way several times."

САМИЗДА́Т, -а, *m., obs.* The hand copy-ing and underground circulation of the writings of forbidden authors under the Soviet regime (lit., self-publication; by imitation of the names of official Soviet publishing houses such as "Politizdat"). ◆*В самиздате все тогда прочитали Солженицына.* "In those days everyone read Solzhenitsyn in samizdat."

САМОВО́ЛКА, -и, *f., army.* A deliberate absence without official leave (from самовольная отлучка).

САМОКА́Т, -а, *m., army* (lit., scooter or soap-box racer; a wordplay on самоход and самоволка). See **самово́лка** and **самохо́д**.

САМОПА́Л, -а, *m., neg.* Homemade cloth-ing sold under commercial labels (lit., a homemade cap gun). ◆*Эти джинсы самопал, они не "Левис."* "Those jeans aren't real Levi's; they're just imitations."

САМОСТРО́ЧНЫЙ, -ая, -ое, *neg.* Homemade (cf. **самопа́л**). ◆*Это само-строчная рубашка, а никакой не Кар-ден.* "There's no way that shirt is a real Cardin. It's just a homemade fake."

САМОХО́Д, -а, *m., army.* Absence from one's unit without leave. ◆*Ты решил в субботу пойти в самоход?* "Did you decide to go AWOL on Saturday?"

САМУРА́Й, -я, *m., neg.* A Japanese (lit., samurai). ◆*Этот самурай Москвы совсем не знает.* "That Jap doesn't know Moscow at all."

СА́ПА: Ти́хой са́пой, see under **ти́хой.**

САПО́Г, -а́, *m., army.* Lit., boot. **1.** *neg.* An army officer responsible for ideological training. ◆*Тихо, сапог идёт!* "Quiet! Here comes the 'boot'!" **2.** *joc.* An infantry officer. ♦*Он не авиатор, он — сапог.* "He's no air force man — he's a 'boot.'" •**Обта́чивать/обточи́ть сапоги́,** see under **обта́чивать.**

САПО́ЖНИК, -а, *m., neg.* An incompetent worker (lit., a shoemaker, from the idea that shoemakers tend to be drunkards). ♦*Видно, сапожник чинил твой телевизор: опять не работает.* "It looks like the repairman who fixed your TV is a real 'shoemaker' — here it is on the fritz again."

САРДЕ́ЛЬКА, -и, *f., rude.* A penis (lit., a sausage). ♦*У тебя, кажется, сарделька стоит.* "You seem to have an erection."

СА́РРА, -ы, *f., neg.* A Jewish woman (lit., Sarah). ♦*А кто она, русская или Сарра, сразу не поймёшь.* "It's hard to tell whether she's Russian or Jewish."

САТАНА́ В Ю́БКЕ, *idiom, neg.* An aggressive, pushy woman (lit., a devil in a skirt). ♦*Чего эта сатана в юбке ругается?* "What's that devil in skirts cursing about?"

САТАНЕ́ТЬ/ОСАТАНЕ́ТЬ, *neg.* To lose one's self-control. ♦*Он без курева сатанеет.* "He goes crazy without tobacco."

СА́ХАР: Что-л. не са́хар, *idiom.* Something is unpleasant, difficult. ♦*Да, сейчас жизнь — не сахар.* "Life is no bowl of cherries these days."

СА́ХЕР, -а, *m., joc.* Sugar (by wordplay on сахар and **хер**). ♦*Сахер в чай положил?* "Did you put sugar in the tea?" •**Са́хер, шма́хер, обжима́хер,** *rhyming phrase, joc.* A swindle, a gyp. ♦*У них там в магазине сахер, шмахер, обжимахер.* "You'll get swindled in that store."

САЧКОВА́ТЬ/САЧКАНУ́ТЬ. To shirk, avoid work, goof off (from **сачо́к**). ♦*Любишь ты сачковать, а кто вместо тебя это сделает?* "If you keep goofing off who do you think is going to get the job done?"

САЧКОДРО́М, -а, *m., joc.* A place for hanging around idly (by wordplay on **сачо́к** and аэродром). ♦*Пойдём на сач-*кодром, покурим.* "Let's go have a smoke at the hangout."

САЧО́К, сачка́, *m.* A lazy person, a do-nothing (lit., a [butterfly-]net). ♦*Ну и сачок же ты!* "What a lazybones you are!" •**Дави́ть сачка́,** see under **дави́ть.**

СА́ША С УРАЛМА́ША, *idiom, joc.* A simple or naive person, a provincial (lit., Sasha from the Urals Automobile Factory, the popular hero of the 1940s movie *Two Soldiers*). ♦*Эх ты, Саша с Уралмаша, эти сапоги стоят намного дешевле, зачем ты купил их?* "You country bumpkin! These boots aren't worth anything near what you paid for them!"

СБИВА́ТЬ/СБИТЬ це́лку, *idiom, rude.* **1.** To deflower, take a girl's virginity. ♦*Он с ней возится уже месяц, всё целку сбить не может.* "He's been dating her for a month and still hasn't managed to deflower her." **2.** To initiate into adulthood. ♦*Ты уже начал пить: на заводе тебе сбили целку.* "I see you're drinking; apparently they initiated you at the factory."

СБЛЕДНУ́ТЬ, *perf. only, neg.* To become frightened (by wordplay on бледный, "pale," and **блядь**). ♦*Он сразу сбледнул, когда нас увидел.* "He got scared when he saw us." •**Сбледну́ть с лица́,** *neg., rude.* To turn pale with fright. ♦*Что это ты сбледнул с лица, тебе плохо?* "You've turned white as a ghost — are you feeling ill?"

СБО́НДИТЬ, *perf. only, neg.* To steal, make off with. ♦*Кто у меня кошелёк сбондил?* "Who lifted my wallet?"

СБРЕ́НДИТЬ, *perf. only, neg.* To lose one's senses, to lose one's judgment. ♦*Он от старости совсем сбрендил.* "He's completely lost his judgment in his old age."

СВА́ДЬБА: До сва́дьбы заживёт, see under **до. Соба́чья сва́дьба,** see under **соба́чья.**

СВА́ЛИВАТЬ/СВАЛИ́ТЬ. To leave, go, go away. ♦*Они давно свалили за бугор.* "They went abroad long ago."

СВАЛИ́ТЬ экза́мен, *idiom, students.* To

pass an examination. ♦*Я уже свалил все экзамены, теперь — свобода!* "I've passed all my exams; now I'm free!"

СВА́РКА, -и, *f., army.* A large-caliber machine gun (lit., welding). ♦*За той стеной у них сварка работает, туда нельзя.* "There's a machine gun sputtering behind that wall, so we can't go in that direction."

СВАТ, -а, *m., crim.* A police officer (lit., a matchmaker). ♦*Ты этого свата знаешь?* "Do you know this cop?"

СВА́Я, -и, *f., joc.* A tall, thin man (lit., a pole). ♦*Для этой сваи диван мал будет.* "The couch won't be long enough for that beanpole to sleep on."

СВЕЖА́К, -á, *pred. use.* Very fresh or very sleek-looking. ♦*Это мясо — свежак!* "This meat is really fresh!"

СВЕЖА́ТИНА, -ы, *f., pos.* Something fresh and new (lit., fresh game). ♦*Этот фильм — свежатина.* "This movie is really original."

СВЕ́ЙКА, -и, *f., crim.* A penis. ♦*Мне по свейке мячом попали: всё болит.* "They hit me in the crotch with the ball; it really hurts."

СВЕРБЕ́ТЬ/ЗАСВЕРБЕ́ТЬ, *neg.* To want (lit., to itch). ♦*Тебе так и свербит бежать на танцы.* "You're just itching to go out dancing."

СВЕРКА́ТЬ/СВЕРКНУ́ТЬ го́лым за́дом, *idiom, rude.* To walk around naked (lit., to flash one's bare behind). ♦*Иди оденься, не сверкай голым задом, гости пришли.* "Go and get dressed, the guests have arrived."

СВЕРНУ́ТЬСЯ, *perf. only, joc., neg.* To die (lit., to spoil, turn sour). ♦*Сейчас свернуться тоже дорого, похороны стоят больших денег.* "These days even dying is expensive; funerals cost an awful lot."

СВЁРТОК, свёртка, *m., joc.* A turn, a crossroad. ♦*Где-то здесь должен быть свёрток к дому.* "Somewhere around here there must be a turn toward the house."

СВЕРЧО́К, сверчка́, *m., army.* One who decides to do an extra period of army ser-

vice (lit., a cricket; playing on сверхсрочник). ♦*Сколько у нас в роте сверчков?* "How many 'crickets' are there in our unit?"

СВЕТ: Свет в конце́ туне́ля, *idiom, pos.* An escape from difficulties, a solution to problems (lit., light at the end of the tunnel). ♦*То, что ты предлагаешь, уже свет в конце тунеля.* "Your proposal offers some light at the end of the tunnel." **В све́те реше́ний...,** *idiom, joc.* Lit., "In light of the decisions that have been made," a cliché of the "years of stagnation" under Brezhnev, now used jocularly. ♦*Ну, что надо делать в свете решений?* "Well, what should we do in light of the decisions that have been made?" **«Да бу́дет свет!» — сказа́л монтёр и сде́лал замыка́ние,** see under **да. Крыть на чём свет стои́т,** see under **крыть. Туши́(те) свет!,** see under **туши́(те).**

СВЕТИ́ТЬ: Что-л. све́тит кому́-л., *idiom, pos.* Something is in the cards for someone; someone has a good chance of something. ♦*Мне получить эту работу не светит.* "I haven't got a chance of getting that job."

СВЕТИ́ТЬСЯ/ЗАСВЕТИ́ТЬСЯ, *idiom, neg.* To be caught doing something wrong. ♦*Смотри, не засветись на этом деле.* "Watch out that you don't get caught."

СВЕ́ТКА — ПИПЕ́ТКА, *idiom.* A rhyming phrase used to tease girls named Svetlana (lit., Svetka is a pipette).

СВИДА́НКА, -и, *f., joc.* A date. ♦*Ты идёшь на свиданку сегодня?* "Do you have a date today?"

СВИНОМА́ТКА, -и, *f., neg.* A fat woman (lit., a sow). ♦*Смотри, эта свиноматка опять себе новое платье купила.* "Look, that fat pig has bought herself another new dress!"

СВИНОФЕ́РМА, -ы, *f., neg.* A mess, messy quarters (lit., a pigsty). ♦*Весь дом вы превратили в свиноферму, а кто убирать будет?* "You've turned the whole house into a pigsty. Who do you think is going to clean it up?"

СВИНТИ́ТЬ, *perf.* To leave, to escape (lit., to unscrew). ♦*Мне надо из Москвы свинтить, меня милиция ищет.* "I've got to get out of Moscow, the police is after me."

СВИ́НТУС, -а, *т., joc.* **1.** A pig, swine. ♦*А ты что, свинтус, после себя убрать не можешь, всю посуду бросил на столе?* "You pig, can't you clean up after yourself? You've left all the dirty dishes on the table." **2.** A selfish person. ♦*Этот свинтус бросил её с ребёнком.* "That swine abandoned her and the baby."

СВИНЯ́ЧИТЬ/НАСВИНЯ́ЧИТЬ, *neg.* To make a mess. ♦*Кто это так насвинячил на столе?* "Who made this mess here on the table?"

СВИСТ, -а, *т., neg., joc.* Lying, a lie (lit., whistling). ♦*Это всё свист.* "That's a big lie."

СВИСТЕ́ТЬ, *imperf. only, neg., joc.* To tell a lie. ♦*Не свисти, этого не было.* "Don't lie! That never happened."

СВИ́СТНУТЬ, *perf. only, neg., joc.* To steal. ♦*Кто свистнул мой свитер?* "Who lifted my sweater?"

СВИСТО́К, свистка́, *т., army.* A fighter plane. ♦*Опять свисток летит, учения у них, что ли?* "There goes another fighter plane. They must be doing maneuvers."

СВИСТОПЛЯ́СКА, -и, *f.* Fuss, confusion, to-do. ♦*В правительстве идёт свистопляска, каждый день меняют министров.* "The government is all at sixes and sevens; they replace the ministers every day."

СВИСТУ́Н, -а, *т., neg.* A liar. ♦*Ты этому свистуну не верь.* "Don't believe that liar."

СВИ́ХИВАТЬСЯ/СВИХНУ́ТЬСЯ из-за́ чего́-л., *idiom.* To be crazy about something. ♦*Мои ребята совсем свихнулись из-за компьютера, играют всё время в игры.* "My kids have completely flipped over the computer. Now they're always playing computer games."

СВОБО́ДА: Век свобо́ды не вида́ть, see under **век.**

СВОЛО́ТА, -ы, *f., collect., rude, neg.* Worthless people, bastards, bums. ♦*Там у них собралась одна сволота.* "The people they're hanging out with are just a bunch of bums."

СВО́ЛОЧЬ, -и, *f.* Scum, swine (used as a term of abuse). ♦*Ты, сволочь, зачем сюда пришёл?* "You scum, what did you come here for?"

СВЯЗИ́СТКА, -и, *f.* A girlfriend or female lover (lit., a telephone worker, a wordplay on связь, communication, and любовная связь, love affair).

СДАВА́ТЬ/СДАТЬ, *youth.* **1.** To sell. ♦*Я эти шузы сдал вчера джоржу.* "I sold those shoes to a Georgian yesterday." **2.** To betray, hand over. ♦*Они решили его сдать, чтобы уйти от наказания.* "They decided to turn him in so as to escape punishment themselves."

СДВИГ, -а, *т., neg.* A quirk, eccentricity, abnormality. ♦*У каждого свой сдвиг.* "Everyone's got his own quirks."

СДВИГ ПО ФА́ЗЕ, *idiom.* Odd or quirky behavior (lit., an electric change of polarity). See **сдвиг.**

СДВИ́НУТЫЙ, -ая, -ое, *neg.* Crazy, abnormal. ♦*Только сдвинутый мог на ней жениться.* "Only a crazy man could marry that woman."

СДВИ́НУТЬСЯ, *perf. only, neg.* To go crazy, go out of one's mind. ♦*Он у нас совсем сдвинулся.* "He's gone clean out of his mind."

СДЕ́ЛАЛ ДЕ́ЛО, СЛЕЗА́Й С ТЕ́ЛА, *rhyming phrase, rude.* Lit., "You've done the deed, now get off the body," from the saying Сделал дело, гуляй смело, "You've done your task; you're free to go have some fun." **1.** A sardonic reference to having sex, like "wham-bam-thank-you-ma'am." ♦*Сделал дело, слезай с тела, надевай штаны.* "Finished? Okay, put on your pants." **2.** In nonsexual contexts, an authorization to take a break, take the rest of the day off, and so on. ♦*Сделал дело? Покрасил окно? Слезай с тела, можно поспать.* "You've finished painting the window? Well, get off the body — go take a nap."

СДЕ́ЛАТЬ, *perf. only, youth, neg.* To punish someone, get one's own back against someone. ♦*Я этого не забуду, я тебя ещё сделаю.* "I won't forget this, and I'll get you for it." •**Сде́лать козу́,** *idiom.* **1.** To behave strangely (lit., to make a goat). ♦*Ну ты и сделал козу, зачем ты эту грязную кошку домой притащил?* "What a weird thing you did! Why did you bring home this dirty cat?" **2.** To take revenge, to get back at. ♦*Я тебе ещё сделаю козу за это!* "I'll get even with you for what you've done to me!" •– **Сде́лать ру́чкой,** *idiom.* To say goodbye, to leave. ♦*Сделай папе ручкой, он уходит на работу.* "Say bye-bye to daddy, he's going to work."

СДИРА́ТЬ/СОДРА́ТЬ, *youth.* To copy, cheat (lit., to skin). ♦*Дай содрать лекции.* "Let me copy your notes."

СЕ ЛЯ ВИ, *idiom.* "That's life," an expression of resignation (Fr. "c'est la vie"). ♦*Ты знаешь, они развелись. — Ну что ж, се ля ви.* "Did you hear that they've divorced? — Well, c'est la vie."

СЕ́ВЕРНОЕ СИЯ́НИЕ, *idiom, joc.* A drink made of vodka, cognac, and champagne (lit., aurora borealis). ♦*Сделай для хохмы «северное сияние».* "Just for the fun of it, make us some 'aurora borealis.'"

СЕДЛО́: Как коро́ве седло́, see under **как.**

СЕЗО́НКА, -и, *f.* A season pass for a suburban train. ♦*У меня сезонка кончилась.* "My season pass has expired."

СЕЙЧА́С ЗУ́БЫ ПРОГЛО́ТИШЬ!, *idiom.* A threat to hit in the face (lit., You'll swallow youth teeth!) ♦*Сейчас у меня зубы проглотишь, если не заткнёшься.* "I'll hit you in the face if don't shut up."

СЕЙЧА́С МО́ЖНО ДЕ́ЛАТЬ ВСЁ, НО НЕ ВСЕМ, *idiom, joc.* A sardonic summing-up of post-Soviet lawlessness in Russia (lit., Everything's permitted now, but not to everybody).

СЕКАНУ́ТЬ ДУБАРЯ́, *idiom.* To die (from дать дуба, to die, and дубарь, cold weather). ♦*От такой еды секануть*

дубаря недолго. "You can croak from this slop they're feeding us."

СЕКА́РЬ, -а, *m.* A clever, hard-working student (cf. **сечь**). ♦*Этот секарь уже готов к экзаменам, мне далеко до него.* "That bookworm is already prepared for the exams, but I've still got a long way to go."

СЕКА́ТОР, -а, *m., army, joc.* A smart, knowledgeable person (see **сечь**). ♦*Спроси секатора, он всё тебе объяснит.* "Ask the expert. He'll explain everything to you."

СЕ́КЕЛЬ, -я, *m., rude.* Clitoris. ♦*Она, знаешь, как возбуждается, если её за секель потрогаешь.* "She gets excited if you touch her on her button."

СЕКРЕ́ТКА, -и, *f.* A locking or alarm device for protecting an automobile from theft. ♦*У меня машина с секреткой, её так просто не угонишь.* "My car has got an anti-theft device, so it wouldn't be so easy to steal it."

СЕКСОКОСИ́ЛКА, -и, *f., joc.* A sexy woman (by wordplay on сенокосилка, "mowing machine," and секс, "sex").

СЕКСУА́Л-ДЕМОКРА́Т, -а, *homosex., joc.* A homosexual (by wordplay on социал-демократ, "social democrat"). ♦*Это кафе только для сексуал-демократов.* "This cafe is only for gays."

СЕКСУА́ЛЬНЫЙ ЧАС, *idiom, joc.* A scolding from the bosses (lit., a sex session). ♦*Ты куда? — Сейчас начнётся сексуальный час, собирают насчёт трудовой дисциплины.* "Where are you off to? — It's time for my sex session. I'm going to be disciplined for breaking the rules."

СЕКУ́Н, -а́, *m., youth.* An expert, a knowledgeable person (from **сечь**). ♦*Он секун в литературе.* "He's an expert on literature."

СЕЛЁДКА, -и, *f., joc.* A necktie (lit., a herring). ♦*Поправь селёдку, съехала набок.* "Straighten your tie — it's listing to one side."

СЕМЕ́ЙНЫЕ ТРУСЫ́, *idiom, joc.* Kneelength cotton undershorts, considered very unfashionable (lit., family undershorts). ♦*Зачем ты купила опять семейные трусы, их уже никто не носит!* "What did you buy me more 'family undershorts' for? No one wears them anymore!"

СЕМЁРА, -ы, *f., obs.* Seven rubles. ♦*Давай ещё семёру.* "Let me have another seven."

СЕМЕРИ́ТЬ/ПОСЕМЕРИ́ТЬ. To eat. ♦*Посемерить не выйдет—в холодильнике один электрический свет.* "There's no nothing to eat in this fridge except the electric light."

СЕМЁРКА, -и, *f.* A model 7 Zhiguli automobile. ♦*Чья эта «семёрка»?* "Whose model 7 is that?"

СЕ́МЕЧКИ: Для кого́-л. се́мечки, *idiom, joc.* Easy (lit., sunflower seeds) for someone. ♦*Для него это сделать — семечки.* "For him it'll be easy as pie to do that."

СЕМИТАБУРЕ́ТОВКА, -и, *f.* A home brew of bad quality (lit., made from seven stools). ♦*Это не водка, а семитабуретовка, из чего она сделана?* "This home brew tastes like wood alcohol, what is it made of?" See **табуре́товка.**

СЕМЬ НА ВО́СЕМЬ, *idiom, joc.* Very large (lit., seven by eight). ♦*Морда у него — семь на восемь.* "Look at the huge mug on that guy."

СЕНЬО́Р-ПОМИДО́Р, -а, *m. joc.* A jocular mode of address (lit., "Señor Tomato"). ♦*Ну, сеньор-помидор, есть будешь?* ""Well, Sir, will you have somet hing to eat?"

СЕПАРА́ТКА, -и, *f., youth.* A private or reserved supply of liquor (from Eng. "separately"). ♦*Не хочу всю водку ставить на стол, будет сепаратка — выпьем сами.* "I'm not going to put all the vodka on the table; we'll keep a reserve of ourselves."

СЕРГЕ́Й-ВОРОБЕ́Й, *idiom.* A rhyming phrase used to tease boys named Сергей (lit., Sergey the sparrow).

СЕРЕДНЯ́К, -á, *m.* Someone or something average, unremarkable. ♦*Он как учёный ничего? — Середняк.* "How is

he as a scholar? — So-so."

СЕРИ́ЙНЫЙ УБИ́ЙЦА, *idiom, prof.* A serial killer. ♦*Опять в Москве появился серийный убийца, девочек убивает в лифтах.* "There's another serial killer operating in Moscow now. He's killing girls in elevators."

СЕРО-БУРО-МАЛИ́НОВЫЙ, -ая, -ое, *joc.* Of an unidentifiable color. ♦*Кофты она какие-то носит серо-буро-малиновые.* "She wears some sort of gray-brown–berry jackets."

СЕ́РЫЙ, -ая, -ое. Illegitimate, illegal, or semi-legal (lit., gray). ♦*Все наши банковские операции становятся серыми, надо бы нам быть осторожней.* "Our bank operations are heading into a gray area. We should be careful what we do."

СЕ́РЫЙ ТЕЛЕФО́Н, *idiom, business.* A telephone protected against bugging (lit., a grey telephone). ♦*Это серый телефон, можешь звонить мне в любое время.* "You can call me anytime at this number — it's a grey phone."

СЕРП: Как серпо́м по я́йцам, see under **яйцо́.**

СЕ́РЫЙ, -ая, -ое, *neg.* Boring, uninteresting (lit., gray). ♦*Человек он довольно серый.* "He's a pretty boring fellow."

СЕРЬГА́, -и́, *f., crim.* A padlock (lit., an earring). ♦*Там на гараже серьга, надо пилить.* "There's a padlock on the garage — we'll have to saw it through."

СЕРЬЁЗ: На по́лном серьёзе, *idiom.* Seriously, no kidding. ♦*Ты это на полном серьёзе говоришь?* "Do you mean that seriously?"

СЕЧЬ/ПОСЕ́ЧЬ, *youth, joc.* To understand, be knowledgeable about, be at home with (lit., to cut). ♦*Ты в компьютерах сечёшь?* "Do you understand computers?"

СЖИРА́ТЬ/СОЖРА́ТЬ с потроха́ми, *idiom, neg.* To humiliate, persecute (lit., to devour, innards and all). ♦*Зачем ты поссорился с директором? Теперь он тебя сожрёт с потрохами.* "Why did you argue with the director? Now he's going to eat you alive."

СИВУ́ХА, -и, *f., neg.* Cheap liquor of poor

quality (from сивый, "gray"). ♦*Как ты пьёшь эту сивуху?* "How can you drink that mud?"

СИГА́ТЬ/СИГАНУ́ТЬ. To jump. ♦*Смотри, как он сиганул метра на три в длину.* "Look, he jumped a distance of about three meters."

СИГНА́ЛКА, -и, *f., army.* A stretch of borderland which has been plowed so as to reveal footprints (from сигнал, a signal).

СИДЕ́ЛКА, -и, *f.* Behind, buttocks (from сидеть, "to sit"). ♦*Всю сиделку отсидел, пока переводил эту статью.* "My behind got numb by the time I finished translating the article."

СИДЕ́ТЬ/СЕСТЬ, ПОСИДЕ́ТЬ: Сиде́ть в печёнках, *idiom, neg.* To be irritating, annoying (lit., to settle in one's liver). ♦*Когда он уедет, его замечания сидят в печёнках?* "When is he leaving? His remarks are getting under my skin." **Сиде́ть/посиде́ть на бло́ке,** *idiom, army.* To man a roadblock (lit., to sit on a block). ♦*Тут ещё всю зиму будем сидеть на блоках, боевиков в этом районе полно.* "We'll have to be on guard duty at this barrier all winter, the Chechens use this road whenever they can." **Сиде́ть/посиде́ть на спине́,** *idiom.* To sleep (lit., to sit on your own back). ♦*Ты посиди на спине, я постою на часах.* "Have a snooze, I'll stand the first watch and you can sleep on your feet". **Сиде́ть на винте́/сесть на винт,** *idiom, youth.* To use narcotics regularly, to be a drug addict. ♦*Он уже год сидит на винте.* "He's been addicted to the stuff for a year already." **Сиде́ть на нуле́/сесть на нуль,** *idiom.* To have no money (lit., to be sitting on zero). ♦*Я уже три дня сижу на нуле.* "I've been broke for three days." **Сиде́ть/посиде́ть на очке́,** *idiom.* To sit on the toilet. ♦*Ты долго будешь сидеть на очке?* "How long are you going to be sitting on the can?" **Сиде́ть на тра́вке,** *idiom, youth.* To smoke dope (lit., to sit on the grass). ♦*Он давно сидит на травке.* "He's been smoking dope for a long time."

СИДЕ́ТЬ/ВЫ́СИДЕТЬ СОБА́КУ, *idiom,* army. To be on duty from 3 to 9 A.M. (lit., to sit dog hours, from собачий, damned, bad). ♦*Не люблю я сидеть собаку, в сон клонит всё время.* "I can't stand the dog watch, I have a hard time keeping my eyes open."

СИ́ДОР, -а, *m.* A bag, string bag. ♦*Что у тебя там в сидоре?* "What have you got there in your bag?"

СИКИЛЬДЯ́ВКА, -и, *m. & f., neg.* See **креве́тка.**

СИ́КОСЬ-НА́КОСЬ, *idiom, joc., neg.* In a careless, slapdash way (from косой, "crooked"). ♦*Ты всё привык делать сикось-накось.* "You've got into the habit of doing everything in a half-baked way."

СИ́ЛА: От си́лы, *idiom.* At the most. ♦*Ему от силы 50 лет.* "He's no more than 50 years old." **Со стра́шной си́лой,** *idiom.* Intensely, devotedly. ♦*Он занимается бизнесом со страшной силой.* "He puts his whole heart into his business."

СИЛОВИ́К, -а, *m.* A member of a government department authorized to use coercive force, e.g., defense, the army, the police. A minister of such a department.

СИЛОВИ́К-НАСТА́ВНИК, -а, *m., army.* A soldier sadistically applying brute force against recently enlisted men (from сила, power, strength, and наставлять, to teach).

СИМПАПУ́ЛЕЧКА, -и, *f., joc.* A sympathetic, attractive girl or woman. ♦*Она у тебя симпапулечка!* "Your girl is a real darling!"

СИМПАТЯ́ГА, -и, *m. & f., joc.* An attractive person or animal. ♦*Эта собака — такая симпатяга!* "That dog is such a darling!"

СИМПО́ТНЫЙ, -ая, -ое, *youth.* Attractive, pleasing. ♦*Этот симпотный костюм я куплю.* "I'm going to buy that nice-looking suit."

СИНАГО́ГА, -и, *f., neg.* A large proportion of Jews in one office, department, or the like (lit., a synagogue). ♦*У нас не кафедра, а синагога.* "Our department is a regular synagogue."

СИНЕГЛА́ЗКА, -и, *f.* Lit., blue-eyed. **1.** *youth.* A police car. ♦*На каждом углу по синеглазке, ловят кого, что-ли?* "There's a police car at every corner, what's going on, are they trying to catch someone?" **2.** A type of potato. ♦*Надо бы ещё ведро синеглазки купить.* "We better buy another bushel of potatoes."

СИ́НИЙ, -яя. A thief, convict (lit., blue, meaning tattooed). ♦*У него татуировок больше, чем чистой кожи, типичный синий.* "He has tattoos all over his body; I think he used to be in prison."

СИНЯ́К, -а́, *m., neg.* A drunkard (from синий, "blue" [in the face]). ♦*Ты этого синяка знаешь?* "Do you know that drunk?"

СИНЯ́ЧКА, -и, *f., neg.* A woman drunkard (from синяк, "a bruise"). ♦*Синячка опять приходила деньги просить.* "That drunk came asking for money again."

СИСТЕ́МА: В систе́ме, *idiom.* Belonging to an official or party organization, the police, and so on. ♦*Скажи, в какой он системе?* "Which service does he work for?"

СИСТЕ́МНЫЙ, -ая, -ое. Cf. **систе́ма. 1.** Belonging to an official or party organization, the police, and so on. ♦*Ты знаешь, её муж системный?* "Do you know that her husband is a secret police agent?" **2.** *youth.* Belonging to a street gang. ♦*Он системный чувак.* "That guy belongs to a gang."

СИ́СЬКА, -и, *f., rude.* Bosom, breast (lit., nipple). ♦*Что-то одна сиська болит.* "I've got a pain in one of my boobs." •**Пья́ный в си́ську,** see under **пья́ный.**

СИСЯ́СТЫЙ, -ая, -ое, *rude.* Big-bosomed. ♦*Кто эта сисястая, вон там сидит?* "Who's that busty woman sitting over there?"

СИТА́ТЬ/ЗАСИТА́ТЬ, *youth, obs.* To sit (from Eng. "sit"). ♦*Сколько ещё ситать, времени больше нет.* "I can't sit here any longer, I've got no time."

СИФ, -а, *m., neg.* Syphilis. ♦*На юге сиф.* "There's an outbreak of syphilis in the

south."

СИФА́К, -а́, *m., neg.* See **сиф.**

СИФО́Н, -а, *m.* **1.** A draft, breeze. ♦*Тебе надо заклеить окна, в квартире такой сифон, сидеть нельзя.* "You'd better stuff the cracks in the windows. There's such a draft in this apartment that you just can't sit here." **2.** *neg.* See **сиф.**

СИФО́НИТЬ/ЗАСИФО́НИТЬ, *neg.* **1.** To blow, be drafty. ♦*Закрой окно, так и сифонит.* "Shut the window. There's too much of a draft." **2.** To leak, drip. ♦*Почему вода сифонит из крана?* "How come water is dripping from the tap?"

СИЯ́НИЕ: Се́верное сия́ние, see under **се́верное.**

СКАДРОВА́ТЬСЯ, *perf. only, youth, joc.* To become acquainted with a girl (cf. **кадр**). ♦*Хочешь скадроваться вон с той блондинкой?* "Do you want to meet that blond over there?"

СКАЖИ́ ДА ПОКАЖИ́! *idiom, neg., joc.* Never mind; it's none of your business (lit., "tell and show!", disparagingly mimicking the other's curiosity). ♦*Скажи, ты будешь завтра на приёме? — Скажи да покажи!* "Tell me, are you going to the reception tomorrow? — None of your business." **Скажи́ да покажи́, да дай потро́гать,** *idiom, neg., joc.* A lengthened version of the foregoing; lit., "tell and show and let me touch!"

СКАЗА́ТЬ как в лу́жу пёрднуть, *neg., rude.* To say something unsuitable, out of place (lit., to talk as if farting in a pool). ♦*Ну, ты сказал как в лужу пёрднул, никто этого делать не будет.* "What you said is completely out of line — no one would do a thing like that."

СКА́ЗОЧНИК, -а, *m., army.* A military correspondent (lit., a fairy tale teller). ♦*В зону боевых действий сказочников приказано не пускать.* "We have orders; you 'fairy tale tellers' aren't allowed in the combat zone."

СКАКА́ТЬ/ЗАСКАКА́ТЬ, *neg., joc.* To dance (cf. **ска́чки**). ♦*Дай я немного посижу, скакать надоело.* "Let me take a break; I'm tired of dancing." •**Скака́ть как вошь на гребешке́,** *idiom, neg.* To fuss around, bustle about, be fidgety (lit., to jump around like a louse on a comb). ♦*Что ты вертишься, скачешь как вошь на гребешке? Успокойся!* "Why are you jumping around like a chicken without its head? Calm down!"

СКА́ЛИТЬ/ПОСКА́ЛИТЬ зу́бы, *idiom, neg.* To laugh (lit., to bare one's teeth). ♦*Кончай скалить зубы, ничего в этом смешного нет.* "Stop laughing — there's nothing funny about it."

СКАМЕ́ЙКА, -и, *f., crim.* A horse (lit., a bench). ♦*Где твоя скамейка? — Пасётся.* "Where's your horse? — Grazing."

СКА́ТЫВАТЬ/СКАТА́ТЬ, *youth.* To copy (lit., to roll). ♦*Дай скатать зада́чу по математике.* "Let me copy your math homework."

СКА́ЧКИ, ска́чек, *pl., youth, joc.* Lit., a horse race. 1. A date, a tryst. ♦*У него сегодня скачки с Людкой.* "He's got a date with Lyudmila today." 2. A dance. ♦*Пойдём на скачки вечером?* "Shall we go to the dance this evening?"

СКВОЗАНУ́ТЬ, *perf. only.* 1. To go quickly. ♦*Сквозани в магазин, купи поесть.* "Dash into the store and get something to eat." 2. To pass by, pass through. ♦*Пока ты спал, мы уже сквозанули пару городов.* "We already passed through a couple of towns while you were asleep."

СКВОРЕ́Ц, скворца́, *m., joc.* A person carrying building materials to a dacha in a car (lit., a starling, with reference to nest building). ♦*Дорога в субботу забита скворцами, все что-то везут на дачи.* "The traffic on Saturdays is heavy because of all the 'starlings' taking stuff to their dachas."

СКВОРЕ́ЧНИК, -а, *m., neg.* A many-storied, crowdedly arranged apartment building; esp. the type built during Khrushchev's time (lit., a starling house; cf. **хрущо́ба**). ♦*Надоело мне жить в скворечнике, хочу построить себе дом за городом.* "I'm sick of living in a birdhouse; I want to build myself a house

in the suburbs."

СКЕЛЕ́Т: Ходя́чий скеле́т, see under **ходя́чий.**

СКЕНТОВА́ТЬСЯ, *youth.* To make friends, become friendly (cf. **кент**). ♦*Ты давно с ним скентовался?* "Have you been friends with him for long?"

СКИ́ДЫВАТЬ: Дава́й, скидыва́й!, see under **дава́й.**

СКИ́НУТЬ: Ски́нуть това́р, *idiom, youth.* To sell something at a good profit. ♦*Вчера скинул товар, есть навар.* "Yesterday I made a fat sale, so now I've got a wad."

СКИ́НХЕД, -а, *m.* A skinhead, punk. ♦*Вот не думал, что сын твой скинхедом станет!* "I never imagined that your son would turn into a skinhead!"

СКИПА́ТЬ, *imperf. only, youth.* To leave, run away (from Eng. "skip" or "escape"). ♦*Пора скипать отсюда.* "It's time to get out of here."

СКЛЕ́ИТЬ ТА́ПОЧКИ, *idiom.* To die (lit., to glue up one's slippers). ♦*Все мы склеим тапочки в своё время.* "We'll all die when our number is up."

СКЛИФ, -а, *m., Moscow.* The Sklifosovsky Institute, an emergency clinic in Moscow. ♦*Вези его в Склиф: у него перелом ноги.* "You'd better take him to the Sklif — his leg is broken."

СКЛОНЯ́ТЬ, *imperf. only, joc., neg.* To curse, abuse. ♦*Все сейчас склоняют правительство.* "Everyone's bad-mouthing the government these days."

СКОЗЛИ́ТЬ, *perf.* To say something stupid (from коза, "goat"). ♦*Ты как всегда скозлил.* "As usual, you put your foot in your mouth."

СКОКА́РЬ, -я́, *m., crim.* A robber who specializes in apartment robberies. ♦*Это работа скокаря. Кто у тебя проходил по квартирным кражам?* "This is the work of professionals. Do we have anything in the files on this MO?"

СКОЛОПЕ́НДРА, -ы, *f., neg.* A nasty person. ♦*Эта сколопендра слова доброго не скажет.* "You can't expect a kind word from that snake."

СКО́ЛЬКО ВО́ЛКА НИ КОРМИ́, А У

СЛОНА́ ВСЁ РАВНО́ (Я́ЙЦА) БО́ЛЬШЕ, *idiom, rude.* You can't change the nature of someone or something (lit., "No matter how much you feed a wolf, an elephant still has bigger [balls]"). This is a playful distortion of the proverb "No matter how much you feed a wolf, he'll still look to the woods" (. . . он всё равно в лес смотрит).

СКОММУНИ́ЗДИТЬ, *perf. only, joc.* To steal, "communize". By rhyme play on **спи́здить** and коммунизм, "communism." The expression reflects the sardonic popular stance on stealing from plants and factories: there is nothing dishonest in it since, according to communist doctrine, property belongs to all, that is, to no one. ♦*Кто скоммуниздил мои часы?* "Who 'communized' my watch?"

СКОПЫ́ТИТЬСЯ, *perf. only, joc.* **1.** To lie down. ♦*Он пришёл с работы, сразу скопытился, сейчас ещё спит.* "He lay down as soon as he got home from work, and he's still asleep now." **2.** To die. ♦*От этого спирта скопытиться можно.* "You could drop dead from this liquor."

СКО́РОСТЬ СТУ́КА ПРЕВЫША́ЕТ СКО́РОСТЬ ЗВУ́КА, *idiom, joc.* Lit., "The speed of denunciation exceeds the speed of sound," a rhyming expression of sardonic resignation to the process of denunciation. ♦*Директор уже знает, как ты выступил против него на собрании. — Ничего странного. Скорость стука. . . .* "The director already knows that you spoke against him at the meeting. — That's no surprise. After all, the speed of denunciation exceeds the speed of sound."

СКОРПИО́Н, -a, *m.* A strap with spikes placed across a road to bar traffic (lit., a scorpion).

СКОСОЁБЛИВАТЬСЯ/СКОСОЁ-БИТЬСЯ, *rude.* **1.** To be twisted, distorted. ♦*Почини дверь в туалете, совсем скосоёбилась.* "Fix the bathroom door! It's all warped." **2.** To make faces, grimace. ♦*Когда ему сказали, что его не избрали в академики, он весь скосо-*

ёбился. "When they told him he hadn't been elected to the Academy, he grimaced."

СКОТОБА́ЗА, -ы, *f., rude.* A worthless or bad person. ♦*Какая скотобаза испортила пишущую машинку?* "Who's the bastard who broke the typewriter?"

СКОТОВО́З, -a, *m., neg.* A large bus (lit., a cattle car). ♦*Вот скотовоз идёт, всех заберёт на остановке.* "There comes a cattle car — it'll be able to take all of us at this bus stop."

СКРИП, -a, *m.* **1.** *crim.* A basket (from the squeaking sound made by woven baskets). ♦*Что ты там положил в скрип, слишком тяжело нести.* "What did you put in this basket? It's too heavy to carry." **2.** Whining, complaining (cf. **скрипе́ть**[1]). ♦*Мне твой скрип надоел до чёртиков.* "I'm sick and tired of your whining." •**Со скри́пом,** *idiom.* Difficult, slow and painful (lit., with creaking). ♦*Сегодня торговля идёт со скрипом.* "Business is slow today."

СКРИПЕ́ТЬ[1]**/ЗАСКРИПЕ́ТЬ,** *neg.* To whine, complain. ♦*Перестань скрипеть, лучше займись делом.* "Stop whining and do something about it."

СКРИПЕ́ТЬ[2]**/ПРОСКРИПЕ́ТЬ.** To survive with difficulty, barely stay alive. ♦*Она совсем постарела, видно, недолго скрипеть осталось.* "She's aged a lot; it looks like she won't be able to squeak along much longer."

СКРИПУ́ЧИЙ, -ая, -ее, *neg.* **1.** Squeaky. ♦*Дверь у нас такая скрипучая, сил нет.* "That door of ours is so squeaky, I can't stand it." **2.** Dissatisfied, complaining. ♦*Что ты такой скрипучий сегодня?* "How come you're so grouchy today?"

СКУКОТА́, -ы́, *f.* Insipidity, dullness, tedium. ♦*Какие-нибудь интересные выступления в Думе были? — Сегодня нет, одна скукота.* "Did anything interesting happen in Parliament today? —No, it was just the usual boring routine."

СКУЛ, -a, *m., youth, obs.* School (from Eng. "school"). ♦*Я в скул сегодня не* *пойду.* "I'm not going to school today."

СКУЛА́, -ы́, *f., crim.* An inner coat pocket (lit., a cheekbone). ♦ *Положи деньги в скулу и не показывай.* "Put the money in your inside pocket and don't let anyone see it."

СКУЛО́ВЫЙ, -ая, -ое, *youth, obs.* Of or pertaining to school, school-. ♦ *Это моя ещё скуловая герла.* "This is my old girlfriend from school."

СКУПЕРДЯ́Й, -я, *m., neg.* A stingy or greedy person. ♦ *Это такой скупердяй, ты его ещё не знаешь.* "He's a real tightwad, believe me — you don't know him yet."

СКУПЛЯ́ТЬСЯ, *imperf., south.* To buy food supplies, to shop. ♦ *Они пошли скупляться на праздник.* "They went to stock up on food for the holidays."

СКУ́РВЛИВАТЬСЯ/СКУ́РВИТЬСЯ, *rude, neg.* To change for the worse, go downhill, turn rotten (from **ку́рва**). ♦ *Он совсем скурвился, старых друзей не признаёт.* "He's really gone bad; he doesn't even say hello to his old friends any more."

СЛАБА́ НА ПЕРЕДО́К, *idiom, neg.* Promiscuous, sexually available (of a woman) (lit., weak in the pussy). ♦ *Ты уж больно слаба на передок.* "You're awfully soft in the pussy — you can't say no to any man."

СЛАБА́К, -а́, *m., neg.* A weakling. ♦ *Ты что, слабак, даже мешок поднять не можешь?* "What are you, some kind of weakling? Can't even lift that sack?"

СЛАБО́: Слабо́ кому́-л. сде́лать что-л., *idiom, neg.* Someone can't do something. ♦ *Спорим, что тебе слабо догнать меня!* "I bet you can't catch up with me!" **Не слабо́,** *idiom, joc.* Good, well. ♦ *Не слабо ездит, смотри, он уже обошёл троих гонщиков.* "He's racing very well. Look — he's already passed three other drivers."

СЛЕДА́К, -а́, *m.* A crime scene investigator (from **след**, trace). ♦ *Мы следов не оставляем, потому и следаков не боимся.* "We didn't leave any clues, so we are not afraid of any detectives."

СЛЕЗА́ТЬ/СЛЕЗТЬ: Слеза́ть/слезть с де́рева, *idiom, neg.* To become civilized or cultured (lit., to come down from the trees). ♦ *Они только что с дерева слезли, куда им демократия.* "They just came down from the trees! How do you expect them to cope with democracy?" **Слеза́ть/слезть с иглы́,** *idiom, youth.* To stop using drugs (lit., to dismount from the needle). ♦ *Говорят, он давно слез с иглы.* "They say he's quit taking drugs." **(Сесть и) не слеза́ть/не слезть с кого́-л.,** *idiom.* To bother, harass, annoy (lit., to [sit on someone and] not get off). ♦ *Они сели на родителей и не слазят, а им уже за тридцать.* "They're over thirty, but they're still constantly leaning on their parents." **Не слеза́ть с ба́бы,** *idiom, rude.* To have sex with women frequently. ♦ *Он с бабы не слезает.* "He's always sleeping with someone."

СЛЕ́САРЬ ПО ХЛЕ́БУ, *idiom, neg.* A lazy, incompetent worker (lit., a metalworker who specializes in bread). ♦ *Сын тебе помогает по хозяйству? — Нет, он в основном слесарь по хлебу.* "Does your son help out around the house? — No, he's really quite a loafer."

СЛЕСАРЮ́ГА, -и, *m.* A metalworker. ♦ *Он работает слесарюгой.* "He does metalwork."

СЛИ́ВА, -ы, *f., joc.* A blue nose as a sign of drunkenness (lit., a plum). ♦ *По его сливе сразу скажешь, сколько он пьёт.* "You can tell by his nose what a drinker he is."

СЛИВА́ТЬ/СЛИТЬ, *neg.* Lit., to pour out. **1.** To lose, be defeated. ♦ *Вчера наши немцам в футбол слили.* "Our soccer team lost to the Germans yesterday." **2.** *perf. only.* To get rid of someone. ♦ *Куда бы его слить на вечер?* "How can we manage to lose him for the evening?" ♦**Слива́ть/слить во́ду,** *idiom.* To finish, stop (lit., to pour out the water). ♦ *Сливайте воду, пора домой!* "Okay, finish up. It's time to go home!"

СЛИВА́ТЬСЯ/СЛИ́ТЬСЯ в экста́зе, *idiom, joc.* **1.** To have sex. ♦ *И потом он тебе, конечно, предложил слиться в* *экстазе.* "So then I suppose he suggested having some ecstasy." **2.** *neg.* To be carried away, be transported by emotion. ♦ *Опять они там сливаются в экстазе, свой рок слушают.* "There they are going into ecstasies over their rock music again."

СЛИВКИ, сливок, *pl., business.* Winnings from gambling (lit., cream). ♦ *Большие сливки делают в казино, а налоги не платят.* "They're making a bundle at the casino, and they don't pay any taxes on it."

СЛИМОНИТЬ, *perf. only.* To steal. ♦ *Кто слимонил мои часы?* "Who stole my watch?"

СЛИПАТЬ/ЗАСЛИПАТЬ, *youth, obs.* To sleep, take a nap (from Eng. "sleep"). ♦ *Хорошо бы сейчас заслипать.* "Now would be a good time for a nap."

СЛИПАТЬСЯ: (Жопа) не слипнется? see under **жопа.**

СЛОВО НЕ ДОКУМЕНТ, К ДЕЛУ НЕ ПОДОШЬЁШЬ, *idiom.* A mere promise can't be trusted (lit., a person's word isn't a document; it can't be entered into the file). ♦ *Слово даю, отдам долг в пятницу. — Слово не документ. . . .* "I give you my word that I'll pay you back on Friday. — A word isn't a document, it can't be entered in your file."

СЛОН, -а, *т.* Lit., elephant. **1.** *army.* A new recruit, a soldier in his first year of service. ♦ *Слоны все идут чистить картошку.* "All the new guys are going to peel potatoes." **2.** A big, akward man. ♦ *Для такого слона, как ты, нужна мебель побольше.* "This furniture is too small for a mammoth like you."

СЛОНИК, -а, *т., crim.* A method of police interrogation by regulating airflow through a gas mask (lit., baby elephant). ♦ *Неси противогаз, будем слоник ему делать.* "Bring in the gas mask, and we'll give him the treatment."

СЛУПИТЬ, *perf. only, joc., neg.* To eat something quickly or greedily (lit., to beat). ♦ *Сколько ты яиц слупил?* "How many eggs have you wolfed down?"
•**Слупить с кого-л. деньги,** *neg.* To

overcharge, cheat. ♦ *Сколько с тебя слупили за эти сапоги?* "How much did they con out of you for those boots?"

СЛУЧАЙ: Аналогичный случай был..., see under **аналогичный. Клинический случай,** see under **клинический. Тяжёлый случай,** see under **тяжёлый.**

СЛУЧКА, -и, *f., neg., rude.* A sexual encounter, sexual act. ♦ *Пойти к девкам в общагу на случку, что ли?* "I wonder if I should go over to the girls' dorm and have a roll in the hay."

СЛУШАЙ УХОМ, А НЕ БРЮХОМ, *rhyming phrase, rude.* Pay more attention (lit., Listen with your ear, not with your belly). ♦ *Я сто раз повторять не буду, слушай ухом, а не брюхом.* "Listen up! I don't want to have to repeat this a hundred times."

СЛЮНТЯЙ, -я, *т., neg.* An irresolute, spineless person (from слюна, "saliva"). ♦ *Ты на него не надейся в трудную минуту, он — слюнтяй.* "You can't count on him in difficulties; he's too indecisive."

СМАТЫВАТЬ/СМОТАТЬ удочки, *idiom.* To leave, get away from danger (lit., to reel in one's line). ♦ *Ну, сматываем удочки, скоро родители придут, они не любят, когда в доме курят.* "Let's pull out. My parents will be home soon, and they don't like it when people smoke in the house."

СМАТЫВАТЬСЯ/СМОТАТЬСЯ. See **смываться.**

СМЕНА: По хлопку — смена партнёров, see under **по.**

СМЕНКА, -и, *f.* Indoor shoes for school. ♦ *Ты сменку не забыл?* "Did you remember to take your indoor shoes?"

СМЕРТНИЧЕК, смертничка, *т., army.* A metal dog tag with a personal ID number (from смерть, death). ♦ *Тост у меня. Давайте выпьем за то, чтобы смертнички болтались на наших шеях до самого конца войны.* "Here's my toast: May our dog tags remain around our necks until the war is over."

СМЕСЬ БУЛЬДОГА С НОСОРОГОМ, *idiom, joc.* A strange or hybrid thing (lit., a cross between a bulldog and a rhinoceros). ♦ *Он сам спроектировал свою дачу, вот и получилась смесь бульдога с носорогом.* "He designed his country house himself, so it turned out neither fish nor fowl."

СМЕТА́ТЬ/СМЕСТИ́. To eat up quickly (lit., to sweep, to clean up). ♦ *Когда ты успел смести всё мясо?* "When did you manage to eat up all the meat?"

СМЕХ БЕЗ ПРИЧИ́НЫ — ПРИ́ЗНАК ДУРАЧИ́НЫ, *rhyming phrase, neg.* Lit., "Laughter without cause is a mark of stupidity," a rhyming phrase used in disparagement of inappropriate laughter. ♦ *Разве я сказал что-то смешное? Смех без причины — признак дурачины.* "What's so funny? Laughter without cause is a mark of stupidity!"

СМЕХУЁЧКИ, -ов, *pl., rude.* Tricks, jokes, fooling around. ♦ *Вам одни смехуёчки, а дело серьёзное.* "You keep kidding around, but this is a serious matter."

СМЕШИ́НКА В РОТ ПОПА́ЛА, *idiom.* To have the giggles, a bout of inappropriate laughter (lit., a funny thing got into someone's mouth). ♦ *Не пойму, чего ты так смеёшься, смешинка в рот попала?* "What are you laughing at? Having a fit of the giggles?"

СМИТИНГОВА́ТЬСЯ, *perf. only, youth.* See **забива́ть ми́тинг.**

СМОК, -а, *m., youth.* Cigarettes, tobacco products (from Eng. "smoke"). ♦ *Смок кончился.* "I have no more cigarettes."

СМОЛИ́ТЬ/ЗАСМОЛИ́ТЬ. To smoke (from смола, "pitch," "tar"). ♦ *Не смоли как паровоз.* "Don't smoke like a locomotive."

СМОРО́ЗИТЬ глу́пость, *idiom, neg.* To say or do something stupid (lit., to freeze a silly thing). ♦ *Какую я глупость сморозил, что вас послушал.* "What a stupid mistake I made by listening to you!"

СМОРЧО́К, сморчка́, *m., neg.* Lit., morel (mushroom). **1.** A cheeky young person, worthless kid. ♦ *Сморчок, как ты смеешь так разговаривать с матерью.* "You cheeky kid, how dare you talk

to your mother that way!" **2.** A small, weak person. ♦ *В любовниках у неё ходит какой-то сморчок.* "Her boyfriend is a 90-pound weakling."

СМОТРЕ́ЛКИ, смотре́лок, *pl., joc.* Eyes. ♦ *Закрывай свои смотрелки, детям уже спать пора.* "Close your peepers; it's time for little children to go to sleep."

СМОТРЕ́ТЬ/ПОСМОТРЕ́ТЬ на кого́-л., как бу́дто кто-л. до́лжен сто рубле́й, *idiom, neg.* To give someone hostile or threatening looks. ♦ *Что ты на меня смотришь, как будто я тебе сто рублей должен.* "Why are you looking at me as if I owe you a hundred rubles?"

СМОТРИ́БЕЛЬНЫЙ, -ая, -ое, *joc.* Worth seeing, interesting. ♦ *Как фильм? — Смотрибельный.* "How was the movie? — Worth seeing."

СМУР, -а, *m., neg.* A bad mood. ♦ *Сейчас у него смур, оставь его в покое.* "Leave him alone. He's in a bad mood right now." ●**Смур нахо́дит на кого́-л.,** *idiom.* Someone has the blues, is depressed. ♦ *На него смур нашёл, он бросил институт.* "He got into a funk and quit the Institute."

СМУРНЕ́ТЬ/ЗАСМУРНЕ́ТЬ, *joc.* To be gloomy, downhearted. ♦ *Да не смурней ты, будут скоро деньги.* "Don't mope — you'll have some money soon."

СМУРНО́Й, -а́я, -о́е. Gloomy, depressed. ♦ *Какой-то ты сегодня смурной.* "Why are you so gloomy today?"

СМУРЬ, -и, *f., neg.* **1.** A bad mood. ♦ *Опять у тебя смурь, ничего делать не хочешь.* "You're in a bad mood again; you just don't feel like doing anything." **2.** Bad weather. ♦ *На улице смурь, выходить не хочется.* "The weather's foul. I don't feel like going out."

СМЫВА́ТЬСЯ/СМЫ́ТЬСЯ. To leave, slip away, make off (lit., to wash off). ♦ *Давай смоемся с уроков!* "Let's slip out of school."

СМЫЧО́К: Драть/отодра́ть в два смычка́, see under **драть².**

СНАРЯ́Д, -а, *m., joc.* A large liquor bottle

(lit., [artillery] shell). ♦*Куда ты купил столько снарядов?* "How come you bought so many big bottles?"

СНЕГ, -а, *m., crim.* Bed linens (lit., snow). ♦*Вчера мы взяли снега штук на 50.* "Yesterday we stole about 50,000 rubles' worth of linens."

СНЕСТИ́СЬ, *perf. only, neg.* To say something inappropriate, out of place (lit., to lay an egg). ♦*Ну ты и снеслась, разве можно такие вещи говорить в лицо?* "Wow, you really laid an egg! Don't you know better than to say such things to someone's face?"

СНИ́КЕРС, -а, *m.* A foreigner (lit., Snickers, a brand of candy). ♦*Откуда эти сникерсы, из Франции?* "Are they from France, these foreigners?"

СНИМА́ТЬ/СНЯТЬ. To pick up a woman, make a casual acquaintance with a woman. ♦*Надо в ресторане баб снять на вечер.* "Let's pick up some dames for the evening at that restaurant." •**Снима́ть/снять пе́нки,** *idiom.* To get the best of a situation (lit., to take off the cream). ♦*Они первыми стали печатать порнографическую литературу, сняли все пенки.* "They were the first to start publishing pornography, and they skimmed the cream off that business." **Снима́ть/снять стру́жку с кого́-л.,** *idiom.* To bawl out, scold, give a tongue-lashing (lit., to take shavings off someone). ♦*За то, что они разбили окна в школе, с них сняли стружку.* "They got bawled out for breaking the windows at school." **Снима́ть/снять шку́ру,** *idiom, rude.* To beat severely (lit., to take the skin off). ♦*Я с тебя шкуру сниму, если ты его хоть пальцем тронешь.* "I'll flay you alive if you so much as touch him with your little finger." **Снять штаны́ и бе́гать,** *idiom, joc.* Lit., take off your pants and run; used as an impatient or dismissive answer to the question "What should I do?" ♦*Что делать? — Снять штаны и бегать.* "What should I do? — Take off your pants and run!"

СНИМА́ТЬСЯ/СНЯ́ТЬСЯ с ручника́, *idiom, army.* To start thinking (lit., to release the hand brake). ♦*Скорей сни-*майся *с ручника, говори, правильно идём?* "Start thinking fast: are we on the right road?"

СНОСИ́ТЬ/СНЕСТИ́, *sports.* To knock someone off his feet. ♦*Его снесли на штрафной площадке и заработали пенальти.* "They knocked him down in the penalty zone and were penalized."

СНОША́ТЬ/ПОСНОША́ТЬ, *rude.* **1.** To have sex with a woman. ♦*Он давно её сношает.* "He's been sleeping with her for a long time." **2.** To scold, bawl out. ♦*Вчера начальник всех сношал за опоздания.* "Yesterday the boss bawled out the whole staff for being late."

СНОША́ТЬСЯ/ПОСНОША́ТЬСЯ, *rude, neg.* To have sex. ♦*Тебе сношаться не надоело? Пора бы и о деле подумать.* "Aren't you tired of sleeping around? It's time to get serious!"

СНЮ́ХИВАТЬСЯ/СНЮ́ХАТЬСЯ, *neg.* To conspire, collaborate in shady dealings (lit., to sniff one another out). ♦*Они снюхались на этих махинациях.* "They conspired in these intrigues."

СНЯ́В(ШИ) ШТАНЫ́, ПО ВОЛОСА́М НЕ ГЛА́ДЯТ, *idiom, rude.* Lit., "once you've taken off your pants, it's too late to look at your hair"; used in reference to situations where one step necessarily leads to another. (This expression is a play on the proverb Снявши голову, по волосам не плачут: "When your head's been cut off, you don't cry about your hair.") ♦*Не знаю, правильно я сделала, когда решила с ним развестись. — Сняв(ши) штаны, по волосам не гладят.* "I'm not sure I should have decided to divorce him. — Well, after a certain point there's really no choice."

СОБА́КА: На соба́ках, *idiom, youth.* To travel by the Moscow suburban electric trains (lit., by dog team). ♦*Он в Москву на собаках ездит.* "He gets to Moscow by 'dog team.'"

СОБА́ЧИТЬСЯ/ПОСОБА́ЧИТЬСЯ, *neg.* To argue, quarrel, scold (from собака, "dog"). ♦*Перестаньте собачиться, лучше давайте пойдём погуляем.* "Stop arguing and let's go out for a while!"

СОБА́ЧЬЯ РА́ДОСТЬ, *idiom:* Cheap meat pies sold in the street (lit., dog's delight). ♦*Собачью радость будешь есть?* "Will you have a 'doggy-treat'?"

СОБА́ЧЬЯ СВА́ДЬБА, *idiom.* A casual love affair (lit., a dog's wedding). ♦*У него опять собачья свадьба.* "He's having another one of his flings."

СОВА́: Не пьёт то́лько сова́: она́ днём спит, а но́чью магази́ны закры́ты, see under **не.**

СОВА́ТЬ/СУ́НУТЬ нос куда́ не сле́дует, *idiom, neg.* To meddle, be nosy (lit., to poke one's nose in inappropriate places). ♦*Ты опять читал мои письма, не суй нос куда не следует.* "You've been reading my mail again! Don't be so nosy!"

СОВДЕ́ПИЯ, -и, *f., obs., neg.* Soviet Russia, the Soviet Union (from Советские депутаты). ♦*Ты читал газеты, как там дела в Совдепии идут?* "Have you read the papers? What's new in the Sov. Dep.?"

СОВДЕ́ПОВСКИЙ, -ая, -ое, *neg.* Soviet (cf. **Совде́пия**). ♦*Мне надоели ваши совдеповские порядки: того нельзя, этого нельзя.* "I'm sick of your Soviet setup — with you everything's forbidden!"

СОВКО́ВЫЙ, -ая, -ое, *neg.* Soviet (see **сово́к**). ♦*Совковую одежду сразу видно.* "You can recognize Soviet-made clothes instantly."

СОВО́К, совка́, *m., neg.* By wordplay on совок, "dustpan," and советский, "Soviet." **1.** The Soviet Union. ♦*Как жить в нашем совке, не понимаю.* "I can't figure out how to survive in this Soviet dustpan of ours." **2.** A Soviet type of person, an ignorant, narrowminded, doctrinaire person. ♦*Он никогда не поймёт, что хотят демократы, он же совок!* "He'll never be able to grasp what the democrats are after; he's a Soviet-dustpan type!"

СОВРЁТ — НЕ ПОМО́РЩИТСЯ (НЕ ЧИХНЁТ), *idiom, neg.* Lit., "He can lie without grimacing"; an expression used to blame someone as a habitual liar. ♦*He*

слушай её, соврёт — не поморщится.* "Don't listen to her! She'll lie at the drop of a hat."

СОЕДИНЯ́ТЬ/СОЕДИНИ́ТЬ МА́МУ С ПА́ПОЙ, *idiom.* Connecting a plug to a socket (lit., to connect a mom and a pop). ♦*Здесь нет света, ты можешь соединить маму с папой?* "The light's still not on here. Can you get the male end into the female socket?"

СОЗРЕВА́ТЬ/СОЗРЕ́ТЬ. To be ready or eager to do something (lit., to be ripe). ♦*Ты знаешь, я уже созрел выпить. Столько волнений было за день, пора расслабиться.* "Well, I'm ready for a drink. After all today's troubles it's time to relax."

СОЙДЁТ, *idiom.* It's okay, it'll do. ♦*Тебе не холодно будет в плаще? — Ничего, сойдёт.* "Won't you be cold in that raincoat? — No, it'll be fine." ●**Сойдёт для се́льской ме́стности,** *idiom, joc.* Lit., "It'll do for village life." ♦*Как моя новая причёска? — Сойдёт для сельской местности.* "How do you like my new haircut? — It'll do for down on the farm!"

СОЛДАФО́Н, -а, *m., neg.* A rough, rude, military type of person. ♦*Да это же солдафон, всё время орёт, командует.* "He's a real soldier type — always yelling and ordering people around."

СОЛОВЕ́Й, вья́, *m., joc.* A policeman (lit., nightingale, referring to the similarity of the bird's warbling and the police whistle). ♦*Наш соловей сначала свистнет, потом грабит.* "Our police start by whistling at you and end up robbing you."

СОЛО́МА, -ы, *f., youth.* Chopped poppyheads for use as a narcotic (lit., stubble). ♦*Солому заготовил?* "Have you got the 'stubble' ready?"

СО́ЛОП, -а, *m., rude.* A penis. ♦*Тебе солоп покою не даёт, всё время на баб тянет.* "Your prick never lets up — it's always hankering after women." ●**Со́лоп тебе́ на́до?** *idiom, rude.* What more do you want? Why do you keep bothering me? ♦*Всё у тебя есть, солоп тебе надо?* "Isn't that enough for you? What do you want, a prick?"

СОЛЯ́НКА, -и, *f., neg.* A confused mixture (lit., the name of a type of soup). ♦ *Это не концерт, а солянка: и классика, и джаз в одном стакане.* "This isn't a concert, it's a soup of classical and jazz."

СÓННАЯ ТЕТÉРЯ, *idiom, neg.* Someone who prefers sleeping to doing anything (lit., a sleepy grouse). ♦ *Эх ты, сонная тетеря, всю рыбалку проспал!* "Hey, sleepyhead! You missed the whole fishing trip!"

СОНЬЁ, -я́, *n., joc.* A product of the Sony Company (by wordplay on "Sony" and **санье́**). ♦ *Чей это телевизор? — Это соньё.* "What kind of TV is that? — A Sony."

СООБРАЖÁЛКА, -и, *f., joc.* Mind, intelligence. ♦ *Если есть у тебя соображалка, на новой работе не пропадёшь.* "If you've got any sense you won't miss work at your new job."

СОПÁТКА, -и, *f., neg.* Nose (from сопеть, "to breathe noisily through the nose"). ♦ *Твоему дружку сопатку разбили.* "They punched your buddy in the nose."

СОПЛÉВИЧ, -а, *m., youth, joc.* Narcotics, drugs (from сопля, "snot"). ♦ *Ещё немного соплевича осталось.* "There's still a little dope left."

СОПЛЕГЛÓТ, -а, *m., colloquial, neg.* (From сопля, "snot.") **1.** A person of weak character. ♦ *Эти соплеглоты никогда не пойдут против начальства.* "Those snivelers will never stand up against the bosses." **2.** Someone with the sniffles, with a runny nose. ♦ *Возьми с собой платок, соплеглот несчастный.* "Don't forget to take a handkerchief, you poor sniffler."

СÓПЛИ: На сопля́х, *idiom, neg.* Weakly, barely, with difficulty (lit., [held together] by snot). ♦ *Дверь у меня в квартире держится на соплях.* "The door to my apartment is just barely attached to its hinges." **Сóпли-вóпли,** *idiom, neg.* Whining, moaning and groaning (cf. сопля, "snot"). ♦ *Ну нет денег и*

ладно. Мне эти сопли-вопли о нищете надоели. "There's no money and that's all there is to it. I don't want to hear your moaning and groaning about being so poor." **Разма́зывать со́пли по забо́ру,** see under **разма́зывать.**

СОПЛИ́ВЫЙ, -ая, -ое, *neg.* Too young, green, inexperienced (lit., snot-nosed). ♦ *Ты ещё сопливый мать учить.* "You're too young to be telling your mother what to do." •**Обходи́ться/обойти́сь без сопли́вых,** see under **обходи́ться.**

СОПЛИ́ВЫЙ, -ого, *m., rude.* A penis (lit., drippy fellow; from сопля, "snot"). ♦ *Холодно. У меня сопливый чуть не отмёрз.* "It's so cold my 'dripper' is half frozen."

СÓПЛО, -а, *n., neg., joc.* A nose. ♦ *Хочешь в сопло, чтоб не выступал?* "You're going to get it in the nose if you don't cut out that behavior!"

СОПЛЮ́ШКА, -и, *f., neg., joc.* A young, inexperienced girl (from сопля, "snot"). ♦ *Что ты, соплюшка, понимаешь в жизни?* "What do you know about life, you little chit?"

СОПЛЯ́, -и́, *f., army, neg.* An epaulet-stripe as a sign of rank (lit., snot). ♦ *Ему дали ещё одну соплю.* "They gave him another stripe."

СОПЛЯ́К, -á, *m., neg.* A young, inexperienced person (from сопля, "snot"). ♦ *Чего этот сопляк выпендривается? Мал ещё.* "What's that little brat showing off about? He's still a baby."

СОПЛЯ́ЧКА, -и, *f., neg.* See **соплю́шка.**

СОРВÁТЬ резьбу́, *idiom, neg.* To go on a drinking spree, to get completely drunk (lit., to strip the threads of a screw). ♦ *Он опять сорвал резьбу, на работу не ходит уже три дня.* "He's on another drinking bout; he hasn't been to work in three days."

СОРОКÓВНИК, -а, *m.* **1.** Forty years. ♦ *Ему уже сороковник.* "He's already forty years old." **2.** *obs.* Forty rubles. ♦ *Дай сороковник до зарплаты.* "Let me borrow forty rubles until payday." **3.** Forty thousand rubles.

СОРОКОПЯ́ТКА, -и, *f., obs.* A 45-rpm record. ♦ *Эта песня есть только на сорокопятке.* "That song is only available on a 45."

СОСА́ТЬСЯ/ПОСОСА́ТЬСЯ, *rude.* To kiss (from сосать, "to suck"). ♦ *Они сосались целый вечер.* "They've been kissing away all evening."

СОСИ́СКА: Пья́ный в соси́ску, see under **пья́ный.**

СОСКА́КИВАТЬ/СОСКОЧИ́ТЬ. *Lit.,* to jump off. **1.** To leave. ♦ *Он соскочил минут пять назад.* "He just left about five minutes ago." **2.** To leave alone, stop bothering. ♦ *Ты с меня соскочишь со своими просьбами?* "Get off my back with your constant demands!"

СОСКО́К, *interj., neg.* Scram! Buzz off! (cf. **соска́кивать**). ♦ *Ну-ка, быстро соскок отсюда!* "Hey, get out of here!"

СОСТОЯ́НИЕ НЕСТОЯ́НИЯ, *rhyming phrase, neg., joc.* Sexual impotence (by wordplay on **стоя́ть**; lit., a condition of nonstanding). ♦ *У тебя опять состояние нестояния?* "What's with you? Again you're in a nonstanding condition?"

СОСТЫКО́ВАТЬСЯ/СОСТЫКО-ВА́ТЬСЯ, *joc.* To meet, to join (lit., to dock [spacecraft]). ♦ *Стыкуемся за полчаса до отхода поезда.* "We'll meet half an hour before the train leaves."

СОСУНО́К, сосунка́, *m., neg.* A young, innocent, inexperienced person (lit., a suckling). ♦ *Тебе, сосунку, ещё рано такие фильмы смотреть.* "Aren't you still a little wet behind the ears to be watching that sort of movie?"

СОТВОРЯ́ТЬ/СОТВОРИ́ТЬ шлазь, *idiom, crim.* To slap in the face. ♦ *Если тебе сотворить шлазь, думаешь, не обидно?* "You think it's not an insult to be slapped in the face?"

СОХА́ТЫЙ, -ого, *m., crim., neg.* Lit., a moose. **1.** A cuckold. ♦ *Кто сделал его сохатым?* "Who cuckolded him?" **2.** A fool. ♦ *Сохатый он и есть сохатый, ничего толком сказать не может.* "He's a prize fool; he never says anything that makes any sense."

СОЦИАЛИ́СТ(Ы), -а (-ов), *m., obs.* Citizen(s) of socialist (Soviet-bloc) countries. ♦ *Я работаю переводчиком у социалистов.* "I'm working as a translator in countries of the Soviet bloc."

СОЦНАКОПЛЕ́НИЕ, -я, *n., neg., obs.* A potbelly (from социалистическое накопление; lit., a Socialist savings account, i.e., a savings account in a state bank). ♦ *Да, у тебя приличное соцнакопление.* "That's quite a potbelly you've got there."

СПАГЕ́ТТИ: Ве́шать/пове́сить спаге́тти на́ уши, see under **ве́шать.**

СПАЛИ́ТЬСЯ, *perf. only.* To get caught doing something wrong (lit., to get burned). ♦ *Они спалились на взятках.* "They got caught taking bribes."

СПА́ЛЬНЫЙ РАЙО́Н, *idiom.* A residential region on the outskirts of a city (lit., a sleeping region). ♦ *Все её друзья живут в спальных районах.* "All her friends live way out in the bedroom communities."

СПАСИ́БО: Спаси́бо — некраси́во, надо де́нежки плати́ть, *idiom, joc.* Professions of gratitude aren't enough; gratitude isn't a sufficient reward. ♦ *Ну, спасибо за всё. — Спасибо — некрасиво, надо денежки платить.* "Thanks for everything! — Thanks are worthless without a cash payment." **За спаси́бо,** *idiom.* Gratis, for free (lit., for a thank-you). ♦ *За спасибо никто теперь работать не будет.* "These days no one's going to work for nothing."

СПАТЬ: Не спи, замёрзнешь, see under **не.**

СПЕКУЛЬНУ́ТЬ, *perf. only, neg.* To sell, trade. ♦ *Спекульнуть надо часами, чтоб немного подзаработать.* "I've got to do some trade in watches to earn a little extra money."

СПЕРМАТОЗА́ВР, -а, *youth, joc.* Sperm (by wordplay on сперматозоид, "spermatozoon," and динозавр, "dinosaur"). ♦ *От моих сперматозавров только сыновья получаются.* "My sperm makes only sons."

СПЕРМОНАЧА́ЛЬНО, *adv., joc.* From

the beginning, to begin with, at once (by wordplay on сперма and первоначально). ♦*Ты скажи спермоначально, куда ты собираешься нас везти отдыхать.* "To begin with, tell us where you're planning to take us for vacation."

СПЕЦУ́ХА, -и, *f., youth.* A student's major subject in an institution of higher education. ♦*Когда у нас спецуха?* "When does the class in our major subject meet?"

СПЕШУ́ И ПА́ДАЮ, *idiom, neg., joc.* No way; I certainly won't do that (lit., "I'll hurry [to do what you say] so fast that I'll fall down"). ♦*Иди учить уроки! Хватит смотреть телевизор. — Спешу и падаю.* "You've watched enough television. Now go do your homework! — Not a chance!"

СПИДО́МЕТР, -а, *m., joc., neg.* A blood test for AIDS (from СПИД, "AIDS," by wordplay on "speedometer"). ♦*Тебе делали спидометр?* "Did you have your AIDS test?"

СПИДОНО́СЕЦ, спидоно́сца, *m., neg.* An AIDS carrier, someone who has AIDS (-носец, "carrier"). ♦*Бери эту ложку, спидоносцев у нас нет, не бойся.* "Don't worry about using the spoon — no one here has AIDS."

СПИНА́: Пони́же спины́, *idiom, joc.* On the buttocks (lit., below the spine). ♦*Дать бы тебе пониже спины за эти слова.* "You deserve a spanking for what you said."

СПИНОГРЫ́З, -а, *m., joc.* A child (lit., a spine-gnawer). ♦*У неё двое спиногрызов.* "She's got a couple of children."

СПИОНЕ́РИВАТЬ/СПИОНЕ́РИТЬ, *joc.* To steal (from пионер, member of a junior Komsomol youth group; cf. **скоммуни́здить**). ♦*Сколько колбасы спионерили?* "How much sausage did they steal?"

СПИ́ХИВАТЬ/СПИХНУ́ТЬ экза́мен, *idiom, youth.* To pass an examination. ♦*Никак не могу спихнуть английский.* "There's no way I can pass the English exam."

СПИХОТЕ́ХНИКА, -и, *f., neg.* The art of passing the buck, leaving the decision to someone else (from спихивать, "to put off" [as a decision]). ♦*Он полностью овладел спихотехникой.* "He's a past master of the art of passing the buck."

СПИ́ЧИТЬ/ЗАСПИ́ЧИТЬ, *joc.* To speak, to speechify (from Eng. "speech"). ♦*Что он там спичет о светлом будущем?* "What's he speechifying about the bright future for?"

СПЛАВЛЯ́ТЬ/СПЛА́ВИТЬ, *neg.* Lit., to float (logs) down a river. **1.** To sell. ♦*Эти вещи надо срочно сплавить.* "We'd better sell this stuff quickly." **2.** To get rid of. ♦*Она мужа сплавила на дачу.* "She sent her husband packing off to the dacha."

СПЛЫ́ТЬ: Был да сплыл, see under **был**.

СПОК: Будь спок!, see under **будь**.

СПОКУ́ХА, -и, *f., youth.* Calm down, don't get excited (lit., peace and quiet). ♦*Спокуха, ничего ещё не произошло, а вы в панике.* "Calm down! Nothing's happened yet, and you're already in a panic!"

СПО́РИТЬ: Кто спо́рит, тот говна́ не сто́ит, see under **кто**.

СПО́РИТЬ С НАЧА́ЛЬСТВОМ, ЧТО ССАТЬ ПРО́ТИВ ВЕ́ТРА, *idiom, rude.* Arguing with the boss only leads to trouble for yourself (lit., "Arguing with the management is like pissing into the wind"). ♦*Зачем ты его критикуешь? Спорить с начальством, что...* "Why do you criticize him? Arguing with the boss can only get you into trouble."

СПОРТИ́ВНЫЙ ИНТЕРЕ́С, *idiom.* Lit., a sporting interest, that is, disinterested motives. ♦*Он это делает из спортивного интереса или как?* "Is he doing this out of a purely sporting interest, or what?"

СПРОСИ́ О ЧЁМ-НИБУ́ДЬ ПОЛЕ́ГЧЕ, *idiom, joc.* I haven't the faintest idea (lit., ask me about something easier). ♦*Скажи, будет повышение цен? — Спроси о чём-нибудь полегче.* "Tell me, do you think prices are about to go up? — I haven't the faintest idea."

СПРЫ́ГИВАТЬ/СПРЫ́ГНУТЬ, *youth.* **1.** To leave. ♦*Спрыгни отсюда!* "Get out of here!" **2.** To stop, quit. ♦*Он спрыгнул с кайфа.* "He quit drinking."

СПУСК, -а, *m., rude.* An orgasm. ♦*Когда же у тебя спуск будет?* "When are you going to come?"

СПУСКА́ТЬ/СПУСТИ́ТЬ, *rude.* To have an orgasm (lit., to let down). ♦*Я не могу спускать по пьянке.* "I can't come when I'm drunk." •**Спуска́ть/спусти́ть на тормоза́х,** *idiom.* To hush something up, prevent something from coming to trial (lit., put the brakes on something). ♦*Случай с твоим товарищем надо спустить на тормозах.* "Your friend's situation has to be hushed up."

СПЯ́ТИТЬ, *perf. only, neg.* To go crazy, lose one's mind. ♦*Ты что, спятил что ли? Кто же покупает мясо за такую цену?* "Are you out of your mind? No one spends that much on meat!"

СРА́КА, -и, *f., rude.* Buttocks. ♦*Оторви сраку от стула, помой посуду.* "Get your ass off that chair and wash the dishes." •**До сра́ки,** *idiom, rude.* Of no importance, indifferent. ♦*Мне его слова до сраки.* "What he says doesn't matter to me."

СРА́НЫЙ, -ая, -ое, *rude.* Bad, worthless. ♦*Зачем мне эти сраные подарки?* "What do I need these lousy presents for?"

СРАНЬЁ, -я́, *n., rude.* Shit, a pile of shit. •**Встава́ть/встать сранья́,** see under **встава́ть.**

СРАСТА́ТЬСЯ/СРАСТИ́ТЬСЯ, *impers., youth.* To work out, be arranged (lit, to grow together). ♦*У меня не срастается на каникулы поехать домой.* "I can't manage to go home for the holidays."

СРАТЬ/НАСРА́ТЬ, ПОСРА́ТЬ, *rude.* To shit. ♦*Где тут у вас посрать можно?* "Where can a person take a shit around here?" •**Срать/насра́ть (хоте́ть) на кого-что-л.,** *idiom.* To hold in contempt. ♦*Срать я на него хотел, на его угрозы.* "I shit on him and his threats." **Срать/насра́ть с высо́кой го́рки,** *idiom, rude.* Not to care, to be indifferent (lit., to shit from a high hill). ♦*Тебе попадёт за то, что пропускаешь лекции.· — А мне насрать с высокой горки.* "You're going to get in trouble for missing classes.· — I don't give a shit." **Срать ма́ком кому́-л.,** *idiom, rude.* No matter how hard one tries, in spite of all one's efforts (lit., [even if] one shits poppy seeds). ♦*Тебе срать маком до него, он уже известный учёный, а ты никто.* "You can try your best with him, but after all he's a famous scholar and you're just a nobody." **Срать не про́сишься,** *idiom, neg., rude.* To act independent, grown-up (lit., not to ask permission to shit). ♦*Жениться решил, молодец, срать не просишься, а подумал, где вы будете жить?* "So you've decided to get married! Well, that seems very grown-up of you, except that you haven't given a thought to where you're going to live." **Не сесть ря́дом срать с кем-л.,** *idiom, neg., rude.* To hold someone in contempt, to want nothing to do with someone (lit., not to sit next to someone to take a shit). ♦*Я с этим человеком срать рядом не сяду.* "I wouldn't have anything to do with that fellow." **Во рту как ко́шки насра́ли,** *idiom, rude.* Lit., "It's as if cats took a shit in my mouth." Used to describe a bad taste in the mouth, especially of a hangover. ♦*Проснулись, а во рту как кошки насрали, вчера перекурили и выпили лишнее.* "They woke up with the taste of cat shit in their mouths after smoking and drinking too much last night." **Жрать до по́та, срать до слёз,** see under **жрать.**

СРАЧ, -а, *m., rude.* A mess, disorder. ♦*Я пойду в магазин, а ты весь этот срач в квартире убери.* "I'll go shopping, and you clean up the mess in the apartment."

СРЕ́ДНЕЙ ПАРШИ́ВОСТИ, *idiom.* Of poor quality (lit., of medium lousiness). ♦*Вот купил, а колбаса средней паршивости.* "That sausage I bought is pretty awful."

СРОК: Мота́ть срок, see under **мота́ть.**

СРУБА́ТЬ фи́шку, *idiom, youth.* To

understand (lit., to cut the cards). ♦*Теперь срубаешь фишку, почему они не приехали?* "Now do you understand why they didn't come?"

СРЫВА́ТЬ/СОРВА́ТЬ КРЫ́ШУ, *idiom.* Said of drunk or drugged people (lit., someone's roof has blown away). See **кры́ша.** ♦*У него крышу сорвало после выпитой бутылки, вот он и отправился на танке в город за второй.* "He drank a bottle, flipped his lid, hijacked a tank, and drove it into town for another bottle."

СРЫВА́ТЬСЯ/СОРВА́ТЬСЯ. 1. *youth.* To slip away. ♦*Давай сорвёмся с последнего урока.* "Let's cut the last class." **2.** *perf. only.* To appear unexpectedly. ♦*Ты откуда сорвался?* "Where did you pop up from?"

ССА́КИ, ссак, *pl., rude.* Urine. ♦*Это не пиво, а ссаки.* "This isn't beer, it's just piss."

ССАНЬЁ, -я́, *n., rude.* Piss, a pool of piss, a mess. ♦*Чьё это ссаньё, кота?* "Who made this piss-pool — the cat?"

ССАТЬ/ПОССА́ТЬ, *rude.* To urinate. ♦*Поссать хочется.* "I need to take a piss." •**Ссать кипятко́м,** *idiom, rude.* To be enthusiastic, eager, carried away by someone or something (lit., to piss boiling water). ♦*У нас молодой профессор читал лекцию, все бабы ссали кипятком.* "A young professor came to lecture, and all the girls were peeing in their pants over him." **Не ссы (, прорвёмся)!,** see under **не.**

ССУН, -а́, *m., rude.* **1.** Someone who urinates a lot. ♦*Ну ты и ссун, каждые пять минут в туалет бегаешь.* "What a pisser you are — running to the john every five minutes!" **2.** A coward. *Это ссун известный, всё время дрожит за свою шкуру.* "Everyone knows he's a coward — always worried about saving his own skin."

ССЫКУ́Н, -а́, *m., rude, neg.* **1.** Someone who urinates frequently, or a child who wets the bed or his pants. ♦*Ну ты и ссыкун, все простыни промочил.* "What a

piss pot you are! You've gone and soaked the sheets." **2.** A coward. ♦*Этот ссыкун драться не будет.* "That coward won't fight with you."

ССЫКУ́ХА, -и, *f., neg., rude.* **1.** A girl who wets the bed or her pants. ♦*Эта ссыкуха опять мокрая.* "That little pisser is all wet again." **2.** A woman who urinates frequently. ♦*Ты опять, ссыку́ха, в туалет?* "Off to the john yet again, you pisser?" **3.** An innocent, inexperienced girl. ♦*Ты ещё ссыкуха, чтобы так рассуждать, подрасти сначала.* "You're still too much of a baby to discuss such things; wait till you grow up a little."

СТАБУ́НИВАТЬСЯ/СТАБУНИ́ТЬСЯ, *joc.* To crowd together (lit., to herd). ♦*Опять вы все стабунились на кухне, идите в комнаты.* "Why are you all crowded into the kitchen again? Go to the living room."

СТАВ, -а, *m., business.* Goods, merchandise (from ставить, "to put"). ♦*Ты став принёс?* "Have you brought the goods?"

СТА́ВИТЬ/ПОСТА́ВИТЬ: Ста́вить/поста́вить кли́зму, *idiom, neg.* To scold, abuse, punish (lit., to give an enema). ♦*Сейчас ему ставят клизму за обман.* "Now he's going to get his punishment for the trick he played." **Ста́вить/поста́вить на кно́пку,** *idiom.* (To bug, to monitor covertly (lit., to put on the button). ♦*Его телефон ставьте на кнопку.* "Bug his telephone." **Ста́вить/поста́вить на счётчик,** *idiom.* To set a punitive interest rate for debts not paid on time (lit., to put someone on the meter). ♦*Мы тебя поставили на счётчик, ты уже неделю не отдаёшь деньги.* "We've put you on the meter because you're a week behind in your payments." **Ста́вить/поста́вить писто́н,** *idiom, rude.* To have sex, to have an erection. ♦*Сколько ты можешь поставить пистонов за ночь?* "How many times can you make love to a woman in one night?" **Ста́вить/поста́вить гнило́й писто́н,** *idiom, joc.* To have sex as a remedy for a hangover (гнилой, "rotten").

♦*Сейчас бы неплохо гнилой пистон поставить.* "A little tumble would be just the thing right now." **Ста́вить/поста́вить та́ксу,** *idiom.* To set a price. ♦*Какую вы поставили таксу на сигареты?* "What price have you set for the cigarettes?" **Ста́вить/поста́вить финга́л,** *idiom, joc.* To give someone a black eye. ♦*Кто тебе поставил такой фингал?* "Who gave you that black eye?"

СТА́ВКА, -и, *f., crim.* The headquarters of a mafia boss. ♦*В ставку так просто не попадёшь, её охраняют и ещё как.* "It's not so easy to get into his headquarters, it's heavily guarded."

СТА́ДО, -а, *n., neg.* A crowd (lit., a herd). ♦*В магазине стадо, я в очереди стоять не хочу.* "There's a herd of people in the store, and I don't want to wait in line."

СТАКА́Н, -а, *m., neg.* A traffic-control station (lit., a glass). ♦*Тише, сбавь скорость, впереди стакан.* "Slow down. There's a 'glass' up ahead."

СТАКА́НОВЕЦ, стака́новца, *m., joc.* A drunk, a "hero of the drinking-glass" (by wordplay on стакан, "drinking-glass," and Стаханов, the first "Hero of Socialist Labor," a miner who, in the industrializing years of the 1930s, greatly exceeded his production norm). ♦*Вы все — стакановцы!* "You're a bunch of drunks!"

СТА́ЛИНСКИЙ ТОРТ, *idiom, neg.* A "Stalin cake," a grandiose building of a type favored and often constructed under Stalin (in the so-called Stalin baroque style). ♦*А вот это здание — совсем сталинский торт.* "That building is a real Stalin cake."

СТА́ЛКЕР, -а, *m., youth.* A pimp (from the name of a character in a science fiction story by the Strugatsky brothers). ♦*А он сейчас ещё в сталкерах ходит, не знаешь?* "Is he still working as a pimp these days?"

СТАНОВИ́ТЬСЯ/СТАТЬ ра́ком, *idiom, rude.* To take up a position with rear end up. ♦*Чего ты бошься идти к врачу? Станешь раком, он тебе в зад заглянет, и все дела.* "Why are you so nervous about going to the doctor? You'll take the crab position, he'll look up your ass, and that's all there is to it."

СТАНО́К, станка́, *m., joc.* Lit., a lathe. **1.** A woman's buttocks. ♦*Станок у неё знатный.* "She's got a beautiful ass." **2.** A highly sexed woman. ♦*Это такой станок, только держись!* "Watch out, she's a real sexpot!" **3.** A bed. ♦*Готовь станок, давай ляжем.* "Make the bed so we can lie down."

СТА́НЦИЯ «БЕРЕЗА́Й»! КОМУ́ НА́ДО — ВЫЛЕЗА́Й! *idiom, joc.* Lit., "Berezai Station! All off that's getting off!" A rhyming phrase used to attract the attention of dozing or distracted passengers to arrival at a station. ♦*Вот деревня, автобус здесь стоит две минуты. Станция «Березай»! Кому надо — вылезай.* "There's the village. The bus will only stop here for a minute. 'Berezai Station! All off that's getting off!'"

СТА́РАЯ БОЕВА́Я ЛО́ШАДЬ, *f., idiom, joc.* A loyal wife or girlfriend (lit., an old warhorse). ♦*А это моя старая боевая лошадь.* "Meet my dear old gal."

СТАРИКОВА́ТЬ/ЗАСТАРИКОВА́ТЬ, *army.* To start acting like an experienced soldier (from старик, an old man). ♦*Притормози, больно шустро ты начал стариковать.* "Just yesterday you were a green recruit. Now all of a sudden you're pushing people around, acting like a second-year man."

СТАРЛЕ́Й, -я, *m., army.* A first lieutenant. ♦*Тебе старлей передал письмо?* "Did the lieutenant give you the letter?"

СТАРОПРИЖИ́МНЫЙ, -ая, -ое, *joc.* An inflexible, reactionary person, someone who sticks to the rules and codes of the "old" (i.e., Soviet) regime (by wordplay on старорежимный, "belonging to the old regime," and прижимать, "to oppress" or "to suppress"). ♦*Он таким же староприжимным и остался, хотя сейчас другое время.* "Times have changed, but he's still the same old-regimer he always was."

СТА́РОСТЬ НЕ РА́ДОСТЬ (ДА И МО́ЛОДОСТЬ ГА́ДОСТЬ), *idiom.* A sardonic comment on aging (lit., "Old age is no joy, and youth is pretty awful too.")

СТАРПЁР, -а, *m., rude.* An old man (from <u>стары</u>й <u>пердун</u>; cf. **перду́н**). ♦*В политбюро сидели одни старпёры.* "The guys in the Politburo were all a bunch of old farts."

СТАРШО́Й, -о́го, *m.* A leader, boss, director. ♦*Кто у вас старшой?* "Who's in charge here?"

СТА́РЫЙ КОНЬ БОРОЗДЫ́ НЕ ПО́Р-ТИТ, *idiom.* Lit., an old horse doesn't mess up the furrow; an expression used to sum up the advantages of older men as lovers and, by extension, of older people in any activity. ♦*Ну и что же, что он старый, старый конь борозды не портит.* "So what if he's old! An old horse doesn't mess up the furrow, you know."

СТА́СИК, -а, *m.* A cockroach. ♦*Я этих стасиков не переношу.* "I can't stand these cockroaches."

СТВОЛ, -а́, *m., rude.* Lit., the barrel of a gun. **1.** A penis. ♦*Что это у тебя ствол торчит?* "How come your prick is sticking out like that?" **2.** A gun. ♦*Сколько у нас стволов?* "How many guns have we got here?"

СТЁБ: Поднима́ть/подня́ть стёб, see under **поднима́ть**.

СТЕБАНУ́ТЫЙ, -ая, -ое, *rude, neg.* Crazy, idiotic. ♦*Только стебанутый мог такое учудить.* "Only an idiot could pull off a stunt like that."

СТЕБАНУ́ТЬСЯ, *perf. only, rude.* To go crazy. ♦*От всех переживаний стебануться можно.* "These troubles could drive a person crazy."

СТЕБА́ТЬСЯ¹, *imperf. only, youth, rude.* To mock, ridicule. ♦*Кончай над ним стебаться.* "Stop making fun of him."

СТЕБА́ТЬСЯ²/ПОСТЕБА́ТЬСЯ, *rude.* To have sexual relations (cf. **ёб-**). ♦*Они стебаются уже полгода.* "They've been sleeping together for half a year." •**Стеба́ться — смея́ться,** *idiom, rude.* Incredible! Too much! ♦*Стебаться — смеяться, сколько нас ещё будут накалывать!* "This is unbelievable! How long can they go on cheating us like this!"

СТЕЙТСО́ВЫЙ, -ая, -ое, *youth.* American (from Eng. "the States"). ♦*Стейтсовые фильмы всегда забойные.* "American movies are always interesting."

СТЕЙТСЫ́, -о́в, *pl., youth.* Americans (see **стейтсо́вый**). ♦*Когда стейтсы приедут?* "When are the Americans coming?"

СТЕКЛО́, -а́, *n., youth.* Glass utensils for preparing narcotics. ♦*Стекло у тебя грязное, помой.* "Your glassware is dirty — wash it."

СТЁКЛЫШКО: Трéзвый как стёк-лышко, see under **трéзвый.**

СТЕКЛЯНÉТЬ/ОСТЕКЛЯНÉТЬ, *neg., joc.* To get drunk, become glassy-eyed. ♦*Ты уже совсем остеклянел, ничего перед собой не видишь, того и гляди — упадёшь.* "You're already so drunk that you can't see what's in front of your nose. Watch out that you don't fall!"

СТЕКЛЯ́ШКА, -и, *f.* A type of café with big windows, constructed especially in the days of Khrushchev. ♦*Давай посидим в стекляшке на углу.* "Let's get a corner table in the 'steklyashka.'"

СТÉЛЬКА: Пья́ный в стéльку, see under **пья́ный.**

СТЕНД, -а, *m., youth.* An erection (from Eng. "stand"). ♦*В кои веки у меня стенд, а баб нет.* "Here I am with one of my rare erections, and not a woman in sight!"

СТÉПА, -ы, *f., youth.* A student stipend (lit., a nickname for Stepan). ♦*Наша стёпа у старосты.* "Our group leader has our stipend payments."

СТÉРВА, -ы, *f., rude.* A nasty or worthless woman (cf. **стервятник**, "vulture"). ♦*Такую стерву, как наша комендантша, поискать надо.* "Our house mother is a real stinker."

СТИП, -а, *m., youth.* A student stipend. ♦*Когда выдадут стип?* "When are they going to pay our stipend?"

СТОЛБ: Не пьёт тóлько телегрáфный столб (, у негó чáшки вниз), see under **не.**

СТОЛИ́ЦА, -ы, *f.* **1.** A Stolichnaya brand

cigarette. ♦*Ты что куришь, "столи- цу"?* "What are you smoking, a Stolich- naya?" **2.** Stolichnaya brand vodka. ♦*Почём "столица"?* "How much is a bottle of Stolichnaya?"

СТОЛО́ВКА, -и, *f.* A cafeteria, dining hall. ♦*Столовка уже открыта?* "Is the cafeteria open yet?"

СТО́ЛЬНИК, -а, *m.* **1.** *obs.* A hundred- ruble bill. ♦*Ты не забыл, что надо стольник отдать соседу?* "Did you forget to pay our neighbor the hundred we owe him?" **2.** A hundred thousand rubles.

СТОН СО СВИ́СТОМ, *idiom, youth.* Excellent, wonderful (lit., a groan with a whistle). ♦*Он анекдоты рассказы- вает — прямо стон со свистом.* "He's fantastic at telling jokes."

СТОП: Éхать сто́пом, see under **éхать.**

СТОПА́РИК: Вре́зать по стопа́рику, see under **вре́зать.**

СТОПА́РЬ, -я, *m., army.* A useless soldier (from стоп, a stop, meaning that this per- son lets a unit down by poor perfor- mance). See **ручни́к.** ♦*Мне его и даром в роту не надо, все знают, какой он стопарь.* "I don't want him in my com- pany, he's a fuck-up."

СТО́ПИТЬ/ЗАСТО́ПИТЬ, *youth.* To stop a car in order to hitch a ride or, more likely, in order to negotiate payment for a ride (from Eng. "stop"). ♦*Поехали, я за- стопил машину.* "Come on! I've flagged down a car."

СТО́ПОР, -а, *m., neg.* Dullness, stupor, mental sluggishness (from Eng. "stop"). ♦*На меня стопор напал, ничего не соображаю.* "A mental shutdown has come over me; I can't think at all."

СТОПОРИ́ЛА, -ы, *m., crim., neg.* A ban- dit, armed robber. ♦*Когда этого стопо- рилу возьмут?* "When are they going to catch that bandit?"

СТОРЧА́ТЬСЯ, *perf. only, youth, neg.* To die from an overdose of narcotics. ♦*Ты знаешь, Николай вчера сторчался.* "Yesterday Nick died from an overdose."

СТОЯ́К, -á, *m.* **1.** A beer bar without seats. ♦*Там посидеть можно или это*

стояк? "Can we sit down in that bar or is it a 'stander'?" **2.** *rude.* An erection. ♦*По утрам у него стояк — двумя руками не согнёшь.* "In the mornings he gets such an erection you couldn't get your hands around it!" ●**В стояка́,** *idiom, rude.* In a standing position (esp. of sex). ♦*Пришлось с ней в стояка мучиться — хаты нет.* "There was no room in the apartment so I had to screw her standing up."

СТОЯ́ТЬ/СТА́ТЬ, ВСТАТЬ, ПОСТО- Я́ТЬ: Стоя́ть/стать на ата́се (на ва́с- сере, на стрёме, на ци́нке, на шу́хере), *idiom, crim. & youth.* To stand guard. ♦*Ты стой на вассере, а мы сыграем в очко.* "You stand guard while we play a game of blackjack." **Стоя́ть/постоя́ть пешко́м,** *idiom, joc.* To remain standing, decline to sit (lit., to stand in a walking position). ♦*Садитесь. — Ничего, я пешком постою.* "Have a seat. — That's all right. I'll stand." **Стоя́ть/ стать ра́ком,** *idiom, rude.* **1.** To stand bent over. ♦*Что это ты раком сто- ишь? — Да иголку уронила, не могу найти.* "Why have you got your ass in the air like that? — I'm looking for a nee- dle I dropped." **2.** To work hard, espe- cially in a bent-over position. ♦*Я тоже не бездельничаю, целый день стою раком над корытом.* "I haven't exactly been idle — ass-up over a washtub all day." **Стоя́ть/постоя́ть у марте́на,** *idiom, joc.* To cook, prepare food (lit., to stand at the furnace). ♦*Я стою у мар- тена уже час, скоро обед будет готов.* "I've been working at the furnace for an hour already; dinner will be ready soon." **Стоя́ть на кого́-л.,** *idiom, rude.* To desire sexually (lit., to have an erection toward). ♦*У меня на неё не стоит.* "I'm not attracted to her." ♦**Стоя́ть на уша́х,** *idiom, joc.* To work very hard, make a great effort (lit., to stand on one's ears). ♦*Последнюю неделю я стою на ушах, заканчиваю книгу.* "This past week I've been knocking myself out to finish the book." **Стоя́ть на что-л.,** *idiom, rude.* To like, feel like, be attracted to. ♦*Сегодня у меня на работу не* *стоит.* "I don't feel like working today." **Стоя́ть у кого́-л.,** *idiom, rude.* Someone has an erection. ♦*У него́ уже́ давно́ не стои́т.* "It's been ages since the last time he had a hard-on." **Встать на́ уши,** *idiom.* To make a great effort, put oneself out. ♦*Вчера́ мы все вста́ли на́ уши, что́бы купи́ть ему́ хоро́ший пода́рок.* "We all knocked ourselves out yesterday getting him a good present."

СТОЯ́ЧКА, -и, *f., neg., joc.* A beer bar without seats (cf. **стоя́к** 1). ♦*Тут недалеко́ стоя́чка есть, мо́жно по-бы́строму вы́пить.* "There's a 'stander' not far from here where we can have a quick beer."

СТРАТЕ́Г, -а, *m., army.* A strategic bomber pilot (lit., strategist). ♦*Сейча́с всем не пла́тят то́лком, да́же страте́гам.* "Everybody's underpaid these days, even those strategic bomber pilots."

СТРАШИ́ЛО, -а, *n., neg.* Un ugly person (from **страшный,** "frightening"). ♦*Ваш друг тако́е страши́ло, присни́ться мо́жет.* "Your friend is nightmarishly ugly."

СТРА́ШНЫЙ: Стра́шный как война́, *idiom, neg.* Extremely ugly. ♦*Мужи́к у неё стра́шный как война́.* "Her boyfriend is ugly as sin." **Стра́шная как моя́ жизнь,** *idiom, joc.* Very ugly (of a woman; lit., dreadful as my life). ♦*Кто её за́муж возьмёт? Она́ же стра́шная как моя́ жизнь.* "Who would marry her? She's ugly as sin." **Страшне́й а́томной войны́,** *idiom, neg.* Ugly, terrible. ♦*Ба́ба у него́ страшне́й а́томной войны́.* "His girlfriend is uglier than atomic war."

СТРЕЙТ, -а, *m.* A heteresexual man (from Eng. "straight"). ♦*Он не голубо́й, настоя́щий стрейт.* "He's not gay, he's completely straight."

СТРЕЙТОВИ́К, -а, *m.* See **стрейт.**

СТРЕКОЗЁЛ, стрекозла́, *m., joc.* A light-minded, frivolous, scatterbrained person (from **стрекоза,** "dragonfly," and **козёл,** "goat"). ♦*Э́тот стрекозёл не уме́ет вести́ перегово́ры.* "That scatterbrain wouldn't be able to conduct negotiations."

СТРЕ́ЛКА, -и, *f., youth.* A meeting, date, appointment (lit., the hand of a watch). ♦*Стре́лка, как всегда́, в на́шем кафе́.* "We'll meet at our cafe as usual." •**Забива́ть/заби́ть стре́лку,** see under **забива́ть.**

СТРЕЛЯ́ТЬ/СТРЕ́ЛЬНУТЬ. To bum, sponge (as a cigarette) (lit., to shoot). ♦*Стрельни́ сигаре́ту, а то у нас ко́нчились.* "We're out of cigarettes. See if you can bum one for us."

СТРЕЛЯ́ТЬСЯ/ЗАСТРЕЛИ́ТЬСЯ: Что мне, стреля́ться/застрели́ться? see under **что.**

СТРЁМ, -а, *m., crim., youth.* Danger, tension. ♦*Дава́й без стрёма обойдёмся.* "Let's talk calmly."

СТРЕМА́К, -а, *m., youth, neg.* Danger, unpleasantness. ♦*С тобо́й всё вре́мя стремаки́ происхо́дят.* "Bad things are always happening with you."

СТРЕМА́ТЬ/ПОСТРЕМА́ТЬ, *youth, neg.* To frighten, scare. ♦*Ты меня́ не стрема́й.* "Don't scare me."

СТРЕМА́ТЬСЯ/ЗАСТРЕМА́ТЬСЯ, *youth, neg.* To be frightened. ♦*Не на́до стрема́ться, ничего́ тебе́ не сде́лаем.* "There's nothing to be afraid of. We're not going to hurt you."

СТРЁМНЫЙ¹, -ая, -ое, *crim. & youth.* Dangerous. ♦*Это стрёмное де́ло.* "That's a dangerous business."

СТРЁМНЫЙ², -ого, *m., crim. & youth.* One who stands guard. ♦*Ты сего́дня бу́дешь стрёмным.* "You'll be on guard duty today."

СТРЁМОПА́ТИЯ, -ии, *f., youth.* An obsessive, unaccountable fear, anxiety without manifest cause. ♦*У меня́ начина́ется стрёмопа́тия.* "I'm having an anxiety attack."

СТРИПТИ́З, -а, *m., neg.* An intimate, open conversation (lit., striptease). ♦*Мне надое́л э́тот стрипти́з о твои́х любо́вниках.* "I've had enough of your true confessions about all your lovers!"

СТРИПТИЗЁРКА, -и, *f., neg.* **1.** A striptease performer. ♦*Она́ уе́хала на за́пад, там рабо́тает стриптизёркой.* "She went to the West, where she's been working as a striptease artist." **2.** A woman who speaks with inappropriate or unconventional openness. ♦*Ты настоящая стриптизёрка, об этом обычно не говорят.* "You're quite a stripteaser. You know, people don't usually talk about those things."

СТРИТ, *f., indecl., youth.* Street (from Eng. "street"). ♦*На какой стрит ты живёшь?* "What street do you live on?"

СТРОГА́Ч, -а́, *m., obs.* A harsh punishment, a tough sentence (esp. a Party reprimand). ♦*Ему вынесли строгача на общем собрании за пьянку на работе.* "They gave him a harsh one at the general meeting for drinking on the job."

СТРОЙТЕЛЬ, -я, *m., neg.* A man who likes to have sex with two women at a time. ♦*Опять поволок к себе двух девок, вот заядлый строитель!* "Again he's gone off with two girls at the same time — he's really an inveterate threesome artist!"

СТРО́ИТЬ/ПОСТРО́ИТЬ. To torment, mock (lit., to form, line up). ♦*Сейчас я вас строить буду, пока не скажете, кто украл мобилу.* "I'm going to stick it to you until you tell me who stole the cell phone."

СТРО́ИТЬ из себя це́лку, *idiom, neg.* To pretend to be innocent and naive (lit., to make oneself out to be a virgin). ♦*Не строй из себя целку, можно подумать, ты никогда не брал подарки.* "Don't put on that innocent pose, as if you had never accepted a little gift."

СТРОЧИ́ТЬ/ЗАСТРОЧИ́ТЬ, *youth, rude.* To have fellatio performed on one (lit., to fire away, bang away). ♦*Он строчит всем подряд.* "He gets them all to give him blow jobs."

СТРУГА́ТЬ/НАСТРУГА́ТЬ, *joc.* To produce a lot (lit., to plane, from the idea of producing a lot of shavings). ♦*Они уже настругали полный дом детей.* "They've already produced a houseful of children."

СТРУ́МЕНТ, -а, *m., rude.* A penis (from инструмент, "instrument"). ♦*У меня струмент для баб всегда готов.* "My

tool is always ready for a woman."

СТРУНА́, -ы́, *f., youth.* The needle of a syringe (lit., a string). ♦*У меня струна сломалась.* "My needle's broken."

СТРУЧО́К, стручка́, *m., neg., joc.* A small penis (lit., a pod). ♦*С твоим стручком с ней делать нечего.* "You'll never be able to satisfy her with that little pod of yours."

СТРУЯ́ЧИТЬ/ЗАСТРУЯ́ЧИТЬ. From струя, "stream of water". **1.** To beat up. ♦*Ты сам напросился, вот тебя и заструячили.* "You were asking for the beating they gave you." **2.** To do something intensively. ♦*Мы струячили в карты всю ночь.* "We played cards all night." **3.** To drink.

СТРЯСТИ́, *perf., youth.* To borrow money (lit., to shake off). ♦*Стряси у него на пиво.* "Borrow some money from him to buy some beer."

СТУ́ДЕНЬ, -дня, *m., joc.* Lit., meat-jelly. **1.** A fat, flabby person. ♦*Тебе спортом надо заняться, совсем в студень превратился.* "You'd better take up some sport, you've turned into a fatso." **2.** A student.

СТУК: Ско́рость сту́ка превыша́ет ско́рость зву́ка, see under **ско́рость.**

СТУКА́Ч, -а́, *m., neg.* An informer (lit., a knocker; cf. **стуча́ть**). ♦*Ты с ним поосторожнее, он — стукач.* "Be more cautious with him — he's an informer."

СТУКА́ЧЕСТВО, -а, *n., neg.* Informing. ♦*Стукачество у нас на работе сильно в почёте.* "Informing has become a big thing with us at work these days."

СТУКА́ЧКА, -и, *f., neg.* A female informer. ♦*Все знают, что она стукачка.* "Everyone knows that she's an informer."

СТУКЛО́, -а́, *n., neg.* See **стука́ч.**

СТУЧА́ТЬ/СТУ́КНУТЬ, НАСТУЧА́ТЬ, *neg.* To inform. ♦*Кто же на нас настучал?* "Who informed on us?"

СТЫ́ДНО, У КОГО́ ВИ́ДНО, *rhyming phrase, joc.* I'm not ashamed (lit., it's shameful [only] for someone whose [private parts] are showing). ♦*Как тебе не стыдно материться при детях!* —

Стыдно, у кого видно. "You should be ashamed of yourself, swearing like that in front of the children! — There's nothing shameful about it."

СТЫДНЯ́К, -а, *m., youth.* Shame, disgrace. ♦*Какой стыдняк, ни одного экзамена не сдал.* "What a disgrace! I haven't passed a single exam."

СТЫДО́БА, -ы, *f., neg.* **1.** A shame, a disgrace. ♦*Разве это не стыдоба быть нудистом?* "Isn't it disgraceful to be a nudist?" **2.** *m. & f.* A shameless, disgraceful person. ♦*Как ты можешь так ходить, стыдоба!* "How can you go around like that?! You should be ashamed."

СТЫКОВА́ТЬСЯ/СОСТЫКОВА́ТЬ-СЯ. To meet (lit., to dock, join, as in spaceflight). ♦*Вы стыкуетесь сегодня на работе?* "Are you having a meeting at work today?"

СТЫКО́ВКА, -и, *f.* A meeting. ♦*Где у нас сегодня стыковка?* "Where are we holding our meeting today?"

СТЭЙТСО́ВЫЙ, -ая, -ое, *youth.* See **стейтсо́вый.**

СТЭЙТСЫ, -ов, *pl., youth.* See **стейтсы́.**

СТЭНД, -а, *m., youth.* See **стенд.**

СУББО́ТА: Чёрная суббо́та, see under **чёрная.**

СУГРЕ́В: Для сугре́ву, *idiom, joc.* For warmth, to warm up. ♦*Хорошо бы немного выпить для сугреву.* "Let's have a little something to drink, just to warm us up."

СУЕТИ́ТЬСЯ: Не суети́сь под кли-е́нтом, see under **не.**

СУ́КА, -и, *f., neg., rude.* Lit., a bitch. **1.** A term of abuse or reproach (used of both men and women). ♦*Ну и сука же ты, опять нас заложил.* "You bastard! You've betrayed us again!" **2.** *crim.* A thief who breaks the thieves' code of honor. ♦*Ты не врёшь случаем? — Ты что, меня за суку держишь, говорю вам, магазин — без охраны.* "Are you sure you're not lying? — Do you think I'm a rat? I'm telling you, the store is really unguarded."

СУ́КА-КУКУ́ШКА, -и, *f., army.* A female mercenary (from сука, bitch, and кукушка, a cuckoo). See **куку́шка.** ♦*Доносят, где-то здесь сука-кукушка работает, надо её снять.* "We have reports that a sharpshooter bitch is active in this area, we have to get her."

СУКОВА́ТЫЙ, -ая, -ое, *neg.* Stubborn, difficult (lit., knotty, as of wood; cf. **су́ка**). ♦*Ты совсем суковатым стал, с тобой трудно договориться.* "You've become awfully stubborn! It's hard to reach an agreement with you."

СУ́КОЙ БУ́ДУ! *crim., rude.* Lit., "I'll be a bitch (if I do that)," a form of oath. ♦*Придёшь ночью к реке? — Сукой буду! Как договорились.* "Will you come to the river tonight? — Cross my heart! Just as we agreed!"

СУЛТЫ́ГА, -и, *f., army.* Liquor diluted with 30% water. ♦*Султыга осталась? Похмелиться надо.* "Have you still got some 'sultyga'? I need something for my hangover."

СУ́МЕРЕЧНОЕ ЗРЕ́НИЕ, *idiom, army.* A night vision scope (lit., twilight vision).

СУНДУ́К, -а, *m., neg.* A big, tall man (lit, a trunk). ♦*У него брат — чистый сундук.* "His brother is a real giant."

СУНЬ ХУЙ В ЧАЙ (И ВЫНЬ СУ-ХИ́М), see under **хуй.**

СУП: А пото́м — суп с кото́м, see under **а.**

СУ́ПЕР, -а, *m., pos.* Someone or something outstanding, excellent (from Eng. "super"). ♦*Она специалист — просто супер!* "She's a really outstanding expert."

СУПЕРКЛА́СС, -а, *m., pos.* Outstanding, remarkable. ♦*У него сегодня лекция — суперкласс.* "His lecture today was terrific."

СУ́ПНИК, -а, *m., neg.* A faithful lover, a one-woman man (cf. суп). ♦*Опять к ней супник пошёл.* "Her lover came to see her again."

СУРЛЯ́ТЬ/ПОСУРЛЯ́ТЬ. To drink. ♦*Что у тебя сурлять есть?* "What have you got to drink?"

СУРО́ВО, *adv., youth.* Too much, excessive. ♦*Это слишком сурово так пить.* "It's excessive to drink like that." •**Не**

СУРО́ВО? *idiom, youth.* It's too much, too expensive. ♦*А тебе не сурово будет столько денег просить?* "How can you ask for such a sum? It's far too much."

СУСА́НИН, -а, *m., army, joc.* From Susanin, the hero of Musorgsky's opera *Иван Сусанин,* who led Polish invaders to their death in a Russian forest. **1.** A guide who doesn't know the way or whom others suspect of not knowing the way. ♦*А ты, Сусанин, знаешь, куда мы идём?* "Hey, guide, do you know where we're going?" **2.** An air force navigator. ♦*Скоро вылет, где наш Сусанин?* "We're scheduled for takeoff. Where's our navigator?"

СУ́ТОЧНИК, -а, *m., neg.* Someone sentenced to a 15-day term for hooliganism (from сутки, "twenty-four hours). ♦*Где тут суточники работают?* "Where are the 15-day guys working?"

СУХА́РИК, -а, *m.* See **суха́рь.**

СУХА́РЬ, -я́, *m.* Dry wine (from сухой). ♦*Там продаётся сухарь, сколько хочешь.* "They've got lots of dry wine on sale there."

СУХА́Ч, -а́, *m.* Dry wine (from сухой). ♦*Где сухач покупали?* "Where did you get the dry wine?"

СУ́ХЕ, *n., indecl.* Dry wine (by wordplay on сухой, "dry," and Сухе Батор, the Mongolian revolutionary leader). ♦*Возьми пару бутылок сухе.* "Buy a couple of bottles of dry wine."

СУХОДРО́ЧКА, -и, *f., rude.* **1.** Masturbation. ♦*Здесь на корабле женщин нет, все суходрочкой занимаются.* "There are no women on this ship; everyone masturbates." **2.** Futile work, a pointless job. ♦*Без инструментов — это суходрочка, мы не сможем починить трактор.* "Without tools this is useless work — we'll never get the tractor fixed."

СУЧА́РА, -ы, *m. & f., neg., rude.* A bitch, bastard (from су́ка). ♦*Как ты с этой сучарой можешь разговаривать?* "How can you stand to even talk to that bitch?"

СУ́ЧИЙ: Су́чий сын, *idiom, rude.* A worthless person (lit., son of a bitch).

♦*Ты, сучий сын, заткнись, слушать тебя не желаю.* "Shut up, you son of a bitch! I don't want to hear another word out of you." **Су́чья ла́па,** *idiom, rude.* A bastard, scoundrel (lit., bitch's paw). ♦*Ты, сучья лапа, долг отдавать будешь?* "You bastard, are you going to pay what you owe me?"

СУЧКИ́, -ов, *pl., joc.* Hands (lit., twigs).

СУ́ЧНИК, -а, *m., army.* A dog breeder (from сука, "bitch"). ♦*Ты собак не любишь, работа сучника не для тебя.* "You shouldn't be a dog breeder if you don't like dogs."

СУЧО́К, сучка́, *m., neg.* **1.** Cheap vodka of poor quality (lit., knotty wood, alluding to wood alcohol). ♦*В магазине только сучок.* "They've only got cheap vodka at the store." **2.** *rude.* A bastard, scoundrel (from су́ка). ♦*Ты кому, сучок, грубишь?* "Hey, who do you think you're yelling at, you son of a bitch?"

СУШИ́ТЬ/НАСУШИ́ТЬ: суши́ть/насуши́ть сухари́, *idiom.* To get ready to go to prison (lit., to dry biscuits). ♦*За все твои дела тебе пора сушить сухари.* "After what you've done, you'd better start drying biscuits." **Суши́ть вёсла,** *idiom.* **1.** To stop doing something (lit., to dry one's oars). ♦*Суши вёсла, кончай работу.* "Well, it's time to stop work." **2.** An expression of surprise, shock. ♦*А потом началось такое! Суши вёсла: они все полезли в драку.* "Then all hell broke loose. Dry your oars — they all got into a fistfight." **Суши́ть мозги́,** *idiom, neg.* To pester, annoy (lit., to dry someone's brains). ♦*Она мне весь день сушила мозги, всё рассказывала о своих страданиях.* "She addled my brains all day with her stories about her troubles."

СУШНЯ́К, -а́, *m.* Dry wine. ♦*Под мясо сушняк ничего идёт.* "Dry wine goes well with meat." ●**Сушня́к проби́л кого́-л.,** *idiom.* Someone wants to drink (lit., dryness [thirst] has attacked someone). ♦*Меня совсем сушняк пробил, где бы хоть вина достать?* "I'm dying for something to drink. Where can I get some wine?"

СФЕ́РА, -ы, *f., army.* A helmet (lit., sphere). ♦*Надень сферу, хочешь без башки остаться?* "Put on your helmet or you'll lose your head."

СХАРЧИ́ТЬ, *perf. only, neg.* To mistreat, humiliate, persecute maliciously. ♦*Эх, такого человека схарчили! Его уволили, а был хороший учёный.* "The way those people persecuted that man! In the end they fired him, though he was a fine scholar."

СХВАТИ́ТЬ: (У кого-л.) всё схва́чено, see under **всё.**

СХЛОПОТА́ТЬ, *perf. only, joc.* To be punished, get what's coming to you. ♦*Сейчас схлопочешь, прекрати шуметь.* "You're going to get it if you don't stop making that racket."

СХОДИ́ТЬ: Ка́ждый схо́дит с ума́ по-сво́ему, see under **ка́ждый.**

СХО́ДКА, -и, *f., joc.* A meeting (lit., a secret or revolutionary meeting). ♦*На работе у нас сходка в 5 часов, я буду дома попозже.* "I'll be home a little late today. We're having at meeting at work at 5 o'clock."

СХУЁБНИЧАТЬ, *perf. only, rude.* To make a mistake. ♦*Ты, конечно, схуёбничал, когда согласился им помочь.* "You made a big mistake when you promised to help them."

СЧА́СТЬЕ: Не в де́ньгах сча́стье, а в их коли́честве, see under **не.**

СЧЁТ: За мой счёт, за твой де́ньги, see under **за.**

СЧИТА́ТЬ/ПОСЧИТА́ТЬ зу́бы, *idiom, rude.* To beat someone up (lit., to count someone's teeth). ♦*Я слышал, ему посчитали зубы за все его проделки.* "I heard they beat him up for the things he did."

СЪЁБЫВАТЬСЯ/СЪЕБА́ТЬСЯ, *rude.* Cf. **ёб-. 1.** To overindulge in sex. ♦*Он совсем съебался, похудел.* "He's really been overdoing it in the sex department — look how much weight he's lost!" **2.** To leave, go. ♦*Когда съёбываемся по домам?* "When are we going home?"

СЪЕ́ЗДИТЬ, *perf.* To hit (lit., to drive into). ♦*Съездили друг друга пару раз в*

морду и хватит. "You've punched each other in the face twice, cut in out now."

СЪЕЗДЮ́К, -а, *m., joc., rude.* A delegate of the People's Deputy Congresses of the perestroika period (by wordplay on съезд, "congress" and **пиздю́к**).

СЪЕЗЖА́ТЬ/СЪЕ́ХАТЬ, *neg.* To go crazy. ♦*Он, похоже, совсем съехал от жадности.* "He seems to have gone crazy from greed."

СЪЁМ, -а, *m., youth.* **1.** An opportunity or occasion for meeting girls. ♦*Как прошёл съём? Скольких сняли?* "How was the party? How many girls did you get to meet?" **2.** A date, tryst. ♦*Когда у тебя с Лизаветой съём?* "When's your date with Liz?"

СЫГРА́ТЬ в я́щик. See under **игра́ть.**

СЫНО́К, сынка́, *m., army, neg.* A young, inexperienced soldier, a raw recruit. ♦*А ну, сынок, быстро за водой.* "Come on, sonny-boy, get us some water on the double!"

СЫ́ПАТЬ/СЫПАНУ́ТЬ. 1. To leave, get out. ♦*Сыпь отсюда!* "Get out of here!" **2.** To run. ♦*Все сыпанули в магазин: там спиртное дают.* "Everyone ran to the store where there was liquor for sale."

СЫ́ПАТЬСЯ/ЗАСЫ́ПАТЬСЯ. To fail an examination. ♦*Он засыпался на математике.* "He failed the math exam." •**Песо́к сып(л)ется из кого-л.,** see under **песо́к.**

СЫ́РОСТЬ, -и, *f.* Blood (lit., dampness). ♦*Весь пол в сырости, видать, здесь серьёзная потасовка была.* "Looks like there was a big fight here, There's goo all over the floor."

СЫ́РОСТЬ: Завести́сь (взя́ться) от сы́рости, see under **завести́сь. Разводи́ть/развести́ сы́рость,** see under **разводи́ть.**

СЭ́ЙШН, -а, *m., youth.* A party, gathering (from Eng. "session"). ♦*Намечается сэйшн, ты пойдёшь?* "There's going to be a party. Will you come?"

СЮР, -а, *m., joc.* Strangeness, unintelligibility, craziness (from сюрреализм, "surrealism"). ♦*Не жизнь, а сюр сплошной.* "Our life these days is something completely weird."

СЮ́РНЫЙ, -ая, -ое, *joc.* Strange, unintelligible. ♦ *Это сюрная история.* "That's a weird story."

СЮСЮ́КАТЬ/ЗАСЮСЮ́КАТЬ, *neg.* To speak fawningly or in baby talk, to coo. ♦ *Я не люблю, когда со мной сюсюкают.* "I don't like being crooned at."

СЯ́ВКА, -и, *m., crim., neg.* **1.** A young, inexperienced thief. ♦ *Тут работа не для меня, пусть это сявки делают.* "That's no job for me — give it to the small fry." **2.** A homeless beggar, a pauper. ♦ *У него ничего нет, у этого сявки.* "That poor beggar has absolutely nothing."

ТАБА́К: Де́ло таба́к, see under **де́ло.**

ТАБЛО́, *n., indecl., youth, rude, neg.* Face, mug. ♦*Тебе дать в табло?* "You looking for a punch in the face?" •**Намы́ливать/намы́лить табло́ кому-л.,** see under **намы́ливать.**

ТАБУРЕ́ТОВКА, -и, *f., joc.* Home brew (from табуре́тка, "wooden stool"). ♦*Кто тебе дал табуретовку?* "Who did you get that moonshine from?"

ТАЗ: Накрыва́ться/накры́ться ме́дным та́зом, see under **накрыва́ться.**

ТАК: За так, *idiom.* Gratis, for nothing. ♦*За так тебе никто не будет помогать, надо платить или ставить выпивку.* "Nobody's going to help you for nothing — you have to pay them or at least offer them something to drink."

ТАК ДАМ: Так дам, всю жизнь на апте́ку бу́дешь рабо́тать, *idiom.* A threat of a severe beating; lit., "I'll give it to you so that you'll be paying the medical bills for the rest of your life." ♦*Не приставай, а то так дам, всю жизнь на аптеку работать будешь.* "Get off my case or I'll give it to you so that you'll never see the end of the medical bills." **Так дам, ни оди́н до́ктор не почи́нит,** *idiom.* A threat of a severe beating. ♦*Ещё раз с ней будешь танцевать, так дам, ни один доктор не починит.* "If you dance with her again I'll give it to you so that no doctor will be able to fix you." **Так дам, ни одна́ больни́ца не при́мет,** *idiom.* A threat of a severe beating. ♦*Ещё раз нас родителям заложишь, — так дам, ни одна больница не примет.* "If you tell on us to our parents again, I'll give it to you so that no hospital will admit you."

ТАК НА ТАК МЕНЯ́ТЬ, ТО́ЛЬКО ВРЕ́МЯ ТЕРЯ́ТЬ, *rhyming phrase, joc., euph.* Lit., "To exchange this for that is just a waste of time"; an expression for declining a proposed swap or barter (cf. **ху́й на ху́й меня́ть . . .** under **ху́й**). ♦*Давай менять бензин на масло! — Так на так менять, только время терять.* "Let's trade your gas for my oil. — A deal like that is just a waste of time."

ТАК НЕ ТАК, ПЕРЕТА́КИВАТЬ НЕ БУ́ДЕМ, *idiom, joc.* Used in reply to the expression "Так, так," in the sense "There's nothing to be done," "It can't be changed." ♦*Так, так, понятно, мы никуда не идём. — Так не так, перетакивать не будем.* "Well, that's it. We're not going." — "Right or wrong, we're not going to change it."

ТАК ОНИ́ И ЖИ́ЛИ, гу́бы кра́сили, а ног не мы́ли, *rhyming phrase, joc.* Lit., "So they lived: they painted their lips, but didn't wash their feet." Used in sardonic response to the difficulties of life. ♦*Опять цены выросли вдвое. Так они и жили. . . .* "Prices have doubled again. Well, so they lived. . . ." •**Так они́ и жи́ли, спа́ли врозь, а де́ти бы́ли,** *rhyming phrase, joc.* Lit., "So they lived: they slept separately, but still they had children." Used in ironic resignation to the difficulties of life: "What can you do?" "C'est la vie!" ♦*Скоро нам на пенсию уходить, а не хочется. Так они и жили. . . .* "We're going to be pensioned off soon, though we aren't ready to retire. Well, so they lived. . . ."

ТАКИ́Е ПИРОГИ́! *idiom.* That's the way it is; that's how things stand (lit., "What pies!"). ♦*Опять не платят вовремя зарплату, такие пироги!* "There's going to be another delay in paying our salaries. Well, that's the way the cookie crumbles."

ТАК-ПЕРЕТА́К, *idiom, neg.* A euphemism for swearwords or abusive language. ♦*Так-перетак! Сколько можно тебе повторять: не бери чужие вещи!* "Sugar! How many times do I have to tell you not to take other people's things!"

ТАКО́Й ХОЛО́ДНЫЙ, КАК КРОКОДИ́Л ГОЛО́ДНЫЙ, *rhyming phrase, joc.* Very cold (lit., as cold as a crocodile is hungry). ♦*Что, на улице мороз? Ты такой холодный, как крокодил голод-*

ный. "It must be awfully cold out — you're as cold as a crocodile is hungry."

ТАКОЙ-СЯКОЙ-НЕМАЗАННЫЙ, *idiom, joc.* A nonsense phrase used as a euphemism for swearing or obscenity. ◆*Где это тебя угораздило так вываляться в снегу, такой-сякой-немазанный?* "How did you manage to get all covered with snow like that, dang you!"

ТАЛДЫЧИТЬ/ЗАТАЛДЫЧИТЬ, *neg.* To speak repetitively or droningly. ◆*Скучно с ним: он всегда талдычит о своих проблемах.* "It's boring to be around him; he just keeps droning on and on about his own problems."

ТАЛИТЬ/ПОТАЛИТЬ, *rude.* To have sex with a woman. ◆*Ты нашёл место, где её талить?* "Have you found someplace where you can take her to bed?"

ТАЛМУД, -а, *m., neg.* A long, difficult, boring book (lit., Talmud). ◆*Этот талмуд по истории мне надо прочитать до понедельника.* "I've got to read this whole history tome by Monday."

ТАЛМУДИСТИКА, -и, *f., neg.* A boring, pedantic, or obscure field of study (lit., Talmud studies; cf. **мудистика**). ◆*Он занимается какой-то талмудистикой: то ли историей КПСС, то ли философией.* "He's studying some sort of Talmudistics — the history of the CPSU, or philosophy, or something like that."

ТАМБОВСКИЙ ВОЛК ТЕБЕ ТОВАРИЩ, *idiom.* You're not my comrade; don't call me "comrade" (lit., "A Tambov wolf is your comrade"). This idiom arose in Soviet prison life as a response of authorities to detainees who accidentally addressed them as "comrade" — a status of which their arrest had deprived them — instead of using the approved term "citizen."

ТАМИЗДАТ, -а, *m., obs.* Russian literature banned in the Soviet Union and therefore published abroad (lit., therepublication, by analogy with **самиздат**). ◆*Ты читал в тамиздате Войновича?* "Did you read Voinovich in a 'tamizdat' edition?"

ТАНКИ ГРЯЗИ НЕ БОЯТСЯ, *idiom.* Said of any dirty vehicle (lit., tanks are not afraid of any dirt). ◆*Ты помоешь свою машину или танки грязи не боятся?* "Are you going to wash that old car, or do you think that tanks aren't afraid of dirt?"

ТАНКОМ НЕ ОСТАНОВИШЬ кого-л., *idiom, joc.* Someone is very determined, persistent, energetic (lit., you can't stop him with a tank). ◆*Она всё равно своего добьётся: её и танком не остановишь.* "She'll get what she wants no matter what; she couldn't be stopped even by a tank."

ТАНЦПОЛ, -а, *m., youth.* A dance floor, hall (from танцы, "dances," and пол, "floor"). ◆*На танцпол пойдём сегодня?* "Are we going dancing today?"

ТАНЦЫ-ШМАНЦЫ, танцев-шманцев, *pl., joc.* A dance, dancing (esp. crowded and noisy). ◆*А потом начались, как всегда, танцы-шманцы.* "Then they started up with the dancing, as usual."

ТАНЬГА, -й, *f., joc.* Money. ◆*Таньга есть? Пойдём в ресторан.* "If you've got money, let's go eat in a restaurant."

ТАРАБАРЩИНА, -ы, *f.* Gibberish, unintelligible speech. ◆*Ничего не пойму, что он говорит? Какая-то тарабарщина.* "I can't make out a word of it, he's just talking giberrish."

ТАРАКАН, -а, *m.* **1.** A nickname for Stalin (lit., cockroach). ◆*Таракан народа погубил — жутко!* "It's awful how many people the Cockroach murdered." **2.** *m., neg.* A mustached man (e.g., Stalin; lit., a cockroach). ◆*Ты знаешь этого таракана?* "Do you know that guy with the mustache?" ●**С тараканами,** *neg.* Having marked peculiarities, eccentricities, touches of madness (lit., with cockroaches). ◆*Он с большими тараканами.* "He's got bats in his belfry."

ТАРАКАНОВКА, -и, *f., joc., neg.* Cheap, strong liquor (based on the idea of cockroach poison). ◆*Как нужно себя не уважать, чтобы пить такую таракановку.* "You'd have to be really depraved to drink that sort of rotgut."

ТАРА́НИТЬ/ПРИТАРА́НИТЬ. To bring. ♦*Притарань мне книги.* "Bring me the books."

ТАРАНТА́С, -а, *m., neg., joc.* An old car, jalopy (lit., a type of wagon). ♦*Как ты на таком тарантасе ездишь?* "How can you drive that old jalopy?"

ТАРАХТЕ́ЛКА, -и, *m. & f., neg., joc.* From тарахтеть, "to rattle," "to rumble.") **1.** A garrulous person. ♦*Ну, ты всё уже успела рассказать, тарахтелка?* "So, have you managed to tell the whole story yet, chatterbox?" **2.** A noisy old car. ♦*Заводи свою тарахтелку, да поедем.* "Crank up the old rattletrap and let's get going."

ТАРАХТЕ́ТЬ/ЗАТАРАХТЕ́ТЬ ПО́ПОЙ, *idiom, army.* To be scared, frightened (lit., to rattle one's behind). ♦*Тарахтеть попой потом будем, сейчас думаем только о задании.* "Now let's think about what we have to get done, we can have a shit fit later."

ТАРА́ЩИТЬСЯ/ВЫ́ТАРАЩИТСЯ, *neg.* To stare. ♦*Ну, что она на меня вытаращилась?* "How come she was staring at me like that?"

ТАРЕ́ЛКА, -и, *f.* A flying saucer; a UFO (lit., a plate). ♦*Все сейчас только и говорят, что о тарелках.* "All everyone's talking about these days is flying saucers."

ТАРЕ́ЛОЧНИК, -а, *m., joc.* Someone interested in or attracted by UFOs. ♦*Я не понимаю всех этих тарелочников.* "I don't understand all these flying-saucer nuts."

ТАРЧ, -а, *m., youth.* Drug-induced intoxication. See **торч.**

ТА́РЫ-БА́РЫ, *idiom, neg.* Chatter, empty talk. ♦*Вчера мы встретились и вели тары-бары до утра.* "We got together last night and chewed the rag until morning."

ТАСК, -а, *m., youth.* Drunkenness, drug-induced intoxication (from тащиться, "to drag oneself about"). ♦*У тебя таск, я вижу.* "I see you're high."

ТА́СКА, -и, *f., youth.* Pleasure (from тащиться, "to be pleased"). ♦*Погово-*

рить с тобой такая таска всегда. "It's always a pleasure to talk with you."

ТА́ССОВКА, -и, *f., journalism, obs.* Information from the news agency TASS. ♦*Ты уже просмотрел тассовку?* "Have you looked at the TASS report yet?"

ТАЧА́НКА, -и, *f.* An automobile. ♦*У тебя тачанка на ходу?* "Is your car running?"

ТА́ЧКА, -и, *f.* A automobile, a taxi. ♦*Бери тачку и на самолёт.* "Hail a cab and let's go to the airport."

ТАЧКОДРО́М, -а, *m., joc.* A taxi stand. ♦*Пойдём на тачкодром, там можно взять машину быстрее.* "Let's go over to the taxi stand — we'll get a cab quicker there."

ТАШКЕ́НТ, -а, *m., joc.* Intense heat (from Ташкент, the capital of Uzbekistan). ♦*У вас тут в комнате Ташкент, а на улице совсем холодно.* "It's hot as an oven in your room, even though it's cold outdoors."

ТАЩ, -а, *m., youth.* Pleasure. See **таска.**

ТАЩИ́ЛОВКА, -и, *f., youth.* Something wonderful. ♦*Итальянская эстрада — просто тащиловка!* "That Italian show is simply terrific!"

ТАЩИ́ТЬ, *imperf., youth.* To please, to delight. ♦*Меня тащат деньги и ещё как!* "I adore money."

ТАЩИ́ТЬСЯ, *imperf. only, youth.* **1.** To use drugs. ♦*Сколько лет он уже тащится?* "How many years has he been taking dope?" **2.** To be high on drugs. ♦*Я уже сильно тащусь, мне больше не надо.* "I'm already pretty high; I don't need any more stuff." ●**Тащи́ться от кого-л.,** *youth, pos.* To be crazy about, in love with, ecstatic about someone. ♦*Я от него просто тащусь.* "I'm just crazy about him." **Тащи́ться как лом в говне́,** see under **говно́.**

ТАЮ́ХА, -и, *f., youth, obs.* A necktie (from Eng. "tie"). ♦*Таюху не забудь надеть.* "Don't forget to wear a tie."

ТВО́РЧЕСКИЙ ЗАПО́Р, *idiom, neg.* Inability to work, writer's block (lit., constipation of the creative faculties). ♦*Не* *трогай его, он нервный, у него творческий запор.* "Don't bother him. He's got writer's block and he's very touchy."

ТВОЮ́ ДУ́ШУ ТАК, *rude.* Damn you! Damn it! ♦*Говори, что натворил, твою душу так!* "Tell me what you've been up to, damn you!"

ТЕБЕ́ ЗУ́БЫ НЕ ЖМУТ? *idiom, neg.* I'll knock your teeth out (lit., "Aren't your teeth feeling a little tight? [I'll loosen them for you]"). ♦*Ты слишком обнаглел, тебе зубы не жмут?* "You're out of line. I'm going to knock your teeth out."

ТЕКСТА́, -о́в, *pl., music.* (Written) lyrics of songs, esp. rock songs (distorted from тексты, "texts"). ♦*У тебя есть текста последних групп?* "Do you have the lyrics of the new groups' songs?"

ТЕКУ́ЧКА, -и, *f., neg.* From течь, "to flow". **1.** Routine, daily life. ♦*Текучка совсем заела.* "I'm sick of this daily routine." **2.** Turnover, change of personnel. ♦*У них на заводе большая текучка.* "They have a very high turnover at that plant."

ТЕЛЕ́ГА, -и, *f.* Lit., a cart. **1.** Denunciation, informing. ♦*Кто-то на меня телегу за телегой пишет.* "Someone keeps writing denunciations against me." **2.** An official report of someone's arrest or detainment. ♦*На него телега из милиции пришла: ночевал в вытрезвителе.* "There's been an official report about him from the police: he spent the night in the sobering-up tank." **3.** *youth, neg.* A tall story, lie. ♦*Всё это телеги.* "I don't believe those tall tales." •**Гнать/ прогна́ть теле́гу,** see under **гнать².**

ТЕЛЕ́ЖКА: Ваго́н и ма́ленькая теле́жка, see under **ваго́н.**

ТЕЛЕ́ЖНИК, -а, *m., youth, neg.* A liar, someone who tells dubious tales. ♦*Не верь ему, он известный тележник.* "Don't believe him. He's a well-known liar."

ТЕ́ЛЕК, -а, *m.* Television. ♦*Что сегодня по телеку?* "What's on TV today?"

ТЕЛЕМА́Н, -а, *m.* Someone who likes to watch TV or watches TV a lot. ♦*Он книг не читает, совсем превратился в телемана.* "He doesn't read books any more; he's turned into a regular couch potato."

ТЕ́ЛЕ-МО́ТО-БА́БА-ЛЮБИ́ТЕЛЬ, -я, *m., joc.* A skirt-chaser, playboy. ♦*Мне кажется, этот теле-мото-баба-любитель никогда не женится.* "I think he's too much of a skirt-chaser to ever get married."

ТЕЛЁНОК, телёнка, *m.* A inexperienced young man (lit., calf). ♦*Как ты будешь жить без родителей? Ты ещё совсем телёнок.* "How are you going to live without parents? You're still wet behind the ears."

ТЕЛЕПА́ТЬ/ПРОТЕЛЕПА́ТЬ, *joc.* To guess, divine, intuit (from телепатия, "telepathy"). ♦*Как ты протелепал, что сегодня не будет занятий?* "How did you guess that there would be no classes today?"

ТЕЛЕПА́ТЬСЯ¹, *imperf. only, neg.* To lag behind. ♦*Что вы телепаетесь сзади, догоняйте!* "How come you're lagging behind like that! Catch up!"

ТЕЛЕПА́ТЬСЯ²/ПРОТЕЛЕПА́ТЬСЯ. To waste time, to spend time uselessly. ♦*Мы протелепались в городе целый день, но так и ничего не купили, что хотели.* "We wasted the whole day in town without finding any of the things we intended to buy."

ТЕЛЕСА́, теле́с, *pl., neg.* A human body, usually a fat body. ♦*Телеса-то прикрой.* "Put some clothes on your body."

ТЕЛЕФО́Н: Испо́рченный телефо́н, see under **испо́рченный.**

ТЕЛЕФО́ННОЕ ПРА́ВО, *idiom.* Lit., telephone right. The ability of highly placed government officials to interfere in or influence affairs by telephoning their highly placed friends and connections. ♦*Пока существует телефонное право, ни о каком правовом государстве не может быть и речи.* "So long as the 'telephone right' exists, there can be no question of any legitimate government."

ТЕЛИ́ТЬСЯ/ПРОТЕЛИ́ТЬСЯ, *neg.* To delay, go slowly, shilly-shally (lit., to calve). ♦ *Что вы телитесь? Ведь мы уже опаздываем на поезд!* "What are you dilly-dallying for? We're already late for the train."

ТЁЛКА, -и, *f., neg.* A girl, a girlfriend (lit., a calf). ♦ *Мы были там вчетвером: я с другом и две тёлки.* "There were four of us — my friend and I, and the two chicks."

ТЕЛОДВИЖЕ́НИЕ: Де́лать телодвиже́ния, see under **де́лать.**

ТЕ́ЛЬНИК, -а, *m.* A sailor's striped t-shirt or "wife-beater" (from тело, body).

ТЕМАТИ́ЧЕСКИЙ ВЕ́ЧЕР, *idiom.* A party for close friends. ♦ *Чужих не приводи, вечер строго тематический.* "Don't bring any outsiders to the party, it's strictly for friends."

ТЕ́МЕЧКО: Долби́ть по те́мечку, see under **долби́ть.**

ТЁМНАЯ: Устра́ивать/устро́ить тёмную кому́-л., see under **устра́ивать.**

ТЕМНИ́ЛА, -ы, *m. & f., neg.* Someone who purposely hides or distorts information. ♦ *Он такой темнила, ты от него ничего не добьёшься.* "He's such an obfuscator — you'll never get anything out of him."

ТЕМНИ́ТЬ, *imperf. only, neg.* To hide or distort information. ♦ *Не темни! Скажи, что ты решил делать в этой ситуации.* "Don't be so secretive! Tell me what you've decided to do."

ТЕМНОТА́, -ы́, *f., neg.* Lit., darkness. **1.** *crim.* A liar, deceiver. ♦ *Он же темнота, а вы уши развесили.* "He's a liar, and you went and believed him!" **2.** An ignoramus. ♦ *Ну и темнота ты, элементарных вещей не понимаешь.* "What an ignoramus you are! You don't know the simplest things." **3.** *crim.* Tranquilizers, narcotics. ♦ *Дай немного темноты.* "Give me a little 'darkness.'"

ТЁМНЫЙ, -ая, -ое, *neg.* Ignorant, stupid (lit., dark; alluding to the standard pre-revolutionary characterization of the Russian peasants as тёмный народ). ♦ *Василий у нас тёмный совсем, плохо*

соображает что к чему. "Our Vasily is a complete numskull; he has no idea what's what." **•Тёмный лес,** *idiom.* Something unintelligible (lit., a dark forest). ♦ *Для меня ваши рассуждения об экономике, об инфляции — тёмный лес.* "Your discussions of economics and inflation are Greek to me."

ТЕМП: В те́мпе, *idiom.* Quickly, energetically. ♦ *Собирайся в темпе, в кино опаздываем.* "Get ready quickly. We're late for the movie."

ТЕНЕВИ́К, -а́, *m., neg.* A member of the "shadow economy," an operator, a shady character (from тень, "shadow"). ♦ *Теневики — люди непростые, они умеют использовать ситуацию.* "Those operators are tricky people — they know how to exploit a situation."

ТЕ́НИ ИСЧЕЗА́ЮТ В ПО́ЛДЕНЬ, *idiom, army.* Said of privates heading for absence without leave (lit., shadows disappear at noon, from the title of a popular movie). ♦ *Смотри, тени исчезают в полдень,—через забор и в городе.* "Look, they're climbing over a fence, those AWOLs disappearing like shadows at noon."

ТЁПЛЕНЬКИЙ, -ая, -ое. 1. Ripe for action, ready to go (lit., warm). ♦ *Я его долго уговаривал поехать на юг, он уже тёпленький.* "I've been working on him for a long time, persuading him to take a trip to the south; now he's all hot to trot." **2.** Drunk. ♦ *Вы, я вижу, уже тёпленькие.* "I see you guys are drunk already."

ТЁПЛЫЙ, -ая, -ое. 1. *neg.* Drunk. ♦ *Да ты совсем тёплый, я с тобой никуда не пойду.* "I'm not going anywhere with you — you're completely drunk!" **2.** *army, joc.* Stupid. ♦ *Ты что, совсем тёплый?* "What are you, some kind of idiot?"

ТЕРЕ́ТЬ, *imperf. only.* Lit., to rub. **1.** To paint a picture, work on a painting. ♦ *Он уже год всё трёт одну картину.* "He's been smearing away at that same painting for a year already." **2.** *rude.* To have sex with a woman. ♦ *Я её всю ночь тёр, ничего, понравилось.* "I made love with her all night — it was great."

ТЕРЕ́ТЬСЯ/ПОТЕРЕ́ТЬСЯ, *rude.* To spend time in a certain circle, to associate with certain people. ♦ *Что ты тут трёшься, тебе здесь делать нечего.* "How come you keep hanging out around us? There's nothing for you here."

ТЕРПЁЖ: Не в терпёж, *idiom.* Very impatient. ♦ *Мне не в терпёж поехать в лес за грибами.* "I can't wait to go mushroom hunting in the woods."

ТЕРПЁЖКА, -и, *f., joc.* Patience, endurance. ♦ *Так жить трудно, никакой терпёжки не хватает.* "It's hard to live like this; the patience of a saint isn't enough."

ТЕРПЕ́Ц УРВА́ЛСЯ, *idiom, Ukr.* I have no patience, I've lost my patience (from терпение, "patience," and рваться, "to break"). ♦ *Терпец урвался ждать, пока вы болтать кончите.* "I have no patience to wait for you to finish your gabbing."

ТЕРРОРИ́СТ, -а, *m., joc.* A playboy, seducer, Don Juan. ♦ *Ты у нас известный террорист, ни одну юбку не пропустишь.* "Everyone knows you're an awful womanizer — you're after every skirt you see."

ТЕСА́ТЬ: Хоть кол на голове́ теши́, see under **хоть**.

ТЕ́СТО: Из друго́го те́ста, *idiom, neg.* Different, outside the norm (lit., from a different dough). ♦ *Ты что, из другого теста, почему не помогаешь нам?* "What do you think you are, some superior sort of being? Why don't you give us a hand?" **Жени́х и неве́ста объе́лися те́ста**, see under **жени́х**.

ТЕТЕ́РЯ: Глуха́я тете́ря, see under **глуха́я. Со́нная тете́ря**, see under **со́нная**.

ТЁТКА, -и, *f., youth, joc.* A girl (lit., an aunt). ♦ *А там тётки на всех будут?* "Will there be enough girls to go around?"

ТЕХНА́РЬ, -я, *m.* Someone with a technical education. ♦ *Нет, он технарь, не филолог.* "He studied technical subjects, not humanities."

ТЕ́ХНИК: ю́ный те́хник, see under **ю́ный**.

ТЕ́ХНИКА: под те́хникой, *idiom.* On tape, under electronic surveillance (lit., under technical devices). ♦ *Я под техникой говорить не буду.* "I'm not saying anything on tape."

ТЕХНИ́ЧНО, *adv.* Well, elegantly, successfully. ♦ *Ты над ним технично пошутил.* "That was a clever trick you played on him."

ТЕ́ЧКА, -и, *f., rude.* Lit., estrus. **1.** Sexual excitement, availability. ♦ *У тебя что, течка, на всех мужиков бросаешься?* "What are you, in heat or something? How come you're throwing yourself at all the men?" **2.** Menstruation. ♦ *У неё течка, она не даёт.* "She's got her period, so she won't sleep with me."

ТЕЧЬ В КРЫ́ШЕ, *idiom, joc.* Strange behavior, eccentricity (lit., a leak in the roof). ♦ *У него течь в крыше, всё время что-то бормочет вслух.* "Has he got a screw loose or something? How come he's always muttering to himself?"

ТИГРИ́ЦА, -ы, *f.* A strong, energetic woman (lit, tigress). ♦ *Ей палец в рот не клади, настоящая тигрица.* "Don't mess with her, she's a real tigress."

ТИ́КАЛКА, -и, *f., youth., joc.* A heart (from тик-так, the sound of a clock). ♦ *Что-то тикалка стучит.* "For some reason my ticker is thumping very hard."

ТИ́КАТЬ/НАТИ́КАТЬ. To tick, to make the sound of time passing (from тик-так, a watch sound). ♦ *Сколько на твоих натикало?* "What time does your watch say (tick)?"

ТИКА́ТЬ/УТИКА́ТЬ. To run, escape (from Ukrainian). ♦ *Тикать некуда, за нами река, всех перебьют, будем держаться.* "There's no way to get out of here, the river's behind us and they can get a shot at us from there. We have to stay where we are."

ТИ́КЕТ, -а, *m., youth, obs.* Ticket (from Eng. "ticket"). ♦ *Тикет достал?* "Did you manage to get a ticket?"

ТИ́КИ-ТАК, *adv., joc. Ukr.* **1.** Just right, just so, exactly. ♦ *Ты это делай тики-*

так, и всё будет хорошо. "If you do it just exactly like that, everything will be fine." **2.** Well, fine. ♦*У нас всё будет тики-так, посмотришь.* "Wait and see — everything will turn out fine."

ТИПУ́Н ТЕБЕ́ НА ЯЗЫ́К, *idiom, neg.* Lit., "(May you get) a blister on your tongue." An expression for objecting to the uttering of negative predictions. ♦*Вот заболеешь, тогда узнаешь, что значит быть одному. — Типун тебе на язык, я пока здоров.* "When you get sick, you'll find out what it really means to be on your own. — Bite your tongue! So far I'm just fine!"

ТИ́ПЧИК, -а, *m., neg., joc.* An unpleasant or suspicious character (lit., a type). ♦*Ну и типчик твой друг, такого грубияна я ещё не видела.* "Your friend is quite an unpleasant character. I've never seen such rudeness!"

ТИРА́Ж: Выходи́ть/вы́йти в тира́ж, see under **выходи́ть.**

ТИ́СКАЛО, -а, *n.* A liar (from тиснуть, to cheat). See **ти́снуть.** ♦*Всё, что говорит этот тискало, брехня.* "The man is telling you a pack of lies, he's a bullshit artist."

ТИ́СНУТЬ, *perf. only.* Lit., to squeeze, press. **1.** To print, publish. ♦*Он недавно тиснул пару статей.* "He published a couple of articles recently." **2.** *youth.* To steal. ♦*Кто тиснул деньги со стола?* "Who stole the money that was on the table?"

ТИ́ТИ-МИ́ТИ, *idiom, neg., joc.* A woman's breasts. ♦*Прикрой свои тити-мити, а то сюда могут войти.* "Cover your titties — someone could walk in here anytime." •**Разводить/ развести́ ти́ти-ми́ти,** see under **разводи́ть.**

ТИ́ТЬКА, -и, *f., neg., joc.* A woman's breasts. ♦*Смотри, у неё уже выросли титьки!* "Look, she's starting to get titties!"

ТИХА́РЬ, -я́, *m., crim., neg.* A plainclothes police officer. ♦*Посмотри, там не тихарь за углом топчется?* "Go see if that's a plainclothes cop over there in the corner."

ТИ́ХИЙ (-ая, -ое), как сто обезья́н в кле́тке, *idiom, joc.* Naughty, noise (lit., as calm as hundred monkeys in a cage). ♦*Какой у Вас сын спокойный мальчик. — Как же тихий, как сто...* "What a well-behaved boy you have!" — "Oh, yeah, quiet as a barrel of monkeys."

ТИ́ХИЙ У́ЖАС! *idiom.* Terrible! Incredible! (lit., speechless horror). ♦*Тихий ужас! Наш банк лопнул.* "Oh, my God! Our bank has collapsed."

ТИ́ХО КАК В ТА́НКЕ, *idiom.* Calm, normal, orderly (lit., quiet as in a tank). ♦*Как дела на работе: спорите, наверное, перестраиваетесь? — Что ты, у нас всё тихо как в танке.* "How are things at work? Are they trying to apply the perestroika policies in your office? — Are you kidding? Everything's just chugging along as usual."

ТИ́ХОЙ СА́ПОЙ, *idiom.* Calmly, without haste (lit., with a quiet hoe). ♦*Куда нам спешить, тихой сапой к вечеру всё закончим.* "What's the hurry? We can do the job calmly and still finish by evening."

ТОВАРНЯ́К, -а́, *m.* A freight train. ♦*Это не электричка, товарняк идёт.* "That's not our train; it's a freight train."

ТОГО́: Кто-л. того́, *idiom, neg.* Crazy. ♦*Он что, того?* "What's with him? Is he out of his mind?"

ТОК, -а, *m., youth, obs.* Talk (from Eng. "talk"). ♦*Мне этот ток не нравится.* "I don't like that kind of talk." •**Дави́ть/ продави́ть ток,** see under **дави́ть.**

ТО́КАРЬ-ПЕ́КАРЬ, то́каря-пе́каря, *m., neg.* An incompetent worker (lit., a turner-baker). ♦*Если ты не знаешь, как ремонтировать утюг, токарь-пекарь, то зачем тогда полез?* "You bungler, if you don't know how to fix an iron, why did you even start up?"

ТОЛК ВЫ́ШЕЛ, БЕ́СТОЛОК ОСТА́Л-СЯ, *idiom, joc.* An apotropaic expression used to show uncertainty about the cleverness or success of someone or something (playing on the positive idiom толк вышел, "someone/something has become a success"). ♦*Как твои дети? Из них* вышел толк? — *Толк вышел, бестолок остался.* "How are your kids doing? Has anything good come of them? — Well, what can you expect from kids like that?"

ТОЛКА́ТЬ/ТОЛКНУ́ТЬ. To sell (lit., to push over). ♦ *Я уже толкнул все свои доллары.* "I've already sold all my dollars." •**Толка́ть/толкну́ть речу́гу,** *idiom, neg.* To give a speech, deliver a speech. ♦ *Он опять толкает речугу об экономике.* "He's giving another speech on economics."

ТОЛКА́ТЬСЯ, *imperf. only, rude.* To have sexual relations. ♦ *Он с ней давно толкается?* "Has he been sleeping with her for long?"

ТОЛКУ́ЧКА, -и, *f., neg.* **1.** A crowd. ♦ *В метро сегодня такая толкучка.* "The subway was awfully crowded today." **2.** A market, an open-air bazaar. ♦ *Пойдём на толкучку, сапоги купить надо.* "Let's go down to the flea market. I need to buy some boots."

ТОЛСТОМЯ́СЫЙ, -ая, -ое, *neg.* Fat, obese. ♦ *Ты этого толстомясого знаешь?* "Do you know that fat fellow?"

ТОЛЧО́К, толчка́, *m.* **1.** A toilet. ♦ *А вот и толчок, давай зайдём.* "Let's stop in the bathroom over there." **2.** An open-air market, flea market (cf. **толку́чка 2**). ♦ *Ты был на толчке сегодня? Пластинки продавали?* "Were you at the market today? Were they selling records there?" •**Толчо́к с педа́лями,** *idiom, neg.* A car in bad condition, a worthless automobile (lit., а толчок with pedals). ♦ *Это не машина, а толчок с педалями.* "That's not a car, it's a can on wheels."

ТО-МИ́МО-ТО-КО́СО, *idiom, army.* Said about a poor marksman (from мимо, wide of the mark, and косо, askew). ♦ *Хоть раз в мишень попади, всё время у тебя то-мимо-то-косо.* "Try to hit the target, why don't you? You're shooting here, there, and everywhere."

ТО́ННА, -ы, *f., youth.* A thousand rubles. ♦ *Вот две тонны, купи себе водки.* "Here's two thousand. Buy yourself some vodka."

ТО́НУС: Жить в то́нусе, see under **жить.**

ТО́НЬКА, -и, *f., youth, joc.* Tonic water (lit., a nickname for Antonina). ♦ *Ты джин с тонькой пьёшь?* "Can I offer you a gin and Tonya?"

ТО́ПАТЬ/ПОТО́ПАТЬ, *joc.* To go (lit., to stamp one's feet). ♦ *Топай в магазин.* "Go over to the store."

ТОПИ́ТЬ/ПРИТОПИ́ТЬ НА МА́ССУ, *idiom.* To sleep (lit., to apply someone's weight). ♦ *Не орите, дайте притопить на массу хоть часок.* "Stop making so much noise, I'm trying to hit the sack."

ТОПО́Р: Хоть топо́р ве́шай, see under **хоть.**

ТОПОТУ́НЧИК, -а, *m., joc.* A fussbudget, a bustling person. ♦ *Какой у неё муж топотунчик, всё сразу сделал, кофе принёс, купил конфет.* "Her husband is quite a busy beaver — bringing the coffee, getting the candy, just seeing to everything."

ТОПТА́ТЬ/ПОТОПТА́ТЬ, *rude.* **1.** To have sex with a woman. ♦ *Не ходи туда, там Петька топчет бабу.* "Don't go in there. Pete is screwing a girl." **2.** To beat, win a victory over. ♦ *Нас потоптали в футбол.* "They beat us in soccer."

ТОПТА́ТЬ ГРАНИ́ЦУ, *idiom, army.* To patrol a border (lit., to trample a border). ♦ *Мне осточертело топтать границу, уже десять лет я здесь.* "I'm sick and tired of this guard duty. I've been marching up and down this stretch of the border for ten years."

ТОПТА́ТЬ МУМУ́, *idiom, army.* To bother (lit., to trample Mumu the dog). ♦ *Кончай топтать муму, никто тебя в разведку не возьмёт и не мечтай.* "For the tenth time, I won't take you on this reconnaissance mission. You're beating a dead horse!" See **муму́.**

ТОПТУ́Н, -á, *m., neg.* A detective, sleuth, plainclothes officer. ♦ *Там за углом топтун.* "There's a detective over there in the corner."

ТО́РБА, -ы, *f., crim.* Solitary confinement, isolation cell (lit., a bag). ♦ *А за что* *тебя в торбу определили?* "How come you got put into solitary?"

ТО́РБИТЬСЯ/ПОТО́РБИТЬСЯ, *crim.* To be in solitary confinement (cf. **то́рба**). ◆*Сколько ты здесь торбишься?* "How much time do you have to do in solitary?"

ТОРГА́Ш, -а́, *m., neg.* **1.** A dishonest dealer, a speculator. ◆*Эти торгаши совсем обнаглели, мясо продают по немыслимой цене.* "Those operators are completely shameless, selling meat at crazy prices like that!" **2.** A store clerk. ◆*Он торгаш, в винном магазине работает.* "He's a clerk in a liquor store."

ТОРГОВА́ТЬ/СТОРГОВА́ТЬ, *crim.* To steal. ◆*Ну что, удалось сторговать машину?* "So did you manage to steal the car?"

ТОРЕ́Ц: Дать в торе́ц, see under **дать**.

ТОРМА́ШКИ: Вверх торма́шками, *idiom, joc.* **1.** Topsy-turvy, in disorder. ◆*Пришла с работы, хотела отдохнуть, а в доме всё вверх тормашками.* "I came home from work exhausted and wanted a rest, but everything was in a mess." **2.** *usu. in children's speech.* Head over heels, somersaulting. ◆*Я ему как дал, он и полетел вверх тормашками.* "I gave him a punch and he went flying head over heels."

ТО́РМОЗ, -а, *m.* A stupid person (lit., a brake pedal). ◆*Такому тормозу не объяснить самых простых вещей.* "I can't explain it any more simply. Slowpokes like you are never going to understand. Your brain must have brakes on it."

ТО́РМОЗ: Спуска́ть/спусти́ть на тормоза́х, see under **спуска́ть**.

ТОРМОЗИ́ТЬ/ТОРМОЗНУ́ТЬ. To stop someone suddenly or unexpectedly. ◆*Он перестал делать карьеру, кто его тормознул?* "It looks like his career got stalled. Who put the brakes on him?"

ТОРМОЗИ́ТЬСЯ/ТОРМОЗНУ́ТЬСЯ. To stop, halt, cease. ◆*Я тормознусь, больше пить не буду, завтра рано вставать.* "I'm stopping now. I have to be up early tomorrow, so I'm not going to drink another drop."

ТОРМОЗНО́Й, -а́я, -о́е, *youth, neg.* **1.** Empty, inane, stupid (of things). ◆*Что ты всё читаешь тормозные книги?* "Why do you keep reading those inane books?" **2.** Thickheaded, stupid (of people). ◆*Ты сегодня какой-то тормозной, ничего не понимаешь.* "You're being such a numskull today! You don't seem to understand anything."

ТОРМОЗО́К, тормозка́, *m., obs.* A worker's lunch bag. ◆*Доставай тормозок, пора перекусить.* "Get out your lunch bag. It's time for a bite."

ТОРМОЗУ́ХА, -и, *f.* Brake fluid (from тормоз, brake). ◆*Тормозуху долей, не видишь, у тебя течёт трубка.* "You need some brake fluid. I think there's a leak in the line."

ТОРОПИ́СЬ НЕ СПЕША́ (, поспеша́й ме́дленно), *idiom.* Slow down, don't be in such a rush (lit., make haste slowly). ◆*Давай быстрее, опаздываем! — Торопись не спеша.* "Come on, we're late! — Don't be in such a rush."

ТОРОПЛЮ́СЬ, АЖ ВСПОТЕ́Л, *idiom, neg., joc.* Lit., "I'm hurrying, I'm in a sweat"; used sarcastically in refusing to do what someone else requests. ◆*Вали отсюда, пока жив! — Тороплюсь, аж вспотел.* "Get out of here before I beat you up! — The hell with you and your threats."

ТОРПЕ́ДА, -ы, *f.* A medicinal ampule implanted under the skin for the treatment of alcoholism (lit., a torpedo). ◆*Он с торпедой, ему пить нельзя.* "He's got a torpedo so he can't drink at all." ◆**Зашива́ть/заши́ть торпе́ду,** see under **зашива́ть**.

ТОРТ: Ста́линский торт, see under **ста́линский**.

ТОРЧ, -а, *m., youth.* See **торчо́к**.

ТОРЧА́ТЬ/ЗАТОРЧА́ТЬ. To be drunk, high on drugs (lit., to protrude, stick out). ◆*Ты уже торчишь.* "You're high already."

ТОРЧЁННЫЙ, -ая, -ое. Intoxicated or "high" (from торчать). See **торча́ть**. ◆*С ним бесполезно говорить,* *торчённый дальше некуда.* "Don't try to talk to him, he's stoned out of his mind."

ТОРЧÓК, торчка́, *m., youth, neg.* **1.** A drug addict. ♦ *Этот торчок всё забывает.* "That dopehead forgets everything." **2.** Delight, enjoyment. ♦ *Эта музыка — такой торчок!* "That music is fantastic!"

ТОЧИ́ЛО, -а, *n., neg.* A taxi (lit., a grindstone). ♦ *Бери точило быстрей, а то опоздаем.* "Get a taxi or we'll be late."

ТОЧИ́ТЬ/ПОТОЧИ́ТЬ, *army.* To eat (lit., to sharpen, to gnaw). ♦ *Тащи на стол всё, что поточить можно.* "Put everything edible out on the table."

ТÓЧКА: Тóчка сопротивлéния, *idiom, joc., obs.* A liquor store (lit., a point of resistance; referring to the period of Gorbachev's anti-alcohol policies). *А ты знаешь, где здесь точка сопротивления?* "Do you know if there's a 'point of resistance' around here?" **Пя́тая тóчка,** see under **пя́тая. Упа́сть на четы́ре тóчки,** see under **упа́сть.**

ТОЧНЯ́К, *pred. use.* Accurate, exact. ♦ *Раз он сказал, значит, это точняк.* "If he said so, you can be sure it's exactly so."

ТОШНИ́ЛОВКА, -и, *f., neg.* A cafeteria, dining hall (from тошнить, "to be nauseous"). ♦ *Ты опять в перерыв идёшь в эту тошниловку, давай лучше пойдём в другое место перекусить.* "Are you going back to that greasy-spoon for lunch? Let's go someplace else to have a bite."

ТОШНÓТИК, -а, *m., neg.* An annoying, unpleasant person (from тошнить, "to be nauseous"). ♦ *Этого тошнотика трудно выдержать более пяти минут.* "It's hard to take that guy for more than five minutes."

ТОШНЯ́К, *pred. use, youth, neg.* Something disgusting, terribly bad (from тошнить, "to be nauseous"). ♦ *Этот спектакль — тошняк и больше ничего.* "That play is simply awful."

ТПРУ: Ни тпру, ни ну, see under **ни.**

ТРÁБЛЫ, -ов, *pl., youth, joc.* Troubles, difficulties (from Eng. "trouble"). ♦ *Ну чего ты плачешь, какие у тебя трабблы?* "What are you crying about? What's the trouble?"

ТРАВИ́ТЬ/ПОТРАВИ́ТЬ, *neg., joc.* To tell tall tales, to lie (lit., to give slack, give play to rope). ♦ *Он мастер травить.* "He's a past master of spinning yarns."

ТРÁВКА, -и, *f., youth.* Drugs, marijuana (from трава, "grass"). ♦ *Хочешь травку покурить?* "Do you want to smoke some grass?"

ТРАКТОВÁТЬ/ЗАТРАКТОВÁТЬ, *neg., joc.* To explain the obvious, to be pedantic (from трактат, "treatise"). ♦ *Не надо так долго трактовать, и так ясно, что нужно делать.* "There's no need to lecture about it — it's perfectly clear what needs to be done."

ТРÁКТОР: Пусть рабóтает трáктор — он желéзный, see under **пусть.**

ТРÁЛИ-ВÁЛИ, *idiom, neg., joc.* **1.** Long-drawn-out conversations. ♦ *Кончай по телефону бесконечные трали-вали.* "Enough of your eternal yakkety-yak on the telephone." **2.** Intimate relations, a love affair. ♦ *Ты что, не знаешь, у них трали-вали и причём давно.* "Didn't you know? They've been lovers for a long time."

ТРАМВÁЙ: Я не такáя, я жду трамвáя, see under **я. Попадáть/попáсть под трамвáй,** see under **попадáть.**

ТРАНДÉТЬ/ЗАТРАНДÉТЬ, *neg.* To babble on, to talk nonsense. ♦ *Не транди, кто в это поверит?* "Don't babble such nonsense, no one will believe it."

ТРАНДЕЧИ́ХА, -и, *f., joc.* An overtalkative woman (cf. **трандéть**). ♦ *Я устаю с этой трандечихой разговаривать.* "I'm tired of talking with that magpie."

ТРАНЖИ́РА, -ы, *m. & f., neg.* A big spender, spendthrift. ♦ *Ты у нас в семье один такой транжира, опять у тебя нет денег.* "You're the biggest spendthrift in our family; here you are out of money again!"

ТРАНК, -а, *m., youth.* A tranquilizer, tranquilizers. ♦ *У кого ещё транк остался?* "Who has some more 'tranq'?"

ТРАНКСИБИ́РСКИЙ ЭКСПРЕ́СС, *idiom, youth, joc.* The Trans-Siberian Express train, considered as a drug-trafficking locale (by wordplay on **транк** and транссибирский экспресс, "Trans-Siberian Express"). ♦*На транксибирском экспрессе ездят все нарки.* "All the druggies ride the Trans-Siberian Express."

ТРАНС: В тра́нсе, *idiom, neg.* In shock, struck dumb. ♦*После его выходки я хожу в трансе. Как можно было ударить девушку?!* "I'm shocked by his behavior. How could he hit a girl?!"

ТРА́УР ПОД НОГТЯ́МИ, *idiom, joc.* Dirty nails, dirt under the fingernails (lit., mourning under the fingernails). ♦*У тебя под ногтями траур, как не стыдно.* "You should be ashamed to go around with such dirty fingernails."

ТРА́ХАЛЬ, -я, *m., neg.* A sexually predatory man, a Don Juan. ♦*Этот трахаль всех девок перепортил в деревне.* "That Don Juan has been to bed with all the girls in the village."

ТРАХА́ЛЬЩИК, -а, *m., neg.* See **тра́халь.**

ТРА́ХАНЬЕ, -я, *n., rude.* 1. Sex, sexual activity. ♦*У тебя на уме одно траханье.* "Sex is all you've ever got on your mind." 2. *neg.* Difficult, painstaking work. ♦*Мне уже невмоготу это траханье со словарем.* "I've had it with this grueling work on the dictionary."

ТРА́ХАТЬ/ТРА́ХНУТЬ, *rude.* To have sex with a woman. ♦*Он её трахнул год назад, и все об этом знают.* "He screwed her last year, and everyone knows about it."

ТРА́ХАТЬСЯ/ПОТРА́ХАТЬСЯ, *rude.* To have sex. ♦*Ты с ней уже трахался?* "Have you been to bed with her?"

ТРА́ХНУТЫЙ, -ая, -ое, *neg.* Crazy, strange, abnormal. ♦*Что с тобой, ходишь какой-то трахнутый.* "What's with you? You're going around like some kind of maniac." •**Из-за угла́ мешко́м тра́хнутый,** *idiom, neg., rude.* Dazed, crazed (lit., hit with a sack from the corner). ♦*С ним нельзя дело иметь, он же*

из-за угла мешком трахнутый. "You can't do anything with him, he's completely bonkers."

ТРАХОДРО́М, -а, *m., joc.* A bed (lit., a sex field). ♦*Ложись в траходром, пообнимаемся.* "Get into bed and let's have some embraces."

ТРЕБУХА́, -и́, *f., neg.* Unreliable information (lit., entrails). ♦*Это требуха, не верь ему.* "That's a bunch of nonsense — don't believe him."

ТРЕ́ЗВЫЙ КАК СТЁКЛЫШКО, *idiom, joc.* Sober (lit., sober as a piece of glass). ♦*Завтра все должны быть трезвыми как стёклышко.* "Tomorrow everyone's got to stay sober as a judge."

ТРЕЙДИ́ТЬ(СЯ)/ПОТРЕЙДИ́ТЬ(СЯ), *youth, neg.* To bargain, dicker, haggle about prices (from Eng. "trade"). ♦*Не надо трейдиться, давай штуку и разойдёмся.* "Let's not dicker about it; call it a thousand and it's a deal."

ТРЁКАЛО, -а, *n., neg.* A chatterbox, leg-puller, spinner of tall tales, liar. ♦*Ну и трёкало ты, я тебе не верю.* "You're a fibber. I don't believe you."

ТРЁКАТЬ/ПОТРЁКАТЬ, *neg.* To chatter idly, talk nonsense. ♦*Вам не надоело ещё трёкать?* "Haven't you had your fill of chatter yet?"

ТРЕКЛЯ́ТЫЙ, -ая, -ое. Damned, cursed ("thrice damned," from проклятый and три). ♦*Где же этот треклятый галстук?* "Where is that damned necktie?"

ТРЕНДИ́ТЬСЯ¹, *youth, joc.* To flirt, carry on a courtship. ♦*Вы тут решили трендиться целый день, так не пойдёт: у нас ещё много дел.* "If you guys are planning to bill and coo all day, that won't do! We've got a lot of work to do!"

ТРЕНДИ́ТЬ(СЯ)²/ПОТРЕНДИ́ТЬ(СЯ), *youth, neg.* To bargain, trade (cf. **трейди́ться**). ♦*Он, как всегда, на Арбате трендит, картинки продаёт.* "He's on the Arbat as usual, trading in pictures."

ТРЁП, -а, *m., neg.* Long, pointless conversations; babbling. ♦*Мне ваш трёп надоел ужасно, от него голова пухнет.* "Your chatter is driving me crazy. My head is spinning from it."

ТРЕПА́К, -á, *m., neg.* Gonorrhea (by wordplay on триппер and the name of a Ukrainian dance). ♦*Будешь по бабам ходить, трепак схватишь.* "You could get the clap if you sleep around."

ТРЕПА́ТЬ: Жизнь трепану́ла (потрепа́ла) кого́-л., see under **жизнь.**

ТРЕПА́ТЬСЯ/ПОТРЕПА́ТЬСЯ, *neg.* To talk long and pointlessly, to chatter on. ♦*Не трепись! Если не знаешь наверняка, то и говорить незачем.* "Don't babble. If you don't know for sure, then don't talk about it."

ТРЕПА́Ч, -á, *m., neg., rude.* A big talker, boaster. ♦*Ты этого трепача не слушай.* "Don't listen to that windbag."

ТРЕПЕТУ́ЛЬКА, -и, *f., youth, joc.* A romantic, sentimental young girl. ♦*Ты давно с этой трепетулькой ходишь?* "Have you been dating that doting girl for long?"

ТРЕПЛО́, -á, *n., neg., rude.* See **трепа́ч.**

ТРЕ́СКАТЬ/ПОТРЕ́СКАТЬ, *neg.* To eat greedily (lit., to crunch). ♦*Сколько можно конфеты трескать?* "Don't wolf down so much candy."

ТРЕ́СКАТЬСЯ/ВТРЕ́СКАТЬСЯ, *youth.* To take drugs. ♦*Они в другой комнате трескаются.* "They're doing some drugs in the other room."

ТРЁХА, -и, *f., neg., obs.* Three rubles, a three-ruble piece. ♦*Дай ему трёху, не больше.* "Don't give him more than a three."

ТРЁХМЕСТКА, -и, *f., crim., obs.* Thirty rubles. ♦*С тебя трёхместка.* "Give me thirty rubles."

ТРЁХНУТЬСЯ, *perf. only, neg.* To go crazy, become crazed. ♦*От ваших закидонов трёхнуться можно.* "Your pranks could drive someone crazy."

ТРЁШКА, -и, *f., neg.* See **трёха.**

ТРЕЩА́ТЬ: Голова́ трещи́т у кого́-л., *idiom.* Someone has a splitting headache (lit., someone's head is making a cracking sound). ♦*У меня голова трещит.* "I've got a splitting headache." **За уша́ми трещи́т,** *idiom.* To have a hearty appetite. ♦*Сначала отказывался*

есть, а сейчас ест так, что за ушами трещит. "At first he refused to eat, but now he's packing it away with a hearty appetite."

ТРИДЦА́ТНИК, -a, *m.* **1.** Thirty years. ♦*Ему завтра тридцатник.* "He'll be thirty years old tomorrow." **2.** *obs.* Thirty rubles. ♦*Вот тебе тридцатник и хватит.* "Here's thirty, and that's the end of it."

ТРИ́ППЕР, -a, *m.* Gonorrhea. ♦*Я, кажется, подхватил триппер.* "I seem to have caught the clap." •**Как за́йцу три́ппер,** see under **как.**

ТРО́ГАТЬ ма́му, *idiom, neg., rude.* To hold in contempt, despise, spit on (lit., to touch someone's mother; euph. for **ёб твою мать**). ♦*Я его маму трогал, пусть не грозит.* "The hell with him and his threats."

ТРО́Е СУ́ТОК И ВСЁ ЛЕ́СОМ, *idiom, joc.* Too far away (lit., it's a three-day trip and all forest). ♦*Живут они где-то на западе Москвы, трое суток и всё лесом.* "They live somewhere out in the boondocks of western Moscow."

ТРОМБО́Н, -a, *m., army.* A rifle with a telescopic sight (lit., trombone). ♦*Вчера задело осколком тромбон, хорошо бы новый достать.* "My sniper scope was damaged by a piece of shrapnel and I need a new one."

ТРО́НУТЫЙ, -ая, -ое, *neg.* Crazy (lit., touched). ♦*Ты что, тронутый? Такие деньги потратил на чепуху!* "Are you crazy, spending all that money on this crap?"

ТРО́НУТЬСЯ, *perf. only, neg.* To go crazy, lose one's mind. ♦*После аварии на заводе он совсем тронулся.* "After the accident at the plant he went completely bonkers."

ТРОЯ́К, -á, *m.* **1.** *neg.* See **трёха. 2.** *youth, school.* An "average grade", a "3". ♦*Опять трояк схлопотал по математике.* "I got a C in math again."

ТРУБА́, -ы́, *f., neg.* Lit., pipe. **1.** Trouble, disaster. ♦*Мне труба будет, если родители об этом узнают.* "It'll be curtains for me if my parents find out about this." **2.** *youth.* An underground passageway (for crossing city streets). ♦*Купи газеты в трубе.* "Buy the newspaper in the tube." •**Труба́ де́ло,** *idiom, neg.* It's all over, it's the end, it's gone. ♦*Всей работе — труба дело.* "All that work is down the tubes."

ТРУБЕ́НЬ, -и, *f.* The end (lit., a tube). ♦*Талибам без помощи Пакистана— трубень.* "Without Pakistan's help, the Taliban would be down the tubes."

ТРУБИ́ТЬ/ПРОТРУБИ́ТЬ. To work long and productively. ♦*Я в институте уже протрубил 15 лет.* "I've been working at the Institute for 15 years."

ТРУДИ́ТЬСЯ как Зо́лушка, *idiom.* To do hard and menial work (lit., to work like Cinderella). ♦*Я тружусь как Золушка, никто спасибо не скажет.* "Here I am slaving away like Cinderella and not a word of thanks from anyone."

ТРУДОГО́ЛИК, -а, *m.* **1.** *obs.* An inmate of a labor-camp-cum-detox-institution for alcoholics. ♦*Ну, трудоголики, когда план будем выполнять?* "Well, workaholics, when are we going to get this job done?" **2.** *joc.* Someone who drinks at work. ♦*Трудоголики, когда вы домой пойдёте, хватит пить!* "Well, you workaholics, it's about time to stop drinking and go home."

ТРУЗЕРА́, -о́в, *pl., youth.* Slacks, trousers (from Eng. "trousers"). ♦*Цвет у этих трузеров не тот.* "Those pants are the wrong color."

ТРУП, -а, *m., neg.* A very drunk person (lit., a corpse). ♦*Смотри, вон ещё два трупа идут.* "Look, there go two more dead-drunk guys."

ТРУСЫ́: Семе́йные (Балти́йские) тру-сы́, see under **семе́йные.**

ТРУХА́ТЬ, *imperf. only, rude.* **1.** To have an orgasm. ♦*Ты собираешься трухать или нет?* "Well, are you going to come or not?" **2.** To be cowardly. ♦*Не трухай, всё будет в порядке.* "Don't be such a scaredy-cat. Everything's going to be all right."

ТРЫНДЁЖ, -а, *m., youth, neg.* Prattle, lies. ♦*Это трындёж, ничего больше.*

"That's just a bunch of lies."

ТРЫНДИ́ТЬ/ПОТРЫНДИ́ТЬ, *neg.* To chatter idly, to lie. ♦*Потрындили, хватит.* "Enough tall tales."

ТРЫ́НКАТЬ/ЗАТРЫ́НКАТЬ. To play a stringed instrument without skill or training. ♦*Он на гитаре не умеет играть, просто трынкает.* "He doesn't really know how to play the guitar; he just diddles around on it."

ТРЫН-ТРАВА́, *idiom.* Unimportant, all the same. ♦*Все волнуются, переживают, опоздаем на самолёт или нет, а ему всё трын-трава.* "Everyone else is in a tizzy about whether we're going to miss the plane, but it's all the same to him."

ТРЮК: Выки́дывать/вы́кинуть трюк, see under **выки́дывать.**

ТРЮМ, -а, *m., joc.* A stomach, belly (lit., a ship's hold). ♦*Трюм пустой с утра, надо перекусить чего-нибудь.* "I've been running on empty all day, I've got to get a bite."

ТРЮ́НДЕЛЬ, -я, *m., joc., obs.* Three rubles. ♦*Трюндель на пиво есть?* "Have you got a three for a beer?"

ТРЮ́ХАТЬ/ПОТРЮ́ХАТЬ, *joc.* To go softly, slip out. ♦*Давай отсюда трюхать потихоньку.* "Let's slip out of here on the quiet."

ТРЯПИ́ЧНИК, -а, *m., neg.* A man who is very concerned about fashion and clothing. ♦*Не знала я, что ты такой тряпичник.* "I didn't know you were such a clothes-horse."

ТРЯ́ПКА, -и, *f., neg.* A person of weak will, weak character (lit., [mere] cloth[es]). ♦*Он тебя не поддержит, он — тряпка.* "He won't be able to support you; he's just a rag."

ТРЯ́ПКИ, тря́пок, *pl., neg.* Clothing. ♦*Куда тебе столько тряпок?* "What do you need all those clothes for?"

ТРЯ́ПОЧКА: Молча́ть/замолча́ть в тря́почку, see under **молча́ть.**

ТРЯСТИ́СЬ/ПОТРЯСТИ́СЬ, *joc.* To dance (lit., to shake). ♦*Иди потрясись! Что ты весь вечер сидишь?* "Come dance! Don't just sit there all evening!"

ТРЯХОМУ́ДСТВО, -а, *n., neg.* Stupid behavior, stupidity (cf. **муда́к**). ♦*Тряхомудство такие деньги платить за джинсы.* "It's lunacy to pay that much for jeans."

ТРЯХОМУ́НДИЯ, -и, *f., rude.* Confusion, hubbub, fuss. ♦*Сколько может продолжаться эта тряхомундия с зарплатой, её повысят или нет?* "How long are they going to keep up this confusion about our salaries? Are we getting raises or not?"

ТУ́БЗИК, -а, *m., joc.* A toilet. ♦*Тебе не пора в тубзик?* "Do you need to go to the john?"

ТУ́ГО, *adv., youth.* Excellent, very well (lit., tightly). Cf. **круто.**

ТУГОПЛА́ВКИЙ, -ая, -ое. Stupid, slow to react (lit., of low malleability). ♦*Ну, решайся, идёшь с нами, какой-то ты сегодня не такой, тугоплавкий.* "Make up your mind whether you're coming with us or not! You're being very indecisive today."

ТУ́ГРИКИ, -ов, *pl.* Money (from Mongolian). ♦*Сколько у тебя тугриков, хватит на яблоки?* "How much money do you have on you? Will it be enough to buy apples?"

ТУДА́, ГДЕ НЕТ ТРУДА́, *idiom, joc.* Where life is easy, where the work isn't hard (a rhyming phrase; lit., where there's no work). ♦*Куда твой отпрыск поступил учиться? — Туда, где нет труда.* "Where is your son going to college? — On easy street."

ТУДА́/ТУДЫ́ ЕГО́ (ЕЁ, ИХ) В КА-ЧЕ́ЛЬ, *idiom, rude.* Damn him (her, them) (a euphemistic phrase; lit., there onto a swing). ♦*Значит, она бросила сына, туда её в качель.* "So she abandoned her son, damn her."

ТУЗ, -а́, *m., crim.* Buttocks (lit., ace). ♦*Убери свой туз, сесть негде.* "Move your ass. There's no room to sit."

ТУЛИ́ТЬСЯ/ПРИТУЛИ́ТЬСЯ. 1. To live in crowded conditions or in a small space. ♦*Надоело здесь тулиться в углу.* "I'm sick of living in this hole in the wall." **2.** To lean up against someone.

♦*Притулись ко мне, теплее будет.* "Lean against me; it'll be warmer that way."

ТУ́МБА-Ю́МБА, ту́мбы-ю́мбы, *f., collect., joc.* **1.** Africans. **2.** An exotic language. ♦*На каком языке он говорит? Я эту тумбу-юмбу не понимаю.* "What language is he speaking? I don't follow that mambo-jumbo."

ТУ́МКАТЬ/ПОТУ́МКАТЬ, *joc.* **1.** To think. ♦*Сижу и тумкаю, как дальше быть.* "I'm sitting here thinking what I should do next." **2.** *imperf. only.* To understand, to know. ♦*Он в алгебре что-нибудь тумкает?* "Does he know any algebra?"

ТУ́НДРА, -ы, *f., youth, joc.* An ignorant, uneducated person (lit., tundra). ♦*А ты, тундра, так ничего и не понял, что произошло?* "You ignoramus, you just haven't figured out what happened, have you?"

ТУПА́РЬ, -я́, *m., neg.* An ignorant, stupid, awkward person (from тупой, "blunt"). ♦*Тупарь ты, больше никто, если мог такое натворить.* "You're just a dumbbell, to do a thing like that."

ТУПИ́ТЬ/ЗАТУПИ́ТЬ, *army.* To act stupid, to play the fool (cf. **тупа́рь**).

ТУПО́Й КАК СИБИ́РСКИЙ ВА́ЛЕ-НОК, *idiom, joc.* Stupid, ignorat (lit., as dull as a Siberian felt boot).

ТУПОРЫ́ЛЫЙ, -ая, -ое, *neg., rude.* Stupid, dumb. ♦*Не знал я, что он таким тупорылым окажется.* "I had no idea he'd turn out to be so thickheaded."

ТУРБОВИНТОВО́Й, -а́я, -о́е, *joc.* Energetic, efficient (lit., prop jet). ♦*Он турбовинтовой, он всё устроит.* "He'll arrange everything — he's a regular powerhouse."

ТУРИ́СТ, -а, *m., army.* A soldier absent without leave (lit. a tourist). ♦*Давай-ка документы у вон того мужика проверим, сдаётся мне—явный турист.* "Let's check that guy's papers, I think he's AWOL."

ТУРМАЛА́Й, -я, *m., youth, neg.* A Finn. ♦*Приехал автобус с турмалаями, сейчас начнётся пьянка.* "A busload of

Finns has just arrived; now the drinking will really begin!"

ТУ́РОК, НЕ КАЗА́К, *idiom, neg.* A weak, cowardly person (lit., a Turk, not a Cossack). ♦ *Эх ты, турок, не казак, не можешь даже прыгнуть с парашютом!* "Hey, you Turk, you can't even bring yourself to do a parachute jump!"

ТУ́РОК НЕДОРЕ́ЗАННЫЙ, *idiom, neg.* A Turk (lit., an incompletely killed Turk). ♦ *Вот турки недорезанные, опять они лезут в наши дела.* "There go those damned Turks interfering in our affairs again."

ТУРУ́СЫ НА КОЛЁСАХ, *idiom, neg.* Untruth. ♦ *Всё это турусы на колёсах. Хватит слушать эту ерунду!* "That's a crock! I don't want to hear that crap."

ТУСМА́Н, -а, *m., youth.* A crowd, a gathering. ♦ *По какому случаю на улице тусман?* "Why is there such a crowd out on the street?"

ТУСНЯ́К, -а, *m., youth.* See **тусо́вка**.

ТУСОВА́ТЬСЯ/ПОТУСОВА́ТЬСЯ, *youth.* To meet, to get together, to spend time together (lit., to shuffle [cards]). ♦ *Мы обычно в кафе тусуемся по вечерам.* "We usually get together at the café in the evenings."

ТУСО́ВКА, -и, *f., youth.* A get-together. ♦ *А где у них тусовка?* "Where do they usually get together?"

ТУСО́ВЩИК, -а, *m., youth.* A party-goer, playboy, good-time Charlie. ♦ *Его работать не заставишь, это — тусовщик, каких поискать надо.* "You'll never get him to work — he's such a playboy."

ТУФТА́, -ы́, *f., crim.* Nonsense, falsehood. ♦ *Не слушай эту туфту.* "Don't listen to that nonsense." •**Гнать/погна́ть туфту́,** see under **гнать**[2].

ТУФТИ́ТЬ/ЗАТУФТИ́ТЬ, *youth and crim.* To lie (cf. **туфта́**).

ТУ́ХАС, -а, *m., neg.* Buttocks (from Heb./Yiddish "tukhas"). ♦ *Подвинь тухас, а то пройти нельзя в дверь.* "Move your behind — you're blocking the door."

ТУ́ХЛЫЙ, -ая, -ое, *neg., joc.* In a bad mood, depressed. ♦ *Что ты ходишь целый день какой-то тухлый?* "How come you've been going around in such a funk all day?"

ТУ́ЧА, -и, *f.* A bazaar, a secondhand market (lit., a cloud). *Ты был сегодня на туче?* "Did you go to the flea market today?"

ТУШЕВА́ТЬСЯ/СТУШЕВА́ТЬСЯ. To be shy, shrinking (lit., to shade in a drawing). ♦ *Не тушуйся, здесь все свои.* "Don't be shy! You're among friends here."

ТУШИ́(ТЕ) СВЕТ! *idiom.* Lit., "Turn off the light." **1.** *neg.* Something terrible, an awful situation. ♦ *Мы сидим, пьём. Вдруг заходит начальник — туши свет!* "We were sitting there drinking when the boss walked in — horrors!" **2.** *pos.* Excellent! Wonderful! ♦ *Вчера были на его концерте — тушите свет!* "We went to his concert last night — it was terrific!"

ТЫ И МЁРТВОГО ИЗНАСИ́ЛУЕШЬ (подни́мешь), *idiom, neg.* Lit., you would rape (resurrect) a corpse; used in protest against excessive insistence on anything. ♦ *Ты меня достал своими просьбами. От тебя не отстанешь, ты и мёртвого изнасилуешь.* "There's no getting away from your constant demands; you would rape a corpse."

ТЫ МНЕ НЕ ТЫЧЬ, *idiom.* Don't address me with ты; don't take liberties with me. ♦ *Ты мне не тычь, я тебя в первый раз вижу.* "Don't call me ты! I don't even know you."

ТЫК: Ме́тод ты́ка, see under **ме́тод**.

ТЫ́КАТЬ/ТКНУТЬ но́сом, *idiom, neg.* To point out someone's mistakes, criticize. ♦ *Что ты меня тыкаешь носом в мои ошибки?* "Why are you always rubbing my nose in my mistakes?"

ТЫ́КВА, -ы, *f., joc.* A head (lit., pumpkin). ♦ *У тебя есть тыква на плечах?* "Haven't you got a head on your shoulders?" •**Вса́живать/всади́ть по ты́кве,** see under **вса́живать**. **Дава́ть/дать по ты́кве,** see under **дава́ть**.

ТЫЛ, -а, *m.* Connections, protection,

influence. ♦ *Какие у тебя тылы, что-бы устроить его в институт?* "What kind of connections do you have, that you were able to get him into the institute?"

ТЫ́РИТЬ/СТЫ́РИТЬ. To steal. ♦ *Ты пойдёшь ночью тырить тюльпаны?* "Are you coming with us tonight to steal some tulips?"

ТЫ́РКАТЬСЯ/ПОТЫ́РКАТЬСЯ, *neg.* **1.** To bustle around, make a fuss. ♦ *Она уже неделю со мной тыркается, тре-бует, чтобы я бросил курить.* "She's been fussing at me for a week, trying to get me to stop smoking." **2.** To try some-thing unsuccessfully. ♦ *Я потыркался в дверь и ушёл.* "I fiddled with the door but couldn't open it, so I left."

ТЫР-ПЫР, *idiom, joc.* Any which way, pointlessly, unsuccessfully. ♦ *Отвечаю на экзамене, тыр-пыр, вижу, говорю не то.* "I was just answering at random on the exam; I could see that what I was saying wasn't right."

ТЫР-ПЫ́Р-НАШАТЫ́РЬ, *rhyming phrase, joc.* In vain, pointlessly, unsuc-cessfully (an absurd rhyming phrase from **тыр-пы́р** and нашатырь, "smelling salts"). ♦ *Попытались завести маши-ну, она долго стояла на морозе, тыр-пыр-нашатырь — не получилось.* "We tried to start the car after it had been standing out in the cold, but nothing doing."

ТЫРС(А)НУ́ТЬ, *perf., south.* To hit, to strike (from тырса, "sawdust").

ТЫ́ЩА, -и, *f.* A thousand roubles. ♦ *Одолжи тыщу.* "Lend me a thou-sand."

ТЬМУТАРАКА́НЬ, -и, *f.* An out-of-the-way place, a distant, obscure place. ♦ *Он живёт где-то в тьмутаракани, ехать к нему часа два.* "He lives somewhere out in the sticks. It takes two hours to get there."

ТЭН, -а, *m., youth.* Ten rubles (from Eng. "ten"). ♦ *Дай мне тэн.* "Give me a ten."

ТЭНО́К, тэнка́, *m.* See **тэн.**

ТЭТЭ́ШНИК, -а, m. A pistol (from пистолет ТТ, a type of officer's gun).

ТЮ́ЛЯ, -и, *f., joc.* An awkward, clumsy person. ♦ *Эх ты, тюля, ничего делать не умеешь.* "You clumsy oaf, you can't do anything right!"

ТЮ́ЛЬКА, -и, *f.* Lies, tall talk. **Гнать/по-гна́ть тю́льку,** *idiom.* To lie. ♦ *Ну ты и мастер гнать тюльку.* "You're so good at making up tall tales."

ТЮ́РЯ, -и, *f., crim.* Bread moistened with vodka (reputedly a way of getting more drunk on less vodka). ♦ *Он потребляет только тюрю.* "He takes vodka only with bread."

ТЮРЯ́ГА, -и, *f.* A prison (from тюрьма). ♦ *Он в тюряге уже больше года.* "He's been in jail for over a year."

ТЮ́ТЕЛЬКА В ТЮ́ТЕЛЬКУ, *idiom.* Just right, just exactly. ♦ *Ну что, сапоги при-шлись как раз? — Тютелька в тю-тельку.* "So, did you find boots that fit you right? — To a tee."

ТЮФЯ́К, -а, *m., neg.* A passive, ineffec-tual person (lit., a mattress). ♦ *Не будь таким тюфяком, потребуй повыше-ния.* "Don't sit there like a bump on a log, ask for a promotion!"

ТЯ́ГА: Задава́ть/зада́ть тя́гу, see under **задава́ть.**

ТЯЖЁЛЫЙ СЛУ́ЧАЙ, *idiom.* That's hard, that's a difficult situation. ♦ *Не могу сыну купить зимнюю обувь. — Да, тяжёлый случай.* "I can't afford to buy winter shoes for my son. — That's really tough."

ТЯНИ́-ТОЛКА́Й, *idiom.* Any mechanism that can only be operated by human power (lit., push-pull). ♦ *Это не машина, а тяни-толкай, уж очень часто ломается.* " Half the time my car won't run on its own power, you have to push it to get anywhere."

ТЯНУ́ТЬ¹/ВЫ́ТЯНУТЬ. To drink. ♦ *Мы не успели оглянуться, он вытянул целую бутылку водки.* "Before we could even look around, he had already drunk up a whole bottle of vodka."

ТЯНУ́ТЬ²/ПОТЯНУ́ТЬ. Lit., to drag, pull. **1.** *crim.* To accuse, blame. ♦ *Что ты на меня тянешь, не брал я твои деньги.* "What are you blaming me for? I didn't take your money." **2.** To cost. ♦ *На* *сколько эта куртка тянет?* "How much does this jacket cost?" •**Тяну́ть/потяну́ть пусты́шку,** *idiom.* To fail, to come to nothing (lit., to draw an empty one). ♦*В который раз му не можем найти убийцу, тянем пустышку за пустышкой.* "Again we haven't been able find the killer. We keep drawing a losing ticket." •**Тяну́ть/потяну́ть рези́ну,** *idiom, neg.* To stall, hold back, be reluctant (lit., to stretch the rubber). ♦*Не*

тяни резину, говори, в чём дело! "Don't beat around the bush — say what's the matter." **Не тяни́ кота́ за хвост,** see under **не.**

ТЯНУ́ТЬ ФА́ГУ, *idiom.* To smoke. ♦*Кто хочет тянуть фагу, на всё про всё—5 минут.* "If anyone wants to take a drag you have five minutes."

ТЯ́ПАТЬ/ТЯ́ПНУТЬ, *joc.* To drink (lit., to hoe). ♦*Давай ещё по одной тяпнем.* "Let's have another round."

У МАТРО́СОВ НЕТ ВОПРО́СОВ, *rhyming phrase, joc.* What you said is clear, there are no questions (lit., "the sailors have no questions," an absurd rhyming phrase). ♦*Задача понятна? Вопросы есть? — У матросов нет вопросов.* "Is the assignment clear? Are there any questions? — Perfectly clear. No questions."

УБА́ЛТЫВАТЬ/УБОЛТА́ТЬ. To convince, to persuade (from болтать, "to chat"). ♦*Не убалтывай меня, не пойду.* "Don't try to talk me into it, I'm simply not going."

УБЕ́ЙСЯ ВЕ́НИКОМ, *idiom, joc.* Leave me alone, stop bothering me (lit., kill yourself with a broom). ♦*Убейся веником, не мешай читать!* "Leave me alone, I'm trying to read!"

УБИРА́ТЬ/УБРА́ТЬ бе́льма, *rude.* To turn one's eyes away, look away from something. ♦*Убери бельма!* "Stop looking at me!"

УБЛЮ́ДОК, ублю́дка, *m., neg.* Idiot (lit., bastard). ♦*У тебя знакомые — одни ублюдки.* "Your friends are a bunch of idiots."

УБО́Й, *pred. use, youth.* Great! Wonderful! ♦*Статья в газете о реформе — убой!* "There's a terrific article in the paper about the reforms." •**На убо́й,** *idiom.* **1.** To death, to slaughter. ♦*Сколько людей отправили на убой в Афганистан и никто за это не ответил.* "Look how many people went to their deaths in Afghanistan with no one taking responsibility for it." **2.** For slaughter. ♦*Что вы кормите детей как на убой, они же растолстеют, а это вредно.* "Why are you stuffing the children like turkeys for slaughter? They'll just get fat, and that's no good for them."

УБО́ЙНЫЙ, -ая, -ое, *youth.* Excellent, wonderful. ♦*Купи эту пластинку, советую, убойная вещь.* "Buy that record — believe me, it's really great!"

УБЫ́ТЬ: Кого́-л. не убу́дет, *idiom.* Nothing bad will happen to someone. ♦*Лад-но, я сегодня вместо него поработаю, меня не убудет.* "Okay, I'll take his place at work today. No harm will come to me by it."

УВА́ЛИВАТЬ/УВАЛИ́ТЬ, *army.* To head into town on liberty. See **отва́ливать.** ♦*В роте оставить половину состава, остальные пусть уваливают.* "Half of the company must stay here on duty and the other half is authorized to go out on libbo for the night."

УВИ́ДЕТЬ: Пожуём — уви́дим, see under **пожуём.**

УВОДИ́ТЬ/УВЕСТИ́. To steal. ♦*У меня только что сумку увели.* "My purse was just stolen."

УГА́Р, *pred.\ use, youth, pos.* Excellent! Wonderful! ♦*Ну и автомобиль у тебя, полный угар!* "What a terrific car you've got!"

УГОВА́РИВАТЬ/УГОВОРИ́ТЬ (бу-ты́лку, литр), *idiom.* To drink (a lot). ♦*Когда вы успели уговорить целую бутылку?* "When did you manage to drink up the whole bottle?"

У́ГОЛ, угла́, *m.* **1.** *obs.* Twenty-five rubles. ♦*С тебя ещё угол.* "You still owe me twenty-five." **2.** A suitcase. ♦*Ставь свой угол сюда.* "Put your suitcase here." •**Из-за угла́ мешко́м уда́ренный (приби́тый, тра́хнутый),** see under **тра́хнутый.**

УГОЛЁК, уголька́, *m., youth.* A black person (lit., a charcoal). ♦*А что делает сегодня наш уголёк?* "What's our black friend up to today?"

УГОРА́ТЬ/УГОРЕ́ТЬ, *youth.* To be delighted, amazed (lit., to have carbon monoxide poisoning). ♦*Я просто угорел, когда узнал, что поступил в вуз.* "I was just thrilled when I found out I got accepted to college."

УГОРЕ́ЛЫЙ: Как угоре́лый, see under **как. Как угоре́лая ко́шка,** see under **как.**

УГРО́ХАТЬ, *perf. only, neg.* Lit., to thud,

thump. **1.** To kill. ◆*Они его рано или поздно угрохают.* "They're going to kill him sooner or later." **2.** To spend, waste. ◆*Я угрохал все деньги на мебель.* "I blew all the money on furniture."

УГРЮ́М-РЕКА́, *idiom, army.* Said of soldiers' bad mood after detention in a guardhouse (from the title of popular novel Угрюм-река, lit., a gloomy river). ◆*Угрюм-реку полечим просто: два раза по двести и всё пройдёт.* "We'll take care of your bad mood right quick. Drink two glasses of vodka and you'll feel like a new man."

УДА́ВКА, -и, *f., joc.* A necktie (lit., a noose). ◆*Ты забыл надеть удавку.* "You forgot to wear a tie."

УДАРЯ́ТЬ/УДА́РИТЬ: Ударя́ть/уда́рить в бо́шку (в го́лову), *idiom.* To intoxicate, make drunk. ◆*Он не пил давно, вино сразу ударило в голову.* "He hasn't drunk for a long time, so the wine went to his head very quickly." **Ударя́ть/уда́рить по ба́бам,** *idiom, joc.* To go out with girls, go looking for girls (playing on the Soviet exhortation ударять/ударить по пьянству [по прогулам, etc.], "to strike a blow in the field of drunkenness [absenteeism, etc.]). ◆*Пора нам по бабам ударить.* "It's about time we went and struck a blow in the field of girls." **Ударя́ть/уда́рить по пи́ву,** *idiom.* To drink beer, to drink in a beer bar (lit., to hit a beer). ◆*Неплохо ударить по пиву, жарко!* "It sure would be nice to knock back a couple of beers in this heat!" **Ударя́ть/уда́рить по петуха́м,** see under **держа́ть.**

УДЕ́ЛЫВАТЬ/УДЕ́ЛАТЬ, *neg.* Lit., to knock down. **1.** To beat, win a victory over. ◆*Ты его вчера хорошо уделал в теннис.* "You really whipped him in that tennis game yesterday." **2.** To hit, beat up. ◆*Скорей, там Кольку уделывают за забором.* "Hurry up. They're beating up on Nick behind the fence there."

УДОВО́ЛЬСТВИЕ: Все три́дцать три удово́льствия, see under **все.**

УДО́Й, -а, *m.* Income (lit., yield of milk). ◆*Неплохой удой за два дня!* "Quite a good income for two days' work!"

У́ДОЧКА: Сма́тывать/смота́ть у́дочки, see under **сма́тывать. Учи́ться на у́дочку,** see under **учи́ться.**

УЕБА́ТЬ, *perf. only, rude.* To hit, beat (cf. **ёб-**). ◆*Кто тебя так уебал, не лицо, а синяк.* "Who beat you up like that? Your whole face is one big black-and-blue mark."

УЁБЫВАТЬ/УЕБА́ТЬ, *rude.* To leave (cf. **ёб-**). ◆*Пора уёбывать.* "It's time to leave."

УЁБЫВАТЬСЯ/УЕБА́ТЬСЯ, *rude.* To leave, go away (cf. **ёб-**). ◆*Куда они уебались?* "Where did they go?"

УЕДА́ТЬ/УЕ́СТЬ, *neg.* To criticize or rebuke sharply, assail harshly (lit., to bite). ◆*Ельцина сильно уели в прессе за его пьянство.* "Yeltsin was stingingly rebuked in the press for his drunkenness."

УЖИРА́ТЬСЯ/УЖРА́ТЬСЯ, *neg.* To get very drunk. ◆*Ты вчера совсем ужрался.* "You got completely smashed yesterday."

УЖИРО́Н, -а, *m., youth, neg.* A drinking bout. ◆*После ужирона голова трещит.* "My head is splitting after that drinking party."

УЗКОПЛЁНОЧНЫЙ, -ого, *neg.* A Mongolian or Asian person (lit., narrow film, referring to the shape of the eyes). ◆*В Иркутске деваться нельзя от узкоплёночных.* "There's no escape from the slant-eyes over there in Irkutsk."

УЗЮЗЮ́КИВАТЬСЯ/УЗЮЗЮ́КАТЬ-СЯ, *joc.* To get very drunk. ◆*Как только ты с ним встретишься, обязательно узюзюкаешься.* "Whenever you get together with him you get roaring drunk."

УИКЭ́НД (ВИКЭ́НД), -а, *m.* Weekend (from Eng. "weekend"). ◆*Что ты делаешь на уикэнд?* "What are you doing over the weekend?"

УЙТИ́ кого́-л., *idiom.* To get rid of, fire. ◆*Он сам ушёл, или его ушли с работы?* "Did he leave voluntarily, or did they fire him?"

УКА́КИВАТЬСЯ/УКА́КАТЬСЯ. 1. To shit in one's pants. ◆*Ты уже большой, а* укакался. "You're too old to soil your pants!" **2.** To get scared. ◆*Чего вы все укакались, это всего лишь гром.* "What are you all so scared of? It's just thunder."

УКА́Т, *pred. use, youth.* Good! Excellent! ◆*Слушай, анекдот знаю, укат!* "Listen to this joke — it's terrific!"

УКОРА́ЧИВАТЬ/УКОРОТИ́ТЬ. To put someone in his place, bring someone down a peg (lit., to shorten). ◆*Надо её укоротить, она делает, что хочет.* "She's got to be put in her place — she thinks she can do just whatever she feels like."

У́КСУС, -а, *m., neg.* Sour wine (lit., vinegar). ◆*Я этот уксус пить не буду.* "I'm not going to drink this vinegar."

УКУСИ́ТЬ: Кака́я му́ха тебя́ укуси́ла?, see under **кака́я.**

УЛА́МЫВАТЬ/УЛОМА́ТЬ, *joc.* To persuade. ◆*Тебе его уломать не удастся.* "You won't manage to talk him into it."

УЛЕПЁТЫВАТЬ/УЛЕПЕТНУ́ТЬ, *joc.* To flee. ◆*Почему они так улепётывают, боятся нас, что ли?* "Why are they taking to their heels like that? Are they afraid of us?"

УЛЁТ! *pred. use, youth.* Good! Wonderful! ◆*Этот фильм — ну просто улёт!* "This movie is out of this world!" •**В улёте,** *idiom.* Happily drunk, high. ◆*Я совсем в улёте, больше не пью.* "I'm high as a kite already; no more for me."

УЛЕТА́ТЬ/УЛЕТЕ́ТЬ, *youth.* Lit., to fly away. **1.** To be delighted, thrilled, full of admiration. ◆*Пальто у тебя, я улетаю!* "I'm crazy about that coat of yours." **2.** To be amazed, shocked. ◆*Улететь можно, ты слышал, цены выросли в три раза.* "I'm in shock — have you heard that prices have just tripled?"

УЛЁТНЫЙ, -ая, -ое, *youth.* Amazing, wonderful. ◆*Таких улётных вестернов давно не видел.* "It's been ages since I've seen such terrific Westerns!"

УМ: Не для сре́днего ума́ (сре́дних умо́в), see under **не. Не по уму́,** see under **не.**

УМА́Т, -а, *m., youth, pos.* A wonder, something or someone wonderful. ◆*Эта герла — умат!* ◆"That girl is wonderful."

УМА́ТНЫЙ, -ая, -ое, *youth, pos.* Amusing, entertaining. ◆*Он уматный чувак.* "He's a very amusing fellow."

УМА́ТЫВАТЬ/УМОТА́ТЬ, *joc.* **1.** To bore, weary. ◆*Он умотает кого хочешь своими разговорами.* "He'd bore anyone to tears with his stories." **2.** To go away, go out. ◆*Куда дети умотали?* "Where have the children gone to?"

УМА́ТЫВАТЬСЯ/УМОТА́ТЬСЯ. To be on one's feet, be running around (cf. мотать, "to wind" [wool, a bobbin, etc.]). ◆*Дай я полежу, умотался за целый день.* "Let me lie down for a while — I've been running around all day."

УМЕ́ЮЧИ ДО́ЛГО, *idiom, joc.* An off-color reply to the idiom Долго ли имеючи?, "It doesn't take long for someone who knows how," alluding to the idea that sex *is* something that takes a long time precisely for someone who knows how. ◆*Вы успеете сделать это до завтра? — Долго ли умеючи? — Умеючи долго.* "Can you get this done by tomorrow? — I'm a professional! I'll be quick. — A *real* professional takes some time over it."

УМИНА́ТЬ/УМЯ́ТЬ. To eat quickly and hungrily (lit., to knead, press). ◆*Пироги уже умяли, пейте чай.* "Now that you've gobbled up all the pastries, why don't you have some tea."

УМО́РА, -ы, *f., pred. use.* Someone or something killingly funny. ◆*Это не человек — одна умора.* "That fellow could make you die laughing."

УМЫВА́ТЬ/УМЫ́ТЬ, *neg.* **1.** To deceive, cheat (lit., to wash). ◆*Опять меня умыли на 1000 рублей.* "They've cheated me out of another thousand rubles." **2.** To win, show superiority, get the upper hand. ◆*Вы вчера их хорошо умыли в футбол.* "You guys really creamed them in the soccer game yesterday."

УМЫКА́ТЬ/УМЫКНУ́ТЬ. To steal, lift

(lit., to abduct). ♦*Кто мою ручку умык-нул, отдавайте!* "Whoever made off with my pen, give it back!"

УПА́Д, *indecl., pred., youth.* Something wonderful (from падать, "to fall"). Cf. **отпа́д**.

УПА́ДНЫЙ, -ая, -ое, *youth.* Excellent, fine (cf. **па́дать**). ♦*Это упадный чу-вак.* "He's a great guy."

УПАКО́ВАННЫЙ, -ая, -ое. Well dressed. ♦*Ты откуда такой упакован-ный, из Штатов?* "Where's your sharp outfit from, the States?" •**Упако́ванный от и до,** *idiom.* Dressed very fashion-ably, dressed to the nines. ♦*Эта девоч-ка упакованная от и до.* "That gal is dressed to kill."

УПАКО́ВЫВАТЬ/УПАКОВА́ТЬ, *joc.* To imprison. ♦*Всех путчистов упако-вали за решётку.* "They've put all the putschists behind bars."

УПАКО́ВЫВАТЬСЯ/УПАКОВА́ТЬ-СЯ. To dress well or fashionably. ♦*Ты неплохо упаковался.* "You've really decked yourself out."

УПА́Л, ОТЖА́ЛСЯ! *Idiom.* Do what was ordered (lit., drop, do some push-ups).

УПА́СТЬ, *perf. only, youth.* Lit., to fall. **1.** To be at a loss, understand nothing, be disoriented. ♦*Ты что, упал, не знаешь, сколько стоит водка?* "Where'd you come from, Mars, not to know the price of vodka?!" **2.** To fall in love. ♦*Я на те-бя упал.* "I've fallen for you." •**Упа́сть в коло́дец,** *idiom, joc.* Lit., to fall into a well; used of strange or unexpected behavior. ♦*Ты что, упал в колодец, ма-теришься при детях?* "What's wrong with you? Have you lost your mind, swearing like that in front of the chil-dren?" **Упа́сть на четы́ре то́чки,** *idiom, joc.* To land on all fours. ♦*Хорошо, я упал на четыре точки, а то бы ногу сломал.* "It's a good thing I landed on all fours; otherwise I could have broken a leg." **Упа́сть с луны́,** *idiom, neg.* To lose one's sense of reality (lit., to fall out of the moon). ♦*Ты, видно, упал с луны, ничего не знаешь, что у нас происхо-дит.* "Are you in another world? You don't seem to have any idea what's going on."

УПЕКА́ТЬ/УПЕ́ЧЬ. To imprison (from печь, "to bake"). ♦*Его упекли в тюрь-му на 5 лет за махинации.* "He was sentenced to five years for swindling."

УПЁРТОСТЬ, -и, *f.* Stubbornness. ♦*Твоя упёртость всем известна.* "Everyone knows how stubborn you are."

УПЁРТЫЙ, -ая, -ое, *neg., Ukr.* Stubborn. ♦*Нельзя быть таким упёртым.* "Don't be such a stubborn ass."

УПИ́ЗЖИВАТЬ/УПИ́ЗДИТЬ, *rude.* To leave. ♦*Когда он упиздил в кино?* "When did he leave for the movies?"

УПИРА́ТЬСЯ/УПЕРЕ́ТЬСЯ, *joc.* **1.** To make an effort, make a push. ♦*Надо упереться и быстро закончить эту работу.* "We have to make a big push and finish up this job." **2.** To be stubborn, dig in one's heels. ♦*Он упёрся, не хочет ехать с нами и всё.* "He's dug in his heels about it — he won't come with us and that's that." •**Упира́ться/упе-ре́ться ро́гом,** *idiom, joc.* Lit., to push with one's horn. **1.** To work very hard. ♦*Там надо упираться рогом, не поси-дишь.* "You really have to slave on that job — no fooling around." **2.** To be stub-born. ♦*Он упёрся рогом, не думаю, что его можно убедить.* "Now that he's dug in his heels, I don't think it'll be possible to persuade him."

УПИ́САТЬСЯ МО́ЖНО, *idiom, joc.* Lit., one could pee from it (i.e., from amaze-ment, admiration). ♦*Он такие анек-доты рассказывал, уписаться можно.* "The stories he told! You could pee in your pants!"

УПО́Р: В упо́р не ви́деть, see under **ви́деть.**

УПЫ́ХАННЫЙ, -ая, -ое, *youth.* High on drugs, stoned. ♦*Они каждый день здесь бродят упыханные.* "They go around stoned here every day."

У́РКА, -и, *m., neg.* A thug, a hoodlum. ♦*Страшно по улицам ходить, везде урки.* "The streets are so full of hood-lums, it's scary to go for a walk."

УРЛА́, -ы́, *f., collect., neg.* Hooligans, ruf-fians. ♦*Опять во дворе урла* *собралась.* "Those hooligans are hanging out in the yard again."

УРЛОБА́Н, -а, *m.* A nasty person (from ур**л**а, a hooligan, and <u>банди</u>т, a gangster). ♦*Если кто-то из урлобанов тронет тебя, то будет дело иметь со мной.* "If any of those hoodlums mess with you, they're going to have to deal with me."

УРЛО́ВЫЙ, -ая, -ое, *neg.* Of or pertaining to thieves, bandits, gangsters (cf. ур**л**а́). ♦*Это урловые дела, мы здесь ни причём.* "We had nothing to do with this — it was the work of gangsters."

У́РНА ПРИВОКЗА́ЛЬНАЯ, *idiom, neg.* A cheap woman, slut (lit., a railroad-station trash can). ♦*Ты бы помолчала, урна привокзальная.* "Shut up, you slut."

У́РОВЕНЬ: На у́ровне, *idiom.* Of the highest quality, superior. ♦*Он хороший преподаватель? — На уровне.* "Is he a good teacher? — Tops."

УРО́Д, -а, *m., army.* A soldier in his first month of service (lit., a freak, monster). ♦*Это урод пришёл после наряда, пусть спит, всё равно толку от него никакого.* "Let the private sleep, he's worthless now, he's just come off duty."

УРОНИ́ТЬ, *perf. only, youth.* To beat up (lit., to drop). ♦*За это тебя мало уронить.* "After what you did, beating's too good for you."

УРЫВА́ТЬ¹/УРВА́ТЬ, *neg.* To get, grab, pick up (lit., to tear out). ♦*Смотри, какое платье я вчера себе урвала на распродаже.* "Look at the dress I got myself at the sale yesterday."

УРЫВА́ТЬ²/УРЫ́ТЬ, *neg.* To hit, beat to death (cf. рыть могилу, "to dig a grave"). ♦*Ещё слово и я тебя урою.* "One more word out of you and I'll kill you."

УРЫВА́ТЬСЯ/УРЫ́ТЬСЯ, *youth.* **1.** To make a mistake, to disgrace oneself. ♦*Видишь, как он урылся, не знает, как работать с компьютером.* "Look how he messed up! He doesn't know how to use a computer. **2.** To shut up. ♦*Уройся, не твоё это дело!* "Shut up! This is

none of your business!"

УРЫ́ЛЬНИК, -а, *m., youth.* A washbasin. ♦*Где здесь у вас урыльник, руки сполоснуть надо.* "Where's a washbasin around here? I need to wash my hands."

УРЮ́К, -а, *neg.* A person from the eastern republics of the former Soviet Union; a Kazakh, Uzbek, Tadjik, and so on (lit., a dried apricot). ♦*За сколько этот урюк продаёт дыни?* "How much is that 'apricot' asking for his melons?"

УСА́ТАЯ КОНСТИТУ́ЦИЯ, *idiom, joc.* The Stalin Constitution of the 1930s (lit., the mustachioed constitution). ♦*Усатая конституция на словах была самая демократичная.* "The words of the Stalin Constitution sounded very democratic."

УСА́ТЫЙ, *m.* Joseph Stalin (lit., the mustachioed fellow). ♦*Когда усатый был в Кремле, то был порядок.* "When Mustaches was in the Kremlin, at least we had law and order."

УСЕКА́ТЬ/УСЕ́ЧЬ. To understand. ♦*Ты усёк, что тебе сказали?* "Did you understand what they said to you?"

УСЁР: До усёру, *idiom, rude.* Too much (lit., to the point of shitting in one's pants). ♦*Я не могу здесь сидеть до усёру, у меня дела.* "I can't sit around too long — I've got work to do."

УСИ́ЖИВАТЬ/УСИДЕ́ТЬ. To drink a lot. ♦*Вчера мы с тобой литр усидели.* "Yesterday you and I drank a whole liter."

УСИРА́ТЬСЯ/УСРА́ТЬСЯ, *rude.* To shit in one's pants. ♦*Ты знаешь, он усрался от страха.* "He shit in his pants from terror." •**Усра́ться мо́жно!** *idiom, rude.* Incredible! Wow! ♦*У него сейчас квартира, усраться можно!* "What an apartment he's got! You could wet your pants!"

УСРА́ЧКА: До усра́чки, *idiom, rude.* See до усёру under **усёр.**

УССЫВА́ТЬСЯ/УССА́ТЬСЯ, *rude.* To pee in one's pants. ♦*Сколько можно менять тебе штаны! Ты опять уссался.* "How many times a day can I change your pants! You've peed all over yourself again." •**Уссыва́ться/усса́ться от смеха,** *idiom.* To piss from laughter. ♦*Он такие пишет юморные рассказы, уссаться можно от смеха.* "The stories he writes are so funny, you'll pee in your pants." •**Усса́ться мо́жно!** *idiom, rude.* See **усра́ться мо́жно** under **усира́ться.**

УСТРА́ИВАТЬ/УСТРО́ИТЬ: Устра́ивать/устро́ить нервотрёпку, *idiom, neg.* To make people nervous. ♦*На работе идут проверки, устроили нервотрёпку всем без исключения.* "We're being audited at work — it's making absolutely everybody nervous." **Устра́ивать/устро́ить пропердо́н,** *idiom, rude.* To abuse, insult. ♦*Сейчас нам устроят пропердон за то, что ковёр прожгли.* "We're going to get a scolding for burning the carpet." **Устра́ивать/устро́ить тёмную кому́-л.,** *idiom, neg.* To beat someone unconscious (lit., to make [the room] dark for someone). ♦*Он нас предал, надо ему устроить тёмную.* "He betrayed us, so we'll have to beat him to a pulp." **Устра́ивать/устро́ить хорово́д,** *idiom, youth.* To beat up (an individual) as a gang (lit., to arrange a circle dance). ♦*Мы тебя ещё поймаем, устроим хоровод.* "We'll catch you yet, and when we do we'll beat you up." **Устра́ивать/устро́ить барда́к,** see under **разводи́ть/развести́ барда́к.**

УСЫ́ПКА-УТРУ́СКА, -и, *f., joc.* Theft of merchandise in transit or by store personnel (lit., spillage and leakage). ♦*А где 20 бутылок, усыпка-утруска?* "What happened to the other 20 bottles? A little 'spillage and leakage'?"

УСЫХА́ТЬ/УСО́ХНУТЬ. To get thin (lit., to dry out). ♦*За лето ты совсем усохла.* "You lost a lot of weight over the summer." •**Усыха́ть/усо́хнуть от сме́ха,** *idiom.* To laugh hard and long. ♦*Мы все просто усохли от смеха.* "We all died laughing."

УТЕРЕ́ТЬ нос кому́-л., *idiom.* To show one's superiority, get the better of someone. ♦*Эти лётчики в воздухе хоть кому утрут нос.* "These pilots are better fliers than anyone else."

УТИРА́ТЬСЯ/УТЕРЕ́ТЬСЯ, *neg.* To be victimized, humiliated, taken advantage of (lit., to wipe spit off one's face). ♦*Ну что, утёрся, твои деньги сгорели в банке?* "So are you another victim of the bank's collapse?"

УТРЯ́НКА: По утря́нке, *idiom.* In the morning. ♦*По утрянке вставать неохота.* "I don't feel like getting up in the morning."

УТЮ́Г, -а́, *m., youth.* A dealer in hard currency (lit., an iron). ♦*Сколько этот утюг возьмёт и за сколько?* "How much is he willing to buy and at what rate?"

УТЮ́ЖИТЬ/ПРОУТЮ́ЖИТЬ карма́ны, *idiom, crim.* To pick pockets, be a pickpocket (lit., to iron pockets). ♦*Он при деле: утюжит карманы в трамваях.* "He's on the job, picking pockets on the tram."

УХАЙДА́КИВАТЬ/УХАЙДА́КАТЬ. To kill. ♦*Сколько парней ухайдакали в Афганистане?* "How many of our boys were killed in Afghanistan?"

УХЛЁСТЫВАТЬ/УХЛЕСТНУ́ТЬ. To make advances, to flirt (from хлестать, "to lash"). ♦*Этот за каждой юбкой ухлёстывает.* "He goes running after every skirt."

УХЛО́ПЫВАТЬ/УХЛО́ПАТЬ. 1. To kill. **2.** To spend a lot of money. ♦*Я все деньги ухлопал на презенты.* "I've spent all my money on presents." **У́ХНУТЬ,** *perf. only, neg.* To spend a lot of money (lit., to crash, fall). ♦*Знаешь, сколько мы ухнули денег за неделю?* "Do you realize how much money we've blown in one week?"

У́ХО: по́ уху, *idiom.* I don't care. ♦*А мне по уху, что ты говоришь.* "Just lock it up, I really don't care what you have to say." See **до ла́мпочки**

УХОДИ́ТЬ/УЙТИ́ в то́чку, *idiom, youth.* To leave, vanish, hide (lit., to turn into a dot). ♦*Не уходи в точку, ты мне будешь нужен.* "Don't disappear on me. I'm going to need you."

УХРЮ́КИВАТЬСЯ/УХРЮ́КАТЬСЯ, *joc.* To drink, get drunk (lit., to oink like a pig). ♦*С кем это ты так ухрюхался?* "Who was that you were drinking so much with?"

УХУЕ́Л? *idiom, rude.* Are you crazy? (distorted from охуел [see **охуе́ть**]; by wordplay on Уху ел "Did you eat fish soup?"). ♦*Ты что, ухуел?* "Are you out of your mind?"

УЧИ́СЬ, ПОКА́ Я ЖИВ(А́), *idiom, joc.* Don't just praise me — follow my example! (lit., learn [from me] while I'm still alive). ♦*Ты отлично готовишь борщ! — Учись, пока я жив!* "What delicious borscht you make! — Well, you'd better learn my technique while I'm still among the living!"

УЧИ́ТЬ: Не учи́ меня́ жить (, лу́чше помоги́ материа́льно)!, see under **не.**

УЧИ́ТЬСЯ на у́дочку, *idiom, youth.* To be a C student, to get average grades. ♦*Он у вас, наверное, отличник? — Да нет, учится так себе, на удочку.* "I suppose he's a real whiz-kid. — Far from it! He's only getting C's."

У́ШИ: У́ши вя́нут, *idiom, neg.* I'm tired of listening (lit., my ears are fading). ♦*Не хочу тебя слушать, ты такую чушь несёшь, уши вянут.* "I don't want to listen to your nonsense. It's wearing out my ears." **У́ши пу́хнут,** *idiom, neg.* Someone is tired of listening (lit., someone's ears are swollen). ♦*От ваших разговоров уши пухнут.* "You've talked my ears off." **И у́ши у тебя́ холо́дные,** *idiom, joc.* You're a fool (lit., even your ears are cold). ♦*Эх ты, и уши у тебя холодные, зачем ты решил продавать дом?* "You fool, how come you decided to sell your house?" **По са́мые у́ши,** *idiom.* Very much, to an extreme degree (lit., up to one's ears). ♦*Ему дали срок по самые уши.* "They sentenced him to an extremely long prison term." **По́ уши в дерьме́,** *idiom, rude.* In a lot of trouble (lit., up to one's ears in shit). ♦*Из-за твоих ошибок мы оказались по уши в дерьме.* "Now we're up to our ears in it because of your mistakes." **Стоя́ть на уша́х,** see under **стоя́ть.**

У́ШКИ: Держа́ть у́шки топо́риком, see under **держа́ть.**

УЩУ́ЧИВАТЬ/УЩУ́ЧИТЬ. To catch someone lying (from щука, "a pike"). ♦*Здорово ты его ущучил, не будет больше врать.* "You caught him out beautifully! Now he won't tell any more lies."

ФАЗА́Н, -а, *m., army, joc.* A soldier enlisted in the spring enlistment period (lit., a pheasant). ◆*Сколько фазанов в роте?* "How many 'pheasants' are there in this unit?"

ФАЗАНА́РИЙ, -я, *m., army.* An autumn draftee. (lit., a pheasant school). See **фаза́н.**

ФАЗЕ́НДА, -ы, *f., joc.* A dacha, a country house (from a popular Latin American television series). ◆*Надо ехать на фазенду картошку копать.* "I've got to go out to my hacienda to dig some potatoes."

ФА́ЗЕР, -а, *m.* Father (from Eng. "father"). ◆*Где твой фазер работает?* "Where does your father work?"

ФАЙФ, -а, *m., youth, obs.* Five rubles (from Eng. "five"). ◆*Дай ещё файф и хватит.* "Give me another five and we're even."

ФАК, -а, *m., youth, rude.* Lay, fuck (from Eng. "fuck"). ◆*Тебе нужен хороший фак.* "What you need is a good lay." •**Констати́ровать фак,** see under **констати́ровать.**

ФА́КАТЬСЯ/ЗАФА́КАТЬСЯ, *youth, rude.* Cf. **фак. 1.** To sleep with someone. ◆*Он факается с Любкой?* "Is he sleeping with Lyubka?" **2.** To become exhausted, worn out. ◆*Мы зафакались с твоим мотором.* "We're sick and tired of trying to fix your motor." •**Чем бы дитя́ ни те́шилось, лишь бы не фа́калось,** see under **чем.**

ФАКИ́Р БЫЛ ПЬЯ́Н И ФО́КУС НЕ УДА́ЛСЯ, *idiom, joc.* Lit., "The fakir was drunk and the trick didn't work"; used in evasive explanation of a failure or disappointment. ◆*Почему ты не покажешь видео? — Факир был пьян и фокус не удался, видак сломался.* "Why don't you show a movie? — The fakir was drunk and the trick didn't work. The television is broken."

ФА́КМЕН, -а, *m., youth, rude.* A womanizer, skirt chaser (cf. **фак**). ◆*У этого факмена на уме одни бабы.* "That womanizer has nothing but dames on his mind."

ФАК-СЕ́ЙШН, -а, *m., youth, rude.* Group sex (from Eng. "fuck session"). ◆*У них сегодня вечером фак-сейшн затевается.* "They're getting up a group-sex session for this evening."

ФАЛОВА́ТЬ/ЗАФАЛОВА́ТЬ. From фал, a sailor's rope. **1.** To pick up, make the acquaintance of (a girl, woman). ◆*Я её зафаловал, она придёт в пять.* "That girl I picked up is coming over at five." **2.** To persuade, win over. ◆*Мне никак его не зафаловать на покупку дачи.* "I'll never be able to persuade him to buy a dacha."

ФАНА́Т, -а, *m.* A sports fan (from фанатик). ◆*Вчера фанаты устроили драку после матча.* "The fans got into a fistfight after yesterday's match."

ФАНА́ТЕТЬ/ЗАФАНАТЕ́ТЬ. To be a sports or music fan. Cf. **фана́т.**

ФАНЕ́РА, -ы, *f., joc.* Money (lit., veneer, plywood). ◆*С фанерой сейчас туго.* "Money's tight right now." •**Пролета́ть/пролете́ть как фане́ра над Пари́жем,** see under **пролета́ть.**

ФАНО́, *indecl.* An upright piano (from фортепиано, "piano"). ◆*А фано куда ставить?* "Where should we put the piano?"

ФАРМАЗО́Н, -а, *m., crim.* A big-time robber. ◆*Это тебе не какой-нибудь карманник, это фармазон.* "He's no pickpocket — he's a bigtimer."

ФАРТ, -а, *m.* Good luck, a good break. ◆*Каждому в жизни нужен фарт.* "Everyone needs a lucky break in life."

ФАРТИ́ТЬ/ПО(Д)ФАРТИ́ТЬ кому-л. To turn out well, go well, be fortunate for someone. ◆*Ему сильно пофартило, он выиграл крупное дело.* "Things went really well for him — he won that big case."

ФАРЦА́, -ы́, *m.* See **фарцо́вщик.**

ФАРЦЕВА́ТЬ/СФАРЦЕВА́ТЬ. To trade, traffic, buy and sell (esp. with foreigners).

♦*Он фарцует всю свою жизнь, так и дежурит у «Интуриста».* "He spends all his time trading; right now he's working at the Intourist Hotel."

ФАРЦÓВЩИК, -а, *m., neg.* One who trades with foreigners, dealing in clothing, currency, and the like. ♦*У него куча денег, он же фарцовщик.* "He's made heaps of money trafficking with foreigners."

ФÁРЫ, фар, *pl., neg.* Eyes (lit., headlights). ♦*Ну что ты фары вылупил?* "What are you staring at?"

ФАСÁД, -а, *m., joc.* A face (lit., facade). ♦*Посмотри, у меня фасад не грязный?* "Is my face dirty?"

ФАСÓН: Держáть фасóн, see under **держáть.**

ФАТÉРА, -ы, *f., joc.* An apartment, flat. ♦*Какой у неё номер фатеры?* "What's the number of her apartment?"

ФА-ФÁ, *idiom, youth, neg.* Chatter, chitchat, empty talk. ♦*Опять вы тут фафа?* "Are you guys yakking away again?"

ФÁФА И ФИ́ФА, *idiom, joc.* Conceited, spoiled girls. ♦*Кто эти фафа и фифа?* "Who are those stuck-up girls?"

ФÁЧИТЬ/ЗАФÁЧИТЬ, *youth, rude.* See **Фáкать.**

ФÁШИК, -а, *m., youth.* A fascist (from фашист). ♦*Он ходит в фашиках.* "He's joined the fascists."

ФЕДЕРÁЛ, -а, *m.* A serviceman (from <u>федеральные</u> войска, federal armed forces). ♦*Федералы не полиция, не надо нам зачистками заниматься.* "We are soldiers, dammit, and we shouldn't have to be bothered with police matters." See **зачи́стка.**

ФЕЙС, -а, *m., youth.* A face (from Eng. "face"). ♦*Умой фейс, ты грязный.* "Wash your face — you're filthy!"

ФЕН, -а, *m., youth.* A drug, narcotic. ♦*Фен принёс?* "Did you bring the dope?"

ФÉНЕЧКА, -и, *f., youth.* **1.** Decorative beadwork or leatherwork. ♦*Кто подарил тебе эту фенечку?* "Who gave you the fancy beadwork?" **2.** An entertaining story. ♦*Расскажи ещё раз эту фенечку.* "Spin us that yarn again."

ФÉНЯ, -и, *f.* **1.** *crim.* Thieves' cant. ♦*Я не знаю феню.* "I don't speak the argot." **2.** *joc.* Buttocks. ♦*Отрастил себе феню, в брюки не влезаешь.* "You've got so broad in the beam that you'll never fit into these pants." •**До фéни,** *idiom, neg.* It doesn't matter to someone, it's all the same. ♦*Мне ваши проблемы до фени.* "I don't give a damn about your problems." **К ядрёной фéне,** *idiom, rude, neg.* To hell, to the devil (euph. for к ёбаной фене). ♦*Пошли его к ядрёной фене и дело с концом.* "Tell him to go to hell, and that's the end of the matter."

ФИГ, -а, *m., rude.* A fig (an obscene gesture). •**Фиг вам! (расходи́тесь по дома́м),** *idiom, joc.* No; no way; too bad for you. ♦*Я вас не повезу в Москву, так что фиг вам, расходитесь по домам.* "I'm not taking you to Moscow, so too bad for you." **Фиг с ним (с ней, с ни́ми),** *idiom, neg.* The hell with, too bad for him (her, them). ♦*Ты их не позвал, они обидятся. — Да фиг с ними, пусть обижаются!* "They'll be offended that you didn't call them. — The hell with them! So let them be offended." **Фиг кому́-л. на пóстном ма́сле,** *idiom, neg.* Too bad for someone, the hell with someone. ♦*Фиг ему на постном масле, а не книгу.* "Too bad for him — I'm not giving him the book." **Нá фиг,** *idiom, rude.* **1.** To the devil, to hell. ♦*Иди ты на фиг, надоел.* "Go to hell. I'm sick of you." **2.** Unnecessary, useless. ♦*Сам подумай, на фиг мне это надо.* "Can't you see I need this like a hole in the head!" **На фигá,** *idiom, rude.* What the hell for for? ♦*На фига мне эта работа.* "What do I need that job for?" **На фигá козé ба́ян,** *idiom, rude.* It's inappropriate, unnecessary, out of place (lit., a goat doesn't need an accordion). ♦*Я подарю ему цветы. — На фига козе баян, он же не девушка.* "I'm going to bring him flowers. — What the hell for? He's not a girl!" **Ни фигá,** *idiom, neg.* Nothing. ♦*Дома ни фига нет поесть.* "There's not a thing to eat in the house." **Ни фигá**

себе́!, *idiom.* Incredible! Are you kidding? ♦ *Ни фига себе сказал!* "What did you say!" **Фи́га с два́ кому́-л.**, *idiom, neg.* By no means; no; no way. ♦ *Фига с два ему, а не премию.* "He's certainly not getting a bonus."

ФИ́ГА, -и, *f., rude.* A fig (an obscene gesture). ♦ *Фигу тебе, а не загранкомандировку.* "Up yours! You're not getting to go on a trip abroad." •**Фи́гу с ма́слом,** *idiom, joc.* No, no way, nothing. ♦ *Я думал получить зарплату, а получил фигу с маслом.* "I was supposed to get my salary, but I got exactly nothing." **Держа́ть фи́гу в карма́не,** see under **держа́ть.**

ФИГАНУ́ТЫЙ, -ая, -ое, *neg.* Crazy, abnormal (cf. **фиг**). ♦ *Что он ходит какой-то фиганутый?* "Why is he going around as if he's off his rocker?"

ФИГА́ЧИТЬ/ЗАФИГА́ЧИТЬ. Cf. фиг. 1. To hit, throw. ♦ *Куда вы зафигачили мяч?* "Where did you throw the ball?" **2.** To do something intensely, strongly. ♦ *Какой дождь фигачит!* "It's raining cats and dogs."

ФИГЕ́ТЬ/ОФИГЕ́ТЬ. Cf. фиг. 1. To be amazed. ♦ *Я с тебя фигею, как ты мог такое сделать.* "I'm surprised at you! How could you do such a thing!" **2.** To be exhausted, worn out. ♦ *Офигел я от модных песен.* "I'm sick of the popular songs."

ФИ́ГЛИ-МИ́ГЛИ, -ей, *pl., neg.* Nonsense, idle chatter; sweet nothings (cf. **фиг**). ♦ *Ну, начались тут фигли-мигли, он ей комплименты, она глазки строит.* "So now they've starting with the billing and cooing — he gives her compliments; she makes eyes at him."

ФИГНЯ́, -й, *f., neg.* Nonsense, rubbish (cf. **фиг**). ♦ *Это сплошная фигня, что он говорит.* "What he's saying is a bunch of crap."

ФИГО́ВИНА, -ы, *f., joc.* A gadget, thing (cf. **фиг**). ♦ *Вот ещё какая-то фиговина от мотора.* "Here's another thingummy from the motor."

ФИГО́ВЫЙ, -ая, -ое, *neg.* Bad (cf. **фиг**). ♦ *Фонарь у тебя фиговый, не светит*

ни черта. "Your flashlight is lousy. It doesn't give any light at all."

ФИГУ́ЛЕЧКА, -и, *f., joc.* A fig (an obscene gesture; cf. **фиг**). ♦ *Фигулечку тебе, а не апельсин.* "Up yours! No, you can't have an orange!"

ФИГУ́ЛЕЧКУ ТЕБЕ́ НА РОГУ́ЛЕЧКУ, *rude.* Up yours! The hell with you! ♦ *Продай мне эту книгу! — Фигулечку тебе на рогулечку.* "I'd like to buy that book. — The hell with you! I'm not selling."

ФИГУРИ́СТЫЙ, -ая, -ое. Having an attractive figure (esp. of a woman). ♦ *Жена у него ничего, фигуристая.* "His wife is really stacked."

ФИГУРЯ́ТЬ/ФИГУРНУ́ТЬ, *joc.* **1.** To show off clothes, model clothes. ♦ *Она любит фигурять в новых платьях.* "She likes to show off new dresses." **2.** To appear. ♦ *Его имя фигуряет во всех газетах.* "His name is showing up in all the papers."

ФИ́ЗИЯ, -и, *f., joc.* A face (from физиономия, "physiognomy"). ♦ *Кто это так тебе разукрасил физию?* "Who made up your face like that?"

ФИ́КСА, -ы, *f.* A metal false tooth. ♦ *У него фикса из золота.* "He's got a gold tooth."

ФИКСА́ТЫЙ, -ая, -ое. Having a metal tooth or teeth. ♦ *А как я его узнаю? — Он высокий, чернявый, фиксатый.* "How will I recognize him? — He's tall and dark and has a metal tooth."

ФИЛО́Н, -а, *m., neg.* An idler, lazy person. ♦ *Он не будет работать, это же филон.* "He's too lazy to work."

ФИЛО́НИТЬ/ПРОФИЛО́НИТЬ, *neg.* To be idle, lazy. ♦ *Ты всё лето профилонил, пора искать работу.* "You've idled away the whole summer; now it's time to look for a job."

ФИЛЬТРОВА́ТЬ/ОТФИЛЬТРОВА́ТЬ, *youth.* To weigh one's words, speak cautiously (lit., to filter out). ♦ *Фильтруй при нём, ему об этом знать не надо.* "Speak carefully when he's around — I don't want him to find out about this."

ФИЛЬТРУ́Й БАЗА́Р! *idiom, neg.* Stop

yelling, stop scolding. ♦*Не тебе его ругать, фильтруй базар!* "Stop yelling at him!"

ФИНА́НСЫ ПОЮ́Т РОМА́НСЫ, *idiom.* "There's no money" (lit., The finances are singing romances). ♦*У всех сейчас финансы поют романсы.* "Everyone has money problems these days."

ФИНГА́Л, -а, *m., joc.* A black eye. ♦*Он ходит с фингалом уже неделю.* "He's had that black eye for a week already." •**Ста́вить/поста́вить финга́л,** see under **ста́вить.**

ФИ́НИК, -а, *m., joc.* A Finn (lit., a date [fruit]). ♦*У фиников до сих пор сухой закон?* "Do the Finns still have dry laws?"

ФИ́НКА, -и, *f.* A Finnish knife (a weapon popular with mobsters). ♦*Даже не думай финку достать.* "don't you even think of getting a finka."

ФИНТ, -а́, *m., neg.* A trick, ruse. ♦*Это его обычный финт — пообещать и не сделать.* "Well, that's his usual trick, to promise and then not deliver." •**Финт уша́ми,** *idiom, neg.* A trick (lit., a trick with ears). ♦*Опять ты делаешь финт ушами.* "There you go again with your nasty tricks."

ФИНТИ́ЛЬ, -я, *m.* A black eye (lit., wick). See **фона́рь.**

ФИНТИ́ТЬ/ЗАФИНТИ́ТЬ, *neg.* To be tricky, to talk one's way out of something. ♦*Его не спрашивай, он начнёт финтить!* "Don't bother questioning him — he'll find a way to wriggle out of it."

ФИНТИФЛЮ́ШКА, -и, *f., neg.* **1.** Adornment, jewelry. ♦*Зачем ты надела эти финтифлюшки, не на бал, на работу идёшь.* "What are you wearing all those baubles for? You're going to work, not to a ball." **2.** A silly, light-headed woman. ♦*Не женись на этой финтифлюшке, толку не будет.* "Don't marry that silly girl! You'll never hear a sensible word from her."

ФИОЛЕ́ТОВО, *adv.* All the same, I don't care (from фиолетовый, lilac, pale purple, meaning the color of little attraction).

♦*А мне фиолетово, хочешь ты идти на пост или нет, всё равно пойдёшь, точка!* "I don't care whether you want to man your post or not. You're gonna do it and you're gonna do it now!"

ФИРМА́, -ы́, *f.* **1.** *youth.* Foreigner(s). ♦*В этом доме только фирма живёт.* "The only people living in this building are foreigners." **2.** *pos.* A brand-name item, something with a (usually foreign) label. ♦*Этот плащ — фирма!* "That raincoat has a foreign label."

ФИРМА́Ч, -а́, *m.* **1.** A businessman, a company employee. ♦*Он фирмач, работает в совместном предприятии.* "He's a businessman working for a joint-venture company." **2.** A fashionable person. ♦*Какой фирмач идёт, всё по последней моде!* "What a fashion plate he is — always in the latest style."

ФИТИ́ЛЬ, -я, *m.* Lit., a wick. **1.** *neg.* A weakling. ♦*Этот фитиль по дороге сломается, его нельзя брать с собой.* "We can't take that weakling on the trip with us; he'll collapse on the way." **2.** A tall person. ♦*Ну и фитиль ты! Сколько у тебя росту?* "What a beanpole you are! How tall *are* you, anyhow?" •**Вставля́ть/вста́вить фити́ль,** see under **вставля́ть.**

ФИТЮ́ЛЬКА, -и, *f., joc.* **1.** A gadget, contraption, thing. ♦*А где отсюда такая фитюлька, без этого телевизор работать не будет.* "Where's that gadget that was here? The TV won't work without it." **2.** A small, weak-looking man. ♦*Это разве мужик? Так, фитюлька.* "You call that 90-pound weakling a man?" **3.** A silly, flighty woman. ♦*Сам он человек серьёзный, а жена у него фитюлька какая-то.* "He himself is a serious person, but his wife is a bimbo."

ФИ́ФА, -ы, *f., neg.* A fashion-crazy girl. ♦*Давно он с этой фифой ходит?* "Has he been going with that fashion-plate for a long time?"

ФИ́ФТИ-ФИ́ФТИ, *idiom.* Fifty-fifty (from Eng.). ♦*Ты уверен, что он нас поддержит? — Не знаю, фифти-фифти.* "Are you sure he'll support us? — I don't know, it's really fifty-fifty."

ФИ́ШКА, -и, *f.* A playing card. ♦*Посмотри, кажется, одной фишки не хватает.* "Look — there's a card missing from the deck." •**Как фи́шка ля́жет,** *idiom.* It depends on fate; it's in the stars; there's no way of knowing beforehand (lit., it's lying hidden like a card). ♦*Я не знаю ещё, где я буду работать, как фишка ляжет.* "I still don't know where I'll be working; we'll see what kind of a hand fate deals me." **Сруба́ть фи́шку,** see under **сруба́ть.**

ФИ́ШКИ, фи́шек, *pl., youth.* Eyes. ♦*Протри фишки, не видишь, куда идёшь.* "Rub your eyes! You're not looking where you're going."

ФЛАЖО́К, флажка́, *т., army.* A safety (lit., a flag), referring to the shape of a safety on an automatic rifle. ♦*Флажки проверьте, а то перестреляете друг друга.* "Check your safeties before you hit the barracks so you don't end up shooting each other."

ФЛАКО́Н, -а, *т., youth.* A bottle. ♦*У тебя ещё булькает в флаконе?* "Do you have anything left in that bottle?"

ФЛЭТ, -а, *т., youth.* An apartment (from Eng. "flat"). ♦*На чей флэт пойдём слушать диски?* "Whose apartment should we go to to listen to the records?"

ФЛЭТО́ВЫЙ, -ая, -ое, *youth.* Domestic, of the home, homemade. ♦*Я люблю флэтовую еду.* "I like home cooking."

ФОЛЬКЛО́Р, -а, *т., joc.* Swearing, abuse (lit., folklore). ♦*А дальше все услышали такой фольклор, хоть уши затыкай.* "Then they heard the kind of swearing that could make your ears turn red."

ФОНАРЕ́ТЬ/ОФОНАРЕ́ТЬ, *neg.* To become exhausted. ♦*Я офонарел от занятий, сходить в кино, что ли?* "I'm knocked out from all this studying. What do you say we go to the movies?"

ФОНА́РЬ, -я́, *т., joc.* A black eye (lit., a torch, lantern, streetlight). ♦*У тебя фонарь под глазом, откуда?* "Where did you get that black eye?" •**До фонаря́,** *idiom, neg.* Indifferent, immaterial, unimportant. ♦*Мне цены эти до фонаря.* "The prices don't matter to me." **От фонаря́,** *idiom, neg.* Out of the blue; without forethought, unintentionally. ♦*Он это сказал от фонаря, не думай об этом.* "He didn't mean anything by what he said. Don't give it a second thought."

ФОНД НЕЗАВИ́СИМОСТИ, *idiom, joc.* A hidden stash of money (lit., an independence fund). ♦*Жена об этих деньгах не знает, это фонд независимости.* "My wife doesn't know about this money — it's my 'independence fund.'"

ФОНИ́ТЬ/ЗАФОНИ́ТЬ, *neg.* To interrupt, make noise (lit., of distortions in amplifying systems). ♦*Не фони, когда взрослые разговаривают.* "Don't make such a racket when the grown-ups are talking."

ФОНТА́Н: Закрыва́ть/закры́ть фонта́н, see under **закрыва́ть.**

ФОНТАНИ́РОВАТЬ/ЗАФОНТАНИ́РОВАТЬ, *neg.* To talk much and continuously (cf. **фонта́н**). ♦*Слушай, он начал фонтанировать, это часа на два.* "Now that he's started spouting off, he'll go on for two hours."

ФО́РИН, -а, *т., youth.* A foreigner (from Eng. "foreign"). ♦*Она ходит только с форинами.* "She only goes out with foreigners."

ФОРСИ́ТЬ/ПОФОРСИ́ТЬ, *neg.* To flaunt new and fashionable things (clothes, cars). ♦*Любит она пофорсить, каждый день у неё новые сапоги.* "She just loves to show off her stylish things! It seems as though she wears a new pair of boots every day."

ФО́РТЕЛЬ, -я, *т., neg.* Surprising behavior; a stunt, trick. ♦*Это что за фортель?* "What sort of stunt is that!" •**Выки́дывать/вы́кинуть фо́ртель,** see under **выки́дывать.**

ФРА́ЕР, -а, *т., crim.* A noncriminal. ♦*Кто этот фраер, что ему нужно?* "What does that straight fellow want here?" •**Жа́дность фра́ера погу́бит,** see under **жа́дность. Желе́зный фра́ер,** see under **желе́зный.**

ФРАЕРНУ́ТЬСЯ, *perf. only, crim., neg.*

To be taken in, to be conned (cf. **фра́ер**). ♦*Ты знаешь, как мы фраернулись, поверили ему, а он нас заложил.* "Do you realize how we've been taken in? We trusted him, and he betrayed us."

ФРИЛА́ВНИК, -а, *youth.* Someone who follows the beliefs and practices of free love (from Eng. "free love"). ♦*Они живут вместе — уже женатые? Нет, они — фрилавники.* "They're living together — are they married? — No, they believe in free love."

ФРУКТ, -а, *т., neg.* An unpleasant or bad person (lit., a fruit). ♦*Ну ты и фрукт, предал друга.* "What a rat you are, betraying your friend like that." •**Вся́кому о́вощу свой фрукт,** see under **вся́кому.**

ФРЭНД, -а, *т., youth.* A friend (from Eng. "friend"). ♦*У тебя есть фрэнд?* "Do you have a friend?"

ФРЭНДО́ВЫЙ, -ая, -ое, *youth.* Of a friend (from Eng. "friend"). ♦*Это фрэндовые книги.* "These are my friend's books."

ФРЭНЧ, -а, *т., youth.* A Frenchman (from Eng. "French"). ♦*Этот фрэнч когда приехал?* "When did that Frenchman get here?"

ФРЯ, -и, *f., neg.* A girl, woman (from Ger. "Frau"). ♦*Что это за фря сидит в углу?* "Who's that dame sitting over there in the corner?"

ФУГА́С, -а, *т., neg.* A large (more than half-liter) bottle of usually low-quality wine (lit., a high-explosive bomb). ♦*Возьми пару фугасов, нам на троих хватит.* "Get a couple of wine bombs — that'll be enough for the three of us."

ФУГОВА́ТЬ/ФУГАНУ́ТЬ. 1. To work (lit., to plane). ♦*Мы фуговали всю неделю, а получили всего ничего.* "We worked hard all week and got paid practically nothing." **2.** To throw out, to kick out. ♦*Фугани его отсюда!* "Kick him out of here!"

ФУ́ЛИ НА́ДО? *idiom, rude.* What are you up to? (euph. for **ху́ли на́до**; an indignant response to cheating or aggression). ♦*Фули надо? Чего без очереди прёшь?*

"What do you think you're doing, cutting ahead in line like that?"

ФУНТ: Не фунт изю́му, see under **не.**

ФУНЯ́ТЬ/НАФУНЯ́ТЬ. To fart. ♦*Здесь здорово кто-то нафунял.* "Someone farted here."

ФУ́РА, -ы, *f., army.* An army cap (from фуражка). ♦*Фуру свою никак не найду, ты не брал?* "Did you take my cap? I can't find it anywhere."

ФУРГО́Н, -а, *т.* A cap (lit., a carriage, from a horse and carriage and wagon).

ФУРЫ́ЧИТЬ/ЗАФУРЫ́ЧИТЬ. To be operating, to function, work (from the sound of a motor). ♦*У меня телевизор не фурычит.* "My TV is on the fritz."

ФУТБО́ЛИТЬ/ОТФУТБО́ЛИТЬ, *neg.* To pass on to someone else (as a memo, request). ♦*Мою рукопись футболят от редактора к редактору, а решения не принимают.* "They've passed my manuscript like a hot potato from one editor to another without reaching any decision."

ФУ́-ТЫ, НУ́-ТЫ (, ЛА́ПТИ ГНУ́ТЫ), *rhyming phrase, neg.* Well, well! What's going on! ♦*Фу-ты, ну-ты, какой серьёзный, давно таким стал?* "Well, well, what's with the long face? Has this been going on for a long time?"

ФУФЛО́, -а́, *п., neg.* **1.** Goods of poor quality, junk, trash. ♦*Я это фуфло не куплю.* "I'm not going to buy that junk." **2.** A worthless person, bastard. ♦*Не ожидал, что он такое фуфло.* "I didn't expect him to be such a bastard." •**Дви́гать фуфло́,** see under **дви́гать.**

ФУ-ФУ́: На фу-фу́, *idiom.* For nothing, wastefully, pointlessly. ♦*Мать из кожи лезет, помогает тебе, а ты всё на фу-фу пускаешь.* "Your mother's knocking herself out to help you, and you go and spend everything on useless stuff."

ФЭЙС, -а, *т., youth.* A face (from Eng. "face"). ♦*Побрей фэйс.* "Shave your face."

ФЭЙСОВА́ТЬ/ФЭЙСАНУ́ТЬ, *youth.* To slap or punch in the face (cf. **фейс**). ♦*Кто тебе так фэйсанул?* "Who punched you in the face like that?"

ФЭЭРГÉШНИК, -a, *m.* A German (from the abbreviation ФРГ, Федеративная Республика Германия). ♦*Да, фээргеш-ники умеют делать машины!* "Those Germans sure know how to make cars!"

◆ X ◆

ХАБА́ЛКА, -и, *f., neg.* A loud, pushy woman. ◆*Откуда такие хабалки берутся?* "Where did those shrews come from?"

ХАБА́РИК, -а, *m.* A hidden cigarette which was partly smoked and then put out (from хабарь, a greedy person). ◆*У кого есть хабарики, умираю курить хочу.* "Does anyone have any butts I can bum, I'm dying for a smoke." See **хаба́рь.**

ХА́ВАЛКА, -и, *f., joc.* A mouth. ◆*У тебя когда-нибудь хавалка закрывается?* "Don't you ever shut your mouth?"

ХА́ВАЛО, -а, *n., rude.* A mouth. ◆*Закрой хавало!* "Shut your mouth!"

ХА́ВАТЬ/СХА́ВАТЬ. 1. To eat. ◆*Кто схавал всё мясо?* "Who ate up all the meat?" **2.** To understand, to know one's way around in something (lit., to chew). ◆*Ты в шахматах хаваешь?* "Do you understand chess?"

ХА́ВКА: Проры́в на ха́вку, see under **проры́в.**

ХА́ЗА, -ы, *f.* A house. ◆*На хазе кто будет?* "Who's going to be at the house?"

ХАЙ, -я, *m., neg.* Noise, uproar. ◆*Что за хай?* "What's the ruckus?"

ХАЙВЭ́Й, -я, *m., youth.* Road, street (from Eng. "highway"). ◆*Этот хайвэй по вечерам забит машинами.* "This road has a lot of traffic in the evenings."

ХАЙР, -а, *m., youth.* Hair (from Eng. "hair"). ◆*Когда хайр будешь стричь?* "When are you going to get your hair cut?"

ХАЙРА́ТЬ/ОБХАЙРА́ТЬ, *youth.* To cut hair. ◆*Кто тебя так коротко обхайрал?* "Who cut your hair so short?"

ХАЙФА́Й, -я, *m., youth.* Stereo equipment (from Eng. "hi-fi"). ◆*У тебя хайфай есть?* "Have you got a hi-fi?"

ХАЛДА́, -ы́, *f., neg.* An uneducated, vulgar woman. ◆*Что с неё взять, она же халда!* "What can you expect from a bimbo like that?"

ХАЛТУ́РИТЬ/ПОХАЛТУРИ́ТЬ. To earn money at a supplementary job, to moonlight. ◆*Она халтурит по вечерам, даёт уроки английского языка.* "She earns extra money by giving English lessons in the evenings."

ХАЛУ́ПА, -ы, *f., neg.* A poor, shabby house or apartment, a hut or slum. ◆*В этой халупе нет даже туалета.* "There isn't even a toilet in this hovel."

ХАЛЯ́ВА, -ы, *f.* Something free, given gratis. ◆*В самолёте можно на халяву выпить.* "Complimentary drinks are served on the plane." •**На халя́ву и у́ксус сла́дкий,** see under **на.**

ХАЛЯ́ВИТЬ/ПОХАЛЯ́ВИТЬ, *neg.* To work carelessly, to do things sloppily. ◆*Кто привык халявить, того трудно научить работать хорошо.* "When someone is used to doing sloppy work, it's hard to train him to work well."

ХАМ ТРАМВА́ЙНЫЙ, *idiom, rude.* A boor, lout, a rough, ignorant person. ◆*Других слов от тебя и не ждали, хам трамвайный.* "You lout, you can't even use decent language."

ХАНА́, *pred. use, neg.* The end, curtains, disaster. ◆*Мне хана, если я это не сделаю.* "It'll be curtains for me if I don't get this done."

ХА́НКА, -и, *f.* Vodka. ◆*Я ханку с утра жрать не буду.* "I don't drink vodka in the morning."

ХАНЫ́ГА, -и, *m., neg.* A drunkard (cf. **хань**). ◆*Этот ханыга уже пьян с утра.* "That boozer has been drunk since this morning."

ХАНЬ, -и, *f.* A drink. ◆*Давай сначала дело сделаем, а потом будем хань глотать.* "Let's do the job first, and then we'll have ourselves a drink."

ХА́ПАЛКА, -и, *f., neg.* A hand (cf. **ха́пать**). ◆*Убери свои хапалки, это не твои вещи.* "Get your hands off those things, they're not yours."

ХА́ПАТЬ/ХА́ПНУТЬ, *neg.* **1.** To steal. ◆*Он, знаешь, сколько хапнул, пока в магазине работал?* "Do you know how much he managed to steal while he was working at the store?" **2.** To touch, take. ◆*Не хапай, не твоя книга.* "Don't touch that book — it's not yours." **3.** To eat greedily. ◆*Что ты хапаешь, ешь аккуратно.* "Why are you gobbling it down like that? Eat properly!"

ХА́ПКА, -и, *f.* A homemade liquor (from хапнуть, to drink with thirst. ◆*Жаль, у нашей хозяйки хапки нет, но она знает, где взять.* "Unfortunately, out hostess doesn't make her own moonshine anymore but she said she knows where to get some good juice."

ХАРИТО́Н, -а, *m., youth, joc.* A face. ◆*Харитон у тебя кирпича просит.* "That face of yours is just begging to be hit with a brick."

ХА́РИТЬ/ОТХА́РИТЬ, *rude.* To have sex with a woman. ◆*Хорошо бы её отхарить.* "I'd like to go to bed with her."

ХАРКОТА́, -ы́, *f., collect., neg.* Negligible, contemptible people (lit., spittle). ◆*Зачем ты водишь с этой харкотой, не друзья они тебе.* "Why do you hang around with those nobodies? They're not for you."

ХАРЧ, -а, *m.* Food. ◆*Ты харч с собой взял?* "Did you bring the grub with you?" •**Мета́ть харчи́,** see under **мета́ть.**

ХАРЧЕВА́ТЬСЯ/ПОХАРЧЕВА́ТЬСЯ. To eat (cf. **харч**). ◆*Где вы харчуетесь в обед?* "Where do you eat lunch?"

ХАРЭ́, *adv.* From хорошо. **1.** That's enough, stop. ◆*Харэ ржать.* "Stop laughing." **2.** All right, agreed. ◆*Ты пойдёшь с нами? — Харэ.* "Are you coming with us? — Okay."

ХА́РЯ: Мять ха́рю, see under **мять.**

ХА́ТА, -ы, *f.* An apartment (from Ukr. word for a house). ◆*У тебя хата трёх-комнатная?* "Do you have a three-room apartment?"

ХА́ХАЛЬ, -я, *m., neg.* A sweetheart, suitor, beau. ◆*К кому, интересно, этот хахаль с цветами пошёл?* "I wonder who that beau is going to court with those flowers."

ХА́ХАНЬКИ-ХИ́ХОНЬКИ, *pl., neg.* Jokes, tricks. ◆*Вам бы только хаханьки-хихоньки, а дело стоит.* "With you it's just a barrel of laughs but no work."

ХА́ЧИК, -а, *m., neg.* A Caucasian (from a Caucasian proper name). ◆*Хачики у себя всё время воюют, что им надо, не пойму.* "Those Caucasians are always at war among themselves; I can't understand what they're trying to achieve."

ХА́ЯЛЬНИК, -а, *m., rude.* A mouth (from хаять, "to bad-mouth"). ◆*Сейчас дам в хаяльник за такие слова.* "I'm going to give it to you in the mouth for what you said."

ХВА, *interj., youth.* Enough; stop it (shortened from хватит). ◆*Хва, не хочу слушать твою ругань.* "Cut it out. I don't want to listen to your yelling."

ХВАТА́ТЬ/СХВАТИ́ТЬ за я́йца, see under **яйцо́.**

ХВОРА́ТЬ/ЗАХВОРА́ТЬ, *joc.* To suffer the effects of a hangover. ◆*Он хворает, налей ему сто грамм.* "He's hung over — pour him a hundred grams."

ХЕ́ВРА, -ы, *f., youth & crim.* A group, set, company (from Hebr. hevrah, a group of friends). ◆*Чья это хевра там стоит, курит?* "Who are those guys standing over there smoking?"

ХЕ́ЗАТЬ/ПОХЕ́ЗАТЬ, *rude.* To defecate. ◆*Убери за котом, он в углу похезал.* "Clean up after the cat — he pooped over there in the corner."

ХЕР, -а, *m., rude.* A penis. •**Хер дра́ный,** *idiom, rude.* An idiot, bastard (драный, "worn-out"). ◆*Хер драный, вали отсюда!* "Get out of here, you idiot!" For the following expressions, see under **хуй:** Хер (хуй) с горы́; Хер (хуй) це́лых, ноль деся́тых; Хер (хуй) зна́ет что; Кака́я хер (хуй) ра́зница; Меня́ учи́ть, то́лько хер (хуй) тупи́ть; Языко́м хоть хер (хуй) лижи́, а рука́м во́ли не дава́й; На́ хер (хуй); Хоте́ть и ры́бку съесть и на́ хер (хуй) сесть; Ни хера́ (хуя́) себе́; Ста́рый хер (хуй); Хер (хуй) моржо́вый; Не́ хер (хуй); Оди́н хер (хуй); Хоть бы хер (хуй); Хер (хуй) в жо́пу; Хер (хуй) его́ зна́ет; Чтоб мне хер (хуй) пти́цы склева́ли; Сра́внивать/сравни́ть хер (хуй) с па́льцем; То́чить/наточи́ть хер (хуй); На́ хер (хуй) (не на́до); Посыла́ть/посла́ть на́ хер (хуй); Хоте́ть/захоте́ть и ры́бку (и ка́шку) съе́сть, и на́ хер (хуй) сесть; До хера́ (хуя́); Како́го хе́ра (ху́я) тебе́ на́до?; Ни хера́ (хуя́) себе́!; На хера́ (хуя́) козе́ бая́н (попу́ гармо́нь)?; За каки́м хе́ром (ху́ем)?

ХЕРНЯ́, -и, *rude.* Cf. **хуйня́.** 1. Semen. 2. Nonsense, rubbish. ♦*Всё, что ты сказал — херня́!* "Everything you said is just nonsense." •**Херня́ жи́же,** *idiom, rude.* See **хуйня́ жи́же** under **хуйня́.**

ХЕРОВА́ТЫЙ, -ая, -ое, *rude.* Bad (cf. **хер**). ♦*Что-то пироги какие-то херова́тые получились.* "For some reason the pastries came out terrible."

ХЕРО́ВИНА, -ы, *f., rude.* Cf. **хер.** 1. Whatchamacallit, thingamajig. ♦*Подай мне вон ту херовину и отвёртку.* "Hand me the screwdriver and that thingamabob over there." 2. An unpleasant occurrence. ♦*Какая-то херовина получается, никто нас не предупредил, что переговоры отменяются.* "There's been a screwup — no one told us that the meetings had been postponed."

ХЕРОМА́НТИЯ, -и, *f., joc.* Nonsense (by wordplay from хиромантия, "palmistry," and **хер**). ♦*Он на работе занимается какой-то херомантией.* "He's involved in some sort of nonsense at work."

ХИЛЯ́ТЬ/ПОХИЛЯ́ТЬ, *joc.* To go, walk. ♦*Слушай, друг, хиляй отсюда.* "Listen, buddy — get out of here."

ХИМИ́ЧИТЬ/НАХИМИ́ЧИТЬ, *neg.* To do or produce something illegally or secretly; to adulterate goods (from химия, "chemistry"). ♦*Они давно в этом банке химичат с валютой, хотя у них нет лицензии.* "They've been speculating in currency at that bank for a long time even though they aren't licensed."

ХИППА́РЬ, -я́, *m., neg.* A person who dresses and acts strangely (from Eng. "hippie"). ♦*Что там за хиппарь стоит, весь в лохмятьях.* "What sort of weirdo is that over there, all dressed in rags?"

ХИППОВА́ТЬ/ЗАХИППОВА́ТЬ, *joc.* Cf. **хиппа́рь.** 1. To live an idle life. ♦*Сколько можно хипповать, пора за ум браться.* "Enough hanging around doing nothing; it's time to get serious." 2. To wear sloppy clothes and long hair, to dress like a hippie. ♦*Ну и вид у тебя, хиппуешь, я вижу, и бороду отпустил.* "I see you're all decked out in hippie gear and you've let your beard grow."

ХИП-ХА́П: на хип-ха́п, *idiom.* Carelessly, casually (from хапать, to grab, to use fast, uncontrolled motions). ♦*Привыкли всё делать на хип-хап, вот и авария за аварией.* "You do everything half-ass and that's why you have to deal with accidents one after another."

ХИТРОВА́Н, -а, *m., joc.* A sly, tricky person. ♦*Он думает, что он хитрован, а все его хитрости сразу видно.* "He thinks he's a real slyboots, but his tricks are completely transparent."

ХИТРОЖО́ПЫЙ, -ая, -ое, *rude.* Sly, cunning (lit., sly-assed; cf. **жо́па**). ♦*Ему особенно не верь, слишком уж он хитрожопый.* "Don't trust that guy — he's a real sly-ass."

ХЛЕБ: И то хлеб, see under **и.**

ХЛЕБА́ЛО, -а, *n., rude.* A mouth. ♦*Не лови хлебалом мух.* "Pay attention" (lit., don't catch flies with your mouth).

ХЛЕБА́ЛЬНИК, -а, *m., rude.* A mouth. ♦*Что ты хлебальник раскрыл, тут нечему удивляться.* "What are you gaping at? There's nothing so strange here!"

ХЛОБЫСТА́ТЬ/ХЛОБЫСТНУ́ТЬ, *neg.* To slurp up, drink much or noisily. ♦*После солёной рыбы хлобысшешь воду как сумасшедший.* "After the salt fish you'll drink like crazy."

ХЛО́ПАТЬ/ХЛО́ПНУТЬ. To drink (liquor) quickly. ♦*Хлопни рюмку и беги в магазин.* "Have a quick one and run over to the store."

ХМУ́РОЕ У́ТРО, *idiom, army.* Reveille (lit., gloomy morning, after the title of a popular novel). ♦*В этом мире лучше всего отбой, но потом хуже всего— хмурое утро.* "In a soldier's world the best part of the day is taps, and the worst is reveille."

ХМЫРЬ, -я́, m., neg. 1. An unpleasant person. ♦*Зачем ты пригласил этого хмыря?* "What did you invite that sourpuss for?" **2.** *army.* Food sent from home. ♦*Получил хмырь, делиться надо.* "Divvy up what you got from home."

ХО́БОТ: Брать/взять за хо́бот, see **брать/взять за жа́бры** under **брать.**

ХОДИ́ТЬ/ПОЙТИ́, ЗАХОДИ́ТЬ, СХО-ДИ́ТЬ: Ходи́ть/пойти́ до ве́тру, *idiom.* To urinate (lit., to go into the wind.) ♦*Надо сходить до ветру.* "I have to take a leak." **Ходи́ть как поёбаный,** *idiom, rude.* To be in a bad mood, in low spirits. ♦*Сейчас жарко, ходишь как поёбаный.* "It's so hot it makes you feel really low." **Ходи́ть/пойти́ на бля́дки,** *idiom, rude.* To have promiscuous sexual relations with women, to sleep around with various women (cf. **блядь**). ♦*Тебе не надоело каждый день ходить на блядки?* "Aren't you sick of constantly sleeping around?" **Ходи́ть/пойти́ нале́во,** *idiom.* To be sexually unfaithful, cheat on someone (lit., to go left). ♦*Жена всё время налево ходит, а муж ничего не замечает.* "His wife is always cheating on him, but he never notices a thing." **Ходи́ть/пойти́ на размагни́чивание,** *idiom, army.* A sailor's shore pass (from размагнититься, to relax, to take everything easy). ♦*На размагни́чивание пойдёте без меня, у меня денег нет.* "You're going to have to go on shore duty alone, I can't go, I'm broke." **Ходи́ть/заходи́ть на ци́рлах,** *idiom, neg.* To be submissive (lit., to walk on tiptoe). ♦*Муж у неё забитый, ходит на цирлах.* "Her husband is completely submissive to her." **Ходи́ть/пойти́ по ба́бам,** *idiom, neg.* To have frequent affairs, be a skirt-chaser. ♦*У него уже дети взрослые, а он всё по бабам ходит.* "He's got grown children already, but he's still chasing skirts." **Ходи́ть/сходи́ть по-бы́строму,** *idiom.* To urinate, take a leak. *Где здесь можно сходить по-быстрому?* "Where can a person take a leak around here?" **Пойти́**

по рука́м, *idiom, neg.* To become a prostitute. ♦*И давно она пошла по рукам?* "Has she been a prostitute for long?"

ХОДО́К, -а́, m., joc. A lady-killer, Don Juan (cf. **ходи́ть по ба́бам**). ♦*Он у нас известный ходок, у него каждую неделю новая баба.* "He's quite the Don Juan around here, going out with a new girl every week."

ХОДЯ́ЧИЙ СКЕЛЕ́Т, neg., joc. A very skinny person (lit., a walking skeleton). ♦*У него не жена, а ходячий скелет.* "What he's got isn't a wife, it's a walking skeleton."

ХОЖДЕ́НИЕ ПО МУ́КАМ, idiom, army. A drill (lit., a march on torments, after the title of a popular novel). ♦*Слыхал, не будет хождения по мукам, а будет снегоуборка.* "Thank God there's so much snow today, that means we won't have to run the obstacle course."

ХОЖДЕ́НИЕ ПО ТО́НКОМУ ЛЬДУ, idiom, army. AWOL (lit., a walk on a thin ice). See **самохо́д.**

ХОККЕ́Й!, idiom. Okay (a word play on хоккей, hockey, and Engl. okay).

ХОЛОДРЫ́ГА, -и, f., neg. Very cold weather (from холод, "cold," and дрожать, "to shiver"). ♦*Ну и холодрыга сегодня.* "We're having a real cold snap today."

ХОМУ́Т, -а́, m., youth, neg. A police officer (lit., horse collar). ♦*Хомутов на улицах сегодня много.* "There are a lot of cops on the streets today."

ХОМУТА́ТЬ/ЗАХОМУТА́ТЬ, neg. From хомут, "horse collar." **1.** To force someone to do something. ♦*Меня захомутали переводить статью.* "They roped me into translating the article." **2.** To try to induce someone to marry oneself. ♦*Она давно хочет его захомутать, он богатый жених.* "She's been trying to collar that rich fellow for a long time." **3.** *youth.* To arrest. ♦*Вчера двоих наших захомутали.* "Yesterday two of our people were collared."

ХОРЁК, хорька́, m., neg. A scoundrel, bastard (lit., polecat). ♦*Чтобы я этого* *хорька в доме больше не видел.* "I don't ever want to see that bastard in my house again."

ХОРОВО́Д: Устра́ивать/устро́ить хорово́д, see under **устра́ивать.**

ХОРОНИ́ТЬ/ПОХОРОНИ́ТЬ ОКУ́-РОК, *idiom, army.* A punishment for soldiers who drop their cigarette butts on the ground. When even one such butt is found all soldiers are woken up in the middle of the night and forced to spend hours digging deep holes to bury individual cigarette butts.

ХОРО́ШЕГО ЧЕЛОВЕ́КА ДОЛЖНО́ БЫТЬ МНО́ГО, *idiom, joc.* Lit., there *should* be a lot of a good person; used in affectionate defense of plumpness. ♦*Я после родов сильно поправилась. — Ничего, хорошего человека должно быть много.* "I put on a lot of weight after having the baby. — Never mind. There *should* be a lot of a good person."

ХОРОШЕ́ТЬ/ЗАХОРОШЕ́ТЬ кому́-л., *impersonal.* To get high, drunk. ♦*Тебе захорошело уже?* "Are you feeling good yet?"

ХОРО́ШИЙ, -ая, -ое, *joc.* Drunk. ♦*Вчера вы были хорошие.* "Yesterday you guys were good and drunk."

ХОТЕ́ТЬ/ЗАХОТЕ́ТЬ: Хоте́ть/захоте́ть и ка́ку и ма́ку, *idiom, joc.* To want too much, to want something impossible (lit., to want both the shit and the poppies). ♦*Ты хочешь и каку и маку: и много зарабатывать и ничего не делать.* "You're asking for the moon, wanting to earn a lot of money without doing any work." **Хоте́ть/захоте́ть на горшо́к,** *idiom.* To have to go to the bathroom (lit., to want to go on the potty). ♦*Я опять захотел на горшок, где здесь туалет?* "I need to go again — where's the john around here?" **Хоте́ть не вре́дно,** *idiom, joc.* Lit., "There's no harm in wanting"; used in the sense of "You can't have what you want." ♦*Я хочу разбогатеть. — Хотеть не вредно.* "I wish I were rich. — Well, go ahead and wish." **Че́рез не хочу́,** see under **че́рез. Хоте́ть/захоте́ть и ры́бку (и ка́шку) съесть и на́ хуй (на́ хер) сесть,**

see under **хуй. Я то́же хочу́, но ма́ма спит и я молчу́,** see under **я.**

ХОТЬ КОЛ НА ГОЛОВЕ́ ТЕШИ́, *idiom.* Lit., even if you sharpen a stake on his/her head, meaning no matter what you do, no matter how hard you try to persuade soneone. ♦*Не хочет он учиться, хоть кол на голове теши, не убедишь его.* "You can beat him black and blue and he still won't study."

ХОТЬ ТОПО́Р ВЕ́ШАЙ, *idiom, neg.* It's stuffy, it's smoky (lit., [you could] hang an ax [from it]). ♦*Открыли бы форточку, а то накурили — хоть топор вешай.* "You'd better open the window — it's so smoky in here, you could hang an ax from it."

ХОХЛОБА́КС, -а, *m., joc.* Ukrainian currency used before the last monetary reform (from **хохо́л** and **бакс**). ♦*Хохлобаксов у меня целая куча, а стоит это ничего.* "I've got piles of Ukrainian money, but it's not worth a thing."

ХОХЛЯ́НДИЯ, -и, *f., joc.* Ukraine (from **хохо́л**). ♦*В хохляндии сейчас жить не сладко, цены растут как сумасшедшие.* "It's no picnic living in Ukraine these days. Prices there are going up like crazy."

ХО́ХМА, -ы, *f.* A joke, witticism (from Heb. "wisdom," *khochma*). ♦*Хочешь, хохму расскажу?* "Do you want me to tell a joke?" •**Отка́лывать/отколо́ть хо́хму,** see under **отка́лывать.**

ХОХМА́Ч, -а́, *m.* A jokester (cf. **хо́хма**). ♦*Он такой хохмач, с ним не соскучишься.* "He's such a comedian. There's never a dull moment with him."

ХОХМИ́ТЬ/ПОХОХМИ́ТЬ. To play jokes, be mischievous (cf. **хо́хма**). ♦*Они любят похохмить.* "They like to play jokes."

ХОХО́Л, хохла́, *m.(f.* **хохлу́шка, -и**). A Ukrainian (lit., a topknot, referring to the Cossack hairstyle). ♦*На базарах полно хохлов, они торгуют всем, чем можно.* "The open-air markets are full of Ukrainians trading in every conceivable kind of goods."

ХОХОТА́ЛЬНИК, -а, *m., neg.* A mouth

(from хохотать, "to guffaw"). ♦*Закрой хохотальник, чтоб я тебя больше не слышал.* "Shut your mouth — I don't want to hear another word out of you."

ХО́ЧЕШЬ ЖИТЬ —УМЕ́Й ВЕРТЕ́ТЬ-СЯ, *idiom.* You have to be flexible to survive (lit., If you want to survive, you'd better learn to spin around).

ХО́ЧЕШЬ ЖИТЬ —УМЕ́Й РАЗДЕ́ТЬ-СЯ, *idiom, joc.* A sardonic twist on the foregoing: "If you want to survive, you'd better learn to take your clothes off."

ХО́ЧЕШЬ СКАЗА́ТЬ? СТОЙ И МОЛЧИ́! *Idiom.* Shut up! (Lit., if you want to say something, stand at attention and keep silent).

ХОШ, -а, *m.* A wish, desire. ♦*У тебя хош есть погулять?* "Do you feel like going out?"

ХРЕН, -а, *m., rude.* A penis (lit., horseradish). •**Хрен мочёный,** *idiom, rude.* An idiot, fool (lit., pickled horseradish). ♦*А ты, хрен мочёный, что здесь дела-ешь?* "What are you doing here, you idiot!" For the following expressions, see under **хуй: Хрен (хуй) с горы́; Хрен (хуй) це́лых, ноль деся́тых; Хрен (хуй) зна́ет что; На́ хрен (хуй); Ни хрена́ (ху́я) себе́; Ста́рый хрен (хуй); Не́ хрен (хуй); Оди́н хрен (хуй); Хоть бы хрен (хуй); Хрен (хуй) его́ зна́ет; На́ хрен (хуй) не на́до; До хрена́ (хуя́); Како́го хре́на (ху́я) тебе́ на́до? Ни хрена́ (ху́я) себе́!; За каки́м хре́ном (ху́ем)?**

ХРЕНА́ЧИТЬ/ЗАХРЕНА́ЧИТЬ. Cf. **хрен. 1.** To beat up. ♦*За углом наших хреначат.* "They're beating up our boys over in the corner." **2.** To do something quickly. ♦*Я эту работу должен захре-начить за день.* "I've got to get this whole job churned out in one day."

ХРЕНО́ВИНА, -ы, *f., joc.* Cf. **хрен. 1.** Nonsense. ♦*Ты веришь в эту хрено-вину по радио?* "You mean you believe that rubbish that was on the radio?" **2.** Thingamajig, gadget. ♦*Здесь была такая хреновина, карандаши точить.* "There was a whatchamacallit over here — you know, for sharpening pencils."

ХРЕНО́ВЫЙ, -ая, -ое, *neg.* Bad, poor (cf. **хрен**). ♦*Это дело очень хреновое.* "That's a very bad business."

ХРЕНОТЕ́НЬ, -и, *f., rude.* Nonsense (by wordplay on **хрен** and тень, "shadow"). ♦*Ты опять эту хренотень про шпи-онов читаешь?* "Are you reading that junk about spies again?"

ХРЕ́НУШКИ, хре́нушек, *pl., joc.* No, no way (cf. **хрен**). ♦*Хренушки вам, а не мясо.* "No, you can't have any meat."

ХРОМА́ТЬ/ПОХРОМА́ТЬ, *neg.* To go, walk (lit., to limp). ♦*Хромай отсюда, пока цел.* "Get out of here while you still can."

ХРОНЬ, -и, *f., collect., neg.* Drunks, drinkers (from хронический алкоголик, "chronic drunkard"). ♦*Смотри, хронь с утра у магазина стоит, чего-то ждут.* "Those drunks have been hanging around the store since morning — they must be expecting something."

ХРУ́МКАТЬ/ПОХРУ́МКАТЬ, *joc.* To eat (esp. cabbage or other common food). ♦*Что на обед мне похрумкать?* "What sort of chow is there for dinner?"

ХРУСТА́ЛЬ, -ля́, *m., collect., joc.* Empty bottles (lit., crystal). ♦*Где здесь хрус-таль принимают?* "Where do they take empties around here?"

ХРУСТЫ́, -о́в, *pl., joc.* Money (lit., sounds of rustling). ♦*Все любят хрусты.* "Everyone likes money."

ХРУЩО́БА, -ы, *f., neg.* Shabby, cheap apartment buildings put up under Khrushchev in an attempt to solve the infamous Russian housing shortage (by wordplay on трущоба, "slum," and Хрущёв, "Khrushchev"). ♦*Квартиры в хрущобах стоят сейчас сравнительно недорого.* "Apartments in the Khru-shchev tenements are relatively cheap these days."

ХРЮ́КАТЬ/ХРЮ́КНУТЬ, *joc., rude.* Lit., to grunt. **1.** To talk. ♦*Тебя не спра-шивают, не хрюкай.* "Shut up, no one's asking you." **2.** To drink. ♦*Пора нам с тобой хрюкнуть как следует.* "It's time for you and me to have a proper drink together."

ХРЯ́ПАТЬ/СХРЯ́ПАТЬ, *joc.* To eat (lit., to crunch, munch). ♦*Что ещё есть поесть, я уже всё схряпал.* "What else is there to eat? I've already wolfed down everything you gave me."

ХРЯ́ТЬ/ПОХРЯ́ТЬ. To go, run. ♦*Ну, похряли, туда ходу часа два.* "Let's go, step it out, it'll take us two hours if we walk."

ХУЁВНИЧАТЬ/ПРОХУЁВНИЧАТЬ, *rude.* Cf. **хуй. 1.** To waste time, do nothing. ♦*Опять день прохуёвничали, а работа стоит.* "Again we've wasted the whole day without doing any work." **2.** To be stubborn, capricious. ♦*Кончай хуёвничать, тебя просят помочь, так помоги.* "Stop being difficult — you're being asked to help out, so help out."

ХУЕГЛО́Т, -а, *m., rude.* A worthless person (lit., cock-swallower, cf. **хуй**). ♦*Этот хуеглот только и думает о деньгах.* "All that bastard ever thinks about is money."

ХУЁ-МОЁ, *n., indecl., rude.* Etcetera, etcetera, nonsense, chatter (cf. **хуй**). ♦*Он ещё рассказывал о загранице и всякое хуё-моё.* "He kept on telling about his trip abroad and all that."

ХУЕПЛЁТ, -а, *m., rude.* A chatterbox (from плести, "to braid" or "weave," and **хуй**). ♦*Ну что ещё нарассказал этот хуеплёт?* "So what else did that chatterbox say?"

ХУЕСО́С, -а, *m., rude.* An idiot, worthless person (lit., cocksucker, cf. **хуй**). ♦*Этот хуесос с нами больше не играет в команде.* "That bastard isn't going to play on our team any more."

ХУЕТА́, -ы́, *f., rude.* Fuss, bother, useless bustle (by wordplay from суета and **хуй**). ♦*Хватит заниматься хуетой, давай делать деньги!* "Enough fooling around with nonsense — let's make some money!" •**Хуета́ из-под ногтей,** *idiom, rude.* Nonsense, trash, garbage. ♦*Эта не хлеб, а хуета из-под ногтей.* "This isn't bread. It's some kind of garbage." **Хуета́ хуе́т,** *idiom, rude.* Nonsense (distorted from суета сует, "vanity of vanities"). ♦*Всё, что они говорят про тебя — хуета хует.* "Everything they say about you is nonsense."

ХУЕТЕ́НЬ, -и, *f., rude.* A mess, foul-up (cf. **хуй**). ♦*С расписанием поездов творится какая-то хуетень.* "There's some screwup with the train schedule."

ХУЙ, -я, *m., rude.* A penis. •**ХУЙ** *(пот.)*: **Ста́рый хуй,** *idiom, rude.* An old man. ♦*А ты, старый хуй, что здесь делаешь?* "What are you doing here, old fellow?" **Хуй моржо́вый,** *idiom, rude.* An idiot (lit., a walrus's prick). ♦*Не спорь с ним, этот хуй моржовый ничего не поймёт.* "Don't argue with that idiot. He'll never understand." **Хуй соба́чий,** *idiom, rude.* A worthless person. ♦*Значит, ты шпионишь за нами, хуй собачий?* "So you're spying on us, are you, you bastard?" **Я́сный хуй,** *idiom, rude.* It's perfectly clear, it's obvious. ♦*Ясный хуй, он не придёт.* "He obviously won't come." **Хуй в жо́пу,** *idiom, rude.* Up yours; the hell with you. ♦*Хуй в жопу, а не долг тебе!* "The hell with you! I'm not paying you back." **Хуй в жо́пу вме́сто укро́пу,** *rhyming phrase, rude.* Rhyming elaboration on the preceding idiom (укроп, "dill"). ♦*Он просится переночевать, хуй в жопу вместо укропу, пусть домой идёт.* "He wants to sleep at our place? The hell with him. Let him go home to sleep." **Хуй на ны,** *idiom, rude.* To bad, nothing doing. ♦*Хуй на ны нам, а не зарплата в этом месяце.* "Too bad for us, we're not getting any salary this month." **Хуй на па́лочке,** *idiom, rude.* A worthless person. ♦*Кто он такой, чтобы его слушать, хуй на палочке и всё.* "Why do you listen to him? He's a complete nobody." **Хуй на по́стном ма́сле,** *idiom, rude.* A bastard, scoundrel, worthless fellow. ♦*А этому хую на постном масле скажи, что ты его знать не хочешь.* "Tell that bastard that you don't even want to know him." **Хуй с бугра́,** *idiom, rude.* A nobody, an unknown person. ♦*Никакой он не министр, просто хуй с бугра.* "He's no minister — he's a complete nobody." **Хуй с горы́,** *idiom, neg.* An unknown person (lit., a prick from the mountains). ♦*Кто это? — Хуй с горы.*

"Who's that? — Some nobody." **Ху́й там**, *idiom, rude.* No; you're wrong; I refuse. ♦ *Ты купишь мне пиво? — Хуй там.* "Will you buy me a beer? — Hell, no." **Хуй це́лых, ноль деся́тых**, *idiom, joc.* Very little, not much ("one prick-unit, no tens"). ♦ *Я получил гонорар хуй целых, ноль десятых.* "The honorarium I got was pretty small — one unit, no tens." **А хуй не мя́со?** *idiom, rude.* Of course not, obviously not (lit., "Isn't a prick a piece of meat?") ♦ *Ты хочешь взять мой магнитофон, а хуй не мясо?* "You want to borrow my tape recorder? Hell, no!" **Весь хуй до копе́ечки**, *idiom, rude.* That's all, that's everything down to the last detail. ♦ *Неужели всё так и было? — Конечно, весь хуй до копеечки.* "Is that really how it happened? — Yes, down to the last detail." **Вот-те ху́й!**, *idiom, rude.* Incredible! (of unpleasant surprises). ♦ *Вот-те хуй, опять денежная реформа!* "Oh, no, not *another* monetary reform!" **Два дру́га — хуй да у́ксус**, *idiom, rude.* Incompatible (lit., a prick and vinegar). ♦ *Какие они друзья, два друга — хуй да уксус.* "What sort of friends are they? — They can't endure each other." **За таки́е ре́чи хуй (член) тебе́ на пле́чи**, *idiom, rude.* You're talking nonsense (lit., "For such words, a prick on your shoulder"). ♦ *Ты сказал, он не наш человек, за такие речи хуй тебе на плечи.* "You don't know what you're talking about when you say he's not one of us." **Здра́вствуй, здра́вствуй, хуй морда́стый**, *rhyming phrase, rude.* Response to the greeting Здравствуй (cf. under **мо́рда**). **Или хуй попола́м, или пизда́ вдре́безги**, *idiom, rude.* An exhortation to risk everything (lit., either a broken prick or a shattered cunt). ♦ *Давай сыграем на все деньги, или хуй пополам, или пизда вдребезги.* "Let's put all our money on it — nothing ventured, nothing gained." **На ка́ждую хи́трую жо́пу есть хуй с винто́м**, *idiom, rude.* He who cheats will be cheated (lit., for every smart-ass there's a prick with a bolt). **Не́ хуй**, *idiom, rude.* Don't, one shouldn't (cf. **Не́ хуй выёбы-**

ваться under **выёбываться**). ♦ *Не хуй туда ходить.* "Let's not go there." **Оди́н хуй**, *idiom, rude.* It doesn't matter, it's all the same. ♦ *Мне один хуй, что делать, идти в цирк или в кино.* "I don't care whether we go to the circus or to the movies." **Хоть бы хуй**, *idiom, rude.* It doesn't matter, it has no effect. ♦ *Его ругают, а он хоть бы хуй.* "They scold him, but it has no effect on him." **Хуй его знает**, *idiom, rude.* I don't know, no one knows. ♦ *Хуй его знает, когда они приедут.* "Heaven only knows when they'll arrive." **Хуй и пизда́ из одного́ гнезда́**, *rhyming phrase, rude.* It doesn't make any difference, it doesn't matter. ♦ *Что коньяк покупать, что водку. Хуй и пизда из одного гнезда.* "Should I buy cognac or vodka? Oh, well, it really makes no difference."

•**ХУЙ** (*acc. sg. with verbs*): **КЛАСТЬ**: **Класть/положи́ть хуй**, *idiom, rude.* To despise, scorn. ♦ *На твои угрозы я хуй положил.* "I spit on your threats." **МЕНЯ́ТЬ**: **Хуй на́ хуй меня́ть, то́лько вре́мя теря́ть**, *idiom, rude.* It's pointless (lit., it's a waste of time to exchange one prick for another). ♦ *Давай поменяемся часами. — Хуй на хуй менять, только время терять.* "Let's exchange watches. — It's pointless. They're both pretty much the same." **СКЛЕВА́ТЬ**: **Чтоб мне хуй пти́цы склева́ли**, *idiom, rude.* An expression of surprise, incredulity (lit., may birds peck out my pecker). ♦ *Чтоб мне хуй птицы склевали, она опять не пришла.* "Well, I'll be damned — again she hasn't shown up!" **СОСА́ТЬ**: **Соси́ хуй в прокурату́ре**, *idiom, rude.* Things aren't going well (rhyming answer to the question Всё в ажуре? "Is everything okay?" or Ты что, в натуре! "Are you crazy?"; lit., suck a cock in the prosecutor's office). ♦ *Как твои дела, всё в ажуре? — Соси хуй в прокуратуре.* "Are things going okay with you? — No." **СРАВНИ́-ВАТЬ**: **Сра́внивать/сравни́ть хуй с па́льцем**, *idiom, rude.* To compare incommensurable things (lit., to compare a prick with a finger). ♦ *Вспомни, как* *было при Брежневе. Жили нормально. — Сравнил хуй с пальцем, зато тогда каждый сидел и молчал.* "Remember how good things were under Brezhnev? — You're comparing apples and oranges. In those days everyone kept his mouth shut." **СУ́НУТЬ: Сунь хуй в чай (и вынь сухи́м),** *idiom, neg., rude.* A Chinese (lit., "Dip your prick in tea [and take it out dry]," an absurd imitation of the way Chinese names sound to Russians). ♦*У меня в группе новый студент — сунь хуй в чай.* "The new student in my group is a wonton." **ТОЧИ́ТЬ: Точи́ть/ наточи́ть хуй,** *idiom, rude.* To get ready for an erotic encounter (lit., to sharpen one's prick). ♦*Ты, я вижу, хуй наточил, у тебя свидание?* "You must have a date — I see you're all sharpened up." **ХОТЕ́ТЬ: А хуй не хо́чешь?** *idiom, rude.* You expect too much. ♦*Дай мне твой компьютер на наделю. — А хуй не хочешь?* "Let me borrow your computer for a week. — You're asking for the moon."

•**ХУЙ** (*acc. sg. with prepositions*): **ЗА: Не счита́ть за́ хуй,** *idiom, rude.* To consider worthless, not to respect. ♦*Его на работе за хуй не считают.* "They don't respect him at work." **НА: На́ хуй (не на́до),** *idiom, rude.* No one needs it, to hell with it, it's beside the point, it's irrelevant, it doesn't matter. ♦*В такое время твои книги и на хуй не надо.* "The hell with your books at a time like this." **Посыла́ть/посла́ть на́ хуй,** *idiom, rude.* To refuse, reject. ♦*Пошли его на хуй с его подарками.* "The hell with him and his presents." **Хоте́ть/захоте́ть и ры́бку (и ка́шку) съесть и на́ хуй (на́ хер) сесть,** *rude.* To eat one's cake and have it too; to have the impossible (lit., to eat fish and sit on a prick; an absurd rhyming phrase). ♦*Ты хочешь и рыбку съесть и на хер сесть — и работать и отдыхать одновременно, так не бывает.* "You can't be at work and on vacation at the same time! You want to eat your cake and have it too." **ПОД: Ру́ки под хуй зато́чены,** *idiom, rude.* Clumsy (lit., hands shaped like a prick). ♦*У тебя*

руки под хуй заточены, даже гвоздь забить не можешь. "You're all thumbs — you can't even hammer in a nail." **С: С гу́лькин хуй,** *idiom, rude.* Very little, just a tiny bit (lit., about the size of a pigeon's prick). ♦*Воды осталось с гулькин хуй, а пить хочется.* "I'm thirsty, but we have very little water left." **Два тайме́ня, оди́н с хуй, друго́й поме́нее,** *rhyming phrase, rude.* I didn't catch any fish, the fishing was bad (lit., I caught two, one about the size of a prick, and the other a little smaller; таймень, the name of a Siberian fish).

•**ХУЙ** (*acc. pl.*): **Наве́шивать/наве́шать хуй,** *idiom, rude.* To abuse, swear at (lit., to hang pricks on). ♦*Подожди навешивать хуи, я не виноват.* "Don't be so quick to swear at me! I didn't do it." **Раздава́ть/разда́ть хуи́,** *idiom, rude.* To scold, verbally abuse. ♦*Не ходи к нему, он всем раздаёт хуи.* "Don't go near him — he curses everyone out."

•**ХУ́Я** (*gen. sg.*): **До худ,** *idiom, rude.* Lots, a great deal. ♦*Там пива до хуя.* "There's lots of beer there." ♦*Людей на остановке до хуя и больше, не сядешь в автобус.* "There are so many people at the bus stop you won't get a seat on the bus." **Како́го ху́я тебе́ на́до?,** *idiom, rude.* What more do you want? ♦*Я тебе всё сказал, что знаю, какого хуя тебе ещё надо?* "I've told you everything I know; what more do you want?" **На хуя́ козе́ ба́ян (попу́ гармо́нь)?,** *idiom, rude.* It's useless, irrelevant, beside the point (lit., "What does a goat [a priest] need an accordion for?"). ♦*Ты предлагаешь мне эту работу, а на хуя козе баян?* "I need that job you're offering me like a hole in the head." **Ни ху́я осо́бенного,** *idiom, rude.* Nothing special (distorted from ничего особенного). ♦*Ну как балет? — Ни хуя особенного.* "So, how was the ballet? — Nothing special." **Ни ху́я себе́!** *idiom, rude.* Incredible! What next! ♦*Ни хуя себе! Где-то стреляют.* "What the hell is going on! There's shooting somewhere." **От ху́я у́шки,** *idiom, rude.* No, nothing doing, like hell I will (lit., ears from a prick).

♦*От хуя ушки тебе, а не компьютер.* "There's no way you're going to get a computer." **Срыва́ться/сорва́ться с ху́я,** *idiom, rude.* Lit., to slip off a prick. **1.** To be stunned, shocked. ♦*Ты что, с хуя сорвался, не слышал, что Союза больше нет?* "What's wrong with you? Haven't you heard there's no more Soviet Union?" **2.** To make a quick or unexpected movement. ♦*Вы что, с хуя сорвались, куда вы несётесь?* "Where are you rushing off to?"

•**ХУЁВ** *(gen. pl.):* **Хуёв та́чку,** *idiom, rude.* Nothing doing, there's no chance (lit., a wheelbarrow full of pricks). ♦*Хуёв тебе тачку, а не новую машину.* "There's no way you're going to get a new car."

•**ХУ́Ю** *(dat. sg.):* **Я не о́хаю, мне всё по́ хую,** *rhyming phrase, rude.* I don't care, it doesn't bother me. ♦*Жизнь, конечно, непростая сейчас, но я не охаю, мне всё по хую.* "Life is a little complicated right now, of course, but it doesn't bother me."

•**ХУЯ́М** *(dat. pl.):* **Иди́ к хуя́м,** *idiom, rude.* Go to hell! ♦*Иди к хуям со своими просьбами!* "The hell with you and your demands!" **Не годи́ться ни к хуя́м,** *idiom, rude.* To be useless, good for nothing. ♦*Эта лампа не годится ни к хуям.* "This lamp is completely useless."

•**ХУ́ЕМ** *(instr. sg.):* **За каки́м ху́ем?** *idiom, rude.* Why? What for? ♦*За каким хуем я туда пойду?* "What should I go there for?" **Окола́чивать ху́ем гру́ши,** *idiom, rude.* To be at leisure, take it easy (lit., to shake pears out of the trees with one's prick). ♦*Пока вы на юге хуем груши околачивали, мы здесь дом построили.* "While you were taking it easy down south, we built a house here."

•**ХУЯ́МИ** *(instr. pl.):* **Обве́шивать/обве́шать хуя́ми,** *idiom, rude.* To abuse, cover with abuse. ♦*Я только к нему вошёл, а он сразу меня обвешал хуями.* "The minute I walked into his room, he started heaping abuses on me."

•**ХУЮ́** *(loc. sg.):* **Ви́деть/уви́деть на хую́,** *idiom, rude.* To despise, reject. ♦*Я видел все твои обещания на хую.* "I

spit on your promises." **Я и так на хую́, то́лько ла́пки све́сил,** *idiom, rude.* Used in reply to the expression Иди на хуй!, "Go to hell!" (lit., "I'm already there, hanging my legs over the side").

ХУЙЛО́, -а́, *n., rude.* Idiot, bastard (cf. **хуй**). ♦*Это хуйло никогда не поможет.* "That bastard will never help out."

ХУЙНУ́ТЬ, *perf. only, rude.* Cf. **хуй. 1.** To hit, beat. ♦*Хуйни его ногой, пора вставать.* "Hit him in the foot to wake him up." **2.** To sell. ♦*Может быть, хуйнуть ему рубашку?* "Maybe you can sell him a shirt."

ХУЙНЯ́, -и́, *f., rude.* Nonsense (lit., semen; cf. **хуй**). ♦*Твои планы — хуйня.* "Your plans are nonsense." •**Хуйня́ война́, гла́вное манёвры,** *idiom, rude.* Never mind, it doesn't matter (lit. "the war is nonsense; all that matters is the maneuvers"). **Хуйня́ жи́же,** *idiom, rude.* You're wrong, that's not true (lit., semen is more watery; used in protesting reply to **хуйня́**). ♦*Всё, что ты говоришь — хуйня. — Хуйня жиже.* "What you're saying is a lot of nonsense. — No, it's not." **Это всё хуйня́ по сравне́нию с мирово́й револю́цией,** *idiom, rude.* Never mind, it doesn't matter (lit., "it's all nonsense in comparison with world revolution").

ХУЙНЯ́-МУЙНЯ́, хуйни́-муйни́, *f., rude.* Nonsense (cf. **хуйня́**). ♦*Что читаешь? — Всякую хуйню-муйню, детектив.* "What are you reading? — Some nonsense or other, a detective story."

ХУ́ЛИ, *adv., rude.* What for? (cf. **хуй**). ♦*А хули ты сюда припёрся?* "How come you came crashing in here?"

ХУ́ТОР: На ху́тор ба́бочек лови́ть, see under **на.**

ХУХРЫ́-МУХРЫ́, *idiom, joc.* Nonsense. ♦*Это дело серьёзное, не хухры-мухры.* "Don't joke around; this is serious business."

ХУ-ХУ́ НЕ ХО-ХО́? *idiom, rude.* You're expecting too much, you can't have what you want (cf. **А хуй не хо́чешь?**). ♦*Ты хочешь жениться на его дочери, а ху-*

ху не хо-хо? "You want to marry his daughter? You're asking for the moon!"

ХУ́ЮШКИ! *pl., rude.* Nothing doing, no way (cf. **ху́й**). ♦*Хуюшки ему, а не зарплата!* "Nothing doing! I'm not paying him any salary."

ХУЯ́К, -а́, *m., rude.* A quick motion or sound (cf. **ху́й**). ♦*Он его хуяк по морде.* "He smacked him one in the face." •**Хуя́к, хуя́к, гони́ троя́к,** *idiom, rude.* Words of protest against a sudden change of plans (lit., bang-bang, give me back three rubles). ♦*Собирайся, едем в Крым. — Хуяк, хуяк, гони трояк.* "Get ready. We're going to the Crimea. — Huh? Out of the blue like that?"

ХУЯ́КАТЬ/ХУЯ́КНУТЬ, *rude.* To hit, smash, shatter (cf. **ху́й**). ♦*Он хуякнул чашку.* "He smashed the teacup."

ХУЯ́КНУТЬСЯ, *perf. only, rude.* Cf. **ху́й**. **1.** To fall. ♦*Здесь хуякнуться можно, нет ступенек.* "Watch out you don't fall here. There's a step missing." **2.** To go crazy. ♦*Вы ещё не хуякнулись здесь от безделья?* "Haven't you gone crazy from boredom out here?"

ХУЯ́РИТЬ/ОТХУЯ́РИТЬ, *rude.* Cf. **ху́й**. **1.** To work. ♦*Я хуярил всю неделю, устал.* "I'm exhausted, I've been working all week." **2.** To go. ♦*Куда мы хуярим?* "Where are we going?" **3.** To hit. ♦*Его хуярили целый час.* "They beat on him for a whole hour." **4.** To drink. ♦*Он хуярит водку всю жизнь.* "He's been drinking vodka all his life." •**Ве́тер в ха́рю, а мы хуя́рим,** *idiom, rude.* We're not discouraged by difficulties (lit., the wind's in our face, but we carry on). ♦*Как вы поедете на охоту? Там же мороз градусов 40. — А, ветер в жарю, а мы хуярим.* "How can you go hunting? It's 40 below zero! — That won't prevent us."

ХЭЙР, -а, *m., youth.* Hair (from Eng. "hair"). ♦*У меня длинный хэйр, надо сходить в парикмахерскую.* "My hair is too long. I'd better go to the hairdresser's."

ХЭНДЫ́, -о́в, *pl., youth.* Hands, arms (from Eng. "hand"). ♦*У него все хэнды в наколках.* "His arms are all covered with tattoos."

◆Ц◆

ЦА́ПАТЬ/ЦА́ПНУТЬ, *neg.* To touch, take (lit., to snatch). ◆*Не цапай, не твоя рубашка.* "Don't touch that shirt! It's not yours."

ЦА́ПАТЬСЯ/ПОЦА́ПАТЬСЯ, *neg.* To quarrel, argue. ◆*Они опять поцапались из-за денег.* "They've had another quarrel about money."

ЦА́ПЛЯ, -и, *f., neg.* An unattractive, skinny woman (lit., a heron). ◆*Вон, смотри, цапля идёт, кто это?* "Who's that scarecrow over there?" ●**Но́ги как у ца́пли**, see under **но́ги.**

ЦА́РСКОЕ СЕЛО́, *idiom, joc.* A luxurious residential area for New Russians and high officials (from the name of the summer residence of the tsars).

ЦАРЬ: Без царя́ в голове́, *idiom, neg.* Thoughtless, foolish (lit., with no czar in one's head). ◆*Ты не думай, что он без царя в голове, хоть и одевается как панк.* "Don't imagine that he's a fool just because he dresses like a punk."

ЦА́ЦКА, -и, *f.* **1.** A toy. ◆*Бросай свои цацки, идём гулять.* "Put away your toys and let's go for a walk." **2.** A bauble, trinket. ◆*Посмотри, какие цацки я тебе купил.* "Look at the trinkets I've bought you."

ЦА́ЦКАТЬСЯ/ПОЦА́ЦКАТЬСЯ, *neg.* To spoil, fuss over, overindulge. ◆*С ним надо перестать цацкаться, кто он такой, пусть работает как все.* "You've got to stop indulging him. Who the hell is he, that he shouldn't work like everyone else?"

ЦВЕТО́К АСФА́ЛЬТА, *idiom, joc.* Lit., pavement flower. **1.** A prostitute. ◆*Не приставай к мужикам, как цветок асфальта.* "Don't run after the guys like a prostitute." **2.** A pale, weak girl or woman. ◆*Не бери себе в жёны этот цветок асфальта, она всё время болеет.* "Don't marry that pavement flower — she's sick all the time."

ЦВЕТО́К В ПЫ́ЛИ, *idiom, joc., army* A sweeper (lit, flower in the dust, the title of a popular movie). ◆*Ну ты, цветок в пыли, мети побыстрее, скоро отбой.* "Hurry up with the sweeping, it'll soon be time for taps."

ЦЕ, *pred. use, rude.* A virgin (abbr. of **це́лка**). ◆*Она ещё це?* "Is she still a virgin?"

ЦЕ́ЛКА, -и, *f., rude.* Lit., intact hymen. **1.** A virgin. ◆*Разве она целка?* "You mean she's really a virgin?" **2.** A prude, hypocrite. ◆*Ты что, целка, что ли, даже вина не пьёшь.* "What sort of prude are you, making as if you don't even drink wine?" ●**Как це́лка по́сле семи́ або́ртов**, *idiom, neg.* Acting prudishly, posing as an innocent (lit., like a virgin after seven abortions). ◆*Что ты как целка после семи абортов, не знаешь, что в этих случаях дают взятку?* "How can you act so naive? Even you must know that in cases like this a bribe is called for." **Стро́ить из себя́ це́лку**, see under **стро́ить.**

ЦЕ́ЛКИЙ, -ая, -ое, *joc.* Deft, adroit, crafty (playing on **це́лка** and цель, "goal" or "purpose"). ◆*Ты парень целкий, не пропадёшь.* "You're a smart fellow. You'll do all right."

ЦЕЛОВА́ТЬСЯ/ПОЦЕЛОВА́ТЬСЯ с две́рью, *idiom, joc.* To find no one at home (lit., to exchange kisses with the door). ◆*Я к тебе пришёл, как договорились, поцеловался с дверью и ушёл.* "I went to your place as we agreed, but you weren't there, so I left."

ЦЕМЕНТОВО́З, -а, *m., joc.* A police car (by wordplay on цемент, "cement," and **мент**).

ЦЕНТР, *pred. use, crim., pos.* Good, excellent. ◆*Эти сапоги — центр! Покупай.* "These boots are super! Buy them."

ЦЕНТРОВО́Й, -о́го, *youth.* A chief, head (as of a gang). ◆*Кто на вашей улице центровой?* "Who's the leader on your street?"

ЦЕНТРЯ́К, -а́, *m., youth.* **1.** A major vein. ◆*У тебя центряк не виден, не попаду.* "Your 'central' isn't visible; I can't find it with the needle." 2. A chief, boss. ♦*В их компании центряк — это Володя.* "Volodya is the leader of their group."

ЦЕПАНУ́ТЬ, *perf. only.* To pick up (a girl), make a girl's acquaintance (lit., to hook). ♦*Цепани эту, вон там стоит, вроде ничего.* "Try to pick up that one over there — she's awfully good-looking."

ЦЕПАНУ́ТЬ дизу́, *idiom.* 1. To get dysentery (lit., to catch dysentery). ♦*На востоке—цепануть дизу—раз плюнуть.* "In the East, getting dysentery is as easy as one, two, three." 2. To receive false information. ♦*Все факты надо проверять по сто раз, а то можно цепануть дизу.* "That data must be analyzed another hundred times, it could very well be misinformation."

ЦЕПЛЯ́ТЬ/ЗАЦЕПИ́ТЬ. To be intoxicating, give a high. ♦*А пиво это хорошее, цепляет.* "This is good beer; it gives you a real buzz."

ЦЕПЛЯ́ТЬСЯ, *imperf. only.* To insist on, keep harping on. ♦*Не цепляйся к словам, может быть, я и не так сказал.* "Don't keep harping on what I said. Maybe I was wrong."

ЦЕПУ́РА, -ы, *f., youth.* Decorative chain, necklace. ♦*Сколько ты цепур нацепила, не тяжело?* "Look at all those chains you're wearing! Aren't they heavy?"

ЦЕРЭУ́ШНИК, -а, *m.* A CIA agent (ЦРУ, Центральное разведывательное управление). ♦*Он, наверно, церэушник.* "Apparently he's a CIA agent."

ЦЕХОВИ́К, -á, *m., obs.* Someone working in illegal production of merchandise (from цех, "workshop"). ♦*Он известный цеховик, подпольно делал женские кофточки.* "He's known to be an underground producer — he's been manufacturing women's blouses illegally."

ЦИВИ́Л, -а, *m. youth, neg.* A square, a conformist, a conventional person (from Eng. "civilian"). ♦*Он из цивилов, с нами не поедет.* "He won't come with us, he's a square."

ЦИВИ́ЛЬ, -я, *m., army.* Civilian clothes. ♦*У тебя есть цивиль переодеться?* "Have you got a set of civvies to change into?"

ЦИВИ́ЛЬНЫЙ, -ая, -ое, *youth, pos.* Good, rich, luxurious. ♦*Закажи цивильный обед, есть хочется.* "Order a good meal. I'm hungry."

ЦИКЛ, -а, *m.* 1. *neg.* An obsession, fixed idea. ♦*У него на чувихах — цикл.* "He's obsessed with girls." 2. Menstrual period. ♦*У меня цикл, отстань от меня.* "Leave me alone. I've got my period." 3. *youth.* A drug, a narcotic. ♦*Ты мой цикл не брал?* "Did you take my 'cyclo'?"

ЦИ́МЕС!, *idiom.* Very good, nice, tasty (from Yid. tzimmes). ♦*Будешь в увольнительной, попробуй местную жратву, цимес!* "When you get liberty you should try the local food, it's really good."

ЦИНК, -а, *m., army.* A coffin, a death (lit., zinc). ♦*После этих боёв будет много цинка.* "There are going to be a lot of casualties from these battles."

ЦИНКА́, -и, *f., army.* A box with cartridges (from цинк, zinc, meaning the metal that boxes were made of). ♦*Цинки три возьми, не больше, а то тяжело тащить по горам.* "If you take more than three boxes of cartridges your load would be too heavy for the mountain terrain."

ЦИ́НКОВАЯ ПАРА́ДКА, *idiom, army.* A coffin (lit., a zinc parade uniform). ♦*Главное,—в цинковую парадку не приодеться.* "There is one parade uniform I don't ever want to try on and that's the 'zinc' one!"

ЦИНКА́Ч, -а, *m., army.* A serviceman in a zinc coffin (lit., a zinc man). See **ци́нковая пара́дка**.

ЦИ́РЛЫ: Ходи́ть на ци́рлах, see under **ходи́ть**.

ЦИСТЕ́РНА, -ы, *f., joc.* Someone who drinks a lot (lit., a cistern). ♦*Тебя не напоишь, ты настоящая цистерна.* "No one can get you drunk — you're such a bottomless pit."

ЦИФЕРБЛА́Т, -а, *m., joc.* A face (lit., clock face). ♦*Поверни циферблат, ка-*

жется, тебе надо умыться. "Show me your face — it looks like you need a wash."

ЦУ́ЦИК, -a, *m.* A puppy. ♦ *Где ты взял этого цуцика?* "Where did you get that puppy?" •**Мёрзнуть/замёрзнуть как цуцик,** see under **мёрзнуть.**

ЦЫГА́НИТЬ/НАЦЫГА́НИТЬ, *neg.* To beg, to mooch (from цыган, "gypsy"). ♦ *Пойду на улицу цыганить сигареты, все кончились.* "I'm going out to mooch some cigarettes — I haven't got any left."

ЦЬ́ІПКА, -и, *f.* A pretty, attractive girl (lit., a chick). ♦ *Вон стоит неплохая цыпка.* "There's a nice-looking chick over there."

♦ Ч ♦

ЧА́ВКА, -и, *f.* A mouth (from чавкать, to eat noisily). ♦*Чавка у тебя не закрывается, ты молчать умеешь?* "You don't ever shut your trap, do you? Do you ever know how to keep quiet?"

ЧАЙКО́ВСКИЙ: Пить/вы́пить чайко́вского, see under **пить.**

ЧАЙЛД, -а, *m., youth.* A child (from Eng. "child"). ♦*Чей это чайлд ещё не спит?* "Whose child is that who's still awake?"

ЧА́ЙНИК, -а, *m.* Lit., a teapot. **1.** *neg.* A fool, a stupid person. ♦*Не прикидывайся чайником.* "Don't act like an idiot." **2.** *neg.* A driver who stores his car in the winter; an inexperienced driver (cf. **подснежник**). ♦*Осторожно, впереди едет чайник.* "Watch out! There's an out-of-practice driver ahead of us." **3.** *crim.* Gonorrhea. ♦*Если у тебя чайник, то надо пить пенициллин.* "If you've got the clap, you should take penicillin." •**Навари́ть ча́йник,** see under **навари́ть.**

ЧА́ЛИТЬ/ПОЧА́ЛИТЬ, *crim. & youth.* To have sexual relations with a woman. ♦*Ты знаешь, кто её чалит?* "Do you know who's sleeping with her?"

ЧА́ЛИТЬСЯ/НАЧА́ЛИТЬСЯ, *crim.* **1.** To serve time in prison. ♦*Они чалятся уже два года.* "They've served two years already." **2.** To be convicted of a crime. ♦*Они чалились по восемьдесят восьмой.* "They were convicted on Article 88" (a well-known political article of the criminal code).

ЧА́ЛЫЙ, -ого, *crim.* A recidivist. ♦*Он свой, чалый.* "He's one of us; this isn't the first time he's been in prison."

ЧАН, -а, *m., neg.* A head (lit., vat, tub). ♦*У тебя чан совсем не варит, пойди отдохни.* "Your mind isn't working — go take a rest."

ЧА́О-КАКА́О. See **ча́о с кака́вой!**

ЧА́О С КАКА́ВОЙ! *idiom, joc.* So long! See you later! ♦*Ну, чао с какавой! Не забывай!* "So long! Don't forget!"

ЧАП, -а, *m., youth.* Fellow, guy (from Eng. "chap"). ♦*Он наш чап, не подведёт.*

"He's one of our guys. You can rely on him."

ЧА́ПАТЬ/ПОЧА́ПАТЬ, *joc.* To walk slowly, unhurriedly. ♦*Ну, почапали потихоньку.* "Well, let's amble along."

ЧАПО́К, чапка́, *m.* **1.** A tea house. **2.** Any shop or store. ♦*Чапок закрылся, у нас ни пива, ни сигарет, что делать будем?* "The store has already closed for the night and we're out of beer and smokes. Got any ideas?"

ЧА́РНЫЙ, -ая, -ое, *youth, pos.* Good, good-looking. ♦*У тебя чарная подруга.* "Your girlfriend is really good-looking."

ЧЕБУРА́ХАТЬСЯ/ЧЕБУРА́ХНУТЬ-СЯ, *joc.* To fall. ♦*На улице скользко, можно чебурахнуться.* "The streets are so slippery it would be easy to fall."

ЧЕБУРА́ШКА, -и, *f.* A small bottle for juice, water, and so on (from the name of a popular cartoon character of diminutive size). ♦*Вы принимаете чебурашки?* "Can I return bottles here?"

ЧЕГО́-ТО ХО́ЧЕТСЯ, а кого — не зна́ешь, *idiom, joc.* "I feel horny" (lit., I want something, but I don't know who).

ЧЕЙНДЖ, -а, *m., youth.* An exchange, a swap (from Eng. "change"). ♦*Давай чейндж сделаем на куртки.* "Let's swap jackets."

ЧЕЙНДЖАНУ́ТЬСЯ, *perf., youth.* To exchange, swap. ♦*Мы уже чейнджанулись трузерами.* "We've exchanged slacks."

ЧЕКАНА́ШКА, -и, *m. & f., youth, neg.* A crazy person (from чека, "linchpin"). ♦*Ты у нас чеканашка.* "You're a nut."

ЧЕКАНУ́ТЫЙ, -ая, -ое, *youth, neg.* Crazy. ♦*Неужели ты, чеканутый, женился?* "You mean you actually got married, you maniac?!"

ЧЕКАНУ́ТЬСЯ, *perf. only.* To go crazy. ♦*Он совсем чеканулся, всю мебель порубил.* "He went out of his mind and hacked up all the furniture."

ЧЕКУ́ШКА, -и, *f.* A quarter of a liter of

vodka. ♦*Возьми чекушку, нам хватит.* "Just get a quarter-liter; that'll be enough for us."

ЧЕЛНÓК, -á, *m.* A merchant who buys goods abroad and sells them in Russia (lit., a shuttle). ♦*Кожу надо покупать у челноков, у них дешевле.* "Leather coats are cheaper when you buy from a 'shuttle'."

ЧЕЛОВÉК-АМФÍБИЯ, *idiom, army.* A soldier on dish-washing duty (lit., an amphibian man, after the title of a popular SF novel, meaning that there's plenty of water around him). ♦*Не стоит на кухне человеком-амфибией оставаться, кожа с рук слазит через неделю.* "You don't want to get stuck with dishwashing duty on the ship, the skin on your hands will start to peel off after a week."

ЧЕЛОВÉК ИЗ ОБÓЙМЫ. An influential person, party boss, and the like (lit., someone belonging to a cartridge clip, i.e., a member of a set). ♦*Видно сразу, он человек из обоймы, дача, машина, власть — всё у него есть.* "It's obvious he's one of the big wheels with his dacha, his car, and all his power — he's got everything." **Как бéлый человéк,** see under **как.**

ЧЕЛОВÉК-НЕВИДÍМКА, *idiom, army, joc.* A lazy soldier (lit., an invisible man). ♦*Это настоящий человек-невидимка, сразу исчезает, ничего не делает.* "He's a slacker, he gets out of everything because he disappears whenever there's work to be done."

ЧЕМ БЫ ДИТЯ́ НИ ТÉШИЛОСЬ, ЛИШЬ БЫ НЕ ФÁКАЛОСЬ, *idiom, rude.* A distortion of the common saying Чем бы дитя ни тешилось, лишь бы не плакало, "Let the kid amuse himself any way he wants, just so he doesn't cry." The distorted version, referring to teenagers, replaces the ending with "just so he or she doesn't have sex" (cf. **фáкаться**). ♦*Моя дочь без ума от тяжелого рока. — Да, ну и ладно. Чем бы дитя ни тешилось, лишь бы не факалось.* "My daughter is crazy about hard rock. — Well, let the kid have her fun, as long as she doesn't get laid."

ЧЕМ ДÁЛЬШЕ ВЛЕЗ, ТЕМ БÓЛЬШЕ ИНТЕРÉС, *rhyming phrase, joc.* "The deeper you penetrate, the more interesting it gets." An off-color parody of the proverb Чем дальше в лес, тем больше дров, "The further you go into the woods, the more firewood there is." ♦*Ты знаешь, мне нравится эта работа. — Чем дальше влез, тем больше интерес.* "You know, I'm getting to like this work. — Sure, the more you get into it, the more interesting it is."

ЧЕНЧ, -а, *m.,* An exchange, a swap (from Eng. "change"; cf. **чейндж**). ♦*Давай сделаем ченч, ты мне часы, а я тебе — сумку.* "Let's make a swap — you take my bag, and I'll take your watch."

ЧЕПÉЦ, чепцá, *m.* Emergency situation (from чрезвычайное, extreme, and происшествие, accident). ♦*Как дежурство?—Нормально, ни чэпэ, ни чепца.* "How was your watch? Normal, no incidents, no accidents."

ЧЕПУХÁ: Чепухá на пóстном мáсле, *idiom.* Nonsense, rubbish. ♦*Это чепуха на постном масле.* "That's completely absurd." **Нестú чепухý,** see under **нестú.**

ЧЕРВÓНЕЦ, -а, *m.* A ten-ruble bill.

ЧЕРВÓНЧИК, -а, *m.* From червонец. **1.** A ten-ruble bill. **2.** *pl.,* money. ♦*Вы мне верные друзья, с вами я и сыт и пьян, милые червончики мои!* "Darling chervonchiki, you're my true friends; with you I've got plenty to eat and drink" (from a popular song).

ЧЕРДÁК, -á, *m.* Lit., attic. **1.** *joc.* The head, brain. ♦*У меня совсем чердак не работает.* "My brain has completely shut down." **2.** *crim.* An outer breast pocket. ♦*Не клади деньги в чердак, можно их легко вытянуть.* "Don't put your money in your outer pocket — it could easily be stolen."

ЧÉРЕЗ ДЕНЬ НА РЕМÉНЬ, *idiom, army.* A rhyming phrase describing contempt for duties without a break (lit., to have a rifle belt in a day).

ЧÉРЕЗ НЕ МОГÝ, *idiom.* In spite of one's weakness; by way of overcoming oneself (lit., in spite of "I can't"). ♦*Ты должна сделать это через не могу.* "You've got to outdo yourself and bring this off."

ЧЕ́РЕЗ НЕ ХОЧУ́, *idiom.* In spite of disinclination (lit., in spite of "I don't want to"). ♦*Давай, делай это через не хочу.* "Come on — do it even if you don't want to."

ЧЕРЕПО́К, черепка́, *m., joc.* Skull, head (lit., shard, crock; by wordplay on череп, "skull"). ♦*Там иди осторожно, а то сверху кирпичом по черепку попадёт.* "Be careful over there — a brick could fall on your head." •**Черепо́к (черепу́шка) не ва́рит у кого́-л.,** *idiom, joc.* Someone's brain isn't working; someone isn't thinking clearly. ♦*У тебя что, черепок не варит, зачем ты их привёл сюда?* "Have you got a screw loose or something? What did you bring them here for?"

ЧЁРНАЯ БА́БОЧКА, *idiom, business.* A dummy company (lit., black butterfly). ♦*Фирму свою он окружил ещё чёрными бабочками, чтобы деньги прятать.* "He's surrounded his company with dummy firms to hide his income."

ЧЁРНАЯ СУББО́ТА, *neg., obs.* Lit., black Saturday. A Soviet arrangement whereby one Saturday a month was a compulsory workday. ♦*Сегодня я работаю до пяти, у нас чёрная суббота.* "I'll be at work until five today — it's our black Saturday."

ЧЕРНИ́ЛА, черни́л, *pl., joc.* Red wine of poor quality (lit., ink). ♦*Ты, я вижу, большая любительница чернил.* "I see you really go for that red rotgut."

ЧЕРНОЖО́ПЫЙ, -ого, *m., neg., rude.* A person from the Caucasus (lit., a black-assed fellow). ♦*В Москве черножопые обнаглели, делают всё, что хотят, — убивают, спекулируют.* "The black-asses have gotten very uppity in Moscow lately — they speculate, murder, whatever they feel like."

ЧЕРНОЗЁМ: Под ногтя́ми чернозём, это зна́чит агроно́м, see under **под**.

ЧЕРНОМА́ЗЫЙ, -ого, *neg., rude.* A

black person (lit., smeared black; cf. **чёрный**³). ♦*Зачем тебе нужен этот черномазый?* "Why do you associate with that black guy?"

ЧЕРНОРО́ТЫЙ, -ого, *neg.* Foulmouthed, obscene, nasty (lit., blackmouthed). ♦*Черноротый ты, от тебя слова доброго не дождёшься.* "You have a nasty tongue — you never have a kind word to say."

ЧЕРНОТА́, -ы́, *f., coll., neg.* Caucasians and/or Asians (lit., blackness). ♦*Откуда столько черноты в Москве?* "How come all these black people are in Moscow?"

ЧЕРНУ́ХА, -и, *f., neg.* Art or literature showing the negative side of life. ♦*Сейчас в кино одну чернуху показывают, смотреть не хочется.* "The movies nowadays are only showing the dark side of things; I don't feel like watching that stuff."

ЧЕРНУ́ШКА, -и, *f.* A black-humor joke (wordplay on частушка, a popular rhyme, and чёрный юмор, "black humor"; cf. **черну́ха**).

ЧЁРНЫЙ¹**: по-чёрному,** *neg.* Excessively, uncontrolledly. ♦*Он давно пьёт по-чёрному.* "His drinking has been out of control for a long time."

ЧЁРНЫЙ²**, -ого,** *m., youth.* **1.** Opium, an opium preparation. ♦*У меня чёрный давно кончился.* "My 'blackie' is all gone." **2.** Crystalline iodine. ♦*Разведи чёрного немного.* "Dissolve some 'blackie' for me."

ЧЁРНЫЙ³**, -ого,** *m., rude.* A black person.

ЧЁРНЫЙ⁴**, -ого,** *m., neg.* A person from the Caucasus. ♦*Чёрные уже торгуют виноградом?* "Are the blackies selling grapes yet?"

ЧЁРНЫЙ ТЮЛЬПА́Н, *idiom, army.* A transport aircraft for soldiers killed in action (lit., black tulip). ♦*Не хотелось бы, чтобы за нами чёрный тюльпан прилетел.* "I'd hate to see a black tulip coming for us."

ЧЕРНЯ́ШКА, -и, *f.* **1.** Black bread. ♦*У нас к обеду черняшка есть?* "Do we have any black bread for dinner?"

2. *crim.* Opium. ♦*Почём черняшка?* "How much is opium selling for?"

ЧЕРПА́К, -á, *m., army.* A soldier in his second year of service (lit., a ladle). ♦*Он уже черпак, всё знает, что надо и не надо делать.* "He's in his second year already — he knows which are the good jobs and which aren't."

ЧЁРТ, -a, *m.* Lit., devil. **1.** Used as a term of abuse or disgust. ♦*Чёрт, сколько можно повторять, отстань от меня.* "Damn it, how many times do I have to tell you to leave me alone!" **2.** *crim., neg.* Someone who does not belong to the criminal world. ♦*Он здесь лишний, он же чёрт.* "He's straight — he doesn't belong here." •**ЧЁРТ** *(nom. sg.)*: **Чёрт лы́сый,** *idiom, rude.* A bald fellow. ♦*Наш директор, чёрт лысый, так и не сделал, что обещал.* "Our director didn't do what he promised, that bald devil." **Чёрт зна́ет что,** *idiom, neg.* Lit., the devil knows what; used to express disapproval or dislike. ♦*Это чёрт знает что! Везде беспорядок, грязь.* "What the hell is this! Filth and confusion everywhere!" **Чёрт его́ зна́ет,** *idiom, neg.* Lit., the devil knows; used to express complete ignorance of something. ♦*Чёрт его знает, когда будет порядок.* "The devil knows when we'll have law and order." **Чёрт му́тной воды́,** *crim., neg.* A crook, cheat (lit., a devil of muddy water). ♦*Ты всё же с ним будь поосторожней, он чёрт мутной воды.* "Be a little more cautious with him. He's a crook." **Чёрт чи́стой воды́,** *crim., neg.* A naive person, a fool (lit., a devil of clean water). ♦*Только дурак может его принять за вора в законе, он же чёрт чистой воды.* "How could you take him for a real criminal? He's just a dupe." **Чёрт-те что,** *idiom.* No one can understand, the devil only knows. ♦*Сейчас в экономике чёрт-те что творится.* "The devil only knows what's going on in the economy these days." **Кой чёрт дёрнул кого́-л.,** *idiom, neg.* What got into someone? What possessed someone? (lit., What devil grabbed someone?). ♦*Кой чёрт тебя дёрнул сказать ему об*

этом? Это же секрет. "What possessed you to tell him about it? It's a secret!" **ЧЕ́РТИ** *(nom. pl.)*: **Где тебя́ че́рти носи́ли?** *idiom.* Where have you been? (lit., where did the devils take you?). ♦*Мы тебя ищем целый день. Где тебя черти носили?* "We've been looking for you all day. Where the hell have you been?" **ЧЁРТА** (gen. sg.): **Чёрта лы́сого,** *idiom.* It's impossible; nothing will come of it (lit., of a bald devil). ♦*Ты хочешь отдыхать на юге? Чёрта лысого, туда нет билетов.* "You want to take a vacation in the south? Nothing doing — there aren't any tickets." **(А чёрта) лы́сого не хо́чешь?,** *idiom, neg.* You're expecting too much, you're indulging in wishful thinking (lit., Do you want a bald devil?). ♦*За это вы все будете уволены! — А чёрта лысого не хочешь?* "You'll all be fired for that! — Don't get your hopes up!" **Чёрта с два,** *idiom.* No, not, never. ♦*Чёрта с два я ему дам машину.* "No way I'm going to let him have the car." **Како́го чёрта?,** *idiom.* Why? ♦*Какого чёрта ты припёрся так поздно?* "Why did you come so late?" **На чёрта?,** *idiom.* Why? What for? ♦*На чёрта мне нужен этот ребёнок?* "What do I need that kid for?" **ЧЁРТОМ** *(instr. sg.)*: **За каки́м чёртом?,** *idiom.* Why? What for? ♦*За каким чёртом вы туда поехали? Там нечего делать.* "What did you go there for? There's nothing to do there."

ЧЁРТОВА КУ́КЛА, *idiom, neg.* A female idiot, fool. ♦*Если эта чёртова кукла ещё раз такое скажет, я ей покажу.* "I'll teach that ninny a lesson if she ever says such a thing again."

ЧЕСА́ТЬ¹/ПОЧЕСА́ТЬ язык(и́), *idiom, joc.* To gossip, chatter (lit., to scratch one's tongue). ♦*Вы любите чесать языки.* "You guys are too fond of gossiping." **Чеса́ть ре́пу,** *idiom, joc.* To deliberate, think over carefully (lit., to scratch one's head; cf. **ре́па**. ♦*Быстрее чеши репу, идёшь с нами или нет.* "Make up your mind already! Are you coming with us or not?"

ЧЕСА́ТЬ²/ЧЕСАНУ́ТЬ, *joc.* **1.** To run, go

quickly. ♦*Что ты так чесанул, ты что, спешишь?* "Why did you run off like that? Are you in a hurry?" **2.** To speak a foreign language fluently. ♦*Она чешет по-русски как русская!* "She speaks Russian like a real Russian."

ЧЕСА́ТЬСЯ: Ру́ки че́шутся, see under **ру́ки.**

ЧЕСНО́К, -а́, *m., crim.* A thief, a criminal (lit., garlic). ♦*Это наш человек, чеснок.* "He's one of ours — a criminal like us."

ЧЕСНЯ́К, -а́, *m., crim.* A thief, criminal. ♦*Если ты чесняк, то не должен выходить на работу в тюрьме, это против воровских законов.* "If you're a criminal you mustn't work in prison — it's against the criminal code."

ЧЕТВЕРТА́К, -а́, *m.* Twenty-five rubles (lit., a quarter).

ЧЕТВЕРТИ́НКА, -и, *f.* A bottle of vodka containing 250 grams (cf. **четверта́к**). ♦*Сейчас уже не продают четвертинок.* "These days they're not selling those quarter-liters any more."

ЧЁТКО, *adv., youth.* Well, very well. ♦*Пока всё идёт чётко.* "So far everything's going fine."

ЧЕХО́Л, чехла́, *m., joc.* A condom (lit., a cover, slipcover). ♦*У кого есть чехол? Иду к тёлке, есть подозрение, что к ней без чехла нельзя.* "Who's got a condom? I'm afraid the girl I'm going out with may have a disease."

ЧЕШУЯ́, -и́, *f., neg.* Nonsense, rubbish (lit., fish scale; by wordplay on **чепуха**). ♦*Всё это чешуя, не обращай внимания на сплетни.* "That's rubbish — don't pay any attention to such gossip."

ЧИ́КИ-БРИ́КИ, *pl., joc.* **1.** Commotion, fuss. ♦*Сейчас идут всякие чики-брики насчёт приватизации.* "There's a lot of commotion going on about privatization these days." **2.** An affair, a sexual connection. ♦*И давно у них эти чики-брики?* "Have they been sleeping together for long?"

ЧИК-ФА́ЭР, -а, *m., youth.* A cigarette lighter (from **чик**, the sound of lighting a match, and Eng. "fire"). ♦*У кого мой*

чик-фаэр? "Who's got my lighter?"

ЧИН: Заче́м мне чины́, когда́ нет ветчины́, see under **заче́м.**

ЧИНА́РИК, -а, *m.* A cigarette butt. ♦*Сигарет больше нет, будем курить чинарики.* "There are no cigarettes left; we'll have to smoke butts."

ЧИПО́К, чипка́, *m., joc.* A discount store, a store that sells inexpensive goods (esp. abroad; from Eng. "cheap"). ♦*Пиво почём в чипке?* "How much does beer cost at the cut-rate store?"

ЧИ́РИК, -а, *m., obs.* Ten rubles (from червонец).

ЧИРИ́КАТЬ/ЗАЧИРИ́КАТЬ, *neg.* To chatter, babble. ♦*Тебя не спрашивают, не чирикай.* "Cut out your chattering; no one asked your opinion."

ЧИ́СТИТЬ/НАЧИ́СТИТЬ фейс, *idiom, youth, neg.* To hit, beat (lit., to clean someone's face). ♦*Тебе давно пора начистить фейс за твои дела.* "You've had a beating coming to you for a long time for the things you've been up to."

ЧИТА́БЕЛЬНЫЙ, -ая, -ое. Worth reading (from читать, "to read," and Eng. "-able"). ♦*А это читабельная книга? — Вполне.* "Is this book worth reading? — Oh, very much so."

ЧИФ, -а, *m.* A boss, chief (from Eng. "chief"). ♦*Чиф уже на работе?* "Is the boss in yet?"

ЧИФА́Н, -а, *m.* Food. ♦*Чифан здесь неважнецкий, а так жить можно.* "The food sucks here, but other than that life's OK."

ЧИФА́НИТЬ/ПОЧИФА́НИТЬ, *youth.* To eat, have something to eat. ♦*По-быстрому почифанили и пошли.* "Let's have a quick bite and get going."

ЧИФИРИ́ТЬ/ПОЧИФИРИ́ТЬ. To drink strong tea (cf. **чифи́рь**). ♦*Давай почифирим.* "Let's have some good strong tea."

ЧИФИ́РЬ, -я́, *m.* Strong tea. ♦*Сделай-ка чифирь, а то спать хочется.* "Make some strong tea or I'll fall asleep."

ЧИ́ЧА, -и, *f., neg.* A Chechen fighter (abbr. of чечен). ♦*Чичи настоящие звери, никто так не воюет и никто не* *умеет так выжить в горах.* "These Chechens are like animals, the way they maneuver, fight, and survive in the mountains is unreal."

ЧЛЕН, -а, *m.* A penis (lit., member). ◆*У него член до колен.* "He's got a prick down to his knees."

ЧЛЕНОВÓЗ, -а, *m., neg.* An official government car (lit., member-transporter or prick-transporter, compounded from член, "member [of the government or the Party]", but also "penis," and возить, "to convey." These cars are usually large black Volgas or ZILs, which give their occupants privileged treatment in city traffic). ◆*Перекрыли движение, сейчас поедут членовозы.* "They've stopped traffic to let some prick-conveyers go by."

ЧМО, *n., indecl., youth, neg.* A worthless or unpleasant person (from acronym of человек московской области, "a person of the Moscow district"). ◆*Я с этим чмо дела не буду делать.* "I wouldn't have any dealings with that creep."

ЧМОК, -а, *m., youth, neg.* A worthless or unpleasant person. ◆*Отойди отсюда, чмок, видеть тебя не хочу.* "Get out of here, you schmuck! I don't want to see your face."

ЧМÓРИТЬ/ЗАЧМÓРИТЬ, *youth.* To frighten, terrify. ◆*Рэкетиры его совсем зачморили, требуют деньги, грозятся избить.* "Those racketeers have got him completely terrorized with their demands for money and their threats of violence."

ЧМÓШНИК, -а, *m., youth, neg.* An unpleasant, dirty person. ◆*Этот чмошник загадил всю квартиру.* "That slob has messed up the whole apartment."

ЧМÓШНЫЙ, -ая, -ое, *youth, neg.* Unpleasant, dirty. ◆*Там у вас чмошная компашка, туда не пойду.* "Those friends of yours are such slobs, I wouldn't want to go to their place."

ЧМУР, -á, *m., neg.* A person who acts strangely, an eccentric or crazy person. ◆*Этот чмур всё делает не так, как люди.* "That weirdo doesn't do anything in the normal way."

ЧМЫ́РИТЬ/ЗАЧМЫ́РИТЬ, *army.* **1.** To drill too much. ◆*Новый ротный всех зачмырил, выслуживается, скотина.* "That jackass drills us to death because he thinks it's gonna get him promoted." **2.** To insult, tease recruits. ◆*Хватить их чмырить, мы их всё же научили стрелять.* "Don't harass them too much, we've already taught them how to fire their weapons."

ЧМЫРЬ, -я́, *m., army.* A recruit. See **салáга.** ◆*Раз они чмыри, правила простые: нам сапоги чистить, гладить, отбивать койку.* "We have very simple rules around here, the new recruits polish our shoes, iron our uniforms, and make our racks, understand?"

ЧÓКАТЬСЯ/ЧÓКНУТЬСЯ, *joc.* To go crazy (lit., to clink glasses in a toast). ◆*Ты совсем у нас чокнулся?* "Have you gone completely out of your mind?"

ЧÓКНУТЫЙ, -ая, -ое, *joc.* Crazy. ◆*Чего ты кричишь, чокнутый, что ли?* "What are you shouting for? Are you crazy?"

ЧПÓКАТЬ/ЧПÓКНУТЬ, *joc.* To have sex with someone (from the sound of opening bottles). ◆*Так ты её всё же чпокнул или нет?* "Well, did you go to bed with her or not?"

ЧПÓКНУТЫЙ, -ая, -ое, *youth, neg.* Strange, crazy, abnormal. ◆*Не обращай на него внимание, он давно чпокнутый.* "Don't pay any attention to him; he's completely crazy."

ЧТИ́ВО, -а, *n., joc.* Easy reading, something to read for entertainment (from чтение). ◆*Я купил пару детективов, у меня теперь хорошее чтиво на воскресенье.* "I bought myself a couple of detective stories, so I've got some easy reading for Sunday."

ЧТО ВЫ́РОСЛО — ТО ВЫ́РОСЛО, *idiom.* Don't complain! (lit., What's grown has grown). ◆*Говоришь, что правительство слабое? Чему здесь удивляться, что выросло — то выросло.* "You say the government is powerless. What is there to be surprised at? We have what we have."

ЧТО ЗА ШУМ, А ДРА́КИ НЕ́ТУ, *idiom.* What's the argument about? (lit., How come all the noise, and no fight?)

ЧТО МНЕ, СТРЕЛЯ́ТЬСЯ/ЗАСТРЕ-ЛИ́ТЬСЯ? *idiom.* Lit., "What should I do, shoot myself?" Used in response to an accusation, in the sense "Yes, I did it, but it's not the end of the world." ♦*Ты опять разбил машину. — Ну и что мне, стреляться?* "You've gone and wrecked the car again! — Well, yeah. What should I do, shoot myself?"

ЧТО НА́ДО, *idiom, pos.* Very good. ♦*Он парень что надо.* "He's a terrific guy."

ЧТО ПОСМЕ́ЕШЬ, ТО И ПОЖМЁШЬ, *idiom, joc.* Lit., "Whatever you dare, that's what you'll squeeze"; distorted from the proverb Что посеешь, то и пожнёшь, "As you sow, so shall you reap." ♦*У него опять новая женщина. — Что посмеешь, то и пожмёшь.* "He's got another new girlfriend. — Well, as you dare, so shall you squeeze."

ЧТОБ КОМУ́-Л. ПОВЫЛА́ЗИЛО!, *idiom, neg.* Used as a threat or a curse (lit., May s.o.'s eyes pop out!) ♦*Чтоб им повылазило за все их реформы!* "May they fry in hell for all their reforms!"

ЧТОБ МНЕ ЛО́ПНУТЬ, *idiom.* I'll be damned (if I'm not telling the truth) (lit., may I explode). ♦*Я сам видел, как он взял деньги, чтоб мне лопнуть.* "On my word, I saw him take the money — may I burn in hell if it's not true!"

ЧТО́-ТО СТА́ЛИ НО́ЖКИ ЗЯ́БНУТЬ, НЕ ПОРА́ ЛИ НАМ ДЕРЯ́БНУТЬ, *idiom, joc.* An invitation or suggestion to have a drink. Lit., "My feet are freezing — isn't it time for a little nip?"

ЧТО́-ТО СТА́ЛО ХОЛОДА́ТЬ, НЕ ПОРА́ ЛИ НАМ ПОДДА́ТЬ?, *rhyming phrase, joc.* An invitation or suggestion to have a drink. Lit., "It seems to be getting a little chilly — shouldn't we have a drink?"

ЧУВА́К, -а́, *m., youth, obs.* A fellow, guy. ♦*Чувака этого знаешь?* "Do you know that guy?"

ЧУВИ́ХА, -и, *f., youth, obs.* A girlfriend, female friend. ♦*Это твоя чувиха?* "Is she your friend?"

ЧУВСТВИ́ТЕЛЬНЫЙ, -ая, -ое, *youth, joc.* Good, tasty (lit., sensitive, sentimental). ♦*Да, это чувствительный шашлык!* "Wow, that's delicious shashlik!"

ЧУ́ВСТВО ЗАРНИ́ЦЫ, *idiom, army.* Intuition (a feeling for a summer lightning, from озарение, sudden insight). ♦*Что тебе чувство зарницы шепчет, будет бой или обойдётся в этот раз?* "What's your gut telling you? Are they going to ambush us before dawn or not?"

ЧУВЫ́РЛА, -ы, *f., neg.* An unattractive woman. ♦*Где он эту чувырлу откопал?* "Where did he dig up that dog?"

ЧУДА́К НА БУ́КВУ «МЭ», *idiom, joc.* An idiot (playing on чудак and муда́к). ♦*Что хочет этот чудак на букву «мэ»?* "What does that idiot want?"

ЧУ́ДО В ПЕ́РЬЯХ, *idiom, joc.* A strange, eccentric person. ♦*Ну ты, чудо в перьях, кто так жарит мясо?* "Hey, you weirdo, what kind of way is that of cooking meat?"

ЧУ́КЧА, -и, *т., neg.* An idiot, fool (lit., a Chukcha [Eskimo]). ♦*Почему ты такой чукча, даже свой телефон не можешь запомнить.* "Why are you such an idiot! You can't even remember your own phone number!"

ЧУМА́, -ы́, *т. & f., youth.* An entertaining person (lit., a plague). ♦*Ты просто чума, с тобой обхохочешься.* "What a comedian you are! You make people split their sides with laughter."

ЧУМИ́ЧКА, -и, *f., neg.* A slovenly woman. ♦*Не ходи как чумичка, надень новое платье.* "Don't go around like a slut. Put on some nice clothes."

ЧУМНО́Й, -а́я, -о́е. Slowed down, stuporous. ♦*Сегодня все ходят как чумные, жарко.* "Everyone's going around like zombies in this heat today."

ЧУРБА́Н, -а, *т., neg.* A stupid, dull person (lit., a log). ♦*Это чурбан, как ему не объясняй, ничего не понимает.* "He's a blockhead — no matter how many times you explain it to him, he doesn't get it."

ЧУ́РКА, -и, *т. & f., rude.* Lit., a piece of

wood. **1.** A non-Russian, mainly from the eastern part of the former Soviet Union. ♦ *Этот чурка не говорит по-русски.* "That eastern guy doesn't speak Russian." **2.** An idiot. ♦ *Этой чурке ничего не объяснишь.* "It's impossible to explain anything to that idiot."

ЧУ́ТКИЙ, -ая, -ое, *youth, pos.* Good, tasty. ♦ *Чуткое мороженое, на, попробуй.* "This is good ice cream — have a taste!"

ЧУХ, -а, *m., youth, neg.* An insignificant or unknown person. ♦ *Что хочет этот чух?* "What does that fellow want?"

ЧУХА́Н, -а, *m., army.* A recruit (from чухаться, to act slowly). See **чмырь.**

ЧУ́ХАТЬСЯ/ПОЧУ́ХАТЬСЯ, *neg.* **1.** To tarry, dawdle. ♦ *Не чухайтесь, пора на работу.* "Stop dawdling. It's time to get to work." **2.** To scratch oneself. ♦ *Что ты всё время чухаешься, блохи завелись?* "Why do you keep scratching yourself? Have you got fleas?"

ЧУХЛО́, -а́, *n., youth, neg.* A face. ♦ *Умой своё чухло.* "Wash your face."

ЧУ́ЧЕЛО ГОРО́ХОВОЕ, *idiom, neg.* An awkward, ugly, unattractive person (lit., a rag doll, stuffed animal). ♦ *Вот чучело гороховое, опять всё сделал не так, чуть не устроил пожар.* "That scarecrow did everything wrong again and practically started a fire in the process."

ЧУЧМЕ́К, -а, *m., rude.* See **чу́рка.**

ЧУ́-ЧУ ЗАМАНДРЮ́ЧУ, *rhyming phrase, joc.* I'll give it to you, I'll beat you up. ♦ *А хочешь, чу-чу замандрючу за такие слова.* "I'm going to give it to you for what you said."

ША! Hush! Order! ◆*Ша, ребята, заканчиваем базар.* "Quiet down, children! Stop the hullaballoo!"

ШАБИ́ТЬ/ЗАШАБИ́ТЬ. To smoke. ◆*Давай зашабим твои сигареты.* "Let's smoke those cigarettes of yours."

ША́ВКА, -и, *f., neg.* Lit., a type of dog. **1.** A quarrelsome woman. ◆*Опять эта шавка ругаться будет.* "That scold is about to let loose with another tonguelashing." **2.** An unattractive woman. ◆*Она шавка по сравнению с тобой.* "She's a dog compared to you."

ШАГА́ЛОВКА, -и, *f., army.* A drill (from шагистика, a square-bashing). ◆*Шагаловка всех достала, каждый день муштруют.* "Everyone is getting fed up with daily parade drill."

ША́ЙБА, -ы, *f.* A small washbasin in a steam bath (lit., a hockey puck). ◆*Бери шайбу, пойдём сполоснёмся.* "Take the basin and let's go get rinsed."

ША́ЙКА-ЛЕ́ЙКА, -и, *f., joc.* A group, company, set (by wordplay on шайка, "gang" or "pail," and лейка, "bucket"). ◆*Здесь была их шайка-лейка с гитарой?* "Was that group with the guitar here?"

ШАЙТА́Н-АРБА́, -ы, *f., joc.* (From шайтан, "devil," and арба, "cart"). **1.** A new, unknown, uncomprehensible device. ◆*Ты знаешь, как работает этот микроскоп? — Нет, это для меня шайтан-арба.* "Do you know how this microscope works?" "No, it's a mystery to me." **2.** A vehicle.

ШАКА́Л, -а, *m., neg.* A sneaky, cowardly person (lit., a jackal). ◆*Этот шакал тебя подведёт, вот посмотришь.* "You'll see — that jackal will let you down."

ШАКА́ЛИТЬ/НАШАКА́ЛИТЬ, *neg.* To ask someone for something, esp. drink or tobacco; to mooch, sponge. ◆*На тебе сигарету и хватит шакалить.* "Okay, here's a cigarette; now stop mooching off me."

ШАЛА́ВА, -ы, *f., neg.* A prostitute; a promiscuous woman. ◆*Эта шалава тебе ещё навредит.* "That whore is going to get you into trouble." ●**Залётная шалава,** see under **залётная.**

ШАЛА́НДАТЬСЯ/ПРОШАЛА́НДАТЬСЯ, *joc.* To wander around, be in motion (from шаланда, a flat-bottomed boat). ◆*Где ты шаландался всю ночь?* "Where have you been gallivanting around all night?"

ШАЛАШО́ВКА, -и, *f., crim.* A prostitute (from шалаш, a rude forest shelter). ◆*Давно она в шалашовки пошла?* "Has she been a prostitute for long?"

ШАЛМА́Н, -а, *m., neg.* A rude eating place, café. ◆*В этом шалмане водку дают?* "Do they serve vodka in this dive?"

ШАЛУПЕ́НЬ, -и, *f., neg.* **1.** Nonsense, rubbish. ◆*И ты веришь в эту шалупень?* "Do you mean to say you believe that nonsense?" **2.** Worthless people, bad company. ◆*Брось ты водиться с разной шалупенью.* "Stop going around with that trashy crowd."

ША́МАТЬ/ПОША́МАТЬ. To eat. ◆*Давно ничего не шамал, пойдём в столовую.* "I haven't had a thing to eat in ages — let's go over to the cafeteria."

ШАМПУ́НЬ, -я, *f., joc.* Sparkling wine, champagne (lit., shampoo; by wordplay on шампанское, "champagne"). ◆*На Новый год надо достать пару бутылок шампуня.* "We have to get a couple of bottles of champagne for New Year's."

ША́НЕЦ, ша́нца, *m., joc.* A chance, opportunity. ◆*Это хороший шанец подзаработать.* "This is a good chance to earn a little extra."

ШАНТРАПА́, -ы́, *f., collect., neg.* Hoodlums, hooligans. ◆*В подъезде у нас одна шантрапа собирается по вечерам: пьют, курят, матерятся.* "Hooligans hang around our building in the evenings, drinking, smoking, and swearing."

ШАНХА́Й, -я, *m., joc.* A poor neighborhood, slum (lit., "Shanghai"). ◆*Как они* *в этом "шанхае" живут, не представляю: ни воды, ни газа нет.* "I can't imagine how people can live in this slum without water or fuel."

ША́ПКА: Дава́ть/дать по ша́пке, see under **дава́ть.**

ШАПЭ́, *f., indecl., youth.* A girl or woman accepted as "one of the boys" in male company. ◆ *При ней всё можно говорить, она — шапэ.* "You can say anything in front of her — she's a regular guy."

ША́РА: На ша́ру, *idiom, joc.* **1.** Without paying; on someone else's account. ◆ *Мы на шару доехали до Москвы.* "We got as far as Moscow without paying." **2.** Without preparation, off the cuff. ◆ *Я пошёл экзамен сдавать на шару.* "I went to take the exam without studying." **Прое́хаться на ша́ру,** see under **прое́хаться.**

ШАРАБА́Н, -а, *m., joc.* A head (lit., chariot). ◆ *На твой шарабан эта шапка не налезет.* "This hat will never fit your head."

ШАРА́ГА, -и, *f., neg.* A small factory, workshop. ◆ *Сколько ты получаешь на своей шараге?* "How much do you make at your workshop?"

ШАРА́П, -а, *m., neg.* Noise, confusion, tumult. ◆ *Я в этом шарапе ничего не слышал, кто куда идёт и когда.* "In that hubbub I couldn't make out who was going where and when." ●**Поднима́ть/ подня́ть шара́п,** see under **поднима́ть.**

ШАРА́ПЩИК, -а, *m., neg.* A loud person. ◆ *Не приводи этого шарапщика больше, от него один шум, а толку мало.* "Don't bring that loudmouth here any more — he just makes a lot of noise without any sense."

ШАРА́ШИТЬ/НАШАРА́ШИТЬ, *joc.* To do something quickly. ◆ *Ну ты и шарашишь, скоро так и закончишь ремонт.* "You're really chugging along — at that rate you'll have the repairs finished very soon."

ШАРА́ШКИНА КОНТО́РА, *idiom, neg.* A disreputable business, shady concern. ◆ *Он всю жизнь работает в шараш-*

киных конторах. "He's been working in fly-by-night businesses all his life."

ША́РИКИ ЗА РО́ЛИКИ ЗАХО́ДЯТ, *idiom, joc.* To be unable to think straight (lit., one's ball bearings are behind one's rollers). ◆ *У меня шарики за ролики заходят от усталости.* "I'm so tired I can't think straight." ●**Крути́ть ша́рики,** see under **крути́ть.**

ША́РИТЬ, *imperf. only, pos.* To have a good grasp of something, understand something well (lit., to feel, grope). ◆ *Он в математике шарит ещё как.* "He really knows his way around in mathematics."

ША́РНИК, -а, *m.* An informer. See **стука́ч.**

ШАРУ́Н, -á, *m., army.* A lazybones (from на шару, at someone's expense). ◆ *В этой роте шаруны работают как миленькие, у нашего капитана не забалуешь.* "Even the deadbeats work like good little boys in our company, our captain rules with an iron fist."

ШАРЫ́, -о́в, *pl.* Lit., balls. **1.** Eyes. ◆ *Убери шары.* "Get your eyes off me." **2.** Brain, mind (alluding to шарики, "ball bearings"). ◆ *Шары не работают.* "My brains aren't working." ●**Дава́ть/ дать по шара́м,** see under **дава́ть.**

ШАССИ́-КОНЬЯ́К, *idiom, joc.* Brake fluid used for drinks (lit., landing-gear cognac). ◆ *Здесь шасси-коньяк как воду пьют.* "They drink the liquid like water here."

ШАССИ́-ЛИКЁР, *idiom.* Lit., landing gear liqueur. See **шасси́-конья́к.**

ША́СТАТЬ по де́вкам, *idiom, neg.* To run after girls, chase girls. ◆ *Тебе не надоело шастать по девкам?* "Aren't you tired of running after girls?"

ША́ХЕР-МА́ХЕР, *idiom, neg.* Shady dealings, machinations. ◆ *Они на складе с продуктами давно шахер-махер делают, пускают товар налево.* "They've been up to some shady business at the warehouse for a long time, siphoning off goods on the side."

ШАХНА́, -ы́, *f., rude.* Female genitals; women. ◆ *Ты без шахны жить не* *можешь.* "You can't live without getting laid."

ШАШЛЫ́К, -á, *m., joc.* A person from the Caucasus (lit., shashlik, shish-kebab). ♦*Шашлыки очень любят шашлыки.* "Shashliks really like shashlik."

ШВА́БРА, -ы, *f., neg.* A skinny, unattractive woman (lit., a mop). ♦*Что этой швабре надо?* "What does that scarecrow want?"

ШВА́РКАТЬ/ШВА́РКНУТЬ, *neg.* **1.** To throw, smash. ♦*Он все тарелки шваркнул на пол.* "He threw all the dishes onto the floor." **2.** To hit, beat. ♦*Он его как шваркнет в зубы!* "He up and punched him in the mouth." **3.** To drink. ♦*Вчера шваркнули литр и не заметили.* "Yesterday we drank a whole liter without even noticing it."

ШВО́РИТЬ/ПОШВО́РИТЬ, *rude.* To have sex with a woman. ♦*Её шворят все кому не лень.* "Everyone who wants to can screw her."

ШЕБУТНО́Й, -а́я, -о́е, *neg.* Noisy, bustling, restless. ♦*Ты у нас какой-то шебутной, всё тебе не сидится на месте.* "You're so restless you can't sit still in your seat."

ШЕВЕЛИ́ТЬ/ПОШЕВЕЛИ́ТЬ: Шевели́ть/пошевели́ть мозга́ми, *idiom, joc.* To think, consider (lit., to move one's brains). ♦*Над этим делом надо пошевелить мозгами.* "I'll have to think this matter over." **Шевели́ть/пошевели́ть помидо́рами,** *idiom, joc.* To move quickly (lit., to move one's tomatoes). ♦*Шевели помидорами, уже недолго идти.* "Shake a leg. We don't have far to go." **Шевели́ть/пошевели́ть поршня́ми,** *idiom.* To run, move fast (lit., to move someone's pistons). ♦*Устали или нет, мне всё равно, но шевелить поршнями вы будете.* "I don't care how tired you are, you'd better beat feet."

ШЕКАЛДЫ́КНУТЬ, *perf. only, joc.* To drink a little, have a little something to drink. ♦*Ну что, пора и нам шекалдыкнуть немного.* "What do you say, shall we have a little something to drink?"

ШЕЛЕСТУ́ХА, -и, *f.* Money (lit., rustling). ♦*Шелестухи не подкинешь, не дотяну до получки.* "Can you loan me some money? I'm not going to make it to payday."

ШЕЛУПО́НЬ, -и, *f., neg.* Nonsense, rubbish. ♦*Он всегда рассказывает всякую шелупонь.* "He's always telling all sorts of ridiculous stories."

ШЕПТА́ТЬ: Пого́да ше́пчет, see under **пого́да.**

ШЕПТУ́Н: Пуска́ть/пусти́ть шепту́на, see under **пуска́ть.**

ШЕ́РОЧКА С МАШЕ́РОЧКОЙ, *idiom, joc.* An inseparable pair (from Fr. "cher," "ma chère"). ♦*Опять эти шерочка с машерочкой идут.* "Here come those lovebirds again."

ШЕРСТИ́ТЬ/ПОШЕРСТИ́ТЬ, *joc.* To win from, defeat (lit., to ruffle, rub). ♦*Мы их вчера хорошо пошерстили в карты.* "We gave them quite a drubbing at cards last night."

ШЕРУДИ́ТЬ/ПОШЕРУДИ́ТЬ. 1. To rustle about, make a rustling noise. ♦*Хватит шерудить бумагами, ты мне мешаешь читать.* "Stop rustling around like that. I'm trying to read." **2.** To search, look around. ♦*Пошеруди в ящике, там должны быть ключи.* "Look in the drawer. I think the keys must be there." •**Шеруди́ть/пошеруди́ть мозга́ми,** *idiom.* To think over, consider (lit., to move one's brains). ♦*Надо хорошо пошерудить мозгами, чтобы не остаться в дураках.* "I have to think this over very carefully to make sure I don't get cheated."

ШЕРША́ВЫЙ, -ого, *rude.* A penis (lit., rough, horny). ♦*Ты слишком много гуляешь, не отсохнет шершавый?* "Won't your dick shrivel up if you play around so much?" •**Загоня́ть/загна́ть шерша́вого под ко́жу,** see under **загоня́ть.**

ШЕСТЕРИ́ТЬ/ЗАШЕСТЕРИ́ТЬ, *neg.* To serve, be subordinate, run errands. ♦*Ему уже надоело для них шестерить.* "He's tired of being their errand boy."

ШЕСТЁРКА, -и, *m., neg.* A subordinate, a

gofer (cf. **шестери́ть**). ♦*Я вам не шес-тёрка бегать в магазин.* "I'm not your gofer, to do your shopping for you."

ШЕСТИДЕСЯ́ТНИК, -а, *т.* A member of the generation of the 1960s, who had democratic, pro-Western ideas. ♦*Шес-тидесятников сейчас в политике нет.* "There are no 60s people in politics these days."

ШЕ́Я: Гнать в ше́ю (в три ше́и), see under **гнать**[1].

ШИБАНУ́ТЬ, *perf.* To hit. ♦*Кто тебя так шибанул? Весь глаз заплыл.* "Who hit you? Your whole eye is swollen."

ШИ́БЗДИК, -а, *т., neg.* A small, imma-ture man (cf. **бздеть**). ♦*Что это за шибздик к тебе ходит?* "Who's that lit-tle fart who visits you?"

ШИЗ, -а, *т., neg.* A crazy or bizarre person (from **шизофреник**, "schizophrenic"). ♦*Он настоящий шиз.* "He's a real men-tal case."

ШИЗА́: Шиза́ идёт (ко́сит) у кого́-л., *idiom, neg.* (Someone) is crazy (cf. **шиз**). ♦*Чего он орёт? — У него шиза пошла, не обращай внимания.* "What's he yelling about? — He's gone crazy, don't pay any attention."

ШИЗАНУ́ТЫЙ, -ая, -ое, *youth, neg.* Insane (cf. **шиз**). ♦*У тебя все друзья шизанутые.* "All your friends are crazy."

ШИЗАНУ́ТЬСЯ, *perf., youth, neg.* To go crazy (cf. **шиз**). ♦*Он давно шизанул-ся?* "How long ago did he go schizo?"

ШИЗО́, *n., indecl., crim., obs.* A mental ward, insane asylum, esp. as used for con-finement of political dissidents (cf. **шиз**). ♦*Попадёшь в шизо, тогда узнаешь, что это такое.* "Only if you land in a mental ward yourself will you realize what it's really like."

ШИЗО́ИД, -а, *т., neg.* See **шиз**.

ШИ́ЛО, -а, *n.* Spirits (lit., an awl, referring to the severe and sharp taste of liquor). ♦*Шило надо пить на выдох, а то горло сожжёшь.* "If you don't drink that on the inhale (while you inhale) and then afterwards slowly exhale you're going to burn your throat."

ШИПЕ́ТЬ/ЗАШИПЕ́ТЬ, *neg.* To scold, yell. ♦*Не шипи, всё равно я тебе не слушаю.* "Stop yelling! I'm not listening to you anyhow."

ШИ́РЕВО, -а, *n., youth.* Narcotics for use by injection (from **ширять**, "to inject"; cf. **ширя́ться**). ♦*Всё ширево у тебя осталось.* "You've got all the dope."

ШИ́РКА, -и, *f., youth.* Drugs, narcotics (cf. **ши́рево**). ♦*Дай дёрнуть ширки.* "Let's smoke some dope."

ШИ́РМА, -ы, *f., crim.* A pocket. ♦*Про-верь у него ширму.* "Check out his pocket."

ШИРМАЧО́К: На ширмачка́, *idiom, neg.* For free, without paying. ♦*С ними на ширмачка выпить не выйдет.* "You won't get away with drinking on their account."

ШИРОКО́ ШАГА́ЕТ, ШТАНЫ́ ПОР-ВЁТ, *idiom, neg.* Someone will get his come-uppance (lit., if he takes broad strides, he'll rip his pants). ♦*Смотри, как он быстро идёт вверх. — Ничего, широко шагает, штаны порвёт.* "Look how quickly he's progressing in his career. — Don't worry. He'll get his come-uppance."

ШИРЯ́ТЬСЯ/НАШИРЯ́ТЬСЯ. To take drugs by injection. ♦*Он давно ширя-ется?* "Has he been shooting up for long?"

ШИ́ТО-КРЫ́ТО, *idiom.* Secretly. ♦*Всё надо сделать тихо, шито-крыто.* "This has to be kept hush-hush."

ШИТЬ де́ло, *idiom, crim.* To accuse falsely, frame, pin someone else's crime on a person (lit., to sew a case, a phrase used originally of putting together a crim-inal file on someone). ♦*Не шейте мне это дело!* "Don't pin that crime on me!"

ШИШ, -а́, *т., neg.* An obscene gesture (cf. **фиг, фи́га**). •*Ни шиша́,* *idiom, neg.* Nothing. ♦*Есть хочется, а в кармане ни шиша.* "I'd like to eat, but I haven't got a penny in my pockets." **Шиш с ма́с-лом,** *idiom, neg.* No way, certainly not. ♦*Шиш тебе с маслом, а не деньги.* "I certainly won't give you any money." **На каки́е шиши́?** *idiom.* By what means?

With what resources? ♦ *На какие шиши ты собираешься идти в ресторан?* "How do you intend to pay for a meal in a restaurant?"

ШИШ ДА КУМЫ́Ш, *a rhyming phrase.* Nothing, few. ♦ *На обед—шиш да кумыш, кухня где-то застряла.* "We are having nothing for lunch, our field kitchen is lost someplace."

ШИ́ШКА, -и. 1. *f., rude.* A penis (lit., a bump, lump). ♦ *Вода холодная, даже шишка замёрзла.* "The water's too cold — it's frozen my prick." **2.** *m., joc.* A boss, an important or influential person. ♦ *На таких машинах только шишки ездят.* "That's the kind of car that only VIPs drive."

ШИШКАТУ́РА, -ы, *f., neg.* The nomenklatura, the bosses (cf. **ши́шка**). ♦ *Шишкатура о народе никогда и не думала.* "The political bosses have never cared about the people."

ШИШКОВО́З, -а, *m., neg.* A limousine for VIPS. See **членово́з**.

ШКАНДЫБА́ТЬ/ПОШКАНДЫБА́ТЬ, *joc.* To limp. ♦ *Нога болит, еле шкандыбаю.* "My foot is so sore I can barely hobble around."

ШКА́РЫ, -ов, *pl.* Slacks, pants. ♦ *Эти шкары мне в самый раз.* "These slacks fit me just right."

ШКАФ, -а, *m.* A tall, strong man (lit., a wardrobe). ♦ *А что это за шкаф с ней пришёл?* "Who is the big guy who came with her?

ШКВА́РКИ, шква́рок, *pl.* **1.** Leftovers, remains of food. ♦ *От гуся остались одни шкварки.* "There are just a few leftovers from the goose." **2.** Nonsense, rubbish. ♦ *Всё это шкварки, несерьёзно.* "That's all nonsense, beside the point."

ШКВОРЧА́ТЬ/ЗАШКВОРЧА́ТЬ, *joc.* **1.** To sizzle. ♦ *Что у тебя на сковородке шкворчит?* "What's that sizzling in your frying pan?" **2.** To scold. ♦ *Чего так на тебя мать шкворчит?* "How come your mother keeps scolding you like that?"

ШКЕ́РА, -ы, *f.* A secretive place to hide things. ♦ *В шкере у меня самогон,*

вечером приходи, покурим, выпьем. "I've got a little bit of home-made liquor, let's grab a few smokes and have a drink."

ШКЕТ, -а, *m.* A short boy. ♦ *Эй, шкет, ты можешь помыть мне стёкла в машине?* "Hey, shortie, can you wash my windshield?"

ШКИ́РКА: Брать/взять за шки́рку, see under **брать**.

ШКО́ДНИК, -а, *m., neg.* A mischief maker, a naughty boy. ♦ *Какой шкодник разбил все лампочки в подъезде?* "Where's the troublemaker who broke all the lightbulbs in the entrance hall?"

ШКУ́РНИК, -а, *m., neg.* A greedy, selfish person (from шкура, "skin"). ♦ *Какой ты шкурник, никому помочь не хочешь.* "How can you be so selfish! You won't help anybody."

ШЛАНГ, -а, *m.* A penis (lit., hose). ♦ *Ну у тебя и шланг!* "What a prick you've got!" ●**Шла́нги горя́т,** *idiom, joc.* To feel the need of a drink as a remedy for a hangover (lit., one's tubes are burning). ♦ *Надо пива купить, шланги горят.* "I need to get some beer — my throat is burning." **Прики́дываться/прики́нуться шла́нгом,** see under **прики́дываться**.

ШЛАНГОВА́ТЬ/ЗАШЛАНГОВА́ТЬ, *neg.* To play truant, dodge work. ♦ *Тебе не надоело шланговать?* "Aren't you tired of playing truant?"

ШЛЁНДРА, -ы, *m., neg.* A playboy, debauchee, party-goer. ♦ *Куда ты опять собрался, шлёндра?* "Where are you off to now, playboy?"

ШЛЁНДРАТЬ, *imperf. only, neg.* To party, devote oneself to pleasure and entertainment (cf. **шлёндра**). ♦ *Ты всё шлёндраешь, а жена что скажет?* "What will your wife say about all your partying?"

ШЛЁПНУТЬ, *perf. only.* Lit., to slap. **1.** To kill, shoot. ♦ *Там могут и шлёпнуть, смотри в оба.* "Watch out. They could kill you." **2.** To drink quickly. ♦ *Шлёпни стакан водки, сразу согреешься.* "Toss down a glass of vodka. It'll warm you up."

ШЛИФОВА́ТЬ/ПОШЛИФОВА́ТЬ, *youth, joc.* To go, leave (lit., to grind, polish). ♦*Куда он пошлифовал?* "Where's he gone to?"

ШМАЛИ́ТЬ/ЗАШМАЛИ́ТЬ, *neg.* To smoke. ♦*Хватит шмалить, дышать нечем!* "Stop smoking — I can't even breathe in here."

ШМАЛЬ, -и́, *f.* Drugs for smoking. ♦*У кого шмаль есть?* "Does anyone have any dope?"

ШМЕЛЬ, -я́, *m., youth.* A wallet (lit., bumblebee). ♦*Где мой шмель?* "Where's my wallet?"

ШМОКОДЯ́ВКА, -и, *m. & f., neg.* A small, weak, unimpressive person. ♦*Кому ты грозишь, шмокодявка?* "Who do you think you're threatening, you shrimp?"

ШМОЛЯ́ТЬ/ПЕРЕШМОЛЯ́ТЬ. To shoot. ♦*Ты сегодня ночью на часах, да смотри, своих в темноте не перешмоляй с испуга.* "You are standing sentry watch tonight. Do me a favor and don't shoot any of our guys because it's dark and you get spooked."

ШМОН, -а, *m.* A search of premises, investigation. ♦*У него вчера на квартире был шмон.* "They searched his apartment yesterday." ●**Наводи́ть/навести́ шмон,** see under **наводи́ть.**

ШМО́ТКИ, шмо́ток, *pl., neg.* Clothes. ♦*Ты только о шмотках думаешь.* "All you ever think about is clothes."

ШМОТЬЁ, -я́, *n., joc.* See **шмо́тки.**

ШМЫ́ГАТЬ/ШМЫ́ГНУТЬ. To go (lit., to whisk, to flip). ♦*Ты не заметил, в какую дверь он шмыгнул?* "Did you notice which door he went out?"

ШМЯ́КАТЬ/ШМЯ́КНУТЬ, *joc.* To drink (lit., to thud, plop). ♦*Давай шмякнем рюмочку другую водки.* "Let's knock off a vodka or two."

ШНИФТ, -а́, *m., crim.* **1.** A window. ♦*Открой шнифт, душно стало.* "Open the window; it's stuffy in here." **2.** An eye. ♦*Отверни свои шнифты, что уставился?* "What are you staring at? Get your eyes off me!"

ШНО́БЕЛЬ, -я, *m., neg.* A large, ugly nose (from Ger. "Schnabel"). ♦*Шнобель её сильно портит.* "That schnozzle of hers ruins her looks."

ШНУРКИ́, -о́в, *pl., youth.* Parents (lit., shoe laces). ♦*Где работают твои шнурки?* "Where do your parents work?" ●**Шнурки́ в стака́не,** *idiom, youth.* (Someone's) parents are at home. ♦*У меня шнурки в стакане, ко мне нельзя.* "My folks are at home, so we can't go to my place." **Гла́дить/погла́дить шнурки́,** see under **гла́дить.**

ШНУРКОВА́ТЬСЯ, *imperf.* In driving, to change lanes frequently and unreasonably (lit., to lace boots). ♦*Идиота видно на дороге сразу, смотри, как шнуркуется.* "You can see he's an idiot. Look how he's weaving in and out of traffic."

ШНУРОВА́ТЬ/ЗАШНУРОВА́ТЬ грызо́льник (гры́зло), *idiom.* To be silent, to stop talking (lit., to lace up one's mouth). ♦*Молод ещё выступать, шнуруй грызольник.* "You're too young to speak up, shut your mouth."

ШНУРО́К, шнурка́, *m., army.* A recruit (lit., a shoelace, meaning something insignificant). See **сала́га, уро́д.** ♦*Если шнурок хочет что-то сказать, он должен стоять и молчать.* "As a private you have one option when you have something you want to say, you can stand at attention and shut your mouth."

ШНЫРЬ, -я́, *m., neg.* A nosy person. ♦*От этого шныря некуда деться, всё уже разузнал обо всех.* "There's no getting away from that busybody — he knows everything about everybody."

ШНЫРЯ́ТЬ/ЗАШНЫРЯ́ТЬ, *neg.* To bustle around, meddle. ♦*Смотри, кто там шныряет в зале, не наш ли общий знакомый.* "Look who's bustling around the room over there. Isn't that our mutual acquaintance?"

ШО́БЛА, -ы, *f., neg.* A group, set, company. ♦*Их шобла вся курит.* "Their whole group smokes."

ШО́МПОЛ, -а, *m., army.* A corporal (lit., ramrod). ♦*Давай, шомпол, ложись спать.* "Okay, corporal, time for bed."

ШОП, -а, *m.*, *youth.* A store, shop (from Eng. "shop"). ◆*Ты в шоп пойдёшь?* "Are you going to the store?"

ШОРКАТЬСЯ/ШОРКНУТЬСЯ. (To go, to move (lit., to shuffle). ◆*Ты не знаешь, в какой ресторан лучше шоркнуться?* "Do you know which restaurant we should go to?"

ШОРОХ, -а, *m.* Noise, confusion, disorder (lit., rustling). ◆*Что там за шорох?* "What's the hubbub over there?" •**Без шороха,** *idiom.* Quietly. ◆*Только делать это надо с умом, без шороха.* "This has to be done carefully and discreetly."

ШПАГА, -и, *f.* Spirits that have previously been used for technical purposes (lit., a rapier, referring to a sharp taste). ◆*Шпагу профильтруй, чёрт знает, что в нём техники мыли.* "Filter those spirits before you drink them, God only knows what the tech guys have already washed in them."

ШПАКЛЕВАТЬСЯ/НАШПАКЛЕВАТЬСЯ. To put on makeup (lit., to caulk). ◆*Сейчас нашпаклююсь и пойдём.* "I'll just put on my makeup and then we'll go."

ШПАКЛЁВКА, -и, *f.*, *neg.* Makeup, cosmetics. ◆*На тебе шпаклёвки килограмм.* "You must be wearing a pound of makeup."

ШПАЛА, -ы, *m. & f.*, *neg.* A tall, thin person (lit., a railroad tie). ◆*У тебя подруга — шпала.* "Your girlfriend's quite a beanpole."

ШПАНА, -ы, *f.*, *collect, neg.* Thugs, hoodlums.

ШПАРИТЬ/ЗАШПАРИТЬ. To talk fast (from шпарить, "to scald"). ◆*Ты шпаришь по-английски, как и по-русски.* "You babble away in English as fluently as in Russian."

ШПИЛИТЬ/ПОШПИЛИТЬ, *rude.* To have sex with a woman (from шпилька, "hairpin"). ◆*Он её давно шпилит?* "Has he been sleeping with her for long?"

ШПИНГАЛЕТ, -а, *m.*, *joc.* A teenager, young person (lit., a door latch). ◆*В каком классе учится твой шпингалет?* "What grade is your boy in?"

ШПОКАТЬ/ШПОКНУТЬ, *joc.* **1.** To break, shatter. ◆*Кто эту вазу шпокнул?* "Who broke this vase?" **2.** To have sex with a woman. ◆*Он шпокает всех девок подряд.* "He sleeps with all the girls one after another."

ШПРИЦ, -а, *m.* A reprimand (lit., a syringe, referring to an unpleasant procedure like an injection). ◆*Не переживай, шприц воткнули, бодрее будешь.* "Chill out, you're sure to feel like a new man after the commander chews you out."

ШПЫНЯТЬ/ЗАШПИНЯТЬ. To tease, to bait, to nag (from шпынь [*obs.*], "thorn"). ◆*Хватит меня шпынять, устал я от твоих придирок.* "Stop nagging me, I'm tired of your carping."

ШРАПНЕЛЬ, -и, *f.*, *army.* Pearl barley or oatmeal or porridge (lit., shrapnel, referring to the rough texture and bad taste). ◆*У меня в горло не лезет шрапнель без куска масла.* "There is no way I can down that shrapnel or porridge without a load of butter in it."

ШТАНЫ: Наложить в штаны, see under **наложить. Снять штаны и бегать,** see under **снимать.**

ШТАТНИК, -а, *m.* An American. ◆*Штатники без машины жить не могут.* "Americans just can't live without their cars."

ШТОПАТЬ/ЗАШТОПАТЬ, *joc.* **1.** To repair surgically, perform an operation on someone (lit., to darn). ◆*После аварии его быстро заштопали, сейчас выздоравливает.* "They sewed him up right after the accident, and now he's recovering." **2.** To apprehend, catch. ◆*Их заштопали на месте, воровали машины.* "They were caught red-handed stealing cars."

ШТОПОР: В штопоре, *idiom, neg.* Lit., in a spin. **1.** On a drinking spree. ◆*Он в штопоре уже неделю.* "He's been on a binge for a week already." **2.** Intensely occupied with something, very busy. ◆*Я всю неделю был в штопоре, не мог даже позвонить.* "I've been so busy all week I didn't even have time to phone."

ШТРЯ́ВКАТЬ/ПОШТРЯ́ВКАТЬ. To eat. ♦ *Поштрявкать бы сейчас было в самый раз.* "A bite to eat would really hit the spot right now."

ШТУ́КА, -и, *f.* A thousand rubles, a thousand-ruble bill. ♦ *Сейчас диван стоит 300 штук.* "A sofa costs 300,000 these days." •**Вот так шту́ка!** *idiom.* Incredible! I can hardly believe it! ♦ *Значит, он не придёт, вот так штука!* "You mean he's not coming? How can that be?"

ШТУКАТУ́РКА, -и, *f., joc.* Makeup, cosmetics (lit., plaster). ♦ *Не много на мне штукатурки?* "Have I got too much makeup on?"

ШТУРМ ЗИ́МНЕГО, *idiom, army.* The mass rush for the "head" or toilet in the morning (lit., the storming of the Winter Palace). ♦ *Если встать на 5 минут раньше, то никакого ещё штурма Зимнего не будет, если опоздать, будешь стоять в очереди, чтобы отлить.* "If you get up 5 minutes early you'll miss the mass dash to the head, if you don't, you're gonna have to wait in line just to take a piss."

ШТУ́ЦЕР: большо́й шту́цер, *idiom.* (From штуцер, "connecting pipe"). **1.** A specialit, an expert. ♦ *Он большой штуцер в моторах.* "He's an expert with motors." **2.** A boss. ♦ *Не знал, что он у вас такой штуцер.* "I didn't realize he's such a big wheel among you."

ШТУ́ЧКИ-ДРЮ́ЧКИ, *pl., joc.* Tricks, mischief, annoying behavior. ♦ *Что за штучки-дрючки? Почему все ложки лежат в холодильнике?* "What sort of stupid trick is this? How come all the spoons are in the refrigerator?"

ШУБНЯ́К, -а, *m.* Fear (from шуба, fur coat, referring to how people shiver from cold or fear). ♦ *Ему надо к доктору, каждую ночь у него шубняк, кричит, вскакивает, дрожит.* "He needs to go see the shrink, he wakes up every night screaming and shaking with fear."

ШУГА́ЛОВО, -а, *n., youth.* Fear, horror (from шугать, "to scare, to frighten").

♦ *На улицах ночью шугалово, лучше дома сидеть.* "It's too scary on the streets at night, better stay home."

ШУГА́ТЬ/ШУГАНУ́ТЬ. To drive away, to scare away. ♦ *Ну-ка шугани собак с нашего двора!* "Get these dogs away from our yard!"

ШУГНЯ́К, -а, *m.* Nagging, harassing. See **шуга́ть.**

ШУМ: Изобража́ть/изобрази́ть шум морско́го прибо́я, see under **изобража́ть.**

ШУМИ́ХА, -и, *f.* A brouhaha, a sensation (from шум, "noise"). ♦ *Вокруг болезни президента как всегда шумиха в газетах.* "As usual, the papers are making a sensation about the president's illness."

ШУ́МНЫЙ КАК ВОДА́ В УНИТА́ЗЕ, *idiom, rude.* Lit., noisy as a toilet flushing; used to describe a noisy, energetic person. ♦ *Я от него устал, он шумный как вода в унитазе.* "I'm sick of him — he kicks up too much dust."

ШУМО́К: Под шумо́к, *idiom, neg.* Secretly, unnoticed, under cover of confusion. ♦ *Во время перестройки, под шумок, они сделали большие деньги.* "During the perestroika years they made a lot of money without anyone noticing."

ШУРОВА́ТЬ/ПОШУРОВА́ТЬ, *joc.* To look, look for something, search (lit., to dig). ♦ *Пошуруй в ящиках, там должны быть сигареты.* "Dig around in the drawers. The cigarettes must be in there somewhere."

ШУРУ́ПИТЬ/ЗАШУРУ́ПИТЬ. To understand (from шуруп, "screw"). ♦ *Ты шурупишь, в чём тут дело?* "Do you get the point?"

ШУРША́ТЬ/ЗАШУРША́ТЬ, *neg.* Lit., to rustle. **1.** To babble, to speak out of turn. ♦ *Сиди тихо, не шурши!* "Sit quietly and stop chattering!" **2.** To bustle, meddle, make unnecessary fuss. *Он всё шуршит в парламенте.* "He's always making some to-do in Parliament."

ШУ́РЫ-МУ́РЫ, *pl., indecl., joc.* Flirting, love games, endearments. ♦ *Они не работают как надо, у них на уме шуры-муры.* "Those two aren't doing their work properly; all they can think of is billing and cooing."

ШУСТРИ́ТЬ/ПОДШУСТРИ́ТЬ, *joc.* To make a fuss, bustle around. ◆*Зря ты так шустришь, всё равно тебе не дадут квартиру.* "It's no use making all that fuss; you're still not going to get the apartment."

ШУСТРЯ́К, -á, *m., neg.* An energetically self-promoting person. ◆*Это такой шустряк, он всё для себя сделает.* "He's a real go-getter — always looking out for Number One."

ШУ́ТКИ ШУ́ТКАМИ, *rhyming phase.* Joking aside, seriously. ◆*Шутки шутками, но кто всё же будет отвечать за эту работу?* "Seriously, though, who's going to be accountable for this job?" **Шу́тки шу́тками, а полхуя́ в желу́дке,** *idiom, rude.* Joking aside; it's no joke any more (lit., joking is one thing, but half a prick in the belly; cf. **хуй**). ◆*Шутки шутками, а полхуя в желудке, его всё же задержала милиция.* "This is no joke any more — he's been picked up by the police."

ШУТКОВА́ТЬ/ПОШУТКОВА́ТЬ, *joc.* To joke, play tricks, be mischievous (from Ukr.). ◆*Пошутковали и будет.* "You've had your little joke. Enough now."

ШУ́ХЕР, а, *m., crim.* Danger, alarm (from шухать, "to frighten"). ◆*Сейчас шухер будет, надо уходить.* "Now they're going to raise the alarm — we'd better get out of here."

ШУХЕРИ́ТЬ/ЗАШУХЕРИ́ТЬ. 1. To behave badly. ◆*Это вы шухерили и все фонари побили на улице?* "Was it you that acted up like that, knocking out all the street lights." **2.** To arrest. ◆*Кого ещё зашухерили вчера?* "Who else was arrested yesterday?" **3.** To betray, to let down, to report. ◆*Кто же нас зашухерил?* "Who told on us?"

ШУ́ШЕРА, -ы, *f., neg.* Worthless people (lit., old clothes, rags).

ШУШУ́КАТЬСЯ/ЗАШУШУ́КАТЬСЯ. To whisper, to exchange whispered secrets. ◆*Что вы там шушукаетесь?* "What are you whispering about over there?"

ЩА! Contracted from сейчас. **1.** Right away, right now. ♦*Ща приду!* "I'm coming right away!" **2.** No; no, I won't. ♦*Так я тебе и дал, ща!* "I certainly won't give it to you."

ЩАС. See **ЩА.**

ЩЕГÓЛ, щеглá, *m., neg.* A young, inexperienced person (lit., a goldfinch). ♦*А этот щегол сумеет сделать всё, как надо?* "But will that puppy be able to do it right?"

ЩЕКÁ: Давáть/дать зá щеку, see under **давáть.**

ЩЁКИ ВИДÁТЬ ИЗ-ЗА СПИНЫ́, *idiom, neg.* Lit., your cheeks can be seen from behind your back; used to reproach someone for being overweight. ♦*Меньше надо есть, уже щёки из-за спины видать.* "You shouldn't eat so much — your cheeks can be seen from behind your back."

ЩЕКÓЛДА, -ы, *f., joc.* A big jaw (lit., a latch). ♦*Ну и щеколда у неё!* "What a big jaw she's got!"

ЩЕКОТÚН, -á, *m., rude.* A small penis (lit., tickler). ♦*Твоим щекотуном с ней делать нечего.* "With that little thing of yours you won't get anywhere with her."

ЩЕКОТÚНЧИК, -a, *m., business.* A device for detecting electronic bugs (from щекотать, "to tickle"). ♦*Доставай свой щекотунчик, проверим номер.* "Get your 'tickler' and let's check out the room."

ЩЕЛИ́ТЬ/ПОЩЕЛИ́ТЬ, *army.* To sleep (lit., to make a chink). ♦*Что ещё делать остаётся, только щелить до утра.* "There's nothing for it but to catch some z's before morning."

ЩЁЛКАТЬ¹/ЩЁЛКНУТЬ. To photograph (lit., to click, snap). ♦*Щёлкни меня на фоне Кремля.* "Take a snap of me with the Kremlin in the background."

ЩЁЛКАТЬ/ПРОЩЁЛКАТЬ ТАБЛÓМ, *idiom.* To miss, fail to see (from табло, a face, and щёлкать, to snap, click). See **щёлкать щеколдой.**

ЩЁЛКАТЬ²/ПРОЩЁЛКАТЬ щекóлдой (чéлюстью), *idiom, joc.* To miss out on something (lit., to crack one's latch [jaw]). ♦*Вы уже всё съели, а я? — Не надо щёлкать челюстью.* "You guys already ate it all?! What about me? — Well, you shouldn't have missed the moment."

ЩИ—ХОТЬ НÓГИ ПОЛОЩИ́, a rhyming phrase. A watery, thin soup (lit., this soup would make a good footbath).

ЩИПÁТЬ/ПОЩИПÁТЬ, *joc.* Lit., to pluck, pinch. **1.** To win money at a game. ♦*Мы их хорошо пощипали в покер.* "We really cleaned them out in the poker game." **2.** To borrow money. ♦*Ты всё родителей щипал, а когда сам зарабатывать будешь?* "You've been constantly borrowing money from your parents, but when are you going to earn some of your own?"

ЭГОЍСТИК, -а, *m., youth.* A personal tape player with headphones. ♦*Я надену в метро эгоистик, сижу, слушаю музыку, хорошо!* "I take my Walkman on the subway and listen to music while I'm traveling."

«ЭЙ», — ЗОВУ́Т ЛОША́ДЕ́Й, *rhyming phrase, joc.* "Hey" is what they call horses (used in protesting response to being rudely hailed). ♦*Эй, куда ты идёшь? — "Эй," — зовут лошадей.* "Hey! Where are you going? — Hay is for horses."

ЭКЗЕМПЛЯ́Р, -а, *m., neg.* A scoundrel, a bad person. ♦*Это такой экземпляр, поискать надо!* "That bastard is in a class by himself."

Э́КСТРА, -ы, *f.* A brand of vodka. ♦*У меня есть бутылка Экстры.* "I've got a bottle of Extra."

Э́КСТРА-КЛАСС, *idiom, pos.* First-class, outstanding. ♦*Он певец — экстра-класс!* "He's a terrific singer."

Э́КТИВ, -а, *m., youth, neg.* A homosexual who plays the active role. ♦*По всему видно, это эктив.* "Apparently he's an 'active'."

ЭЛЕКТРОСВА́РКА, -и, *f., army.* Illumi-native rockets, illum (lit., an electric welding machine). ♦*Мы видны как на ладони, подождём, пока электросварка погаснет, а потом перебежками в лес.* "We're too visible in this light, only when it subsides can we dash to the forest."

ЭЛЕМЕ́НТ: В элеме́нте, *idiom.* Easily, simply. ♦*Это в элементе можно сделать за пять минут.* "It'll be a cinch to do that in five minutes."

Э́НТОТ, *pronoun, joc.* This, that. ♦*Кто энтот человек?* "Who's that fellow?"

ЭРЕКТОРА́Т, -а, *m., joc.* Voters (by wordplay on эрекция, "erection," and электорат, "electorate"). ♦*У него эректорат — одни комсомольские бабушки.* "His whole constituency is made up of Komsomol grandmothers."

Э́ТАКАЯ, РАЗЭ́ТАКАЯ МАТЬ, *idiom, euph.* Damn it! ♦*Он, этакая, разэтакая мать, не верит мне и всё.* "Damn it, he just doesn't believe me!"

ЭТО КОГО́-Л. НЕ КОЛЫ́ШЕТ, *idiom.* It doesn't bother (someone) (lit., it doesn't shake someone in the wind). ♦*Это меня не колышет.* "That doesn't bother me."

◆Ю◆

ЮБОЧНИК, -а, *m., neg.* A womanizer (from юбка, "skirt"). ◆*Он известный юбочник.* "Everyone knows he's a skirt-chaser."

ЮГ, -а, *m., youth.* A Yugoslavian. ◆*Когда юги уезжают?* "When are the Yugoslavians leaving?"

ЮГО́ВЫЙ, -ая, -ое, *youth.* Yugoslavian. ◆*Это чья обувь, юговая?* "Are those shoes from Yugoslavia?"

ЮДА, -ы, *m., neg.* A Jew. ◆*Он носит русскую фамилию, но меня не обманешь, он чистый юда.* "He has a Russian surname but that doesn't fool me a bit; I can see he's an out-and-out Jew."

Ю́ЗАТЬ, *imperf., youth.* To use (a computer) (from Eng. "use"). ◆*Кто юзал мой компьютер?* "Who's been using my computer?"

ЮЗЕР, -а, *m., youth.* A computer user (from Eng. "user"). ◆*Я не программист, простой юзер.* "I'm no programmer, I'm just a user."

ЮЛИ́ТЬ/ЗАЮЛИ́ТЬ, *neg.* **1.** To fawn, flatter. ◆*Он перед всеми юлит.* "He kowtows to everyone." **2.** To be evasive, avoid answering. ◆*Не юли, говори, что случилось.* "Don't be evasive. Tell me what happened."

Ю́НЫЙ ТЕ́ХНИК, *idiom, joc.* Someone who is always tinkering, constructing, inventing things (from the name of a Soviet youth organization that encouraged technically gifted children). ◆*А этот телевизор мне мой юный техник, муж, построил.* "My technical genius of a husband built me this television himself."

ЮС, -а, *m. & f., youth.* An American (from U.S.). ◆*У нас преподавательница — юс.* "Our teacher is an American."

Ю́ШКА, -и, *f.* Blood (from Ukr.; lit., a type of soup). ◆*Смотри, тебе юшку пустят, если будешь так себя вести.* "Watch out, they'll bloody you up if you act like that."

Я ЛЮБЛЮ́ ТЕБЯ́, ЖИЗНЬ, *idiom, army*. Taps. From the title of a popular song (lit., I'm in love with life, meaning that for a soldier it's the best time because it's time to hit the rack).

Я НЕ ТАКА́Я, Я ЖДУ ТРАМВА́Я, *rhyming phrase, joc.* Lit., "I'm not that sort of a girl; I'm just waiting for the tram." Used in mocking mimicry of a woman's refusal to accept casual advances. ◆*Девушка, как вас зовут? — Я на улице не знакомлюсь. — Подумаешь, я не такая, я жду трамвая.* "Hey, what's your name? — Excuse me, I don't talk to strangers on the street. — Oh, really! Not that sort, just waiting for the tram?"

Я ПА́ДАЮ, *idiom*. I'm fainting, falling (from delight, amazement, laughter, etc.). ◆*Ну и анекдот, я падаю!* "That joke has me in stitches!"

«Я» — ПОСЛЕ́ДНЯЯ БУ́КВА АЛФАВИ́ТА, *idiom, joc.* Lit., "Ya" ('I') is the last letter of the alphabet; used to disparage egoism or boasting. ◆*А я всегда это знал. — «Я» — последняя буква алфавита.* "I knew it all along. — Oh, sure! Ya is the last letter of the alphabet."

Я ТЕ! I'm going to give it to you! I'll teach you a lesson! (short for я тебе задам). ◆*Ты будешь материться, я те!* "I'm going to give it to you if you keep swearing like that!"

Я ТО́ЖЕ ХОЧУ́, НО МА́МА СПИТ И Я МОЛЧУ́, *rhyming phrase, joc.* You can't have what you want; your wish is impossible (lit., "I want it too, but mama's asleep and I'm keeping quiet"). ◆*Я хочу торт. — Я тоже хочу, но мама спит и я молчу.* "I want some cake. — Me too, but it's out of the question."

ЯВИ́ЛИСЬ, НЕ ЗАПЫЛИ́ЛИСЬ, *idiom, joc.* Lit., they've shown up without even getting dusty; used of the quick or unexpected arrival of guests.

ЯДРЁНА ВОШЬ (ПА́ЛКА), *idiom, rude.* Used as a general expletive — damn it!; lit., robust, vigorous louse (stick). ◆*Ты будешь, ядрёна вошь, работать или нет!* "Goddamit — are you going to work or not?"

Я́ЗВА, -ы, *f., neg.* An unpleasant or malicious person (lit., an ulcer). ◆*Ну ты, язва, хватит ругаться.* "Cut out the abuse, you ulcer."

ЯЗЫ́К: Болта́ть (чеса́ть, трепа́ть) языко́м, see under **болта́ть.**

ЯИ́ШНИЦА: Сде́лать яи́шницу, see under **де́лать.**

ЯЙЦО́, -а́, *n.* A testicle (lit., egg). **ЯЙЦЕ́** *(distorted acc. sg.)*: **Кака́я му́ха це-це́ укуси́ла за яйце́?** *idiom, joc.* What's got into you? (lit., "What tsetse fly bit you in the balls?"). **Я́ЙЦА** *(nom. pl.)*: **Я́йца седы́е**, *idiom, rude.* Experience, seniority (lit., gray balls). ◆*У меня уже яйца седые, а всё бегаю на побегушках.* "I'm already an old hand but they keep using me as a gofer." **Кру́че тебя́ быва́ют то́лько я́йца!** *idiom.* "Only eggs could be more hard-boiled than you!" **Кру́че тебя́ то́лько я́йца, вы́ше тебя́ то́лько звёзды**, *idiom, youth, joc.* Lit., "Only eggs (balls) are harder than you; only the stars are higher than you." Used in disparagement of boasting. **Я́ЙЦА** *(acc. pl.)*: **Воробью́ по я́йца**, *idiom, rude.* Shallow (lit., up to a sparrow's balls). ◆*Плыви, не бойся, здесь воробью по яйца.* "Don't be afraid to swim here. It's very shallow." **Заса́живать/засади́ть по са́мые я́йца**, see въеба́ть по са́мые я́йца under **въеба́ть. Крути́ть я́йца**, *idiom, rude.* To irritate, bore, nag (lit., to twist someone's balls). ◆*Что ты ему яйца крутишь, не пойдёт он с нами.* "Why do you keep nagging him? He's not going to come with us." **Моро́чить/заморо́чить я́йца**, *idiom, rude.* To bore, wear out. ◆*Не морочь мне яйца своей рыбалкой.* "Don't bore me with your fishing stories." **Отрыва́ть/оторва́ть я́йца кому́-л.**, *idiom, rude.* To punish severely (lit., to tear off someone's balls). ◆*Ему за эти слова мало яйца оторвать.* "Torture is too good for him after what he said." **Хвата́ть/схвати́ть за я́йца,** *idiom, rude.* To catch in the act, catch red-handed (lit., by the balls). ♦*Наконец этого жулика схватили за яйца.* "They finally caught that thief in the act." **Я́ЙЦАМ** *(dat. pl.):* **Как серпо́м по я́йцам,** *idiom, rude.* Very unpleasant, painful (lit., like a sickle through one's balls). ♦*Эта новость об обмене денег всем как серпом по яйцам.* "This news about the exchange rates is going to hit everyone hard." **ЯЙЦА́МИ** *(instr. pl.):* **Он лежи́т и е́ле ды́шет, то́лько я́йцами колы́шет,** *rhyming phrase, rude.* He's exhausted, he can hardly move (lit., "He's lying there are barely breathing; only his balls are stirring"). **Я́йцами по воде́ пи́сано,** *idiom, rude, joc.* Unclear, uncertain (lit., written on water with one's balls). ♦*Не знаю, приедет он или не приедет. Всё это яйцами по воде писано.* "I don't know whether he'll come or not, it's entirely up in the air."

ЯНГО́ВЫЙ, -ая, -ое, *youth.* Young (from Eng. "young"). ♦*Он не очень янговый чувак.* "He's not such a young fellow."

ЯПО́НА МАТЬ! *rude,* Damn it! (euph. for **ёб твою́ мать***).* ♦*Япона мать, ты мо-* жешь не толкаться? "Damn it. Can't you stop nudging me?"

ЯПО́НСКИЙ БОГ! *idiom, euph.* Damn it! (lit., Japanese God). ♦*Японский бог, руку обварил!* "Damn it, I've burned my hand!"

ЯПО́НСКИЙ ГОРОДОВО́Й! *idiom, euph.* Damn it! (lit., Japanese police officer).

ЯПО́ШКА, -и, *m., neg.* A Japanese. ♦*Япошки думают, что они самые умные.* "The Japs consider themselves the cleverest people in the world."

ЯСНЕ́Е Я́СНОГО, *idiom.* Entirely clear (lit., clearer than clear). ♦*Дело наше яснее ясного, а никак не решится.* "Our problem is as clear as could be, but there's no solution."

Я́СНО И ЕЖУ́, *idiom.* Simple, easy to understand (lit., clear even to a hedgehog). ♦*Как это делать, ясно и ежу.* "Any fool could see how to do that."

Я́ЩИК, -а, *m.* A secret, unauthorized factory. ♦*Он работает в ящике, ракеты делает.* "He's running quite a racket, operating an unauthorized factory." •**Сыгра́ть в я́щик,** see under **игра́ть.**

NOTES

NOTES

NOTES

3 Foreign Language Series From Barron's!

The **VERB SERIES** offers more than 300 of the most frequently used verbs.
The **GRAMMAR SERIES** provides complete coverage of the elements of grammar.
The **VOCABULARY SERIES** offers more than 3500 words and phrases with their foreign language translations. Each book: paperback.

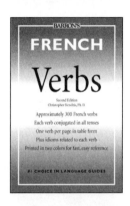

FRENCH GRAMMAR ISBN: 978-0-7641-1351-2	**ITALIAN VERBS** ISBN: 978-0-7641-2063-3
GERMAN GRAMMAR ISBN: 978-0-8120-4296-2	**SPANISH VERBS** ISBN: 978-0-7641-1357-4
ITALIAN GRAMMAR ISBN: 978-0-7641-2060-2	**FRENCH VOCABULARY** ISBN: 978-0-7641-1999-6
JAPANESE GRAMMAR ISBN: 978-0-7641-2061-9	**GERMAN VOCABULARY** ISBN: 978-0-8120-4497-3
RUSSIAN GRAMMAR ISBN: 978-0-8120-4902-2	**ITALIAN VOCABULARY** ISBN: 978-0-7641-2190-6
SPANISH GRAMMAR ISBN: 978-0-7641-1615-5	**JAPANESE VOCABULARY** ISBN: 978-0-7641-3973-4
FRENCH VERBS ISBN: 978-0-7641-1356-7	**RUSSIAN VOCABULARY** ISBN: 978-0-7641-3970-3
GERMAN VERBS ISBN: 978-0-8120-4310-5	**SPANISH VOCABULARY** ISBN: 978-0-7641-1985-9

Barron's Educational Series, Inc.
250 Wireless Blvd., Hauppauge, NY 11788
Call toll-free: 1-800-645-3476

In Canada: Georgetown Book Warehouse
34 Armstrong Ave., Georgetown, Ontario L7G 4R9
Call toll-free: 1-800-247-7160

Please visit **www.barronseduc.com**
to view current prices and to order books

(#26) R 12/08

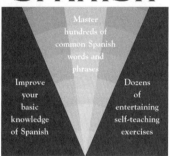